# Studies in Early Medi

Series Editor: Joanna Story, Univer

*About the series*

*Studies in Early Medieval Britain* illuminates the history of Britain from the start of the fifth century to the establishment of French-speaking aristocracies in the eleventh and twelfth centuries, for historians, archaeologists, philologists and literary and cultural scholars.

*Studies in Early Medieval Britain* explores the origins of British society, of communities, and political, administrative and ecclesiastical institutions. It was in the early Middle Ages that the English, Welsh and Scots defined and distinguished themselves in language, customs and territory and the successive conquests and settlements lent distinctive Anglo-Saxon, Scandinavian and Norman elements to the British ethnic mix. Royal dynasties were established and the landscape took a form that can still be recognised today; it was then too that Christian churches were established with lasting results for our cultural, moral, legal and intellectual horizons.

*Studies in Early Medieval Britain* reveals these roots and makes them accessible to a wide readership of scholars, students and lay people.

*About this volume*

Christian theology and religious belief were crucially important to Anglo-Saxon society, and are manifest in the surviving textual, visual and material evidence. This is the first full-length study investigating how Christian theology and religious beliefs permeated society and underpinned social values in early medieval England. The influence of the early medieval Church as an institution is widely acknowledged, but Christian theology itself is generally considered to have been accessible only to a small educated elite.

This book shows that theology had a much greater and more significant impact than has been recognised. An examination of theology in its social context, and how it was bound up with local authorities and powers, reveals a much more subtle interpretation of secular processes, and shows how theological debate affected the ways that religious and lay individuals lived and died.

This was not a one-way flow, however: this book also examines how social and cultural practices and interests affected the development of theology in Anglo-Saxon England, and how 'popular' belief interacted with literary and academic traditions. Through case-studies, this book explores how theological debate and discussion affected the personal perspectives of Christian Anglo-Saxons, including where possible those who could not read. In all of these, it is clear that theology was not detached from society or from the experiences of lay people, but formed an essential constituent part.

*Also in this series*

**Veiled Women**
**Volume I: The Disappearance of Nuns from Anglo-Saxon England**
Sarah Foot

**Veiled Women**
**Volume II: Female Religious Communities in England, 871–1066**
Sarah Foot

**Carolingian Connections**
**Anglo-Saxon England and Carolingian Francia, c. 750–870**
Joanna Story

**Alfred the Great**
**Papers from the Eleventh-Centenary Conferences**
Edited by Timothy Reuter

**St Wulfstan and his World**
Edited by Julia Barrow and Nicholas Brooks

**Early Medieval Studies in Memory of Patrick Wormald**
Edited by Stephen Baxter, Catherine Karkov, Janet L. Nelson and David Pelteret

**Sustaining Belief**
**The Church of Worcester from c. 870 to c.1100**
Francesca Tinti

**Women's Names in Old English**
Elisabeth Okasha

**Bede and the End of Time**
Peter Darby

# HEAVEN AND EARTH IN
# ANGLO-SAXON ENGLAND

*To my parents*

# Heaven and Earth in Anglo-Saxon England

## Theology and Society in an Age of Faith

HELEN FOXHALL FORBES
*Durham University, UK*

Routledge
Taylor & Francis Group

LONDON AND NEW YORK

First published 2013 by Ashgate Publishing

2 Park Square, Milton Park, Abingdon, Oxfordshire OX14 4RN
52 Vanderbilt Avenue, New York, NY 10017

*Routledge is an imprint of the Taylor & Francis Group, an informa business*

First issued in paperback 2020

**British Library Cataloguing in Publication Data**
A catalogue record for this book is available from the British Library.

**Library of Congress Cataloging-in-Publication Data**
Foxhall Forbes, Helen.
    Heaven and earth in Anglo-Saxon England : theology and society in an age of faith / by Helen Foxhall Forbes.
      pages cm. -- (Studies in early Medieval Britain)
    Includes bibliographical references and index.
    ISBN 978-1-4094-2371-3 (hardcover) 1. England--Church history--449-1066. 2. Theology--England--History--Early church, ca. 30-600. 3. Theology--England--History--Middle Ages, 600-1500. I. Title.

    BR749.F69 2013
    274.2'03--dc23
                                                                    2012049943

ISBN 978-1-4094-2371-3 (hbk)
ISBN 978-0-367-60123-2 (pbk)

# Contents

*List of Figures and Tables*                                                    *ix*
*Foreword*                                                                       *xi*
*Acknowledgements*                                                              *xiii*
*Abbreviations*                                                                  *xv*


1   I Believe in One God                                                          1

2   Creator of All Things, Visible and Invisible                                 63

3   And He Will Come Again to Judge the Living and the Dead                     129

4   The Communion of Saints and the Forgiveness of Sins                        201

5   The Resurrection of the Body and the Life Everlasting                      265

    Epilogue                                                                   329


*Bibliography*                                                                  *335*
*General Index*                                                                 *385*
*Index of Manuscripts*                                                          *393*

# List of Figures and Tables

**Figures**

2.1   The 'Harley Psalter' © The British Library Board
      (Harley 603, fol. 72r, detail)                                    95

5.1   Cambridge, Corpus Christi College, 41, p. 433, detail            295

**Tables**

2.1   Anglo-Saxon manuscripts containing liturgical forms for baptism   105
2.2   Anglo-Saxon manuscripts containing rites for the sick             114

3.1   Anglo-Saxon manuscripts containing rituals for ordeals            163
3.2   Manuscripts containing material collected by and associated
      with Archbishop Wulfstan of York, and works written by him        174
3.3   The effects of Wulfstan's injunctions forbidding oaths and
      ordeals on days and seasons of feasting and fasting
      (I Cnut 16–17), as applied to the year 1020                       191

5.1   Anglo-Saxon manuscripts containing funerary rites and rituals
      for the dead                                                      284

# Foreword

The *Studies in Early Medieval Britain* are intended to illuminate the history, society and culture of the island of Britain and of its various regions between the fifth and twelfth centuries. The series will include volumes devoted to different aspects and phases of that long period between the collapse of Roman imperial authority and the establishment of French-speaking aristocracies in the eleventh and twelfth centuries. It is a forum for interdisciplinary collaboration between historians, archaeologists, philologists, literary and cultural scholars that respects the differences between their diverse disciplines, and facilitates communication between them. A very substantial body of evidence survives from the Early Middle Ages, but much of it is fragmentary and scattered across a wide range of scholarly domains. The task of an early medievalist is to master the necessary technical skills and to convey the fascination of their subject. There is a large public, lay and academic, whose interest in the origins of our society, culture and institutions has been whetted at school, college or university, by local studies, in adult education, by dramatic archaeological discoveries or through television programmes. *Studies in Early Medieval Britain* seek to reach this public by avoiding inaccessible jargon and by interpreting the early medieval past with the help of good illustrations. We aim to maintain the highest standards of scholarship and exposition. The series is therefore open both to works of general synthesis and to monographs by specialists in particular disciplines attempting to reach a wider readership. It also includes collaborative studies by groups of scholars.

Dr Foxhall Forbes brings great erudition combined with a lightness of touch to her book on *Heaven and Earth in Anglo-Saxon England*. Her work is profoundly historical, but draws deeply on theology, as well as literary studies, archaeology, art history, and topographical and place-name research. Her mastery of the Old English as well as Latin sources, and her familiarity with contemporary continental evidence, means that this book is more wide ranging and rooted in hard evidence than any study of early English beliefs and practices that has gone before. Her goal is to explore the social context of theology among the Anglo-Saxons; how Anglo-Saxons experienced Christianity and put it into practice in everyday life (and death). She targets in the primary evidence those 'meeting points between theology and real life', where the voices of the educated elite discuss or allude to the everyday practices and beliefs of Anglo-Saxon Christians. She examines the formal theological sources that reveal what the intellectuals of the age thought ought to happen, and identifies variations in theological 'theory' over time. She argues too that theology is not just normative (describing what should happen) but that it can reflect and respond to real beliefs and events, and to changes in attitudes.

Dr Foxhall Forbes problematises the evidence that remains to us, reading beyond its immediate meaning to think hard about the contexts in which it was recorded, preserved and read by the Anglo-Saxon audience, and about the oral prehistory of the textual source. In this way she is able to include in her discussion those who could not read or who did not have direct access to the world of learning.

Dr Foxhall Forbes's book focuses on the four hundred or so years from the eighth to eleventh century. She engages us with the theology through a series of case studies, analysing it through historical sources and scenarios: she investigates the gap between monasticism and the wider world through a discussion of the role of angels and devils in Anglo-Saxon liturgy; she shows how theological ideas about mercy and judgement shaped the practice of Anglo-Saxon law and capital punishment; she investigates gift-giving practices as evidence for the communication of theological ideas about the afterlife, the fate of the soul and purgatory; she shows us how extant evidence relates to 'popular belief and culture', and analyses the institutional contexts in which Christian beliefs were communicated to Anglo-Saxon audiences. Dr Foxhall Forbes's use of diverse genres of evidence is ground-breaking, and her book opens up a much wider range of sources for the study of 'real life' and religious practices in Anglo-Saxon England than any that has gone before. It will be widely consulted by medievalists of many periods and places, and makes a major contribution to scholarship and to our understanding of the religious and cultural history of Anglo-Saxon England.

*Joanna Story*
*University of Leicester*

# Acknowledgements

This book is the result of an Early Career Fellowship funded by the Leverhulme Trust and the University of Leicester, to whom I am profoundly grateful for financial (and other) support. Some of the research was undertaken during my doctoral studies, funded by the Arts and Humanities Research Council, at the Department of Anglo-Saxon, Norse and Celtic in the University of Cambridge, and the Theologische Fakultät in the Albert-Ludwigs-Universität, Freiburg-im-Breisgau. In the course of research and writing, a huge number of people have been incredibly kind and generous in offering advice, comments, support and above all their time to help me. In particular, I would like to thank Richard Buckley, John-Henry Clay, Roy Flechner, Richard Flower, Sarah Foot, Thom Gobbitt, Catherine Karkov, Simon Keynes, Steve Ling, Rosalind Love, Levi Roach, Owen Roberson, Richard Sowerby, Jo Story, Roey Sweet, Francesca Tinti, Elaine Treharne, and David Woodman for comments and advice on many matters; and especially Elizabeth Boyle, Giles Gasper, and James Palmer for their patience in reading multiple chapters and answering many queries. Thanks are also due to Suzanne Paul at the Parker Library for her help with manuscripts; and to Turi King and Alex Woolf for being unfailingly brilliant. Finally, I owe a huge amount to my parents, without whom this book could never have been written, and to whom I am immensely grateful for their support over the years. I am sure they now know much more about Anglo-Saxon theology and history than they ever wanted to.

# Abbreviations

| | |
|---|---|
| *Abing* | S.E. Kelly (ed.), *Charters of Abingdon Abbey, Part 1*, Anglo-Saxon Charters 7 (Oxford, 2000) |
| | S.E. Kelly (ed.), *Charters of Abingdon Abbey, Part 2*, Anglo-Saxon Charters 8 (Oxford, 2001) |
| *ASC* | *Anglo-Saxon Chronicle* |
| BCS | *Cartularium Saxonicum: A Collection of Charters Relating to Anglo-Saxon History*, ed. W. de Gray Birch (3 vols, London, 1885–99) – cited by charter number |
| *Bur* | P.H. Sawyer (ed.), *Charters of Burton Abbey*, Anglo-Saxon Charters 2 (Oxford, 1979) |
| *CantStA* | S.E. Kelly (ed.), *Charters of St Augustine's Abbey, Canterbury and Minster-in-Thanet*, Anglo-Saxon Charters 4 (Oxford, 1995) |
| CCSL | Corpus Christianorum Series Latina |
| *CH* | *Catholic Homilies* |
| *Councils and Synods*, I.i | D. Whitelock, M. Brett and C.N.L. Brooke (eds), *Councils and Synods with Other Documents Relating to the English Church, I, part i (871–1066)* |
| *Councils and Synods*, I.ii | *I, part ii (1066–1204)* (Oxford, 1981) |
| CSEL | Corpus Scriptorum Ecclesiasticorum Latinorum |
| *DCD* | *De civitate Dei* |
| EEMF | Early English Manuscripts in Facsimile |
| EETS, OS | Early English Text Society, Original Series |
| EETS, SS | Early English Text Society, Supplementary Series |
| Fleming, 'Christ Church' | R. Fleming, 'Christ Church Canterbury's Anglo-Norman Cartulary', in C. Warren Hollister (ed.), *Anglo-Norman Political Culture and the Twelfth-Century Renaissance: Proceedings of the Borchard Conference on Anglo-Norman History, 1995* (Woodbridge, 1997), 83–55 |
| HBS | Henry Bradshaw Society |
| *HE* | *Historia ecclesiastica gentis Anglorum* |
| K | J.M. Kemble (ed.), *Codex diplomaticus aevi Saxonici* (6 vols, London, 1839–48) – cited by charter number |
| *LME* | *Letter to the Monks of Eynsham* |
| *LS* | *Lives of Saints* |

| | |
|---|---|
| *Malm* | S.E. Kelly (ed.), *Charters of Malmesbury Abbey*, Anglo-Saxon Charters 11 (Oxford, 2006) |
| MGH | Monumenta Germanica Historiae (volumes now available online at http://www.dmgh.de) |
| *North* | D.A. Woodman (ed.), *Charters of Northern Houses*, Anglo-Saxon Charters 16 (Oxford, 2012) |
| *Pet* | S.E. Kelly, *Charters of Peterborough Abbey*, Anglo-Saxon Charters 14 (Oxford, 2009) |
| *PL* | J.P. Migne (ed.), *Patrologia Latina* (221 vols, Paris 1844–64) |
| *RC* | *Regularis Concordia* |
| Robertson, *Anglo-Saxon Charters* | A.J. Robertson (ed.), *Anglo-Saxon Charters*, Cambridge Studies in English Legal History (Cambridge, 1956) |
| *Roch* | A. Campbell, *Charters of Rochester*, Anglo-Saxon Charters 1 (Oxford, 1973) |
| S | P.H. Sawyer, *Anglo-Saxon Charters: An Annotated List and Bibliography* (London, 1968) – cited by charter number (available in an electronic and updated form at http://www.esawyer.org.uk) |
| *Sel* | S.E. Kelly (ed.), *Charters of Selsey Abbey*, Anglo-Saxon Charters 6 (Oxford, 1998) |
| *Shaft* | S.E Kelly (ed.), *Charters of Shaftesbury Abbey*, Anglo-Saxon Charters 5 (Oxford, 1996) |
| *Sherb* | M.A. O'Donovan (ed.), *Charters of Sherborne*, Anglo-Saxon Charters 3 (Oxford, 1988) |
| *StAlb* | J. Crick (ed.), *Charters of St Albans*, Anglo-Saxon Charters 12 (Oxford, 2007) |
| *Wells* | S.E. Kelly (ed.), *Charters of Bath and Wells*, Anglo-Saxon Charters 13 (Oxford, 2007) |
| Whitelock, *Wills* | D. Whitelock (ed.), *Anglo-Saxon Wills*, Cambridge Studies in English Legal History (Cambridge, 1930) |
| *WinchNM* | S. Miller (ed.), *Charters of the New Minster, Winchester*, Anglo-Saxon Charters 9 (Oxford, 2001) |

# Chapter 1
# I Believe in One God

… every man should learn so that he knows and understands the pater noster
and creed, if he wants to lie in hallowed ground or be worthy of the Eucharist,
because he is not a good Christian who will not learn it … [1]

In the early decades of the eleventh century, Archbishop Wulfstan of York
(d.1023) declared that those who were ignorant of the creed and the pater noster
were not good Christians, and therefore should be deprived of certain Christian
rights such as burial in consecrated ground. Wulfstan was a scholar: he was
widely read, his ideas were informed by theology and canon law, and he was one
of the leading English clergy. Perhaps unsurprisingly, he presents a top-down
approach of what it meant to be Christian: he stands high up in the institutional
ecclesiastical hierarchy, with the responsibility for many souls, and he was a
vigorous advocate for reform and high standards.[2] Scholars like Wulfstan viewed
beliefs and practices surrounding death and burial in the light of Christian
theology, learning and tradition, but these were of course never isolated from
the world in which they existed. Wulfstan's decree highlights the tensions which
might occur as theology negotiated and influenced the social context in which
it was worked out, just as it also throws up many questions which illustrate
the complexities of early medieval religious belief. How far, for example,
does this decree reflect a response to a genuine problem of people who lacked
basic Christian knowledge but still sought inclusion in Christian practices? Are
knowledge and understanding of the creed and pater noster enough to consider
someone a Christian, if there is not also belief, faith or conviction? Why would
someone who did not know such basic Christian prayers have any desire for
burial in hallowed ground in any case? What did this mean to Wulfstan, and to
those who sought it? And, ultimately and perhaps most importantly, what did it
mean to be a Christian (or to be a good Christian) in the changing social contexts
of Anglo-Saxon England?

The details of the answers to these questions depended in the early Middle
Ages, as they depend today, on who was asked, when, and in what context. The
priest and monk Bede (d.735) also insisted that Christians should know the pater

---

[1]  Wulfstan, *Canons of Edgar*, 22, ed. R. Fowler, *Wulfstan's 'Canons of Edgar'*, EETS,
OS 266 (London, 1972), 6: ' … ælc man leornige þæt he cunne pater noster and credon, be
þam þe he wille on gehalgodan licgan oððe husles wyrðe beon; forðam he ne bið wel cristen
þe þæt geleornian nele … '.

[2]  See the essays in M. Townend (ed.), *Wulfstan, Archbishop of York: The Proceedings
of the Second Alcuin Conference* (Turnhout, 2004).

noster and creed.[3] But while Bede seems to have accepted the value of burial in a monastic cemetery, he probably would not have understood the concept of hallowed ground in precisely the way that Wulfstan did, since it does not seem to have existed in the eighth century.[4] This highlights the fact that neither belief nor practice is static and it is not always clear which came first, as in the case of hallowed ground. From an early stage in the history of Christianity, burial near saints' relics or in a church was considered to be important or spiritually valuable, and perhaps this ultimately gave rise to the practice of burying bodies in ground which had been consecrated and therefore marked out as holy. But since burial near saints' relics or in churches or church cemeteries was in early centuries a privilege afforded to the wealthy and to those in religious life, it might also be that this practice led to a desire to be buried in places which were understood to identify prestige and inclusion in a Christian community, and to a belief that this practice was somehow spiritually valuable.[5] In reality, these beliefs and practices probably developed in parallel and were mutually reinforcing, illustrating the reciprocal nature of the relationship between theological discussion and the societies in which this was carried out, as well as the fact that in some cases it can be difficult to disentangle theological and social factors.

This book explores the relationship between Christian theology and societies in Anglo-Saxon England, and is concerned in particular with how theology was mediated from the scholarly contexts in which it was discussed and developed to situations in which it affected or more directly influenced the lives of Christian Anglo-Saxons (or Anglo-Saxons who thought they were Christians, good or otherwise). And, since the relationship works both ways, this book also considers how social practices and interests in Anglo-Saxon England affected the development of theology. This means that much of the theology explored here is pastoral or pastorally oriented, in that it focuses on topics which were communicated to congregations or individuals with the aim of helping souls to achieve their own salvation, topics such as eschatology – the study of death, the afterlife and the Last Judgement – or the beginnings of sacramental theology in the rituals of baptism. The practicalities of pastoral care itself have been explored in some detail in recent scholarship: the work of John Blair, Katy Cubitt, Sarah

---

[3]    Bede, *Epistola ad Ecgberhtum*, 5, ed. C. Plummer, *Venerabilis Baedae Historiam ecclesiasticam gentis Anglorum: Historiam abbatum, Epistolam ad Ecgberctum, una cum Historia abbatum auctore anonymo, ad fidem codicum manuscriptorum denuo recognovit, Epistola ad Ecgberctum* (2 vols, Oxford, 1896), 408–9. For information about Bede, see the essays in S. DeGregorio, *The Cambridge Companion to Bede* (Cambridge, 2011); and G.H. Brown, *A Companion to Bede* (Woodbridge, 2009).

[4]    See below, 273–8.

[5]    For the development of the rites and rituals for consecrated cemeteries, see H. Gittos, 'Creating the Sacred: Anglo-Saxon Rites for Consecrating Cemeteries', in S. Lucy and A.J. Reynolds (eds), *Burial in Early Medieval England and Wales* (London, 2002), 195–208.

Foot and Francesca Tinti has been particularly important here in pinning down the details of ecclesiastical organisation and structures across the Anglo-Saxon period, as well as developments in practice.[6] This focus on institutions and organisational structures has allowed for investigation of 'the Church', but has meant that the impact of theology specifically has received much less attention. Discussion of pastoral theology was based on, and worked out in relation to, the evidence of Holy Scripture and the body of tradition inherited from earlier theologians, especially the 'Greats' such as Pope Gregory I (d.604), who had sent Christian missionaries to England from Rome, or Augustine of Hippo (d.430), who has been called the Father of western theology. But what was explored or considered in a speculative or abstract theological discussion might not be immediately suitable for communication to lay Christians, especially those who had little formal learning, and who could not read for themselves. It is at the meeting-point between the more speculative and the practical that it is possible to glimpse this pastoral dialogue, which on one side comprises the ways that preachers and teachers dealt with the challenges of conveying what was necessary for salvation to their congregations, and on the other how those people responded to what they were taught.

The surviving sources which reveal this dialogue seem to present a fragmented picture, and it is notoriously difficult to understand both sides: the vast majority of people in the early Middle Ages have not left any personal expression of belief, most often because they were unable to read or write. While Bede explains what he believes, and what he thinks good Christians ought to believe, the beliefs of the Northumbrian peasants of Bede's day do not survive in their own words, and Bede's correspondents and dedicatees as well as many of the people he describes are ecclesiastical or noble rather than 'ordinary'. However, the interpretation of sources for Anglo-Saxon theological thought and discussion presents its own difficulties, especially in terms of understanding whose ideas they represent, how widely these ideas circulated, and in what contexts. It is not always easy to understand whether earlier ideas were repeated by Anglo-Saxon authors because that is what those Anglo-Saxon authors specifically believed, or whether the authority of tradition dictated what was communicated without that necessarily being representative of the thoughts of either the preacher or the congregation. Nevertheless, there is a considerable amount of textual, material and pictorial evidence which throws light on this dialogue, and which reveals the tensions and concerns which were played out in belief and in practice, and in a wide variety of cultural and social contexts.

---

[6] See for example J. Blair, *The Church in Anglo-Saxon Society* (Oxford, 2005); C. Cubitt, 'The clergy in early Anglo-Saxon England', *Historical Research* 78:201 (2005): 273–87; C. Cubitt, 'Bishops, priests and penance in late Saxon England', *Early Medieval Europe* 14:1 (2006): 41–63; S. Foot, *Monastic Life in Anglo-Saxon England, c. 600–900* (Cambridge, 2006); F. Tinti, *Sustaining Belief: The Church of Worcester from c. 870 to c. 1100* (Farnham, 2010).

Some areas are more difficult to access than others, and so because of the nature of the evidence as well as for reasons of space, this study focuses on Christian communities in Anglo-Saxon England rather than on conversion or on religious beliefs held prior to conversion. The primary concern here is how theology was developed and used in Christian contexts, rather than the process of Christianisation itself.[7] This means that although the key issues explored in this book are considered as far as possible in relation to Anglo-Saxon England in general, the discussion centres on the period from the eighth century, by which time much of England was Christianised, to the eleventh, when Anglo-Saxon England gradually became an Anglo-Norman realm and ecclesiastical structures and interests also saw significant change. Within this chronological period, geographical coverage is uneven because of the patchiness of the surviving evidence. The traditional problems of Anglo-Saxon sources are reflected here: the eighth century is dominated by Northumbrian sources while in the ninth century evidence is comparatively scarce until the reign of King Alfred (871–99). Scandinavian migration into northern England in the ninth and tenth centuries seems ultimately to have resulted in re-Christianisation and conversion of some areas, but there is comparatively little written evidence available for understanding how theology was developed or used in these communities in this period, and these communities are not considered in detail.[8] In the tenth and eleventh centuries the majority of the surviving sources originated in southern England, with the exception of the booming voice of Archbishop Wulfstan of York, who at times threatens to drown out other contributors to the picture.

Theological and religious texts form a large proportion of the extant written evidence from Anglo-Saxon England, and almost all surviving textual evidence was written down, if not authored, by men and women in religious life or those who had been trained by them. Even texts which might seem to be more documentary than 'religious', such as records of the transfer of property, usually survive because they were copied in the archives of religious houses, and might represent an event which was motivated as much by religious concern as by economic, social or cultural interests. This has two major implications for this study. The first is simply to underline yet again the difficulties of written evidence for accessing the beliefs of people who were illiterate and who were not wealthy or influential enough to have people to write for them. The second is more subtle, and forms one of the methodological strands taken here. Some texts such as sermons were

---

[7]    For studies of Christianisation, see H. Mayr-Harting, *The Coming of Christianity to Anglo-Saxon England* (London, 1972); B. Yorke, *The Conversion of Britain: Religion, Politics and Society in Britain, c.600–800* (Harlow, 2006); J.-H. Clay, *In the Shadow of Death: Saint Boniface and the Conversion of Hessia, 721–54*, Cultural encounters in Late Antiquity and the Middle Ages 11 (Turnhout, 2010); see also the essays in R. Gameson (ed.), *St Augustine and the Conversion of England* (Stroud, 1999).

[8]    On this topic see further L. Kopar, *Gods and Settlers: The Iconography of Norse Mythology in Anglo-Scandinavian Sculpture* (Turnhout, 2012).

intended to teach or communicate theological ideas, but even texts with a different primary purpose often contain information which is either pertinent to theological discussion, or which indicates how the complexities of theology were negotiated in other contexts. By setting this kind of information alongside the more formal discussions found in more straightforwardly theological texts, it is possible to gain another perspective on the meeting-point between theology and the 'real life' contexts in which it functioned. This perspective can in turn be supplemented by other sorts of evidence, such as archaeological material, images, or in some cases topographical or place-name evidence. This approach to theology is unusual but it is only in this comparison of a wide range of different types of evidence that it is possible to begin to explore the workings of early medieval theology in its social context. Ultimately, despite their limitations and fragmentary nature, the combination of different types of evidence also opens up possibilities in the range of perspectives gained, and the resulting picture is not so much fragmented as refracted.

It is also worth noting that Anglo-Saxon theology is, in some respects, different both from the theology of the patristic tradition which preceded it, and from the scholastic tradition which followed it. Most Anglo-Saxon theological texts are not treatises examining specific issues and subjecting these ideas to sustained questioning, although a few Anglo-Saxon writers did produce works of this sort: one example is the discussion of the nature of the soul by Alcuin (d.804), an Anglo-Saxon scholar who was trained at York but who spent much of his working life away from England, at the court of Charlemagne.[9] Instead, a considerable proportion of the texts which reveal the theological discussions of Anglo-Saxon scholars are either catechetical, and so focus on the basics of the faith; or they are exegetical, and so provide commentary on passages of Scripture; or they are both of these. In the tenth and eleventh centuries in particular, many of the texts which reveal theological and religious thought were written as homilies or sermons, for private reading as well as (or sometimes instead of) public delivery, and usually in the vernacular. The homilies of Ælfric of Eynsham (d.1009/1010), an abbot who was an older contemporary of Archbishop Wulfstan's, are tied closely to their liturgical contexts and often expound the Scriptural passages set for the day; but Ælfric also tied catechesis into exegetical commentary, as for example in his homily for Epiphany, which narrates and explains Christ's baptism before discussing the necessity of baptism and other rituals such as the Eucharist for salvation.[10] Here the pastoral purposes of catechism and exegesis together are clear, and stand in some contrast, for example, to the large number of Latin exegetical works written by Bede which were probably intended for monastic audiences.

Many of the tenth- and eleventh-century homilies are quite heavily dependent on their patristic sources, but their production for late Anglo-Saxon audiences

---

[9]   Alcuin, 'De animae ratione liber ad Eulaliam virginem', *PL* 101.639–47.

[10]   For information about Ælfric, see the essays in H. Magennis and M. Swan (eds), *A Companion to Ælfric* (Leiden, 2009).

does show one way in which theology was undertaken at this time, with varying degrees of adaptation for their new contexts.[11] To some extent, religious poetry also reflects the adaptation of ideas to a particular medium and context, but is frequently descriptive rather than speculative.[12] In contrast, more direct engagement with specific questions is found in other contexts such as letters which raise or deal with particular questions, even if sometimes only one half of an exchange survives: a wealth of information about the pressing theological issues of the day is to be found, for example, in the letters of Bede or Alcuin, or in the collection of letters associated with the eighth-century missionary Boniface (d.754), who wrote to many different people to ask for guidance or advice.[13] Some of these letters clearly continued to be valued for the theological (and other) advice they contained, as shown by their preservation in later manuscripts. Other exchanges show not only the depth of thinking which went into the discussion of some topics, but also that these could rouse the tempers of some of the participants in such debates: a surviving personal letter from Ælfric to Wulfstan, and the letters which Ælfric wrote for Wulfstan to be read publically to priests, indicate that Ælfric was infuriated by some of the opinions and questions which Wulfstan had sent him.[14] Even though Wulfstan's part of this debate no longer survives, his own opinions are clear both from Ælfric's responses and from his many other writings, including law codes and quasi-political tracts, as well as from the materials collected by him for use in his own writings.

Gradual changes in theology are also visible in penitential handbooks, liturgical texts, law codes, and in the canons of church councils, all of which are related in their attempts to regulate certain types of behaviour or events. Penitential handbooks set out the range of penances required to atone for particular sins, and seem to have been used in England in some form as early as the late seventh century, since penitential texts survive which may represent some of the teachings of Theodore, Archbishop of Canterbury (d.690).[15] This material continued to be

---

[11]    M.M. Gatch, 'The unknowable audience of the Blickling Homilies', *Anglo-Saxon England* 18 (1989): 99–115.

[12]    See for example *Dream of the Rood*, ed. G.P. Krapp, *The Vercelli Book*, Anglo-Saxon Poetic Records 2 (New York, 1932), 61–5.

[13]    E.L. Dümmler, *Epistolae Karolini aevi*, MGH, Epistolae Karolini aevi II (Berlin, 1895); M. Tangl, *Die Briefe des Heiligen Bonifatius und Lullus*, MGH, Epistolae Selectae 1 (Berlin, 1916); see also C.E. Fell, 'Some Implications of the Boniface Correspondence', in H. Damico and A.H. Olsen (eds), *New Readings on Women in Old English Literature* (Bloomington, IN, 1990), 29–43; A. Orchard, 'Old sources, new resources: Finding the right formula for Boniface', *Anglo-Saxon England* 30 (2001): 15–38.

[14]    B. Fehr (ed.), *Die Hirtenbriefe Ælfrics in altenglischer und lateinischer Fassung*, Bibliothek der angelsächsischen Prosa 9 (Darmstadt, 1966, reprinted with supplementary introduction by P. Clemoes [orig. pub. 1914]); see also below, 177–84.

[15]    This material is extremely complicated: for discussion see T.M. Charles-Edwards, 'The Penitential of Theodore and the "Iudicia Theodori"', in M. Lapidge (ed.), *Archbishop*

used and was eventually translated (with some adaptation) into Old English: by the tenth and eleventh centuries, a range of vernacular penitential handbooks seems to have been in circulation alongside Latin texts, and some of the changes in their stipulations reflect developments in theology.[16] Many penitential injunctions were drawn directly from canon law, the decisions made at ecclesiastical councils in response to current issues; and in some cases canon law was also influential in secular law codes.[17] The developments which are visible in the decrees of ecclesiastical councils and secular law are often matched by changes in liturgical rituals, or in some cases by the production of liturgies for specific rituals, as in the case of ordeals, or consecrated ground.

These texts are quite helpful in understanding theology as the discussion of belief, but because they are all normative (and so state what ought to happen, rather than what actually happened), they reveal much less about actual practice. More useful information about belief and practice on the ground, and thus also for the existence of theological ideas in non-normative contexts, can sometimes be found in chronicles, or more often in narrative sources such as histories and hagiographies. The distinction between these last two genres is sometimes loose, and all three are most often concerned with nobility or with those in religious life. But for hagiographical texts in particular, the heavy reliance on earlier models and the lack of information available to some authors can make it difficult to know how to interpret beliefs, practices and events described in these texts.[18] Perhaps the most notable example of this is found in the Northumbrian *Life of Gregory the Great*, written probably in the late seventh or early eighth century at Whitby, in which the author explains that on account of the limited information available, some of the miracles described may not in fact have been performed by Gregory: the author concludes that these are 'universal truth' and it should not be considered problematic if the miracles were in fact performed by some other saint, because

---

*Theodore: Commemorative Studies on his Life and Influence* (Cambridge, 1995), 141–74; R. Flechner, 'The making of the Canons of Theodore', *Peritia* 17/18 (2004): 121–43; and for the texts P.W. Finsterwalder (ed.), *Die Canones Theodori Cantuariensis und ihre Überlieferungsformen* (Weimar, 1929); see also A.J. Frantzen, *The Literature of Penance in Anglo-Saxon England* (New Brunswick, NJ, 1983); A.J. Frantzen, 'The tradition of penitentials in Anglo-Saxon England', *Anglo-Saxon England* 11 (1983): 23–56.

[16] See A.J. Frantzen (ed.), *The Anglo-Saxon Penitentials: A Cultural Database* (2008), http://www.anglo-saxon.net/penance, accessed November 2012.

[17] See C. Cubitt, *Anglo-Saxon Church Councils, c.650–c.850*, Studies in the early history of Britain (London, 1995).

[18] F. Lifshitz, 'Beyond positivism and genre: "Hagiographical" texts as historical narrative', *Viator: Medieval and Renaissance Studies* 25 (1994): 95–113; R.C. Love, 'Hagiography', in M. Lapidge et al. (eds), *The Blackwell Encyclopaedia of Anglo-Saxon England* (Oxford, 1999), 226–8; E.M. Treharne, 'Ælfric's Account of St Swithun: Literature of Reform and Reward', in R. Balzaretti and E.M. Tyler (eds), *Narrative and History in the Early Medieval West* (Turnhout, 2006), 167–88.

like the limbs of the body, 'we are all members one of another'.[19] Hagiography is an imitative genre, and as the Whitby *Life* shows, in some cases the episodes described may in fact owe more to their predecessors than to early medieval reality.

Other narrative material can sometimes be found in charters, documents which arrange and formalise transactions and donations of property and which may include accounts of disputes, or explain how the land became available to be granted.[20] In addition to this narrative material, charters in particular sometimes include theological information in the proem – the introductory section – but it is worth remembering too that charters are quite formulaic and that in many cases the existence of the document seems to have been more important than what it said.[21] However, charters as well as wills and writs are important because they represent the end-product of a much longer process of engagement and interaction between lay people and religious houses, and this itself probably afforded opportunities for the communication of ideas. And although formulae were used in creating the texts, this does not mean that those formulae were 'empty' or insincere: in some cases it is possible to hear the echoes of the voices of those who wished to donate property or portable objects for the good of their souls. Charters and wills primarily represent the transactions of extremely wealthy individuals, and although they reveal far more than the simple fact of a transaction of land, it is difficult to know how far the concerns that they illustrate were a reality further down the social scale. But other types of documentary evidence such as guild statutes also reveal these kinds of concerns, and while these are still not representative of all levels of society, they go at least some way towards attempting to redress the balance.

Some of the difficulties of written evidence are also reflected in material and visual culture. The pictorial and visual evidence of stone sculpture and illustrations in manuscripts or on church walls (either surviving or described) are, like written evidence, primarily associated with religious houses and elites. It is possible, if unlikely given the preservation history of most manuscripts, that

---

[19]  *Vita S. Gregorii*, 30, ed. and trans. B. Colgrave, *The Earliest Life of Gregory the Great* (Cambridge, 1985 [orig. pub. 1968]), 128–35.

[20]  S. Keynes, *The Diplomas of King Æthelred 'the Unready' 978–1016: A Study in their Use as Historical Evidence*, Cambridge Studies in Medieval Life and Thought, 3rd series, 13 (Cambridge, 1980), 97, 130 and n. 168, 200–1; S. Keynes, 'Royal Government and the Written Word in Late Anglo-Saxon England', in R. McKitterick (ed.), *Uses of Literacy in Early Mediaeval Europe* (Cambridge, 1990), 226–57, at 245–52; P. Wormald, *The Making of English Law: King Alfred to the Twelfth Century* (Oxford, 1999), 143–53; S. Foot, 'Reading Anglo-Saxon Charters: Memory, Record, or Story?', in E.M. Tyler and R. Balzaretti (eds), *Narrative and History in the Early Medieval West* (Turnhout, 2006), 39–65, at 53; see also P. Wormald, 'A handlist of Anglo-Saxon lawsuits', *Anglo-Saxon England* 17 (1988): 247–81.

[21]  See for example D.F. Johnson, 'The fall of Lucifer in Genesis A and two Anglo-Latin royal charters', *Journal of English and Germanic Philology* 97:4 (1998): 500–21; see also S.E. Kelly, 'Anglo-Saxon Lay Society and the Written Word', in McKitterick (ed.), *The Uses of Literacy in Early Mediaeval Europe*, 36–62, at 44.

some of the surviving illustrated books were associated with lay people: David F. Johnson suggests that the early eleventh-century illustrated copy of the Old English Hexateuch, now London, British Library, Cotton Claudius B.iv, might be a contender here, although on balance it seems more likely that this book belonged to a religious house.[22] But whether lay or religious, manuscript art is essentially private because it is contained in books and viewed by small groups of people, unlike the 'public' images painted on walls or carved into stone sculptures. It is difficult to know how to interpret public visual representations too, because it is not always clear how visible such images were, or how far people might have understood the theological complexities that lay behind them.[23] And although archaeological evidence is valuable in understanding practices which were not necessarily limited to quite such a small number of noble or ecclesiastical individuals, this too has difficulties of interpretation. While texts describe practice and state belief, even if the reliability of these is variable, archaeological remains only reveal practices, so that belief must always be conjectured.[24] Moreover, the most useful archaeological evidence for the issues discussed in this book comes from burials and cemeteries, and the archaeology of death brings its own problems of interpretation: it is difficult to know whose practices burials represent, especially when these are tied up with aspects of social or religious control, as in the case of the burial of criminals.[25]

The importance of theology for understanding all of these sources is the extent to which it lies behind them. The evidence that now survives in Anglo-Saxon texts and images, and in the archaeology of Christian death, was primarily written, designed, commissioned and orchestrated by people who were part of, or influenced by, a tradition of Christian learning. Anglo-Saxon theology

---

[22]  D.F. Johnson, 'A Program of Illumination in the Old English Illustrated Hexateuch: "Visual Typology"?', in R. Barnhouse and B.C. Withers (eds), *The Old English Hexateuch: Aspects and Approaches* (Kalamazoo, MI, 2000), 165–99, at 194–5; in contrast, for the suggestion that a female audience may have been intended for the manuscript, see C.E. Karkov, 'The Anglo-Saxon Genesis: Text, Illustration, and Audience', in R. Barnhouse and B.C. Withers (eds), *The Old English Hexateuch: Aspects and Approaches* (Kalamazoo, MI, 2000), 201–37, at 206–7. There are also exceptional cases of Latin manuscripts in lay ownership, as for example the book of patristic Latin texts owned by Æthelweard the Younger (see S. Keynes, 'Cnut's Earls', in A.R. Rumble (ed.), *The Reign of Cnut: King of England, Denmark and Norway* (London, 1994), 43–88, at 67–70; C. Cubitt, 'Ælfric's Lay Patrons', in Magennis and Swan (eds), *A Companion to Ælfric*, 165–92, at 182.

[23]  See below, 101–3.

[24]  See below, 265–7.

[25]  See below, 278–313; also M. Parker Pearson, 'The powerful dead: Archaeological relationships between the living and the dead', *Cambridge Archaeological Journal* 3:2 (1993): 203–29, at 203–7; M. Parker Pearson, *The Archaeology of Death and Burial* (Stroud, 1999), 11–17; A.J. Reynolds, *Anglo-Saxon Deviant Burial Customs* (Oxford, 2009), 34–60.

has sometimes been viewed as static or derivative,[26] but the imagination and innovation of Anglo-Saxon authors has been stressed in recent years, and this is significant: Aron Gurevich observed that 'theological thought, which is apparently constrained by tradition, does not nevertheless remain stationary, but is constantly developing as it responds to changes in social world understanding'.[27] While this is undoubtedly true, the flipside of this is that society and social world understanding are also influenced by changes in theological thought. It is clear too that Christian beliefs, or perhaps better, the beliefs of Christians, are not limited to the formal tenets of the Christian faith because they encompass, incorporate and exist within the broader realm of culture and lived experience. Moreover, much of what might be termed 'culture', or cultural ideas or beliefs, is not transmitted through explicit tuition, but rather is absorbed, acquired or inferred from social situations, practices or interactions.[28] The close examination of a wide variety of sources undertaken in this study therefore sheds light both on Anglo-Saxon theology and on Anglo-Saxon society, so that homilies can help to make sense of charters, archaeological evidence can help to interpret anecdotal accounts in saints' lives, or place-names can cast a different light on the rituals of baptism and the funerary liturgy as well as on the homilies that describe these rituals. Although not always easy to read, real or attempted communications of ideas and beliefs are visible in the surviving sources, as are decisions over how practices were determined, undertaken or enforced. Theology is woven in and out of these, where it is found informing particular approaches, or pressed into action to interpret a given situation.

Of course, some areas of theology were undoubtedly remote from the daily lives of Anglo-Saxon Christian communities: Bede's careful and complex discussion of what precisely was meant in a particular passage of Isaiah probably would not have seemed immediately relevant (or comprehensible) to most Anglo-Saxon men and women.[29] But this study shows that theology did form part of the experience of Anglo-Saxon Christian communities, often in the way it shaped or responded to events or practices, and this is explored here through case studies which focus on particular theological ideas, or on specific contexts which allow a way into understanding how theology was developed in, and responded to, different contexts in Anglo-Saxon England. Considering creation and the role of angels and devils in liturgy and landscape helps to bridge the gap between monasticism and the wider world in which monasteries were located (Chapter 2); a discussion of theology and the law reveals how theological ideas about mercy and judgement

---

[26]    See for example C.L. Wrenn, 'Some Aspects of Anglo-Saxon Theology', in E. Bagby Atwood and A.A. Hill (eds), *Studies in Language, Literature and Culture of the Middle Ages and Later* (Austin, 1969), 182–9, at 182.

[27]    A. Gurevich, 'Popular and scholarly medieval cultural traditions: Notes in the margins of Jacques Le Goff's book', *Journal of Medieval History* 9:2 (1983): 71–90, at 88.

[28]    P. Boyer, *The Naturalness of Religious Ideas: A Cognitive Theory of Religion* (Berkeley, 1994), 24.

[29]    Bede, *De eo quod ait Isaias 'Et claudentur'* (*Epistola* XV), *PL* 94.702–10.

shaped the ways that methods of proof such as oaths and ordeals and penalties such as capital punishment were understood and used (Chapter 3). Changing ideas about the immediate fate of the soul after death and especially the concept of purgatory are revealed through the gift-giving practices of Anglo-Saxon men and women and provide evidence for the communication of beliefs about the afterlife (Chapter 4); and the practical and theological responses to concerns over the body and its relationship to the soul attest to lively debates about eschatological ideas, and show how different beliefs might affect practices (Chapter 5). The rest of this chapter considers in more detail how the surviving evidence relates to 'popular' belief and culture, before setting out the institutional contexts in which Christian beliefs were communicated to Anglo-Saxon audiences between about 700 and 1100, and exploring the broader contexts of life and lived experience which also contributed to the range of beliefs of Christian Anglo-Saxons.

## Understanding Belief in the Early Middle Ages

Interpretations of early medieval religious beliefs have, unsurprisingly, changed significantly in the centuries that they have been scrutinised by scholars, as have the particular issues which most concerned those who have explored this topic. In the sixteenth century, both Protestant and Catholic scholars in England looked to early medieval religious belief and practice in Britain to provide evidence that their interpretation of Christianity was 'correct' and had the weight of antiquity on its side, and especially in the islands where religious beliefs and practices were being deliberated and challenged.[30] By the nineteenth century, scholars no longer looked for evidence that early medieval English or British people were like them in their faith, as the sixteenth-century antiquarians had done. Instead, many sought to demonstrate precisely the opposite, that early medieval belief was marked by credulity and gullibility and was therefore markedly different from the contemporary modern world. Henry Lea's study of ordeals and other legal practices in the early Middle Ages, entitled *Superstition and Force*, exemplifies

---

[30]    B. Gordon (ed.), *Protestant History and Identity in Sixteenth-Century Europe: Vol. 1, The Medieval Inheritance* (Aldershot, 1996); D. Nussbaum, 'Reviling the Saints or Reforming the Calendar? John Foxe and his 'Kalender' of Martyrs', in C.J. Litzenberger and S. Wabuda (eds), *Belief and Practice in Reformation England: A Tribute to Patrick Collinson from his Students* (Aldershot and Brookfield (VT), 1998), 113–36; B.S. Robinson, 'John Foxe and the Anglo-Saxons', in C. Highley and J.N. King (eds), *John Foxe and his World* (Aldershot, 2002), 54–72; F. Heal, 'What can King Lucius do for you? The Reformation and the early British Church', *English Historical Review* 120:487 (2005): 593–614; F. Heal, 'Appropriating History: Catholic and Protestant polemics and the national past', *Huntington Library Quarterly* 68:1/2 (2005): 109–32; A.J. Kleist, 'Anglo-Saxon Homiliaries in Tudor and Stuart England', in A.J. Kleist (ed.), *The Old English Homily: Precedent, Practice, and Appropriation* (Turnhout, 2007), 445–92; C. Highley, *Catholics Writing the Nation in Early Modern Britain and Ireland* (Oxford, 2008).

this approach: Lea argued that 'it is only in an age of high and refined mental culture that man can entertain an adequate conception of the Supreme Being', contrasting his own day with the 'limited reason' of the early medieval period, an age of 'comparative simplicity', in which 'miracles come to be expected as matters of every-day occurrence, and the laws of nature are to be suspended whenever man chooses to tempt his God with the promise of right and the threat of injustice to be committed in His name'.[31]

This kind of impression of early medieval religious belief was based on a rather uncritical reading of the surviving sources and informed primarily by the top-down picture presented by them, so that the early medieval period was perceived as an age of faith marked by credulity and mindless adherence to Christian teachings.[32] There were also attempts to consider belief more from the bottom up, but from some quarters this resulted in the rather extreme view that except in learned and elite contexts, paganism survived or was appropriated, so that 'Christianity' for many people was syncretistic, imperfectly learned or somehow detached from 'true Christianity'.[33] This too is problematic: although syncretism does seem to have occurred at various points in the early Middle Ages in England and elsewhere, as in Bede's description of the seventh-century East Anglian King Rædwald (who may or may not have been buried in Mound 1 at Sutton Hoo),[34] documented cases of prolonged syncretism (of the kind suggested by the proposed sharp division between learned and popular beliefs) are rare. Even more importantly, in the early Middle Ages as later there is no evidence that 'paganism' was deliberately maintained so that it existed in secret as a religion which was self-consciously opposed to Christianity.[35] In turn, therefore, this view too was rejected by many

---

[31]   H.C. Lea, *Superstition and Force: Essays on the Wager of Law – The Wager of Battle – The Ordeal – Torture* (Philadelphia, 1870), 86, 201.

[32]   This view has been completely discredited in scholarly literature but unfortunately still seems to exist in 'popular' works: see for example C. Freeman, *The Closing of the Western Mind: The Rise of Faith and the Fall of Reason* (New York, 2003), and as a useful corrective introduction, the essays in S.J. Harris and B.L. Grigsby, *Misconceptions about the Middle Ages* (London, 2008).

[33]   See for example J. Delumeau, *Le catholicisme entre Luther et Voltaire, Nouvelle Clio* (Paris, 1971).

[34]   Bede, *HE* II.15, ed. M. Lapidge, P. Monat and P. Robin, *Histoire ecclésiastique du peuple anglais = Historia ecclesiastica gentis Anglorum*, Sources chrétiennes 489–91 (3 vols, Paris, 2005), I.372–6; S. Keynes, 'Raedwald the Bretwalda', in C.B. Kendall and P.S. Wells (eds), *Voyage to the Other World: The Legacy of Sutton Hoo* (Minneapolis, MN, 1992), 103–23; M. Parker Pearson, R. Van de Noort and A. Woolf, 'Three men and a boat: Sutton Hoo and the east Saxon kingdom', *Anglo-Saxon England* 22 (1993): 27–50.

[35]   J. Arnold, *Belief and Unbelief in Medieval Europe* (London, 2005), 115–16; on what clerical writers meant by 'pagans', see R.A. Markus, 'Gregory the Great's Pagans', in R. Gameson and H. Leyser (eds), *Belief and Culture in the Middle Ages: Studies Presented to Henry Mayr-Harting* (Oxford, 2001), 23–34; J.T. Palmer, 'Defining paganism in the Carolingian world', *Early Medieval Europe* 15:4 (2007): 402–25; see also below, 57–9.

scholars in favour of a blurrier distinction between elite and clerical circles of belief and culture on the one hand, and unlearned or lay ('popular') circles on the other, as spheres of interest which were to some degree separate, but constantly in contact and certainly not isolated from each other.[36]

But as a number of scholars have pointed out, the key problem with this model of connected but rather compartmentalised circles of belief is that it assumes that 'types', 'classes' or 'social categories' of people held different beliefs, which implies in turn that these social groups were internally coherent and at the same time relatively distinct from one another.[37] Local priests are particularly good examples of why this is problematic, because as clergy they might be (and of course in the sources, often are) presented as a separate group from the laity; but many local priests were drawn from the communities which they served and their education may often have been basic or patchy, so that they might have shared more in common with their congregations than with bishops or highly educated monks.[38] And just as it is clear that some clergy were well educated and others were not, some laity (primarily elites) seem to have attained a considerable level of learning while others did not.[39] At the same time, the relationships between priests and those they served may also have been quite variable. The tenth-century will of Æthelgifu, an Anglo-Saxon noblewoman, illustrates precisely how the sharing of religious culture is not dependent on social or clerical status alone. Æthelgifu was a high-ranking lady who seems to have led some kind of quasi-religious life outside the cloister, and perhaps she could read, at least a little. In her will, she freed 'Eadwine, my priest', and asked that he offer three masses for

---

[36] J.-C. Schmitt, 'Au Moyen Age: culture folklorique, culture clandestine', *Revue du Vivarais* (1979): 143–8; J.-C. Schmitt, 'Les traditions folkloriques dans la culture médiévale. Quelques réflexions de méthode', *Archives de sciences sociales des religions* 52:1 (1981): 5–20; J. Le Goff, 'The Learned and Popular Dimensions of Journeys in the Otherworld in the Middle Ages', in S.L. Kaplan (ed.), *Understanding Popular Culture: Europe from the Middle Ages to the Nineteenth Century*, New Babylon Studies in the Social Sciences 40 (Berlin, 1984), 19–37, and the essays in J. Le Goff, *The Medieval Imagination*, trans. A. Goldhammer (Chicago, 1992).

[37] M. Rubin, *Corpus Christi: The Eucharist in Late Medieval Culture* (Cambridge, 1991); K.L. Jolly, *Popular Religion in Late Saxon England: Elf Charms in Context* (Chapel Hill, NC, 1996); C. Cubitt, 'Sites and sanctity: Revisiting the cult of murdered and martyred Anglo-Saxon royal saints', *Early Medieval Europe* 9 (2000): 53–83, at 54–8; C.S. Watkins, '"Folklore" and "popular religion" in Britain during the middle ages', *Folk-Lore* 115:2 (2004): 140–50.

[38] Cubitt, 'Sites and sanctity', 58; Watkins, '"Folklore" and "popular religion"', 141–2.

[39] See Kelly, 'Anglo-Saxon Lay Society and the Written Word'; E.M.C. van Houts, 'Women and the writing of history in the early middle ages: The case of Abbess Matilda of Essen and Æthelweard', *Early Medieval Europe* 1 (1992): 53–68; S. Ashley, 'The Lay Intellectual in Anglo-Saxon England: Ealdorman Æthelweard and the Politics of History', in J.L. Nelson and P. Wormald (eds), *Lay Intellectuals in the Carolingian World* (Cambridge, 2007), 218–45.

her each week.[40] Eadwine might have been Æthelgifu's confessor, and/or able to discuss with her such religious topics as she wanted, but it is not clear how well educated he would have been himself, and he was not even a free man.[41]

Recognition of these difficulties has led to acceptance by many scholars that medieval and early modern European 'popular' and 'elite' or 'clerical' belief and culture were much more closely integrated than once thought, and especially that elites (both lay and ecclesiastical) shared and participated in the beliefs and practices of non-elites to a significant degree, although there are differences of opinion over precisely how this may have worked. Karen Jolly presents Anglo-Saxon 'popular' and 'formal' religion as two overlapping spheres in which almost all 'formal' religion exists within the sphere of the 'popular': she argues that 'popular religion' is essentially the common Christian worldview which incorporates almost all aspects of Christianity broadly construed, including the formal practices of the Church and excluding only a few complex theological ideas such as *homoousios* (the idea that Christ is the same essence or substance as God), which she suggests was known to 'only a few scholars in the early Middle Ages'.[42] A similar (but perhaps more clearly defined) model is proposed by Carl Watkins, who argues that broadly speaking the spectrum included 'official beliefs', the core systematic teachings of the Church, and 'unofficial beliefs', which often varied locally and were much more fluid.[43] To a greater or lesser extent, he suggests, everyone held both official and unofficial beliefs, and that these 'existed within the interstices of official faith and ritual and churchmen did not *necessarily* see them as pagan, unChristian, heretical or erroneous',[44] although this does not mean there were no tensions between different beliefs or cultural values. He cautions, however, that although the distinction between 'official' and 'unofficial' beliefs might be clear to modern scholars, those living in local communities as well as local and diocesan clergy may not always have perceived such clear-cut distinctions.[45]

---

[40]    S 1497, ed. D. Whitelock, *The Will of Aethelgifu: A Tenth Century Anglo-Saxon Manuscript* (Oxford, 1968), and see 33–4: 'mon eadwine preost'; see also D.A.E. Pelteret, *Slavery in Early Mediaeval England: From the Reign of Alfred until the Twelfth Century*, Studies in Anglo-Saxon History (Woodbridge, 1995), 115; S. Foot, *Veiled Women: 1, The Disappearance of Nuns from Anglo-Saxon England; 2, Female Religious Communities in England, 871–1066* (Aldershot, 2000), I.139–41, II.183–6.

[41]    As a slave, Eadwine should in theory not have been allowed to be a priest: see Pelteret, *Slavery*, 115–18, 248.

[42]    Jolly, *Popular Religion*, 18–19. '... Deum verum de Deo vero, natum [genitum], non factum, consubstantialem Patri; per quem omni facta sunt' ('true God of true God, born, not created, of the same substance/essence as the Father').

[43]    Watkins, '"Folklore" and "popular religion"', 145–7.

[44]    Ibid., 146.

[45]    Ibid., 146. The idea that the distinction between 'official' and 'unofficial' beliefs could be rather fuzzy on the ground is borne out by anthropological research, which supports the idea that such distinctions are not always clear-cut to members of Christian

These are only two examples of a considerable body of scholarship, and these models and others like them are helpful in acting as a reminder that the experience of religious belief for many people was not simplistic, and consisted of more than either a tradition based on learning, or beliefs based on superstition.[46] But they are only helpful up to a point, and in considering religious belief and practice in Anglo-Saxon England it is important to bear in mind the significant social, religious and intellectual developments of the eleventh century, which would fundamentally change the way that the regulation of Christian belief and practice were conceptualised, and it is essential to remember how the situation was different before this. In this context the changing nature and perception of papal authority in the eleventh century (and subsequently) was particularly important. The pope had been held to be the spiritual head of all Christians since well before the Christianisation of the Anglo-Saxons, but effective institutional control from the papacy in matters of jurisdiction and belief was only really achieved fairly late in the eleventh century.[47] Before this time, the papacy was essentially responsive and reactive rather than active in its approach to questions of belief and practice: the pope might act as final arbiter in certain kinds of disputes, or show papal authority in the grants of privileges or immunities, or confirm (but perhaps not appoint) certain candidates for archbishoprics or bishoprics, but the extent to which successive popes were concerned with more general belief and practice for Christians outside Rome was fairly limited.[48] This is not to say that the pope was

---

communities who hold and practise those beliefs. See for example the study of a rural community in modern Greece, where it was observed that people did not distinguish clearly between the central tenets of their denomination of Christianity and other beliefs (such as the evil eye) which are not officially part of Orthodox teaching: H.A. Forbes, *Meaning and Identity in a Greek Landscape: An Archaeological Ethnography* (New York, 2007), 350–2.

[46] See also (for example) B. Scribner, 'Is a history of popular culture possible?', *History of European Ideas* 10:2 (1989): 175–91; Cubitt, 'Sites and sanctity'; P. Burke, 'History and folklore: A historiographical survey', *Folk-Lore* 115:2 (2004): 133–9; C. Cubitt, 'Folklore and Historiography: Oral Stories and the Writing of Anglo-Saxon History', in R. Balzaretti and E.M. Tyler (eds), *Narrative and History in the Early Medieval West* (Turnhout, 2006), 189–223; E. Duffy, 'Elite and popular religion: the Book of Hours and lay piety in the later Middle Ages', in K. Cooper and J. Gregory (eds), *Elite and Popular Religion: papers read at the 2004 Summer Meeting and the 2005 Winter Meeting of the Ecclesiastical History*, Studies in Church History 42 (Woodbridge, 2006): 140–61; N.P. Tanner, *The Ages of Faith: Popular Religion in Late Medieval England and Western Europe* (London, 2009).

[47] See for example H.E.J. Cowdrey, *Pope Gregory VII, 1073–1085* (Oxford, 1998), 423–80, 520–9; K.G. Cushing, *Reform and the Papacy in the Eleventh Century: Spirituality and Social Change*, Manchester Medieval Studies (Manchester, 2005), 55–81.

[48] See for example J.M. Wallace-Hadrill, *The Frankish Church*, Oxford History of the Christian Church (Oxford, 1983), 110–22, 276–8, 295–7; B.H. Rosenwein, *Negotiating Space: Power, Restraint, and Privileges of Immunity in Early Medieval Europe* (Manchester, 1999), 106–12, 133–4, 156–83; J. Moorhead, 'Bede on the papacy', *Journal of Ecclesiastical History* 60:2 (2009): 217–32; F. Tinti, 'England and the Papacy in the Tenth Century', in

insignificant or had no influence at all, but it is reasonable to say that in the early Middle Ages the active identification and enforcement of correct Christian belief and practice for the whole Church was not usually one of the major tasks of either the pope, or the papal organisation.[49]

In the early Middle Ages, questions of belief and practice were often considered more in the context of theological discussion rather than as official statements from the papacy or from papal councils.[50] It is worth bearing in mind that the effects of the significant developments in theology from the later eleventh century means that here too there are quite striking differences between the earlier and later Middle Ages. In some cases there are clear distinctions in approach which help to explain why these theological changes are significant in understanding how belief was set down and perceived. An early example of this is *Sic et Non*, a text put together by Peter Abelard (d.1142): this presented contradictory statements from patristic texts, inviting (but not offering) resolution, and was intended as an exercise for students.[51] But this was foreign to the working methods of many early medieval writers: Ælfric, for example, was inclined to treat conflicting statements in separate works rather than to deal directly with apparently divergent opinions, at least partly because he was often quite closely dependent on the Scriptural and patristic authorities that he used.[52] Even here though there are visible differences among Anglo-Saxon authors. Bede at least occasionally explained and resolved apparent contradictions, or analysed and corrected the opinions of previous authors.[53] Ultimately, the pastoral focus of much early medieval theology means that when Anglo-Saxon authors treated theological topics, they were often trying to set them down as they applied to their congregations, and what was discussed or determined was frequently reactive or recapitulative, and responded to the point raised without trying to examine an issue from all angles.[54] In contrast, scholars

---

C. Leyser, D.W. Rollason and H. Williams (eds), *England and the Continent in the Tenth Century: Studies in Honour of Wilhelm Levison (1876–1947)* (Turnhout, 2011), 163–84.

[49]   Blair, *The Church*, 506–7; Cushing, *Reform and the Papacy in the Eleventh Century*, 60–86.

[50]   See M.L. Colish, 'The Early Scholastics and the Reform of Doctrine and Practice', in M.B. Christopher and I.H. Louis (eds), *Reforming Church before Modernity* (Aldershot, 2005), 61–8.

[51]   See *Sic et Non*, prol., ed. B.B. Boyer and R. McKeon, *Sic et Non: A Critical Edition* (Chicago, 1977), 89–104, for Abelard's explanation of the purpose and function of the work.

[52]   See for example M.M. Gatch, *Preaching and Theology in Anglo-Saxon England: Aelfric and Wulfstan* (Toronto, 1977), 4–17; and the discussion of Ælfric's theology in L. Grundy, *Books and Grace: Ælfric's Theology*, King's College London Medieval Studies 6 (London, 1991).

[53]   See for example the essays in S. DeGregorio, *Innovation and Tradition in the Writings of the Venerable Bede* (Morgantown, 2006).

[54]   This was the case often but not always: see for example the discussion in M.L. Colish, 'Carolingian debates over nihil and tenebrae: A study in theological method',

like Abelard and those who followed him often invited questions from both sides, at least partly in an attempt to explore and to systematise belief, and so also to determine what should be considered as correct belief.

The effects of these ecclesiastical and intellectual developments were significant, because it means that from the latter part of the eleventh century there were two key changes in how belief was discussed and considered. On the one hand scholars were attempting to explore and elucidate belief in new ways, while on the other the papacy was more actively seeking to establish and mandate belief from the top. This is quite different from the situation in earlier centuries, and there are three key points here. Firstly, there are a number of areas where it is impossible for the modern scholar – let alone local communities in the early Middle Ages – to identify one official line which represents the beliefs of 'the Church' on such issues. Secondly, even for topics where there is more clearly an official or more universally accepted line, this does not always mean that 'the Church' attempted to mandate that belief, given the limits of the papacy before the later eleventh century. And thirdly, it is questionable how useful the concept of 'the Church' even is in this period, given that for most people the experience of religion and belief was profoundly local or regional, and based in small communities.[55] In particular, it is worth noting that some clergy simply took a harder line than others in terms of what they would or would not accept, so that horizontal variance in belief within one 'group' or 'type' of people is at least as significant as vertical variance in belief across different levels of society.[56] The cumulative effect of all this is that what was believed and practised in any given local area may have been quite variable, both in terms of what was taught by the priest or other ecclesiastics, and in terms of what other beliefs might have circulated locally. Medieval theologians, clerics and religious writers may have liked to think that they had a monopoly on belief, but it is clear that this was never the case.

The difficulty of identifying an official line of belief is exemplified in the range of beliefs about the afterlife, especially the concept of purgatory and the fate of the soul immediately after death and before the Last Judgement. There are few systematic explanations or discussions of purgatory in surviving Anglo-Saxon (or other early medieval) texts, whether intended for lay education or as academic theological discourse. Bede and Ælfric discussed purgatory, but the works of other Anglo-Saxon scholars do not consider purgatory in any detail.[57] Archbishop

*Speculum: A Journal of Medieval Studies* 59:4 (1984): 757–95.

55 See P. Brown, *The Rise of Western Christendom: Triumph and Diversity, AD 200–1000* (Oxford, 2003), 355–79.

56 See for example see R.A. Markus, 'From Caesarius to Boniface: Christianity and Paganism in Gaul', in J. Fontaine and J.N. Hillgarth (eds), *Le Septième siècle: Changements et continuités. Actes du Colloque bilatéral franco-britannique tenu au Warburg Institute les 8–9 juillet 1988*, Studies of the Warburg Institute 42 (London, 1992), 154–72.

57 See below, 203–12.

Wulfstan seems not to have referred to purgatory in his entire corpus of writings, and one sixteenth-century reader of his sermons noted approvingly that Wulfstan appears to express the idea that souls go only to heaven or hell after death, with no possibility of an alternative interim condition.[58] It has been argued that purgatory emerged from 'popular belief' and that theologians and ecclesiastics were simply forced to accept it, sanction it, and make it official, and that purgatory did not exist at all in this period and would be 'born' only in the late twelfth century.[59] Chapter 4 examines belief in purgatory as one of the case studies for the transmission and effect of theological ideas, and concludes not only that it did exist in this period, but also that it was quite widely believed. But widespread or not, it is difficult to determine from the surviving evidence whether purgatory counted as official teaching in this period since it is so infrequently mentioned, even if it is only discussed by those who were the academic and orthodox giants of their day. In this the contrast between the early and high or late Middle Ages is marked.

The surviving sources show that what was determined, promoted or objected to depended on local context and particular individuals, sometimes simply those who shouted the loudest, and here it is significant that some concepts which were rejected by Anglo-Saxon authors would in due course be established as canonical or be considered mainstream doctrine. The passage of time determined that Ælfric was over-cautious in a number of areas, such as his apparent rejection of the concept that would become transubstantiation.[60] This issue had already caused

---

[58]    See the marginal note in Cambridge, Corpus Christi College, 201, p. 20, printed and discussed in D. Bethurum, *The Homilies of Wulfstan* (Oxford, 1957), 225, 339, see also 25: 'Hic Archiepiscopus Wulfstanus diserte negat tertium locum post hanc vitam'.

[59]    Gurevich, 'Popular and scholarly'; J. Le Goff, *The Birth of Purgatory*, trans. A. Goldhammer (Chicago, 1984), 1–14 and *passim*; see also C.S. Watkins, 'Sin, penance and purgatory in the Anglo-Norman realm: The evidence of visions and ghost stories', *Past and Present* 175:1 (2002): 3–33; C.S. Watkins, *History and the Supernatural in Medieval England* (Cambridge, 2007), 180–5, 230–1.

[60]    Ælfric, *CH* II.1, ll. 86–148 (and esp. 124–8), ed. M. Godden, *Ælfric's Catholic Homilies: The Second Series Text* EETS, SS 5 (Oxford, 1979), 152–4: 'Micel is betwux þære ungesewenlican mihte þæs halgan husles. and þam gesewenlican hiwe agenes gecyndes; Hit is on gecynde brosniendlic hláf. and brosniendlic wín. and is æfter mihte godcundes wordes. soðlice cristes lichama and his blód. na swa ðeah lichamlice. ac gastlice' ('There is a great difference between the invisible power of the holy Eucharist and the visible appearance of its own nature: in nature it is corruptible bread and corruptible wine, and after the power of the divine word, it truly becomes Christ's body and his blood, not bodily, however, but spiritually'); *Pastoral Letter* I. 138–40, ed. Fehr, *Die Hirtenbriefe Ælfrics*, 30: 'þæt husel is Cristes lichama, na lichamlice ac gastlice. Na se lichama, þe he on þrowode, ac se lichama, þe he embe spræc. Þa-þa he bletsode hlaf and win to husle anre nihte ær his þrowunge ... ' ('the Eucharist is Christ's body, though not bodily but spiritually. Not the body in which he suffered, but the body which he spoke about when he blessed bread and wine for the Eucharist, the night before his passion ... '). See also H. Magennis, 'Ælfric Scholarship', in Magennis and Swan (eds), *A Companion to Ælfric*, 5–34, at 9–11.

serious disagreement in the Carolingian world in the ninth century, and, like purgatory, continued to be the subject of much discussion: even in the later Middle Ages when the general premise was accepted, there was still significant debate over the details. Transubstantiation was widely accepted later, but many people (both highly educated and less well educated) evidently found transubstantiation a difficult belief to accept, and perhaps also to understand.[61] The nature of the surviving Anglo-Saxon evidence makes it almost impossible to determine how widely accepted was the belief that when bread and wine was consecrated in the mass it turned literally and physically into the body and blood of Christ, but the evidence of Ælfric's over-cautiousness (as it would turn out) acts as a warning that some of his objections ought perhaps to be taken with a pinch of salt since his claims for orthodoxy may in fact have gone against the grain, even if he genuinely had found little evidence for some of the beliefs to which he objected in the works he read. This highlights too how access to resources, or library books, might in some cases affect which beliefs were accepted or rejected by learned local authorities.

It is worth noting too that the complaints of vociferous clergy were not always held up on appeal, highlighting both the multiplicity of beliefs and the rather random nature of what was, or was not, determined to be acceptable in any given local context. A clear example of this is found in an incident discussed in a letter of 746 written to Boniface by Pope Zacharias, who complained about Boniface's decision to rebaptize certain individuals who had already been baptized by a priest whose Latin was poor. The priest had mangled the Latin words so that instead of baptizing 'in nomine patris et filii et spiritus sancti' ('in the name of the Father, the Son, and the Holy Spirit'), he baptized instead 'in nomine patria et filia et spiritus sancti' ('in the name of the Holy Spirit with the fatherland and the daughter'). Boniface's objections were not received well by Pope Zacharias, who wrote as his immediate superior to inform him that since poor Latin was not (quite) akin to heresy, it was unnecessary to insist on rebaptism, itself unorthodox if not performed for appropriate reasons.[62] This disagreement may have arisen in part because in the early Middle Ages sacramental theology had not really been explored in detail as it would be later, and in this period the number of sacraments, their nature, and even what made something a sacrament was not a matter of universal agreement, so that the theology of the sacraments was itself subject to debate.[63] Perhaps more

---

[61]    See for example C. Chazelle, 'Exegesis in the Ninth-Century Eucharist Controversy', in C. Chazelle and B.v.N. Edwards (eds), *The Study of the Bible in the Carolingian Era* (Turnhout, 2003), 167–87; and Rubin, *Corpus Christi*, 30–7, 53–5, 121–4, 327–8.

[62]    *Epistola* 68, ed. Tangl, *Die Briefe*, 140–2.

[63]    Pope Zacharias seems to take the approach which would later become standard, that the intention and matter (water) were crucial for the sacrament and so confusion in the wording would not immediately invalidate it (e.g. Augustine, *Tractatus in Iohannis euangelium*, 80.3, ll. 5–6, ed. R. Willems, *Sancti Aurelii Augustini in Iohannis Euangelium*

importantly, it is worth considering too how this must have been received on the ground and the confusion that this may have caused for new Christians attempting to learn about their faith and the purpose of baptism.

This instance of disagreement is also important as a cautionary reminder about the nature of the extant evidence. As in so many cases, only one side of the story survives: neither Boniface's original instructions in his own words, nor his response to this letter, are now extant. If the letter from Pope Zacharias had not survived, and instead a manuscript preserved a letter from Boniface instructing that rebaptism was necessary in such cases of priestly incompetence in Latin, modern scholars might assume that Boniface's letter represented the belief of 'the Church', since Boniface was the local figure of authority and by 746, he was also archbishop and papal legate. The surviving letter, like Ælfric's comments on the Eucharist, underlines the variability of theological belief in different places and how much this was dependent on local ecclesiastical officials, even extremely learned ones. This is significant in remembering that theological beliefs cannot be cast as rigid, unchanging and monolithic in comparison to fluid and flexible local 'popular' beliefs. One of the dangers in the various models put forward for understanding beliefs is therefore that in looking for the popular, the role and nature of more academic beliefs and the variability of theology is forgotten. People living in an area with a Boniface or an Ælfric might have been told more categorically and perhaps more frequently what was, and was not, deemed acceptable, but this may have been more limited, or simply different from, what higher authorities expected.

These tensions also point to another difficulty with many of the models for understanding belief. Ultimately, even while recognising that the dividing lines are not clear-cut, they tend to perpetuate a top-down perspective because they continue to distinguish between 'what is certainly acceptable to the Church', usually linked to literate and scholarly traditions, and 'what may be, but may not be, acceptable to the Church', some of which may be linked to local or place-bound traditions. Certain types of beliefs evade easy categorisation and sit uncomfortably in models like those proposed by Jolly or Watkins, because it is not easy to know where to place them or how to fit them into the categories which these models include. For example, heretical beliefs cut across the division between learned and unlearned, 'popular' and 'formal', or the beliefs of the masses and the beliefs of the few; they are identified in opposition to another tradition, and from the outside – in that the heretic assumes that he or she holds correct belief – but where beliefs were identified as heretical they were not discussed by contemporaries in ways which allow easy categorisation. It has been argued that the reason that so few

---

*Tractatus CXXIV*, CCSL 36 (Turnhout, 1954), 529: 'accedit verbum ad elementum et fit sacramentum'). In contrast, Boniface's rigid insistence on the correct wording of the liturgy suggests that he believed the performative aspect of the sacrament to be critical, so that pronouncing the correct formula effected sacramental change, almost like 'magic words'. See also H. Vorgrimler, *Sacramental Theology* (Collegeville, MN, 1992), 43–55.

cases of heresy are recorded in the early Middle Ages is precisely because official beliefs were not universally identified and uniformity was not demanded from the top, whether out of disinclination or inability.[64] Many beliefs which did provoke complaints of heresy from groups or individuals had originated in learned contexts, and/or were held (at least initially) by small groups of people: it is therefore not particularly useful to consider these as 'popular' or 'unofficial' beliefs in the usual sense, and they are not place-bound in the sense of being tied to the landscape.

A good example of these different kinds of beliefs side by side is found in the condemnation of two heretics in the mid eighth century, first at a provincial synod in Francia and later at a Roman synod, and recorded in the collected correspondence associated with Boniface.[65] Here it is also possible to see the objections of local figures of authority, like Boniface, to the beliefs which they identified as problematic in their areas of jurisdiction, and it is clear that such issues were identified at local or regional level and passed upwards when further problems were encountered, rather than being determined in the first instance by universalising or top-downward decrees. The individuals condemned for heresy were Aldebert, a Gaul, and Clemens, an Irishman, and the letter from Boniface to Pope Zacharias recorded that although they differed in the form of the error, they were alike in the weight of their sins.[66] Aldebert was accused of all manner of wickedness and seems to have sparked some popular following as a miracle-worker: among other offences, he apparently dedicated oratories to himself, gave out his fingernails and hair as relics, and declared that there was no need for confession, because he knew all hidden sins.[67] In contrast, Clemens is reported to have denied the writings of the holy fathers (Jerome, Augustine and Gregory are specifically mentioned), to have revived Jewish law and thus to have insisted that it is right for a Christian to marry his brother's widow, and to have declared that when Christ descended to hell he released all who were there, worshippers of God and idols alike.[68]

The beliefs of Clemens are described as the 'incorrect' interpretation of written texts, and at least some of what was attributed to him seems to have originated from a reading of Scripture and patristic writings. This suggests that despite the

---

[64]   R.I. Moore, *The Formation of a Persecuting Society: Authority and Deviance in Western Europe, 950–1250* (Oxford, 2007), 66–8.

[65]   *Epistolae* 57, 59, 62, ed. Tangl, *Die Briefe*, 102–5, 108–20, 127–8.

[66]   *Epistola* 59, ed. Tangl, *Die Briefe*, 110, ll. 2–5: 'Unus, qui dicitur Eldebert, natione generis Gallus est, alter, qui dicitur Clemens, genere Scottus est; specie erroris diversi, sed pondere peccatorum conpares'.

[67]   *Epistola* 59, ed. Tangl, *Die Briefe*, 111, l. 11 – 112, l. 12.

[68]   *Epistola* 59, ed. Tangl, *Die Briefe*, 112, ll. 13–29. He apparently meant the liberation of souls at the harrowing of hell rather than universal salvation: see M.M. Gatch, 'The harrowing of Hell: A liberation motif in medieval theology and devotional literature', *Union Seminary Quarterly Review* 36 Suppl. (1981): 75–88; K. Tamburr, *The Harrowing of Hell in Medieval England* (Cambridge, 2007).

inevitable polemic and stereotyping which accompany such accusations of heresy, the disagreement here arose in the context of learning and interpretation of Scripture rather than out of 'unofficial' or 'popular' beliefs, and Clemens is not recorded as having had any kind of popular following. This is rather different from Aldebert, who has sometimes been associated with nature worship and paganism,[69] although this is probably wishful thinking. It is clear that what Aldebert was accused of was perceived as Christian heresy and incorporated Christian structures and hierarchies (Aldebert himself was ordained bishop, for example) even if he presented an alternative to the religious beliefs and practices espoused by Boniface and others. On the other hand, the reported actions of Aldebert do give some insight into the more place-bound beliefs which might be associated with local saints' cults, for example. It is also clear that while Aldebert's reported beliefs have elements which might be deemed or identified as 'popular', he was not utterly detached from the world of learning. A number of written texts were brought as evidence against Aldebert, including what was purportedly a *Life* written about him; a letter supposedly used by Aldebert which he said was from Jesus and fell down from heaven; and a prayer including the names of many angels.[70] These clearly show contact with Christian liturgy, learning and apocryphal traditions, although it is of course possible that they were simply found (or invented) by his opponents and attached to his name without good reason.

Boniface and the various councils did not reject the beliefs of either Aldebert or Clemens because these were 'popular' or outside the world of formal religion, or because they were at the wrong end of a spectrum of official and unofficial belief, or because they were 'pagan'. The beliefs of Aldebert and Clemens were rejected by Boniface and other figures of authority because they did not agree with what was perceived by that select group to be the correct interpretation of Christianity, but this apparent unity of belief should not overshadow the fact that Boniface also did not always agree with his superiors, as the correspondence over rebaptism indicates. Moreover, while the Frankish and Roman councils which condemned Aldebert and Clemens were unified in their agreement that the beliefs of these men were not unacceptable, there is no recorded attempt to identify and set down the appropriate beliefs about these matters. This is significant because the identification of unacceptable belief does not necessarily determine what is considered to be correct or acceptable belief, and in extreme cases like those of Aldebert or Clemens it might have been perfectly clear that these beliefs were not acceptable to any of the bishops involved even if in fact individual episcopal interpretations of some aspects of a particular belief, such as the harrowing, might not have agreed in all the details. This contrasts significantly with later approaches: the first canon of IV Lateran, for example, is an expanded version of the creed which identifies

---

[69]   V.I.J. Flint, *The Rise of Magic in Early Medieval Europe* (Oxford, 1991), 168–72.

[70]   *Epistola* 59, ed. Tangl, *Die Briefe*, 114, l. 14 – 115, l. 29, 116, l. 35 – 117, l. 19.

the accepted interpretation of some of the credal statements,[71] but this highlights how difficult it is to take even the credal statements as clear evidence for 'Church teaching' or 'official' belief, because the bare bones of the creeds are not absolute and are subject to interpretation.

It is also significant that in some cases there was little difference between beliefs and practices which occurred locally and to which local figures of authority objected, and the beliefs that those same local figures of authority held themselves. One example is in the context of the cults of saints and the local veneration of saints. In summary, theological belief about sanctity and the cults of saints held that miracles might occur at the places where the bodily remains of certain holy individuals rested, or at places which were somehow associated with them or with their deeds in life. This belief underpins the veneration of established saints such as St Peter or St Oswald (in later Anglo-Saxon England) as much as it underpinned the veneration of newer saints such as St Eadburh, or those about whom little was known. Somtimes local veneration of individuals or places seem to have caused clerical condemnation; importantly, however, this was not always based on different beliefs, but could rather stem from a different understanding of how particular beliefs should be applied, and in some cases perhaps also political exigency. One example of this is the growing cult of Waltheof, an English earl who had been executed in 1076 and whose body had been translated after it was found incorrupt in 1085.[72] In 1102, the Council of Westminster condemned new veneration of the bodies of the dead, or springs or other things, without episcopal authority, and it is possible that this canon applied at least partly to Waltheof's cult.[73] Archbishop Anselm of Canterbury (d.1109) also wrote to the nuns at Romsey (and to Stephen, the archdeacon of Winchester) in 1102 to forbid their veneration of an unnamed man as a saint.[74]

---

[71] IV Lateran (1215), 1, ed. N.P. Tanner, *Decrees of the Ecumenical Councils* (2 vols, London, 1990), I. 230. This is too long to quote in full but for example, this expanded creed specifically affirms belief in transubstantiation, the indivisibility of the Holy Trinity, and that the bodies which will be resurrected are the same as those fleshly bodies that we have now – none of which is outlined specifically in the creed.

[72] See E. Cownie, *Religious Patronage in Anglo-Norman England, 1066–1135* (Woodbridge, 1998), 119–21, at 126; P.A. Hayward, 'Translation-narratives in post-conquest hagiography and English resistance to the Norman Conqest', *Anglo-Norman Studies* 21 (1998): 67–93, at 92.

[73] Council of Westminster (1102), 27, *Councils and Synods*, I.ii, no. 113: 'Ne quis temeraria novitate corporibus mortuorum aut fontibus aut aliis rebus, quod contigisse cognovimus, sine episcopali auctoritate reverentiam sanctitatis exhibeat'. See also the Council at London (25 December 1074 x 28 August 1075), 8, *Councils and Synods*, I.ii, no. 92.

[74] *Epistolae* 236, 237, ed. F.S. Schmitt, *S. Anselmi Cantuariensis Archiepiscopi, opera omnia* (Edinburgh, 1946–61), IV.144–5; Hayward, 'Translation-narratives in post-conquest hagiography', 92.

What this example shows is of course not an objection to the cults of saints, nor to the theological beliefs which underpinned the practices surrounding the veneration of saints. Anselm and his colleagues all believed in saints, in their miracles, and in the veneration which was due to them. What they objected to was people or places being venerated as holy when they had not been approved by episcopal sanction and brought under ecclesiastical control.[75] Similar examples are visible throughout the Middle Ages, from the dubious individual venerated by locals but discredited by St Martin in the fourth century, to the three local cults which the fourteenth-century bishop of Exeter, John Grandisson, sought to eradicate.[76] And although in some cases they simply repeat or translate earlier proscriptions, some of the earlier Anglo-Saxon objections to local practices should probably be viewed in this light. Ælfric's complaints about holy wells, trees or stones echo and repeat those of writers from late Antiquity, and such objections continued throughout the Middle Ages, but it is possible that some of what Ælfric, like Anselm or John Grandisson, disliked was the fact that these had grown up outside local ecclesiastical control. Crucially, what this means is that in many cases local or 'popular' belief must in fact have been incredibly close to the beliefs of local clergy and figures of authority, whether those individuals were the most learned or the most ignorant ecclesiastical officials. Differentiating between these beliefs is a question of shades of grey, not the black and white distinctions of 'correct' or 'incorrect' that the surviving sources often present.

In understanding how a local figure of authority like a Boniface or an Ælfric might have perceived the range of beliefs he encountered, it is useful to compare the status accorded to different types of visions by the modern Roman Catholic Church. Private revelations to individuals do not have the status of Scripture, which is the public Revelation of God to humanity, but the Church may accept (or simply not discredit) the validity of certain revelations without considering them as fundamental to Catholic belief.[77] Thus Scripture is 'proved' or 'approved';

---

[75]   A. Walsham, *The Reformation of the Landscape: Religion, Identity, and Memory in Early Modern Britain and Ireland* (Oxford, 2011), 38–9, 66–9; see also Hayward, 'Translation-narratives in post-conquest hagiography', 81–3 for discussion of the possible lack of episcopal validation for the translation of saints by Abbess Ælfgifu at Barking; and P. Fouracre, 'The Origins of the Carolingian Attempt to Regulate the Cult of Saints', in J. Howard-Johnston and P.A. Hayward (eds), *The Cult of Saints in Late Antiquity and the Middle Ages: Essays on the Contribution of Peter Brown* (Oxford, 1999), 143–65, at 143–50.

[76]   N. Orme, 'Bishop Grandisson and popular religion', *Devonshire Association Report and Transactions* 124 (1992): 107–18.

[77]   *Catechism of the Catholic Church: Popular and Definitive Edition* (London, 2000), 22–3 (*c*.67): 'Throughout the ages, there have been so-called "private" revelations, some of which have been recognized by the authority of the Church. They do not belong, however, to the deposit of faith. It is not their role to improve or complete Christ's definitive Revelation, but to help live more fully by it in a certain period of history. Guided by the Magisterium of the Church, the *sensus fidelium* knows how to discern and welcome in these

private revelations may be 'unproved' or 'unverified' even if they are widely accepted (such as the apparition of the Virgin Mary at Fatima in 1917);[78] and still further visions are disapproved of, and rejected outright (such as those reported by Joseph Smith in 1823–1827, which ultimately led him to found the Church of Jesus Christ of Latter-Day Saints).[79] This tripartite distinction can also be found in the early Middle Ages even if it is not expressed in exactly this way, and even if these distinctions were identified personally and individually rather than institutionally. Thus for Boniface as for the modern Church, beliefs found in Scripture were 'proved' or 'approved'. A vision of the otherworld shown to a brother of the monastery of Wenlock was 'unproved' and 'unverified' in the sense that it was a private vision to an individual and not recorded in Scripture, but clearly Boniface accepted it as useful and considered it worth publicising, since he recorded it and took care to stress the closeness of his account to the visionary. In contrast, the visions of Aldebert were 'disapproved of' and emphatically rejected as contrary to 'correct' belief.

These are just three points in a personal perspective which would of course encompass and make judgements about many different beliefs encountered in the course of life, and there were presumably also some areas of belief which provoked less strong opinions, or where there was little consideration of which side of a line a particular issue might fall. Personal perspectives such as these are important because the exact range and variety of beliefs held by any one individual, and in turn the relative significance attached to different aspects of religious belief, are unlikely to be exactly replicated even by another follower of the same religion.[80] Aldebert, for example, clearly did not share precisely the same perspective as Boniface. Even those who were not in positions of authority to approve or disprove beliefs might have a clear idea of which beliefs they personally accepted or rejected. In this connection, the few cases of unbelief described in early medieval sources indicate that the rejection of beliefs of any kind was not limited to those who had been highly educated, and this is important too because although the transmission of Christian ideas (that is, Christian education in the

---

revelations whatever constitutes an authentic call of Christ or his saints to the Church'; K. Rahner, 'Über Visionen und verwandte Erscheinungen', *Geist und Leben* 21 (1948): 179–213; P. de Letter, 'Revelations, Private', *New Catholic Encyclopedia* 12 (Washington, DC, 2003), 202.

[78] M. O'Carroll, 'Apparitions', *Theotokos: A Theological Encyclopedia of the Blessed Virgin Mary* (Wilmington, DE, 1982), 47–8.

[79] See J. Smith, *The Book of Mormon: An Account Written by the Hand of Mormon upon Plates taken from the Plates of Nephi* (Liverpool, 1854); G. Hardy, *Understanding the Book of Mormon: A Reader's Guide* (Oxford, 2010).

[80] Examples from the modern world suggest that members of the same denomination of Christianity can apparently hold completely contradictory beliefs and yet to a certain extent negotiate the tensions arising from them, as illustrated by the issue of women's ordination in the Church of England.

broadest possible sense) is an important prerequisite for Christian belief, the fact that people were exposed to Christian education does not *prima facie* mean that they necessarily believed everything that they were taught.[81]

The surviving sources might give the impression that if preachers could only hammer in the right kind of information, heresy and unorthodoxy would be stamped out; but this is in large part because they often originated from clergy who were keen to push a reformist agenda, and in practice attempts to understand or refine theology and beliefs might in fact themselves be interpreted as heresy or heterodoxy (although a later example, Martin Luther is a case in point here). Ascertaining instances of unbelief or irreverence from the surviving evidence is difficult, but they are occasionally found in miracle stories as proof of the power of God or the saints. Context makes it difficult to trust these at one level since the purpose of the story is frequently to demonstrate divine or saintly power, but as Susan Reynolds cogently argues, such anecdotal accounts of unbelief would not be there if they did not bear some relation to reality.[82] One such account is found in Ælfric's *Life of St Swithun*, and Ælfric seems to have added this himself because it does not appear in his sources. Ælfric tells of a funeral wake at which someone joked and mocked Swithun by pretending to be him, until he fell down, senseless, and did not recover until he had been taken to St Swithun and begged forgiveness for his silliness.[83]

Another anecdote is found in the *Life of Ecgwine*, written in the early eleventh century by Byrhtferth, the school-master of Ramsey: this records the attempt by a 'rustic' to claim ownership of land which the monks claimed belonged to the saint.[84] The 'rustic' was required to swear an oath asserting his right to the land, and attempted to pervert the course of justice by placing in his shoe some earth from lands which were genuinely his own: this way, when he swore that he was standing on his own lands, he felt he was (near enough) telling the truth. The point of the story is to demonstrate St Ecgwine's sanctity and power, and so the 'rustic' was not allowed to escape unscathed but accidentally cut off his own head with his scythe, which indicated clearly that he had sworn the oath falsely. The story itself is a combination of literary construct and hagiographical intent, but is possible that behind these some elements of truth are buried. Byrhtferth had little information about St Ecgwine, who had lived in the late seventh/early eighth century, but this event is of course not supposed to have happened during Ecgwine's lifetime, and instead is recorded as having taken place while one Wigred was prior of Evesham.

---

[81]    S. Reynolds, 'Social mentalities and the case of medieval scepticism', *Transactions of the Royal Historical Society*, 6th series 1 (1991): 21–41, at 25–31.

[82]    Reynolds, 'Social mentalities and the case of medieval scepticism', Ibid., 29.

[83]    Ælfric, *Life of Swithun*, 19, ed. and trans. M. Lapidge, *The Cult of St Swithun*, Winchester Studies 4.ii (Oxford, 2003), 600–1.

[84]    *Vita S. Ecgwini*, iv.10, ed. M. Lapidge, *The Lives of St Oswald and St Ecgwine* (Oxford, 2009), 290–6 and see lxxxii–lxxxiii for the date; the anecdote is discussed in Wormald, *Making of English Law*, 158–9; Cubitt, 'Folklore and Historiography', 199–200.

Wigred himself is another figure about whom little is known but later writers placed this episode in a chronology which suggests that it took place in the late tenth or early eleventh century, and so perhaps roughly contemporaneously with Byrhtferth's composition of the *Life*, if the later chronology can be trusted.[85]

It is worth stressing again that the accounts that Byrhtferth and other writers presented did need to be credible to their audiences, even if these were audiences predominantly made up of well-educated men and women in religious life. Early medieval hagiographies often present those who scoffed at the power of the saints as stupid or delusional rather than atheistic, and true atheism in the modern sense seems unlikely in the early Middle Ages, at least on the basis of the present evidence.[86] On the other hand, while Byrhtferth's context for writing did not admit the possibility that someone could get away with such a trick, clearly the peasant thought otherwise, or he would not have tried it.[87] Seeing through accounts of the miraculous like this one in order to find evidence of 'what actually happened' is challenging, and understanding how these miracles appeared to contemporaries is also difficult. It is clear that there were no pervading early medieval *mentalités* which made all people think in a particular way (specifically, one which is supposedly different from modern people or modern scholars).[88] In the same way, it is inappropriate and inaccurate to assume that events which look peculiar in different societies might seem quite normal to people within those societies because of their worldview.[89] Whether people believed in (for example) invisible spirits or not, it did not mean that they considered these spirits 'normal' or unfrightening, that they ever expected to see them, or even that they did not find the idea of angels and devils as unsettling as many people might do today: they

---

[85]   Lapidge (ed.), *The Lives of St Oswald and St Ecgwine*, 291, n. 81.

[86]   There are few discussions of medieval atheism, but those studies which have been undertaken usually focus on the later Middle Ages. See for example F. Niewöhner and O. Pluta, *Atheismus im Mittelalter und in der Renaissance* (Wiesbaden, 1999); O. Pluta, 'Atheismus im Mittelalter', in K. Kahnert and B. Mojsisch (eds), *Umbrüche: Historische Wendepunkte der Philosophie von der Antike bis zur Gegenwart. Festschrift für Kurt Flasch zu seinem 70. Geburtstag* (Amsterdam, 2001), 117–30, and most usefully Reynolds, 'Social mentalities and the case of medieval scepticism'.

[87]   It is interesting too that Byrhtferth's account stands in such contrast to some of the later literary constructions of those who swore oaths or undertook ordeals falsely by reframing the question, or answering (like the peasant here) in such a way that they did not directly tell a lie. In a twelfth- or thirteenth-century romance, someone pulling such a stunt might have escaped with land and life, especially if he were noble or royal rather than 'rustic', but in tenth-century hagiography, apparently not. See J.W. Baldwin, 'The crisis of the ordeal: Literature, law, and religion around 1200', *Journal of Medieval and Renaissance Studies* 24:3 (1994): 327–53.

[88]   Reynolds, 'Social mentalities and the case of medieval scepticism', esp. 21–9. In the same way, it is clearly nonsense that people in the early Middle Ages had no sense of individuality (for example): see Arnold, *Belief and Unbelief in Medieval Europe*, 186.

[89]   Boyer, *The naturalness of Religious Ideas*, 34–6.

demand and receive attention in the surviving sources precisely because they are unusual and disruptive in the pattern of daily life.[90]

A useful comparison here is William Dalrymple's account of the experience of twentieth-century monks in the monastery of Mar Saba, in the West Bank. One Fr. Theophanes described a frightening experience that he had on a windy night:

> As I prayed I heard footsteps coming up the corridor. It was the noise of a monk walking: I could hear the rustling of his habit. The footsteps came closer and then stopped outside my room. I waited for the monk to speak, but nothing happened. Suddenly I heard very clearly the noise of many feet tripping down the stairs from the opposite direction. They were like madmen, jumping down the steps very quickly – loud, irregular footsteps: there were maybe nine or ten of them, all running.[91]

On leaving his cell, Fr. Theophanes saw nothing, and thinking that thieves had come to the monastery, he and his companion Fr. Evdokimos spent an hour searching for them. But afterwards when they had found no one, they discussed the matter with their superior, the Archimandrite, and eventually understood what had happened. 'The first set of footsteps were those of St Sabas. The rabble were demons coming to turn Fr. Theophanes into a Freemason.[92] St Sabas knew what they were planning, so he stood in front of Fr. Theophanes' door to guard it. Then he chased the demons away.'[93]

What is significant here is that while Fr. Theophanes might have believed that demons were a continual threat and that St Sabas was always present in the monastery, he did not initially interpret what he had experienced as a demonic attack thwarted by St Sabas until after he had re-evaluated the episode with input from their superior, and only then when other logical explanations had been excluded. Accounts from the early Middle Ages also suggest that the surviving interpretations as recorded in sources were sometimes reached in a similar way. One such episode comes from the *Life* of Leoba, an English missionary abbess of Tauberbischofsheim (Baden-Württemberg) who had died in 782, although the *Life* itself was written at Fulda (Hessen) in the ninth century.[94] This text gives an account of the disappearance of keys that belonged to a nun at Wimbourne

---

[90]     Ibid., 34–5.

[91]     W. Dalrymple, *From the Holy Mountain: A Journey in the Shadow of Byzantium* (London, 1997), 292.

[92]     Freemasons appear sometimes to be equated with Catholics (see Dalrymple, *From the Holy Mountain*, 280). In other Orthodox monasteries, Dalrymple was apparently asked whether he was 'Orthodox or heretic'.

[93]     Dalrymple, *From the Holy Mountain*, 293.

[94]     See S.J. Hollis, *Anglo-Saxon Women and the Church: Sharing a Common Fate* (Woodbridge, 1992), 271–6.

(Dorset), the community where Leoba had been trained.[95] The nun assumed that she had lost the keys and begged forgiveness from the abbess, but the abbess informed her that she had not lost them, insisting instead that they must have been taken by the devil. The nuns prayed and the keys eventually turned up in the mouth of a dead fox, which confirmed the suspicions of the abbess.[96] In reality, the identification of demonic power or influence may not have been made as early as the account suggests, as in the case of Fr. Theophanes and the devils. Many of the incidents now attributed in early medieval written accounts to demonic, angelic or saintly spirits must also have been re-evaluated after the event, and once interpreted in this way, it was precisely their unusual nature which made them worthy of recording.

The interpretations of Fr. Theophanes and Wimbourne's abbess were made in monastic contexts that were consciously or unconsciously informed by written texts which record similar events and interpretations: it is not at all clear how many believers in the same region (whether the West Bank in the twentieth century, Wimbourne in the eighth, or Fulda in the ninth) but who lived in non-monastic contexts would have accepted the same analysis of the episode. Perhaps some would have agreed with the interpretation, while others, like Byrhtferth's 'rustic', would have been more sceptical of the powers of the saint than were his devoted monastic followers. And yet, on the other hand, there are many people in modern 'rational' societies who are quite happy to accept beliefs which other members of those societies might consider superstitious, such as the evil eye; or lone magpies as a portent (or cause?) of sorrow; or even, depending on the viewpoint, organised religion. In the early Middle Ages as in the twentieth or twenty-first century, these complexities of belief are elided unless the roles played by individuality, agency, context and circumstances are understood. Early medieval sources do show differences between the beliefs and practices of peasants and clergy, and the objections of clergy to beliefs held by non-clerical communities, but they also show differences between abbesses and their nuns, and between scholars such as Ælfric and Wulfstan. In the case of theological disagreement, as in the case of local saints, the overwhelming impression is that many of the beliefs involved were not so different as they are sometimes made out to be, but were simply justified or understood in slightly different ways which were nonetheless held to be crucially distinct.

Understanding the beliefs of every individual in the early Middle Ages is clearly impossible. Even the beliefs of almost all educated Anglo-Saxons are no longer discernible by modern scholars, because there are so few authors whose names are known and whose works survive to the present day, while those at the bottom of the social scale may even be as invisible archaeologically as they are

---

[95]    Rudolf, *Vita Leobae*, 5, ed. G. Waitz, 'Vita Leobae abbatissae Biscofesheimensis auct. Rudolfo Fuldensi', *Supplementa tomorum I–XII, pars III*, MGH, Scriptores in Folio 15.1 (Hannover, 1887), 118–31, at 124.

[96]    See also below, 72–3.

in the textual record.[97] One approach to this is, as Sarah Tarlow argues, 'to accept that personal interiority, especially in the past, may ultimately be inaccessible'.[98] And yet it remains true that that the acceptance or rejection of a particular belief is ultimately down to the individual, and models which seek to analyse belief in a structural way where 'the Church' or 'official belief' is at one end of a spectrum, or forms one circle, still in a sense take an ecclesiastical perspective. What people believed was determined to some degree by personal choice and decision as much as it was governed by local circumstances including place-bound beliefs and practices, or affected by the views of the local religious and secular authorities on the matter, or the specific context, as well as the way in which an interpretation or belief was formed – and recorded. As the example of the monks of Mar Saba or the nuns of Wimbourne suggests, some of the beliefs which are presented as *faits accomplis* in the surviving texts are clearly far more complex, and probably required much more interpretation after the fact, than is generally obvious in the surviving sources.

This is not to suggest, however, that the evidence which survives is so person- or place-specific that it can never be informative about ideas or beliefs more generally in the period, and here Tarlow proposes the concept of 'belief discourses'. This involves recognising that people accept a variety of beliefs, some of which may be inconsistent or contradictory, and almost all of which are context-specific: belief discourses may represent belief indirectly through practice rather than providing direct evidence of it, and incorporate material practices as well as through textual statement, discussion or narrative.[99] In examining the richness and variety of early medieval beliefs about issues like angels and devils, or the dead body, and the practices which went hand-in-hand with these beliefs, it is possible to see the range of ideas in circulation and in dialogue, even if it is ultimately fruitless to try to identify one belief as 'popular' or 'unofficial', or another as 'formal' or 'official'. The importance of specific context is highlighted by Watkins too: he shows that the twelfth-century author Gerald of Wales seems to have adjusted his approach depending on whether he was writing manuals of instruction or attending local festivals.[100] In some cases, such specific context is not easy to identify for the surviving texts; and it is difficult to imagine that someone like Ælfric would have budged much to 'negotiate' Christian values, since he was something of a hardliner and a stickler for orthodoxy: Ælfric quite unnecessarily uses the example of the man who mocked Swithun as an opportunity to complain about wakes, and

---

[97]    See H. Hamerow, 'Overview: Rural Settlement', in S. Crawford, H. Hamerow and D.A. Hinton (eds), *The Oxford Handbook of Anglo-Saxon Archaeology* (Oxford, 2011), 119–27, at 125–6.

[98]    S. Tarlow, *Ritual, Belief, and the Dead Body in Early Modern Britain and Ireland* (Cambridge, 2010), 15; see also S. Tarlow, *Bereavement and Commemoration: An Archaeology of Mortality*, Social Archaeology (Oxford, 1999), 47.

[99]    Tarlow, *Ritual, Belief, and the Dead Body*, 15–18.

[100]    Watkins, '"Folklore" and "popular religion"', 142–4.

about the practices of eating and drinking around a corpse instead of offering prayers.[101] Perhaps in Ælfric's writings it is possible to access personal interiority, although he and others like him are certainly the exception rather than the rule.

Conceptualising belief in terms of multiple individual perspectives requires acknowledging that all beliefs may be received differently, and accepted or rejected by individuals, wherever such beliefs originated, and in this sense it is reasonable to argue that personal interiority is inaccessible in the early Middle Ages. But the significance of conceptualising belief in this way is that both Ælfric and the man who mocked Swithun, who clearly accepted and rejected different beliefs, are thus placed on the same level. Ecclesiastical officials like Ælfric himself would argue that he and the man who mocked Swithun should not be placed on the same level, because Ælfric was highly educated in the ways of theology, and the man who mocked Swithun was not. Taking a step back, it seems that this too is to misunderstand what Christian belief is, and what it means to be a Christian. Those at the top of the hierarchy thought that what they determined, based on learned tradition, was Christian belief, although as the discussion of examples like Boniface and the issue of rebaptism has shown, this was not always secure or fixed. But Christian belief is more complex than this. Vincent of Lérins observed that Catholic belief is 'what has always been believed everywhere, by all' ('quod ubique, quod semper, quod ab omnibus creditum est').[102] It seems likely that even in the fifth century, this was not as straightforward as Vincent suggests, and it was certainly not straightforward in Anglo-Saxon England (and is still less so in the twenty-first century).

The ability of all Christians to assert their own beliefs – as in the case of burgeoning saints' cults, or Aldebert and Clemens, or theological discussions – means that these must all be examined as instances of Christian belief, even while recognising that some contemporaries identified them as incorrect, invalid or objectionable, and that the ecclesiastical hierarchy retained the last word – although not the only word – on belief. This range of Christian beliefs and the different ways in which they were perceived by contemporaries surrounds the dialogue between priests and their congregations, in which pastoral theology was communicated to wider audiences and was required to engage with the societies which made up those audiences. Understanding the fact of this variety is therefore the first step in understanding this process of communication. The next section of this chapter turns to the second step, and explores the range of circumstances in which Christians learned and expressed

---

[101]  Ælfric, *Life of Swithun*, 20, ed. Lapidge, *Cult of St Swithun*, 602.

[102]  *Commonitorium*, II.5, ll. 25–6, ed. R. Demeulenaere, 'Vincentius Lerinensis, Commonitorium', in R. Demeulenaere and J. Mulders (eds), *Foebadius, Victricius, Leporius, Vincentius Lerinensis, Evagrius, Ruricius: Liber contra Arrianos; De laude sanctorum; Libellus emendationis; Epistulae; Commonitorium. Excerpta ex operibus s. Augustini; Altercatio legis inter Simonem Iudaeum et Theophilum christianum*, CCSL 64 (Turnhout, 1985), 127–95, at 149.

their faith in Anglo-Saxon England, both within and outside churches, as well as the changing institutional contexts and opportunities in which teaching might take place. It is also important to consider the materials used for teaching – not only the texts which were used to teach and the authors who wrote them, but the written form in which these circulated; and to consider the teachers themselves, how (and how much) they were trained and what were the aspirations (if not always the actualities) of the pastoral mission. To say that within this dialogue the responses of the laity were clear would be to overstate the case, but it is possible sometimes to hear the echoes of lay experience or to postulate how such teaching was received.

## Learning the Faith in Anglo-Saxon England

In the broadest and most basic sense, and in the early Middle Ages as today, Christians are those who are initiated into the faith through baptism;[103] and again in the early Middle Ages as today, a good Christian might be said to be someone who keeps to the promises made in baptism, both in the beliefs which are held and in the performance of practices which express and form part of Christian belief. From the perspective of ecclesiastical officials, the formal responsibility of informing and educating people about Christian belief and practice fell to priests and bishops, in the contexts of preaching or the services of routine pastoral care such as baptism and confession. However, the context in which this pastoral work was undertaken was not static: the ecclesiastical landscape which supported pastoral care changed and developed significantly between the late sixth century and the eleventh century. Missionaries from Rome and Iona came to England from the late sixth century, and Irish and European contacts continued to be influential in subsequent centuries, so that reforms instigated abroad were taken up and put into practice in English contexts too.[104] Understanding the variety of local ecclesiastical arrangements which sustained both clergy and laity is extremely

---

[103]    See S.A. Keefe, *Water and the Word: Baptism and the Education of the Clergy in the Carolingian Empire*, Publications in Mediaeval Studies (Notre Dame, IN, 2002), I.2–6.

[104]    H.M. Taylor, 'Tenth Century Church Building in England and on the Continent', in D. Parsons (ed.), *Tenth-Century Studies: Essays in Commemoration of the Millennium of the Council of Winchester and Regularis Concordia* (London, 1975), 141–68, 237; V. Ortenberg, *The English Church and the Continent in the Tenth and Eleventh Centuries: Cultural, Spiritual, and Artistic Exchange* (Oxford, 1992); Blair, *The Church*, 8–49; Foot, *Monastic Life*, 265–8; J.T. Palmer, *Anglo-Saxons in a Frankish World, 690 – 900*, Studies in the Early Middle Ages 19 (Turnhout, 2009); S. Hamilton, 'The Early Pontificals: The Anglo-Saxon Evidence Reconsidered from a Continental Perspective', in C. Leyser, D.W. Rollason and H. Williams (eds), *England and the Continent in the Tenth Century: Studies in Honour of Wilhelm Levison (1876–1947)* (Turnhout, 2011), 411–28.

important for understanding how Christian belief and practice may have worked on the ground, and how these were shaped and influenced by local circumstances.

Here it is important also to understand the development of the settled landscape in which these ecclesiastical structures and arrangements existed, and in which pastoral work was carried out. Anglo-Saxon society was predominantly rural: early Anglo-Saxon settlements were mainly quite small and dispersed rather than nucleated (although there is regional variation), and in the late seventh and early eighth centuries there is evidence that some settlements shifted gradually across the landscape rather than remaining stable.[105] By the late seventh or early eighth century there were also other larger centres where churches or ecclesiastics might be found, including proto-urban trading places known as 'wics' and probably under royal or ecclesiastical control, such as Ipswich or Hamwic (modern Southampton); royal palaces, such as Bamburgh; and major religious centres such as Jarrow (Northumberland), or Whitby or Ripon (Yorkshire), many of which also seem to have been sites of trade and production, to judge from the material assemblages found there.[106]

From the ninth century, rural settlements seem to have stabilised to some degree, and some continued to be occupied as before, while there was also an increase in urbanisation and urban settlements.[107] From this time there is more evidence for smaller, local churches, both in towns and in the surrounding localities, apparently at least partly due to a growing desire among Anglo-Saxon nobility to

---

[105] H. Hamerow, 'Settlement mobility and the middle Saxon shift: Rural settlements and patterns in Anglo-Saxon England', *Anglo-Saxon England* 20 (1991): 1–17; H. Hamerow, 'The development of Anglo-Saxon settlement structure', *Landscape History* 31:1 (2010), 5–22.

[106] R.A. Hall and M. Whyman, 'Settlement and monasticism at Ripon, North Yorkshire, from the 7th to 11th centuries A.D', *Medieval Archaeology: Journal of the Society for Medieval Archaeology* 40 (1996): 62–150; J.D. Richards, 'What's so special about "productive sites"? Middle Saxon settlements in Northumbria', *Anglo-Saxon Studies in Archaeology & History* 10 (1999): 71–80; Blair, *The Church*, 255–6; T. Pestell, 'Markets, Emporia, Wics, and "Productive" Sites: Pre-Viking Trade Centres in Anglo-Saxon England', in S. Crawford, H. Hamerow and D.A. Hinton (eds), *The Oxford Handbook of Anglo-Saxon Archaeology* (Oxford, 2011), 556–79, and see the essays in D. Hill and R. Cowie (eds), *Wics: The Early Medieval Trading Centres of Northern Europe* (Sheffield, 2001) and T. Pestell and K. Ulmschneider (eds), *Markets in Early Medieval Europe: Trading and Productive Sites, 650–850* (Macclesfield, 2003).

[107] D. Hill, 'Athelstan's urban reforms', *Anglo-Saxon Studies in Archaeology & History* 11 (2000): 173–86; M.O.H. Carver, *The Birth of a Borough: An Archaeological Study of Anglo-Saxon Stafford* (Woodbridge, 2010); Hamerow, 'The development of Anglo-Saxon settlement structure'; R.A. Hall, 'Burhs and Boroughs: Defended Places, Trade, and Towns. Plans, Defences, Civic Features', in Crawford, Hamerow and Hinton (eds), *The Oxford Handbook of Anglo-Saxon Archaeology*, 600–24.

have churches on their own estates.[108] Early episcopal seats were often located in old Roman towns (such as York), although in the early centuries of Anglo-Saxon Christianity these were not urban in the way that they would come to be later; other sites founded as monasteries were more isolated (such as Lindisfarne).[109] While church-building accompanied urbanisation and the construction of towns in some cases, for example the early tenth-century defensive towns built by Æthelflæd, Lady of the Mercians (d.918), in other cases churches or bishoprics were founded away from towns.[110] From the later tenth century, following the monastic reform movement, a number of cathedrals were served by monastic communities, so that the urban centre of Winchester (for example) held the episcopal seat, male and female monastic communities, and a number of smaller town churches.

It has been suggested that before about the late ninth or early tenth century, the key ecclesiastical centres in this landscape were 'minsters', a term which covers religious foundations or communities whether monastic or non-monastic: these minsters may have provided much of the routine pastoral care which Christians needed, such as baptism, the mass, or confession.[111] Some of the larger minsters seem also to have had smaller satellites dependent on them, and in some places groups of monasteries seem to have formed 'clusters'; in some cases there is evidence for communities of various types which grew up around them.[112] It is clear that there were significant variations in size and purpose, from large double foundations like Wearmouth-Jarrow through to the women's house at Nazeing (Essex), which seems from the archaeological evidence to have been extremely small indeed. In later centuries it is possible to see the proliferation

[108]    Blair, *The Church*, 368–425; see also S. Wood, *The Proprietary Church in the Medieval West* (Oxford, 2006), 645–51.

[109]    Blair, *The Church*, 66–73, 249; see also M. Henig, 'The Fate of Late Roman Towns', in Crawford, Hamerow and Hinton (eds), *The Oxford Handbook of Anglo-Saxon Archaeology*, 515–33.

[110]    J. Barrow, 'Churches, Education and Literacy in Towns 600–1300', in D.M. Palliser (ed.), *The Cambridge Urban History of Britain: Vol. 1, 600–1540* (Cambridge, 2000), 127–52, at 130–1; G.G. Astill, 'Overview: Trade, Exchange, and Urbanization', in Crawford, Hamerow and Hinton (eds), *The Oxford Handbook of Anglo-Saxon Archaeology*, 503–14, at 508–10.

[111]    There is a considerable body of literature on the institutional arrangements for pastoral care in early medieval England. See for example Blair, *The Church*; S. Bassett, 'Boundaries of knowledge: Mapping the land units of late Anglo-Saxon and Norman England', in W. Davies, G. Halsall and A.J. Reynolds (eds), *People and Space in the Middle Ages, 300–1300* (Turnhout, 2006), 115–42, at 115–19; Foot, *Monastic Life*; C. Cubitt, 'The Institutional Church', and 'Pastoral Care and Religious Belief', in P. Stafford (ed.), *A Companion to the Early Middle Ages: Britain and Ireland c.500–1100* (Oxford, 2009), 376–94, and 395–413; T. Pickles, 'Church Organization and Pastoral Care', in Stafford (ed.), *A Companion to the Early Middle Ages*, 160–76.

[112]    I.N. Wood, 'Monasteries and the geography of power in the age of Bede', *Northern History* 45:1 (2008): 11–25.

of smaller churches, either founded by and dependent on the 'old minsters' as part of their efforts to ensure effective pastoral care across the large areas for which they were parochially responsible, or founded by local aristocracy on their own lands and perhaps also taking some public pastoral role, as well as serving as the private chapels of land-owners.[113] According to the 'minster model' or 'mother-church model', the earlier minsters retained their significance as 'mother churches', often receiving dues from the smaller local churches or controlling them in some other way.[114] This argument is based on a range of detailed and complex evidence, including archaeological and topographical information as well as written material, and this cannot be discussed here at length; the idea of the enduring influence of the earlier 'mother churches' finds support (for example) in the tenth-century legal decrees which enjoin that 'old minsters' should receive certain types of tithes and a proportion of the dues paid to smaller churches founded with their jurisdictional areas.[115]

This 'minster model' has received widespread support from a number of scholars, but aspects of it have been queried.[116] The extent to which the larger minsters in any part of the period were driven by a perceived need to provide pastoral care has been questioned, and it has been argued that small churches may have been far more numerous even in the seventh and eighth centuries than has often been assumed, so that even in the early centuries of the Anglo-Saxon Church, some clergy may have lived with their families in lay settlements rather than in religious communities.[117] The surviving evidence shows that the relationships between, and even the number of, smaller churches and larger ecclesiastical centres seem to have varied a great deal between different regions, and it is clear

---

[113]   Jolly, *Popular Religion*, 35–70; Blair, *The Church*, 291–504; Tinti, *Sustaining Belief*, 225–314.

[114]   S. Foot, 'Parochial ministry in early Anglo-Saxon England: The role of monastic communities', in W.J. Sheils and D. Wood (eds), *The Ministry: Clerical and Lay: papers read at the 1988 Summer Meeting and the 1989 Winter Meeting of the Ecclesiastical History Society*, Studies in Church History 26 (Oxford, 1989): 43–54, at 43; Blair, *The Church, passim*, esp. 4–5, 156, 162–3, 491.

[115]   II Edgar 1.1–3.1, ed. F. Liebermann, *Die Gesetze der Angelsachsen* (3 vols, Halle, 1903–1916), I.196–9; and Blair, *The Church*, 442–3.

[116]   See for example E. Cambridge and D.W. Rollason, 'Debate: The pastoral organization of the Anglo-Saxon Church: A review of the "Minster hypothesis"', *Early Medieval Europe* 4 (1995): 87–104; D.W. Rollason, 'Monasteries and Society in Early Medieval Northumbria', in B. Thompson (ed.), *Monasteries and Society in Medieval Britain: Proceedings of the 1994 Harlaxton Symposium*, Harlaxton Medieval Studies, n.s. 6 (Stamford, 1999), 59–74.

[117]   C. Cubitt, 'Images of St Peter: The Clergy and the Religious Life in Anglo-Saxon England', in P. Cavill (ed.), *The Christian Tradition in Anglo-Saxon England: Approaches to Current Scholarship and Teaching* (Woodbridge, 2004), 41–54; Cubitt, 'The clergy in early Anglo-Saxon England'. See also E. Cambridge, 'The early church in County Durham: A reassessment', *Journal of the British Archaeological Association* 137 (1984): 65–85.

that no one arrangement can have been in place for the whole of England at a stage when local circumstances varied so greatly between different regions. Even towards the end of the period when England was politically unified (at least in theory), it seems that there was no common Anglo-Saxon experience: evidence from the Domesday Book suggests that the number of churches in different dioceses varied greatly, although in some cases this may owe more to the way in which information was recorded rather than to reality; and in the main, smaller churches appear to have played a greater role in eastern England than in western England, where minsters may have retained rather more influence.[118] But even in one diocese relationships between smaller churches and 'old minsters' were not uniformly construed: Francesca Tinti's detailed study of the Worcester diocese reveals that older minsters retained their importance where successive bishops were influential, but areas where lay or monastic patrons were stronger tended to see the proliferation of smaller churches.[119]

This variety of circumstances in which lay people related to the institutional Church, and how these circumstances may have changed over the centuries, is significant in understanding that there was an attendant variation in what might have been expected, communicated and performed in terms of practice and perhaps also belief, and how this too may have varied or changed according to local situations. It seems that by about 800, the number of churches in the landscape was such that most people would have lived within three to five miles of one: if someone had a desire to visit a church to request pastoral services he could probably find one within reasonable walking distance, although what was available locally might have varied as much (or more) as between a community like Jarrow or a community like Nazeing.[120] It is not always easy to establish the relationship of surviving early churches to the communities for which they may have been responsible. It is possible that the prominent hill-top locations of some churches in the landscape, such as Breedon on the Hill (Leicestershire) or Brixworth (Northamptonshire), may have made them somewhat isolated from other settlements;[121] in other cases churches were founded in central positions near core settlement areas, and were perhaps central to the communities they served.[122]

The personal and communal experience of religion which required laity to seek out churches at some distance must have been quite different from religious experience in settlements which either contained small churches, such as the

---

[118]   V. Thompson, *Dying and Death in Later Anglo-Saxon England* (Woodbridge, 2004), 29; J. Barrow, 'The Clergy in English Dioceses c. 900–c. 1066', in F. Tinti (ed.), *Pastoral Care in Late Anglo-Saxon England*, Anglo-Saxon Studies 6 (Woodbridge, 2005), 17–26, esp. 24–5.

[119]   Tinti, *Sustaining Belief*, 225–314.

[120]   Blair, *The Church*, 152.

[121]   Foot, *Monastic Life*, 99–101.

[122]   See in particular S. Turner, *Making a Christian Landscape: The Countryside in Early Medieval Cornwall, Devon and Wessex* (Exeter, 2006).

late Saxon church at Raunds Furnells (Northamptonshire), or which had grown up near or around larger ecclesiastical centres; or in the urban areas of the tenth and eleventh centuries which might contain several small churches as well as a religious community (or communities) of varying sorts, and perhaps an episcopal seat, as for example Worcester or Winchester.[123] The different types of religious establishment point also to the range of experiences of the clergy and those in religious life, and this is important too because at the heart of routine pastoral care were sacramental offices such as baptism, the mass, or the imposition of penance, which could be performed only by priests. Even in the early period when religious communities at minsters may have provided many of these services, it is clear that priests were allocated this duty: in his letter to Archbishop Ecgberht of York, Bede assigns the role of basic Christian teaching to priests when he complains that he had to provide translations of the creed and pater noster for them.[124]

Some priests were also monks, as Bede himself was, but distinguishing between monk-priests, priests who were not monks, and monks who were not priests, is not always easy in the surviving sources, because in many cases men are described either as monk or as priest even when they were both.[125] This means that it can be difficult to ascertain the precise status of the priests who undertook pastoral care, and how and where they might have been educated and trained, but it is clear that there were many different possibilities. Some priests do seem to have lived in communities which had both (contemplative) monastic and pastoral functions, as the 'minster model' suggests: according to Bede, members of the monastic community at Lindisfarne travelled throughout the countryside to perform baptisms, masses and other duties of pastoral care.[126] The author of the *Life* of Boniface suggests that Wessex in the late seventh century likewise saw travelling priests.[127] In the later period, especially after the monastic reforms of the tenth century, an increasing number of cathedral communities were staffed by monastic personnel. In the late tenth and early eleventh centuries, records show that a large proportion of the monks at Winchester's cathedral (the Old

---

[123]   For discussion see A. Boddington, G. Cadman and J. Evans, *Raunds Furnells: The Anglo-Saxon Church and Churchyard* (London, 1996); Tinti, *Sustaining Belief*; H. Foxhall Forbes, 'Squabbling siblings: Gender and monastic life in late Anglo-Saxon Winchester', *Gender & History* 23:3 (2011): 653–84.

[124]   Bede, *Epistola ad Ecgbertum*, 5, ed. Plummer, *Venerabilis Baedae Historiam ecclesiasticam*, 409.

[125]   Cubitt, 'The clergy in early Anglo-Saxon England'.

[126]   Bede, *Vita S. Cuthberti prosa*, 9, ed. and trans. B. Colgrave, *Two Lives of Saint Cuthbert: A Life by an Anonymous Monk of Lindisfarne and Bede's Prose Life* (Cambridge, 1985 [orig. pub. 1940]); *HE* III.26.4, ed. Lapidge, Monat and Robin, *Histoire ecclésiastique*, II.164–6; Foot, *Monastic Life*, 292–6.

[127]   Willibald, *Vita S. Bonifatii*, 1, ed. R. Rau, *Briefe des Bonifatius: Willibalds Leben des Bonifatius, nebst einigen zeitgenössischen Dokumenten* (Darmstadt, 1968), 460, ll. 19–21.

Minster) were ordained as priests and deacons: they were presumably responsible for providing services of pastoral care for those who came to the cathedral, but there is little evidence that they travelled widely to offer the sacramental offices to those who did not come to them.[128] Other cathedrals such as Exeter (or Sherborne before Bishop Wulfsige's reforms in 998) were staffed by communities of secular clergy;[129] and there were probably secular communities without bishops whose priested personnel undertook pastoral services for the surrounding areas, who may have had greater resources in the form of books and liturgical equipment than lone priests at local churches.[130]

Access to resources and learning is a crucial factor in considering how belief or practice might have been shaped and affected by local contexts and circumstances. The *Regularis Concordia*, produced in Winchester probably in the early 970s, as well as the tenth- and eleventh-century records of the members of the Winchester communities suggest that child oblation was a reality in the tenth century as it had been in the late seventh century when the seven-year-old Bede was given to the community at Jarrow:[131] boys who grew up in monasteries which were wealthy and with good resources – centres of academic excellence – might more easily become priests who were highly educated scholars. Evidence for cathedral schools is more difficult to recover, but it seems that there was little substantial difference between monastic and cathedral schools in this period, and it is possible that priests trained in the school at one community might be sent elsewhere after ordination, although whether to other communities or to serve at the churches of nobles or kings is unclear.[132] Some local churches and their patrons seem to have been able to support communities of clergy rather than a lone priest, and although it is usually impossible to recover how well resourced these small communities might have been, it is possible that lay patrons may have provided less in the way of books and liturgical equipment than was

---

[128]    See Stowe 944, fols. 18r–20r (Old Minster), 20v–22r (New Minster); S. Keynes (ed.), *The Liber Vitae of the New Minster and Hyde Abbey, Winchester: British Library Stowe 944: Together with leaves from British Library Cotton Vespasian A. VIII and British Library Cotton Titus D. XXVII*, EEMF 26 (Copenhagen, 1996), 64–5.

[129]    Barrow, 'The clergy in English dioceses'.

[130]    J. Wilcox, 'Ælfric in Dorset and the landscape of pastoral care', in Tinti (ed.), *Pastoral Care in Late Anglo-Saxon England*, 52–62, at 57–8.

[131]    Bede, *HE*, V.24.2, ll. 6–14, ed. Lapidge, Monat and Robin, *Histoire ecclésiastique*, III.188; *Regularis Concordia*, 11, 20, 22, 31, 36–7, 62, ed. T. Symons, *Regularis Concordia: The Monastic Agreement of the Monks and Nuns of the English Nation* (London, 1953), 7–8, 17, 18. 28, 35–6, 61; Stowe 944, fols. 19r–20r, 21r–22r (although it is not clear in all cases what exactly 'puer' (literally 'boy') means in these lists). See also M. de Jong, 'Growing up in a Carolingian monastery: Magister Hildemar and his oblates', *Journal of Medieval History* 9:2 (1983): 99–128.

[132]    F. Barlow, *The English Church 1000–1066: A History of the Later Anglo-Saxon Church* (London, 1978), 277–8; C.S. Jaeger, *The Envy of Angels: Cathedral Schools and Social Ideals in Medieval Europe, 950–1200*, Middle Ages Series (Philadelphia, 1994), 26.

found in churches supported by monastic or episcopal patrons.[133] Records of local churches which were inherited by the children of priests suggest that some trainee priests may have learned by helping their fathers, although in other cases they might perhaps have assisted their uncles, and presumably other boys in the area could also learn in the same way.[134]

Clergy in all these different contexts were theoretically responsible to their bishop, whose duty it was to assess their suitability as candidates for ordination and who could theoretically refuse to ordain them if they lacked the requisite knowledge; and yet it is also difficult to establish the education and beliefs of bishops in this period. Post-conquest sources paint a bleak picture of the Anglo-Saxon Church and its bishops in some areas: William of Malmesbury reports that one Denewulf was appointed as bishop of Winchester in the ninth century despite being unable to read or write.[135] It is difficult to assess the veracity of William's account, but the importance of bishops as political players suggests that it is not impossible that such appointments were made if they were deemed to be strategic for some reason.[136] However, many bishops were trained in and ruled over major churches which were centres of learning and which produced many manuscripts, and some sense of the possible levels of episcopal learning can be gleaned from the professions made by southern English bishops to successive archbishops of Canterbury.[137] The professions rework and expand upon the creed,[138] and their contents suggest that some English bishops may have mastered advanced levels of theology, if they wrote in their own words as is sometimes claimed.[139] However,

---

[133] Barrow, 'The clergy in English dioceses', 22–3; Wood, *The Proprietary Church in the Medieval West*, 519–20, 530. See for example the details of the equipment apparently belonging to a church in Sherburn-in-Elmet listed in the York Gospels: J.J.G. Alexander and N. Barker (eds.), *The York Gospels: A Facsimile with Introductory Essays by Jonathan Alexander [et al.]* (London, 1986), 96–7.

[134] H. Gittos, 'Is there any Evidence for the Liturgy of Parish Churches in Late Anglo-Saxon England? The Red Book of Darley and the Status of Old English', in Tinti (ed.), *Pastoral Care in Late Anglo-Saxon England*, 63–82, at 63–4.

[135] II.75.22, ed. M. Winterbottom and R.M. Thomson, *William of Malmesbury, Gesta pontificum Anglorum* (Oxford, 2007), I.256.

[136] See below, 172–85.

[137] These are edited and discussed in M. Richter and T.J. Brown, *Canterbury Professions* (Torquay, 1973), and see also N. Brooks, *The Early History of the Church of Canterbury: Christ Church from 597 to 1066*, Studies in the early history of Britain (Leicester, 1984), 164–7.

[138] See for example the professions of Tidfrith, bishop of Dunwich, and Denebeorht, bishop elect of Worcester (nos. 2–3, ed. Richter and Brown, *Canterbury Professions*, 2–4).

[139] For example, a profession to Ceolnoth, probably by Cynefrith, bishop of Lichfield, includes the following statement: 'Moreover, I will explain in a few words the orthodox, catholic and apostolic faith, just as I have learned it from [my teachers and predecessors]' (see no. 17, ed. Richter and Brown, *Canterbury Professions*, 14–16: 'Insuper et orthodoxam catholicam apostolicamque fidem, sicut ab illis didici, paucis uerbis exponam'). The

some of the bishops used standard formulae or recycled a profession written by one of their predecessors, and it is not clear whether in some cases bishops simply affirmed a profession that was given to them and therefore did not have to write it themselves; others seem to have had poor Latin grammar, suggesting that language may have posed difficulties even if their learning might have been stronger in other respects.[140]

The resources or circumstances within some dioceses were probably not ideal, although this might have been noted more by bishops with greater learning: the questions for ordinands in Oxford, Bodleian Library, Junius 121 (a Worcester manuscript dating from the third quarter of the eleventh century whose contents are primarily associated with Archbishop Wulfstan), allow the ordination of a 'half-learned' priest if the need is great, suggesting that ordination was not only conferred on those who had achieved high levels of education.[141] Clearly, those who learned in environments with greater access to resources were more likely to have more secure and more extensive knowledge of the complexities of Christian teachings, although the effort which some tenth- and eleventh-century churchmen in particular put into providing materials for use by priests of all backgrounds, from well educated but under-confident through to 'half-learned' shows a clear desire to improve standards across the board.[142] Sometimes this may have been from personal experience: Ælfric complained that his teacher, a rural priest, had been unable to interpret Scripture correctly.[143] On the other hand, Ælfric and others were apparently able to learn at least the basics from local clergy, such as Orderic Vitalis (d.*c.*1142), who was taught from the age of five to ten by Siward, a Saxon priest

---

profession of Deorwulf, bishop elect of London, also made to Ceolnoth, notes that he composed and wrote his statement of faith (no. 23, ed. Richter and Brown, *Canterbury Professions*, 19–20).

[140]    Nos. 11, 14, and 15, ed. Richter and Brown, *Canterbury Professions*, 11, 13 are virtually identical; the profession of Helmstan of Winchester (no. 18, ed. Richter and Brown, *Canterbury Professions*, 16) contains numerous grammatical errors (see M. Lapidge, 'Latin learning in ninth-century England', *Anglo-Latin Literature, 600–899* (London, 1996), 409–54, at 434).

[141]    *On the Examination of Candidates for Ordination*, 16, *Councils and Synods*, I.i , no. 57.

[142]    See for example J. Hill, 'Monastic Reform and the Secular Church: Ælfric's Pastoral Letters in Context', in C. Hicks (ed.), *England in the Eleventh Century: Proceedings of the 1990 Harlaxton Symposium*, Harlaxton Medieval Studies 2 (Stamford, 1992), 103–17; J. Hill, 'Archbishop Wulfstan: Reformer?', in Townend (ed.), *Wulfstan, Archbishop of York*, 309–24.

[143]    Ælfric, Preface, ll. 13–42, ed. R. Marsden, *The Old English Heptateuch and Aelfric's Libellus de Veteri Testamento et Novo: Vol. 1, Introduction and Text*, EETS, OS 330 (Oxford, 2008), 3–4; for information about Ælfric's education, see J. Wilcox (ed.), *Aelfric's Prefaces*, Durham Medieval Texts 9 (Durham, 1994), 7–8; Cubitt, 'Ælfric's Lay Patrons', 177; J. Hill, 'Ælfric: His Life and Works', in Magennis and Swan (eds), *A Companion to Ælfric*, 35–66, at 44–9.

at his father's church in Shrewsbury in the latter part of the eleventh century.[144] Siward may have been high-born, and little more is known of Ælfric's teacher, but this does suggest that some learning was available even outside monastic contexts. In practice it is clear that the ways in which religious practices and beliefs were understood, performed and explained by priests, and in turn observed, received and understood by their congregations, must have varied quite significantly according to each priest, where he was working, how he had been trained, and according to the different people within the congregation, and their own experiences.

The basic benchmark for Christian education that priests were supposed to teach their congregations was knowledge of the creed and the pater noster. Wulfstan was only one of many clergy to insist on this, although he was unusual in incorporating the requirement into legal texts.[145] Instructions that all Christians should learn the creed and the pater noster are found in a number of tenth- and eleventh-century homilies, both those by Wulfstan's colleague Ælfric and those whose authors are now anonymous, and this message had been promulgated in England at least from the early eighth century.[146] When Bede wrote to Ecgberht, Archbishop of York, he urged that 'above all, one message should be proclaimed: that the Catholic faith, which is contained in the Apostles' Creed, and the pater noster, which the Scripture of the Holy Gospel teaches us, should be thoroughly committed to the memory of all of those who are under your rule'.[147] Bede made it clear that all Christians – both laity and those in religious life – should learn these prayers, and urged Ecgberht several times in the space of a few lines to ensure that everyone under his charge had done so.[148] The importance of knowledge of these prayers for all Christians was emphasised in the canons of numerous councils, such as the Council of *Clofesho* in 747, which was significant for its attempts to regulate church life and pastoral care at a fairly early stage of the English Church, and addressed many of the concerns identified by Bede.[149] Similar exhortations are found in Christian contexts throughout the Middle Ages.

---

[144] Orderic Vitalis, *Historia Ecclesiastica*, V.1, XIII.41, ed. M. Chibnall, *The Ecclesiastical History of Orderic Vitalis* (6 vols, Oxford, 1969–1980), III.6–9, IV.552–3.

[145] I Cnut 22–2.4, ed. Liebermann, *Gesetze*, I.302–3.

[146] Reynolds, 'Social mentalities and the case of medieval scepticism', 31–2; J.H. Lynch, *Christianizing Kinship: Ritual Sponsorship in Anglo-Saxon England* (Ithaca, NY, 1998), 187–8.

[147] Bede, *Epistola ad Ecgbertum*, 5, ed. Plummer, *Venerabilis Baedae Historiam ecclesiasticam*, 408: 'In qua uidelicet praedicatione populis exhibenda, hoc prae ceteris omni instantia procurandum arbitror, ut fidem catholicam, quae apostolorum symbolo contineatur, et dominicam orationem, quam sancti euangelii nos scriptura edocet, omnium, qui ad tuum regimen pertinent, memoriae radicitus infigere cures'.

[148] Bede, *Epistola ad Ecbertum*, 5–6, ed. Plummer, *Venerabilis Baedae Historiam ecclesiasticam*, 408–10.

[149] Council of *Clofesho* (747), 10, ed. A.W. Haddan and W. Stubbs, *Councils and Ecclesiastical Documents Relating to Great Britain and Ireland* (3 vols, Oxford, 1869),

From a pastoral perspective, for Christians to learn enough of their faith to achieve salvation it was the sense and content of the prayers rather than the Latin words themselves which were important, and so in England from a fairly early stage both laity and priests were advised to learn the prayers in the vernacular if they could not learn them in Latin. Bede instructed Archbishop Ecgberht to make those who did not know Latin learn the creed and pater noster in their own language, and noted that to this end he had frequently provided translations of the creed and pater noster to priests, presumably so that they in turn could teach them to lay learners.[150] Both Ælfric and Wulfstan likewise provided vernacular translations of basic Christian prayers, including them in sermons which instructed that these were the prayers that all Christians should know.[151] Vernacular poetic paraphrases of the Apostles' Creed and pater noster (and the Gloria patri) are incorporated into a liturgical compilation in Oxford, Bodleian Library, Junius 121, a late eleventh-century Worcester manuscript;[152] but it seems that these poems were originally composed for a different purpose and thus theoretically might have been intended as a meditative response to the creed and pater noster or perhaps as a way of making the sense and content more memorable.[153] Another poetic paraphrase of the pater noster is found in Cambridge, Corpus Christi College, 201 (a manuscript containing material associated with Wulfstan), where it was copied alongside penitential poems; and a more straightforward translation is found in the Exeter Book.[154]

The creed was also significant because as the foundation of Christian belief, it has an important role in the rituals of pastoral care which prepared Christian

III.366; see also Cubitt, *Anglo-Saxon Church Councils, c.650–c.850*, 97–124.

[150] Bede, *Epistola ad Ecgbertum*, 5, ed. Plummer, *Venerabilis Baedae Historiam ecclesiasticam*, 409: 'Propter quod et ipse multis saepe sacerdotibus idiotis haec utraque, et symbolum uidelicet, et dominicam orationem in linguam Anglorum translatam optuli'. Bede described the priests who needed such translations as 'stupid' or 'unlearned', but it is not clear whether they were genuinely ignorant of the prayers, or if they could explain the sense and content of the prayers in English but perhaps were only able to memorise or read out the Latin, rather than being able to relate the content of Latin words or phrases to the knowledge required for salvation.

[151] See for example Ælfric: *CH* I.19, I.20 ll. 1–2, ed. P. Clemoes, *Ælfric's Catholic Homilies: The First Series*, EETS, SS 17 (Oxford, 1997), 325–34, 355, and the Ælfrician translations in Cambridge, University Library, Gg.3.28 (Frantzen, *Literature of Penance*, 160–1); Wulfstan, *Hom.* VIIa, ed. Bethurum, *Homilies*, 166–8; *Canons of Edgar*, 17, 22, ed. Fowler, *Canons of Edgar*, 6–7.

[152] These are in C.A. Jones (ed. and trans.), *Old English Shorter Poems: Vol. 1, Religious and Didactic* (Cambridge, MA, 2012), 78–81 (Lord's Prayer III), 82–7 (Apostles' Creed), 88–93 (Gloria Patri).

[153] See Jones, *Old English Shorter Poems*; L. Whitbread, "The Old English Poems of the Benedictine office and some related questions", *Anglia* 80 (1962): 37–49.

[154] See Jones, *Old English Shorter Poems*, 66–7 (Lord's Prayer I, from the Exeter Book), 68–77 (Lord's Prayer II, from CCCC 201).

men and women for salvation. In theory, instruction in the Christian faith was a prerequisite for baptism, the ritual which initiated believers into the Church, and the baptismal ritual included affirmation of the creed, although not necessarily its recitation by the baptismal candidate. The priest put credal statements to the candidate and he had to affirm that he accepted them (by answering 'credo', I believe).[155] Since acceptance of these beliefs was the minimum required for initiation it might seem peculiar that Christians, who by definition had accepted the creed, were encouraged to learn it; but by the late seventh century (or possibly the early eighth), infant baptism seems to have been considered ideal: it may by this time have been usual in some, but probably not all, areas of England.[156] In later centuries the situation must have varied considerably across England: from the ninth century northern England saw significant Scandinavian immigration and an influx of non-Christians, whereas by this time Christianity was well entrenched in the south.[157] The parents and godparents of those who were baptized when they were too young to affirm their own faith were required to affirm these beliefs on his/her behalf, with the attendant promise to instil Christian belief and faith and its significance in the baptismal candidate as he/she grew up.[158] To this end, parents were instructed to teach their children the fundamentals of the faith, and where beliefs or knowledge about beliefs were directly or indirectly passed on, this may have reinforced (or, in some cases, undermined) the messages delivered in more formal contexts.[159]

Surviving penitential and legal texts record a variety of (often quite heavy) penalties for priests who were responsible for children dying without baptism, and especially in the later period and where pastoral care seems to have been undertaken by priests who lived in settlements with the laity they served, it was presumably in the priest's own interest to ensure that he did baptize children quite soon after birth, rather than potentially risk the wrath of angry parents if a child died unbaptized.[160] The laws of King Ine of Wessex (r.688–726) instruct that children should be baptized within 30 days, although since these decrees only survive as an appendix to the laws of King Alfred (d.899) it is difficult to be certain

---

[155] P. Cramer, *Baptism and Change in the Early Middle Ages, c. 200–c. 1150* (Cambridge, 1993), 140–1.

[156] S. Foot, '"By Water in the Spirit": The Administration of Baptism in Early Anglo-Saxon England', in J. Blair and R. Sharpe (eds), *Pastoral Care before the Parish* (Leicester, 1992), 171–92, at 187–8; Foot, *Monastic Life*, 300–1.

[157] See for example the essays in D.M. Hadley and J.D. Richards, *Cultures in Contact: Scandinavian Settlement in England in the Ninth and Tenth Centuries*, Studies in the Early Middle Ages 2 (Turnhout, 2000); and Kopar, *Gods and Settlers*.

[158] Foot, 'Baptism', 187–8; Lynch, *Christianizing Kinship*, 183–8.

[159] Council of *Clofesho* (747), 14, ed. Haddan and Stubbs, *Councils*, III.367; Foot, *Monastic Life*, 301.

[160] Foot, 'Baptism', 192.

about quite how closely they represent a genuine seventh-century tradition.[161] Eighth-century canons recommended that baptism be performed only at Easter and Pentecost, or in cases of emergency, but it seems likely that in reality baptisms were performed throughout the year as required, when children were born or when they came close to death.[162] In later centuries it is difficult to determine precisely what was considered to be ideal because there are so many different regulations. For example, an eleventh-century homily recommends that priests should baptize children within 30 days, apparently without regard for the liturgical season and more because of concerns over infant mortality, and in his *Pastoral Letter* for Bishop Wulfsige, Ælfric insisted that if a priest was presented with unbaptized children he should baptize them immediately so that they did not die without baptism; but canonical prescriptions about the performance of baptisms only at Easter and Pentecost or in cases of emergency were repeated at ecclesiastical councils of the later eleventh century.[163]

Baptism was supposed to be followed up by confirmation performed by the bishop, and if this took place when the candidate was old enough, this would be another opportunity for teaching and perhaps also examination of the faith.[164] In settlements which lay at some distance from cathedrals, the occasion or opportunity for confirmation must have depended primarily on the travels of the bishop or the willingness of the parents to travel.[165] The sources suggest that (unsurprisingly) some bishops were more diligent than others in travelling through their dioceses and performing confirmations, but it remains difficult to establish either how frequently confirmations took place or, more importantly, how assiduous bishops were in examining the faith of candidates when they performed confirmations.[166] The vast areas covered by some dioceses in the early years of English Christianity

[161] Ine, 2–2.1, ed. Liebermann, *Gesetze*, 90–1.

[162] Report on the legatine synod of 786, 2, ed. Haddan and Stubbs, *Councils*, III.448–9; Foot, 'Baptism', 188–9; for Carolingian baptismal instruction, see Keefe, *Water and the Word*.

[163] *Hom.* 24, ed. A.S. Napier, *Wulfstan: Sammlung der ihm zugeschriebenen homilien nebst Untersuchungen über ihre Echtheit*, Sammlung englisher Denkmäler in kritischen Ausgaben 4 (Berlin, 1883), 120, ll. 8–15; Ælfric, *Pastoral Letter* I.71, ed. Fehr, *Die Hirtenbriefe Ælfrics*, 16; e.g. Council at Winchester (1070), 7, *Councils and Synods*, I.ii, no. 86.

[164] Foot, 'Baptism', 178–9, 183–4; see for example Hom. 24, ed. Napier, *Wulfstan*, 120, l. 15 – 121, l. 5.

[165] Foot, *Monastic Life*, 300.

[166] In the early period in particular it seems that baptized individuals were not always confirmed: see U, IV.9, ed. Finsterwalder, *Canones Theodori*, 317; Bede, *Epistola ad Ecgberhtum*, 7, ed. Plummer, *Venerabilis Baedae Historiam ecclesiasticam*, 410; also H. Vollrath, 'Taufliturgie und Diözesaneinteilung in der frühen angelsächsischen Kirche', in P. Ní Chatháin and M. Richter (eds), *Irland und die Christenheit: Bibelstudien und Mission / Ireland and Christendom: The Bible and the Missions* (Stuttgart, 1987), 377–86, at 385–6; Foot, 'Baptism', 179; Cramer, *Baptism and Change in the Early Middle Ages*, 179.

suggests that for some bishops it may simply have been impossible to travel through the entire diocese in a year, although this may have become more manageable in later centuries.[167] An eighth-century vision of the afterlife includes a description of a multitude of children who died unbaptized during the episcopacy of Bishop Daniel of Winchester (*c.*705–44), although whether the blame was to be directly laid at his door or elsewhere is not clear.[168] In any case, the diocese at this stage was huge and the idea that so many children died without baptism is perhaps not unrealistic, although the point here may also be rather political.[169]

The rituals for confession and penance underline the importance of the creed as the basis for Christian knowledge, as do the rites for the sick and the dying since they incorporate the rite of confession.[170] Before confession, the priest was required to ensure that the penitent understood (and believed) the fundamentals of the faith so that he could make a proper confession: as in the case of those who sought Christian burial without knowledge of the creed, it seems that the importance of the ritual of confession (and specifically, absolution) may have been understood even by those whose knowledge of Christianity was rather shaky. Some of the rituals for confession include the incipit for the Nicene Creed, although it is not clear whether penitents were regularly able to recite this. Other confessional rituals examined the penitent's knowledge of the creed through a dialogue in a way similar to the baptismal ritual.[171] These dialogues render the creed more loosely, and especially where the creed is shortened they often emphasise two key ideas which seem to have been considered the most essential knowledge for laity. These are firstly the idea of God the Father, Son and Holy Ghost (one God in three parts), and secondly the idea of life after death and resurrection at judgement day (the immortality of the soul, and reward or recompense according to one's deeds in life).[172] The focus on these ideas is understandable even though essential aspects of Christian belief such as the Crucifixion and Resurrection are omitted, since these underline the monotheistic nature of Christianity and highlight the importance of

---

[167]   Cubitt, *Anglo-Saxon Church Councils, c.650–c.850*, 114–15.

[168]   *Epistola* 115, ed. Tangl, *Die Briefe*, 247–50, at 249, ll. 3–12.

[169]   Cubitt, *Anglo-Saxon Church Councils, c.650–c.850*, 114–15.

[170]   F.S. Paxton, *Christianizing Death: The Creation of a Ritual Process in Early Medieval Europe* (Ithaca, NY, 1990), 92–114.

[171]   Frantzen, 'Tradition', 24–5.

[172]   See for example the ritual for confession in the *Old English Handbook*, 52.01.02, ed. Frantzen, *The Anglo-Saxon Penitentials*, quoted here from CCCC 201 (D): 'ic gelife on drihten heahfæder ealra þinga wealdend. & on þone sunu & on þone halgan gast & ic gelife to life æfter deaðe & ic gelife to arisenne on domes dæge & eal þis ic gelife þurh godes mægen & his miltse to weorðone' ('I believe in the Lord, the High Father, ruler of all things, and in the Son, and in the Holy Ghost, and I believe in life after death, and I believe that I will arise on the day of judgement. And all this I believe will happen through God's power and mercy').

life after death and careful preparation for it, towards which many of the rituals of pastoral care were aimed.

Establishing how frequently early medieval Christians (in England or elsewhere) had recourse to confession is more difficult. Tenth- and eleventh-century Anglo-Saxon homilies contain frequent exhortations to confession, giving the impression that it took place only infrequently, but this may be misleading; conversely the lack of references in narrative sources perhaps indicates in fact that the practice was common enough that it was not considered to merit comment, just as references to the abuse of confession suggest that the practice may have been fairly widespread.[173] Confession may have been more frequent in some sections of society than others, especially in the early period, since even in the eighth century some elite individuals seem to have had their own confessors.[174] It is worth bearing in mind too that at least from the ninth century, if not earlier, the reception of communion was linked with confession, and this had affected the expected frequency of both practices.[175] Early medieval sources from England and from the Continent encourage confession and reception of communion at least annually, and more often if possible, especially in the later period.[176] Neither Bede in the eighth century nor Ælfric in the late tenth would necessarily have expected lay people to receive communion every week, but both recommended reception of communion whenever the soul was in a fit state (that is, following confession), and Ælfric instructed that lay people should receive communion at mass about sixteen times a year.[177] In the eleventh century Wulfstan enshrined in law an exhortation to frequent confession and communion.[178] Long before the Fourth Lateran Council

[173]   Frantzen, *Literature of Penance*, 155–6; R. Meens, 'The Frequency and Nature of Early Medieval Penance', in P. Biller and A.J. Minnis (eds), *Handling Sin: Confession in the Middle Ages*, York Studies in Medieval Theology 2 (Woodbridge, 1998), 35–61, at 53.

[174]   B. Poschmann, *Penance and the Anointing of the Sick*, trans. F. Courtney (Freiburg, 1964), 139.

[175]   S. Hamilton, *The Practice of Penance, 900–1050* (Woodbridge, 2001), 60.

[176]   See, for example Bede, *Epistola ad Ecgbertum*, 15, ed. Plummer, *Venerabilis Baedae Historiam ecclesiasticam*, 419; Council of *Clofesho* (747), 23, ed. Haddan and Stubbs, *Councils*, III.370; *Capitula Bavarica*, VI, ed. R. Pokorny, *Capitula Episcoporum*, MGH (4 vols, Hannover, 1995), III.196; Theodulf, *Capitula*, 36, ed. H. Sauer, *Theodulfi Capitula in England: die altenglischen Übersetzungen, zusammen mit dem lateinischen Text*, Texte und Untersuchungen zur englischen Philologie 8 (Munich, 1978), 376–83; see also Meens, 'Frequency and Nature', 37; Hamilton, *Practice of Penance*, 5.

[177]   Ælfric stated that the laity should receive communion on Sundays in Lent, the three days preceding Easter Sunday, and on Easter Day, the Thursday of Rogation week, Ascension Day, Pentecost and the four days after the four Ember-feasts: see *Hom.* XIX, ll. 119–35, ed. J.C. Pope, *Homilies of Ælfric: A Supplementary Collection*, EETS, OS 259–60 (2 vols, London, 1967–8), II.628–9; Foot, *Monastic Life*, 205, 302.

[178]   e.g. V Æthelred 22, 22.1, ed. Liebermann, *Gesetze*, I.242–3; and see Wulfstan, *De conuersione et penitentia et communione*, ed. T.N. Hall, 'Wulfstan's Latin Sermons', in Townend (ed.), *Wulfstan, Archbishop of York*, 93–139, at 129–30. See also Frantzen,

in 1215, which formally enjoined annual confession and reception of communion upon all adult Christians, some clergy evidently considered that this was an essential part of Christian practice.[179]

Expectations for church attendance were also quite high: from early on, officials of the English Church seem to have assumed that laity would be present at churches on Sundays and feast-days, where they were supposed to attend mass and hear the preaching which priests and abbots were required to undertake, whether or not they received communion at the mass.[180] Similarly, the sermons of the tenth and eleventh centuries assume that preaching is the responsibility of bishops and priests, and that this would take place on Sundays and feast-days. Many of Ælfric's homilies contain a gospel pericope and commentary, indicating that they were expected to be preached at mass, and he provided homilies for most of the Sundays in the Church year.[181] By the tenth century, if not earlier, most preaching to lay congregations seems to have been in the vernacular, although even Bede's Latin homilies seem to refer to the presence of a lay congregation: Bede's Latin would presumably have presented difficulties for most lay people and some clergy, too, although perhaps the homilies might have been used as notes for *ex tempore* vernacular preaching, especially if the texts were glossed.[182] Nonetheless, it is far more difficult to ascertain in reality how frequently laity might have attended churches, or even if they did, how studiously they paid attention: one Old English homily notes that the devil encourages fidgeting in church, suggesting that

*Literature of Penance*, 146–7; S. Keynes, 'An abbot, an archbishop, and the viking raids of 1006–7 and 1009–12', *Anglo-Saxon England* 36 (2006): 151–224, at 177–9.

[179] A. Murray, 'Confession before 1215', *Transactions of the Royal Historical Society*, 6th series 3 (1993): 51–81, at 58, 63, 64–5. Anglo-Saxon secular laws also refer to the performance of penance and decree that those who refused penance could be excommunicated: see Ch. 3, and Foot, *Monastic Life*, 305–6.

[180] Council of *Clofesho* (747), 14, ed. Haddan and Stubbs, *Councils*, III.367; see also Alcuin, *Epistola* 18, ed. Dümmler, *Epistolae*, 52, ll. 31–2: 'laicorum est obedire praedicationi, iustos esse et misericordes' ('[the duty] of the laity is that they should obey preaching, and be just and merciful').

[181] P. Clemoes, 'The Chronology of Ælfric's Works', in P. Clemoes (ed.), *The Anglo-Saxons: Studies in Some Aspects of Their History and Culture Presented to Bruce Dickins* (London, 1959), 213–47, at 214–18; M. Clayton, 'Homiliaries and preaching in Anglo-Saxon England', *Peritia* 4 (1985): 207–42, at 221; Wilcox, 'Ælfric in Dorset', 53.

[182] M.M. Gatch, 'The Achievement of Aelfric and his Colleagues in European Perspective', in P.E. Szarmach and B.F. Huppe (eds), *Old English Homily and its Backgrounds* (Albany, 1978), 43–73, at 60–1; D.G. Scragg, 'The corpus of vernacular homilies & prose saints' lives before Ælfric', *Anglo-Saxon England* 8 (1979): 223–77, at 223; A. Thacker, 'Monks, Preaching and Pastoral Care in Early Anglo-Saxon England', in J. Blair and R. Sharpe (eds), *Pastoral Care before the Parish* (Leicester, 1992), 137–70, at 140–1.

(unsurprisingly) some members of medieval congregations may have been much like their modern counterparts.[183]

This accumulation of evidence presents a complicated and somewhat fragmented picture, in which it is difficult to pin down precisely how, or how often, laity at different times and in different places had access to Christian teaching. The frequent exhortations for people to learn the most basic prayers and tenets of the Christian faith, or to participate in routine Christian practices, might seem to indicate firstly that many people in Anglo-Saxon England neither acquired much knowledge of the Christian faith nor believed much of it, and secondly that only a minimum of knowledge was expected of lay congregations in any case. Comments such as those made by Ælfric about the poor level of learning (or possibly poor attention span) of some of those in his congregations seem to reinforce the picture of limited lay knowledge of the Christian faith.[184] But it is important to remember that (then as now) congregations cannot have been completely static and that at any given time a congregation might have included people with limited knowledge as well as people with much more detailed knowledge. Comments on the creed in particular were especially appropriate in homilies at certain regular times of the year when the creed was a defining part of the liturgy, for example at Easter, or in the context of particular services or offices, such as baptism. It is also clear that Anglo-Saxon clergy did not consider that Christian learning among the laity was (or should be) limited to knowledge of the creed and pater noster, only that this was the minimum basis on which to build more detailed learning: exhortations to learn basic prayers are matched by much more complex and sophisticated discussions of theological topics even in texts which seem to have been directed at lay audiences.

This picture presented by the sources is therefore not only complicated, but rather contradictory, simultaneously insisting on the basics and assuming that more complex and detailed theological discussions will not be lost on the same audience. This is exemplified by one of Wulfstan's sermons which begins by stating that Christian men should know the pater noster and creed, but turns to a careful discussion of Christology and the idea that Christ is both truly divine

---

[183]   *Hom.* XLVI, ed. Napier, *Wulfstan*, 233, ll. 17–20.

[184]   See for example *CH* I.11, ll. 2–7, ed. Clemoes, *Catholic Homilies*, 266: 'Ic wolde eow trahtnian þis godespel þe man nu beforan eow rædde: ac ic ondræde þæt ge ne magon þa miclan deopnesse þæs godspelles swa understandan swa hit gedauenlic sy. Nu bidde ic eow þæt ge beon geþyldige on eowrum geþance oð þæt we þone traht mid godes fylste oferrædan magon' ('I want to explain this gospel to you, which has now been read before you, but I worry that you are unable to understand the great depth of the gospel as is appropriate. Now I ask that you be patient in your thoughts until we can read through the text, with God's help'); or *CH* I.36, ll. 282–4, ed. Clemoes, *Catholic Homilies*, 495: 'We mihton þas halgan rædinge menigfealdlicor trahtnian æfter augustines smeagunge; ac us twynað hwæðer ge magon maran deopnysse þæron þearflice tocnawan' ('we could explain this holy reading in more ways according to Augustine's thinking, but we doubt that you can profitably understand the great depth in it').

and truly human, receiving his divinity from God and his humanity from Mary.[185] Significantly, this kind of inconsistency is not limited to texts intended for use in lay education, but is also found in much of the material produced for priests who were responsible for performing routine pastoral care, or aimed at improving or assessing their knowledge. Thus the questions for ordinands in Junius 121 require the would-be priest to be able to explain the significance of baptism and the mass, even though they conclude with the possibility that a half-learned priest might be ordained.[186] In his *Pastoral Letters* for Wulfstan and Bishop Wulfsige of Sherborne, written in the voice of the bishop and directed at priests who were probably in the bishops' respective dioceses, Ælfric discusses quite complex topics such as what happens when the Eucharist is consecrated, but also takes care to explain that the consecrated Host should not be left in a place where it can go mouldy, or where mice can eat it.[187] Likewise, in his computistical handbook Byrhtferth of Ramsey makes frequent (and often quite sarcastic) jibes at the ignorance of those who struggled with Latin, and then proceeds to explain complex methods of calculation for them in English, so that his subject-matter remained sophisticated even while he berated the 'stupid' priests he addressed.[188]

To some extent this results from the conflict between an ideal situation where all Christians are highly educated about their faith, and the rhetoric of reform which focused on those who displayed any measure of ignorance.[189] In the Anglo-Saxon Church this rhetoric dates at least back to Bede's time, and his complaint

---

[185]   *Hom.* VII, ed. Bethurum, *Homilies*, 157–65. One of the manuscripts which contains this sermon, Cambridge, Corpus Christi College, 201, also preserves a shorter version (VIIa, ed. D. Bethurum, *The Homilies of Wulfstan* (Oxford, 1957), 166–8) where the translation of the creed is much simpler. It is difficult to ascertain the intended purpose of the manuscript, but it seems to have been intended at least partly as a reference book for teaching. The two sermons are also found in two Worcester books which were intended to be companion volumes: the more complex sermon (VII) is included in Hatton 113+114, and the simpler (VIIa) in Junius 121. The collections in CCCC 201 and Junius 121/Hatton 113+114 are closely related, but it may be that in both cases the compilers considered it useful to have two sermons explaining the basics of the faith – one simple and one more complex – which could be used according to the potential audience. See further H. Foxhall Forbes, 'Making Books for Pastoral Care in Late Eleventh-Century Worcester: Oxford, Bodleian Library, Junius 121 and Hatton 113+114', in P.D. Clarke and S. James (eds), *Pastoral Care in the Middle Ages* (Farnham, forthcoming); and cf. Gatch, *Preaching*, 20, for the suggestion that Wulfstan preferred to avoid theological subtlety.

[186]   *Examination of Candidates*, 11–16, *Councils and Synods*, I.i, no. 57; see also the canons of the Council of *Clofesho* (747), 10–11, ed. Haddan and Stubbs, *Councils*, III.366.

[187]   Ælfric, *Pastoral Letter for Wulfsige*, I.133–42, ed. Fehr, *Die Hirtenbriefe Ælfrics*, 29–31; Hill, 'Monastic Reform', 109–11.

[188]   e.g. Byrhtferth, *Enchiridion*, I.1, ll. 137–40, 214–16; I.3, ll. 1–2; II.1, ll. 191–3, ed. P.S. Baker and M. Lapidge, *Byrhtferth's Enchiridion*, EETS, SS 15 (Oxford, 1995), 14–16, 20, 46, 66.

[189]   Hill, 'Monastic Reform', 111.

about 'unlearned' priests, but it is unclear whether these priests were only ignorant of Latin or also of content: it may be that these priests were able to explain at least some of the sense and content of the prayers in English even if they could not read Latin.[190] It is also notable that while Bede makes this complaint to Archbishop Ecgberht he does not complain about the decision by Ecgberht or other bishops to ordain priests who did not know these prayers in Latin. Boniface clearly also faced a scarcity of priests in the mission field, and was instructed by Pope Zacharias that men could be ordained priest before the canonical age of 30, if the situation required it.[191] Boniface's concern is clear in his own letter to Archbishop Ecgberht, where he asks advice about whether to remove a priest who had been restored to the priesthood after performing penance: his letter reveals his anguish over the decision, as he tells Ecgberht 'if I remove him … children will die without the holy water of rebirth [i.e., baptism] because of the scarcity of priests'.[192] In the eighth century as in the eleventh, it seems that half-learned or otherwise inadequate priests were deemed to be better than none at all, but this enjoined a constant process of learning and teaching on priests as on laity, picked up in Byrhtferth's admonition to the priests who used his manual: 'in the sight of the just judge both will be guilty – those who do not wish to learn, and those who do not wish to teach'.[193]

Especially after the middle of the tenth century, such complaints also spring from a specifically monastic rhetoric which presented secular clergy as ignorant, lazy and lax in fulfilling their duties in contrast to those in monastic life, and because so many of the surviving texts and manuscripts seem to have originated from, and survive in manuscripts copied at, the major episcopal or monastic centres (or episcopal centres which were monastic) the picture is coloured in favour of monasticism. But this can overshadow the fact that even while monastic authors complained about the secular clergy, they clearly accepted that these men played an important role in the Christian mission, and in some cases recognition of this role may have led to silence about it rather than complaints.[194] On the other hand, the nature of the evidence means that it is difficult to pinpoint precisely the materials which secular communities and lone priests might have used for teaching, and how these materials might have related to the surviving texts and

---

[190]   Bede, *Epistola ad Ecgbertum*, 5, ed. Plummer, *Venerabilis Baedae Historiam ecclesiasticam*, 408–9.

[191]   *Epistola* 87, ed. Tangl, *Die Briefe*, 369–72.

[192]   *Epistola* 91, ed. Tangl, *Die Briefe*, 376–7.

[193]   Byrhtferth, *Enchiridion*, 4, ed. and trans. Baker and Lapidge, *Byrhtferth's Enchiridion*, 53–4: 'Simul erunt rei in conspectu iusti arbitris: qui nolunt scire et qui nolunt docere'. See also Ælfric's comment in his English preface to his *Grammar*, ed. Wilcox, *Aelfric's Prefaces*, 115 (no. 3b): 'And he se naðor nele ne leornian ne tæcan, gif he mæg, þonne acolað his andgyt fram ðære halgan lare and he gewit swa lytlum and lytlum fram Gode' ('And he who will neither learn nor teach if he is able to, then his understanding of holy learning will become cold, and he will go little by little from God').

[194]   See for example the discussion in Foxhall Forbes, 'Squabbling siblings', 673–4.

manuscripts. Priests were instructed that they should own and be able to use a fairly wide selection of books, including those for the mass and pastoral offices (such as confession and baptism) as well as those for daily services and for calculating Church feasts.[195] It seems probable that not all priests would or could have owned or used all of these different books, but even in the localities some priests may have worked from centres which owned resources in common.[196] It also seems likely that in many cases the material copies of texts used in smaller churches may have been in the form of booklets rather than bound books, whether these were liturgical rituals or homilies for preaching, and some of the surviving manuscripts look as if they might have been intended as reference collections containing the sorts of texts copied in this way.[197]

Apart from the many other reasons why manuscripts do not survive to the present day, the prevalence of bound manuscripts rather than booklets in the surviving record is probably because booklets were used until they fell to bits, or were discarded, reused or recycled (for example as strips for binding other books) as liturgical texts and homilies became outdated or superseded by new material.[198] However, the surviving books do indicate the variety of contexts for pastoral care and education in the range of purposes suggested by the texts and books used and copied within the same centre. For example, similar collections of penitential texts are found in two eleventh-century manuscripts from Worcester, now Oxford, Bodleian Library, Laud misc. 482 and Junius 121, but the two books are noticeably different in character and were clearly for different practical purposes.[199] Laud misc. 482 is a slim and portable volume containing liturgical material and instructions for performing the offices of confession and the rites for the sick and dying, and the absence of the last pages of the volume may point to wear as a result of practical use and being carried about.[200] In contrast, Junius 121 is a fat volume containing catechetical homilies and other instructional material, including information pertinent to the training of priests such as questions which bishops should put to candidates for ordination, and it forms a partner to the homiliary now surviving in two parts as Oxford, Bodleian Library, Hatton 113 and 114.[201] While Laud misc. 482 looks like it was specifically designed to be used in the practical performance of pastoral care, the material found in Junius 121 and Hatton 113+114 is a collection which may have had many purposes, one of which

---

[195]   e.g. Ælfric, *Pastoral Letters*, I.52, II.157, ed. Fehr, *Die Hirtenbriefe Ælfrics*, 13, 126–7; see also Penitential of Ps.-Ecgberht, Prol., ed. Haddan and Stubbs, *Councils*, III.417.

[196]   Wilcox, 'Ælfric in Dorset', 56–60.

[197]   P.R. Robinson, 'Self-contained units in composite manuscripts of the Anglo-Saxon period', *Anglo-Saxon England* 7 (1978): 231–8; Wilcox, 'Ælfric in Dorset', 60–1.

[198]   Gittos, 'Is there any Evidence for the Liturgy of Parish Churches', 63–4.

[199]   N.R. Ker, *Catalogue of Manuscripts Containing Anglo-Saxon* (Oxford, 1957), nos. 338 and 343.

[200]   Thompson, *Dying and Death*, 67–73.

[201]   Ker, *Catalogue*, 399, 412.

seems to have been the education and training of priests, but it might also have been used as a reference book for copying texts into booklets.[202]

Books and booklets as well as the information from book-learning supported priests' duties in performing religious practices for their congregations, and teaching them about Christian beliefs, but once again what might have been offered depended on time and place. Priests at smaller churches seem to have been expected to provide the offices of baptism and mass, as well as offering their congregations the opportunity to confess and to perform penance, or to receive anointing when they were unwell.[203] In later periods they might also have been expected or requested to provide Christian burial rituals, as the place and type of burial seems to have become increasingly important.[204] But what was offered by a lone priest did not cover all the practices which were deemed (or which came to be deemed) necessary. In some cases the bishop's presence was required in the localities, as for consecrating churches (and cemeteries, in the tenth and eleventh centuries), just as confirmations seem to have been performed when bishops toured their dioceses. For other rituals which were performed at cathedrals, priests as well as individuals and congregations were required to travel to the bishop: the rite of public penance, for example, reserved for serious sins and used mainly in the tenth and eleventh centuries, was performed by a bishop and involved the ritual (and literal) expulsion of the offender from the Church on Ash Wednesday before reconciliation on Maundy Thursday.[205] The liturgies for some major feasts (such as Easter) required the participation of more than one person in holy orders, and although it is possible that some priests without deacons needed to know how to perform these rituals, it is also possible that some priests may have gone with their congregations to a larger church such as a minster or cathedral for these feasts.[206]

Such travel as a Christian community is significant in the common sense of religious purpose which may have attended such occasions, but there were also several occasions during the year – indeed, often at these major feasts – which were marked by processions which brought formal religious practices out of churches and into the local landscape, especially in later centuries. On Palm Sunday, the festivities for Holy Week began with a procession recalling the triumphal entry

---

[202]    M. Budny, *Insular, Anglo-Saxon and Early Anglo-Norman Manuscript Art at Corpus Christi College, Cambridge: An Illustrated Catalogue* (2 vols, Kalamazoo, MI, 1997), I.476–7; Tinti, *Sustaining Belief*, 298–301.

[203]    Gittos, 'Is there any Evidence for the Liturgy of Parish Churches', 64–5.

[204]    D.A. Bullough, 'Burial, Community and Belief in the Early Medieval West', in P. Wormald et al. (eds), *Ideal and Reality in Frankish and Anglo-Saxon Society: Studies Presented to J.M. Wallace-Hadrill* (Oxford, 1983), 177–201; Thompson, *Dying and Death*, 57–63, 112–17; Gittos, 'Is there any Evidence for the Liturgy of Parish Churches', 64–5.

[205]    S. Hamilton, 'Rites for Public Penance in Late Anglo-Saxon England', in H. Gittos and M.B. Bedingfield (eds), *The Liturgy of the Late Anglo-Saxon Church* (Woodbridge, 2005), 65–103, at 87–8.

[206]    Gittos, 'Is there any Evidence for the Liturgy of Parish Churches', 65–6.

of Jesus into Jerusalem before his arrest, Crucifixion and Resurrection, events which were commemorated later in the week on Maundy Thursday, Good Friday and Easter Sunday respectively.[207] The evidence for the practicalities of how these processions worked in specific localities is generally rather patchy but eleventh-century Winchester provides a clearer picture than most. Here the monks at the Old Minster (the cathedral) and the New Minster formed a procession and went to a church together to collect the palms, perhaps the church of St James outside the city walls to the west.[208] A similar type of procession took place at Candlemas (2nd February) to mark the presentation of Christ in the temple and in Winchester this too seems to have involved the monks from both the Old and New Minsters and may have involved a station at another church.[209] Processions also took place on Rogation Days and at the celebrations for saints' days, usually whichever saint or saints were culted in the locality.[210]

These kinds of processions were occasions at which cultural ideas shared by communities of believers were expressed and communicated, whether directly or indirectly. Homilies for Palm Sunday explain the event commemorated, but the procession itself was a moment of liturgical drama and recreated a past event and its symbolism: observers of any age (whether or not they were involved in the procession) who did not understand the significance of the event it commemorated may simply have asked those who did.[211] The Rogation processions are a particularly important example here because it seems that at Rogationtide it was assumed that a particularly large number of people would be present, perhaps including those who were less than well catechised: many of the Rogationtide homilies are quite simple and focus on quite basic information.[212] But these processions are also important in that they are one example of religion and religious ritual happening beyond the confines of churches, blurring the boundaries between lay and ecclesiastical space. Another example of this in action is possibly visible from the liturgical blessings which were used for crops and fields, or other areas of the outside world beyond the

---

[207]   For full discussion of these, see M.B. Bedingfield, *The Dramatic Liturgy of Anglo-Saxon England* (Woodbridge, 2002), esp. 90–170.

[208]   *RC*, 33, 36, ed. and trans. Symons, *Regularis Concordia*, 30–1, 34–6; M. Biddle and D. Keene, 'Winchester in the Eleventh and Twelfth Centuries', in M. Biddle (ed.), *Winchester in the Early Middle Ages: An Edition and Discussion of the Winton Domesday* (Oxford, 1976), 241–448, at 268–9.

[209]   Biddle and Keene, 'Winchester in the Eleventh and Twelfth Centuries', 268–9.

[210]   Bedingfield, *The Dramatic Liturgy of Anglo-Saxon England*, 191–6; Blair, *The Church*, 455–6, 486–9.

[211]   See for example *Hom.* VI, ed. R. Morris, *The Blickling Homilies of the 10th Century: From the Marquis of Lothian's Unique MS. A.D.971*, EETS, OS 58 (London, 1874), 71; Bedingfield, *The Dramatic Liturgy of Anglo-Saxon England*, 90–113.

[212]   J. Bazire and J.E. Cross (eds.), *Eleven Old English Rogationtide Homilies*, Toronto Old English Series 7 (Toronto, 1982), 41; Bedingfield, *The Dramatic Liturgy of Anglo-Saxon England*, 196–7.

monastery.[213] These were once understood to be evidence of the accommodation of Christianity to paganism, but recent work has demonstrated that in fact these were closely associated with the institutional Church, and represent ideas and ideals of religious thought more than those of the laity.[214] To try to interpret these as evidence of 'lay piety' would therefore clearly be incorrect, but blessings for crops or wells, for example, may provide another instance of the possibility of liturgical ritual outside church walls, even if once again it is difficult to determine how frequently laity or lay communities attended such blessings.[215]

Celebrations in honour of saints were another opportunity for bringing laity into contact with formal ritual, although again how this occurred, and how frequently, depended according to local context. Major centres often had a large number of relics, some of which might be the remains of saints who were culted universally in Christian cultures, such as the apostles or other people who featured in the gospels: the list of relics at Exeter includes (for example) the beard and hair of St Peter, and the neckbone of St Paul.[216] The documents which record Exeter's relics also provide some information about how the relics came to the minster, apparently by the donation of King Æthelstan in the early tenth century, and this is given in the form of a text which is more likely a sermon than simply a list, perhaps intended for a mass or procession in celebration of the relics.[217] This long list of relics is comparatively unusual and a feature of a major centre rather than a smaller church: comparable relic lists survive for other large religious houses like the New Minster in Winchester, which similarly records the gifts of relics, such as the 'scrin' given by Emma of Normandy (d.1052), who was married first to King Æthelred (d.1016) and then to Cnut (d.1035).[218] Interest in relics gave rise to a couple of texts which record the relics of the saints scattered across England, but again these are primarily for major churches.[219] However, it seems likely that almost all churches, even quite small ones, would have contained relics of a saint

---

[213]   K.L. Jolly, 'Prayers from the field: Practical protection and demonic defense in Anglo-Saxon England', *Traditio: Studies in Ancient and Medieval History, Thought, and Religion* 61 (2006): 95–147; D.A. Rivard, *Blessing the World: Ritual and Lay Piety in Medieval Religion* (Washington, DC, 2009), 41–3, 51–77.

[214]   T. Rowe, 'Blessings for Nature in the English Liturgy, c. 900–1200', PhD thesis, University of Exeter, 2010, 188–94, 214–16, 234–45. I am grateful to Tamsin Rowe for allowing me to see a copy of her doctoral thesis.

[215]   Rowe, 'Blessings for Nature', 42–52, 172–9.

[216]   P.W. Conner, *Anglo-Saxon Exeter: A Tenth-Century Cultural History* (Woodbridge, 1993), 171–209, esp. 176–87.

[217]   F. Rose-Troup, 'The ancient monastery of St Mary and St Peter at Exeter', *Report and Transactions – The Devonshire Association for the Advancement of Science, Literature and Art* 2 (1931): 179–220, at 212–15.

[218]   London, British Library, Stowe 944, fols. 58r–v.

[219]   See D.W. Rollason, 'Lists of saints' resting-places in Anglo-Saxon England', *Anglo-Saxon England* 7 (1978): 61–94.

or saints, although in most cases these saints were probably culted much more locally and were perhaps unique to one place.[220]

Written information about many of these local saints is lacking and for many, possibly never existed, so that only their names (and often, not even that) survive to the present day. One example is the St Ailwine (now Egelwin) culted at Scalford (Leicestershire), about whom nothing further is known (local legend holds that he is buried in the churchyard, but no one seems to know where exactly). The local character of these cults and the landscapes in which they existed are particularly important, because when saints were celebrated in the places where they had lived and died, stations in processions might be made at places where the saint had left a lasting impression in the landscape. Sometimes these were literal impressions in the physical landscape, like the footprints of St Mildred in a slab of rock near Thanet (Kent), but sometimes the natural environment formed part of a saint's legend, like the trees and springs associated with St Kenelm.[221] Where surviving written hagiographical traditions are rooted in local landscapes and topographies it is possible that they represent quite early cult devotion, even when references are found only in much later texts.[222] Moreover, as Katy Cubitt and others have argued, these kinds of local concerns may represent the kinds of cults which grew up outside the formal ecclesiastical legends which sought to represent all saints and their miracles in the models of earlier hagiographical texts.[223]

The number of visitors to the places which were prominent in the life and death of a saint and the miracles performed at such places likewise feature in hagiographies as a means of indicating the power that a saint commanded: the site where Oswald was killed in 642 apparently attracted visitors who scraped up the dust to use in healing people and animals.[224] Oswald was also responsible for erecting a cross at Heavenfield, near Hexham (Northumberland), where he defeated Caedwalla in 633 or 634; and like the site of his death, the cross was apparently visited by people seeking miracles who took little pieces of the wood which were used to cure people and animals.[225] In other cases saints became part of

---

[220]    J. Blair, 'A Saint for Every Minster? Local Cults in Anglo-Saxon England', in A. Thacker and R. Sharpe (eds), *Local Saints and Local Churches in the Early Medieval West* (Oxford, 2002), 455–94.

[221]    Goscelin, *Vita virginis Mildrethae*, 19, ed. D.W. Rollason, *The Mildrith Legend: A Study in Early Medieval Hagiography in England* (Leicester, 1982), 132–3; *Vita S. Kenelmi*, 6, 13, ed. R.C. Love, *Three Eleventh-Century Anglo-Latin Saints' Lives: Vita S. Birini, Vita et Miracula S. Kenelmi, and Vita S. Rumwoldi* (Oxford, 1996), 58, 68; Blair, *The Church*, 475–9.

[222]    J. Blair, *Anglo-Saxon Oxfordshire* (Stroud, 1994), 73–7.

[223]    Cubitt, 'Sites and sanctity'; Blair, *The Church*, 146–9, 475–7; see also F. Lifshitz, *The Name of the Saint: The Martyrology of Jerome and Access to the Sacred in Francia, 627 – 827*, Publications in Medieval Studies (Notre Dame, IN, 2006).

[224]    Bede, *HE*, III.9–10, ed. Lapidge, Monat and Robin, *Histoire ecclésiastique*, 58–64.

[225]    Bede, *HE*, III.2, ed. Lapidge, Monat and Robin, *Histoire ecclésiastique*, 18–24.

the built environment as their relics continued to lie in churches which also formed part of their legends: once rescued from the thorn bush, St Edmund's head was reunited with his body for burial, and a chapel was constructed over his remains.[226] Although saints were especially commemorated in their localities at particular times of year, their presence in the landscape was of course more constant and the use of saints' names in place-names suggests that at least the names of these saints (and perhaps some of their deeds or possessions) were known to those who lived in, visited or travelled through those places, even if in some cases little written tradition now survives for these individuals.[227]

Crosses made of wood or stone, like the one constructed by Oswald, served as a visible and positive marker of Christian sacrality in the landscape, and may have been positioned along routeways or as route markers.[228] In some cases crosses may also have been used as stations in Rogationtide processions.[229] Records of the boundaries of lands contain information about holy features which were used as boundary markers, including what seem to be crosses such as these, as well as trees and wells;[230] but while wooden or stone crosses were holy in and of themselves because of the sign they represented, trees, wells and stones were not. As already noted, some hagiographical accounts explicitly associate springs or wells and trees with saints, and so it may be that some of these features were identified as holy because of now lost traditions that linked them with holy people, although in other cases they might simply have been marked with the sign of the cross.[231] Sometimes there appears to have been tension over what was identified as 'holy', as in the striking example of 'the tree which the ignorant call holy' in a Latin charter copied in the twelfth century, itself forged but perhaps containing a translation of a genuine boundary clause.[232] More general objections to holy wells,

---

[226]     Abbo, *Passio S. Eadmundi*, 11–13, ed. M. Winterbottom, *Three Lives of English Saints* (Toronto, 1972), 79–82; see also XI–XIV, ed. T. Arnold, *Memorials of St Edmund's Abbey* (London, 1890), 16–19. Ælfric, *Passio S. Eadmundi*, LS XXXII, ll. 123–88, ed. W.W. Skeat, *Aelfric's Lives of Saints: Being a Set of Sermons on Saints' Days Formerly Observed by the English Church*, EETS 76, 82 (vol. 1), 94, 114 (vol. 2) (4 vols in 2, London, 1881–1900), II.322–8.

[227]     Blair, 'Saint for Every Minster?', 455–9, 480–1; Blair, *The Church*, 216–17.

[228]     Blair, *The Church*, 478–9.

[229]     C. Neuman De Vegvar, 'Converting the Anglo-Saxon Landscape: Crosses and their Audiences', in A.J. Minnis and J. Roberts (eds), *Text, Image, Interpretation: Studies in Anglo-Saxon Literature and its Insular Context in Honour of Éamonn Ó Carragáin* (Turnhout, 2007), 407–29, at 420–3.

[230]     e.g. S 766 (W.G. Searle, *Ingulf and the Historia Croylandensis*, Cambridge Antiquarian Society Octavo Publications 27 (Cambridge, 1894), 212): 'haliganstan' ('holy stone'); S 544 (*Abing*, no. 43): 'halgan ac' ('holy oak').

[231]     Cubitt, 'Sites and sanctity', 62; Blair, *The Church*, 477–8.

[232]     S 311 (BCS 476): 'ad quendam fraxinum quem imperiti sacrum vocant'; Blair, *The Church*, 477; D. Hooke, *Trees in Anglo-Saxon England: Literature, Lore and Landscape*, Anglo-Saxon Studies 13 (Woodbridge, 2010), 50.

trees or stones are found in the writings of clergy from late Antiquity and right through the Anglo-Saxon period: Ælfric and Wulfstan both complained about the foolishness of those who made offerings at trees, wells or stones.[233]

It has sometimes been argued that such complaints were made in response to beliefs or practices which represent continuity with pre-Christian or 'pagan' ideas, but as already noted, in many cases it was probably the fact that these holy places fell outside ecclesiastical control which upset clerical authorities, rather than because these represented any real (or imagined) 'pagan' behaviour. It is also clear that in some cases certain 'holy' features originated entirely in Christian contexts, and therefore cannot represent continuity of pre- or non-Christian practice. Here many of the 'holy wells' are a good example, because they are located in or near settlements which originated after the Middle Saxon shift and therefore in most places also quite some time after the conversion to Christianity.[234] If these were holy wells, they were perceived as holy in Christian contexts and may never have been considered holy by anyone who did not see himself as a Christian: some of them may have been used for baptism, in any case.[235] The liturgical blessings for wells which were produced and used from the tenth century to the twelfth also show that wells were understood to be Christian by the clergy who wrote and enacted these blessings, since they seem to have been designed as rites of purification for the benefit of Christian communities, and were not intended to 'convert' water features which were perceived to have pagan associations, whatever the actual origins of the wells which received the blessings.[236]

This is particularly important because it is extremely difficult to find any concrete evidence for 'paganism' within Anglo-Saxon Christian communities: the idea that pagan belief or practice survived in these contexts to the extent that it is now visible has been discredited by a number of scholars.[237] This is not to say that people did not (for example) believe in magical practices, because undoubtedly

---

[233]   Ælfric, *De auguriis*, LS XVII, ll. 129–35, ed. Skeat, *Lives of Saints*, 1.372–4; Wulfstan, *Canons of Edgar*, 16, ed. Fowler, *Canons of Edgar*, 4–5.

[234]   M. Jacobsson, *Wells, Meres, and Pools: Hydronymic Terms in the Anglo-Saxon Landscape*, Acta Universitatis Upsaliensis, Studia Anglistica Upsaliensia 98 (Uppsala, 1997), 224–7.

[235]   Rowe, 'Blessings for Nature', 141–9, 171–81.

[236]   R.K. Morris, 'Baptismal Places: 600–800', in N. Lund and I.N. Wood (eds), *People and Places in Northern Europe, 500–1600: Essays in Honour of Peter Hayes Sawyer* (Woodbridge, 1991), 15–24, at 18–20; J. Blair, 'The Prehistory of English Fonts', in M. Henig and N. Ramsay (eds), *Intersections: The Archaeology and History of Christianity in England, 400–1200: Papers in Honour of Martin Biddle and Birthe Kjølbye-Biddle* (Oxford, 2010), 149–77, at 157–60; Rowe, 'Blessings for Nature', 40–4, 172–9.

[237]   See in particular the arguments in C.E. Fell, 'Paganism in Beowulf: A Semantic Fairy-Tale', in T. Hofstra, L.A.J.R. Houwen and A.A. MacDonald (eds), *Pagans and Christians: The Interplay between Christian Latin and Traditional Germanic Cultures in Early Medieval Europe. Proceedings of the Second Germania Latina Conference held at the University of Groningen, May 1992*, Germania Latina, 2; Mediaevalia Groningana, 16

they did. But because the evidence which survives is so overwhelmingly from Christian contexts, it is virtually impossible to uncover any real information about these supposed magical practices, and even where texts survive which look in some way 'dubious' now, it is clear that these texts and the books that contain them originated, and were probably used at, religious centres, often quite important ones.[238] It is also clear that in some cases, representations of paganism appealed to Roman or Greek ideas rather than to a precise reality on the ground; moreover, as James Palmer has shown, modern scholars have sometimes 'translated' these episodes in ways which reflect preconceptions about 'Germanic' paganism without taking full account of the way in which 'real' and imagined paganisms were used by medieval authors to reflect a whole range of (probably also real and imagined) ideas that were perceived to run contrary to acceptable Christian belief or practice.[239] While authors sometimes distinguished between bad Christians and pagans, at other times it seems that the groups or individuals who prompted complaints from clergymen simply practised or believed in ways which some clergy – specifically, those who encountered them and wrote about them – felt was inappropriate behaviour for Christians. Such objections were therefore not always connected specifically with (for example) a particular natural feature which was identified as objectionable.

One example may be found in the complaint made in the late eleventh century by St Wulfstan of Worcester to the tree which overshadowed a church that he dedicated. This has been interpreted as evidence that this was some kind of 'holy tree' in an unChristian sense, but as Alexandra Walsham points out, it is in fact far more likely that the problem was that the priest tended to sit under this tree while he was gambling and drinking.[240] It seems highly unlikely that St Wulfstan, in the overwhelmingly Christian context of late eleventh century southern England, would have recognised a genuine pagan even if one had fallen out of said tree. In the same way, Ælfric's objections to people who feasted and drank around corpses probably arose from his monastic perspective: in his view, a dead body should be watched over quietly, accompanied by the singing of psalms and the offering of prayers. The complaints about feasting, horse-racing, and other games

---

(Groningen, 1995), 9–34; R.I. Page, 'Anglo-Saxon Paganism: The Evidence of Bede', in Hofstra, Houwen and MacDonald (eds), *Pagans and Christians*, 99–129.

[238]  See for example K.L. Jolly, 'Cross-Referencing Anglo-Saxon Liturgy and Remedies: The Sign of the Cross as Ritual Protection', in H. Gittos and M.B. Bedingfield (eds), *The Liturgy of the Late Anglo-Saxon Church* (Woodbridge, 2005), 213–43, at 214, 231–2.

[239]  Palmer, 'Defining paganism'.

[240]  William of Malmesbury, *Vita S. Wulfstani*, ii.17, ed. M. Winterbottom and R.M. Thomson, *William of Malmesbury: Saints' Lives. Lives of SS. Wulfstan, Dunstan, Patrick, Benignus and Indract* (Oxford, 2002), 94–6. See Hooke, *Trees in Anglo-Saxon England*, 35, for the suggestion of pagan continuity; and Walsham, *Reformation of the Landscape*, 38 for the counter-argument.

at Rogationtide in the canons of the Council of Clofesho in 747 are again probably borne out of a sense of what was appropriate at a holy time.[241] As Christine Fell argued, here the sources seem simply to represent 'secular' practices (rather than 'pagan' ones), and as moments at which the community came together these are also moments at which beliefs and cultural expectations were transmitted. If the feasting and recounting of poems and stories described in other Anglo-Saxon texts, perhaps most famously in *Beowulf*, is at all representative of real practice then these situations too fall into this category.[242] The *Beowulf*-poet and Bede (amongst others) suggest that religious ideas and theology were included in what might be communicated at such occasions; if the Old English riddles are also among the sorts of poems that might be performed then, it seems that potential topics could range from God's creation of the world to filthy humour.[243]

Where the surviving evidence for beliefs is primarily represented by practices it is much more difficult to know what to make of them, or how to unpick the specifics. This is the case, for example, with practices like burial, as revealed in the archaeological record. Burials are another context in which beliefs of various sorts might be communicated (although, obviously, not to the person being buried). It is clear that as settlement patterns and ecclesiastical institutional structures varied, so too did burial practices and presumably the attendant beliefs about burials and the dead. Burial practices are discussed in more detail in the final chapter, but it is enough to note here that Christian burial is really a feature of the tenth and eleventh centuries, when local churches began to have graveyards and when churchyard burial became much more usual.[244] By the eleventh century, writers like Archbishop Wulfstan assumed that burial in consecrated ground was something that was considered important, but consecrated ground itself seems to be a development of the late ninth (or perhaps the early tenth) century.[245] With the exception of the individuals buried in monastic cemeteries, usually elites or those living a religious life in that community, burial before this time seems to have been predominantly a local affair, and the attendant rituals which accompanied such

---

[241] Canons of the Council of *Clofesho* (747), 16, ed. Haddan and Stubbs, *Councils*, III.368.

[242] *Beowulf*, ll. 89b–98, 1063–1162, ed. R.D. Fulk et al., *Klaeber's Beowulf and The Fight at Finnsburg*, Toronto Old English Series 21 (Toronto, 2008), 6, 37–41.

[243] See J. Wilcox, '"Tell Me What I Am": Old English Riddles', in D.F. Johnson and E. Treharne (eds), *Readings in Medieval Texts* (Oxford, 2005), 46–59; M. Bayless, 'Humour and the Comic in Anglo-Saxon England', in M.H. Sandra and H. Paul (eds), *Medieval English Comedy* (Turnhout, 2007), 13–30.

[244] See E. Zadora-Rio, 'The making of churchyards and parish territories in the early medieval landscape of France and England in the 7th–12th centuries: A reconsideration', *Medieval Archaeology: Journal of the Society for Medieval Archaeology* 47 (2003): 1–19; D.M. Hadley, 'Late Saxon Burial Practice', in Crawford, Hamerow and Hinton (eds), *The Oxford Handbook of Anglo-Saxon Archaeology*, 288–314 and below, 273–8.

[245] See Gittos, 'Consecrating Cemeteries'; and below, 273–8.

burials are impossible to recover in the absence of written evidence. Many burials of Christian bodies did not contain material possessions, but some did, and again their significance seems to have been variable. The pectoral cross in the coffin of St Cuthbert might have been meant to honour him; in other cases small items may have been included in graves out of personal sentiments or because they were considered to be amuletic – although identifying precisely the beliefs which these practices represent is probably ultimately impossible.[246]

Analysis of Anglo-Saxon cemeteries suggests that in both earlier and later periods some importance was attached to being buried according to family or kin groups, who might have been responsible for preparing the body, although in some cases there may have been specialists within a community who undertook such tasks.[247] Again, before ecclesiastical institutional structures had developed to the point where the widespread use of Christian ritual in death was possible, ideas about how dead bodies should be treated, and what happened to them, may have been even more variable than they were afterwards.[248] Recovering these beliefs accurately is virtually impossible though, just as it is unlikely that the probably numerous and varied religious beliefs associated with domestic life, birth, or 'coming of age' in Anglo-Saxon Christian communities will ever be satisfactorily recovered. Here it is also difficult to know where to draw the line between religious and secular, and it is worth remembering that this is in any case something which is worried about by people like theologians, historians and anthropologists, but was probably far less of a concern on the ground: some beliefs or practices probably were self-consciously identified as religious, such as baptism, but it is difficult to know how far, or precisely how, burial in a small lay community in the eighth century might have counted as a religious moment. Beliefs about invisible beings such as angels and devils, or elves and monsters, which might play a role in religious rituals but also exist in the landscape, blur the boundary between religious and secular because they rather form part of life experience and could be accorded religious meaning or not according to context.[249]

This discussion has attempted to outline what can be learned from the surviving sources about the contexts in which theological beliefs were communicated and

---

[246]    See for example Thompson, *Dying and Death*, 33–5, 107–12; D.M. Hadley and J. Buckberry, 'Caring for the Dead in Late Anglo-Saxon England', in Tinti (ed.), *Pastoral Care in Late Anglo-Saxon England*, 121–47, at 138–41; R. Gilchrist, 'Magic for the dead? The archaeology of magic in later medieval burials', *Medieval Archaeology: Journal of the Society for Medieval Archaeology* 52 (2008): 119–59.

[247]    Hadley and Buckberry, 'Caring', 142–5; Z. Devlin, *Remembering the Dead in Anglo-Saxon England: Memory Theory in Archaeology and History* (Oxford, 2007), 34, 50; see for example the cemetery at Ailcy Hill, Ripon: Hall and Whyman, 'Settlement and monasticism at Ripon, North Yorkshire, from the 7th to 11th centuries A.D'.

[248]    See also É. Rebillard, *The Care of the Dead in Late Antiquity*, Cornell Studies in Classical Philology 59 (Ithaca, NY, 2009).

[249]    See below, 63–127.

transmitted to Anglo-Saxon audiences, and in which Anglo-Saxon audiences could respond to those beliefs, as well as to touch upon some of the other situations for which limited information now survives. While it is impossible to pry into every aspect of belief and to 'uncover the secrets of men's hearts', it is important to remember what is represented by these different moments in the sources.[250] Each one – at baptism, confession, burial, in a Rogationtide procession or at the blessing of a field, or simply walking through the landscape – is an opportunity for questioning or disputing, for learning, for accepting or rejecting one belief or for expressing another, for understanding or misunderstanding. And yet, even though the once impermeable barrier between 'popular' and 'scholarly' has been broken down, it is still generally considered that theology lay outside the experience of the 'common man'. In the absence of detailed evidence from the Anglo-Saxon 'common man', this book takes an alternative approach, exploring through case studies how far theological debate and discussion might have affected the personal perspectives of Christian Anglo-Saxons, including where possible those who could not read or did not have direct access to the world of letters and learning. In all of these case studies, it is clear that theology was not detached from society or from the experiences of people who were not theologians, but formed an essential constituent part.

---

[250]    J.N. Danforth, *Gleanings and Groupings from a Pastor's Portfolio* (New York, 1852), 319.

# Chapter 2
# Creator of All Things, Visible and Invisible

> At the very beginning of creation, heaven, earth, the angels, air and water were
> made from nothing.[1]

## Introduction

The Bible begins with the story of creation, relating that in the first six days God
created heaven and earth and everything that adorned them, before he rested on
the seventh. The biblical account focuses on the visible creation, describing the
heavenly bodies which light up the sky, the animals and plants which live in the
earth, the air and the seas, and finally humankind.[2] The invisible beings created
by God are not mentioned in the first chapters of Genesis, but angels and other
spirits inhabited the late antique and early medieval Christian worlds just as
they appear throughout the Old Testament and in the gospels.[3] Bede's confident
statement that God created heaven, earth and angels draws on Augustine's

---

[1]    Bede, *De natura rerum*, 2, ll. 1–2, ed. C.W. Jones et al., *Opera didascalia, 1. De
orthographia; De arte metrica et de schematibus et tropis; De natura rerum*, CCSL 123A
(Turnhout, 1975), 192: 'In ipso quidem principio conditionis facta sunt caelum, terra,
angeli, aer, et aqua de nihilo'. See also *Hom.* II, ed. R. Morris, *The Blickling Homilies of the
10th Century: From the Marquis of Lothian's Unique MS. A.D. 971*, EETS, OS 58 (London,
1874), 23: 'Geþencean we eac þæt Drihten his englas gesceop, & heofen & eorþan, sæ,
& ealle þa gesceafta þe on þæm syndon' ('Let us also remember that the Lord created his
angels, and heaven and earth, the sea, and all creatures that are in them').

[2]    Gn 1–2.

[3]    See for example J. Daniélou, *Les anges et leur mission: d'après les Pères de l'Eglise*,
Collection Irenikon, n.s. 5 (Paris, 1953); C.A. Mango, 'The Invisible World of Good and
Evil', in C.A. Mango (ed.), *Byzantium: The Empire of New Rome, History of Civilisation*
(London, 1980), 151–65; V.I.J. Flint, *The Rise of Magic in Early Medieval Europe* (Oxford,
1991); B. Caseau, 'Crossing the Impenetrable Frontier between Earth and Heaven', in
R.W. Mathisen and H. Sivan (eds), *Shifting Frontiers in Late Antiquity: Papers from the
First Interdisciplinary Conferences on Late Antiquity, the University of Kansas, March,
1995* (Aldershot, 1996), 333–43; D. Keck, *Angels and Angelology in the Middle Ages*
(Oxford, 1998); H. Mayr-Harting, *Perceptions of Angels in History: An Inaugural Lecture
Delivered in the University of Oxford on 14 November 1997* (Oxford, 1998); D.D. Hannah,
*Michael and Christ: Michael Traditions and Angel Christology in Early Christianity*,
Wissenschaftliche Untersuchungen zum Neuen Testament 2 (Tübingen, 1999); C. Leyser,
'Angels, Monks, and Demons in the Early Medieval West', in R. Gameson and H. Leyser
(eds), *Belief and Culture in the Middle Ages: Studies Presented to Henry Mayr-Harting*
(Oxford, 2001), 9–22.

commentary on Genesis, and reflects the belief recorded in the Nicene Creed that God's creation included everything both visible and invisible, a sentence inserted to counter the heretical idea that angels had created the world.[4] Scripture and canonical tradition held that as God's messengers, angels played key roles at certain moments in Christian history, announcing the conception of Jesus to the Blessed Virgin Mary and his birth to the shepherds, or warning the wise men to return to their country without informing Herod about the child that they had found. But these holy messengers are of course not the only invisible spirits whose presence was felt in the visible world: early medieval theology inherited from patristic tradition the idea that there were also wicked angels, thrown out of heaven after one of them had become over-proud and led a rebellion against God.[5] These fallen angels became devils or demons, and were invisibly present in the visible world as the blessed angels were, but caused trouble for human beings by possessing their minds and bodies, and by tempting and encouraging them to do wicked deeds.[6]

Early medieval texts present creation as comprising both invisible and visible created beings, and 'scientific' texts which treated 'nature' or 'creation' usually included information about both spiritual and physical beings. In Latin, 'natura' could incorporate both the visible and invisible in creation, while Old English does not appear to have developed specific words corresponding to the modern concepts of 'nature' or 'the natural world', suggesting that for Anglo-Saxon writers these too may not have always been clearly defined.[7] It has been suggested that neither the concept of the supernatural (as defined now), nor terminology for this concept, existed before about the twelfth or thirteenth century,[8] although it

---

[4]   There are differences between the first and second versions, but they both include this statement: First Council of Nicaea (325): 'visibilium et invisibilium factorem'; First Council of Constantinople (381): 'factorem caeli et terrae, visibilium omnium et invisibilium', ed. N.P. Tanner, *Decrees of the Ecumenical Councils* (2 vols, London, 1990), I.5, 24; Keck, *Angels*, 17–18.

[5]   Keck, *Angels*, 16–17, 24–7.

[6]   See Flint, *Rise of Magic*; Leyser, 'Angels, Monks, and Demons'; A. Argyriou, 'Angéologie et démonologie à Byzance: formulations théologiques et représentations populaires', *Cuadernos del CEMYR* 11 (2003): 157–84; A. Diem, 'Encounters between Monks and Demons in Latin Texts of Late Antiquity and the Early Middle Ages', in K.E. Olsen, A. Harbus and T. Hofstra (eds), *Miracles and the Miraculous in Medieval Germanic and Latin Literature* (Leuven, 2004), 51–67.

[7]   J. Neville, *Representations of the Natural World in Old English Poetry*, Cambridge Studies in Anglo-Saxon England 27 (Cambridge, 1999), 1–2; and see the discussion of what Bede understood by 'natura' in F. Wallis, 'Si naturam quaeras: Reframing Bede's "Science"', in S. DeGregorio (ed.), *Innovation and Tradition in the Writings of the Venerable Bede* (Morgantown, WV, 2006), 65–99.

[8]   Wallis, 'Si naturam quaeras', 93–8; R. Bartlett, *The Natural and the Supernatural in the Middle Ages: The Wiles Lectures given at the Queen's University of Belfast, 2006*, The Wiles Lectures (Cambridge, 2008), 3–17.

has also been argued that in Old English at least, there was a vocabulary for the strange and 'unnatural'.[9] Nevertheless, recent scholarship has emphasised that the modern distinction between the natural and the supernatural is not easily applied to the early Middle Ages, and that the boundaries between physical and spiritual were blurred.[10] Spiritual beings did visit and inhabit the physical landscape, and special places or objects connected heaven and earth, the invisible and the visible, but the boundaries between the spiritual and physical were perhaps not as blurry as has been suggested.

In his commentary on Genesis, Bede distinguished between the 'invisible and spiritual creation' and the 'corporeal, visible and corruptible creation': clearly he did not think that the physical and the spiritual were as one, and without distinction, even if the entire universe and all that it was contained was God's creation, and what God created was 'natural'.[11] Ælfric of Eynsham likewise noted that 'the creatures which the one Creator created are of many kinds, and of various appearance, and move about differently: some are invisible spirits without a body, like the angels in heaven; some are creeping on the earth with their whole body, like worms do; some go on two feet, some on four feet; some fly with feathers, some swim in waters'.[12] For Bede and Ælfric as for many others in the early Middle Ages, there was a crucial distinction between the invisible and visible aspects of God's creation, even though both invisible and visible were considered to be part of one whole, and not divided along the lines of 'natural' and 'supernatural'. The distinction between visible and invisible is significant because of the specific

---

[9]   A. Hall, *Elves in Anglo-Saxon England: Matters of Belief, Health, Gender and Identity*, Anglo-Saxon Studies 8 (Woodbridge, 2007), 11–12.

[10]   D. O'Sullivan, 'Space, Silence and Shortage on Lindisfarne: The Archaeology of Asceticism', in H. Hamerow and A. MacGregor (eds), *Image and Power in the Archaeology of Early Medieval Britain: Essays in Honour of Rosemary Cramp* (Oxford, 2001), 33–52, 34–7; Bartlett, *The Natural and the Supernatural*, 3–17. See (for example) O'Sullivan, 'Space, Silence and Shortage', 35: 'To separate the physical or natural and the spiritual in the landscape is to impose a post-Enlightenment, Cartesian perspective at odds with early monastic vision. The physical landscape was the spiritual landscape and God's purpose and design was everywhere apparent within it'.

[11]   Bede, *In principium Genesis*, 1.i.2, ll. 137–49, ed. C.W. Jones, *Bedae venerabilis opera, pars II: opera exegetica, 1. Libri quattor in principium Genesis usque ad nativitatem Isaac et eiectionem Ismahelis adnotationum*, CCSL 118A (Turnhout, 1967), 7: Bede compares 'omnem creaturae spiritalis et inuisibilis' and 'corporalem uero, uisibilem et corruptibilem creaturam'.

[12]   Ælfric, *LS* I, ll. 49–55, ed. W.W. Skeat, *Aelfric's Lives of Saints, Being a Set of Sermons on Saints' Days Formerly Observed by the English Church*, EETS 76, 82 (vol. 1), 94, 114 (vol. 2) (4 vols in 2, London, 1881–1900), I.14: 'Ða gesceafta þe þæs án scyppend gescéop synden mænig-fealde. and mislices hiwes. and úngelice farað. Sume sindon ungesewenlice gastas. butan lichoman swá swá synd ænglas on heofonum. Sume syndan creopende on eorðan. mid eallum lichoman. swá swá wurmas doð. Sume gað on twam fotum. sume on feowe fotum. Sume fleoð mid feðerum. sume on flodum swimmað'.

roles of the invisible spirits, and precisely how and when they were understood to appear in the visible world.

Angels and devils feature prominently in many types of early medieval written sources, especially homiletic and hagiographical works and vision literature; they appear in histories too (although more frequently in some histories than in others), while they are usually absent from the sparser records of chronicles. In these contexts their appearance is often part of a narrative: angels take on roles as guides, guardians, protectors, visitors and champions of the blessed, as well as retaining their primary function as messengers, while devils are disruptive, they instigate wicked deeds, damage people mentally and physically as well as spiritually, and are ultimately vanquished, expelled or destroyed by God's saints who are kept guarded by angels. These narratives were sometimes represented in artistic form, whether painted into medieval books or on to church walls, or carved into stone, as were biblical episodes where invisible spirits played a prominent role, so that angels and devils were made visible in the physical world. In medieval theology, angels and devils were particularly important because of the way that they were incorporated into the conceptualisation of the relationship between God and humankind, and the conceptualisation of the spiritual and physical relationships between heaven and earth, but they were more difficult to discuss and to explain than other aspects of God's creation.[13] Ælfric of Eynsham claimed that he was uncertain about how far detailed discussion and analysis of the angelic nature was really appropriate, and he stated that he was afraid 'to speak about them too much, because it is only for God to know how their invisible nature continues in eternal purity, without any pollution or decay'; but these words follow Ælfric's source closely here, and in fact he frequently mentions angels and devils in anecdotal accounts, and discussed them in some detail.[14]

Other authors evidently did not see a need to shrink from considering angels and their nature. The author of the anonymous late seventh- or early eighth-century *Life of Gregory* notes approvingly that Gregory discussed the angels with more skill than those who came before or after him.[15] Bede seems to have viewed angelology as a matter which required careful scrutiny: in his commentary on

[13]  E. Grant, *God and Reason in the Middle Ages* (Cambridge, 2001), 256–7.

[14]  Ælfric, *CH* I.3, ll. 19–21, ed. P. Clemoes, Ælfric's Catholic Homilies: The First Series, EETS, SS 17 (Oxford, 1997), 486: 'Be þam we forhtiað fela to sprecenne. for þan ðe gode anum is to gewitenne hu heora úngesewenlice gecynd buton ælcere besmitennysse oððe wanunge on ecere hluttornysse þurhwunað'. His source is an anonymous Latin sermon for All Saints, ed. J.E. Cross, '"Legimus in ecclesiasticis historiis": A sermon for All Saints and its use in Old English prose', *Traditio: Studies in Ancient and Medieval History, Thought, and Religion* 33 (1977): 101–35; see M. Godden, Ælfric's Catholic Homilies: Introduction, Commentary and Glossary, EETS, SS 18 (Oxford, 2000), 299–300; and cf. M. Fox, 'Ælfric on the creation and fall of the angels', *Anglo-Saxon England* 31 (2002): 175–200.

[15]  *Vita S. Gregorii*, 25, ed. and trans. B. Colgrave, *The Earliest Life of Gregory the Great* (Cambridge, 1985 [orig. pub. 1968]), 118–21.

Genesis he noted the absence of the angels in the account of creation, and explained this by the fact that the invisible and spiritual creation was part of those higher and more powerful matters which should be scrutinised by investigation, as opposed to the commands or promises made by God to humankind which make up much of the biblical creation story.[16] Ælfric was notoriously concerned with authority and orthodoxy,[17] and some of the more complex aspects of angelic theology could be difficult in this regard because they had no clear narrative or explanation in Scripture, but the appearance of angels and devils in other contexts may also have given him cause for concern. Liturgical practices which would have been acceptable to Ælfric (such as baptism, the mass, the anointing of the sick or funeral liturgies) requested the help of angels in keeping devils away, but angels and devils appeared also in contexts which Ælfric would have considered unorthodox, such as quasi-liturgical magical practices, or practices which he might have deemed magical and unChristian. Several ecclesiastical councils decreed that various names of angels or archangels were uncanonical and unsupported by Scripture, but it is not clear whether the clergy who forbade the use of them believed that calling upon these names would conjure devils, or whether they simply objected to uncanonical angelic names: it is sometimes difficult to tell whether the prayers would be acceptable if a canonical angelic name were used instead.[18]

It is fairly typical of Ælfric that he would rather be silent on certain topics than attempt to find a definitive answer where scriptural or other secure information was lacking. However, the importance of angels and devils in early medieval theology was such that theological discussion about them is found fairly frequently, and especially on such key topics as their creation and fall.[19] Here there were a range of interpretations about some details, such as precisely when the angels came into being,[20] and in fact Ælfric contributed to these debates too. Ælfric included the creation of the angels in general terms in his discussion of the creation of the world, since they must have originated in the first six days as all other created beings did, but he declined to identify precisely when the angelic spirits came into

[16] Bede, *In principium Genesis*, 1.i.2, ll. 137–49, ed. Jones, *Opera exegetica, 1,* 7.

[17] M.M. Gatch, *Preaching and Theology in Anglo-Saxon England: Aelfric and Wulfstan* (Toronto, 1977), 14. See also J. Hill, 'Ælfric, Authorial Identity and the Changing Text', in D.G. Scragg and P.E. Szarmach (eds), *The Editing of Old English* (Cambridge, 1994), 179–81.

[18] e.g. Boniface, *Epistola* 59, ed. M. Tangl, *Die Briefe des Heiligen Bonifatius und Lullus*, MGH, Epistolae Selectae 1 (Berlin, 1916). See also M.R. James, 'Names of angels in Anglo-Saxon and other documents', *Journal of Theological Studies* 11 (1909–10): 569–71; Keck, *Angels*, 163–4; Mayr-Harting, *Perceptions of Angels in History*, 10–12.

[19] See Augustine, *DCD* XI.9, 11, 13–15, 19, ed. B. Dombert and A. Kalb, *Sancti Aurelii Augustini. De civitate dei*, CCSL 47–8 (2 vols, Turnhout, 1955), II.328–30, 332–8; *De Trinitate*, III.8, ed. W.J. Mountain and F. Glorie, *Sancti Aurelii Augustini de Trinitate libri XV*, CCSL 50–50A (2 vols, Turnhout, 1968), I.143–6.

[20] For a summary see Keck, *Angels*, 16–17.

existence.[21] In contrast, Bede assumed that in the instant that God created heaven and earth, he also created the angels to fill heaven: 'without doubt as soon as it was created, heaven was filled with inhabitants, that is with the blessed throngs of angels, who were created in the beginning with heaven and earth'.[22] The author of the nineteenth Vercelli homily situated the angels' creation in the beginning with the heavens and earth and seas and all that is in them, but like the author of the second Blickling homily, declined to specify precisely when in this sequence the angels came into existence.[23] In contrast, the late tenth-century chronicle of Æthelweard notes at the beginning that God created the angels on the first day, when light appeared.[24]

Byrhtferth, the school-master at Ramsey, discussed the creation of the angels in his *Enchiridion*, a work intended to teach priests about computus which seems to have been completed by about 1012.[25] Rather puzzlingly, Byrhtferth seems to locate the creation of the angels on the eighth day: he even underlines that the creation of the angels took place on 25 March (which he also notes was the day of the Annunciation, Crucifixion and Pentecost), and since he has identified the first day of creation as 18 March one might assume that this leaves little room for doubt.[26] This is particularly odd because this would mean that the angels were created after everything else had been created and even after God had rested on the seventh day, beyond which point it was normally held that nothing new was created: some authors went to great lengths to argue that nothing had ever been created after the first six days.[27] As it stands, what Byrhtferth has written seems

---

[21]    *CH* I.1, ll. 21–100, ed. Clemoes, *Catholic Homilies*, 179–82; *Letter to Sigeweard*, ll. 56–64, ed. R. Marsden, *The Old English Heptateuch and Aelfric's Libellus de Veteri Testamento et Novo: Vol. 1, Introduction and Text*, EETS, OS 330 (Oxford, 2008), 202; Fox, 'Ælfric on the creation and fall of the angels', 180–1, 183.

[22]    Bede, *In principium Genesis*, 1.i.2, ll. 45–6, ed. Jones, *Opera exegetica, 1*, 4: '… quia nimirum suis incolis mox creatum, hoc est beatissimis angelorum agminibus, impletum est. Quos in principio cum caelo et terra esse conditos…'. See also Isidore, *Sententiae* i.10.3, PL 83.554: 'ante omnem creaturam angeli facti sunt, dum dictum est fiat lux' ('the angels were created before every other creature, when "let there be light" was spoken').

[23]    *Hom.* XIX, ll. 12–13, ed. D.G. Scragg, *The Vercelli Homilies and Related Texts* (London, 1992), 316: 'Ærest on frymþe he geworhte heofonas ꝛ eorðan ꝛ sæ ꝛ ealle þa þinc þe on him syndon, ꝛ ealle þa englas þe on heofonum syndon' ('First in the beginning he created the heavens and the earth and the sea and all the things that are in them, and all the angels which are in heaven').

[24]    I.1, ed. A. Campbell, *The Chronicle of Æthelweard* (London, 1962), 3: 'Primo enim die deus in lucis apparitione condidit angelos'.

[25]    P.S. Baker and M. Lapidge (eds), *Byrhtferth's Enchiridion*, EETS, SS 15 (Oxford, 1995), xxv–xxxiv.

[26]    Byrhtferth, *Enchiridion*, II.1.281–8, ed. Baker and Lapidge, *Byrhtferth's Enchiridion*, 72.

[27]    For an extreme example, see *De mirabilibus sacrae scripturae*, by the seventh-century 'Irish Augustine', *PL* 35.2149–2200; and discussion in M. Smyth, *Understanding*

to be heterodox, but it is possible that he has simply tied himself in knots here with his own over-clever reasoning. Since the week cycles through seven days, the eighth day is the same as the first: Byrhtferth may in fact have meant the first day, like Bede, but placed angelic creation on the eighth day because this day was understood to symbolize the eighth age of eternal blessedness, the heavenly kingdom, and contemplation of the face of God, which was one of the angels' primary roles.[28] Elsewhere, in his discussion of the number eight, Byrhtferth locates the creation of light and the angels on the first day, which he identifies as 18 March, and so it is also possible that what he wrote about angelic creation on 25 March is simply not, in fact, what he actually meant.[29]

To judge from the surviving evidence, the fall of the angels received more attention from Anglo-Saxon authors than did the angels' creation: it was discussed by several named authors, it features in a number of poems, and is often referred to in passing, but it was also represented pictorially in late Anglo-Saxon manuscripts.[30] The greater interest in the fall was probably because of its significance in the role that the devil played in the fall of humankind and in the identification of pride as a deadly sin. Here too there were differences of opinion, although here at least some biblical passages were more easily interpreted with reference to the angelic fall.[31] Bede did not identify clearly when he thought that the fall took place, although he mentions the angelic fall and its effects on many occasions: he notes (for example) that the serpent which tempted Eve was inhabited by one of the fallen angels;[32] and in his scientific works he identifies the air above the earth and below heaven

---

*the Universe in Seventh-Century Ireland*, Studies in Celtic History 15 (Woodbridge, 1996).

[28] Bede, *De temporum ratione*, 71, ed. C.W. Jones, *Opera didascalia, 2. De temporum ratione*, CCSL 123B (Turnhout, 1977), 542–4; Bede, *In principium Genesis*, 1.ii.2, ll. 986–7, ed. Jones, *Opera exegetica, 1*, 32: 'Nam in reuolutione temporum octauus idem qui et primus computatur dies' ('For in the turning of times, the eighth day is reckoned the same as the first'). See also C.W. Jones, 'Some introductory remarks on Bede's Commentary on Genesis', *Sacris erudiri* 19 (1969–70): 115–98, at 191–8.

[29] Byrhtferth, *Enchiridion*, IV.1.180–1, ed. Baker and Lapidge, *Byrhtferth's Enchiridion*, 210.

[30] D. Anlezark, 'The Fall of the Angels in Solomon and Saturn II', in K. Powell and D.G. Scragg (eds), *Apocryphal Texts and Traditions in Anglo-Saxon England* (Woodbridge, 2003), 121–33 (see 122 for a useful list of poetic descriptions of the Fall). See also T.D. Hill, 'The Fall of Angels and Man in the Old English Genesis B', in L.E. Nicholson and D.W. Frese (eds), *Anglo-Saxon Poetry: Essays in Appreciation for John C. McGalliard* (London, 1975), 279–90; C.B. Tkacz, 'Heaven and Fallen Angels in Old English', in A. Ferreiro (ed.), *The Devil, Heresy and Witchcraft in the Middle Ages: Essays in Honor of Jeffrey B. Russell*, Cultures, Beliefs and Traditions: Medieval and Early Modern Peoples 6 (Leiden, 1998), 327–44.

[31] e.g. Is 14:12–13.

[32] Bede, *In principium Genesis*, 1.iii.1, ll. 1875–1880, ed. Jones, *Opera exegetica, 1*, 59. Here Bede follows Augustine, *De Genesi ad litteram*, 11.2, ed. J. Zycha, *Sancti Aureli Augustini De Genesi ad litteram libri duodecim eiusdem libri capitula; De Genesi ad*

as the dwelling place of the apostate angels.[33] Illustrations of the fall represent
the banishment of the angels-turned-devils by placing them in the lower part of
the page, in contrast to the depiction of angels in heaven at the top of the page. A
painted illustration of the fall accompanies an early eleventh-century copy of an
Old English translation of the Hexateuch, now London, British Library, Cotton
Claudius B.iv (at fol. 2r), although the fall itself is not in fact included in the
surrounding text at all: the devils' new state is represented almost as the inverse of
the image of heaven.[34] While beautifully robed angels hold up Christ's mandorla,
naked (or almost naked) devils tumble into hell still gripping the mandorla which
surrounds Lucifer, and a serpent-like beast entwines its tail and wraps its jaws
around the mandorla and the stray limbs of some of the devils.[35]

Three representations of the angelic fall are found in a tenth-century illustrated
book of Old English poetry, now Oxford, Bodleian Library, Junius 11 (at pp. 3, 16,
17). These line-drawn images incorporate a range of complexities and subtleties
but in all three, the devils occupy a lower section, in which Satan is depicted
bound (twice in a hell mouth) as naked devils fall down into torment, and heaven
occupies an upper register.[36] However, the ability of some devils to escape into
the air and wreak havoc is clear from other illustrations in the book, such as those
of the temptation and fall of Adam and Eve (on pp. 20, 24, 28). The Old English
poetic versions of Genesis are copied surrounding these illustrations, and *Genesis*

---

*litteram imperfectus liber; Locutionum in Heptateuchum libri septem*, CCSL 28 (Vienna,
1894), 335–7.

[33]    *De natura rerum*, 25, ll. 4–7, ed. Jones et al., *Opera didascalia, 1*, 216; see also *De
temporum ratione*, 5, ll. 64–7, ed. Jones, *Opera didascalia, 2*, 286.

[34]    For discussion of the date and place of production of the manuscript, see B.C.
Withers, *The Illustrated Old English Hexateuch, Cotton Claudius B.iv: The Frontier of
Seeing and Reading in Anglo-Saxon England* (London, 2007), 53–85.

[35]    For detailed discussion of this image, see B.C. Withers, 'Satan's Mandorla:
Translation, Transformation and Interpretation in Late Anglo-Saxon England', in C.
Hourihane (ed.), *Insular and Anglo-Saxon Art and Thought in the Early Medieval Period*
(Princeton, NJ, 2011), 247–70; for more general discussion of the illustrations in the
manuscript see C.R. Dodwell and P. Clemoes, *The Old English Illustrated Hexateuch:
British Museum Cotton Claudius B. IV*, EEMF 18 (Copenhagen, 1974), 13–73, esp. 17, and
60 (where the editors note with reference to this image in particular that 'the artist seemed
quite incapable of rendering the face in profile').

[36]    For discussion of this image see G. Henderson, 'The Programme of Illustrations
in Bodleian MS Junius XI', in G. Robertson and G. Henderson (eds), *Studies in Memory
of David Talbot Rice* (Edinburgh, 1975), 113–45; B.C. Raw, 'The probable derivation of
most of the illustrations in Junius II from an illustrated Old Saxon Genesis', *Anglo-Saxon
England* 5 (1976): 133–48; N. Howe, 'Falling into Place: Dislocation in the Junius Book',
in M.C. Amodio and K. O'Brien O'Keefe (eds), *Unlocking the Wordhord: Anglo-Saxon
Studies in Memory of Edward B. Irving, Jr.* (Toronto, 1998), 14–37; C.E. Karkov, *Text
and Picture in Anglo-Saxon England: Narrative Strategies in the Junius 11 Manuscript*
(Cambridge, 2001), 19–44, 48–50, 132–3, 62.

*A* has a particularly interesting reading of the fall, locating it prior to the creation of earth: the poet explains that after the wicked angels had been thrown out of heaven, God wanted to repopulate their vacant seats, and so proceeded to create the earth, which was empty and void.[37] Although not without precedent, this idea is unusual, and as David Johnson points out, it is therefore particularly striking that it also appears in two tenth-century charters written at Winchester, one of them probably attributable to Bishop Æthelwold (d.984).[38] It is interesting too that one of Æthelwold's pupils, Ælfric, does not appear to have accepted this interpretation, instead placing the fall of the angels after the creation of the earth but before the creation of Adam and Eve; he seems to have been less certain, however, about whether the transformation from angel to devil occurred before, after, or during the fall itself.[39] The author of the nineteenth Vercelli homily introduces the detail that the wicked angels were blown out of heaven, apparently an echo of the baptismal liturgy which involved blowing on the baptismal candidate to exorcise the devil.[40]

The omission of information about the fall from Genesis did itself cause comment from some quarters. Ælfric noted in the preface to his translation of Genesis that the title of the book meant 'the origin book', because 'it tells of the origin of everything (but not the creation of the angels)'.[41] Alcuin explained that the reason that Genesis is silent about angelic sin but reveals human sin is that God intended to heal the wound caused by man's sin, but not the wound caused by the angels.[42] Bede assumed that as with the creation of the angels, the fall

---

[37] *Genesis A*, ll. 8–102, ed. A.N. Doane, *Genesis A: A New Edition* (Madison, 1978), 109–11; see also D.F. Johnson, 'The fall of Lucifer in Genesis A and two Anglo-Latin royal charters', *Journal of English and Germanic Philology* 97:4 (1998): 500–21, at 501–12.

[38] M. Lapidge, 'The hermeneutic style in tenth-century Anglo-Latin literature', *Anglo-Saxon England* 4 (1975): 67–111, at 88–90; Johnson, 'The fall of Lucifer', 512–16.

[39] Ælfric, *CH* I.1, ll. 21–69, ed. Clemoes, *Catholic Homilies*, 179–81; Letter to Sigeweard, ll. 65–83, ed. Marsden, *The Old English Heptateuch and Aelfric's Libellus de Veteri Testamento et Novo*, 202–3. One of Wulfstan's sermons discusses the topic, following Ælfric, *CH* I.1 quite closely: see *Hom.* VI, ll. 24–33, ed. D. Bethurum, *The Homilies of Wulfstan* (Oxford, 1957), 143–4.

[40] *Hom.* XIX, ll. 13–19, ed. D.G. Scragg, *The Vercelli Homilies and Related Texts*, EETS, OS 300 (London, 1992), 316; T.D. Hill, 'When God blew Satan out of Heaven: The motif of exsufflation in Vercelli Homily XIX and later English Literature', *Leeds Studies in English* n.s. 16 (1985): 132–41, at 132–3, 136–7.

[41] Ælfric, '*Prefatio* to Genesis', ll. 47–9, ed. Marsden, *The Old English Heptateuch and Aelfric's Libellus de Veteri Testamento et Novo*, 5: 'Seo boc ys gehaten Genesis, þæt ys 'gecyndboc', for þam þe heo ys firmest boca ꝸ spricþ be ælcum gecinde. Ac heo ne spricð na be þæra engla gesceapenisse'. See also M.J. Menzer, 'The Preface as Admonition: Ælfric's Preface to Genesis', in R. Barnhouse and B.C. Withers (eds), *The Old English Hexateuch: Aspects and Approaches* (Kalamazoo, MI., 2000), 15–39.

[42] Alcuin, *Interrogationes et responsiones in Genesin*, 3, *PL* 100.517C: 'Quare angelicum peccatum silentio in Genesi absconditum est et hominis patefactum? Quia angelicum vulnus Deus non praedestinavit curare, hominis vero sanare praedestinavit'.

was a deliberate omission because it pertained to the spiritual world, rather than the physical and material world which was the focus of the account in Genesis.[43] These discussions are interesting for what they reveal of the kinds of questions that concerned Anglo-Saxon authors, and the details which were perceived to be important as well as those which were not, although these questions are much less complex than some of the tortuously exhaustive angelology which would be a concern in later centuries.[44] More importantly, the implications of angelology and demonology, especially the purposes and functions of angels and devils as well as where in the physical landscape they might exist or be found, were significant in understanding the roles that spiritual beings played in the daily lives of men and women on earth. Angels and demons had a central function in many pastoral contexts and rituals, and seem to have acted as agents through which complex theological concepts could be reified, so that theological ideas could be communicated in a spiritual framework employing agents which were familiar and recognisable even as they were invisible and probably also disconcerting.[45]

## Visible and Invisible Worlds

While the details of how the angels came into being and how some of them fell may have been the cause of some uncertainty amongst early medieval scholars, there was clear agreement among Christians that angels and fallen angels alike were believed to be continuously present in the air, although usually invisible to normal human eyes.[46] These blessed and wicked spirits are presented as opposing forces of good and evil, frequently fighting with each other and attracted to the good and evil deeds performed by human beings. Miracle stories attribute to angels and devils many of the minor mishaps or marvels of daily life, both mental and physical: accounts of the fourth-century St Martin of Tours record that after he slipped on the altar steps and was badly bruised, his swift healing was the work of

---

[43]   Bede, *In principium Genesis*, 1.1, ll. 146–9, ed. Jones, *Opera exegetica, 1*, 7: 'Vnde etiam consulte de casu praeuaricatoris angeli et sociorum eius penitus reticuit, quia hoc nimirum ad statum inuisibilis illius ac spiritalis creaturae pertinebat' ('Therefore he was determinedly and utterly silent about the fall of the apostate angel and his allies, because this certainly pertained to the condition of the invisible and spiritual creation').

[44]   See for example Keck, *Angels*, 70–92.

[45]   See below, 101–3.

[46]   For studies of this in East and West across the Middle Ages see for example Mango, 'Invisible World'; Caseau, 'Crossing the Impenetrable Frontier between Earth and Heaven'; G. Peers, 'Hagiographic models of worship of images and angels', *Byzantion: Revue internationale des études byzantines* 67:2 (1997): 407–20; Keck, *Angels*; Mayr-Harting, *Perceptions of Angels in History*; Leyser, 'Angels, Monks, and Demons'; M.E.H. Moore, 'Demons and the battle for souls at Cluny', *Studies in Religion / Sciences religieuses* 32:4 (2003): 485–97.

a holy angel sent by God.[47] Devils are supposed to have thrown stones at Cuthbert (d.687) and tried to throw him off high places,[48] just as in the tenth century the devil was believed to be responsible for the post which fell on Bishop Æthelwold and crushed his ribs.[49] Perhaps more prosaically, in the eighth century when a sister at Wimbourne lost her keys one night she assumed that this was because of her negligence, but the abbess determined that this too was the work of the devil: the sisters had to offer their prayers in another building because they could not get into the church, but by these prayers they confounded the devil, and the keys were eventually discovered in the mouth of a dead fox.[50] In this way, beliefs which made sense of how people experienced the world were both reinforced by, and understood with reference to, the theological ideas and interpretations which themselves sought to explain human experience.

Sometimes the spiritual presence was assumed rather than seen, but in other cases the power to see invisible spirits was an indicator of sanctity. Cuthbert was considered worthy to see and to speak with angels and was never denied their help when he asked for it,[51] while Guthlac (d.715) reported that the Lord sent an angel to talk with him every morning and evening,[52] but numerous saints were granted these privileges, a claim to sanctity which borrows first from the example of Christ and then in turn from other saints.[53] Saints were also often granted the power to see devils which were invisible to others, or, like Christ, were assaulted by demons attempting to claim the prize of a holy soul: Ælfric notes that holy men are in particular need of angelic protection to stave off some, if not all, demonic temptation.[54] Like other saints, Dunstan (d.988) was granted visions of angels, but he was also attacked by the devil while he was praying one night, and wrestled with

[47]   See for example Ælfric, *CH* II.XXXIV, ll. 216–19, ed. M. Godden, *Ælfric's Catholic Homilies: The Second Series Text*, EETS, SS 5 (Oxford, 1979), 294.

[48]   Bede, *Vita S. Cuthberti prosa*, 22, ed. and trans. B. Colgrave, *Two Lives of Saint Cuthbert: A Life by an Anonymous Monk of Lindisfarne and Bede's Prose Life* (Cambridge, 1985 [orig. pub. 1940]), 228–9.

[49]   Wulfstan, *Vita S. Æthelwoldi*, 15, ed. and trans. M. Lapidge and M. Winterbottom, *Wulfstan of Winchester: The Life of St Æthelwold* (Oxford, 1991), 28–9.

[50]   Rudolf, *Vita Leobae abbatissae Biscofesheimensis*, 5, ed. G. Waitz, 'Vita Leobae abbatissae Biscofesheimensis auct. Rudolfo Fuldensi', MGH, Scriptores in Folio 15.1 (Hannover, 1887), 118–31, at 124.

[51]   Anon, *Vita S. Cuthberti*, I.4, ed. and trans. Colgrave, *Two Lives of Cuthbert*, 66–9; Bede, *Vita S. Cuthberti prosa*, 6, ed. and trans. Colgrave, *Two Lives of Cuthbert*, 178–9.

[52]   Felix, *Vita S. Guthlaci*, 50, ed. and trans. B. Colgrave, *Felix's Life of Saint Guthlac: Introduction, Text, Translation and Notes* (Cambridge, 1985 [orig. pub. 1956]), 156–7.

[53]   See for example T.D. Hill, 'Imago Dei: Genre, Symbolism and Anglo-Saxon Hagiography', in P.E. Szarmach (ed.), *Holy Men and Holy Women: Old English Prose Saints' Lives and Their Contexts* (Albany, NY, 1996), 35–50; J. Carey, 'Varieties of Supernatural Contact in the Life of Adomnán', in J. Carey, M. Herbert and P. Ó Riain (eds), *Studies in Irish Hagiography. Saints and Scholars* (Dublin, 2001), 49–62.

[54]   Ælfric, *CH* I.11, ll. 65–7, ed. Clemoes, *Catholic Homilies*, 268.

him until he called on God's assistance, at which point the devil left him alone.[55] The author of the *Life* of Dunstan known only as 'B', writing in the late 990s, notes approvingly: 'O how great were the merits of this glorious bishop, who, still living, deserved to see visions of angels and to hear their marvellous voices!'.[56] Guthlac not only saw devils, who tried to tell him how he should undertake his fasting, but was also dragged bodily to the gates of hell with them, and had to be rescued by St Bartholomew.[57] Devils masqueraded as angels in their efforts to tempt the saints, but holy men and women were granted the power to see through these demonic disguises and identify the true nature of the spirits, as Martin did and so too did Juliana, whose encounter with a devil is recorded at some length in an Old English poetic account of her martyrdom (which probably took place in 304), written by Cynewulf probably in the ninth century and preserved in the tenth-century Exeter Book.[58]

These angelic and demonic encounters were important for establishing a claim to sanctity and owe much to the genre of hagiography, but they are also significant in understanding how holiness provided a gateway to the world of God's invisible creation. In this context it is worth noting that angels and devils were not the only spirits which might appear to holy individuals, but that in some circumstances, saints could also see human souls. There are numerous accounts of saints seeing souls led to heaven by angels,[59] but the souls of those longer dead sometimes appeared to holy men and women as well, and often to them alone even when others were present. Bede reports that as Torhtgyth, a particularly devout sister at the monastery in Barking, lay on her deathbed, she saw and spoke with abbess Æthelburh, but no one else who was present was able to see or hear the abbess, who had died three years earlier.[60] Like angelic and demonic spirits, souls were

---

[55]    Byrhtferth, *Vita S. Oswaldi*, V.6, ed. and trans. M. Lapidge, *The Lives of St Oswald and St Ecgwine* (Oxford, 2009), 158–61; B, *Vita S. Dunstani*, 16–17, 31–5, ed. M. Winterbottom and M. Lapidge, *The Early Lives of St Dunstan* (Oxford, 2012), 54–9, 90–101.

[56]    B, *Vita S. Dunstani*, 35.2, ed. Winterbottom and Lapidge, *Early Lives*, 98–100: 'O magnum gloriosi presulis meritum, qui meruit uiuens uidere angelorum uisiones uocesque mirabiles eorundem audire!'; and see p. lxiv for the dating of the work.

[57]    Felix, *Vita S. Guthlaci*, 30–3, ed. and trans. Colgrave, *Felix's Life of Saint Guthlac*, 98–109.

[58]    The Exeter Book is now Exeter, Cathedral Library, MS 3501: *Juliana*, ll. 242b–558, ed. B.J. Muir, *The Exeter Anthology of Old English Poetry: An Edition of Exeter Dean and Chapter MS 3501*, Exeter Medieval English Texts and Studies (2 vols, Exeter, 2000), I.196–208; A.J. Frantzen, *The Literature of Penance in Anglo-Saxon England* (New Brunswick, NJ, 1983), 188–90; M. Lapidge, 'Cynewulf and the Passio S. Iulianae', in M.C. Amodio and K. O'Brien O'Keefe (eds), *Unlocking the Wordhord: Anglo-Saxon Studies in Memory of Edward B. Irving, Jr.* (Toronto, 1998), 147–71.

[59]    e.g. B, *Vita S. Dunstani*, 34, ed. Winterbottom and Lapidge, *Early Lives*, 96–8.

[60]    Bede, *HE*, IV.9.1, ed. M. Lapidge, P. Monat and P. Robin, *Histoire ecclésiastique du peuple anglais = Historia ecclesiastica gentis Anglorum*, Sources chrétiennes 489–91

part of God's invisible creation, and while a soul animated the body it had a visible presence in this world: Ælfric notes in this context that all souls are spirits, although not all spirits are souls; and the anonymous author of an Old English homily copied in an eleventh-century manuscript, almost certainly in Exeter, noted that all the angels and human souls were created together on the same day.[61] The souls of holy men and women continued to 'live' after death, in the miracles that they wrought through God's power, and the body was often referred to as a fleshly prison which kept the soul away from God until death. The power of living saints to see the invisible world indicates that, at least for the hagiographers, the holiness of the saints positioned them somewhere between the visible and the invisible worlds even while they were still alive, and on occasion allowed them to pass between them while living as they would after they were dead.[62]

Although many accounts of invisible spirits owe a significant debt to hagiographical traditions and to the importance of establishing sanctity, this is not to say that there was not a very real belief in these spirits, and in their presence even when they were not seen. Spiritual beings appeared and disappeared in the physical world because they were there all the time, the invisible coexisting with the visible and occupying the same spaces and landscapes. Here a letter written by Boniface to the abbess Eadburga, some time between 716 and 719, is particularly informative.[63] The letter records the deathbed visions of a brother who was an inhabitant of the monastery of Much Wenlock (Shropshire), and Boniface takes pains to stress that he heard the account of the 'marvellous visions' from the brother himself.[64] On leaving the body, the visionary saw the entire world below

---

(3 vols, Paris, 2005), II.242.

[61]   See the discussion of the nature of the soul in Alcuin, 'De animae ratione liber ad Eulaliam virginem', *PL* 101.639–47, esp. 644–5; Ælfric, *LS* I, ll. 188–9, ed. and trans. Skeat, *Lives of Saints*, I.22–3; *Hom.* 57, ed. A.S. Napier, *Wulfstan: Sammlung der ihm zugeschriebenen Homilien nebst Untersuchungen über ihre Echtheit*, Sammlung englisher Denkmäler in kritischen Ausgaben 4 (Berlin, 1883), 293, ll. 5–12; and see also E. Treharne, 'Homilies: London, Lambeth Palace Library, 489', in O. Da Rold et al. (eds), *The Production and Use of English Manuscripts 1060 to 1220* (Leicester, 2010), available at http://www.le.ac.uk/english/em1060to1220/mss/EM.Lamb.489.htm, accessed October 2012. For a more detailed discussion of the relationship between soul and body see below, 313–23.

[62]   P. Brown, *The Cult of the Saints: Its Rise and Function in Latin Christianity* (Chicago, 1981), 50–68.

[63]   Boniface, *Epistola* 10, ed. Tangl, *Die Briefe*, 8–15. For discussion of this letter see P. Sims–Williams, *Religion and literature in Western England, 600–800*, Cambridge Studies in Anglo-Saxon England 3 (Cambridge, 1990), 243–72; S. Foot, 'Anglo-Saxon "Purgatory"', in P.D. Clarke and T. Claydon (eds), *The Church, the Afterlife and the Fate of the Soul: Papers Read at the 2007 Summer Meeting and the 2008 Winter Meeting of the Ecclesiastical History Society*, Studies in Church History 45 (Woodbridge, 2009), 87–96, at 92–4; H. Foxhall Forbes, '"Diuiduntur in quattuor": The interim and judgement in Anglo-Saxon England', *Journal of Theological Studies* 61:2 (2010): 659–84, at 661–7, 673–4.

[64]   Boniface, *Epistola* 10, ed. Tangl, *Die Briefe*, 8, ll. 12–15.

him gathered together, including people who were still living. From this privileged view-point he was able to see things which were normally invisible to human eyes: according to Boniface, 'he said that it was as if the eyes of a seeing and waking man were veiled with a very thick cloth; and suddenly the veil was taken away, and then all things were clear, which before were unknown, veiled, and unseen'.[65]

Those things which were normally unseen included the spiritual presence around human beings who were still living in the world, as well as numerous angels and devils surrounding souls which were leaving their bodies.[66] The brother of Wenlock seems to have been shown the world as the invisible spirits saw it, populated by visible and invisible beings simultaneously as they coexisted in the same landscapes or buildings. The visionary described that he saw the entire world below him gathered together, and that 'those who were good and not guilty of wicked sins were kept safe and defended by angels; on the other hand, those who were sinful and wicked had an enemy spirit [i.e., a devil] always with them, encouraging them to wicked deeds and rejoicing each time a sin was committed'.[67] This description mirrors information found elsewhere, such as Bede's statement that it is 'unconcealed' or 'not hidden' that the elect are surrounded by an invisible angelic presence, especially when they apply themselves to sacred tasks such as prayer or church attendance.[68] The visionary was therefore actually able to see what Bede believed, but had presumably not encountered visibly for himself. The brother of Wenlock also gave specific information about living people and the spiritual and sometimes physical effects of the angels and demons upon them, although invisible to human eyes. A girl saw and coveted a particularly beautiful spindle-whorl, and a wicked spirit urged her to steal it: when she did so, her tempter reported the event to other wicked spirits, and they all rejoiced in her sin.[69]

Most significantly, the visionary saw Ceolred, king of the Mercians (d.716), who was surrounded by angels, protecting him with an angelic 'umbrella'

---

[65]   Boniface, *Epistola* 10, ed. Tangl, *Die Briefe*, 8, ll. 17–21.

[66]   Boniface, *Epistola* 10, ed. Tangl, *Die Briefe*, 8, ll. 21–3; 9, ll. 17–25; 13, ll. 7–21.

[67]   Boniface, *Epistola* 10, ed. Tangl, *Die Briefe*, 13, ll. 8–17.

[68]   *Hom.* II.10, ll. 92–6, ed. D. Hurst, *Bedae venerabilis opera, pars III: opera homiletica*, CCSL 112 (Turnhout, 1955), 248–9; see also Alcuin's sweet (but perhaps apocryphal) story in *Epistola* 284, ed. E.L. Dümmler, *Epistolae Karolini aevi*, MGH, Epistolae Karolini aevi II (Berlin, 1895), 443, ll. 7–10: 'Fertur enim magistrum nostrum et vestrum patronum beatum dixisse Baedam: "Scio angelos visitare canonicas horas et congregationes fraternas; quid, si ibi me non inveniunt inter fratres? Nonne dicere habent: 'Ubi est Baeda? quare non venit ad orationes statutas cum fratribus'?" ' ('It is reported that your teacher and our patron, the blessed Bede, said: "I know that angels visit the canonical hours and the brothers' services: what if they do not find me there among the brothers? Surely they will say: 'where is Bede? why has he not come with the brothers to the regular prayers'?" ').

[69]   Boniface, *Epistola* 10, ed. Tangl, *Die Briefe*, 13, ll. 22–7.

('umbraculum'), opened out like a big book.[70] But Ceolred was a sinner, and so devils tried to attack him, eventually demanding of the angels that they be allowed to torment him on account of his wickedness. When the angels agreed to allow this, a multitude of demons attacked Ceolred, 'tiring him inestimably'.[71] Ceolred evidently did not deserve to receive angelic protection and it is therefore not clear why he received it; but the fact that the angels had to be worn down before handing him over to the devils might indicate that his status as king somehow entitled him to greater spiritual protection, although these angels may also be comparable to the guardian angels which would be described in more detail in the tenth and eleventh centuries.[72] Nonetheless, his unhappy fate in the next world was clear to Boniface at least, since in another letter he describes how Ceolred was eventually driven mad as a result of these devils, and died: 'as those who were present testified, a wicked spirit turned Ceolred, the sinner, to insanity of mind, while he was feasting spendidly with his companions ... so that raving mad, babbling frantically and conversing with devils and bad-mouthing the priests of God, he departed from this light without penance and confession and went to the torments of hell, no doubt'.[73]

The unveiled world, in which both visible and invisible are laid before the eyes in plain sight, is also represented in the illustrations in the Harley Psalter (now London, British Library, Harley 603), a book which seems to have been a collaborative effort of the community of Christ Church, Canterbury, begun in the early eleventh century but never fully finished, so that artists were still adding to the illustrations around a hundred years later.[74] The Harley Psalter is a an early copy of the ninth-century Utrecht Psalter (now Utrecht, Universiteitsbibliotek, MS 32), which was made near Reims and brought to England probably by the end of the tenth century, but as William Noel has argued, Harley is far more than a copy: its illustrations were relevant to the community for which and by which it was created.[75] Page after page of the Harley Psalter shows the role given to angels and devils in the illustration and interpretation of the psalm-verses even when the psalm-texts themselves make no reference to the invisible spirits; and although in many cases Harley's artists copied or reworked the angels or devils of

---

[70] Boniface, *Epistola* 10, ed. Tangl, *Die Briefe*, 14, ll. 1–19: 'Quem ut dixit videbat angelico quodam umbraculo contra impetum demoniorum quasi libri alicuius extensione et superpositione defensum' (p. 14, ll. 3–5).

[71] Boniface, *Epistola* 10, ed. Tangl, *Die Briefe*, 14, ll. 15–19.

[72] See below, 108–10.

[73] Boniface, *Epistola* 73, ed. Tangl, *Die Briefe*, 152, l. 29 – 153, l. 7.

[74] W. Noel, *The Harley Psalter*, Cambridge Studies in Palaeography and Codicology 4 (Cambridge, 1995), esp. 121–49. The illustrated pages are reproduced (in black and white) in T.H. Ohlgren, *Anglo-Saxon Textual Illustration: Photographs of Sixteen Manuscripts with Descriptions and Index* (Kalamazoo, MI, 1992); and in colour on the British Library website (http://www.bl.uk).

[75] Noel, *The Harley Psalter*, 6–12.

Utrecht, in others they added to or adapted, or simply revivified what they found there, indicating the relevance and importance of angels and devils in their own interpretation and representation of the Psalms.

Working perhaps between about 1010 and 1020, Artist A added physical details to his demons such as talons and claws, and genitalia and breasts, making them more ferocious and terrible;[76] Artist G, who probably worked between 1073 and 1076, elaborated on the image provided for Psalm 30 by adding a dynamic illustration of the Psalmist reaching towards an angel while a devil seeks to pull him back with a trident, thus underscoring the Psalmist's cry, 'deliver me from the hands of mine enemies'.[77] Many of Harley's illustrations show the angels in heaven and separated from earth, but they are also frequently to be found at the sides of humans, aiding them and protecting them from devils. The illustration for Psalm 27 (fol. 15v) shows the Psalmist protected by an angel holding an umbrella or canopy, reminiscent of the description of the angelic protection offered to Ceolred before he was given over to demonic spirits. In other cases demons catch hold of people with hooks or snares (fol. 17r), or drag or push people physically and bodily (fol. 23v). While the illustrations are as much metaphorical and allegorical as they are related to the real world, they do also present elements of belief attested elsewhere; and like the brother of Wenlock, the reader of the Harley Psalter views the world as if with the veil of the flesh removed, so that there is hardly a page where invisible spirits are not present.

Tenth- and eleventh-century texts likewise refer frequently to the constant presence of the invisible spirits, and to the attraction of angels and devils to good and bad people as well as to their good and bad deeds, and the continuous invisible struggles between them. Homilies often explain that the angelic presence is a shield or protection, especially to those who contended against devils:[78] the first Blickling homily notes that the Blessed Virgin Mary was surrounded by extra angels while she was pregnant, because they guarded her particularly while she carried Jesus in her womb.[79] In one of the law codes for Cnut, as well as in his discussion of the rights and duties of Christians (the so-called *Institutes of Polity*), Archbishop Wulfstan of York describes the hovering presence of angels which protect certain priestly actions, such as baptism and the Eucharist, and explains that these same actions drive devils away.[80] Other references to the constant

---

[76]  D. Tselos, 'English manuscript illumination and the Utrecht psalter', *The Art Bulletin* 41:2 (1959): 137–49, at 139; Noel, *The Harley Psalter*, 136–7.

[77]  K.M. Openshaw, 'Weapons in the daily battle: Images of the conquest of evil in the early medieval psalter', *Art Bulletin* 75:1 (1993): 17–38, at 29; Noel, *The Harley Psalter*, 139–40; Ps. 30: 16 'libera me et eripe me de manibus inimicorum meorum'.

[78]  *Hom.* III, XVI, ed. Morris, *Blickling Homilies*, 29, 209; see also *Hom.* IV, ll. 308–42, ed. Scragg, *Vercelli Homilies*, 102–4.

[79]  *Hom.* I, ed. Morris, *Blickling Homilies*, 11.

[80]  *Polity*, 130–2, ed. K. Jost, *Die 'Institutes of Polity, Civil and Ecclesiastical'*, Schweizer anglistische Arbeiten 47 (1959), 104; I Cnut 4.2, ed. F. Liebermann, *Die Gesetze*

presence of devils are often quite matter-of-fact, but audiences were advised to be aware of the very real danger that wicked spirits posed. Ælfric mentions 'the invisible devil who flies through the world and sees many things',[81] while in the 'Admonition' at the end of his *Enchiridion*, Byrhtferth of Ramsey warns that the air is full of devils who wander the earth to deceive good men and make them do wicked deeds, but that these devils will back off with the help of the ever-present angels.[82] This 'Admonition' was reworked into a homily which survives now in Cambridge, Corpus Christi College, 421, a book which was probably written at Canterbury in the early eleventh century, and which came to Exeter later in the eleventh century, suggesting that Byrhtferth's warnings about devils were not confined to the audiences of his computistical handbook.[83]

Wandering devils might ultimately imperil the soul, but they also caused trouble on a more mundane level by possessing people and making them insane or unwell, and as in the gospels, miracle stories frequently attribute sickness to demonic possession. The *Dialogues* of Gregory the Great (d.604), a popular text which was translated into English in the late ninth century, includes a story illustrating just how easily devils could afflict the unwary: a nun wanted to eat a lettuce from the garden but neglected to sign herself with the cross beforehand, and was immediately possessed by a devil. An abbot was called, and when he ordered the devil to leave, it complained 'I did nothing! I was sitting on the lettuce and she bit me!'[84] This highlights the perceived importance of Christian ritual in daily life, especially for keeping away invisible and ever-present dangers, and prayers and liturgical texts echo this in their frequent references to devils and requests for protection against them. The story from the *Dialogues* illustrates a long-established belief that the sign of the cross was the most effective way of keeping devils at bay, a belief which recurs frequently in late antique and early

*der Angelsachsen* (3 vols, Halle, 1903–1916), I.284–5; see also Ælfric, *Letter* II.143, ed. B. Fehr, *Die Hirtenbriefe Ælfrics in altenglischer und lateinischer Fassung*, Bibliothek der Angelsaechsischen Prosa 9 (Darmstadt, 1966, reprinted with supplementary introduction by P. Clemoes [orig. pub. 1914]), 143, which may be the source for Wulfstan.

[81]   *LS* XVII, ll. 110–11, ed. and trans. Skeat, *Lives of Saints*, I.372–3: 'se ungesewenlica deofol þe flyhð geond þas woruld. and fela ðincg gesihð'.

[82]   Byrhtferth, *Ammonitio*, ll. 84–8, ed. and trans. Baker and Lapidge, *Byrhtferth's Enchiridion*, 242–9.

[83]   *Hom.* XLVIII, ed. Napier, *Wulfstan*, 246–50, at 250, ll. 2–6. On CCCC 421 see P.W. Conner, *Anglo-Saxon Exeter: A Tenth-Century Cultural History* (Woodbridge, 1993), 4; W. Green and E. Treharne, *Homilies: Cambridge, Corpus Christi College, 421*, in O. Da Rold et al. (eds), *The Production and Use of English Manuscripts 1060 to 1220* (Leicester, 2010), available at http://www.le.ac.uk/english/em1060to1220/mss/EM.CCCC.421.htm, accessed November 2012.

[84]   I.4, H. Hecht, *Bischofs Waerferth von Worcester Übersetzung der Dialoge Gregors des Grossen über das Leben und die Wunderthaten italienischer Väter und über die Unsterblichkeit der Seelen*, Bibliothek der angelsächsischen Prosa 5 (Leipzig, 1900), 30, l. 28 – 31, l. 26.

medieval texts.[85] The prayer book written in the second quarter of the eleventh century for Ælfwine, dean of the New Minster, Winchester, contains devotions to the holy cross and a list of four reasons why the cross should be adored, the second of which is that 'if your first work is to the cross, all the demons, if they are around you, will not be able to hurt you'.[86] Immediately before an image of the Crucifixion, this book also includes a prayer requesting that 'by this sign of the holy cross all my enemies, visible as well as invisible, present as well as absent, and powerful as well as powerless, may be thrown down'.[87]

Prayers like this originated and were used in monastic and clerical contexts and are almost always in Latin, and so although the perceived need to keep oneself safe from demonic assaults was evidently taken for granted in some circles, these prayers on their own cannot absolutely act as evidence for the widespread currency of these beliefs more broadly in society. But the theology of the invisible spirits was pressed into pastoral use and therefore appears in other contexts too, indicating that one of the concerns of preachers and teachers was to ensure that their congregations understood both that these devils were

---

[85]    See for example the essays in C.E. Karkov, S.L. Keefer and K.L. Jolly (eds), *The Place of the Cross in Anglo-Saxon England* (Woodbridge, 2006); K.L. Jolly, C.E. Karkov and S.L. Keefer (eds), *Cross and Culture in Anglo-Saxon England: Studies in Honor of George Hardin Brown* (Morgantown, WV, 2008); S.L. Keefer, K.L. Jolly and C.E. Karkov, *Cross and Cruciform in the Anglo-Saxon World: Studies to Honor the Memory of Timothy Reuter* (Morgantown, 2010), and K.L. Jolly, 'Cross-Referencing Anglo-Saxon Liturgy and Remedies: The Sign of the Cross as Ritual Protection', in H. Gittos and M.B. Bedingfield (eds), *The Liturgy of the Late Anglo-Saxon Church* (Woodbridge, 2005), 213–43. Pseudo-Alcuin, 'De divinis officiis', *PL* 101.1173–1286, incorporates information about the efficacy of the sign of the cross against the enemy into a discussion of the liturgy for Good Friday at Sext, the moment that the Crucifixion took place, noting that Christ was put to death on the cross rather than by the sword or by stoning because it would not be possible to carry swords or stones all the time, whereas the sign of the cross is easily made with the hand (xviii, *PL* 101.1207D–1208B). This has incorrectly been attributed to Alcuin in some recent scholarship (e.g. D.F. Johnson, 'The Crux usualis as Apotropaic Weapon in Anglo-Saxon England', in E.K. Catherine, K. Sarah Larratt and J. Karen Louise (eds), *The Place of the Cross in Anglo-Saxon England* (Woodbridge, 2006), 80–95, at 83, following W.O. Stevens, *The Cross in the Life and Literature of the Anglo-Saxons* (New York, 1904), 29 [33 in the 1977 reprint]), but in fact the text probably dates to the early tenth century [*c*.908]: see J.J. Ryan, 'Pseudo-Alcuin's *Liber de divinis officiis* and the *Liber 'Dominus vobiscum'* of St Peter Damiani', *Mediaeval Studies* 14 (1952): 159–63.

[86]    London, British Library, Cotton Titus D.xxvii, fols. 70r–v, ed. B. Günzel, *Ælfwine's Prayerbook (London, British Library, Cotton Titus D.xxvi + xxvii)*, HBS 108 (London, 1993), no. 46.12: 'Secunda causa est, si primum opus tuum tibi sit ad crucem, omnes demones, si fuissent circa te, non potuissent nocere tibi'.

[87]    Cotton Titus D.xxvii, fol. 64v, ed. Günzel, *Ælfwine's Prayerbook*, no. 44: 'Hoc signaculo sancte crucis prosternantur, Domine, omnes inimici mei, tam uisibiles quam uisibiles, tam presentes quam absentes, tam potentes quam inpotentes'. The illustration of the Crucifixion is on fol. 65v and is reproduced as Fig. I in Günzel's edition.

everywhere present, and also how they imperilled the soul. Homilies thus advocate the use of the cross as an apotropaic sign to prevent harm from wandering and invisible wicked spirits, and stress the need to teach congregations how to keep themselves safe from demonic attack. The fourth Blickling homily instructs that Christians should make the sign of the cross seven times throughout the day, at the times which correspond to the Hours of the Divine Office, on the grounds that when this sign is made the devil will be put to flight.[88] Interestingly, the homilist follows this by saying: 'if the teachers will not firmly command this to God's people, then they will be very guilty before God, because God's people should know how to protect themselves against devils'.[89] It is not clear whether the author of the homily borrowed this injunction from elsewhere or composed it himself because he thought it was important, but it seems to be at least as much an instruction to the preacher as to the congregation, and the author evidently thought that informing a congregation about devils and how to protect against them was a significant priestly duty.[90]

Byrhtferth likewise warns in his 'Admonition' that food and sleep should always be consecrated and blessed with the holy cross, and this is repeated in the homily based on his text,[91] while Ælfric instructs that people should frequently make the sign of the cross over themselves to keep away the devil and his delusions.[92] Ælfric notes specifically that it is important to make the sign of the cross correctly, with three fingers signifying the Holy Trinity, on the grounds that however a man might wave his hands about, only the clear sign of the cross will have the desired effect against the devil.[93] The author of the fourth Vercelli homily likewise informs his audience of the importance of being aware of the devil and providing protection against his attacks, but uses the metaphor of raising up shields of virtues against the devils bows and arrows.[94] This echoes Boniface's account of the brother of Wenlock's vision, which includes a passage (perhaps based more on Boniface's own interests than on the vision itself) describing how the visionary's sins rose up and cried out against him and were seized by wicked spirits, until the sins were countered by his virtues, which were magnified and amplified by the angels who sought to defend him.[95]

---

[88]   *Hom.* IV, VII, ed. Morris, *Blickling Homilies*, 47, 91.

[89]   *Hom.* IV, ed. Morris, *Blickling Homilies*, 47: '& gif þa lareowas þis nellaþ fæstlice Godes folce bebeodan, þonne beoþ he wiþ God swyþe scyldige; forþon þæt Godes folc sceal witon hu hi hi sylfe scyldan sceolan wiþ deoflu'.

[90]   No source for this section is recorded in the Fontes Anglo-Saxonici Project, *Fontes Anglo-Saxonici: World Wide Web Register*, http://fontes.english.ox.ac.uk, accessed November 2012.

[91]   *Ammonitio*, ll. 91–2, ed. and trans. Baker and Lapidge, *Byrhtferth's Enchiridion*, 248–9; *Hom.* XVIII, ed. Napier, *Wulfstan*, 250, ll. 9–10.

[92]   *LS* XVII, ll. 143–6; XXI, ll. 464–9, ed. and trans. Skeat, *Lives of Saints*, I.374–5, 470–1.

[93]   *LS* XXVII, ll. 147–56, ed. and trans. Skeat, *Lives of Saints*, II.152–5.

[94]   *Hom.* IV, ll. 308–42, ed. Scragg, *Vercelli Homilies*, 102–4.

[95]   Boniface, *Epistola* 10, ed. Tangl, *Die Briefe*, 9, l. 26 – 11, l. 2.

Wicked spirits could also be averted by the recitation of the pater noster and the creed, and the full power of the pater noster is explored in the prose *Solomon and Saturn*. This text survives in a mid tenth-century copy which was ultimately bound up with an eleventh-century liturgical book containing masses and other offices (now Cambridge, Corpus Christi College, 422): *Solomon and Saturn* was probably composed somewhere between the late ninth century and about 930, in a learned and most likely monastic context.[96] But like the sign of the cross, the pater noster and creed were recommended for their apotropaic powers in more pastoral contexts too. This is particularly significant given how frequently homilists and others recommended that these prayers should be learned: they both provided the basis of the faith and served as protection against invisible evil. Ælfric advised that people should sing the pater noster and creed when setting out on a journey, and sign themselves with the cross, so that they could travel with God's protection from demonic attack.[97] In one of his homilies on baptism, Wulfstan alludes to the power of the creed in this respect, stating that people should know how to protect against devils before explaining the significance of the words *abrenuntio* and *credo* as the renouncing of the devil and the acceptance of Christian belief in the baptismal ritual, and then exhorting his audience to learn the creed.[98]

In some cases ideas or instructions about the spiritual presences or the apotropaic uses of signs or prayers were first recorded in texts which may have had, or been intended to have, a 'private' audience, like Ælfwine's prayer book. The audiences of the Blickling and Vercelli books are probably ultimately unknowable, but some of the homilies in these books, such as the fourth Vercelli homily with its explanation of the spiritual presence, were copied more widely, indicating that even if the Vercelli book itself was a 'private' book, the homilies themselves were not limited to this one context.[99] Byrhtferth's *Enchiridion* was probably used in a monastic classroom and seems to be aimed also at secular priests, but it is not clear how widely it was used.[100] Other texts may have had a range of possible intended uses: the preface to Ælfric's *Lives of Saints* records that these *Lives* were made for the laymen Æthelweard and Æthelmær, but the (quite numerous) manuscripts which survive

---

[96]    See D. Anlezark, *The Old English Dialogues of Solomon and Saturn* (Woodbridge, 2009), 49–57, for the suggestion of an association with Glastonbury and Dunstan; although cf. also P.P. O'Neill, 'On the date, provenance and relationship of the Solomon and Saturn dialogues', *Anglo-Saxon England* 26 (1997): 139–68; T.A. Bredehoft, 'Old Saxon Influence on Old English Verse: Four New Cases', in H. Sauer, J. Story and G. Waxenberger (eds), *Anglo-Saxon England and the Continent* (Tempe (AZ), 2011), 83–111, at 95–100, 104–6.

[97]    *LS* XVII, ll. 96–9, ed. and trans. Skeat, *Lives of Saints*, I.370–1.

[98]    *Hom.* VIIIc, ll. 116–26, ed. Bethurum, *Homilies*, 181.

[99]    M.M. Gatch, 'The unknowable audience of the Blickling Homilies', *Anglo-Saxon England* 18 (1989): 99–115.

[100]    See R. Stephenson, 'Byrhtferth's *Enchiridion*: The Effectiveness of Hermeneutic Latin', in E.M. Tyler (ed.), *Conceptualising Multilingualism in England, c. 800 – c. 1250* (Turnhout, 2011), 121–43.

come from religious rather than lay contexts, and may have been used for private reading or in more formal contexts such as preaching.[101] Other texts were more clearly aimed at preaching in public to congregations which included lay people, such as Ælfric's *Catholic Homilies* and probably also Wulfstan's homilies.[102] One of Ælfric's comments is interesting and perhaps suggestive in the insinuation that the power of demons to tempt human beings and urge them to commit wicked deeds had perhaps been taken on board rather too well, although incorrectly understood: he emphasises that demonic temptation cannot be used as an excuse for bad behaviour, noting that the devil 'cannot force any man to wickedness, unless a man of his own will bends to his teaching'.[103]

Another context in which these ideas appear is in medicine, and the prayers and remedies used for healing the sick. Illness and healing are attributed in prayers to devils and angels, sometimes by name, such as the prayers recorded in the margins of an eleventh-century copy of the Old English translation of Bede's *Historia Ecclesiastica*, apparently given to Exeter by Bishop Leofric.[104] A prayer headed 'against sore ears' asks God to drive out 'Fandorahel' and for Raphael to heal; another 'against belly sickness' asks God to drive out the evil angel, 'Laniel', who causes stomach aches, and to grant healing through the benevolent angel, 'Dormiel'.[105] The devil's powers to inflict illness sometimes appear in remedies

---

[101] See C. Cubitt, 'Ælfric's Lay Patrons', in H. Magennis and M. Swan (eds), *A Companion to Ælfric* (Leiden, 2009), 165–92.

[102] For the range of possible uses of homilies and the surviving books, see M. Clayton, 'Homiliaries and preaching in Anglo-Saxon England', *Peritia* 4 (1985): 207–42; J. Wilcox, 'The Dissemination of Wulfstan's Homilies: The Wulfstan Tradition in Eleventh-Century Vernacular Preaching', in C. Hicks (ed.), *England in the Eleventh Century: Proceedings of the 1990 Harlaxton Symposium*, Harlaxton Medieval Studies 2 (Stamford, 1992), 199–217; S. Irvine, 'The Compilation and Use of Manuscripts Containing Old English in the Twelfth Century', in M. Swan and E. Treharne (eds), *Rewriting Old English in the Twelfth Century*, Cambridge Studies in Anglo-Saxon England 30 (Cambridge, 2000), 41–61; J. Wilcox, 'The Audience of Ælfric's *Lives of Saints* and the Face of Cotton Caligula A. xiv, fols. 93–130', in A.N. Doane and K. Wolf (eds), *Beatus Vir: Studies in Early English and Norse Manuscripts in Memory of Phillip Pulsiano* (Tempe, AZ, 2006), 229–63.

[103] *CH* I.1, ll. 121–2, ed. Clemoes, *Catholic Homilies*, 183: 'ac he ne mæg nænne man to nanum leahtre geneadian. buton se mon his agenes willes to his lare gebuge'. No source has been identified for this comment. Elsewhere Ælfric argued against the idea that predestination was an excuse for bad behaviour: see *LS* XVII, ll. 222–50, ed. Skeat, *Lives of Saints*, I.378–82.

[104] Cambridge, Corpus Christi College, 41: for discussion of this manuscript and its marginalia, see S.L. Keefer, 'Margin as archive: The liturgical marginalia of a manuscript of the Old English Bede', *Traditio: Studies in Ancient and Medieval History, Thought, and Religion* 51 (1996): 147–77; T.A. Bredehoft, 'Filling the margins of CCC 41: Textual space and a developing archive', *Review of English Studies* 57:232 (2006): 721–32.

[105] Cambridge, Corpus Christi College, 41, p. 326; cf. R.F. Johnson, 'Archangel in the Margins: St Michael in the Homilies of Cambridge, Corpus Christi College 41', *Traditio:*

contained in medical collections, like the *Leechbooks* copied into London, British Library, Royal 12. D. XVII, probably produced in the middle of the tenth century at Winchester, or the collection known as *Lacnunga* in London, British Library, Harley 585, a late tenth- or early eleventh-century book.[106] Sometimes the roles of angels and devils in healing and causing harm are specifically mentioned, as for example in a short text in Harley 585, which seems to be simultaneously a prayer and remedy: 'a devil has harmed; an angel has cured; the Lord has saved'.[107] But most of these remedies are primarily based on the use of particular plants to heal; some incorporate the apotropaic powers of the sign of the cross, and prayers such as the pater noster or creed, or other liturgical elements such as masses; and there are still others which read more like incantations and which have been viewed with some suspicion by modern scholars.[108]

Remedies that employ the sign of the cross or prayers sometimes simply instruct the use of these during the preparation of herbal ingredients, such as a remedy which requires that the pater noster should be said first three times while a mixture of herbs and butter is boiling, and then nine times while it is boiling three more times.[109] In other cases prayers or signs of the cross were incorporated into much lengthier rituals which might also require other prayers or liturgical components, such as the remedy which instructs that before the specified plants are gathered the healer should go to church and sing a litany (a series of invocations of saints and petitions made directly to God), the creed, and the pater noster, and that he should return to the church and say twelve masses after soaking the plants.[110]

---

*Studies in Ancient and Medieval History, Thought, and Religion* 53 (1998): 63–91, at 67–8.

[106]    R.S. Nokes, 'The several compilers of Bald's Leechbook', *Anglo-Saxon England* 33 (2004): 51–76. The manuscript contains three leechbooks, but only the first two (on fols. 1–109) are associated with Bald: see C.E. Wright, *Bald's Leechbook: British Museum Royal Manuscript 12 D.xvii*, EEMF 5 (Copenhagen, 1955), 13–14.

[107]    CLVII, ed. E. Pettit, *Anglo-Saxon Remedies, Charms, and Prayers from British Library Ms Harley 585: The Lacnunga*, Mellen Critical Editions and Translations 6a–b (2 vols, Lewiston, NY, 2001), 109: 'diabolus lignauit, angelus curauit, Dominus saluauit'. On the difficulty of distinguishing clearly between prayers and charms, see R.M. Liuzza, 'Prayers and/or Charms Addressed to the Cross', in Jolly, Karkov and Keefer (eds), *Cross and Culture in Anglo-Saxon England*, 276–320.

[108]    For a detailed discussion, see Jolly, 'Cross-Referencing Anglo-Saxon Liturgy and Remedies: The Sign of the Cross as Ritual Protection'; and 'Tapping the Power of the Cross: Who and for Whom?', in Karkov, Keefer and Jolly (eds), *The Place of the Cross in Anglo-Saxon England*, 58–79.

[109]    *Leechbook* III, lxviii, ed. O. Cockayne, *Leechdoms, wortcunning and starcraft of early England: Being a collection of documents, for the most part never before printed, illustrating the history of science in this country before the Norman Conquest* (3 vols, 1864), II.358.

[110]    *Leechbook* III, lxxxi, ed. Cockayne, *Leechdoms*, II.356. For detailed discussion of litanies see M. Lapidge, *Anglo-Saxon Litanies of the Saints*, HBS 106 (Woodbridge, 1991), 1–61.

There are also remedies which are interesting because of the people or items which they demand, some aspects of which may have been considered to be more essential than others. One example is a remedy which is supposed to be effective against tumours, and which requires a maiden to fetch a water from a spring or stream water-source that flows east, and to sing the creed and the pater noster over several cups of water drawn from this source.[111] Assuming that this did not require a woman in religious life – and the word used does not specifically designate one – it is possible that this suggests that, by the time this was written down, finding a young girl who knew the creed and the pater noster was not too difficult. Since the maiden was required to say the creed and pater noster three times over cups of water and to repeat the ritual for nine days, it seems likely that she would have known the prayers well enough by the end, even if she had not known them before.

Like other written works from Anglo-Saxon England, these remedies survive in books which were probably produced at religious institutions, and although earlier generations of scholars perceived in these rituals remnants of 'Germanic' or unChristian ideas, recent work has emphasised the learned contexts of their preservation.[112] Instructions which require the healer to read significant quantities of text, or more importantly, to offer masses or to use sacramental or blessed materials such as holy oil, salt or water, were almost certainly used primarily by priests, and not by laity. But also like homilies, the existence of ideas about invisible spirits or the apotropaic power of prayer in medical remedies indicates that there was a discourse about them and about the prevalence of invisible spirits in a wide range of contexts, even though it is even more difficult to recover precisely how people outside the literate contexts in which medical texts were produced might have had access to them, or how they might have experienced them in practice. Some clergy are identified in the sources as having had medical knowledge, and some normative texts suggest that medicine was a discipline which clergy should learn if possible, but little is known of Anglo-Saxon healers: doctors are often only

---

[111]    CLXXVI, ed. Pettit, *Anglo-Saxon Remedies, Charms, and Prayers from British Library Ms Harley 585*, 120: 'Gif wænnas eglian mæn æt þeore heortan: gange mædenman to wylle þe rihte east yrne ] gehlade ane cuppan fulle forð mid ðam streame, ] singe þæreon 'Credan' ] 'Pater noster'; ] geote þonne on oþer fæt, ] hlade eft oþre ] singe eft 'Credan' ] 'Pater noster', ] do swa þæt þu hæbbe þreo; do swa nygon dagas; sona him bið sel'.

[112]    M.L. Cameron, 'Bald's leechbook and cultural interactions in Anglo-Saxon England', *Anglo-Saxon England* 19 (1990): 5–12; J.N. Adams and M. Deegan, 'Bald's leechbook and the *Physica Plinii*', *Anglo-Saxon England* 21 (1992): 87–114; K.L. Jolly, *Popular Religion in Late Saxon England: Elf Charms in Context* (Chapel Hill, NC, 1996); A. van Arsdall, *Medieval Herbal Remedies: The Old English Herbarium and Anglo-Saxon Medicine* (London, 2002); Nokes, 'The several compilers of Bald's leechbook'; M.A. D'Aronco, 'How 'English' is Anglo-Saxon Medicine? The Latin Sources for Anglo-Saxon Medical Texts', in C.S.F. Burnett and N. Mann (eds), *Britannia Latina: Latin in the Culture of Great Britain from the Middle Ages to the Twentieth Century* (London, 2005), 27–41; Jolly, 'Tapping the Power of the Cross: Who and for Whom?'

mentioned in passing in saints' *Lives* when their cures were ineffective in contrast to the healing power of a saint.[113]

Undoubtedly there was a considerable medical tradition in Anglo-Saxon England beyond what survives now, but it is probable that the surviving written books and texts represent one strand of the medicine which was sought out and applied to people beyond the confines of religious centres. While the specific situation on the ground probably varied immensely according to the locality, it seems overwhelmingly likely that if certain ecclesiastical individuals or religious institutions were known to have knowledge of healing, this would have been sought out in times of need. One example of this may be found in the cemetery at Nazeing (Essex), where skeletal analysis of the evidence from the excavation of the cemetery suggests that the female religious community had taken in a number of unwell or injured men and women, and had looked after them.[114] One man buried in the cemetery (Burial no. 53) had sustained several broken limbs and his skeleton was significantly damaged by arthritis, to the extent that he would have required a considerable amount of help to move around; some elderly individuals had little tooth wear, suggesting that they had been fed a special diet.[115] While this suggests that the religious community looked after a number of sick people, the skeletal evidence does not reveal what form of medicine (if any) was used on them, nor yet information about the associated beliefs attached to medical practices. But those who sought medical help at a religious community might have observed some of the preparations, or have been instructed to make the sign of the cross or say particular prayers, or have received explanations about devils or other invisible beasties which afflicted the sick, or about the angels which protected them. The fact that some of the individuals had clearly been looked after for some time also suggests that their contact with the religious community was sustained, and not a once-only event.

Nazeing provides one possible example of the response of a religious community to the sick, but the range of responses from ecclesiastical individuals must have been quite variable. Someone like Ælfric might have instructed the sick to pray, to request or to receive the liturgical ritual of anointing, but it is not clear how or whether he might have relied on medical practices. This contrasts with the presence of a remedy for boils and the instructions for blood-letting

---

[113]   M.L. Cameron, 'Anglo-Saxon medicine and magic', *Anglo-Saxon England* 17 (1988): 191–215; S. Rubin, 'The Anglo-Saxon Physician', in M. Deegan and D.G. Scragg (eds), *Medicine in Early Medieval England: Four Papers* (Manchester, 1989), 7–15; M.L. Cameron, *Anglo-Saxon Medicine* (Cambridge, 1993); see also F.S. Paxton, 'Curing bodies-curing souls: Hrabanus Maurus, medical education, and the clergy in ninth-century Francia', *Journal of the History of Medicine and Allied Sciences* 50:2 (1995): 230–52.

[114]   P.J. Huggins, 'Excavation of Belgic and Romano-British farm with Middle Saxon cemetery and churches at Nazeingbury, Essex, 1975–6', *Essex Archaeology and History* 10 (1978): 29–117, at 54–64.

[115]   Ibid., 56–62.

in Ælfwine's prayer book: Ælfwine may have used the book in his role as dean while he travelled around the estates of the New Minster, and this suggests that for certain types of illness or medical problems he might have attempted to help or advocated cures which were not limited to prayer or to liturgical rituals.[116] In either case, and in the many other potential scenarios, the possibilities for explanations of and communication about beliefs, especially about invisible spirits and their role, are clear, even if the details of these discourses are impossible to recover. Specific details of beliefs which might initially have been most prevalent in monastic settings could therefore filter through into other arenas, especially in pastoral contexts, and this is particularly important because the pastoral settings of angelology and demonology are not always fully recognised.[117] It also suggests that these spirits may have been as real to many people outside learned and monastic contexts as they were to those who lived and worked within them.

This 'realness' is an especially important issue given the ultimate origins of these ideas. Christian theology assumed the existence of these spirits not least because they are recorded in Scripture, and monastic texts in particular had long drawn on the idea of demonic attack and angelic protection.[118] Texts written in more 'scientific' genres such as Bede's *De natura rerum*, self-consciously based on earlier texts with the same title, sought to explain the known world with reference to theology as well as to works dealing with the natural world which were inherited from the classical tradition, such as Pliny's *Historia naturalis*.[119] Anglo-Saxon authors also had recourse to a body of post-classical Christian texts which were written in scientific genres but which themselves drew on both Christian and classical learning, and here Isidore's *De natura rerum* and his *Etymologiae* were perhaps the most influential.[120] Bede and Byrhtferth both draw on earlier writers when they explain that demons belong in the air, which technically designates a space below heaven and distinct

[116]    Cotton Titus D.xxvi, fol. 17r, ed. Günzel, *Ælfwine's Prayerbook*, no. 70.

[117]    Keck, *Angels*, 5.

[118]    Leyser, 'Angels, Monks, and Demons'; see for example the *Rule of Benedict* which assigned a personal angel to each monk: *Regula Benedicti*, 7.13–28, ed. J. Neufville and A. de Vogüé, *La règle de Saint Benoît*, Sources chrétiennes 181–6 (6 vols, Paris, 1971), I.476–80.

[119]    Wallis, 'Si naturam quaeras: Reframing Bede's "science"'; F. Wallis, 'Bede and Science', in S. DeGregorio (ed.), *The Cambridge Companion to Bede*, Cambridge Companions to Literature (Cambridge, 2011), 113–26; see also T.R. Eckenrode, 'Venerable Bede as a scientist', *American Benedictine Review* 22:4 (1971): 486–507; T.R. Eckenrode, 'The growth of a scientific mind: Bede's early and late scientific writings', *Downside Review* 94:316 (1976): 197–212; A. Di Pilla, 'Cosmologia e uso delle fonti nel *De natura rerum* di Beda', *Romanobarbarica* 11 (1992): 129–47.

[120]    For information about texts and manuscripts known to the Anglo-Saxons, see H. Gneuss, *Handlist of Anglo-Saxon manuscripts: A List of Manuscripts and Manuscript Fragments Written or Owned in England up to 1100* (Tempe, AZ, 2001); H. Gneuss, 'Addenda and corrigenda to the Handlist of Anglo-Saxon manuscripts', *Anglo-Saxon England* 32 (2003): 293–305; M. Lapidge, *The Anglo-Saxon Library* (Oxford, 2006).

from it, since heaven is the dwelling place of the angels: as Bede notes, devils were forced to live here after they had been cast out of heaven.[121] In the same way, the prose *Solomon and Saturn* dialogue draws on earlier traditions in recording that when a devil gets tired, it looks for the cattle of a guilty person, or an unclean tree, or goes into the mouth or body of an unblessed man.[122]

In interpreting the world around them, these writers drew as much on academic and theological traditions as they did on the physical world itself, and perhaps especially for understanding the invisible spirits, which were by their nature difficult to observe. All the same, there are hints from other contexts that these interpretations of the physical and spiritual world were not limited to those who had absorbed large quantities of book-learning. This is territory in which it is necessary to proceed tentatively and carefully, since almost all of what survives in the written record is mediated through ecclesiastically trained scribes and authors who were often embedded in a literate culture denied to the unlettered, but descriptions of the physical landscape as well as some of the ways in which the landscape was defined and named in Anglo-Saxon England seem to identify the presence of the spirits in the physical world. The most famous description in this context is the otherworldliness of the physical landscape as described in *Beowulf*: the monster Grendel lives in a *mere* in the fens, away from human settlement, and the unearthly character of the place is underlined by its description as a 'secret land', dark and cold, where fire dances on the water at night.[123] A more specific link with devils occurs in the correspondence between the eery mere of Grendel's dwelling and the final passage of the one of the Blickling homilies, which for the most part discusses the legend of St Michael the Archangel at Gargano.[124] After

---

[121]  Bede, *De natura rerum*, 25, ll. 4–7, ed. Jones et al., *Opera didascalia, 1*, 216; Byrhtferth, *Vita S. Oswaldi*, v.7, ed. and trans. Lapidge, *The Lives of St Oswald and St Ecgwine*, 160–1.

[122]  Prose *Solomon and Saturn*, ll. 45–9, ed. and trans. Anlezark, *The Old English Dialogues of Solomon and Saturn*, 74–5, and see also the commentary at 113.

[123]  *Beowulf*, ll. 1357b–1379, ed. R.D. Fulk et al., *Klaeber's Beowulf and The Fight at Finnsburg*, Toronto Old English Series 21 (Toronto, 2008), 47–8. The word 'mere' has a range of meanings, including 'pond', 'pool', and 'lake': see M. Gelling, *Place-Names in the Landscape* (London, 1984), 26–7; A. Cole, 'The distribution and use of mere as a generic in place-names', *Journal of the English Place-Name Society* 25 (1992–3): 51–2; M. Jacobsson, *Wells, Meres, and Pools: Hydronymic Terms in the Anglo-Saxon Landscape*, Acta Universitatis Upsaliensis, Studia Anglistica Upsaliensia 98 (Uppsala, 1997), 21–3, 208–18. For Grendel's mere, see also R. Butts, 'The analogical mere: Landscape and terror in *Beowulf*', *English Studies* 68 (1987): 113–21; M. Gelling, 'The landscape of *Beowulf*', *Anglo-Saxon England* 31 (2002): 7–11; N. Howe, *Writing the Map of Anglo-Saxon England: Essays in Cultural Geography* (New Haven, CT, 2008), 66–9; C. Abram, 'New light on the illumination of Grendel's mere', *Journal of English and Germanic Philology* 109:2 (2010): 198–216.

[124]  The homily is numbered XVII in the edition (Morris, *Blickling Homilies*, 197–211): the homilies that Morris numbered XVII–XIX should be renumbered XVI–XVIII because

noting that angels help people to fight against devils, the author describes a hellish landscape like that depicted in *Beowulf*: it is watery and covered with dark mists, and it is filled with monsters, devils in the likeness of monsters, and other horrible creatures as well as black souls.[125]

The homily was influenced by the description of St Paul's journey to hell recorded in the apocryphal *Visio S. Pauli*, a text which survives in numerous redactions and which was popular in England as across Europe; and it seems likely that the author of *Beowulf* also drew on the *Visio* (or perhaps a version of the homily, or both the homily and the vision), although it is also possible that *Beowulf* influenced the homily.[126] This should act as a warning that even in poetry which might be termed 'secular' (in that its primary overt message or story does not seem to be religious) the influence of religious literate culture was strong. However, aspects of the 'other' as presented in texts are found more concretely in contexts such as the naming of the landscape. Surviving references to actual features named as 'grendles mere'[127] and 'grendles pyt'[128] may refer to the Grendel of *Beowulf* and suggest that the story (or aspects or versons of it) had a currency outside the literate tradition in which the poem now survives, although it is possible that *grendel* might mean something like 'gravelly' here.[129] Significantly, the elements which are often used to describe *mere* seem to designate the types of places which would not be particularly desirable for settlements.[130] Other landscape features such as pools and pits are likewise described in rather undesirable ways and seem in some contexts to have been associated with the monstrous, just as the Old English text known as *Maxims II* records that monsters belong in the fens.[131]

It is not clear though how far the names that survive in textual records are absolute, or represent the only names by which places or features may have been

---

the fragment numbered XVI by Morris has now been identified as part of the homily that he numbered IV; see R. Willard, *The Blickling Homilies*, EEMF 10 (Copenhagen, 1960), 38–40.

[125] *Hom.* XVI, ed. Morris, *Blickling Homilies*, 209–11.

[126] Morris, *Blickling Homilies*, vi–vii; C.D. Wright, *The Irish Tradition in Old English Literature*, Cambridge Studies in Anglo-Saxon England 6 (Cambridge, 1992), 132–6; the various arguments over which way the influence ran are usefully summarised in A. Orchard, *A Critical Companion to Beowulf* (Cambridge, 2003), 155–8.

[127] S 579 (BCS 1023), AD 951 x 955.

[128] S 78 (BCS 120), 255 (BCS 1331); S 1546b (BCS 1332, 1333).

[129] S 1546b. Other names which seem to refer to Grendel the monster may also have some kind of topographical reference, e.g. the reference to *grendel* in S 669 (BCS 1103) may also indicate a gravelly stream: see Jacobsson, *Wells, Meres, and Pools*, 216–17 and n. 7.

[130] Jacobsson, *Wells, Meres, and Pools*, 215–18.

[131] *Maxims II*, ll. 42b–3a, ed. E.V.K. Dobbie, *The Anglo-Saxon Minor Poems*, Anglo-Saxon Poetic Records 6 (London, 1942), 56: 'Þyrs sceal on fenne gewunian ana innan lande'; Hall, *Elves in Anglo-Saxon England*, 66.

known. Literacy may have been less significant in formulating descriptive place-names, even if it is only through textual records that these names survive, but it is worth noting that it is difficult to know exactly what or who is represented by the ways that the landscape is described. Some names or descriptions, such as 'the ditch where Esne dug across the road', recorded in a charter dating from 846, suggest that they are related to perceptions of a changing local landscape.[132] Occasionally, place-names are described as being those that are used by locals, such as a charter of King Cynewulf, dating perhaps from 766 and probably representing an authentic grant, even if some details (such as the beneficiary) have now been altered: this includes phrases like 'a stream which the locals call Saltbrook', suggesting that the author was not himself local.[133] Nicholas Howe argued that this implies that such records of the landscape needed to be comprehensible to local people, although this is not the only reading of such phraseology.[134] If a 'foreigner' could refer to topographical features in a particular area by their accepted names, it suggests that someone identified them for him, but that still might have been someone from a religious house. On the other hand, if boundary clauses were to be at all useful or effective in forestalling disputes, they needed to refer to names which were accepted within the local area, and so not only the preserve of those in religious life.[135]

The contact between religious models and expectations on the one hand, and experiences of real landscapes on the other, is also clear from hagiographical texts. Saints' *Lives* routinely associate certain types of remote places with evil spirits, and here the local character of the landscape is particularly important. A significant model for Anglo-Saxon saints was Anthony, who had lived as a hermit in the Egyptian desert where he was tried and tested by the wicked spirits who lived there: so too in England would-be saints and ascetics sought out places believed to be occupied by wicked spirits so that they also could battle with demons, but since deserts were rather lacking in the English landscape other types of remote places were selected.[136] Cuthbert chose the wilderness of Farne Island, which had

---

[132]   S 298 (BCS 451): 'ðone dic ðær Esne ðone weg fordealf'; Howe, *Writing the Map of Anglo-Saxon England*, 35–6.

[133]   S 262 (BCS 200): 'rivuli quem incolae vocitant Sealtbroc'; Howe, *Writing the Map of Anglo-Saxon England*, 35.

[134]   Howe, *Writing the Map of Anglo-Saxon England*, 35.

[135]   See for example S. Keynes, 'Royal Government and the Written Word in Late Anglo-Saxon England', in R. McKitterick (ed.), *Uses of Literacy in Early Mediaeval Europe* (Cambridge, 1990), 226–57, esp. 233–4; S.E. Kelly, *Charters of Malmesbury Abbey*, Anglo-Saxon Charters 11 (Oxford, 2006), 92–4; D. Pratt, *The Political Thought of King Alfred the Great*, Cambridge Studies in Medieval Life and Thought, 4th series 67 (Cambridge, 2007), 85.

[136]   D. Brakke, *Demons and the Making of the Monk: Spiritual Combat in Early Christianity* (Cambridge, MA, 2006), esp. 23–47; S. Foot, *Monastic Life in Anglo-Saxon England, c. 600–900* (Cambridge, 2006), 99–101.

apparently remained uninhabited precisely because no one could stand to stay there for any length of time on account of the devils who were there and the illusions which they caused.[137] In a letter to Pope Zacharias, Boniface described his foundation at Fulda as being located in a 'wooded place in a wilderness of great loneliness', a description which perhaps owes as much to hagiographical construct as to reality.[138] Guthlac went to the East Anglian fens, which his biographer Felix described as an area which contained marshes, boggy places, and 'black waters covered with fog',[139] and he was then directed to a particularly remote and unpleasant area, accessed through more bogs and marsh, until Guthlac, like Cuthbert, reached a place where no one previously had been able to dwell, because of the devils who inhabited it.[140]

As it is presented in Felix's narrative, Guthlac's demon-infested fen owes much to literary borrowing as well as to a genuine belief in wicked spirits, since Felix borrowed almost verbatim from Bede's account of Cuthbert the statement that demons had previously prevented anyone living in the saint's chosen remote place.[141] Katy Cubitt has argued that Felix's description is 'almost entirely a textual confection', but it is worth bearing in mind that even when accounts like this owed a considerable amount to literary borrowing, this does not mean that such places were not genuinely feared, or believed to be inhabited by wicked spirits.[142] One of the possible practical reasons that places like Cuthbert's island or Guthlac's fenland retreat were uninhabited is that they were fairly inhospitable and not useful for agriculture, but the emptiness of the landscape might have served to reinforce the idea that evil spirits lived there. Similarly, the descriptions of the demons who visited Guthlac in the fens owe much to the account of the demons who tormented St Anthony in the desert, but

---

[137]   Anon, *Vita S. Cuthberti*, III.1, ed. and trans. Colgrave, *Two Lives of Cuthbert*, 94–7; Bede, *Vita S. Cuthberti prosa*, 17, ed. and trans. Colgrave, *Two Lives of Cuthbert*, 214–17.

[138]   *Epistola* 86, ed. Tangl, *Die Briefe*, 193: 'locus silvaticus in heremo vastissimę solitudinis'; see J.-H. Clay, *In the Shadow of Death: Saint Boniface and the Conversion of Hessia, 721–54*, Cultural Encounters in Late Antiquity and the Middle Ages 11 (Turnhout, 2010), 125–7.

[139]   Felix, *Vita S. Guthlaci*, 24, ed. and trans. Colgrave, *Felix's Life of Saint Guthlac*, 86–7.

[140]   Felix, *Vita S. Guthlaci*, 25, ed. and trans. Colgrave, *Felix's Life of Saint Guthlac*, 88–9.

[141]   Felix, *Vita S. Guthlaci*, 25, ed. and trans. Colgrave, *Felix's Life of Saint Guthlac*, 88–9: 'Nullus hanc ante famulum Christi Guthlacum solus habitare colonus valebat, propter videlicet illic demorantium fantasias demonum ... '. See also A.L. Meaney, 'Felix's life of St Guthlac: Hagiography and/or truth', *Proceedings of the Cambridge Antiquarian Society* 90 (2001): 29–48.

[142]   C. Cubitt, 'Memory and narrative in the cult of early Anglo-Saxon saints', in Y. Hen and M. Innes (eds), *The Uses of the Past in the Early Middle Ages* (Cambridge, 2000), 29–66, at 50.

it is also possible that the hallucinations that Guthlac experienced were a result of Anthony's influence in a different way. It has been argued that both Anthony and Guthlac may have experienced hallucinations as a result of eating barley bread infected with the fungus *ergot*, which can induce effects comparable to those of LSD, although if this were the case it might be expected that Guthlac's companions might also have seen visions.[143] If they did, the visions were not reported. But it is worth noting too that those who might have expected to be attacked by demons, based on the reading of earlier saints' *Lives*, might have experienced visions which presented themselves in a form which was recognisable from their reading through a form of 'cultural conditioning', even if 'real' visions were reshaped in their presentation as a literary text.[144]

It is also clear that the fenland landscape described by Felix is not a complete fantasy, and his references to dark and stagnant water or boggy places are matched in other contexts, such as the descriptions of features and landmarks described in the boundaries of estates recorded in charters.[145] Sometimes features such as meres or pools were designated with animal or bird names as qualifiers (such as the 'titmouse mere' in the boundary of an estate given to Abingdon in 956), but watery places in particular might alternatively be designated 'black', 'foul', 'noxious', or 'dark', probably reflecting their actual natural appearance, but perhaps also implying negative connotations.[146] Occasionally places are identified much more specifically with spiritual or monstrous beings, and terms like þyrs ('giant', or 'demon') or *scucca* ('demon', or 'goblin') employed to describe particular features: two estates in Worcestershire include a 'þyrs pyt' in their bounds,[147] two in Berkshire mention a 'þyrs mere' and a 'ðyrses lacu',[148] and an estate boundary in Devon mentions a 'sceoca broces forda' ('demons' brook's ford').[149] This last became Shobrooke, the river giving its name to the settlement, and one or two other modern place-names may preserve elements of these spirits too, such as Thursford (Norfolk, 'þyrs' + 'ford'),[150] or Shincliffe (County Durham), where the

---

[143]   Colgrave, *Felix's Life of Saint Guthlac*, 16–17; M.L. Cameron, 'The visions of Saints Anthony and Guthlac', in S. Campbell and D.N. Klausner (eds), *Health, Disease and Healing in Medieval Culture* (Basingstoke, 1992), 152–8; Meaney, 'Felix's life of St Guthlac', 39–40.

[144]   See further Foxhall Forbes, 'Diuiduntur in quattuor', 665–6.

[145]   For a fuller discussion of charters, see below, 220–30.

[146]   S 607 (*Abing*, no. 57; Hawkridge, Berkshire): 'mase mere'; or e.g. S 1586 (BCS 279A; Purton, Wiltshire) 'blake mere', 'wulf mere'.

[147]   S 222 (BCS 537), S 1591a (K, III, 395–6).

[148]   S 561 (K 1168), S 1208 (*Abing*, no. 28); Jacobsson, *Wells, Meres, and Pools*, 116, 216–17.

[149]   S 1387.

[150]   M. Gelling and A. Cole, *The Landscape of Place-Names* (Stamford, 2000), 75.

first element may be *scinna* ('demon' or 'phantom').[151] Similar references to these spirits are also found in connection with mounds and barrows (*hlæw* or *beorh*), such as Shuckburgh (Warwickshire), which probably incorporates *scucca* and means something like 'goblin hill' or 'demon hill', or Shucklow (Buckinghamshire); Ailcy Hill (North Yorkshire) may refer to an elf barrow, since the first recorded reference to the mound in 1228 is 'elueshou', although how much earlier this name was coined is unclear.[152]

Here it is probably significant too that Felix reports that Guthlac chose to live in the side of a barrow, because whether this detail represents reality or hagiographical construct, Felix was aiming to highlight the demonic in the landscape, and it seems that the barrow may have held specific meaning for his audience.[153] Written evidence suggests that mounds or barrows were sometimes believed to contain dragons and their treasure, such as the hoard-guarding mound-dwelling dragon in *Beowulf* which occupies a burial barrow filled with treasure,[154] or the confident assertion in the Old English *Maxims II* that the dragon belongs in a barrow where it guards its jewels.[155] Place-name evidence may also imply this, if less securely: a charter dated to 942 includes a 'dracan hlaw' ('dragon barrow') in the bounds of the estate, although it is possible that the document was forged; and modern place-names such as Drakelow (Derbyshire) or Drake Howe (Yorkshire) perhaps also reflect the same belief, although it is not always clear how early these names were used.[156] *Beowulf*'s dragon is a large, fire-breathing creature, and 'draca' seems to refer to a range of serpentine

---

[151]    The first reference to this appears to come from the early twelfth century (*c.*1123): see Gelling, *Place-Names in the Landscape*, 136; A.D. Mills, *A Dictionary of British Place-Names* (Oxford, 2003); V.E. Watts, J. Insley and M. Gelling, *The Cambridge Dictionary of English Place-Names: Based on the Collections of the English Place-Name Society* (Cambridge, 2004), 545.

[152]    R.A. Hall and M. Whyman, 'Settlement and monasticism at Ripon, North Yorkshire, from the 7th to 11th centuries A.D', *Medieval Archaeology: Journal of the Society for Medieval Archaeology* 40 (1996): 62–150, at 65; S. Semple, 'A fear of the past: The place of the prehistoric burial mound in the ideology of middle and later Anglo-Saxon England', *World Archaeology* 30:1 (1998): 109–26, at 111–12.

[153]    Felix, *Vita S. Guthlaci*, 28, ed. and trans. Colgrave, *Felix's Life of Saint Guthlac*, 92–6. See Semple, 'A fear of the past'; Meaney, 'Felix's life of St Guthlac', 35–6; S. Semple, 'Illustrations of damnation in late Anglo-Saxon manuscripts', *Anglo-Saxon England* 32 (2003): 231–45. Interestingly, the boundary clause which refers to 'grendles mere' (S 579 (BCS 1023)) goes on immediately to 'in stancofan' ('to the stone chamber'), perhaps some kind of a burial chamber (see Jacobsson, *Wells, Meres, and Pools*, 157).

[154]    *Beowulf*, ll. 2208b–2311, ed. Fulk et al., *Klaeber's Beowulf and The Fight at Finnsburg*, 75–9; Semple, 'A fear of the past', 109–10.

[155]    *Maxims II*, ll. 26b–7a, ed. Dobbie, *The Anglo-Saxon Minor Poems*, 56: 'Draca sceal on hlæwe, frod, frætwum wlanc'; Semple, 'A fear of the past', 109–10.

[156]    S 484 (*Bur*, no. 6; for information about the authenticity of the charter see P.H. Sawyer, *Charters of Burton Abbey*, Anglo-Saxon Charters 2 (Oxford, 1979), 11–12);

or dragon-like beasts, just as 'wyrm' also covers a range of creatures of this type; but 'draca' can also mean 'devil' and these beasts had demonic associations too based on scriptural references, such as the serpent who tempted Eve in the Garden of Eden, or the dragon in Revelation who is identified with the devil and defeated by St Michael and his angels.[157]

Many prehistoric and early Anglo-Saxon burial mounds are prominent and distinctive in the landscape, and presumably deliberately so for the most part, like the seventh-century burial mounds at Sutton Hoo.[158] Felix notes that the barrow chosen by Guthlac had been cut into by people looking for treasure, and this is interesting for what it reveals about early medieval awareness of what might be in such mounds.[159] It is also significant that Anglo-Saxon execution cemeteries were often located on or near prehistoric or early Anglo-Saxon mounds: of the 27 execution cemeteries discussed by Andrew Reynolds, twelve were connected with mounds, eight with linear earthworks, and three with hillforts, and it is particularly striking that at some sites the mounds may have been contemporary constructions.[160] This suggests that although barrows known to contain earlier burials bore substantial meaning as locations for the executed dead, mounds and earthworks themselves held some significance regardless of whether they were former burial sites. Mounds are represented in the landscape in the Harley Psalter, too, and Sarah Semple argues that some of the illustrations made by Artist F, who worked probably between 1010 and 1020, may represent contemporary judicial practice and the landscape context for the burial of executed offenders, as well as thought on their fate: of especial interest here are the illustrations of decapitated individuals enclosed in a mound, and a drawing of men whose feet are amputated, which she suggests show offenders suffering their fate in hell (see Figure 2.1).[161]

Semple, 'A fear of the past', 110. See also S 513 (BCS 817), for a 'drakenhorde' ('dragon's hoard').

[157] V. Thompson, *Dying and Death in Later Anglo-Saxon England* (Woodbridge, 2004), 132–69; A. Cameron, A. Crandell Amos and A. DiPaolo Healey, *Dictionary of Old English: A to G online* (2007), accessed November 2012 at http://tapor.library.utoronto.ca/doe/index.html: 'draca'; Gn 3; Rv 12:7–9.

[158] M.O.H. Carver, *Sutton Hoo: A Seventh-Century Princely Burial Ground and its Context*, Reports of the Research Committee of the Society of Antiquaries of London 69 (London, 2005), 492–9; H. Williams, 'Death, Memory and Time: A Consideration of the Mortuary Practices at Sutton Hoo', in C. Humphrey and W.M. Ormrod (eds), *Time in the Medieval World* (York, 2001), 35–71, at 53; Clay, *In the Shadow of Death*, 72–3, 99–100.

[159] Felix, *Vita S. Guthlaci*, 28, ed. and trans. Colgrave, *Felix's Life of Saint Guthlac*, 92–6.

[160] A.J. Reynolds, *Anglo-Saxon Deviant Burial Customs* (Oxford, 2009), 156–7. The mound at Stockbridge Down may be an example of a contemporary construction (see N.G. Hill, 'Excavations on Stockbridge Down, 1935–36', *Proceedings of the Hampshire Field Club & Archaeological Society* 13 (1937): 247–59).

[161] Harley 603, fol. 72r; Semple, 'Illustrations of damnation in late Anglo-Saxon manuscripts', 237–40.

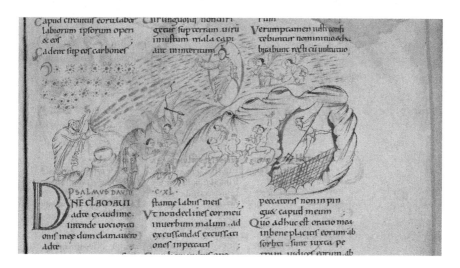

Figure 2.1    The 'Harley Psalter' © The British Library Board (Harley 603, fol. 72r, detail)

The illustrations of Artist F are particularly important in this context because he often departed significantly from his models, although Harley's other artists also illustrated pits, holes, pools and lakes, or simply dark spaces containing demons or monsters, many of which are copied more or less closely from the models in the Utrecht Psalter. The idea that hell was to be found in underground locations and especially in volcanoes is also clear in a range of literate contexts. While the Anglo-Saxon monk Willibald journeyed through the Aeolian Islands in the eighth century, he stopped to climb a volcano because he wanted to look inside 'to see what sort of hell it was', and he presumably knew that hell was found inside volcanoes (and especially Sicilian volcanoes) not least because the *Dialogues* of Gregory recorded that Theoderic was thrown into Etna and thus into hell.[162] The suspicion of dark underground places and their association with the demonic was evidently not limited to monastic contexts though, and the two examples of 'þyrs pyt' in charter bounds suggest that literate culture and local naming practices were not always separated by a huge gulf.[163] On the other hand, the fluidity of beliefs about the afterlife means that pinning down the precise meaning of some of these illustrations is difficult, and not all of them may represent hell quite so neatly as has been assumed.

The depiction of men with amputated feet in the illustration for Psalm 140 is particularly interesting here, since these amputees may in fact have been

[162] *Dialogues* IV.31, ed. A. de Vogüé and P. Antin, *Dialogues de Grégoire le Grand: Livre IV, texte critique et notes*, Sources chrétiennes 265 (Paris, 1980), 104–6; see also Bede, *De natura rerum*, 50, ed. Jones et al., *Opera didascalia, 1*, 233.

[163] See above, 92–3.

understood to be situated in some kind of purgatorial place rather than in hell (see Figure 2.1).[164] The relevant psalm-verse states that 'our bones are scattered next to hell':[165] the mound itself is internally divided so that those with amputated feet sit next to, but separated from and thus juxtaposed with, another area in which there are other men in a net and tormented by a demon, illustrating the verse 'keep me from the snare which they have laid for me ... the sinners fall in his net'.[166] It is those in the net who are probably assumed to be in hell, rather than those whose feet are amputated, and the additional enclosure around those in the net may suggest that they are buried deeper in the mound.[167] Moreover, one of men who is 'next to' hell seems to be lifting his soul, represented as a child, up to one of the vents in the mound, echoing the Psalmist's cry, 'because my eyes are to you Lord, in you I have hoped, do not take away my soul', and perhaps suggesting that these souls are not damned like those in the nets next to them, since they can ultimately be released and join God.[168] This suggests that it should not be assumed that the link between mounds in the landscape and hell or damnation was necessarily straightforward, especially since demons were believed to punish those in purgatorial suffering as well as those in hell: the fourth Blickling homily explains that devils have many souls in their power who will be released from their torments through the prayers and offerings of men and saints.[169]

These complexities and shades of belief are not always clearly visible in the archaeological record, and are often difficult to unpick from texts, with the result that in some cases it is not easy to determine with precision the perceived causes, effects and beliefs which drove particular practices. Although it remains unclear what precise effects the burial of executed men in or near barrows was believed to have on their bodies or on their souls, the pairing of the problematic dead with places that may have had harmful or unholy connotations, or which might have been considered 'haunted' in some way, underlines the fact that both of these were somehow linked in the perceived negativity of their nature.[170] This is reinforced by

---

[164] Harley 603, fol. 72r. For a more detailed discussion see H. Foxhall Forbes, 'O domine libera anima mea! Visualizing Purgatory in Anglo-Saxon England', in J.D. Niles, S.S. Klein and J. Wilcox (eds), *Anglo-Saxon England and the Visual Imagination*, Essays in Anglo-Saxon Studies 6 (Tempe, AZ, forthcoming).

[165] Ps 140:7: 'dissipata sunt ossa nostra secus infernum'.

[166] Ps 140:9–10: 'custodi me a laqueo quem statuerunt mihi ... cadent in retiaculo eius peccatores'.

[167] Cf. also Mt 25:33, in which the sinners are placed on the left, as they are in this illustration from God's perspective (i.e. stage left).

[168] Ps 140:8: 'quia ad te domine domine oculi mei: in te speraui ne auferas animam meam'.

[169] *Hom.* IV, ed. Morris, *Blickling Homilies*, 45–7; see also below, 201–64.

[170] See H. Williams, 'Ancient landscapes and the dead: The reuse of prehistoric and Roman monuments as early Anglo-Saxon burial sites', *Medieval Archaeology: Journal of the Society for Medieval Archaeology* 41 (1997): 1–32; Semple, 'A fear of the past'; H.

the references to 'heathen burials' on the boundaries of legal and administrative units such as counties, hundreds and sometimes estates, which have been discussed in scholarship in some detail and which are usually interpreted with reference to the practice of excluding certain types of offenders from consecrated ground.[171] Textual references to exclusion from consecrated ground are not found until the tenth century, although since these first references are in legal texts and prescribe exclusion as a penalty for some of the worst offences it may be that they confirm, develop or formalise practices which had already been usual for some time.[172]

However, it should be noted that in the context of later Anglo-Saxon England, these 'heathen burials' probably do not indicate the burials of those who were known or believed to follow some kind of organised pagan religion: *hæþen* means 'unChristian' in a much more general sense, and could include unbaptized babies as well as those identified as doing or believing things deemed 'unChristian' by whichever clergyman happened to observe them.[173] This may also be true of the 'heathen barrow' ('Hæþenan beorge') recorded in the boundary clause of one of Cnut's charters dating from 1019, although since the barrow has not been identified in the landscape it is not clear whether what was referred to was a prehistoric or early Anglo-Saxon barrow burial, or something quite different.[174] Those who returned to sin or bad behaviour were likewise assumed to be occupied by or surrounded by devils: the author of the fourth Blickling homily notes that many devils will dwell in anyone who despises God, saying that such a man is 'in the likeness of a heathen', even if he cannot really be one because he has been baptized.[175] This is significant too in considering the references to 'heathen burials' and the treatment of the problematic dead, since these devils might have been considered to stay near dead bodies as well as living ones.

The comparatively frequent location of these burials on boundaries, as well as the fact that so many of the known execution cemeteries are on or near

---

Williams, 'Monuments and the past in early Anglo-Saxon England', *World Archaeology* 30:1 (1998): 90–108; Semple, 'Illustrations of damnation in late Anglo-Saxon manuscripts'; and below, 301–2.

[171] See A.J. Reynolds, 'Burials, Boundaries and Charters', in S. Lucy and A.J. Reynolds (eds), *Burial in Early Medieval England and Wales* (London, 2002), 71–94; Reynolds, *Anglo-Saxon Deviant Burial Customs*, 219–22.

[172] See in particular H. Gittos, 'Creating the Sacred: Anglo-Saxon Rites for Consecrating Cemeteries', in Lucy and Reynolds (eds), *Burial in Early Medieval England and Wales*, 195–208; and further discussion below, 273–8.

[173] See J. Bosworth and T.N. Toller, *An Anglo-Saxon Dictionary, Based on the Manuscript Collections of the Late Joseph Bosworth* (Oxford, 1898), 502: 'hæþen'; Reynolds, 'Burials, Boundaries and Charters', 175–7; Reynolds, *Anglo-Saxon Deviant Burial Customs*, 219–22.

[174] S 956 (*WinchNM*, no. 33).

[175] *Hom.* IV, ed. Morris, *Blickling Homilies*, 49: 'Se þe Godes bebod ofergogaþ, he biþ on hæþenra onlicnesse, & manig deofol on him eardaþ'; see also below, 106–8.

boundaries, has led to the suggestion that the boundary sites themselves are significant because of their liminality.[176] Textual sources and archaeological remains provide evidence that gallows and execution-sites may also have been located on boundaries (as indeed they were located at some of the barrows used for execution burials, for example at Stockbridge Down).[177] It is just possible too that as in the later medieval period, crossroads might also have been used for the burial of problematic bodies, although the evidence here is rather patchy.[178] In many cases the sites of 'heathen burials' are also near major routes of communication such as roads or waterways, raising the possibility that they were significant for the display of heads or bodies: this practice sometimes leaves visible signs in the archaeological record, such as the loss of mandibles (the lower jaw-bone), and seems also to be referred to in some place-names.[179] But it may be too that the location of these sites on boundaries was at least partly connected with a desire to bury the problematic dead as far away as was legally possible, so that perhaps the hundred or county boundary was significant because it was the limit of jurisdiction. Ascertaining whether belief or practice came first is comparable to chickens and eggs, and beliefs in the continuing unsavoury nature of the 'unholy' dead, and their associations with wicked spirits, are quite clear throughout the textual and archaeological record. More importantly, information about the physical presence of the unholy dead in the landscape was evidently remembered and transmitted, and probably widely known, and these kinds of places were presumably discomfiting for those passing through them.

In addition to malevolent beings, the physical landscape also hosted benevolent invisible presences: holy men and women left their traces where they had lived and died in the landscape,[180] but angels too visited earth and certain types of places were often especially connected with them. St Michael the Archangel appeared on mountains, the most famous European sites of angelic appearance being Monte Gargano in southern Italy (Puglia), where Michael left

---

[176]   A.J. Reynolds, 'The Definition and Ideology of Anglo-Saxon Execution Sites and Cemeteries', in G. De Boe and F. Verhaege (eds), *Death and Burial in Medieval Europe: Papers of the 'Medieval Europe Brugge 1997' Conference, 2* (Zelik, 1997), 33–41; Reynolds, *Anglo-Saxon Deviant Burial Customs*, 219–27.

[177]   Hill, 'Excavations on Stockbridge Down, 1935–36'; Reynolds, *Anglo-Saxon Deviant Burial Customs*, 122, 158, 222–6.

[178]   Reynolds, *Anglo-Saxon Deviant Burial Customs*, 212, 216–17; see also below, 301.

[179]   Ibid., 169, 179, 213, 223–4, 233; see also J.L. Buckberry and D.M. Hadley, 'An Anglo-Saxon execution cemetery at Walkington Wold, Yorkshire', *Oxford Journal of Archaeology* 26:3 (2007): 309–29, esp. 314, and Fig. 2; see also S 513 (BCS 817), which records both a 'dragon's hoard' and 'head stakes', although this charter may not be authentic.

[180]   See above, 53–7.

behind his footprints, and Mont-Saint-Michel in Normandy.[181] Michael is also supposed to have appeared in Thuringia when the Anglo-Saxon missionaries were working there, and in response Boniface is supposed to have founded a church dedicated to him.[182] England had its own angelic mountain, St Michael's Mount in Cornwall, although in the surviving record Michael's appearance there in the eighth century is first referred to in a fifteenth-century text.[183] However, the land's association with St Michael appears in an eleventh-century charter of Edward the Confessor, who seems to have granted the land for its symbolic significance, since the land itself was not desperately valuable in economic or political terms: Edward granted 'St Michael's next to the sea' to St Michael and to the brothers who served him at Mont-Saint-Michel.[184]

Angels were believed to inhabit the heavens and the upper air above the earth, and so it is understandable that they were believed to come down on to high places.[185] Churches dedicated to St Michael are sometimes (though by no means always) found on hill-top locations, although how early these dedications were made is not always easy to ascertain.[186] The church of St Michael and All

---

[181]   R.F. Johnson, *St Michael the Archangel in Medieval English Legend* (Woodbridge: Boydell and Brewer, 2005), 36–45.

[182]   A. Heinz, 'Saint Michel dans le "monde germanique". Histoire – Culte – Liturgie', in P. Bouet, G. Otranto and A. Vauchez (eds), *Culto e santuari di san Michele nell'Europa medievale = Culte et sanctuaires de saint Michel dans l'Europe médiévale: atti del Congresso internazionale di studi, Bari, Monte Sant'Angelo, 5–8 aprile 2006* (Bari, 2007), 39–55, at 50.

[183]   N. Orme, 'St Michael and his mount', *Journal of the Royal Institution of Cornwall* n.s. 10:1 (1986–7): 32–43; N. Orme, *The Saints of Cornwall* (Oxford, 2000), 192–5; Johnson, *St Michael*, 68.

[184]   S 1051, ed. S. Keynes, 'The Æthelings in Normandy', *Anglo-Norman Studies* 13 (1991): 173–205, no. 5, at 190–4: 'Tradidi sancto Michaeli archangelo in usum fratrum Deo seruientium in eodem loco Sanctum Michaelem qui est iuxta mare'. Keynes argues that the document is authentic despite some extraordinary features, but does not query (or discuss) the symbolic significance of the land granted.

[185]   Bede, *De natura rerum*, 7, ed. Jones et al., *Opera didascalia, 1*, 197–8; Howe, *Writing the Map of Anglo-Saxon England*, 219–20; for the desirability of hill-top locations for monastic sites see also Foot, *Monastic Life*, 99–101.

[186]   Known early dedications to Michael include the 'clymiterium' near Hexham described by Bede, *HE* V.2.2, ed. Lapidge, Monat and Robin, *Histoire ecclésiastique*, III.18–20, and the church at Bishop's Cleeve, Gloucestershire (S 141 (BCS 246)). It is possible too that there was a seventh-century dedication at Much Wenlock and an eighth-century foundation at St Michael's Mount (M. Clayton, *The Cult of the Virgin Mary in Anglo-Saxon England*, Cambridge Studies in Anglo-Saxon England 2 (Cambridge, 1990), 127, 129); and see also S 50 (*Sel*, 103–6), although Kelly suggests that the king's subscription (which includes the reference to the church of St Michael) may have been revised. For the difficulties with dating church dedications, see N. Orme, *English Church Dedications: With a Survey of Cornwall and Devon* (Exeter, 1996), xii, 56–7.

Angels at Thornhill (Yorkshire) stands on a prominent hill, and although the foundation date is unclear part of a ninth-century cross-shaft survives there, apparently referring to the hill in the inscription it bears: 'Gilswiþ raised up a beacon on a hill in memory of Berhtswiþ, pray for her soul.'[187] The church of St Michael in Stinsford (Dorset) is another possible candidate for an early date, even though documentary evidence is lacking once again. At this church there is a stone carving of St Michael fighting the dragon which probably dates to the early eleventh century, and although the present church is not itself Anglo-Saxon, it is possible that the carving survived from an earlier (Anglo-Saxon) church dedicated to St Michael.[188] There are references to Michael in churches not dedicated to him, too: another image of Michael fighting the dragon, also probably dating to the eleventh century, is accompanied by an Old English inscription and survives now in the church of St Nicholas, Ipswich, where it is incorporated into an interior wall.[189] It is not clear how this stone came to the church, and St Nicholas himself was a comparatively late import into England in any case.[190] But this suggests that while the number of angelic place-names is very limited, churches dedicated to the archangel and depictions in paint or on stone marked out the angelic presence in the visible world.[191]

These markers of the holy and unholy in the landscape are interesting in the broad-brush picture that they reveal of the world beyond constructed Christian narratives, in which religious foundations existed and with which they interacted. The picture revealed through topographical or place-name evidence is much less precise in its details than the information outlined in textual sources, but there are clear meeting-points between the two. The hints of the spiritual in the landscape suggest how information about angels and devils, or about saints, could have been transmitted culturally by implication, or by association, for example, in addition to the formal religious settings in which preachers instructed their congregations

---

[187]    E. Coatsworth and J. Higgitt, *Corpus of Anglo-Saxon Stone Sculpture: Vol. 8, Western Yorkshire* (Oxford, 2008), 258–9, illustrations 728–32: 'Gilsuiþ arærde æft[e] Berhtsuiþe bekum on bergi. Gebiddað þær saule'.

[188]    R. Cramp and C.R. Bristow, *Corpus of Anglo-Saxon Stone Sculpture: Vol. 7, South-West England* (Oxford, 2006), 113–14, ill. 100.

[189]    E. Okasha, *Hand-List of Anglo-Saxon Non-Runic Inscriptions* (Cambridge, 1971), no. 58: 'HER : SĆE [M]IHA[E]L : FEHT ÞIÐ ÐANE : DRACĀ'; 'here St Michael fights (or fought) against the dragon'.

[190]    C.W. Jones, *The Saint Nicholas Liturgy and its Literary Relationships: Ninth to Twelfth Centuries by C.W. Jones; With an Essay on the Music by G. Reaney*, University of California Publications, English Studies 27 (Berkeley, 1963), 120; E.M. Treharne, *The Old English Life of St Nicholas with the Old English Life of St Giles*, Leeds Texts and Monographs, New Series 15 (Leeds, 1997), 36.

[191]    The only place-name to mention an angel seems to be St Michael's Mount: see Watts, Insley and Gelling, *The Cambridge Dictionary of English Place-Names*, 522.

about what they ought to believe.[192] While it may not be possible to reconstruct all the subtleties or shades of belief, the hints of spiritual beings and monstrous creatures allow at least a glimpse into the landscape as it might have been perceived in the course of travel, or in stories, and this in turn reinforces the idea that belief in angels and devils in particular was not limited to contexts of monasticism or great learning. This is important because theological tradition held that invisible spirits responded to certain actions (like the rituals of baptism or the Eucharist) or occasions (like death), and that these spirits could (and should) in turn be affected by the pastoral and liturgical rituals. More importantly still, the expected responses of angels and devils both to human affairs and to each other were often almost an allegorical representation of abstract theological concepts or doctrines, and instruction through the examples of angels and devils seems to have been felt to be an effective way of conveying theological ideas.

## Reification

Angels and devils could aid in the conceptualisation of certain ideas which were crucial to Christian doctrines and Christian theology, such as 'good' and 'evil', or 'sin'. Ælfric borrowed from Alcuin's *Interrogationes Sigewulfi* to explain that evil is nothing in itself, and that its only dwelling is in certain creatures, but he clarified his meaning by including information about the devil which was not found in his source, since Alcuin's original text placed its focus much more in the abstract.[193] This emphasis on the manifestation of evil in a recognisable form is important, because complex and abstract concepts such as 'original sin' may have been more difficult to grasp than the idea of spiritual agents of good and evil which were not always visible, but which could be (and were) represented pictorially and visually. Even if angels or devils themselves were not usually concrete or visible creatures, they were visualisable and could be compared or contrasted to other visible beings, for example in beauty or ugliness. The abilities and nature of

---

[192]   P. Boyer, *The Naturalness of Religious Ideas: A Cognitive Theory of Religion* (Berkeley, 1994), 22–4.

[193]   Ælfric, *Interrogationes Sigewulfi*, XLVII, ll. 309–13, ed. G.E. Mac Lean, 'Ælfric's Version of Alcuini Interrogationes Sigeuuulfi in Genesin', *Anglia* 7 (1884): 1–59, at 32–4: 'Yfel nis nan þing þurh hit sylf. ] nane wununge næfð butan on sumum gesceafte; Se deofol wæs ærest to godum engle gesceapen. ac he wearð yfel þurh modignysse. nu nis yfel nan þing buton godnysse forgægednysse. swa swa þeostru ne synd nan þing buton leohtes forlætennyss' ('Evil is nothing in itself, and it has no dwelling except in some creatures. The devil was created first as a good angel, but he became evil through pride. Now evil is nothing except transgression from goodness, in the same way as darkness is nothing except the absence of light'); *Hom.* I, ll. 190–1, ed. J.C. Pope, *Homilies of Ælfric: A Supplementary Collection*, EETS, OS 259–60 (2 vols, London, 1967–8), I.205: 'Næfð yfel nane wununge þæt hit wesan mæge ahwær buton on gesceaftum þe gode wæron gesceapene'; Fox, 'Ælfric on the creation and fall of the angels', 182–3.

angels and devils were discussed with reference to their similarity to, or difference from, human beings, one of the most significant differences being the power of the spirits to fly through the air. Here Ælfric noted that angels were unlike humans in that they were spirits without bodies, but that like humans and unlike beasts, angels had reason.[194]

Despite being part of God's invisible creation, angels in particular were visibly and visually present to Anglo-Saxon men and women, even those who had no access to books and could not read, in the form of stone representations on churches or monuments, or perhaps in paintings on church walls.[195] Many of the surviving Anglo-Saxon carved stone angels, such as those at Breedon on the Hill (Leicestershire) and Lichfield (Staffordshire), or at Dewsbury and Otley (Yorkshire), belonged to large ecclesiastical centres or religious communities, and some of these latter may have represented complex theological beliefs in a pictorial medium;[196] in contrast smaller churches might have had more ephemeral paintings which no longer survive. This does not, of course, guarantee that everyone could understand the complexity of the theological ideas represented, or even see them: the poor sight and also blindness that must have affected many in a pre-modern population may have meant that some angels were in too lofty a position to be visible from the ground even when they were articulated in stone or paint.[197] It is also worth bearing in mind that without explanation, representations of stories are not necessarily immediately obvious to those whose knowledge of what is depicted is rather patchy.[198] Nonetheless, the potential for visual representations of angels or devils to inform how these spirits were conceptualised, and to reinforce

---

[194]   *CH* I.20, ll. 7–16; I.21, ll. 118–35; I.36, ll. 16–17, ed. Clemoes, *Catholic Homilies*, 335, 349 486.

[195]   The most famous of these are the Lichfield angel (see M.P. Brown, 'The Lichfield angel and the manuscript context: Lichfield as a centre of Insular art', *Journal of the British Archaeological Association* 160 (2007): 8–19; W. Rodwell, 'The Lichfield angel: A spectacular Anglo-Saxon painted sculpture', *Antiquaries' Journal* 88 (2008): 48–108) and the angel at Breedon on the Hill (see D. Parsons, 'A note on the Breedon angel', *Leicestershire Archaeological and Historical Society Transactions* 51 for 1975–1976 (1977): 40–2); but there are a great many: see the volumes in *Corpus of Anglo-Saxon Stone Sculpture*.

[196]   See R.N. Bailey, 'The Winwick Cross and a Suspended Sentence', in A.J. Minnis and J. Roberts (eds), *Text, Image, Interpretation: Studies in Anglo-Saxon Literature and its Insular Context in Honour of Éamonn Ó Carragáin* (Turnhout, 2007), 449–72; J. Hawkes, 'Gregory the Great and Angelic Mediation: The Anglo-Saxon Crosses of the Derbyshire Peaks', in A.J. Minnis and J. Roberts (eds), *Text, Image, Interpretation*, 431–48; T. Pickles, 'Angel veneration on Anglo-Saxon stone sculpture from Dewsbury (West Yorkshire), Otley (West Yorkshire) and Halton (Lancashire): Contemplative preachers and pastoral care', *Journal of the British Archaeological Association* 162 (2009): 1–28, at 7.

[197]   A. Pettegree, *Reformation and the Culture of Persuasion* (Cambridge, 2005), 107–20.

[198]   Ibid., 111–16.

the belief that they were there (if it was ever doubted) is clearly significant, just as the allusions to good or wicked spirits or to the monstrous in the landscape suggests that belief in these spirits did not remain within learned environments. From a theological perspective, presence and response of these spirits to human actions or rituals was particularly important at the beginning and end of mortal life, in the ritual of baptism, and in the dissolution of body and soul at death.

## Baptism

Baptism is not only significant in understanding the development of Anglo-Saxon angelology and demonology, but also in providing a performative context in which knowledge of angelology and demonology might be learned or reinforced. In the ritual of baptism, the soul was cleansed of original sin, the stain on all human souls which existed as a result of the Fall, when Adam and Eve lost their innocence and were evicted from the Garden of Eden. In addition, the baptized individual became a Christian, marked out by and sealed with Christ's cross.[199] Baptism was thus essential, the most important sacrament for all those who believed in Christ, since under normal circumstances only baptized Christians were believed to be able to achieve salvation.[200] The sacrament of baptism was enacted through the visible ritual performed by the priest, but the effect of baptism, which was to make someone a Christian, was performed invisibly, and theological tradition had long held that there were also other significant effects on the spirits present invisibly around all men and women.[201] The surviving Anglo-Saxon manuscripts containing baptismal liturgies are outlined in Table 2.1: the Latin prayers of these liturgies present a vivid image of good and bad spirits around the baptismal candidate, as the priest commands the devils to leave the unbaptized individual and asks God to send his angels to guard the new Christian.[202]

---

[199]   See P. Cramer, *Baptism and Change in the Early Middle Ages, c. 200 – c. 1150* (Cambridge, 1993), 87–8; B.C. Raw, *Trinity and Incarnation in Anglo–Saxon Art and Thought*, Cambridge Studies in Anglo-Saxon England 21 (Cambridge, 1997), 176–86.

[200]   S. Foot, '"By Water in the Spirit": The Administration of Baptism in Early Anglo-Saxon England', in J. Blair and R. Sharpe (eds), *Pastoral Care before the Parish* (Leicester, 1992), 171–92, at 172–3.

[201]   See Daniélou, *Les anges et leur mission: d'après les Pères de l'Eglise*, 95–100; H.A. Kelly, *The Devil at Baptism: Ritual, Theology, and Drama* (Ithaca, NY, 1985); Cramer, *Baptism and Change in the Early Middle Ages*, 11–15, 136, 145–7, 151.

[202]   See for example: 'te quesumus domine ut mittere digneris sanctum angelum tuum ut similiter custodiat hunc famulum tuum et perducat eum ad gratiam baptismi tui. Ergo maledicte diabole recognosce sententiam tuam et da honorem deo uiuo et uero, da honorem iusu christo filio eius et spiritui sancto, et recede ab hoc famulo dei', found (with variants) in Rouen, BM, 274, fols. 64v–65r, ed. H.A. Wilson, *The Missal of Robert of Jumièges*, HBS 11 (London, 1896), 95; CCCC 422, p. 370; CCCC 163, pp. 30–31.

The majority of the liturgy itself took place in Latin, and the dramatic exhortations to the invisible spirits in the liturgical ritual may not have been understood by laity, either because they were too young or because they did not know Latin. It is also not entirely clear that all priests who performed Latin rituals would have understood every word, or whether some were simply able to read Latin words out without complete comprehension. The presence of Old English rubrication for much of the baptismal ritual in manuscripts like the early eleventh-century 'Red Book of Darley' (now Cambridge, Corpus Christi College, 422), probably made at Winchester for use in Sherborne, might suggest that some priests required or preferred additional instructions in Old English for the performance of these pastoral services.[203] But this did not mean that priests and people were completely unaware of the significance of the ritual, even if linguistic difficulties may have meant that in many cases not all of the words of the ritual were immediately understood. The nature of a sacrament such as baptism is that its invisible effects are performed through the visible actions of the priest: Alcuin noted, for example, that 'what the priest performs on the body with water outwardly, the Holy Spirit works invisibly in the soul through faith'.[204] Here the signing of the candidate with the cross is especially important, and some rituals also instructed that the exorcism of the devil should be accompanied (or achieved) by exsufflation, where the priest blows in the face of the candidate to expel wicked spirits.[205] The exorcism is an important part of the baptismal ritual, and homilies written for preaching at baptisms expound the significance of this aspect of the ritual here as well as its specific effects on devils: Wulfstan's homilies for baptism explain that the devil is terrified by the ritual of baptism and is thereby cast out, so that an entrance is left for Christ instead.[206]

---

[203]   The rubrics are printed in R.I. Page, 'Old English liturgical rubrics in Corpus Christi College, Cambridge, MS 422', *Anglia* 96 (1978): 149–58; T. Graham, 'The Old English liturgical directions in Corpus Christi College, Cambridge, MS 422', *Anglia* 111 (1993): 439–46; see also above, 19–20, for the case of the eighth-century priest who was unable to baptize using the correct grammatical formula.

[204]   Alcuin, *Epistola* 113, ed. Dümmler, *Epistolae*, 164, ll. 39–41: 'Quod enim visibiliter sacerdos per baptismum operatur in corpore per aquam, hoc Spiritus sanctus invisibiliter operatur in anima per fidem'; see also Cramer, *Baptism and Change in the Early Middle Ages*, 156–7.

[205]   Alcuin, *Epistolae* 134; 137, ed. Dümmler, *Epistolae*, 202, ll. 15–16, 214, ll. 23–4; Hill, 'When God blew Satan out of Heaven, 136; Foot, 'Baptism', 177; S.A. Keefe, *Water and the Word: Baptism and the Education of the Clergy in the Carolingian Empire*, Publications in Mediaeval Studies (Notre Dame, IN, 2002), 47–50, 63–5, 84–6.

[206]   *Hom.* VIIIa, ll. 36–41; VIIIb, ll. 15–36; VIIIc, ll. 29–35, 54–68, 116–42, ed. Bethurum, *Homilies*, 170, 172–3, 176–9, 181–2; for more general discussion of these homilies and their sources, see K. Jost, 'Einige Wulfstantexte und ihre Quellen', *Anglia* 56 (1932): 265–315, at 301–57; J.T. Lionarons, *The Homiletic Writings of Archbishop Wulfstan: A Critical Study* (Cambridge, 2010), 125–9.

Table 2.1    Anglo-Saxon manuscripts containing liturgical forms for baptism[1]

| Shelfmark | Date and provenance | Edition/facsimile |
|---|---|---|
| Cambridge, Corpus Christi College, 163 | s. xi², probably s. x⁴ᐟ⁴, Worcester, or Old Minster, Winchester, perhaps for the Nunnaminster?[2] | *Parker Library on the web*, http://parkerweb.stanford.edu |
| Cambridge, Corpus Christi College, 422 ('Red Book of Darley'); a sacramentary, collectar, and 'manual'-type book | s. xi^{med}, perhaps written at Winchester for use at Sherborne[3] | *Parker Library on the web*, http://parkerweb.stanford.edu[4] |
| Oxford, Bodleian Library, Bodley 579 ('Leofric Missal')[5] | 'Leofric A': s. x^{1/4}. ?perhaps written for Plegmund (Archbishop of Canterbury, 890–923)[6] 'Leofric B': additions made probably at Canterbury between the second quarter of the tenth century and the end of the century[7] 'Leofric C': additions made during the book's ownership by Leofric (d.1072: Bishop of Crediton (1046) and Exeter (1050))[8] | Orchard, *The Leofric Missal* *Early Manuscripts at Oxford University*, http://image.ox.ac.uk |
| Rouen, Bibliothèque municipale, 274 (Y.6) ('Missal of Robert of Jumièges') | s. xi¹; probably written at Ely or Peterborough[9] | Wilson, *Missal of Robert of Jumièges* |

*Notes*: [1] See further S.L. Keefer, 'Manuals', in R.W. Pfaff (ed.), *The Liturgical Books of Anglo-Saxon England*, Old English Newsletter, Subsidia 23 (Kalamazoo, MI, 1995), 99–109, at 101–2: she notes that these baptismal liturgies come primarily from the Supplement to the Hadrianum (ed. Jean Deshusses, *Le sacramentaire grégorien: ses principales formes d'après les plus anciens manuscrits*, *Spicilegium Friburgense* 16 (Fribourg, 1971), nos. 1065–89). [2] See M. Lapidge, 'The origin of CCCC 163', Transactions of the Cambridge Bibliographical Society 8 (1981), 18–28; M. Budny, *Insular, Anglo-Saxon and Early Anglo-Norman Manuscript Art at Corpus Christi College, Cambridge: An Illustrated Catalogue* (2 vols, Kalamazoo, MI, 1997), I.593–98. [3] A. Corrêa, 'Daily Office Books: Collectars and Breviaries', in Pfaff (ed.), The Liturgical Books of Anglo-Saxon England, 45–60, at 56–7; Keefer, 'Manuals'; Gittos, 'Is there any Evidence for the Liturgy of Parish Churches'; S. Keynes, 'Wulfsige, Monk of Glastonbury, Abbot of Westminster (c 990–3), and Bishop of Sherborne (c 993–1002)', in K. Barker, D.A. Hinton and A. Hunt (eds), *St Wulfsige and Sherborne: Essays to Celebrate the Millennium of the Benedictine Abbey, 998–1998* (Oxford, 2005), 53–94, at 75–6; Rushforth, *Saints in English Kalendars*, 41–2. [4] The liturgical rubrics are printed in Page, 'Old English liturgical rubrics'; Graham, 'The Old English liturgical directions'. [5] This is a very complex, composite book and what is provided here is only the briefest summary. For detailed discussion see N. Orchard, The Leofric Missal, HBS 113–14 (2 vols, London, 2002); R.W. Pfaff, *The Liturgy in Medieval England: A History* (Cambridge, 2009), 72–7, 136–8. [6] See Orchard, The Leofric Missal, 1.23–131; Pfaff, *The Liturgy in Medieval England*, 72–5. [7] Orchard, Leofric Missal, I.132–205; Pfaff, *The Liturgy in Medieval England*, 75–7. [8] Orchard, Leofric Missal, 1.206–33; Pfaff, *The Liturgy in Medieval England*, 136–8. [9] R.W. Pfaff, 'Massbooks: Sacramentaries and Missals', in Pfaff, The Liturgical Books of Anglo-Saxon England, 7–34, at 15–19; Pfaff, *The Liturgy in Medieval England*, 88–91.

Wulfstan's homilies about baptism also reveal a clear concern to explain the significance of the part of the baptismal liturgy which involves dialogues in Latin between the priest and the baptismal candidate or, if the candidate is too young to speak, the priest and the godparents on behalf of the candidate. These dialogues pose three questions about renunciation of the devil, his works and conceits, to which the reply 'abrenuntio' ('I renounce') is given, and then three questions affirming the Christian faith in a short form of the creed which receive the answer 'credo' ('I believe'). In his exposition of the baptismal dialogues, Wulfstan explains and summarises the meaning of 'abrenuntio' and 'credo', providing one written example of how people attending a baptism might have understood the meaning of the ritual and its key dramatic points, even if they did not comprehend the Latin words.[207] Priests were required (at least theoretically) to be able to understand and explain the significance of baptism,[208] and Wulfstan's example may be only one instance of a scenario played out far more frequently but where traces do not survive in the written record. Then as now, the written form of the baptismal liturgy presents a seamless dialogue, but if this is to be enacted properly and without too much prompting the performance of the ritual requires at least minimal preparation beforehand, so that the candidate or his parents know what they are supposed to say and when (especially in the absence of modern printed service-sheets and widespread literacy). If a priest informed a baptismal candidate or his parents of the expected responses, it seems likely that at least some explanation of the terms 'abrenuntio' and 'credo' might also have followed. In a similar vein, Wulfstan's explanation of the terms may have been intended as much to ensure participation in the ritual as comprehension of its meaning.

Information about baptism and its invisible effects also appeared in homilies intended for other occasions. Ælfric too explained the baptismal dialogues in some detail, but not in a homily which was primarily about baptism as Wulfstan's was. Instead, it was the occasion of the Epiphany, a feast associated with Christ's baptism, which prompted Ælfric's discussion.[209] The main point explored by Ælfric is how children who had been baptized before they could understand or speak could be said

---

[207]     *Hom.* VIIIc, ll. 120–6, ed. Bethurum, *Homilies*, 181: 'Ac utan understandan hwæt ða twa word mænan, *abrenuntio* ] *credo*, þe man æt fulluht-þenunge on gewunan hæfð. *Abrenuntio*, þæt is on Englisc, ic wiðsace heononforð æfre deofles gemanan. *Credo*, þæt is on Englisc, ic gelyfe on God ælmihtigne þe ealle ðing gescop ] geworhte. Nage we nane ðearfe þæt we ðyses weorðan lease; ac utan don swa us þearf, gelæstan hit georne' ('let us understand what these two words mean, *abrenuntio* and *credo*, which are usual at the baptismal service: *abrenuntio*, that is in English, I renounce the prompts of the devil from this time on; *credo*, that is in English, I believe in God almighty who created and worked all things. There is no need that we should do this falsely, so let us do as there is need for us, perform it eagerly').

[208]     Canons of Clofesho (747), 10, ed. A.W. Haddan and W. Stubbs, *Councils and Ecclesiastical Documents Relating to Great Britain and Ireland* (3 vols, Oxford, 1869), III.366; *Examination of Candidates for Ordination*, 12, *Councils and Synods*, I.i, no. 57.

[209]     *CH* II.3, ed. Godden, *Catholic Homilies*, 19–28.

to have made baptismal promises. In explaining how the child's godfather made the promises on behalf of the child, Ælfric in fact presents what amounts almost to a full translation of this section of the baptismal ritual, since he gives in English the questions asked by the priest and the answers expected of the child's godfather, before stressing that the child must learn about true Christian belief from the godfather who made the promises and renounced the devil on his behalf.[210] More briefly, Ælfric explained in other homilies 'when a priest baptizes a child, he drives the devil out of that child, because every heathen man belongs to the devil and through baptism he belongs to God',[211] and while he mentions this on several occasions it is interesting to see that this appears in a homily intended for the Ascension, a major feast when Ælfric expected that laity should attend mass and receive communion.[212] Similarly, an Old English penitential homily preserved in a twelfth-century manuscript likewise explains that when a heathen man is baptized he is 'thereby released from devils'.[213]

The homily for Palm Sunday in the Blickling book explains that Christ dwells in the baptized who truly believe in Christ's sacrifice; while those who live wickedly do not have Christ in their hearts, but prepare a dwelling place for devils instead.[214] Similarly, Wulfstan states in his sermon for the dedication of a church that from the time when someone is baptized, the Holy Ghost dwells in him.[215] He borrowed this from Ælfric's homily for the dedication of a church, but added to it the idea that if someone who has been baptized abandons God through demonic instigation, the

---

[210]   *CH* II.3, ll. 245–61, 273–86, ed. Godden, *Catholic Homilies*, 26–7.

[211]   *CH* I.21, ll. 163–7, ed. Clemoes, *Catholic Homilies*, 351: 'Ac ðeahhwæðere godes gelaðung wyrcð gyt dæghwomlice þa ylcan wundru gastlice þe ða apostoli ða worhton lichamlice; ðonne se preost cristnað þæt cild. þonne adræfð he þone deofol of þam cilde: for þan ðe ælc hæþen man bið deofles: ac þurh ðæt halige fulluht he bið godes gif he hit gehylt'; see also *Hom.* IV, ll. 231–4, ed. Pope, *Homilies of Ælfric*, I.277: 'Se deofol bið adræfed þurh ures Drihtnes mihte of þam hæþenan men þonne hine man fullað' ('Through the Lord's might the devil is driven out of heathen men when someone baptizes them').

[212]   Ælfric instructed that laity should receive communion on Sundays in Lent, the three days preceding Easter Sunday, and on Easter Day, the Thursday of Rogation week, Ascension Day, Pentecost and the four days after the four Ember-feasts: *Hom.* XIX, ll. 119–35, ed. Pope, *Homilies of Ælfric*, II.628–9.

[213]   The manuscript is Cambridge, University Library, Ii.1.33 (s.xii²), on which see O. Da Rold, 'Homilies and Lives of Saints: Cambridge, University Library, Ii.1.33', in O. Da Rold et al. (eds), *The Production and Use of English Manuscripts 1060 to 1220* (Leicester, 2010), available at http://www.le.ac.uk/english/em1060to1220/mss/EM.CUL.Ii.1.33.htm, accessed November 2012. The homily is at fols. 219v–222r; *Hom.* IX, ll. 82–4, ed. A.M.L. Fadda, *Nuove omelie anglosassoni della rinascenza benedettina*, Filologia germanica, Testi e studi 1 (Florence, 1977), 183: 'Mycel ælmesse byð þæt man man fullige and to fulluhte nime and swa þonne hæþenan deoflum ætbrede ... '.

[214]   *Hom.* VI, ed. Morris, *Blickling Homilies*, 77.

[215]   Wulfstan, *Hom.* XVIII, ll. 78–80, ed. Bethurum, *Homilies*, 248.

Holy Ghost abandons his dwelling place and devils immediately enter instead.[216] A composite homily in a manuscript from late eleventh-century Worcester borrows from Wulfstan's so-called *Institutes of Polity* to explain that from the time of baptism, angels continually watch over everyone to see how they keep their baptismal promises.[217] It is not entirely clear whom Wulfstan intended or anticipated as an audience for *Polity*, although some of the manuscripts suggest an episcopal context; but the reuse of this and other passages in homilies illustrates one way that the ideas formulated and developed in a text like *Polity* might reappear in other contexts where they might ultimately have been communicated more widely.[218]

Liturgical texts frequently call upon the angels in the context of baptism, and the idea that there is a personal angelic presence from the time of baptism is closely connected with (and indeed forms part of) the concept of guardian angels, whose presence seems to have become increasingly important into the later Middle Ages.[219] Outside sacramental liturgical rituals, this concept is found in England most clearly from the tenth century, although the idea itself is much older.[220] These angels were believed to take responsibility for the people they guarded, in a more specific and personal way than the more general presence of angels described by Boniface as part of the account of the brother of Wenlock's vision. Guardian angels are sometimes mentioned rather casually, as in the case of St Dunstan's guardian angel, who was supposed to have dictated a hymn to him.[221] Ælfric notes that God has set angels over humans as protecting guardians, but

[216]    Ælfric, *CH* II.40, ll. 103–4, ed. Godden, *Catholic Homilies*, 338; Wulfstan, *Hom.* XVIII, ll. 80–2, ed. Bethurum, *Homilies*, 248.

[217]    I *Polity*, 124–5; II *Polity*, 230–1, ed. Jost, *Polity*, 162–3; *Hom.* 30, ed. Napier, *Wulfstan*, 144, ll. 15–20, preserved in Oxford, Bodleian Library, Hatton 113 (s. xi³/⁴, Worcester: see M. Swan and H. Foxhall Forbes, 'St Wulfstan's Homiliary, Part 1: Oxford, Bodleian Library, Hatton 113', in O. Da Rold et al. (eds), *The Production and Use of English Manuscripts 1060 to 1220*, at http://www.le.ac.uk/english/em1060to1220/mss/EM.Ox. Hatt.113.htm, accessed November 2012. See also D.G. Scragg, 'Napier's "Wulfstan" Homily XXX: Its Sources, its Relationship to the Vercelli Book and its Style', *Anglo-Saxon England* 6 (1977): 197–211.

[218]    The copies of *Polity* in Cambridge, Corpus Christi College, 201 (s. xi^med, possibly Winchester) and in Oxford, Bodleian Library, Junius 121 (s. xi³/⁴, Worcester) appear with a number of other texts which suggest that the manuscripts were intended for episcopal use, perhaps for training priests: see N.R. Ker, *Catalogue of Manuscripts Containing Anglo-Saxon* (Oxford, 1957), 399, 412; Budny, *Insular, Anglo-Saxon and Early Anglo-Norman Manuscript Art*, I.298–301; and H. Foxhall Forbes, 'Making Books for Pastoral Care in Late Eleventh-Century Worcester: Oxford, Bodleian Library, Junius 121 and Hatton 113+114', in P.D. Clarke and S. James (eds), *Pastoral Care in the Middle Ages* (Farnham, forthcoming).

[219]    Daniélou, *Les anges et leur mission: d'après les Pères de l'Eglise*, 77–81; Keck, *Angels*, 163–8.

[220]    Keck, *Angels*, 16–17.

[221]    B, *Vita S. Dunstani*, 29.2–6, 30.6, ed. Winterbottom and Lapidge, *Early Lives*, 86–8, 90.

also explicitly states that each believer has his own personal guardian angel to protect him from the attacks of the devil.[222] This seems to be how he understood the angels described by the young man named Stacteus, raised from death by John the Apostle: Stacteus told two brothers that he had seen the angels who were responsible for them weeping, while devils were rejoicing over their destruction.[223]

There seems to have been some variation in precisely how guardian angels were understood, and how they were believed to protect their charges, since some texts suggest that a devil as well as an angel is assigned to each person so that there is a struggle between the two spirits as one urges the person to good thoughts and actions while the other attempts to incite evil. Based on the *Visio S. Pauli*, one anonymous Old English homily records that each man has two 'teachers' in the day, and another two in the night: God's angel teaches the glory of the heavenly kingdom, while the devil teaches hell-punishment.[224] The homilist adds further the more specific vices and virtues that each 'teacher' will encourage, noting that 'God's angel teaches us stillness and appropriate speech and meditation on God's commandments ... the devil teaches us fidgeting and inappropriate laughter and unclean speech ...'.[225] This homily survives in an eleventh-century manuscript perhaps from Canterbury, but with an Exeter provenance,[226] and in a mid-twelfth-century manuscript probably from Worcester or the Worcester region.[227] The fourth Vercelli homily also refers to two 'shepherds' which surround each person every day, although this section of the homily is rather confused: the author states that the second 'shepherd' comes from the heavens to protect each person, using his virtues and good deeds as shields against the attacks of the devil, so that the devil's arrows cannot pierce through this guard.[228] The homily in the Vercelli book was probably written in the tenth century or earlier, but a version of it also survives in the margins of an eleventh-century manuscript of a Old English translation of Bede's *Historia Ecclesiastica*, probably produced in Exeter.[229]

These examples are significant in presenting a wide range of beliefs about angels and devils, because the existence of these beliefs, and especially those about the constant presence of angels and devils (either as specific guardians or more generally), is crucial in understanding the effectiveness of explanations of baptism which incorporated information about the invisible world. The formal theology of

---

[222]   *CH* I.34, ll. 241–58, ed. Clemoes, *Catholic Homilies*, 473–4.

[223]   *CH* I.4, ll. 144–8, ed. Clemoes, 211.

[224]   *Hom.* XLVI, ed. Napier, *Wulfstan*, 233, ll. 2–6.

[225]    *Hom.* XLVI, ed. Napier, *Wulfstan*, 233, ll. 13–18.

[226]   Cambridge, Corpus Christi College, 419: see Lionarons, *The Homiletic Writings of Archbishop Wulfstan*, 14.

[227]   Oxford, Bodleian Library, Bodley 343: see Irvine, 'The Compilation and Use of Manuscripts Containing Old English in the Twelfth Century', 41–2.

[228]   *Hom.* IV, ll. 337–42, ed. Scragg, *Vercelli Homilies*, 104.

[229]   Cambridge, Corpus Christi College, 41: see above, 83 and n. 104.

baptism is that through the baptismal ritual the stain of original sin is washed away,[230] but the homilies which discuss the effects of the priests' actions on unseen good and wicked spirits present a dramatic explanation of what happens in the baptismal ritual, and how the visible actions have invisible consequences. These invisible effects complement the invisible washing away of sin, but may have been much more vivid and real to many people than the abstract idea of sin itself, which has no visible or visualisable form: 'sin' as a concept is far more complex than the idea of 'a sin' as a wicked deed, and the idea of the stain of sin, handed down from Adam and Eve to all subsequent humans, is similarly difficult, so that the precise meaning and effects of these were (and still are) much debated by theologians. The idea that every person is born stained with original sin and becomes sinless through baptism is mirrored in the idea that before baptism every person contains or is associated with a wicked spirit, which is replaced by a good spirit after the ritual has been performed. Whether or not homilists intended the invisible spirits to clarify points of theology in this way, it seems likely that those explanations of baptism which made recourse to invisible spirits may have been more immediately comprehensible to people than were other discussions which did not.

It is also significant that there were probably many opportunities throughout the year in which information about baptism specifically, as well as about the invisible world more generally, might have been communicated in formal contexts of learning. Baptisms were probably performed as and when they were required, although it is possible that they were more frequent at the traditional seasons of Easter and Pentecost, but the baptismal dialogues also form part of the Easter liturgy.[231] The yearly repetition of these dialogues, when all Christians were expected to attend mass, could thus serve as a reminder and reinforcement of baptismal promises as well as an opportunity for the meaning and significance of baptism to be explained again, along with the concomitant theology of the angels and devils. Some (if not all) of Wulfstan's homilies may have been intended to be preached in contexts where the bishop played a major role or at royal or public assemblies, and Easter may have been one of these occasions, although some of the later books in which Wulfstan's homilies were copied indicate that they were valued for the general catechetical information they included.[232] At least in theory,

---

[230]   See for example Bede, *Hom.* II.5, ll. 111–15, ed. Hurst, *Bedae opera homiletica*, 217: 'qui ablutus est fonte baptismatis in remissionum omnium peccatorum non indiget rursus immo non potest eodem modo ablui sed cotidiana tantum mundanae conuersationis contagia necesse habet cotidiana sui redemptoris indulgentia tergantur' ('the one who is washed in the font of baptism in remission of all his sins does not need to be washed again; on the contrary he cannot be washed in the same way, but has need only that the daily contagions of worldly life should be wiped away by the daily forgiveness of his Redeemer').

[231]   See above, 48.

[232]   One good example is Oxford, Bodleian Library, Junius 121, where Wulfstan's homily on the pater noster and creed (*Hom.* VII, ed. Bethurum, *Homilies*, 166–8) was

therefore, adults and children were frequently reminded about the significance of baptism and how the ritual related to the spiritual world around them, whether at Easter, at baptisms themselves, or simply through casual references in homilies or in other contexts. But baptism is only the beginning: all souls would ultimately have to give an account of their deeds before God, and the first step on this journey was made at death, when the invisible spirits played an important role in relocating the soul to its waiting place in the afterlife.

## The Struggle at Death

Anglo-Saxon homilists were anxious to teach their congregations that the state of the soul at death would determine where each person spent the eternal life after death, receiving rewards or punishments according to their deeds in the present life. But Christian theology also held that when the soul left the body at the moment of death, a drama was enacted which was a microcosm of the Last Judgement, determining where and how the soul would exist until such time as that final judgement was made. The idea of an individual judgement at the moment of death seems to have been accepted by some authors as early as the second century, in contrast to earlier notions of the afterlife which presented all souls waiting in some shadowy realm, or even 'sleeping' until they were awakened at the Last Judgement.[233] The individual judgement was also tied into the idea that the soul faced a struggle at death like the passion of the martyrs, entering the invisible world where it was exceptionally vulnerable to attack from devils, so that the need for angelic protection was all the more increased.[234] Growing concern about the sinful nature of humankind meant that this struggle became increasingly important as people became less certain of what awaited the souls of the departed in the afterlife: the earliest Christian funeral liturgies had been joyous in the assurance of salvation for all those who were part of God's elect simply by their acceptance of the Christian faith, but by the sixth century this joy had been replaced by fear for the state of the soul.[235]

---

incorporated into a series of penitential texts, suggesting that it may have been intended for use in the context of penance. This is particularly interesting since the rest of Wulfstan's homilies were copied into the first part of the companion homiliary, Hatton 113. For further discussion, see Foxhall Forbes, 'Making Books for Pastoral Care'.

[233] B. Daley, *The Hope of the Early Church: A Handbook of Patristic Eschatology* (Cambridge, 1991), 220.

[234] C. Vogel, 'Deux conséquences de l'eschatologie grégorienne: la multiplication des messes privées et les moines-prêtres', in J. Fontaine, R. Gillet and S. Pellistrandi (eds), *Grégoire le Grand: Chantilly, Centre culturel Les Fontaines, 15–19 septembre 1982: actes* (Paris, 1986), 267–76.

[235] M. McLaughlin, *Consorting with Saints: Prayer for the Dead in Early Medieval France* (Ithaca, NY, 1994), 34–5.

This fear is visible also in the surviving rituals for the sick and dying from late Anglo-Saxon England (the manuscripts are listed in Table 2.2). These rituals aimed to help the soul pass easily from this world to the next, and were focused primarily on improving the relationship between God and the individual, as the dying person was encouraged to repent and confess to prepare his soul for what would follow after death.[236] It seems that by the eighth century the rites for the sick were often performed only for the dying,[237] and so in the ninth century, Carolingian reformers encouraged anointing as a rite for the sick as well as for the dying, but it may not have been until the tenth century in England that this practice became more frequent.[238] The rituals surviving from Anglo-Saxon England are all found in late tenth- or eleventh-century manuscripts, predominantly from southern England, and in general they comprise both liturgical rites for anointing the sick person's body, and masses to be offered for the sick (sometimes in the house of the invalid). Much of the material in late Anglo-Saxon manuscripts derives from the Carolingian Supplemented Hadrianum, but the arrangement and precise provisions of each manuscript are quite variable, depending at least partly on the intended uses of the books.[239]

The rituals found in Laud misc. 482 and CCCC 422 are quite close and include a substantial amount of Old English material directed at the sick person, while less extensive Old English rubrics are found in Rouen, Bibiliothèque Municipale, 274.[240] The rituals in Oxford, Bodleian Library, Bodley 579, as well as those in CCCC 422 and Laud misc. 482, seem to envisage that the priest will visit the house of the sick person, while the rituals in Orléans, Bibiliothèque Municipale, 105 and Worcester, F. 173 are much more closely connected with the monastic rituals of death.[241] Despite their differences in form, these rituals share material

---

[236]    See for example the Old English instructions in Laud misc. 482 and CCCC 422, printed by B. Fehr, 'Altenglische Ritualtexte für Krankenbesuch, heilige Ölung und Begräbnis', in H. Boehmer (ed.), *Texte und Forschungen zur englischen Kulturgeschichte: Festgabe für Felix Liebermann zum 20. Juli 1921* (Halle, 1921), 20–67; Bodley 579, fol. 319r, ed. N. Orchard, *The Leofric Missal*, HBS 113–14 (2 vols, London, 2002), nos. 2507–14.

[237]    A.G. Martimort, 'Prayer for the Sick and Sacramental Anointing', in A.G. Martimort (ed.), *The Church at Prayer: Vol. 3: The Sacraments* (Collegeville, Minnesota, 1988), 117–37, at 131; F.S. Paxton, *Christianizing Death: The Creation of a Ritual Process in Early Medieval Europe* (Ithaca, NY, 1990), 85–7.

[238]    Paxton, *Christianizing Death*, 128–30.

[239]    Ibid., 128–61; Keefer, 'Manuals', 104–5; Pfaff, *The Liturgy in Medieval England*, 56–7.

[240]    Fehr, 'Altenglische Ritualtexte'; Keefer, 'Manuals', 104; some of the material in Laud misc. 482 is incorporated into the ritual directly from the *Old English Penitential*, about which see A.J. Frantzen, *The Anglo-Saxon Penitentials: A Cultural Database* (2008), http://www.anglo-saxon.net/penance, accessed October 2012.

[241]    Keefer, 'Manuals', 104; see Bodley 579, fols. 319r–324v, ed. Orchard, *Leofric Missal*, nos. 2507–2544; Laud misc. 482, fols. 47r–67v, ed. Fehr, 'Altenglische Ritualtexte', 46–64; CCCC 422, pp. 399–429, ed. Fehr, 'Altenglische Ritualtexte', 48–64; cf. Orléans,

and, more importantly, sentiments: they incorporate prayers invoking angelic protection against the wicked spirits which would try to harm the soul, such as the request in one of the masses for the sick to 'expel from him [i.e., the sick person] the snares of all enemies; Lord, send to him your angel of peace, who may guard this house in perpetual peace'.[242] One prayer asks that Jesus deem it right for his holy angel to visit, make happy, and comfort his servant [i.e., the sick person];[243] and another for protection against the attacks of wicked spirits.[244] In some cases the litanies for the sick specifically request that the sick person be visited by the archangel Raphael, the angel who was frequently invoked for healing.[245] Litanies could be used in other contexts too: many of those found in early medieval English books ask God to send his angel as a protection or guard,[246] and a few others include a petition for freedom from demonic attack.[247]

---

BM, 105, pp. 314–18, ed. A. Davril, *The Winchcombe Sacramentary: Orléans, Bibliothèque municipale, 127 (105)*, HBS 105 (London, 1995), nos. 1778–1790; and Worcester, F. 173, fols. 6v–14r.

[242] This is found before the litany in Laud misc. 482, fol. 49v, ed. Fehr, 'Altenglische Ritualtexte', 49; it comes after the litany in CCCC 422, p. 405; and in Rouen, BM 274, fols. 208v–209r, ed. Wilson, *Jumièges*, 289–90: 'expelle ab eo omnium inimicorum insidias, mitte ei, domine, angelum pacis, qui hanc domum pace perpetua custodiat'.

[243] Bodley 579, fol. 321r, ed. Orchard, *Leofric Missal*, no. 2521; Orléans, BM, 105, p. 318, ed. Davril, *Winchcombe Sacramentary*, no. 1787; Worcester, F. 173, fol. 11v.

[244] e.g. Bodley 579, fol. 319v–320r, ed. Orchard, *Leofric Missal*, no. 2515.

[245] This is found for example in CCCC 422; Laud misc. 482; and Rouen, Bibliothèque municipale, 368; see VIII.ii, XXXIV, XLI.iii, ed. Lapidge, *Litanies*, 130, 246, 279: 'Vt hanc infirmum per angelum tuum Raphaelem uisitare'. For information about Raphael see Keck, *Angels*, 63.

[246] VIII.i, XII, XVI.i, XVIII, XXI, XXIII, XXXII, XXXVI, XLV, ed. Lapidge, *Litanies*, 128, 147, 160, 177, 186, 201, 239, 253, 299: 'Vt angelum tuum sanctum ad tutelam nobis mittere digneris'.

[247] XIII, XXVII, XXXIX, XLIII, ed. Lapidge, *Litanies*, 151, 217, 267, 286: 'Ab infestationibus demonum libera nos Domine'.

Table 2.2        Anglo-Saxon manuscripts containing rites for the sick[1]

| Shelfmark | Date and provenance | Edition/facsimile |
|---|---|---|
| Cambridge, Corpus Christi College, 422 ('Red Book of Darley'); a sacramentary, collectar, and 'manual'-type book | s. xi[med]; perhaps written at Winchester for use at Sherborne[2] | *Parker Library on the web*, http://parkerweb.stanford.edu;[3] partially ed. Fehr, 'Altenglische Ritualtexte' |
| Orléans, Bibliothèque municipale, 105 (127) ('Winchcombe Sacramentary') | s. x[ex]; England, but probably taken to Fleury within a few decades of its production[4] | Davril, *The Winchcombe Sacramentary* |
| Oxford, Bodleian Library, Bodley 579 ('Leofric Missal')[5] | 'Leofric A': s. x[1/4]; ?perhaps written for Plegmund (Archbishop of Canterbury, 890–923)[6] 'Leofric B': additions made probably at Canterbury between the second quarter of the tenth century and the end of the tenth century[7] 'Leofric C': additions made during the book's ownership by Leofric (d.1072; Bishop of Crediton (1046) and Exeter (1050))[8] | Orchard, *The Leofric Missal Early Manuscripts at Oxford University*, http://image.ox.ac.uk |
| Oxford, Bodleian Library, Laud misc. 482 | s. xi[med]; Worcester[9] | partially ed. Fehr, 'Altenglische Ritualtexte' |
| Rouen, Bibliothèque municipale, 274 (Y.6) ('Missal of Robert of Jumièges') | s. xi[1]; probably written at Ely or Peterborough[10] | Wilson, *Missal of Robert of Jumièges* |
| Rouen, Bibliothèque municipale, 368 ('Lanalet Pontifical') | s. xi[in]; St Germans / Wells | Doble, *Pontificale Lanaletense* |
| Worcester, Cathedral Library, F. 173 | s. xi; written for use at Old Minster, Winchester; ?later Worcester provenance[11] | |

*Notes*: [1] See further Keefer, 'Manuals', 104–5. [2] Corrêa, 'Daily Office Books', 56–7; Keefer, 'Manuals'; Gittos, 'Is there any Evidence for the Liturgy of Parish Churches'; Keynes, 'Wulfsige', 75–6; Rushforth, *Saints in English Kalendars*, 41–2. [3] The liturgical rubrics are printed in Page, 'Old English liturgical rubrics'; Graham, 'The Old English liturgical directions'. [4] Pfaff, 'Massbooks: Sacramentaries and Missals', 14–15. [5] For detailed discussion see Orchard, Leofric Missal; Pfaff, *The Liturgy in Medieval England*, 72–7, 136–8. [6] See Orchard, Leofric Missal, I.23–131; Pfaff, *The Liturgy in Medieval England*, 72–5. [7] Orchard, Leofric Missal, I.132–205; Pfaff, *The Liturgy in Medieval England*, 75–7. [8] Orchard, Leofric Missal, I.206–33; Pfaff, *The Liturgy in Medieval England*, 136–8. [9] For detailed discussion of this manuscript and its uses, see Thompson, *Dying and Death*, 57–91. [10] Pfaff, *Liturgical Books*, 15–19; Pfaff, *The Liturgy in Medieval England*, 88–91. [11] Pfaff, 'Massbooks', 25–6.

Although angelic protection was evidently important while someone was sick but still alive, it became much more urgent in the process of dying and death as the soul began its journey from the body.[248] While the archangel Raphael was requested to come to help the sick, the Archangel Michael had been appointed for the dying, as the chief psychopomp who would lead the souls of the blessed from their bodies to rest.[249] Michael's role at death was well-established in the legends associated with him, and he also appears in descriptions of the deaths of other saints, such as the legends associated with the Blessed Virgin Mary, who was reported to have been met by Michael at her death.[250] According to some traditions he was able to help souls even after the Last Judgement: a motif found in later Anglo-Saxon homilies describes Michael, along with SS Peter and Mary, interceding for the souls of the damned after they were condemned to hell, an idea which Ælfric objected to strongly.[251] The dedication of mortuary chapels to Michael, as may have been the case at Worcester, is also a result of the significant role that he was believed to play at death.[252] He was called upon in the prayers which appear in personal and private prayer books, where he is asked to receive the suppliant's soul at death and lead it to the rest of the saints, keeping it from the powers of darkness,[253] and he is invoked frequently in funerary liturgies, where the full force of a monastic community might come together to request his help for the death of one of their own.[254] Here all the angels were important, not just Michael, and funerary rituals request their help both as guides for the soul, and as defenders against demonic attack.[255]

---

[248]   The rites for the dead are discussed in more detail below, 283–94 and see Table 5.1.

[249]   Keck, *Angels*, 38.

[250]   Johnson, *St Michael*, 71–86.

[251]   M. Clayton, 'Delivering the damned: A motif in Old English homiletic prose', *Medium Ævum* 55 (1986): 92–102; Clayton, *The Cult of the Virgin Mary in Anglo-Saxon England*, 253–5.

[252]   J. Barrow, 'The Community of Worcester, 961–c.1100', in N. Brooks and C. Cubitt (eds), *St Oswald of Worcester: Life and Influence* (London, 1996), 84–99, at 89–90.

[253]   See for example the prayer in the book from the latter part of the eleventh century which belonged to St Wulfstan, Bishop of Worcester (d.1095), now Cambridge, Corpus Christi College, 391, p. 585, ed. A. Hughes, *The Portiforium of St Wulstan: Corpus Christi College, Cambridge, MS. 391*, HBS 89–90 (2 vols, Leighton Buzzard, 1958–60), II.3: 'Te rogo et supplico et deprecor sancte michahel archangele qui animas accipiendas accepisti potestatem, ut animam meam suscipere digneris quando de corpore meo erit egressa et libera eam de potestate inimici … ' ('I ask and beg and pray you, St Michael Archangel, who received the power of receiving souls, that you deign to take my soul when it will go out from my body and free it from the power of the enemy').

[254]   See for example Bodley 579, fol. 250v, ed. Orchard, *Leofric Missal*, no. 2228; and the prayers in the funerary liturgy in Worcester, F. 173, fols. 21v and 22v, partially ed. C.H. Turner, 'The churches at Winchester in the early eleventh century', *Journal of Theological Studies* 17 (1916): 65–8, at 66, 68.

[255]   e.g. Bodley 579, fol. 246r, ed. Orchard, *Leofric Missal*, no. 2199; Rouen, BM, 274, fols. 213v–214r, ed. Wilson, *Jumièges*, 297–8; or Orléans, BM, 105, pp. 337–4, ed. Davril,

These rites were developed, transmitted and adapted primarily in monastic or episcopal contexts, and even setting aside for the moment the difficult question of how frequently or widely these rites were used, understanding them would have been difficult or impossible for many people since they were performed almost entirely in Latin, although the extensive provision of English in CCCC 422 and Laud misc. 482 suggests that in these cases, at least, the ritual was intended to take place in two languages.[256] And, of course, those on whom or for whom the rituals were performed might not be in a fit state to hear or understand the liturgy anyway, if they were too sick (or dead), and so the information conveyed in these contexts was probably received by those who performed the rituals and perhaps by some of the bystanders. Although it seems likely that at least by the later Anglo-Saxon period these rites were not performed exclusively for religious personnel,[257] they nonetheless transmit the concerns of religious life and reflect the theological developments which saw demonic attack and angelic protection as the major struggle faced by the soul after death. But these ideas represented in the liturgy are only one manifestation of a belief found in a range of other contexts, and are probably themselves dependent on other texts such as the very influential apocryphal *Visio S. Pauli*, which described the deaths of good and sinful men and the fights which ensued between angels and devils in order to claim the soul and take it to the place to which it belonged by right.[258] The *Visio S. Pauli* was not the only popular and influential vision containing information about the spiritual struggle, however, since these ideas are found in many other texts, such as the *Dialogues* of Gregory the Great and the vision of the brother of Wenlock (to name just two), which may themselves have been influenced by the *Visio S. Pauli*, or have in turn influenced its later redactions.[259]

The liturgical rituals used in Anglo-Saxon England were of course part of a much broader liturgical tradition, just as the recorded visions of St Paul, Fursey and others were popular across Europe and beyond; but the reappearance of the ideas about the angelic and demonic struggle for the soul in the vernacular homilies surviving from later Anglo-Saxon England illustrate one of the ways in which these ideas might have been communicated to people attending church services, as well as to priests or priests-in-training who could pass on the information either

---

*Winchcombe Sacramentary*, nos. 1841–1844; Worcester, F. 173, fols. 16v–17v; see also CCCC 422, pp. 429–35, ed. Fehr, 'Altenglische Ritualtexte', 65–7.

[256]  Keefer, 'Manuals', 104, and see below, 283–94.

[257]  See below, 283–94.

[258]  C. Carozzi, *Eschatologie et au-delà: recherches sur l'Apocalypse de Paul* (Aix-en-Provence, 1994), 81.

[259]  T. Silverstein, 'The "Vision of Leofric" and Gregory's Dialogues', *Review of English Studies* 9 (1933): 186–8; M.P. Ciccarese, 'Alle origini della letteratura delle Visioni: il contributo di Gregorio di Tours', *Studi storicoreligiosi* 5:2 (1981): 251–66; C. Carozzi, *Le voyage de l'âme dans l'au-delà, d'après la littérature latine: V<sup>e</sup>–XIII<sup>e</sup> siècle*, Collection de l'École française de Rome, 189 (Roma, 1994), 91–150; Carozzi, *Eschatologie*, esp. 9–15.

formally or informally. Ælfric's rejection of the *Visio S. Pauli* is at least partly based on Augustine's complaints about the implausibility of the text as a genuine record of St Paul's vision of heaven (because Paul was shown things which he was not allowed to repeat), but the *Visio* and its redactions were certainly popular in Anglo-Saxon England, since numerous homilies borrowed passages from it, and there was an Old English version.[260] The Old English homily which draws on the *Visio* in presenting good and bad 'teachers' of the soul includes a passage describing St Paul's vision of souls leaving their bodies, and depicts the fight in some detail.[261] When Paul saw the wicked soul leaving its body there were a great many angels and devils around it, and the devils listed all the soul's wicked deeds to the angels, who were sorrowful in their hearts, but let the devils lead the soul from its body. In contrast, when many angels and devils congregated around and fought over a soul leaving the body of a good man, the angels overcame the devils with the good deeds which the man had performed, so that the devils went away, and the soul was led to heaven.[262]

Another interesting visionary account is found in slightly different versions in two homilies preserved in eleventh-century manuscripts, firstly the Old English 'Macarius' Homily, and secondly a composite homily which draws upon it. The vision is attributed to 'some holy man' who is not named, but has been identified as Macarius.[263] The homilies describe a soul being forced to leave its body at death, but the soul did not dare to leave the body because it saw wicked spirits waiting for it, ready to snatch it. One of these devils, seemingly quite sarcastically, asked the soul whether it had expected that the Archangel Michael would come with a troop of angels to meet it; another devil responded that it had remained with the soul both day and night and knew its works.[264] This brief exchange contains two particularly important points. The first of these is that the first devil's question indicates what

---

[260] Ælfric, *CH* II.20, ll. 1–18, ed. Godden, *Catholic Homilies*, 190; for Ælfric's sources see Godden, Ælfric's Catholic *Homilies: Introduction, Commentary and Glossary*, 529–38; the Old English translation of the *Visio S. Pauli* is edited by A. diPaolo Healey, *The Old English Vision of St Paul*, Speculum Anniversary Monographs 2 (Cambridge, MA., 1978).

[261] *Hom.* XLVI, ed. Napier, *Wulfstan*, 235, l. 6 – 237, l. 10.

[262] *Hom.* XLVI, ed. Napier, *Wulfstan*, 235, ll. 9–21 (the wicked soul), 236, ll. 20–7 (the good soul).

[263] *Hom.* XXIX, ed. Napier, *Wulfstan*, 140, l. 9 – 141, l. 25 (copied in Oxford, Bodleian Library, Hatton 113: s. xi³/⁴, Worcester); 'Macarius-Homilie', ll. 76–125, ed. H. Sauer, *Theodulfi Capitula in England: die altenglischen Übersetzungen, zusammen mit dem lateinischen Text*, Texte und Untersuchungen zur englischen Philologie 8 (Munich, 1978), 413–15 (copied into Cambridge, Corpus Christi College, 201, part 2 [pp. 179–272]: s. xi^med, Exeter). The homilies also share content with Vercelli Homily IV, but not the vision: see further C.D. Wright, 'The Old English "Macarius" Homily, Vercelli Homily IV, and Ephrem Latinus, *De paenitentia*', in T.N. Hall (ed.), *Via Crucis: Essays on Early Medieval Sources and Ideas in Memory of J.E. Cross* (Morgantown, WV, 2002), 210–34, at 211–29.

[264] *Hom.* XXIX, ed. Napier, *Wulfstan*, 140, ll. 9–19; 'Macarius-Homilie', ll. 77–86, ed. Sauer, *Theodulfi Capitula*, 413–14.

is presented here as a widely expected hope, or for those who were very good even an expectation, that souls would be taken from their bodies by angels, led by the Archangel Michael.[265] The second important point in this discussion is that the second devil's response connects the angels (and devils) assigned to each soul at baptism with the roles that these spirits played throughout life and ultimately at death. While guardian angels protected these souls, this was not their only task: they also announced to God the works and deeds of the humans that they watched over, and kept a record which was used in determining whether angels or devils were allowed to take the soul at the moment of death, as the second devil explains in noting that he had remained with the soul and knew its deeds.[266]

The struggle at death is therefore linked with baptism through the role played by angels and devils at both occasions and during the time in between them, so that invisible spirits are tied to souls all the way through life and beyond. In this context, Byrhtferth's *Ammonitio* (and the homily based on it) warns that every day, the angels assigned to each person at baptism reveal his deeds to God, while devils record his misdeeds; at death all these deeds will be made known, there will be a great battle between devils and angels for the soul, which will be claimed according to the balance of good and evil deeds and led either to punishment or to bliss.[267] The theological interpretation of the struggle at death therefore both reinforces and is reinforced by the interpretation of the effects of baptism on the invisible spirits, and these are two sides of the same coin. This is particularly important in considering the communication of these ideas to congregations. That later Anglo-Saxon writers stressed the significance of the role of the spirits at both of these key moments in the life of the Christian soul indicates that by hearing about one of these, congregations might also learn or relearn information about the other.

Byrhtferth's statement about what was believed to be known of the actions of angels and devils at death is presented in general terms and not tied to a specific vision, matching the impression given by the funeral liturgy that this struggle was believed to take place as a normal part of the process of death rather than being an exceptional occurrence shown only to visionaries. However, for obvious reasons, visions like those already mentioned were exceptionally important in understanding the actions of spirits and the fate of the soul once it had left the body, since these took place in a world which was usually invisible to human eyes. It is therefore interesting to see that while Ælfric objected to the *Visio S. Pauli* he accepted other visions which showed many similar ideas about the struggle at death, and even translated some of these to present them as acceptable alternatives, or used them as exempla after describing the struggle in more general terms. He explicitly offered the vision of Fursey as an alternative to the *Visio S. Pauli*, and in the context of the

---

[265] For Michael as psychopomp, see Johnson, *St Michael*, 71–86.

[266] *CH* I.34, ll. 241–58, ed. Clemoes, *Catholic Homilies*, 473–4.

[267] *Ammonitio*, ll. 55–60, 77–83, ed. and trans. Baker and Lapidge, *Byrhtferth's Enchiridion*, 246–7; *Hom.* 48, ed. Napier, *Wulfstan*, 248, ll. 17–23, 249, ll. 19–27.

*Catholic Homilies* Fursey's vision is presented as the first of a number of exempla about the afterlife.[268] Ælfric seems to have drawn on a text independent of Bede's retelling of the vision of Fursey in the *Historia Ecclesiastica*, although Bede's approval of this vision may have helped to sanction it in Ælfric's eyes: Ælfric also translated two other exempla drawn from Bede's *Historia Ecclesiastica*.[269]

Like the brother of Wenlock, Fursey was granted a vision of the otherworld on his deathbed, and Fursey too experienced the angelic and demonic struggle personally: as three angels began leading his soul from his body, devils came to try to take it, and a battle ensued between the spirits.[270] The angels were ultimately successful in keeping Fursey from the hands of the devils, but the threat of what the wicked spirits had to offer was revealed when they threw a burning soul at him as punishment for receiving goods from a sinful man.[271] Fursey had not known of the man's sins, and the angel prevented him from further harm, but the burn remained on his body as a visible sign from the afterlife.[272] Ælfric presumably hoped that this would be sufficiently interesting to prevent further speculation on the vision of St Paul, but he returned to other visions which echoed these ideas to provide further warnings about what awaited the soul immediately after death. The translation of a passage from the *Vitae patrum* which now survives only in a composite homily was probably also produced by Ælfric, and although it is now quite clumsily inserted into other material on penance, the compiler may thus have ensured that it received wider circulation.[273] This exemplum records a monk's vision of a sinful man giving up his soul: it describes the devils which dragged the soul from his body, and the voice of God condemning the wretched soul.[274] This is contrasted with the death of a good man, to whom the Archangels Michael and Gabriel were sent. When the soul did not want to leave its body, God sent David with his harp and a choir of singers, so that when the soul heard their voices it came out into Michael's hands, whereupon they all went up to heaven.[275]

Ælfric also discussed the spirits at death in his most extended discussion of the afterlife, a sermon written for the octave of Pentecost.[276] Here he borrows from the seventh-century Spanish author, Julian of Toledo, to explain that the devil comes to dying men in an attempt to snatch their souls, and that if someone is dying it is

---

[268]    Ælfric, *CH* II.20, ll. 1–18, ed. Godden, *Catholic Homilies*, 190; three further exempla are included in *CH* II.21, ed. Godden, *Catholic Homilies*, 199–205.

[269]    For detailed discussion of Ælfric's sources for *CH* II.20–21, see Godden, Ælfric's Catholic Homilies: Introduction, Commentary and Glossary, 529–44. CH *II*.21 includes exempla based on Bede, *HE* V.12 and IV.22 (in that order).

[270]    Ælfric, *CH* II.20, ll. 57–171, ed. Godden, *Catholic Homilies*, 192–5.

[271]    Ælfric, *CH* II.20, ll. 203–27, ed. Godden, *Catholic Homilies*, 196–7.

[272]    Ælfric, *CH* II.20, ll. 247–51, ed. Godden, *Catholic Homilies*, 197.

[273]    *Hom.* XXVII, ed. Pope, *Homilies of Ælfric*, II.775–81, and see discussion at 771–4.

[274]    *Hom.* XXVII, ll. 15–47, ed. Pope, *Homilies of Ælfric*, II.775–6.

[275]    *Hom.* XXVII, ll. 48–82, ed. Pope, *Homilies of Ælfric*, II.777–8.

[276]    *Hom.* XI, ed. Pope, *Homilies of Ælfric*, I.415–47.

important that men in holy orders offer prayers for him so that he can escape the devil.[277] Ælfric prefaced this passage with his own reminder that devils are always around us, and followed it with a story about a dying child who saw a dragon ready to consume him, which was vanquished by the prayers of the monks around him.[278] The deaths of good men are discussed just a few lines later, when Ælfric explains that God sends angels to the souls of good men, to lead them into rest where they dwell with Christ.[279] The incorporation of these kinds of visions into Ælfric's own careful explanation of the struggle at death indicates the extent to which he took for granted that this belief was part of orthodox Christian theology, and although these visions stood apart from sacred Scripture, clearly not all visions were suspect if they had significant authority.

Moreover, the retelling of these and other stories in homilies which were designed for public preaching, or which were copied into collections which may have been used for this purpose, indicate how ideas about the roles of angels and devils at death might have been communicated in pastoral contexts, in the same way that information about the roles of angels at baptism was communicated to congregations. Once again, the actions of angels and devils both mirror and reify more abstract theological ideas which explain the 'why' and the 'how' of the soul's existence after death; and although God's omnipotence means that the agency of the invisible spirits is not needed to explain how or why the soul experiences a particular existence after death (or how it travels there), it seems likely that as in the case of baptism and original sin, the spiritual struggle at death may have clarified and helped with the visualisation of complex concepts. However, ideas about angels and devils at the moment of death may not have been conveyed at the occasion itself, and there is a contrast too with the way that ideas about baptism could be communicated at Easter or at other times during the year when the ritual took place. Understanding from the surviving copies of homilies how widely they (and the ideas they contain) might have circulated is therefore quite important, if difficult.

The account of Macarius' vision is interesting here as an example because although the two homilies containing the vision are preserved only in eleventh-century manuscripts, the textual history of this episode suggests that these two homilies represent the end-stage of a wider circulation in the vernacular. The earlier homily is found in Cambridge, Corpus Christi College 201, part 2, a book written at Exeter in the third quarter of the eleventh century, but the text may have been composed well before this, possibly as early as the first half of the tenth century; and it was perhaps written originally in an Anglian dialect, suggesting

---

[277]  *Hom.* XI, ll. 164–7, ed. Pope, *Homilies of Ælfric*, I.423.

[278]  *Hom.* XI, ll. 163, 168–76, ed. Pope, *Homilies of Ælfric*, I.423. The story about the child and the dragon seems to come from the *Dialogues* of Gregory the Great, IV.40.1–5, ed. de Vogüé and Antin, *Dialogues, Livre IV*, 138–42.

[279]  *Hom.* XI, ll. 181–4, ed. Pope, *Homilies of Ælfric*, I.424.

that it did not originate in southern England.[280] This in itself gives some indication that the homily may have circulated more widely, and this text or some version of it was also used in the production of the composite homily which contains this episode. The composite homily now survives in Hatton 113, the first part of a homiliary written in Worcester in the third quarter of the eleventh century.[281] Hatton 113 contains notes showing that it was read and used, and in some cases notes by known authors who were responsible for preaching in Worcester, such as Coleman.[282] However, it also looks like the kind of book which was intended as a reference book from which homilies could be copied into smaller and more portable booklets for use in the field, and so the fact that the version of the homily in this manuscript survives uniquely here does not mean that it reached no further audience than the monks in Worcester.[283] If the book was also used in the context of training priests, this suggests another way in which information might be passed on, whether or not those priests owned a physical copy of the homily. It remains impossible to recover precisely how widely the Macarius episode might have been known or told, but it seems likely that the surviving two copies represent only two fixed moments in a much broader circulation of the story.

Other works survive in greater numbers in any case, such as the homilies by Ælfric, especially his *Catholic Homilies*, which seem to have circulated widely and were promoted by a number of centres.[284] Here it is also significant that many of the visionary accounts recast by Ælfric and others continued to be copied in their original forms as well as in the homilies in which they were reused or reworked, suggesting that there were multiple possibilities for their circulation. Thus the visions which Ælfric borrowed from the *Dialogues* of Gregory the Great and from Bede's *Historia Ecclesiastica* continued to be popular in their Latin originals, and both of these Latin texts were also translated into English in the late ninth century (or perhaps the early tenth).[285] One of the visions which Ælfric borrowed from Bede is particularly interesting in showing the lengthy currency of some of the

[280] Sauer, *Theodulfi Capitula*, 92–4, 210–15, 271–2; D.G. Scragg, 'The corpus of vernacular homilies & prose saints' lives before Ælfric', *Anglo-Saxon England* 8 (1979): 223–77, at 256; Wright, 'Old English "Macarius" Homily', 213–14.

[281] Scragg, 'Corpus', 256; Wright, 'Old English "Macarius" Homily', 213.

[282] N.R. Ker, 'Old English notes signed "Coleman"', *Medium Ævum* 18 (1949): 29–31; W.P. Stoneman, 'Another Old English note signed "Coleman"', *Medium Ævum* 56:1 (1987): 78–82; D.F. Johnson and W. Rudolf, 'More notes by Coleman', *Medium Ævum* 79:1 (2010): 1–13; see also A. Orchard, 'Parallel lives: Wulfstan, William, Coleman and Christ', in J. Barrow and N. Brooks (eds), *St Wulfstan and his World* (Aldershot, 2005), 39–57.

[283] See further Foxhall Forbes, 'Making Books for Pastoral Care'.

[284] Godden, *Catholic Homilies*, lxxvii–lxxviii; Clayton, 'Homiliaries', 235–9; Clemoes, *Catholic Homilies*, 162–8.

[285] Hecht, *Bischofs Waerferth von Worcester Übersetzung der Dialoge Gregors des Grossen*.

ideas discussed here.[286] This concerns a Mercian thegn who was visited by spirits immediately before his death, and who reported this visitation to King Coenred. The thegn was visited first by two young men dressed in white, explained as angels by Bede and Ælfric, who showed him a very small and beautiful book which contained an account of everything good that he had ever done; but they were immediately followed by a whole host of wicked spirits who filled the house, and whose leader presented a huge and horrible book, filled with all the thegn's wicked thoughts and deeds. The devils asked the angels why they stayed with the man when he evidently belonged to the devils, and the angels agreed with them, and left. The devils then struck the thegn with ploughshares, and the thegn reported to Coenred that these blows were travelling through his body, and that when they met, he would die and devils would drag him down to hell.

Ælfric may have ensured that this account had wider currency in the late tenth or early eleventh century by putting it into the mouths of preachers and so into the ears of congregations, but Bede states that in his own time the account served as a prompt for people to perform penance without delay, thereby suggesting that it may have had popular currency beyond the written form in which it is now preserved. It is of course difficult to ascertain how much the account as it appears in Bede's written text has any genuine debt to a report of a vision, especially since one of the other visions recounted by Bede was adjusted so much in the retelling that the details of any earlier account are now almost completely unrecoverable.[287] This means in turn that it is impossible to determine how far, or even whether, the vision which Bede claims to be retelling had any independent oral circulation in the form that it survives in Bede's written text. On the other hand, Bede reports that he learned about the vision from Bishop Pecthelm, who was bishop of Whithorn (now Dumfries and Galloway) when Bede completed his book but who had apparently been a monk and deacon with Aldhelm in south-western England,[288] and this is significant because it begins to show how accounts of visions could travel independently of the written contexts in which they are preserved.

Whether Pecthelm told Bede about this vision in person, or sent him a letter with a written account of it, he presumably told it to other people as well, and his movements around the country from Dorset to Whithorn and elsewhere give an indication of how widely such an account might travel. Throughout the early Middle Ages and beyond, there was clearly a great appetite for accounts of visions, and here it is interesting to note that in the letter sent by Boniface to Eadburg about the vision of the monk of Wenlock, Boniface explicitly states that the abbess had requested information about these visions, which he was now

[286]   Bede, *HE* V.13, ed. Lapidge, Monat and Robin, *Histoire ecclésiastique*, III.84–90; Ælfric, *Hom.* XIX, ll. 136–207, ed. Pope, *Homilies of Ælfric*, II.629–32.

[287]   For a detailed discussion, see Foxhall Forbes, 'Diuiduntur in quattuor', 663–74.

[288]   Bede, *HE* V.13.4, V.18.1, ed. Lapidge, Monat and Robin, *Histoire ecclésiastique*, III.90, 106.

able to supply because he had spoken to the brother himself.[289] As Patrick Sims-Williams notes, Boniface's letter describing Ceolred's unhappy end was supposed to be 'preached' to Æthelbald, and this shows another way that reports of visions might begin to circulate.[290] Accounts of visions were clearly sought after and were sometimes collected into *libri uisionum*, books of visions, and in these contexts the narratives excerpted from larger works sometimes seem to have taken on a life of their own and to have acquired their own independent means of circulation. The letter which Boniface wrote to Eadburg was apparently known and read in late eleventh-century Worcester, because it appears both in the original Latin and with an English translation in a book which also contains Wærferth's translation of Gregory's *Dialogues* and selections from the *Vitae patrum*;[291] and Boniface's letter as well as Bede's account of the vision of Dryhthelm are found together in the *Liber uisionum* compiled by Otloh of Emmeram between 1062 and 1066;[292] they reappear with twelfth-century English visions in a book made for the Cistercian monastery of Louth Park, Lincolnshire.[293]

These works were most certainly 'popular' in the sense that they were best-sellers of the early Middle Ages, but the contexts in which they survive are equally certainly 'scholarly', in the sense that they are part of a literate and literary tradition. It is clear nonetheless that many of these also travelled orally as well as having multiple written versions: Fursey's vision survives in a written version which was used by Bede and then by Ælfric, to name but two, and Fursey seems to have undertaken some kind of preaching tour, since a report of his vision apparently also came to Bede from a man who had met Fursey in East Anglia.[294] The opportunities for information about visions to spread are also highlighted by the cases where those visions were considered by high-ranking clergymen to be unorthodox and problematic, although it is more than likely that

---

[289]   Boniface, *Epistola* 10, ed. Tangl, *Die Briefe*, 8, ll. 5–15.

[290]   Sims-Williams, *Religion*, 271.

[291]   London, British Library, Cotton Otho C.i, vol. 2. K. Sisam, 'An Old English translation of a letter from Wynfrith to Eadburga (A.D. 716–17) in Cotton MS. Otho C.1,' *Modern Language Review* 18 (1923): 253–72, which includes an edition of the letter at 263–72; and Ker, *Catalogue*, no. 182.

[292]   Otloh of Emmeram, *Liber uisionum*, no. 19, ed. P.G. Schmidt, *Otloh von St Emmeram: Liber visionum*, MGH Quellen zur Geistesgeschichte des Mittelalters 13 (Weimar, 1989), 95–101.

[293]   Oxford, Bodleian Library, Fairfax 17: see H. Farmer, 'A monk's vision of purgatory', *Studia Monastica* 1 (1959): 393–7; P. Sims-Williams, 'A Recension of Boniface's Letter to Eadburg about the Monk of Wenlock's Vision', in K. O'Brien O'Keeffe and A. Orchard (eds), *Latin Learning and English Lore*, I (Toronto, 2005), 194–214. These two visions are also copied in Paris, Bibliothèque Nationale, lat. 9376 (s. xi or s. xii): see Sims-Williams, 'A Recension', 199–200.

[294]   Bede, *HE*, III.19, ed. Lapidge, Monat and Robin, *Histoire ecclésiastique*, II.102–14; I. Moreira, *Heaven's Purge: Purgatory in Late Antiquity* (Oxford, 2010), 115–18.

in such cases what survives is exaggerated to a greater or lesser extent. Boniface objected vehemently to Aldebert, who claimed that he was visited by an angel and apparently encouraged 'multitudes' of people to abandon the established churches and to worship with him at crosses and oratories which he had set up instead: how many people really followed him is impossible to determine, but at least in the early period the communication of ideas and beliefs by wandering preachers or visionaries like Aldebert or Fursey seems to have been a reality, and viewed positively or negatively by those in established positions in the ecclesiastical hierarchy according to the substance of what was preached, and the persuasions of the local figures of authority.[295]

Homilies were clearly important in terms of the formal context of communication of beliefs, and accounts of visions evidently provided another way in which people might learn about the afterlife, whether or not they accepted the information they received in either context. But these ideas also appeared in contexts which were not immediately connected with religious belief, or where religious beliefs were not the major concern. The description of Ealdorman Byrhtnoth's death after his (valiant but) unsuccessful attempt to fight the Vikings in 991, versified in *The Battle of Maldon*, states that just before he was hacked down by Viking warriors, Byrhtnoth asked God to allow his soul to pass to the 'Lord of the angels' in peace, so that it should not be harmed by attackers from hell.[296] As J.E. Cross pointed out, this is a paraphrase of the Latin liturgy for the dead, and so it is part of the same tradition which has been discussed here; it is of course also more than possible that Byrhtnoth did not utter such a prayer when faced with a horde of angry Vikings.[297] But even if the poem was written by a man or woman in religious life who felt that such a prayer was appropriate in the time of death, the subject-matter of the poem suggests that it may have received public performance and so have been communicated to a wider audience.[298] Communication about the response to death which was appropriate and necessary in the eyes of ecclesiastics because of the dangers of devils faced by the soul could therefore reappear in poems which might

[295]  *Epistolae* 57, 59, 62, ed. Tangl, *Die Briefe*, 102–5, 108–20, 127–8; for discussion see above, 21–5.

[296]  *The Battle of Maldon*, ll. 175–80, ed. D.G. Scragg, 'The Battle of Maldon', in D.G. Scragg (ed.), *The Battle of Maldon, AD 991* (Oxford, 1991), 1–36, at 24: 'Nu ic ah, milde metod, mæste þearfe þæt þu minum gaste godes geunne, þæt min sawul to ðe siðian mote on þin geweald, þeoden engla, mid friþe ferian'.

[297]  J.E. Cross, 'Oswald and Byrhtnoth: A Christian saint and a hero who is Christian', *English Studies* 46 (1965): 93–109, at 104–6; see also U. Schwab, 'The Battle of Maldon: A Memorial Poem', in J. Cooper (ed.), *The Battle of Maldon: Fiction and Fact* (London, 1993), 63–85, at 75–6.

[298]  The manuscript of the poem was burnt in the Cotton Fire of 1731 and so the text of the poem survives in an eighteenth-century transcript, which means that providing firmer context is difficult, although it is possible that it was copied in a monastic house in eastern England: see Scragg, 'The Battle of Maldon', 1–2, 32–5.

be considered to be 'secular', in the sense that unlike 'religious' poems (such as *The Dream of the Rood*) their overt message does not appear to be primarily about religious belief.[299] This kind of incidental reference simply reiterates how frequently these beliefs might appear, and in how wide a range of contexts.

## Conclusion

In the twelfth century, a woman wrote a prayer addressing her guardian angel into the prayer book which had originally been made for Ælfwine in the second quarter of the eleventh century. The prayer calls upon the 'holy angel, assigned by God Almighty to guard me', and asks 'that you guard me, a weak and unworthy woman, everywhere in this life, and protect and defend me from all evil, and when God orders my soul to depart, that you do not permit demons to have any power over it, but receive it gently from my body and lead it sweetly into the bosom of Abraham'.[300] Angels in general, and guardian angels in particular, became increasingly important in the centuries following the Anglo-Saxon period, and the importance of angelology to theology more generally was sealed by its incorporation into the formal curriculum of the Schools of Paris.[301] Here all manner of aspects of the angelic nature were explored, and some of the discussions would probably have seemed peculiar to Anglo-Saxon authors, as they evidently did to the seventeenth-century scholars who derided the exhaustive questioning of the scholastic theologians and satirised their discussions as the attempt to establish how many angels could dance on the head of a pin.[302] Anglo-Saxon scholars do not seem to have been interested in the same kinds of questions, since many of their concerns were far more pastorally oriented; and some, like, Ælfric, would almost certainly have disapproved of this type of enquiry.

---

[299]  *Dream of the Rood*, ed. G.P. Krapp, *The Vercelli Book*, Anglo-Saxon Poetic Records 2 (New York, 1932), 61–5.

[300]  Cotton Titus D.xxvii, fol. 74r, ed. Günzel, *Ælfwine's Prayerbook*, no. 47: 'Credo quod sis angelus sanctus, a Deo omnipotente ad custodiam mei deputatus, propterea peto, et per illum qui te ad hoc ordinauit, humiliter inploro, ut me miseram fragilem atque indignam semper et ubique in hac uita custodias, protegas a malis omnibus atque defendas, et cum Deus hinc animam meam migrare iusserit, nullam in eam potestatem demonibus habere permittas, sed tu eam leniter a corpore suscipias, et in sinu Habrae suauiter usque perducas iubente ac uiuante creatore ac saluatore Deo nostro, qui est benedictus in secula seculorum. Amen'.

[301]  Keck, *Angels*, 87.

[302]  The question was never posed thus in the Middle Ages (see Keck, *Angels*, 3; Bartlett, *The Natural and the Supernatural*, 73–4), but that has not stopped its frequent repetition; see also A. Sandberg, 'Quantum Gravity Treatment of the Angel Density Problem', *Annals of Improbable Research* 7:3 (2001): http://improbable.com/airchives/paperair/volume7/v7i3/angels-7-3.htm, accessed November 2012.

Angels and devils may not have been viewed in exactly the same way by everyone in England in the early Middle Ages, or even by all Anglo-Saxon scholars, but for once there is no doubt that 'official' belief accorded (and still accords) them clear and critical roles in salvation history. A number of authors explain that those who will ultimately be saved will take the place which the fallen angels had held before they were thrown out of heaven, and there are countless moments in salvation history where angels were essential, such as Gabriel's delivery of the message to Mary about the conception of Jesus.[303] While the perpetual struggles between angels and devils were part of the larger cosmic battle between good and evil, these struggles were played out on an individual basis and specifically with regard to individual souls. The significant quantity of uncanonical material about angels evidently disturbed some clergymen greatly, as did the propensity of devils to disguise themselves as angels and so deceive the unwary, but it should not be assumed that study of angels in the early Middle Ages was necessarily tainted by unorthodoxy or unofficial belief. Even when they expressed reservations, early medieval theologians did discuss angels, not least because understanding angels and devils and their roles was important for understanding a range of other theological topics and concepts such as sin.

Perhaps unsurprisingly, although Anglo-Saxon clergy complained about any number of beliefs which they perceived as objectionable, the denial of the existence of angels or devils was not one of these. People in the early Middle Ages believed in spirits which were usually invisible just as people in the ancient world had done, and just as people would continue to believe in them well into the early modern period and beyond: Protestant writers of the sixteenth and seventeenth centuries may have struggled with how to explain angels, but they certainly did not try to explain them away, even accepting that on very rare occasions angels might still appear visibly in the physical world.[304] The appearance of angels and devils in Anglo-Saxon England may seem surprisingly frequent by comparison, but such appearances are almost always presented as astonishing, disconcerting, or in some way marvellous, and were evidently unexpected when they were believed to have been seen, despite what the hagiographers may have claimed. It is significant in this context that while saints' miracles often occurred in the places where their bodies lay, their power centring on physical places where the saint had lived and died in the landscape, ethereal spirits were said to appear in remote locations, on the margins and isolated from human habitation.

Nonetheless, there are occasional incidental allusions to the possibility that spirits or monsters could appear in more inhabited or habitable areas: one remedy recorded in the eleventh century requires the would-be healer to go to a church

---

[303]    Lk 1:26–38.

[304]    A. Walsham, 'Invisible helpers: Angelic intervention in post-Reformation England', *Past & Present* 208:1 (2010): 77–130, esp. 82–100; see also L. Throness, *A Protestant Purgatory: Theological Origins of the Penitentiary Act, 1779* (Aldershot, 2008), 13–17.

to cross himself and offer himself to God before going to find a plant, but he must go silently, and even if he sees 'some fearful thing or a man coming' he should not speak.[305] Although the remedy does not identify further what kind of fearful thing this might be, it is interesting in the assumption that both men and monsters might be encountered on the way to church. Angels and devils may have been more prominent or more clearly defined in literate contexts than in the wider world, but they seem to have been ubiquitous, and it is this ubiquity which is essential in understanding their significance in such a range of aspects of life in the early Middle Ages. Even if most people were untroubled by these spirits most of the time, their perceived existence was still important. Teachers like Ælfric and Wulfstan, who evidently felt the weight of their own duty to convey information about the meaning of baptism and the responsibilities of Christians, and the fate of the soul after death, clearly tried a whole range of ways to impress 'correct' belief upon their charges. While it is overwhelmingly likely that some people required more convincing than others, it is also probable that the examples of angels and devils may have facilitated understanding in many cases.

From the perspective of the ecclesiastical officials, it was essential that Christians understood baptism and the responsibilities it brought, and what might happen to the soul after death if the personal relationship between every human being and God was not maintained carefully and appropriately. The growing belief in temporary purgation in the afterlife which could be alleviated by the prayers and actions of the living suggests that at least in some quarters Christians not only understood the importance of this personal relationship but also feared the repercussions of sin enough to attempt to make provision for their souls so that they would avoid suffering in the next world if at all possible.[306] The concern to make provision for burial and the increasing regulation of burial in the tenth and eleventh centuries similarly show how practice developed in response to changing ideas and the different weight given to certain beliefs, and suggest that here too, these beliefs were widely understood and accepted.[307] But there were also circumstances in which Christian belief was essential, not for the personal good of the individual but for the effective working of other processes such as law and order, which became entangled with Christian theology in the early Middle Ages. Archbishop Wulfstan thought that it was worth explaining the roles of angels and devils in the laws themselves, and while his laws are famously homiletic, this is still striking: the inclusion of invisible spirits in legal texts which also regulate weights and measures, and property and livestock, is a sharp reminder of how angels and devils infiltrated almost every aspect of life and death.

---

[305]  *Leechbook* III, lxii, ed. Cockayne, *Leechdoms*, 346: 'þeah þe hwæt hwega egeslices ongean cume oþþe man ne cweþ þu him ænig word to ær þu cume to þære wyrte þe þu on æfen ær gemearcodest'.

[306]  See below, 201–64.

[307]  See below, 265–328.

# Chapter 3
# And He Will Come Again to Judge the Living and the Dead

In hell there are thieves, wranglers, misers [ … ], proud men and magicians [ … ]; there are also evil reeves who now judge unjustly, and pervert the just laws of righteous men, which were rightly established before. Christ himself spoke about these judges, he said: 'Judge now as you want to be judged then on the last day of the world'.[1]

## Introduction

Christianity looks towards the end, to the time when Christ will return to judge all the living and the dead. The sense of living in the last age pervades the works of late antique and early medieval authors, and Christians had been waiting for the *parousia*, the Second Coming of Christ, since his Ascension.[2] The Last Judgement, at which the good and the wicked would finally be divided and placed in heaven and hell until the end of time, was one of the most popular topics of discussion amongst ecclesiastical authors in early medieval England, especially among the later Anglo-Saxon homilists.[3] From the perspective of Christian theology, this is the defining moment towards which all human actions should be oriented: at the Last Judgement the good and evil deeds of each and every person will be

---

[1]   *Hom*. V, ed. R. Morris, *The Blickling homilies of the 10th Century: From the Marquis of Lothian's Unique MS. A.D.971*, EETS, OS 58 (London, 1874), 61: 'On helle beoþ þeofas, & flyteras, & gitseras [ … ], þa oformodan men, & þa scinlæcan [ … ]; þær beoþ eac yfele gerefan þa þe nu on wóh demaþ, & rihte domas soþfæstra manna onwendaþ, þa þe ǽr rihtlice gesette wæron. Be þæm demum Crist sylf wæs sprecende; he cwæþ, 'Deme ge nu, swa swa ge willon þæt eow sy eft gedemed on þon ytmæstan dæge þisse worlde'.

[2]   P. Fredriksen, 'Apocalypse and redemption in early Christianity: From John of Patmos to Augustine of Hippo', *Vigiliae Christianae* 45 (1991): 151–83, at 151; R.A. Markus, 'Living within Sight of the End', in C. Humphrey and W.M. Ormrod (eds), *Time in the Medieval World* (Woodbridge, 2001), 23–34, at 31–2; U. Eco, 'Waiting for the Millennium', in R. Landes, A. Gow and D.C. Van Meter (eds), *The Apocalyptic Year 1000: Religious Expectation and Social Change, 950–1050* (Oxford, 2003), 121–35, at 125–6.

[3]   This has frequently been noted: see for example M.M. Gatch, 'Eschatology in the anonymous Old English Homilies', *Traditio: Studies in Ancient and Medieval History, Thought, and Religion* 21 (1965): 117–65, at 164; P. Lendinara, '"*frater non redimit, redimit homo …*": a Homiletic Motif and its Variants in Old English', in E. Treharne and S. Rosser (eds), *Early Medieval English Texts and Interpretations: Studies Presented to Donald G. Scragg* (Tempe, Arizona, 2002), 67–80, at 67.

visible to God and to all humankind and it will no longer be possible to make recompense for sins, so that those who are found wanting will perish. Anglo-Saxon homilists constantly warned about the need to prepare for the Last Judgement, recommending ecclesiastical penance as the most effective means of cleansing the soul in readiness for this final event. Since penance looks ultimately to the salvation of the soul at Judgement Day, its focus is the next world even though penitential actions have to take place in this world. To many people, this must have seemed incomprehensibly remote, especially compared with the more immediate judgements made by men in the context of secular law. But soteriological theology and the interpretation of the Last Judgement also came to shape both the process and content of Anglo-Saxon secular law and judgements, in a number of ways and with lasting consequences.

From the late ninth century, the concept of merciful judgement begins to appear more frequently in Anglo-Saxon legal texts, apparently indicating a growing recognition on the part of legislators and royal advisers that the duties of a Christian king included careful attention to such issues. In particular, the question of the use of judicial execution and the types of judgements handed down by the king and meted out by his officials seems to have been mulled over, with reflexes in legal texts and elsewhere. Another significant way in which consideration of divine judgement shaped legal texts, and perhaps also practice, was the use of oaths and ordeals as means of proof. Oaths and ordeals are common to a number of cultures and do not have to be understood in a Christian context,[4] but it is clear that when they were used in Anglo-Saxon England as part of the process of law they were understood as Christian rituals, and indeed in this context they can only be understood properly with reference to Christian theology. Although the Last Judgement was held up as a model both for merciful judgement and for the problem of proof, this served primarily to highlight the crucial differences between divine and human judgements. By its very nature, divine judgement is always fair and just, since it is performed by God, who is not only good but also omniscient and omnipotent.[5] In contrast, human judgements are beset with problems stemming from human nature: in a world where good and wicked souls have not yet been separated, those who judge or make laws are not always good, and do not always pass judgement mercifully or wisely. And even good judges and lawmakers are faced with the human problem of finding proof, since judges are not omniscient and men and women often do not admit their offences voluntarily, especially when punishment may follow.

Early medieval attempts to resolve these fundamentally human problems often made recourse to theology and consideration of the relationship between humans and God, and especially to the model of the Last Judgement, although what this

[4]   See for example R.W. Lariviere, 'Ordeals in Europe and in India', *Journal of the American Oriental Society* 101:3 (1981): 347–9.

[5]   B. Capelle, 'Valeurs spirituelles de la liturgie des défunts', *Questions liturgiques et paroissiales* 38 (1957): 191–6, at 194–5.

meant in practice varied according to context. Where judges were required to pronounce judgement upon their fellow men, this meant looking to the example of divine mercy, either by incorporating mercy into written laws, or by applying the laws in a merciful way. Those who swore oaths were reminded that God would know whether they swore falsely or not, and that punishment would follow at Judgement Day if not before. In the case of ordeals, judgement was literally handed over to God, on the grounds that he could discern the truth of the matter where humans could not. The making of law and dispensing of justice could therefore both be modelled on the mercy of God – and the knowledge that the actions of judges and lawgivers would be scrutinised at Judgement Day was also significant here, especially when the decisions these people made, or their interpretations of God's judgement in an ordeal, might send people to their deaths.

These themes are often found as related concepts and in associated contexts, but they appear sporadically and only in some of the later Anglo-Saxon sources. The death penalty seems to have been used and discussed quite infrequently before the reign of King Alfred (871–99),[6] and significant information about ordeals only appears in the early tenth century, in the laws of King Æthelstan (d.939) and in liturgical rituals. In contrast, other tenth-century laws (both before and after Æthelstan's) have little concrete information suggesting uncertainty or discussion about the use of capital punishment or ordeals, although some evidence can be gleaned from contemporary hagiographical accounts. The most extensive discussion of the use of capital punishment is found in the works of Archbishop Wulfstan of York (d.1023), especially in the laws which he wrote for Æthelred (d.1016) and Cnut (d.1035), and in his correspondence with Abbot Ælfric of Eynsham (d.1009/1010). Wulfstan also seems to have had serious reservations about the use of ordeals, and because of the weight and volume of his writings, his thoughts on these matters are discussed separately. These case studies are necessarily selective, but they illustrate precisely the importance and effects of theological discussion in the secular world of law and order, and especially the significance of abstract theological ideas in conjunction with religion as lived experience.

## Law and Penance

Ecclesiastical influence on Anglo-Saxon laws is well established, from the decision to record the earliest English laws in writing, perhaps encouraged by the Roman missionaries, to the inclusion in secular laws of high sums of compensation payable to churches and ecclesiastical officials in the case of offences against them.[7] It has also frequently been noted that the close relationship between law

---

[6]   V. Thompson, *Dying and Death in Later Anglo-Saxon England* (Woodbridge, 2004), 181.

[7]   See P. Wormald, 'Lex Scripta and Verbum Regis: Legislation and Germanic Kingship from Euric to Cnut', in his *Legal Culture in the Early Medieval West: Law as*

and penance illustrates the integration of secular and ecclesiastical structures, although quite how the evidence should be interpreted is open to debate.[8] Royal legislation increasingly contained penalties for offences against ecclesiastical custom, and also included occasional references to the performance of penance as a penalty for offences against secular law.[9] Similarly, there are instructions in late Anglo-Saxon penitential books to accept the judgements of secular law, for example the prescription that a man should be excommunicated if he refuses to accept a secular judgement to make peace with someone who has committed an offence against him.[10] The expectation of kings and their advisers may have been, as Elaine Treharne suggests, that ecclesiastical and secular judicial officials should cooperate to punish offences, especially in the period following the Benedictine Reforms of the mid-late tenth century; and it is clear, as Katy Cubitt notes, that royal assemblies attended by ecclesiastical officials were highly significant for the complex relationship between secular law and penance, and for the application of religious penalties in the context of secular law.[11] It is difficult to ascertain precisely how the relationship functioned though: Carole Hough argues that secular law supported the penitential system, but that penitential discipline was

---

*Text, Image and Experience* (London, 1999), 1–44, at 2–3, 8–10, 12–13, 24–37; L. Oliver, *The Beginnings of English Law* (Toronto, 2002), 15–17; see for example Æthelberht 1, ed. and trans. Oliver, *The Beginnings of English Law*, 60–1. The decrees are placed right at the beginning of the code, but it is not clear whether they were originally positioned here or whether this was a final addition (see Oliver, *The Beginnings of English Law*, 44–8, 61 and 83–5).

[8]    T.P. Oakley, *English Penitential Discipline and Anglo-Saxon Law in their Joint Influence* (New York, 1923); T.P. Oakley, 'The cooperation of mediaeval penance and secular law', *Speculum: A Journal of Medieval Studies* 7:4 (1932): 515–24; P. Wormald, *The Making of English Law: King Alfred to the Twelfth Century* (Oxford, 1999); C. Hough, 'Penitential literature and secular law in Anglo-Saxon England', *Anglo-Saxon Studies in Archaeology & History* 11 (2000): 133–42; S. Hamilton, 'Remedies for "Great Transgressions": Penance and Excommunication in Late Anglo-Saxon England', in F. Tinti (ed.), *Pastoral Care in Late Anglo-Saxon England*, Anglo-Saxon Studies 6 (Woodbridge, 2005), 83–105; C. Cubitt, 'Bishops and Councils in Late Saxon England: The Intersection of Secular and Ecclesiastical Law', in A. Grabowsky and W. Hartmann (eds), *Recht und Gericht in Kirche und Welt um 900* (München, 2007), 151–68; R. Meens, 'Die Bußbücher und das Recht im 9. und 10. Jahrhundert: Kontinuität und Wandel', in Grabowsky and Hartmann (eds), *Recht und Gericht in Kirche und Welt um 900*, 217–34.

[9]    e.g. II Æthelstan 26, ed. F. Liebermann, *Die Gesetze der Angelsachsen* (3 vols Halle, 1903–1916), I.164–5.

[10]    *Old English Penitential*, 42.28.01, ed. A.J. Frantzen, *The Anglo-Saxon Penitentials: A Cultural Database* (2008), http://www.anglo-saxon.net/penance, accessed October 2012.

[11]    E.M. Treharne, 'A unique Old English formula for excommunication from Cambridge, Corpus Christi College 303', *Anglo-Saxon England* 24 (1995): 185–211, at 193; Cubitt, 'Bishops and Councils in Late Saxon England'; see also S. Hamilton, 'Rites for Public Penance in Late Anglo-Saxon England', in H. Gittos and M.B. Bedingfield (eds), *The Liturgy of the Late Anglo-Saxon Church* (Woodbridge, 2005), 65–103, at 83–7.

not significant in upholding secular authority.[12] However, the procedures for oaths and ordeals required relics and liturgical rituals, and from at least the tenth century, secular legal process saw ecclesiastical involvement in the presence of bishops at local courts, while in contrast ecclesiastical judgements in the context of penance were matters for priests or bishops and *not* for secular judges.[13]

While this closer integration of the systems of law and penance shows the increasing significance of the Church as an institution in society, it is important to remember that in and of itself this cooperation does not necessarily show the impact of developing theological discussion on secular processes. Theology determines which deeds are considered to be sinful, and which circumstances make deeds more or less sinful, but the system of penance was part of the Church in the world and its institutional structures and procedures, in the same way that the institution and its officials were the recipients of the compensation decreed by secular law for offences committed against the Church as an institution and its personnel. The provision of penalties in secular law for deeds condemned by canon law, such as marriage to a close relation, does not necessarily mean that there has been much engagement on the part of the lawmakers with *why* such a deed should be considered as an offence worthy of punishment, except that an ecclesiastical authority (or authorities) instructs so. Penance may in fact have been most closely linked to the law simply as a related disciplinary system which could integrate secular and ecclesiastical structures together,[14] but in this period it is extremely difficult to distinguish between the concepts of sin and crime, either in law or in penance. A shared vocabulary exacerbates the difficulty, but in any case there is significant overlap in the ground covered by penitential and legal texts, because both dealt with a wide range of aspects of life.[15] It can therefore be difficult to understand whether legislators or the authors of penitentials thought they were setting down the penalties for offences against God or against the king or the kingdom, or even whether such distinctions were really made.

More importantly in this context, the overlap in the coverage of penitential and legal texts makes it difficult to understand how precisely the two systems might have worked in tandem, and especially for offences for which secular law stipulated the death penalty. It is clearer in cases where ecclesiastical penance and secular penalties could have worked side by side, such as the decree in II Cnut which required a convicted perjurer to lose his hand or half his wergeld, and also prevented him from swearing an oath again unless he performed penance.[16] But

---

[12]    Hough, 'Penitential Literature and Secular Law in Anglo-Saxon England', 133–41, esp. 138–9.

[13]    II Æthelstan 23; III Edgar 5.2; Ordal, ed. Liebermann, *Gesetze*, I.162–3, 202–3, 386–7.

[14]    A.J. Frantzen, *The Literature of Penance in Anglo-Saxon England* (New Brunswick, NJ, 1983), 62.

[15]    Wormald, 'Maitland and the Earliest English Law', 61.

[16]    II Cnut 36, ed. Liebermann, *Gesetze*, I.338–9.

where secular law demanded that the offender should lose his life, it is not clear that there is any allowance for the performance of ecclesiastical penances, which could take weeks or years depending on the seriousness and precise circumstances of the offence. For example, penitential decrees in late Anglo-Saxon manuscripts require that theft should be atoned for with periods of fasting lasting anywhere from three weeks to twelve years, depending on the type of theft and type of thief,[17] and it is rather difficult to square this with contemporary instructions that thieves should be killed. Interestingly, it was theoretically possible in some cases for thieves to appeal to the king: in light of the discussions which emphasised mercy as a virtue of Christian kings, and in due course the wording of the king's coronation oath which enshrined this as part of his duty to his people, it is possible that this was an opportunity to allow a thief to live in return for the performance of penance.[18]

In reality though, it seems unlikely that many thieves at a local level were referred to the king, and as with the cooperation of law and penance, this highlights the difficulty of ascertaining the relationship between text and practice. As normative texts, law codes and penitentials state what ought to happen, without necessarily providing confirmation that it actually did. There has been some debate over how far penance was a reality rather than an ideal, and in particular how far the surviving material might have been used in pastoral situations rather than in academic contexts.[19] Perhaps more importantly, the principle of judgement outlined in penitential texts also casts doubt on how far the precise tariffs listed in penitentials should be taken as representative of actual practice. Priests (and bishops) enjoining penance upon those who confessed their offences were encouraged to act with compassion and careful judgement, suiting the penance to the individual as well as to the sin committed, according to the nature of the sin and the circumstances of the sinner. For example, the late tenth- or early eleventh-

---

[17]    According to the *Old English Penitential*, for example, a man who steals food or clothes from need should fast for three weeks if he can return what he stole (44.20.01, ed. Frantzen, *The Anglo-Saxon Penitentials: A Cultural Database*); for stealing items of value a layman should fast for 5 years, whereas a bishop should fast for 12 years (42.25.01, ed. Frantzen, *The Anglo-Saxon Penitentials: A Cultural Database*). According to the *Old English Canons of Theodore*, someone who has often committed theft should fast for seven years if he cannot return what he stole (76.01.02, ed. Frantzen, *The Anglo-Saxon Penitentials: A Cultural Database*).

[18]    See for example III Edgar 7.3, ed. Liebermann, *Gesetze*, I.204–5; and P. Stafford, 'The laws of Cnut and the history of Anglo-Saxon royal promises', *Anglo-Saxon England* 10 (1982): 173–90; M. Clayton, 'The Old English promissio regis', *Anglo-Saxon England* 37 (2008): 91–150.

[19]    See for example R. Meens, 'The Frequency and Nature of Early Medieval Penance', in P. Biller and A.J. Minnis (eds), *Handling Sin: Confession in the Middle Ages*, York Studies in Medieval Theology 2 (Woodbridge, 1998), 35–61; S. Hamilton, *The Practice of Penance 900–1050* (Woodbridge, 2001), 15–76; C. Cubitt, 'Bishops, priests and penance in late Saxon England', *Early Medieval Europe* 14:1 (2006): 41–63.

century *Old English Handbook* instructs the confessor to distinguish according to age, wealth, rank and health, and according to whether misdeeds were intentional, accidental, involuntary or deliberate, and according to the repentance shown by the penitent; the slightly earlier *Old English Penitential* relates the greatness of God's mercy and presents this as the model for confessors, directing that 'priests and bishops should judge mercifully, because no one is without sin'.[20] It is not clear whether this merciful judgement was intended to apply only where the penitentials state that the penance should be assigned according to the discretion of the confessor, or whether this suggests that in fact the entire system of tariffs was intended as a guide rather than a set of immovable rules.

The question of how far written legal texts were actually used in handing down judgements is also a controversial one, and perhaps more so for Anglo-Saxon England than for contemporary continental societies because of the lack of English records of court cases.[21] Part of the difficulty with assessing the application of written legal texts is that the surviving recorded cases are so frequently concerned with land, a topic about which Anglo-Saxon laws are remarkably silent.[22] Anglo-Saxon laws can hardly be called comprehensive, and this too suggests that not all legal judgements were made with reference to written law, presumably indicating instead the existence of a body of oral law or custom for determining the outcome

---

[20]   [Y]41.09.03, ed. Frantzen, *The Anglo-Saxon Penitentials: A Cultural Database*.

[21]   For the argument that early medieval written law was substantially symbolic, see H. Vollrath, 'Gesetzgebung und Schriftlichkeit. Das Beispiel der angelsächsischen Gesetze', *Historisches Jahrbuch* 99 (1979): 28–54; Wormald, 'Lex Scripta and Verbum Regis: Legislation and Germanic Kingship from Euric to Cnut', 79–83. For the view that royal government intended that written law should be used, and/or that it was used, see R. McKitterick, 'Some Carolingian Law-Books and their Function', in B. Tierney and P. Linehan (eds), *Authority and Power: Studies on Medieval Law and Government Presented to Walter Ullman on his Seventieth Birthday* (Cambridge, 1980), 13–27; R. McKitterick, *The Carolingians and the Written Word* (Cambridge, 1989), 23–75; S. Keynes, 'Royal Government and the Written Word in Late Anglo-Saxon England', in R. McKitterick (ed.), *Uses of Literacy in Early Mediaeval Europe* (Cambridge, 1990), 226–57, esp. 198–211; C. Cubitt, '"As the lawbook teaches": Reeves, lawbooks and urban life in the anonymous Old English legend of the seven sleepers', *English Historical Review* 124:510 (2009): 1021–49; A. Rio, *Legal Practice and the Written Word in the Early Middle Ages: Frankish Formulae, c. 500–1000*, Cambridge Studies in Medieval Life and Thought, 4th series 75 (Cambridge, 2009); D. Pratt, 'Written Law and the Communication of Authority in Tenth-Century England', in C. Leyser, D.W. Rollason and H. Williams (eds), *England and the Continent in the Tenth Century: Studies in Honour of Wilhelm Levison (1876–1947)* (Turnhout, 2011), 331–50.

[22]   See A. Kennedy, 'Law and litigation in the Libellus Æthelwoldi episcopi', *Anglo-Saxon England* 24 (1995): 131–83, at 173–83; D. Pratt, *The Political Thought of King Alfred the Great*, Cambridge Studies in Medieval Life and Thought, 4th series 67 (Cambridge, 2007), 217–18.

of some cases.[23] Law codes themselves infrequently refer to judging according to written decrees, although there are some references to written laws and specific kings' codes, suggesting that although these laws may now survive in only a small number of copies, they were available to the compilers of Anglo-Saxon decrees and were intended to be available for judges to use in practice.[24] The instruction by King Edgar (d.975) that one of his codes should be copied and distributed to the ealdormen Ælfhere and Æthelwine for wider promulgation seems to indicate that he intended written law to be circulated and used in practice, but it also highlights the fact that it must have taken time for texts to be copied and circulated, such that some administrative units only received up-to-date laws after some delay.[25]

The question of literacy is also significant, for penance as for law. Theoretically, a penitential was one of the books that priests should own and know how to use, but it is not clear that all priests did own and/or know how to use them,[26] and the repeated injunctions from high-ranking ecclesiastical officials to the clergy in later Anglo-Saxon England may cast doubt on the ability of priests to read the penitentials and impose penance according to their decrees.[27] It is almost impossible to gauge the literacy of local officials and judges, and it is possible that the role of the bishop in the hundred court, as prescribed for example in

---

[23]   Kennedy, 'Law and litigation in the Libellus Æthelwoldi episcopi', 176–8; Wormald, *Making of English Law*, 96, 482; Wormald, 'Lex Scripta and Verbum Regis: Legislation and Germanic Kingship from Euric to Cnut', 9–14.

[24]   I Edward, Prologue, ed. Liebermann, *Gesetze*, I.138–9, states that judges should follow the decrees of written law; other references to previous written laws include II Edward 5; II Æthelstan 5; II Edmund 2; III Edgar 5, ed. Liebermann, *Gesetze*, I.142–3, 152–3, 188–9, 202–3, while references to the laws of specific kings can be found for example at I Edgar 2; VIII Æthelred 43, ed. Liebermann, *Gesetze*, I.192–3, 268–9.

[25]   IV Edgar 15.1, ed. Liebermann, *Gesetze*, I.214–15.

[26]   *Poenitentiale Ecgberhti*, Prologue, ed. A.W. Haddan and W. Stubbs, *Councils and Ecclesiastical Documents Relating to Great Britain and Ireland* (3 vols, Oxford, 1869), III.417; *Pastoral Letters* I.52–4; 2.137–9; II.157–8, ed. B. Fehr, *Die Hirtenbriefe Ælfrics in altenglischer und lateinischer Fassung, Bibliothek der Angelsaechsischen Prosa* (Darmstadt, 1966, reprinted with supplementary introduction by P. Clemoes [orig. pub. 1914]), 13, 51–2, 126–7; A.J. Frantzen, 'The significance of the Frankish penitentials', *Journal of Ecclesiastical History* 30 (1979): 409–21, at 412–13; A.J. Frantzen, 'The tradition of penitentials in Anglo-Saxon England', *Anglo-Saxon England* 11 (1983): 23–56, at 24–5, 31–2; Meens, 'Frequency and Nature', 35–8.

[27]   See for example *Pastoral Letters* I.52–67; II.2, 157, 172, ed. Fehr, *Die Hirtenbriefe Ælfrics*, 13–14, 68–9, 126–7, 130–1; see also S.E. Kelly, 'Anglo-Saxon Lay Society and the Written Word', in McKitterick (ed.), *The Uses of Literacy in Early Mediaeval Europe*, 36–62; J. Hill, 'Monastic Reform and the Secular Church: Ælfric's Pastoral Letters in Context', in C. Hicks (ed.), *England in the Eleventh Century: Proceedings of the 1990 Harlaxton Symposium*, Harlaxton Medieval Studies 2 (Stamford, 1992), 103–17, at 108–11; J. Wilcox, 'Ælfric in Dorset and the Landscape of Pastoral Care', in Tinti (ed.), *Pastoral Care in Late Anglo-Saxon England*, 52–62, esp. 59–60.

Edgar's law codes, could have been at least in part to ensure that the presence of someone literate so that judgements could be made in consultation with the written law.[28] The surviving English books of law and penance also present difficulties, not least because so many of them are associated with Archbishop Wulfstan, whose purposes and rationale with such texts were peculiarly his own. Most of the surviving English manuscripts containing penitential texts are compilations of penitential literature, whereas individual handbooks of penance are comparatively rare.[29] Legal texts too survive in compilations, and the earliest laws are preserved only in twelfth-century copies, probably representing antiquarian rather than practical interest.[30] The utilitarian nature of legal and penitential texts may account for the limited number of surviving copies: like liturgical books, many copies for practical use may have been booklets rather than bound compilations, and they were presumably recycled or discarded once they became outdated and ceased to be useful. The surviving range of manuscripts and the areas for which law codes attempt to legislate also indicate that what survives to the present day is not fully representative of all areas and all periods.[31]

These evidential difficulties suggest that law codes and penitentials may in some cases have been more aspirational than fully representative of actual practice, but the evidence does suggest that in other cases the rules of law or penance were intended to be used and applied as handed down by kings to local judges and by bishops to their priests. It is clear that the increasing cooperation between the systems of law and penance was one symptom of the close involvement of high-ranking ecclesiastics in the production of law codes and probably also in the discussions which preceded the recording of law in writing. This was an avenue through which theological ideas could be transmitted to the makers of secular law, and another symptom can be seen in the incorporation of theological ideas and penitential principles into secular legal texts, both in process and content, and regardless of the institutional Church's system for dealing with those who offended against ecclesiastical law.

---

[28]   III Edgar 5.2, ed. Liebermann, *Gesetze*, I.202–3.

[29]   Frantzen, 'Tradition', 26–7. For example, Oxford, Bodleian Library, Laud misc. 482 (s. xi[med]; Worcester) contains all five of the Old English handbooks of penance edited in Frantzen, *The Anglo-Saxon Penitentials: A Cultural Database*.

[30]   Wormald, *Making of English Law*, 228–36, 244–53, 473–6; S. Irvine, 'The Compilation and Use of Manuscripts Containing Old English in the Twelfth Century', in M. Swan and E. Treharne (eds), *Rewriting Old English in the Twelfth Century*, Cambridge Studies in Anglo-Saxon England 30 (Cambridge, 2000), 41–61, at 42–3.

[31]   Wormald, *Making of English Law*, 93–143.

## Mercy in Judgement and the Treatment of Offenders

At the Last Judgement, God would be terrible and yet merciful, and so mercy was believed to be an important part of earthly judgements too. This was reinforced by Holy Scripture: the author of the letter of James notes, for example, that 'judgement without mercy will be shown to anyone who has not been merciful'.[32] The importance of mercy in judgement was also based on the contrast drawn in the New Testament between the life of Christians and life under the old law, summarised succinctly in the Lord's prayer: 'forgive us our sins as we forgive those who sin against us'.[33] In the context of penance, merciful judgement meant treating different people according to their individual circumstances, and assigning reasonable penances that could be completed by the penitent without them being an impossible burden. Perhaps unsurprisingly, penitentials tend to assume that it is possible to atone for all offences, so that there is nothing which cannot be wiped out by the performance of an appropriate penance.[34] Instead, homiletic and penitential texts emphasise that even if someone only turns to God on the last day of his life, that is enough: the crucial thing is that he should attempt to atone for his sins, or even simply express the desire to do so.[35]

This meant that the stipulation of capital punishment for certain offences in secular law was in fundamental opposition to the way that offenders should be treated according to the theological principles which underlay the penitential system: it is unthinkable that early medieval penitential texts could have stipulated execution rather than fasting or other practices as a means of atoning for sins committed. A careful explanation of this principle is found in a discussion of the gospel of John by Augustine of Hippo (d.430), who explained that there was a distinction between man and sinner, because man was made by God, but a sinner was a man who had put himself in a sinful condition.[36] By placing the emphasis on the sin rather than on the sinner, he highlighted the importance of repentance:

---

[32]   Jas 2:13.

[33]   Mt 6:12, 6:14–15; Lk 6:37; 11.4; see also Paul's distinction between the time of Mosaic law and the time of Christ in Rm 6:14–15; Ga 2:19–21; 3:10–24.

[34]   Theologians did discuss the 'unforgivable sin' mentioned in Mt 12.32, often assuming that it meant blasphemy against the Holy Spirit, but there is no discussion of this in Anglo-Saxon penitentials.

[35]   See for example Ælfric, *CH* II.19, ll. 54–9, ed. M. Godden, *Ælfric's Catholic Homilies: The Second Series Text* (Oxford, 1979), 181–2, and *Hom*. XI, ll. 197–8, ed. J.C. Pope, *Homilies of Ælfric: A Supplementary Collection*, EETS, OS 259–60 (2 vols, London, 1967–8), I.425; also *Old English Penitential*, SXY 41.02.01, ed. Frantzen, *The Anglo-Saxon Penitentials: A Cultural Database*.

[36]   Augustine, *In Iohannis euangelium tractatus*, 12.13, ll. 24–5, ed. R. Willems, *Sancti Aurelii Augustini in Iohannis Euangelium Tractatus CXXIV*, CCSL 36 (Turnhout, 1954), 128: 'Quasi duae res sunt, homo et peccator. Quod audis homo, Deus fecit; quod audis peccator, ipse homo fecit'.

by destroying the sin God's creation would be saved, and the sinner (or criminal) would be able to repent and correct himself. It is also possible to see Augustine exercising this principle in practice. He wrote to the Christian magistrate Apringius, reminding him that judges would also be required to give account of themselves at the divine judgement, and asking for the relaxation of the death penalty in the case of Donatist clerics who had been convicted of murdering and mutilating Catholic priests: Augustine reasoned that lesser punishments would suffice, and that even if they would not, it would be better to let the criminals go free than to avenge the blood of the martyrs by shedding more blood.[37]

But despite God's commandment against murder, Scripture also provided precedent for the permissibility of judicial execution, such as the many offences for which the death penalty is stipulated in Exodus.[38] Patristic authors had discussed these issues too, and especially the exoneration of those who were charged with carrying out capital sentences, a debate to which Augustine had also contributed despite the opinions he expressed elsewhere.[39] Augustine noted that in a judicial execution a man was killed by the law, not by the man who literally and physically put him to death, and he also observed that judicial killing performed by state officials was one of the exceptions to the divine law against human killing.[40] Like Augustine, the patristic writer Jerome (d.420) distinguished between the unlawful killing of the innocent and the use of the death penalty to punish those who committed offences against the law, stating that the punishment of murderers and those who committed sacrilege was the administration of the law and not an outpouring of blood.[41] However, Jerome went further than Augustine, asserting

---

[37] *Epistola* CXXXIV.2–3, ed. A. Goldbacher, *S. Aureli Augustini Hipponiensis episcopi epistulae, pars III, ep. CXXIV–CLXXXIV A*, CSEL 44 (Vienna, 1894), 84–8: 'si ergo nihil aliud constitueretur frenandae malitiae perditorum, extrema fortasse necessitas, ut tales occiderentur, urgeret, quamquam, quod ad nos adtinet, si nihil mitius eis fieri posset, mallemus eos liberos relaxari, quam passiones fratrum nostrorum fuso eorum sanguine uindicari'.

[38] See for example Ex 21:11–30; see also Ex 20:13; Gn 9:6, Rm 13:1–7.

[39] For pre-Constantinian writers, see B. Schöpf, *Das Tötungsrecht bei den frühchristlichen Schriftstellern bis zur Zeit Konstantins*, Studien zur Geschichte der katholischen Moraltheologie 5 (Regensburg, 1958), 64–71.

[40] Augustine, *Quaestiones in heptateuchum libri septem*, III, quaestiones Leuitici, qu. 68, ll. 1663–4, ed. J. Fraipont and D. de Bruyne, *Quaestionum in Heptateuchum, libri VII; Locutionum in Heptateuchum, libri VII; De octo quaestionibus ex Veteri Testamento*, CCSL 33 (Turnhout, 1958), 221: 'quoniam cum homo iuste occiditur, lex eum occidit, non tu'; see also *DCD* I.21, ed. B. Dombert and A. Kalb, *Sancti Aurelii Augustini. De civitate Dei*, CCSL 47–8 (2 vols Turnhout, 1955), I.23.

[41] Jerome, *Comm. in Hierem.* IV.35, ed. S. Reiter, *S. Hieronymi presbyteri opera, pars I. Opera exegetica, 3: In Hieremiam libri VI*, CCSL 74 (Turnhout, 1960), 201: 'Homicidas enim et sacrilegos et uenenarios punire non est effusio sanguinis, sed legum ministerium'.

that the one who struck evil men because they were evil is the Lord's servant.[42] For the worst offenders, therefore, theology and canon law did not exclude the death penalty as the punishment of secular law, and those who enforced the law as part of their duties were not considered to have committed an offence against God.

On the other hand, such statements do not deal with the nature of the law and what it requires, or how far those who made laws demanding death rather than mercy might be responsible for the souls whose lives were taken away as a result of judicial execution. These kinds of questions seem to have been considered by some rulers, but it seems that broadly speaking, in many cases neither the Church as institution nor its officials as individuals (where identifiable) supported judicial execution where alternatives were possible. One significant outcome of this was the right of sanctuary, which seems to have been protected quite carefully throughout the Anglo-Saxon period and beyond, quite probably as a result of ecclesiastical influence upon written law.[43] The late seventh-century laws of Ine, for example, allow that someone who was liable for the death penalty would escape it if he could reach the sanctuary of a church.[44] Alfred's laws allow only seven days' respite, but do state that if anyone takes sanctuary in a church and confesses a previously hidden crime, half the punishment will be remitted: this is particularly significant in the context of the death penalty since it presumably could have meant that the offender might escape with his life.[45] The laws of Æthelstan are notoriously severe, especially with regard to theft, and although one code allows thieves a reprieve of nine days in sanctuary there is an explicit statement that the thief will not be allowed to extend his life beyond that period of time.[46] But even buying time might allow for penance, and in reality it is possible that a delay would have provided the opportunity for negotiation, perhaps forgiveness and a less severe penalty, or maybe even referral of the case to the king.

Hagiographical miracle stories show saints allowing offenders to escape death or other punishments, usually in return for their repentance, and this suggests that the implicit objections to judicial execution in some other contexts might find realisation in other arenas.[47] The protection of sanctuary may have been particularly

---

[42]   Jerome, *Comm. in Ezek.*, 3.ix.1b, ll. 422–4, ed. F. Glorie, *Commentariorum in Hiezechielem libri XIV*, CCSL 75 (Turnhout, 1964), 103: 'qui igitur malos percutit in eo quod mali sunt, et habet uasa interfectionis ut occidat pessimos, minister est domini'.

[43]   G. Rosser, 'Sanctuary and Social Negotation in Medieval England', in J. Blair and B. Golding (eds), *The Cloister and the World: Essays in Medieval History in Honour of Barbara Harvey* (Oxford, 1996), 57–79; J.P. Sexton, 'Saint's law: Anglo-Saxon sanctuary protection in the *Translatio et Miracula S. Swithuni*', *Florilegium* 23:2 (2006): 61–80, at 63.

[44]   Ine 5, ed. Liebermann, *Gesetze*, I.90–1.

[45]   Alfred 5–5.4, ed. Liebermann, *Gesetze*, I.50–3.

[46]   IV Æthelstan 6, ed. Liebermann, *Gesetze*, I.171–2.

[47]   See for example Wulfstan of Winchester, *Vita S. Æthelwoldi*, 46, ed. M. Lapidge and M. Winterbottom, *Wulfstan of Winchester: The Life of St Æthelwold* (Oxford, 1991),

valuable to those who might otherwise have lacked powerful protectors to be their advocates in law, such as those who were unfree, and especially because of this connection to the saints, so that those who reached a church could claim the protection of the saints as well as the negotiating powers of the clergy.[48] According to the eighth-century writer, Bede, Cuthbert (d.687) wanted to be buried away from Lindisfarne precisely to avoid the attention of fugitives seeking his body,[49] and it is clear that saints were believed to play a significant role in defending offenders outside the specific legal context of sanctuary. The late tenth-century accounts of the miracles of St Swithun include an episode about a Frankish thief, detained on account of a serious offence: Swithun's powers, although not his name, were known to this thief, who asked for the saint's help.[50] Swithun released him, but crucially, this was done only in return for the thief's promise to desist from future offences. This is very close to the legal decrees which require convicted offenders to promise not to repeat their offences, but more importantly from the perspective of the hagiographers, the saint had saved a man's life. The clear message is that if souls can be saved, and especially if the outcome of saving an offender's life is that individual's conversion to a more appropriate way of life, then the death penalty should be avoided even if that meant thwarting secular judicial procedures.

The use of execution as part of the process of justice seems to have been subject to some scrutiny from the late ninth century, when King Alfred articulated the importance of mercy in judgement for the first time in Anglo-Saxon law. Alfred located his laws in the context of divine lawgiving, introducing his decrees with a translation of extracts from Mosaic Law as set down in Exodus and followed by selections from the New Testament.[51] He seems to have intended the harsh Mosaic decrees, many of which did demand death as the only suitable penalty, to stand in contrast to the more merciful judgements of the New Testament and of his own laws, informed by Christian theology and ethics and perhaps inspired by the works

---

68; Goscelin's *Vita et translatio S. Edithae,* II.5, ed. A. Wilmart, 'La légende de Ste Edithe en prose et vers par le moine Goscelin', *Analecta Bollandiana* 56 (1938): 5–101 and 265–307, at 272–3; Rosser, 'Sanctuary and Social Negotiation in Medieval England', 61–5; K. O'Brien O'Keefe, 'Body and law in Late Anglo-Saxon England', *Anglo-Saxon England* 27 (1998): 209–32, at 222–4; Sexton, 'Saint's law', 61–2. See also V.I.J. Flint, 'The Saint and the Operation of the Law: Reflections upon the Miracles of St Thomas Cantilupe', in R. Gameson and H. Leyser (eds), *Belief and Culture in the Middle Ages: Studies Presented to Henry Mayr-Harting* (Oxford, 2001), 342–57.

[48]  Sexton, 'Saint's law', 65–78, esp. 76–7.

[49]  Bede, *Vita S. Cuthberti Prosa,* 37, ed. and trans. B. Colgrave, *Two Lives of Saint Cuthbert: A Life by an Anonymous Monk of Lindisfarne and Bede's Prose Life* (Cambridge, 1985 [orig. pub. 1940]), 278–9.

[50]  Lantfred, *Translatio S. Swithuni,* 34, ed. and trans. M. Lapidge, *The Cult of St Swithun,* Winchester Studies 4.ii (Oxford, 2003), 322–5.

[51]  Alfred, Introduction, ed. Liebermann, *Gesetze*, I.26–43.

of the Carolingian author Hincmar of Rheims (d.882),[52] and he marked the change from the Old Testament to the New with the statement that Christ himself came to teach mercy and loving kindness.[53] To a certain extent the presentation of this contrast as a feature of Alfred's laws may have been more ideological than actual, in that before the severe laws decreed by Æthelstan in the tenth century, capital punishment was not in fact stipulated particularly frequently.[54] In the early law codes, theft seems to have been one of the few crimes for which death seems to have been considered an appropriate punishment, either if the thief was caught in the act, or if he was brought to trial and convicted.[55] But it may also be that Alfred's consideration of judicial execution was prompted by how and why he used it, especially because his justification depends heavily on theological arguments.

Alfred's law code prescribes the death penalty for just a few specific and particularly heinous offences such as treachery,[56] but the decrees of Ine's code must also be taken into account because these survive only as an appendix to Alfred's laws. The reasons for the inclusion of this appendix (and its authenticity) have been questioned, but it is quite possible that the two sets of decrees were intended to be used and consulted side by side.[57] Taking the laws of Alfred and Ine together, it is striking that in many of the cases where death is stipulated the offender's fate still lay in the hands of the king, placing the choice between condemnation and death, or forgiveness and life, with the royal person. This is particularly striking given the emphasis in Alfred's introduction on the importance of mercy in judgement. The one rubric for the introduction to Alfred's laws refers to the principle that each man should judge according to how he would himself wish to be judged,[58] and this is placed before the main body of the law code proper, so that the effect is to suggest that this principle lies behind the specific decrees made by Alfred himself. This idea is picked up in the body of the introduction where the hypothetical judge is encouraged to judge no man in such a way that he would not want to be judged by that man afterwards, and this comes in the change from the Old Testament to the New where Christ's mercy (and the necessity of following

---

[52]    M. Treschow, 'The prologue to Alfred's law code: Instruction in the spirit of mercy', *Florilegium* 13 (1994): 79–110, at 102–5; Pratt, *Political Thought*, 230–2.

[53]    Alfred, Introduction, 49, ed. Liebermann, *Gesetze*, I.42–3.

[54]    Thompson, *Dying and Death*, 181; A.J. Reynolds, *Anglo-Saxon Deviant Burial Customs* (Oxford, 2009), 23–9.

[55]    Wormald, *Making of English Law*, 105, 283, 377; Oliver, *The Beginnings of English Law*, 16–17. The decrees of Wihtred and Ine also permit the non-judicial killing of thieves (or those assumed to be thieves) without retribution. See Wihtred 20–21.1, ed. Oliver, *The Beginnings of English Law*, 160–3; Ine 12, 16, 21, and cf. 35, ed. Liebermann, *Gesetze*, I.94–5, 96–7, 98–9, 104–5.

[56]    Pratt, *Political Thought*, 233–4.

[57]    Wormald, *Making of English Law*, 267–9, 278–81.

[58]    Alfred, rubric 1, ed. Liebermann, *Gesetze*, I.16–17; Pratt, *Political Thought*, 229.

his merciful example) is discussed in detail.[59] But significantly, Alfred also explained why he was prepared to use the death penalty in certain circumstances, and this too depended on scriptural and theological precedent. The death penalty was considered to be a suitable response to those who plotted against the king's (or a lord's) life based on the judgement and death of Judas, who betrayed Christ.[60] Like divine mercy, royal mercy therefore had clear limits.

Alfred also dealt specifically with the problem of unjust judgements and bad judges, another trope which appears in hagiographical accounts, where once again saints were pitted against the judicial system as they saved those who had been poorly served by corrupt or careless officials.[61] The king's contemporary biographer, Asser, relates that Alfred had a particular interest in the instruction of magistrates, to the extent that those who were found to be judging poorly were required either to leave office or to study wisdom intensively.[62] Alfred's concern both with wisdom, and with the additional benefits it brought to those who acquired it, is well known, and it is clear from his prose preface to the translation of Gregory's *Pastoral Care* that he intended texts containing wisdom to be used as the basis for his educational reform.[63] It is therefore possible, as Michael Treschow suggests, that the preface to the law code was intended to be available for those who did not understand Latin and who therefore could not access the patristic and scriptural writings upon which Alfred's principles for judgement were based, so that those who could only read English would still be able to learn the wisdom which Alfred recommended.[64] There are passages which seem as if they might have been intended as part of a course of instruction in making judgements, such as the instructions to avoid bribes and idle gossip.[65] Alfred also adapted rather than translated in some instances, such as the statement from Exodus, 'do not refuse to

---

[59]    Alfred, Introduction, 49–9.10 and especially 49.6, ed. Liebermann, *Gesetze*, I.42–7; see also Pratt, *Political Thought*, 299.

[60]    Pratt, *Political Thought*, 232–3; Alfred, Introduction 49.7, and 4–4.2, ed. Liebermann, *Gesetze*, I.44–7, 50–1.

[61]    See for example, Lantfred, *Translatio S. Swithuni*, 26, ed. Lapidge, *Cult of St Swithun*, 310–14; Goscelin's *Vita et translatio S. Edithae*, II.4, ed. Wilmart, 'La légende de Ste Edithe', 272.

[62]    Asser, *Life of Alfred*, 106, ed. W.H. Stevenson, *Asser's Life of King Alfred together with the Annals of Saint Neots, Erroneously Ascribed to Asser* (Oxford, 1904), 92–5; Treschow, 'The prologue to Alfred's law code', 81.

[63]    See for example: T.A. Shippey, 'Wealth and wisdom in King Alfred's Preface to the Old English Pastoral Care', *English Historical Review* 94 (1979): 346–55; J.L. Nelson, 'Wealth and Wisdom: The Politics of Alfred the Great', in J.T. Rosenthal (ed.), *Kings and Kingship* (Binghampton, NY, 1986), 31–52; D. Pratt, 'Persuasion and Invention at the Court of King Alfred the Great', in C. Cubitt (ed.), *Court Culture in the Early Middle Ages: The Proceedings of the First Alcuin Conference* (Turnhout, 2003), 189–222.

[64]    Treschow, 'The prologue to Alfred's law code', 81–2.

[65]    Alfred, Introduction, 40–1, 46, ed. Liebermann, *Gesetze*, I.40–1; Treschow, 'The prologue to Alfred's law code', 101.

give judgement to the poor', which was rendered as a more specific instruction to judge all men equally, rich and poor alike.[66]

However, this adaptation is an indicator that Alfred's main point about mercy may have applied more to the making of law than to the application of law and to the practice of judging: judges were not apparently supposed to make distinctions in judgement but instead were instructed to treat everyone equally, according to the written law which Alfred had set down. As Alfred notes, one might think that no lawbook were needed if all judges followed the principle of judging according to how they would wish to be judged, but this statement is immediately followed by a discussion of how bishops and other wise men came together to discuss merciful laws. In any case, Alfred evidently thought that a lawbook was still necessary since he incorporated these comments into the lawbook that he was writing. Moreover, the introduction contains many excerpts from Exodus which regulate specific practices such as slaves, property or wandering cattle, and which may or may not have been directly relevant in Alfred's kingdom, suggesting that the value of the preface as a guide to judging might have been fairly limited.[67] And even if the putative judges requiring instruction were able to read Old English easily and fluently, it seems unlikely that many of them would have waded through the whole preface frequently if in fact for regular judgements they required the specific decrees of the main law code, although it is significant that the instructions about merciful judgement are placed just before the decrees proper, so that the relevant information was kept closest to the penalties stipulated. In fact, Alfred's selection and adaptation of scriptural texts in the preface seems to be more like the end result of serious consideration about how the process of lawgiving was to be done, so that mercy and merciful judgement were integrated into law at the stage of its production rather than being entirely dependent on the discretion of judges to ensure its application.

Instructions to judges to judge mercifully are found also in the legal treatise known as *Iudex*, which probably dates to the early tenth century; but here too some of the emphasis on mercy may have been intended to apply at the stage of lawmaking rather than, or as well as, in the application of the law.[68] For the most part, *Iudex* is an Old English translation of Alcuin's chapter on judges and judging from his *De virtutibus et vitiis*: both texts begin by warning that each judge should make his judgements with righteousness and with mercy, and note that while some offences require correction, others should be forgiven through mercy.[69] The recommendation to differentiate

---

[66]  Ex 23:6; Alfred, Introduction, 43, ed. Liebermann, *Gesetze*, I.40–1.

[67]  e.g. Alfred, Introduction, 11, 15–17, 28, 35, ed. Liebermann, *Gesetze*, I.28–9, 30–3, 36–7, 38–9.

[68]  See R. Torkar, *Eine altenglische Übersetzung von Alcuins 'De virtutibus et vitiis', Kap. 20 (Liebermanns Judex): Untersuchungen und Textausgabe*, Texte und Untersuchungen zur englischen Philologie 7 (Munich, 1981).

[69]  Iudex, 1–2, ed. Liebermann, *Gesetze*, I.474; ll. 1–10, ed. Torkar, *Altenglische Übersetzung*, 248–9.

between offences, and especially to respond mercifully to some offences, seems to be more important for the lawmaker who set down in written law which offences deserved which penalties; it may also suggest though that both written and unwritten laws might be intended as a flexible guide for judges rather than as a rigid and unbending set of rules. Once again the Last Judgement is held up as the most important model for judges who handed down earthly sentences. Both Alcuin and the Old English *Iudex* quote Jesus's statement, 'with whatever judgement you judge, so you will be judged',[70] and from this Alcuin concludes that the (earthly) judge should fear God as judge, so that in judging he is not damned by God.[71] *Iudex* takes a similar line but warns more explicitly that judges should take care so that at the Last Judgement when they come before God, they are not left dumb and condemned.[72]

According to these texts, the effects of applying the law could therefore potentially be damaging to the souls of judges who passed sentences, and this is discussed in more detail in the Old English *Consolation of Boethius*, one of the texts traditionally attributed to King Alfred's translation programme, although it may in fact have been produced in the early tenth century.[73] The Old English *Boethius* adapts and develops the Latin text in its exploration of the role of the judge, applying penitential language and ideas to the principles and effects of judgements, and ultimately casting the judge in a similar role to the confessor, as Nicole Marafioti shows.[74] The Old English *Boethius* unambiguously treats punishment as a process which benefits the offender by saving his immortal soul, and here the judge's sentences are seen as merciful because ultimately they benefit the offenders, who will suffer less in the next world if they have suffered appropriate punishments in this one.[75] This is striking not only in the simple fact of the translator's adaptation of the Latin text, but also because this seems to be borrowed directly from penitential thought and the way that spiritual atonement and ecclesiastical penance were understood: similar statements are found in the works of patristic authors such as Caesarius of Arles and Augustine.[76] Although it

---

[70]    Mt 7:2.

[71]    Alcuin, *De virtutibus et vitiis*, 20, *PL* 128.628C–629B.

[72]    Iudex, 5–6, ed. Liebermann, *Gesetze*, I.474; ll. 19–26, ed. Torkar, *Altenglische Übersetzung*, 248–51.

[73]    See M. Godden and S. Irvine, *The Old English Boethius: An Edition of the Old English Versions of Boethius's 'De consolatione philosophiae'* (2 vols, Oxford, 2009); N. Marafioti, 'Spiritual Dangers and Earthly Consequences: Judging and Punishing in the Old English *Consolation of Philosophy*', in J. Gates and N. Marafioti (eds), *Capital and Corporal Punishment* (forthcoming). I am grateful to Nicole Marafioti for allowing me to see the text of her article prior to publication.

[74]    Marafioti, 'Spiritual Dangers'.

[75]    *Old English Consolation of Boethius*, B-text, 38, ll. 94–255, ed. Godden and Irvine, *Old English Boethius*, I.352–7; Marafioti, 'Spiritual Dangers'.

[76]    Caesarius, *Sermo* 179.4–5, ed. G. Morin, *Caesarius arelatensis opera pars I,2, Sermones*, CCSL 103–4 (2 vols, Turnhout, 1953), II.726–7; Augustine, *Enarrationes in*

is difficult to find any secure context for the Old English *Boethius*, it is significant that the interpretation of judicial punishment that this text presents would also deflect from the king the burden of stipulating severe penalties in law, whether that king was Alfred or one of his successors.

Principles from penitential theology were also borrowed to interpret how the application of secular law affected the souls of offenders and judges: the translator of *Boethius* presented an interpretation of judicial punishment which had the (rather shocking) effect of allowing that innocent men who were mistakenly punished did not contribute a burden to the soul of the judge. This was because such an injustice was still considered to be less important than making sure that those who required punishment received it, and probably also (although this is not stated) because innocent men who were punished unfairly in this world would also suffer less in the next world as a result.[77] This is not to say that the author was uninterested in just judgements, since it is clear that here as elsewhere, proper justice was a matter of some concern. The punishments referred to in *Boethius* seem to be corporal rather than capital, and so it is difficult to know how severe but non-lethal punishments were squared with judicial execution, when that was demanded. This is especially important in the case of innocent men who were punished incorrectly, and there is evidence that at least from the tenth century, the use of capital punishment in cases where the guilt or innocence of the accused might be unclear or difficult to discern provoked uncertainty and unease from lawmakers and probably also their ecclesiastical advisers.[78] It is precisely these situations in which merciful judgement was so crucial, even though what this meant in practice could be open to multiple interpretations.

In tenth-century laws the mercy which was so carefully recommended by Alfred seems to have become increasingly remote. The laws of Æthelstan in particular are very severe and marked by a determination to deal with the problem of theft, which seems to have become something of an obsession over the course of Æthelstan's reign.[79] Even here though, it is clear that where leading ecclesiastics were involved they advised alternatives to capital punishment, indicating that the hagiographical stories which pitted secular demands for the death penalty against ecclesiastical recommendations of mercy may have had some genuine basis in terms of the attitudes espoused by the different sides. This is illustrated clearly by one of the regional variations of Æthelstan's laws, now surviving only in a Latin translation: the decrees of the bishops and councillors of Kent advocate the pardoning of all offenders who were prepared to perform ecclesiastical penance

---

*Psalmos*, XXXVII.3, ed. E. Dekkers and I. Fraipont, *Sancti Aurelii Augustini enarrationes in Psalmos*, CCSL 38–40 (3 vols, Turnhout, 1956), III.383–4.

[77]     *Old English Consolation of Boethius*, B-text, 38, ll. 210–55, ed. Godden and Irvine, *Old English Boethius*, I.356–7; Marafioti, 'Spiritual Dangers'.

[78]     See below, 149–50.

[79]     Wormald, *Making of English Law*, 305.

and refrain from offending in future.[80] The phrasing of the decree suggests that this was a once-only possibility, since the offenders were required to confess their offences and make amends for them 'between now and August', and the king is thanked for granting this 'gift'; it seems likely though that the impetus for this may have come not from the king himself, but from the bishops and councillors who drew up the decrees.[81]

One of the harshest rulings in Æthelstan's laws is that thieves who were over twelve years old should not be spared if they were caught in the act of stealing goods worth more than eight pence, and this ruling reappears in a modified form in the ordinances drawn up by the bishops and reeves of London, which give the value of the goods as over twelve pence instead.[82] But some time later, another instruction from the king was added to the end of the London ordinances, reconsidering the severity of the decree and changing the age from twelve to fifteen: this is given in the king's voice and states that the king had decided that on balance, he thought it was cruel to put such young people to death for small offences, and therefore sent Bishop Theodred of London to pass on these additional instructions to Archbishop Wulfhelm of Canterbury.[83] At first glance, it seems as if this decision over the use of capital punishment came from the royal person rather than from his ecclesiastical advisers, and as Victoria Thompson notes, the meeting at Whittlebury where this decision was conveyed to the king's councillors is the only one of Æthelstan's meetings which Wulfhelm seems not to have attended.[84]

On closer inspection, the situation is more complex and may reflect the influence of canon law on the process of secular lawmaking. The decree giving twelve as the minimum age for judicial execution (II Æthelstan 1) was promulgated at an assembly at Grately at which Wulfhelm was present and seems to have contributed to the lawmaking process.[85] This decree is paralleled in collections of canon law like the eighth-century *Collectio Canonum Hibernensis*, and in related texts such as the *Excerpta libris romanorum et francorum*, by a statement that twelve was the minimum age at which boys should give restitution.[86] However, there is also a variant version of this statement which stipulates fifteen rather than twelve as

---

[80]   III Æthelstan 3, ed. Liebermann, *Gesetze*, I.170.

[81]   III Æthelstan 3, ed. Liebermann, *Gesetze*, I.170: 'hinc ad Augustum'.

[82]   II Æthelstan 1; VI Æthelstan 1, ed. Liebermann, *Gesetze*, I.150–1, 173.

[83]   VI Æthelstan 12.1, ed. Liebermann, *Gesetze*, I.182–3.

[84]   Thompson, *Dying and Death*, 181.

[85]   Wormald, *Making of English Law*, 291–300, 305.

[86]   It is found in the B-text of the *Collectio Canonum Hibernensis*, LIII.5 ('Paruulus usque annum .xii. pro delicto nihil reddat nisi disciplinam accipiat ...'), and in the A-text of the *Excerpta libris romanorum et francorum*, 26, ed. L. Bieler and D.A. Binchy, *The Irish Penitentials*, Scriptores Latini Hiberniae 5 (Dublin, 1963), 140. The influence seems to run from the *Collectio* to the *Excerpta*, a Breton law code: see D.N. Dumville, 'On the dating of the early Breton lawcodes', *Etudes celtiques* 21:1–2 (1984): 207–21, at 217–20.

the minimum age, a discrepancy caused probably by scribal confusion between the Roman numerals xii and xu or xv.[87] Both versions of these texts seem to have arrived in England from Brittany in the early tenth century along with numerous other books, either during Æthelstan's reign or perhaps even earlier, in the reign of Edward the Elder (d.924).[88] There are four surviving manuscripts containing the *Hibernensis* (or selections from it) which seem to have been imported into England from Brittany at this time, and at least one of them has connections with Canterbury.[89] This means that the version of the canon which gives twelve as the age of restitution was therefore almost certainly available in England and perhaps at Canterbury at the time when this decree was drawn up, and it is therefore possible that this, mediated by Wulfhelm, is the influence behind the minimum age of execution given in II Æthelstan 1.

However, the version which gives fifteen as the minimum age for restitution was evidently also available in England at some stage, not least because it appears as part of the longer (and later) recension of the collection of canon law found in a number of the manuscripts associated with Archbishop Wulfstan of York.[90] The parallels in the minimum age of 'responsibility' found in these variant versions of canons and also in Æthelstan's laws are interesting for the possibility they raise of the influence of canon law on Anglo-Saxon legal texts. In the absence of close verbal parallels, this correspondence does not necessarily imply that there is direct influence here; but at the same time it is still noteworthy because there is

---

[87]   This is the A-text of the *Collectio*, LV.7 ('Paruulus usque ad annos .xv. pro delicto nihil reddat nisi disciplinam recipiet'), and the P-text of the *Excerpta*, 18, ed. Bieler and Binchy, *The Irish Penitentials*, 152–3; see also Dumville, 'On the dating of the early Breton lawcodes', 217–20.

[88]   S. Ambrose, 'The *Collectio Canonum Hibernensis* and the literature of the Anglo-Saxon Benedictine reform', *Viator* 36 (2005): 107–18, at 107–9; see also S. Keynes, 'King Æthelstan's Books', in M. Lapidge and H. Gneuss (eds), *Learning and Literature in Anglo-Saxon England: Studies Presented to Peter Clemoes on the Occasion of his Sixty-Fifth Birthday* (Cambridge, 1985), 143–201, esp. 195–8.

[89]   These are London, British Library, Cotton Otho E.xiii and Royal 5.E.xiii; Oxford, Bodleian Library, Hatton 42; and Cambridge, Corpus Christi College, 279. Shannon Ambrose suggests that in the early 940s Archbishop Oda of Canterbury may have used Otho E.xiii: see Ambrose, 'Collectio Canonum Hibernensis', 110. It is also possible that Hatton 42 was available at Canterbury at some point in the tenth century: see T.A.M. Bishop, 'Notes on Cambridge Manuscripts, Part VI', *Transactions of the Cambridge Bibliographical Society* 3 (1959–63): 412–23; Hatton 42 contains the B-text of the *Collectio* and the A-text of the *Excerpta*, both of which give 12 as the age for 'discipline'.

[90]   Recension B.104, ed. J.E. Cross and A. Hamer, *Wulfstan's Canon Law Collection* (Cambridge, 1999), 139 (for discussion of the canon law collection, see further below, 179–80, and Table 3.1). This is particularly interesting given that Wulfstan used Hatton 42 and made annotations in it: see N.R. Ker, 'The Handwriting of Archbishop Wulfstan', in P. Clemoes and K. Hughes (eds), *England before the Conquest: Studies in Primary Sources Presented to Dorothy Whitelock* (Cambridge, 1971), 315–31, at 318, 328–30.

no other overwhelmingly obvious reason for the specific change from twelve to fifteen recorded in Æthelstan's laws. Given the attitudes of churchmen to capital punishment in other contexts, it seems highly likely that some bishops might have been inclined to use canon law to mitigate capital punishment where possible.

It is may be that the crucial figure here is Bishop Theodred, who, as bishop of London, might have conveyed the London ordinances to Æthelstan. One of the milder stipulations in the London ordinances, the raising of the value of the goods to twelve pence, features also in the instructions which Theodred brought from Æthelstan to Wulfhelm, and it is possible therefore that Theodred had also advised this change so that thieves were not put to death 'for such small offences', as Æthelstan notes.[91] And although the ordinances record what the king had instructed, it is clear that he did not make the decision by himself: he states that 'it seemed to him and to those with whom he had discussed it that no one should slay those who are younger than fifteen years', suggesting that others, perhaps including Theodred, had played a role in raising the age for execution.[92] Theodred is an interesting figure here in any case because he features in a miracle described in the later tenth-century *Life of Edmund* written by Abbo of Fleury (and repeated in Ælfric's translation and adaptation of the *Life*), where he was reported to have insisted on the death penalty for men who were caught trying to steal treasure from Bury St Edmund's. Theodred apparently decided rather belatedly that this was an inappropriate response, and therefore lamented greatly and performed penance for the rest of his life.[93] It is difficult to determine the veracity of the account, and it is of course possible that Abbo's story is less than accurate, but it is striking nonetheless that it is Theodred who is implicated in the king's decision to change the age at which the death penalty could be applied, even if only by merit of acting as the news-bearer.

With the exception of Æthelstan's complaint about young people being put to death, there is scarcely any visible engagement in the laws of his reign with ideas about the use of the death penalty, or why it might (or might not) have been considered an appropriate response to particular crimes. It has been suggested that the swearing of oaths of loyalty, mentioned for the first time at the beginning of Alfred's code, had the effect of setting all offenders against the king, with the result that many more offences (such as theft) could be included in an increasingly broad interpretation of treachery, the crime where divine

---

[91]   VI Æthelstan 12.3, ed. Liebermann, *Gesetze*, I.183.

[92]   VI Æthelstan 12.1, Liebermann, *Gesetze*, I.182–3.

[93]   Abbo's *Passio S. Eadmundi* is ed. M. Winterbottom, *Three Lives of English Saints* (Toronto, 1972), 67–87 (XV, 83–5); and T. Arnold, *Memorials of St Edmund's Abbey* (London, 1890), I.3–25 (XVI, at 20–2); Ælfric's Old English translation of the *Life* is ed. and trans. W.W. Skeat, *Aelfric's Lives of Saints, Being a Set of Sermons on Saints' Days Formerly Observed by the English Church*, EETS 76, 82 (vol. 1), 94, 114 (vol. 2) (4 vols in 2, London, 1881–1900), II.314–35; this episode is at ll. 198–230.

and royal mercy reached its limits.[94] But it may also be simply that kings took a harsher approach to crime for other reasons, such as an increasingly large area of jurisdiction which was more difficult to control, and repeated problems with theft.[95] Tenth- and eleventh-century law codes include decrees limiting direct appeals to the king except where fair judgements had not been obtained, perhaps connected either with changing systems of local government or with the much expanded area for which kings now theoretically had responsibility for jurisdiction.[96] The possibility of appealing to the royal person for mercy was therefore somewhat limited, but in practice decisions on such matters were presumably dependent to a great extent on politics and patronage, in the tenth and eleventh centuries as probably also earlier.[97]

Whatever the reasons behind the apparent increase in the use of capital and corporal punishment in the early tenth century, the effect is that Æthelstan's laws seem exceedingly harsh and draconian, and it is therefore significant that the only other possibilities for evading the death penalty in Æthelstan's law codes are found in the very specific context of cases where proof was uncertain, or difficult to obtain. Æthelstan's laws include the first decrees which provide any significant information about the use of judicial ordeals, which seem to have been used when other forms of evidence or proof were not available, and it is striking to see that those who failed ordeals were not always put to death even when admitting guilt for the same offence would have occasioned execution. In light of concern over the use of the death penalty before, during and after Æthelstan's reign, it seems likely that this too indicates some uncertainty over when judicial execution was appropriate, but it is also significant that ordeals were considered at various times and places to be problematic. Then as now, it could be difficult to prove that someone had actually committed the offence of which he was accused, but in the absence of other evidence, God was the final court of appeal.

## Means of Proof: Oaths and Ordeals

In situations where there was clear-cut evidence, cases were decided on the basis of witnesses and testimony. But where identifying the truth of a matter was not so straightforward, or where the truth was simply disputed, oaths or ordeals could be used as means of proof, or at least of ascertaining some sense of which way

---

[94]   Pratt, *Political Thought*, 233–4. See also *Councils and Synods*, I.i.75–6, for discussion of Theodred.

[95]   Cf. Wormald, *Making of English Law*, 305.

[96]   e.g. II Æthelstan 3; III Edgar 2–2.1, ed. Liebermann, *Gesetze*, I.152–3, 200–1.

[97]   See, for example, S 883; S 1445; N. Brooks, 'The Fonthill Letter, Ealdorman Ordlaf and Anglo-Saxon Law in Practice', in S.D. Baxter et al. (eds), *Early Medieval Studies in Memory of Patrick Wormald* (Farnham, Surrey, 2009), 301–17.

the case ought to be decided.[98] Oaths and ordeals involved a direct appeal to God and made reference to the Last Judgement, and they are particularly interesting case studies for the impact of theology on law because here ecclesiastical and secular interests coincided in a significant way. Moreover, in the eleventh and twelfth centuries it was particularly in the context of ordeals that many theoretical questions concerning the effects of religious belief and practice on secular law began to come under scrutiny, as with the relationship between law and penance and more generally. Developments in penitential theology and in ideas about the effects of sin and guilt from the later eleventh century would have significant implications for how innocence and guilt according to secular law were understood and determined, so that for example in the twelfth century, theologians would wrestle with the difficult problem of the effects of confession on the process of ordeals. One of the questions posed was whether someone would fail an ordeal which sought to prove his guilt or innocence if he had already confessed his sins and thus cleansed himself of them, so that he was no longer 'guilty'; another was whether a secular penalty should be performed for an offence which had been confessed, if the offender was thereby no longer 'guilty'.[99]

These kinds of questions are not explored in surviving English or continental sources dating from before the later eleventh century, although there are objections to ordeals as well as expressions of support for them from contemporary continental writers, often backed up by both theological and practical reasoning.[100] The most famous Carolingian critic of ordeals was Agobard of Lyon (d.840), who argued that God simply did not reveal the secrets of men through the elements of hot iron or water, while Hincmar of Rheims seems to have supported ordeals as much because of political exigency as because of any real faith in their value as means of proof.[101] In contrast, no surviving Anglo-Saxon texts discuss ordeals in an explicitly theoretical or theological way, and so the evidence is limited to legislative texts, liturgical rituals, one hagiographical narrative account, and a couple of hints in charters. The absence of documented cases where ordeals were used is itself interesting,

---

[98]   R. Bartlett, *Trial by Fire and Water: The Medieval Judicial Ordeal* (Oxford, 1986), 26–30. See for example the legal case outlined in S 1454, discussed in Wormald, *Making of English Law*, 151–2; Wormald, 'Giving God and King their Due: Conflict and its Regulation in the early English State'; or the disputes in the Domesday Book, discussed in P. Wormald, 'Domesday Lawsuits: A Provisional List and Preliminary Comment', in Hicks (ed.), *England in the Eleventh Century*, 61–102; R. Fleming, *Domesday Book and the Law: Society and Legal Custom in Early Medieval England* (Cambridge, 1998).

[99]   Bartlett, *Trial by Fire and Water*, 79–80.

[100]   Ibid., 72–86.

[101]   Agobard, *Liber adversus legem Gundobaldi*, 9, *PL* 141.118B–120A; Hincmar, *De divortio Lotharii regis et Theutbergae reginae*, VII–X, ed. L. Böhringer, *Hinkmar von Reims, De divortio Lotharii regis et Theutbergae reginae*, MGH, Concilia IV, Supplementum 1 (Hannover, 1992), 146–74.

especially given the comparatively detailed stipulations in tenth- and eleventh-century legal texts about ordeals as a means of proof. In contrast to the rest of contemporary Europe, ordeals were apparently not employed in Anglo-Saxon England to settle civil cases such as property disputes,[102] and since most of the surviving evidence for disputes concerns property, this may be one reason for Anglo-Saxon silence on recorded cases of ordeals. There is one recorded case where it looks like someone might reasonably have been expected to undergo an ordeal – Helmstan's theft, described in the early tenth-century Fonthill Letter – but the matter was resolved without recourse to this.[103] The evidence for Anglo-Saxon attitudes to ordeals is therefore rather fragmented but there are signs that ordeals were subject to some scrutiny as the death penalty was; more importantly, the evidence for uncertainty or unease over ordeals is also tightly bound up with similar attitudes to the death penalty. Furthermore, the importance of theology to secular judicial process is made abundantly clear in the ways that oaths and ordeals were used, and what was especially important here was whether those who swore oaths and ordeals understood the theology that lay behind them.

*Oaths*

The process of swearing an oath made direct reference to the Last Judgement and to the invisible power of sanctified objects, because oaths were frequently sworn over holy items such as gospel-books, crosses, altars or relics (sometimes themselves contained in altars), and often in churches.[104] Non-judicial oaths could also be sworn over holy items, as illustrated in the Bayeux Tapestry by the famous example of Harold swearing an oath over relics to William of Normandy (and looking rather uncomfortable in the process).[105] By the involvement of sacred

---

[102]    P.R. Hyams, 'Trial by Ordeal: The Key to Proof in the Early Common Law', in M.S. Arnold et al. (eds), *On the Laws and Customs of England: Essays in Honor of Samuel E. Thorne* (Chapel Hill, 1981), 90–126, at 106–7.

[103]    Wormald, *Making of English Law*, 148.

[104]    See for example *ASC* (A), s.a. 876, ed. J. Bately, *The Anglo-Saxon Chronicle: A Collaborative Edition: Vol. 3, MS A: A Semi-Diplomatic Edition with Introduction and Indices* (Cambridge, 1986), 50; *Old English Canons of Theodore*, 76.04.01, 76.04.04–05 and *Old English Scriftboc* 18.01.01–18.02.01, ed. Frantzen, *The Anglo-Saxon Penitentials: A Cultural Database*; Wihtred 18–21, ed. Oliver, *The Beginnings of English Law*, 158–61; and the formulae for oaths, 1–2, ed. Liebermann, *Gesetze*, I.396–7; P.J. Geary, *Furta sacra: Thefts of Relics in the Central Middle Ages* (Princeton, NJ, 1990), 25, 37–8.

[105]    This oath and its nature, as well as how (or if) it took place, has been much discussed: see O.K. Werckmeister, 'The political ideology of the Bayeux Tapestry', *Studi Medievali* 17, 3rd series (1976): 535–95, at 563–79; D. Bernstein, 'The blinding of Harold and the meaning of the Bayeux Tapestry', *Anglo-Norman Studies* 5 (1982): 40–64, at 49–53; J.B. McNulty, *The Narrative Art of the Bayeux Tapestry Master* (New York, 1989), 73; W.R. Lethaby, 'The Perjury at Bayeux', in R. Gameson (ed.), *The Study of the Bayeux Tapestry* (Woodbridge, 1997), 19–20; N.J. Higham, 'Harold Godwinesson: The

items, the judgement of God and the saints is invited upon those who swear, and the formulae for oath-swearing indicate that it was the involvement of God or the saints, and the threat of punishment from them, which was intended to prevent people from swearing oaths falsely.[106] But apart from in exceptional cases, such as the peasant who swore falsely that land belonged to him instead of to St Ecgwine,[107] the judgement and penalty for perjury were expected to be remote, so that the oath 'relied upon God's eventual rather than his immediate judgement'.[108]

This principle is quite straightforward, but understanding how oaths worked in Anglo-Saxon England is rather more complex. The word 'að' refers to a number of types of oath, and the various types might be broken in slightly different ways.[109] Oaths of loyalty were sworn to kings or lords;[110] oaths of allegiance might be sworn by one ruler to another;[111] and oaths might be sworn in the context of drawing up treaties between different parties.[112] From the later tenth century, the king himself had to swear an oath at his coronation ceremony, promising to uphold justice and mercy.[113] Many of these promissory oaths are infrequently referred to before the late ninth century, but it is clear that once instituted such promises were not always kept: homilists and statesman alike frequently urged people to keep their oaths and pledges,[114] or complained that oaths (and pledges) were broken.[115] For the most part, however, promissory oaths were not part of the legal process of ascertaining proof in order to determine the rights or wrongs of a disputed case, because they refer to future behaviour rather than to knowledge about past events or facts.

---

Construction of Kingship', in G.R. Owen-Crocker (ed.), *King Harold II and the Bayeux Tapestry* (Woodbridge, 2005), 19–34, at 19–21.

[106]   The oath formulae are ed. Liebermann, *Gesetze*, I.396–7.

[107]   *Vita S. Ecgwini*, IV.10, ed. M. Lapidge, *The Lives of St Oswald and St Ecgwine* (Oxford, 2009), 290–6; see also above 26–7.

[108]   Bartlett, *Trial by Fire and Water*, 30.

[109]   A. Cameron, A. Crandell Amos and A. diPaolo Healey, *Dictionary of Old English: A to G online* (2007), http://tapor.library.utoronto.ca/doe/index.html, accessed October 2012: 'āþ'.

[110]   e.g. Alfred 1, ed. Liebermann, *Gesetze*, I.46–7; see also above, 149–50.

[111]   Cameron, Crandell Amos and diPaolo Healey, *Dictionary of Old English: A to G online*: 'āþ', definition 1.a.iv (e.g. ASC (C), s.a. 1049, ed. K.O.B. O'Keeffe, *The Anglo-Saxon Chronicle: A Collaborative Edition: Vol. 5, MS C: A Semi-Diplomatic Edition with Introduction and Indices* (Cambridge, 2001), 109–11).

[112]   Alfred and Guthrum, Prol., ed. Liebermann, *Gesetze*, I.126–7; see also Cameron, Crandell Amos and diPaolo Healey, *Dictionary of Old English: A to G online*: 'āþ', definition 1.a.i.a.ii.

[113]   See Stafford, 'The laws of Cnut and the history of Anglo-Saxon royal promises'; Clayton, 'The Old English promissio regis'.

[114]   e.g. Alfred 1; V Æthelred 22:2, ed. Liebermann, *Gesetze*, I.46–7, 242–3.

[115]   e.g. IV Æthelstan 3:2, V Æthelstan Prol 3, ed. Liebermann, *Gesetze*, I.166.

The legal processes of seeking truth where it was not clear relied on oaths of accusation, compurgation or exculpation, and on the oaths which might be sworn by those who gave testimony as witnesses. Depending on period and context, the law might require that one or more people be involved in swearing these oaths, with people of different ranks requiring different numbers of co-swearers, or oath-helpers.[116] The proceedings might be initiated by oaths of accusation, whereas an oath of exculpation was sworn by the accused to deny his involvement in the matter, and in some cases the accused was required to find a certain number of people who would attest to his good character by swearing an oath of compurgation, thereby clearing his name of the accusation.[117] Depending on the circumstances, witnesses might also be asked to swear an oath to support the information they offered, and it is clear from law codes and the surviving formulae for oath-swearing that witnesses' oaths, like oaths of accusation, exculpation or compurgation, were often sworn over relics.[118] There are also references to a 'fore-oath' ('foreað') in legal processes, although the word occurs only twelve times in the Old English Corpus, and again may have held a range of meanings according to context.[119] Alfred's law code describes a process in which the accuser pronounces a 'foreað' in four churches, while the defendant pronounces the 'foreað' in twelve churches.[120] One of Æthelstan's law codes mentions a 'foreað' as part of an ordeal, but it is not clear whether this means the oath sworn by the proband before he undergoes the ordeal, or a preliminary oath of accusation, such as is found in several other legal texts.[121]

It is difficult to ascertain whether the different types of oaths sworn in disputes retained the same meaning or significance by the tenth or eleventh centuries that they had in the seventh or eighth centuries, and certainly aspects of the process had changed by this time. Some decrees suggest that certain types of people were considered to have an innate authority or trustworthiness. One of Æthelstan's codes identifies trustworthy people who can act as witnesses, including priests and reeves, while in the late seventh-century laws of King Wihtred of Kent (d.726), for example, the testimony of bishops and kings was held to be valid

---

[116]   See for example Wihtred 12–19, ed. Oliver, *The Beginnings of English Law*, 158–61; I Æthelred 1–1.13; and *Að*, ed. Liebermann, *Gesetze*, I.216–19, 464–5.

[117]   Cameron, Crandell Amos and diPaolo Healey, *Dictionary of Old English: A to G online*: 'āþ', see for example definitions 1.b, 1.b.ii.e; cf. II Cnut 22–2.3, ed. Liebermann, *Gesetze*, I.324–5.

[118]   III Æthelred 2.1, ed. Liebermann, *Gesetze*, I.228–9.

[119]   Cameron, Crandell Amos and diPaolo Healey, *Dictionary of Old English: A to G online*: 'fore-āþ'.

[120]   Alfred 33, ed. Liebermann, *Gesetze*, I.66–7.

[121]   II Æthelstan 23.2, ed. Liebermann, *Gesetze*, I.162–5; cf. II Cnut 22.1–2; *Dunsæte* 6:2; *Geþyncðo* 3, ed. Liebermann, *Gesetze*, I.324–5, 378–9, 456–7.

without an oath.[122] Wihtred's code also instructs that other members of the clergy should swear oaths with or without helpers according to their rank, and in almost all cases this was to take place over an altar.[123] In contrast, other law codes (especially later codes) prescribe different ways of swearing oaths according to religious status (such as laity or clergy) or rank (within either secular or ecclesiastical hierarchies),[124] but sometimes the procedures are outlined in such a way that they seem (at least theoretically) to have applied to a much wider range of individuals with little regard for their status.[125] And despite procedural changes, the basic principle of how oaths were understood to work, and their effectiveness as methods of determining the truth, seems to have remained the same: retribution would follow at the Last Judgement if not before, either from God or from his saints.

This is important in understanding how the breaking of oaths, or the swearing of false oaths, was perceived in a technical and terminological sense. From a modern perspective, perjury refers either to the act of swearing to information which is known to be false, or (perhaps more technically) to the act of swearing a promissory oath without the intention of keeping it.[126] The concept of 'false oaths' or 'false swearing' seems to cover both of these, but may also include a sense of 'perjury' now rare in modern English, the act of breaking a promise or vow.[127] One of Ine's decrees requires compensation from someone who breaks a pledge which was given in the bishop's presence, although since the word for 'pledge' ('wed') has a range of meanings it is possible that what is referred to here is not the same as the oaths of loyalty or allegiance in later law codes.[128] Anglo-Saxon penitentials and law codes both refer rather vaguely to false oaths or perjury without specifying

---

[122] II Æthelstan 9, ed. Liebermann, *Gesetze*, I.154–5; Wihtred 12, ed. Oliver, *The Beginnings of English Law*, 158–9. There is no information about what should happen in the event of a dispute between two bishops, or between a bishop and a king (for example).

[123] Wihtred 13–17, ed. Oliver, *The Beginnings of English Law*, 158–9.

[124] See Ine 54, ed. Liebermann, *Gesetze*, I.112–15; or for Archbishop Wulfstan's multiple takes on this, compare the procedure for exculpation outlined for ecclesiastics in I Cnut 5–6 with that outlined for those in secular life in II Cnut 30–33.2, and with the compilations *Geþyncðo* and *Að*, ed. Liebermann, *Gesetze*, I.285–9, 330–7, 456–9, 464–5.

[125] e.g. Alfred 4–4.2; I Edward 1–1.5, 3; II Edward 3–3.2, II Æthelstan 9, ed. Liebermann, *Gesetze*, I.50–1, 138–41, 142–3, 154–5.

[126] Oxford English Dictionary, *perjury, n.*, http://www.oed.com/view/Entry/141131, accessed June 2012: see definitions 1a, 1b, 2.

[127] Liebermann, *Gesetze*, II.580–1: *Meineid* [2]; Cameron, Crandell Amos and diPaolo Healey, *Dictionary of Old English: A to G online*: 'āþ', definition 1.a.iii.a, 'man aþ' (or 'manaþ').

[128] Ine 13, ed. Liebermann, *Gesetze*, I.94. For detailed discussion of the word 'wed' in Old English, see M. Ammon, 'Pledges and Agreements in Old English: A Semantic Field Study', PhD thesis, University of Cambridge, 2010, with discussion of Ine 13 at 28, 59, 109.

whether this includes oath-breaking as well as swearing an oath while knowing that the information sworn to is false.[129]

On the other hand, the writings of continental early medieval scholars such as Burchard of Worms (d.1025) indicate that *periurium* encompassed the full range of meanings from oath-breaking to both deliberate and unintentional false swearing, and it seems likely that this Latin term and its Old English equivalents were understood in a similar way in Anglo-Saxon England.[130] It is also clear that unintentional false swearing was a matter of concern in England as elsewhere: several of the penitentials include penances to be prescribed in the event that someone swore an oath falsely but only discovered later that it was false, which would be particularly relevant (for example) in the case of oath-helpers who attested to someone's good character and thus cleared him, but later discovered evidence of his guilt.[131] The law codes themselves seem to indicate that the breaking of promissory oaths and the swearing of false oaths were seen as broadly equivalent or comparable, and that both were understood to bring the soul into danger, because it is in these contexts that the involvement of the bishop or the recommendation of penance is most often visible, often in addition to some form of secular penalty.[132]

In terms of understanding the impact of theology on the law this is highly significant, because it means that the legal process of swearing oaths was utterly dependent for its efficacy on all parties concerned knowing and believing that perjury in all its senses would be punished severely at the Last Judgement, even if perjurers were not discovered during their own lifetimes. The use of oaths in the legal system was therefore completely underpinned by a Christian belief that offenders would not want to risk the danger to the soul that swearing false oaths and breaking promises would bring. Unsurprisingly, those who were prepared to commit serious offences were probably precisely those who were prepared to take that risk: convicted perjurers might be subject to heavy penalties in the worldly systems of law and penance as well as at the Last Judgement, but (then as now) would-be offenders may have assumed that they simply would not be found out

---

[129]     e.g. *Old English Scriftboc*, 18.01.01 (false oath in church, on relics or on a gospel-book), 18.02.01 (false oath on a bishop's or deacon's hand, or on a consecrated cross); *Old English Canons of Theodore*, 76.04.01 (false oath in church), 76.04.04 (false oath on a bishop's or deacon's hand, on a consecrated cross or on an altar); 76.04.05 (false oath on an unconsecrated cross; 76.04.06 (false oaths); *Old English Penitential*, 42.24.01 (swearing falsely and knowing of the perjury), 42.24.02 (being compelled to swear falsely, or not knowing that the oath was false), ed. Frantzen, *The Anglo-Saxon Penitentials: A Cultural Database*.

[130]     Burchard, *Decretum*, 12; G. Austin, *Shaping Church Law around the Year 1000: The Decretum of Burchard of Worms* (Farnham, 2009), 190–6.

[131]     *Old English Penitential* 42.24.02; *Scriftboc* 18.03.01, ed. Frantzen, *The Anglo-Saxon Penitentials: A Cultural Database*.

[132]     e.g. Alfred 1.2, ed. Liebermann, *Gesetze*, I.48–9.

and thus could avoid the workings of justice. Regardless of the closer intertwining of the systems of law and penance, the success of the ecclesiastical systems of pastoral care in conveying the messages of Christian teaching to the populace ought theoretically to have played a significant role in supporting the effectiveness of oaths as a legal process, either by encouraging people to keep the promises that they made or by encouraging them not to take the risk of swearing falsely to clear themselves or their friends and family.

It is more difficult to establish how far the threat of divine punishment really put would-be offenders off perjuring themselves, but there is some evidence to suggest that the terror of the Last Judgement was not entirely lessened by its remoteness. Although the law codes are normative texts rather than records, it is probably significant that several decrees include the phrase 'if he dare' when instructing that the accused may clear himself with an oath, and this perhaps indicates that when faced with the choice between swearing an oath and admitting guilt, some individuals might have felt that admission was the safer option.[133] In some cases the law codes also refer to the possibility that someone might admit guilt rather than swear an oath: Ine's laws give instructions for the correct process in the case that someone admits an offence which he previously denied, when instructed to swear an oath to his innocence.[134] Ine's code also includes a decree demanding double compensation from someone who refuses to swear his oath for a second time, on the grounds that the first oath is considered to be false.[135] A number of Anglo-Saxon decrees explain what should happen in the case of people who do not dare to swear oaths when called as helpers to confirm someone's innocence, and the various outcomes for people whose oaths 'fail' or have 'failed' previously.[136] The latter situations apparently indicate not convicted perjurers but cases where the innocence of the accused was sufficiently doubted that the risk of swearing an oath over holy items was considered to be too great, either by the accused himself or by his oath-helpers.

Despite the threat of the Last Judgement, perjury was clearly a significant problem since it was repeatedly dealt with by lawmakers, and often harshly. This may be partly due to its status as a capital sin: it is frequently listed as such in penitentials and was thus comparable to murder or theft, and the penances for it could be severe, especially for oaths sworn falsely in churches and/or over holy items such as relics.[137] From the tenth century in particular, the offence of perjury is

---

[133] e.g. Ine 17, 46.2; II Cnut 75.1, ed. Liebermann, *Gesetze*, I.96–7, 110–11, 362–3.

[134] Ine 71, ed. Liebermann, *Gesetze*, I.120–1.

[135] Ine 35.1, ed. Liebermann, *Gesetze*, I.104–5.

[136] These often use the word 'berstan', apparently as a technical term: see (for example) I Edward 3; I Æthelred 1.13; II Cnut 22, ed. Liebermann, *Gesetze*, I.140–1, 218–19, 324–5; see also Cameron, Crandell Amos and diPaolo Healey, *Dictionary of Old English: A to G online*: 'berstan', definition 5.

[137] e.g. the penance of 11 years for a false oath sworn in church prescribed in the *Old English Canons of Theodore*, 76.04.01, ed. Frantzen, *The Anglo-Saxon Penitentials: A*

one where law and penance seem to have been closely integrated, and particularly in the imposition of spiritual as well as legal penalties. II Æthelstan decrees that someone who swears a false oath is not to be entitled to swear an oath again, and nor is he entitled to burial in consecrated ground, unless he performs penance as the bishop directs.[138] I Edmund groups perjurers with sorcerers and instructs that they be cast out from the Christian community unless they perform the appropriate penance.[139] But in the context of secular justice, perjury must have been extremely disruptive and this may be the overwhelming reason for it being considered such a serious offence. No matter how well organised the systems of pastoral provision and Christian education were, it seems overwhelmingly likely that some people either did not believe that the Last Judgement was a serious threat, or were more concerned with immediate secular punishment than with remote eternal suffering. It is immediately obvious that if such people were accused of offences and the evidence was sparse, the system of oath-swearing was easily open to abuse. Unsurprisingly, ascertaining the truth from convicted perjurers was known to be a problematic exercise, and this is one of the contexts in which the more immediate judgement of ordeals might be used.

*Ordeals*

Like oaths, ordeals are complex and seem to have been subject to significant variation across the period and perhaps also in different areas of England in the early Middle Ages. Ordeals have received considerably more critical attention than oaths, apparently for two reasons. The first is that modern audiences tend to perceive ordeals as both irrational and barbaric, and scholars have therefore tried to discover why such a practice was employed as part of the practice of 'justice'. The second is that ordeals were the subject of criticism and debate from early on, and ecclesiastical involvement in ordeals was ultimately prohibited at the Fourth Lateran Council in 1215, suggesting that at least some of the problems perceived by modern audiences were also recognisable to medieval audiences.[140] Ordeals

---

*Cultural Database.*

[138]   II Æthelstan 26, ed. Liebermann, *Gesetze*, I.164–5.

[139]   I Edmund 6, ed. Liebermann, *Gesetze*, I.186–7.

[140]   For some recent scholarship on different types of ordeals see Hyams, 'Trial by Ordeal'; Bartlett, *Trial by Fire and Water*; R.M. Fraher, 'IV Lateran's Revolution in Criminal Procedure: The Birth of Inquisitio, the End of Ordeals, and Innocent III's Vision of Ecclesiastical Politics', in R.J. Castillo Lara (ed.), *Studia in honorem eminentissimi Cardinalis Alphonsi M. Stickler*, Pontificia Studiorum Universitas Salesiana, Facultas Iuris Canonici, Studia et textus historiae iuris canonici 7 (Rome, 1992), 97–110; J.W. Baldwin, 'From the Ordeal to Confession: In Search of Lay Religion in Early Thirteenth-Century France', in P. Biller and A.J. Minnis (eds), *Handling Sin: Confession in the Middle Ages*, York Studies in Medieval Theology 2 (Woodbridge, 1998), 191–209; S.L. Keefer, '*Ut in omnibus honorificetur Deus*: The *corsnaed* Ordeal in Anglo-Saxon England', in J. Hill

required not only the presence of holy items such as relics, as oaths did, but also the participation of the clergy to perform the liturgical rituals both for ordeals themselves and for the masses and other preparations which preceded ordeals. Ecclesiastical involvement was therefore strictly necessary for ordeals as part of secular judicial procedure, and so here too ecclesiastical officials supported the laws which were issued by royal decree. And once again, the effectiveness of ordeals was at least partly connected with how far the ideas and Christian theology behind them were understood by those who were accused of offences, although naturally the more physical nature of ordeals as compared to oaths was also significant.

Anglo-Saxon legal and liturgical texts outline the ordeals of hot iron, hot water and cold water in some detail. The ordeal of cold water was similar to the method of 'swimming' witches in later periods, in that the person accused of the offence was thrown into cold water and the outcome was based on whether he sank or floated. If the ritual was performed properly, the water was apparently supposed to reject someone who was guilty: liturgical rites for the cold water ordeal ask the Lord to give the desired sign, so that if the person is guilty he should not be received by the water.[141] Whether or not this meant that the proband drowned anyway, or was deliberately drowned afterwards, is unclear: two tenth-century charters which mention offenders who had drowned

---

and M. Swan (eds), *The Community, the Family and the Saint: Patterns of Power in Early Medieval Europe: Selected Proceedings of the International Medieval Congress, University of Leeds, 4–7 July 1994, 10–13 July 1995* (Turnhout, 1998), 237–64; S.D. White, 'Proposing the Ordeal and Avoiding it: Strategy and Power in Western French Litigation, 1050–1100', in T. Bisson (ed.), *Cultures of Power: Lordship, Status and Process in Twelfth-Century Europe* (Philadelphia, 2005), 89–123; F. McAuley, 'Canon law and the end of the ordeal', *Oxford Journal of Legal Studies* 26:3 (2006): 473–513; S.L. Keefer, 'Ðonne se cirlisca man ordales weddigeð: The Anglo-Saxon Lay Ordeal', in S.D. Baxter et al. (eds), *Early Medieval Studies in Memory of Patrick Wormald* (Farnham, 2009), 353–67; J.D. Niles, 'Trial by Ordeal in Anglo-Saxon England: What's the Problem with Barley?', in Baxter et al. (eds), *Early Medieval Studies in Memory of Patrick Wormald*, 369–82; see also R.V. Colman, 'Reason and unreason in early medieval law', *Journal of Interdisciplinary History* 4:4 (1974): 571–91.

[141]   For example, a prayer used for blessing the water in a number of the rituals for the cold water ordeal, here taken from CCCC 422, p. 325: 'Deus ... uirtutem tue benedictionis his aquis infundere et nouum ac mirabile signum in eis ostendere digneris. ut innocentes a crimine furti uel homicidii uel adulterii. aut alterius neui cuius examinationem agimus more aque in se recipiant et in profundum pertrahant. conscius autem huius criminis a se repellant atque reiciant nec patiantur recipere corpus ...' ('God ... deign to pour out the power of your blessing on these waters and to show a new and marvellous sign in them, so that those whose examination we make, if they are innocent of the crime of theft or murder or adultery or anything else, may the waters according to custom receive them and drag them down to the depths; but the one who has knowledge of this crime, may they [the waters] repel him and throw him out from themselves, nor suffer to receive his body ...'). See also Liebermann, *Gesetze*, I.404, for other versions.

have been interpreted with reference to the cold water ordeal.[142] In contrast, the process for the ordeal of hot water demanded that the accused put his hand into a cauldron of boiling water to remove an object from it, whereas in the ordeal of hot iron the accused was required to hold or carry a piece of heated iron.[143] (It is just possible that one of the illustrations in the late eleventh-century Old English Hexateuch depicts the heating of an iron bar for an ordeal, although since the man is bound and being whipped, it is also possible that the iron was intended for branding.[144]) The two 'hot' ordeals theoretically required a similar process in discerning God's judgement after the ritual: both legal and liturgical instructions indicate that the burned hand of the accused should be bound up and inspected after three days, and that God's judgement was revealed physically once the bandages were taken away.[145]

However, understanding how ordeals worked on the ground is extremely difficult, and for the period before the tenth century in England, virtually impossible. It is not always possible to tell how – or even if – ordeals were really used, and significant changes in the ways that ordeals (and the ways that they were supposed to be used) are described suggest that there was never consistent practice or thought on the matter. Ordeals are mentioned twice in Ine's law code but very little information is given about how they were supposed to work. All that it is really possible to establish from Ine's code is that hot water ordeals were supposed to be used in certain circumstances (since the word used for the process is 'ceac', meaning 'cauldron'); and that at least sometimes it was possible for people to avoid ordeals by making some kind of payment, although whether as a fine or compensation is not quite clear.[146] From the tenth century there is much more evidence: a cluster of references in the first part of the tenth century is followed by a gap of some 40 years until a number of decrees concerning ordeals appear again in the early legislation of Æthelred II.[147] The only narrative account of an ordeal also dates from the tenth century,[148] as do two charters which may (or may not) provide some evidence of the use of ordeals.[149] The eleventh-century evidence is almost entirely dominated by the

---

[142]   See below, 310.

[143]   *Ordal*, ed. Liebermann, *Gesetze*, I.386–7.

[144]   London, British Library, Cotton Claudius B.iv, fol. 80; see Reynolds, *Anglo-Saxon Deviant Burial Customs*, 22 and fig. 4.

[145]   II Æthelstan 23.1, *Ordal*, ed. Liebermann, *Gesetze*, I.162–3, 386–7.

[146]   Ine 37, 62, ed. Liebermann, *Gesetze*, I.104–5, 116–17.

[147]   See in particular I Edward 3; II Æthelstan 4–7; I Æthelred 1–2.1; III Æthelred 3–4.2, ed. Liebermann, *Gesetze*, I.140–1, 152–5, 216–20, 228–31.

[148]   See below, 168–71, for discussion of the narrative account.

[149]   S 1377 (*Pet*, no. 17), AD 963 x 975, records that the land was forfeited by a widow and her son because they were accused of sticking pins into a doll, but the woman drowned at London Bridge: it is possible that this was a result of a cold water ordeal, or mob justice; S 1447, c. AD 950–68; discussed in N. Brooks, *The Early History of the Church of Canterbury:*

voice of Wulfstan, in the later laws of Æthelred and the laws of Cnut, in the *Canons of Edgar* and in other legal texts which show Wulfstan's influence, such as the *Northumbrian Priests' Law*.[150] There is also some post-Conquest evidence which records customs about where ordeals were held, usually in major churches.[151]

In addition to the legal evidence there is also a fairly substantial body of liturgical material for ordeals (outlined in Table 3.1), although as usual with Anglo-Saxon liturgical manuscripts, the close connections of the surviving books with episcopal centres (especially Canterbury and Winchester) make it difficult to establish how widely the texts circulated or were used. Liturgical information about ordeals in Anglo-Saxon England appears first in a late ninth- or early tenth-century southern English book (now Durham, Cathedral Library, A.IV.9), which made its way north during the tenth century and which contains blessings for the elements for ordeals as well as an adjuration to the proband(s).[152] Fuller rituals including the masses and adjurations referred to in law codes occur in a number of books surviving from the later tenth and early eleventh centuries. Many of these are pontificals, books containing the rituals needed by bishops, and it is difficult to know whether these were for reference or for practical performance.[153] There are also two other books containing full ordeal rituals. One is Cambridge, Corpus Christi College, 422, a book containing a number of liturgical offices (including masses, a collectar, offices for baptism, and the anointing of the sick and funerary rites) which was probably written at Winchester in the mid eleventh century but used in Sherborne.[154] The other is Cambridge, Corpus Christi College, 391, which was written in the latter part

---

*Christ Church from 597 to 1066*, Studies in the early history of Britain (Leicester, 1984), 248–9 and below, 172.

[150] Wormald, *Making of English Law*, 208, 396–7; see also below, 172–93.

[151] For the customs at Taunton (Somerset), see Great Domesday Book, fol. 87v, ed. C. Thorn and F. Thorn, *Domesday Book: 8, Somerset* (Chichester, 1980), no. 2.4; and R.W.H. Erskine (ed.), *Great Domesday: a facsimile* (London, 1986–1992); Fleming, *Domesday Book and the Law*, no. 1354. See also J. Blair, *The Church in Anglo-Saxon Society* (Oxford, 2005), 448.

[152] The material for ordeals is found on fols. 48–49v and fols. 53v–55r, ed. A. Corrêa, *The Durham Collectar*, Henry Bradshaw Society 107 (London, 1992), nos. 599–604, 632–40. See also A. Corrêa, 'Daily Office Books: Collectars and Breviaries', in R.W. Pfaff (ed.), *The Liturgical Books of Anglo-Saxon England*, Old English Newsletter, Subsidia 23 (Kalamazoo, MI, 1995), 45–60; Keefer, 'Ðonne se cirlisca man', 362–3.

[153] See S. Hamilton, 'The Early Pontificals: The Anglo-Saxon Evidence Reconsidered from a Continental Perspective', in Leyser, Rollason and Williams (eds), *England and the Continent in the Tenth Century*, 411–28, at 415–28.

[154] See Table 3.1, and above, 82; and Corrêa, 'Daily Office Books', 56–7; S.L. Keefer, 'Manuals', in Pfaff (ed.), *The Liturgical Books of Anglo-Saxon England*, 99–109; R. Rushforth, *Saints in English Kalendars before AD 1100*, Henry Bradshaw Society 117 (Woodbridge, 2008), 41–2.

of the eleventh century at Worcester and which was the personal prayer book of St Wulfstan of Worcester (d.1095).[155] Finally, to the liturgical material can be added the scant information from the archaeological record: some of the surviving wells, pits or cisterns associated with Anglo-Saxon churches (such as those found inside the Old Minster, Winchester) might have been connected with ordeal rituals, although it is difficult to be certain about the purposes of these without additional written evidence.[156]

Recently, scholars have emphasised that ordeals were generally used only in cases where other more usual methods of establishing guilt or innocence, namely oral or written witnesses or the swearing of oaths, were either not possible or were believed to be unreliable.[157] At least in some periods, one of the major implications for convicted perjurers was that in the event of a dispute they were prevented from clearing themselves by swearing oaths, and instead were required to assert their innocence through an ordeal. One of the decrees of Edward the Elder states that perjurers should not be considered 'oath-worthy' (aðwyrðe) but only 'ordeal-worthy' (ordales wyrðe); while one of Æthelstan's decrees removes the right of oath-swearing from convicted perjurers.[158] This perhaps suggests that they may have been required to undergo an ordeal in the event of an accusation against them, although in fact the decrees concerning ordeals do not actually explain whether ordeals were only to be taken by those who were unable or unwilling to swear oaths. The early laws of Æthelred likewise include a process for exculpation which requires that those who are able to should demonstrate their innocence through oath-swearing: those who are unable to do this (or prevented from doing it) because they have previously failed at oath or ordeal are required instead to clear themselves through the ordeal.[159]

---

[155]   See Table 3.1.

[156]   Reynolds, *Anglo-Saxon Deviant Burial Customs*, 22–3; and see M. Biddle, 'Excavations at Winchester 1968: Seventh Interim Report', *Antiquaries Journal* 49 (1969): 295–329, fig. 6. Eadmer of Canterbury (d. in or after 1126) recorded that the old baptistery at the east end of Canterbury Cathedral had been used for trial by ordeal. See the *Life* of Bregwine, 3, ed. B.W. Scholz, 'Eadmer's Life of Bregwine, Archbishop of Canterbury, 761–764', *Traditio* 22 (1966), 124–48, at 139–40: 'Hanc ecclesiam eo respectu fabricauit, ut et baptisteria, et examinationes iudiciorum pro diuersis causis constitutorum quę ad correctionem sceleratorum in ęcclesia dei fieri solent inibi celebrarentur'; see R.W. Southern, *St Anselm: A Portrait in a Landscape* (Cambridge, 1992), 320.

[157]   Hyams, 'Trial by Ordeal', 95–100; Bartlett, *Trial by Fire and Water*, 26–35; Keefer, 'Ðonne se cirlisca man', 353–4.

[158]   I Edward 3; II Æthelstan 26, ed. Liebermann, *Gesetze*, I.140–1, 164–5.

[159]   I Æthelred 1–1.2; III Æthelred 4–4.2; cf. II Cnut 30–30.3, ed. Liebermann, *Gesetze*, I.216–17, 228–31, 330–3.

Table 3.1    Anglo-Saxon manuscripts containing rituals for ordeals[1]

| Shelfmark[2] | Date and provenance | Edition/facsimile |
|---|---|---|
| *Pontificals*[2] | | |
| Cambridge, Corpus Christi College, 146 ('Samson Pontifical') | s. x^ex, Old Minster, Winchester / Canterbury | *Parker Library on the web*, http://parkerweb.stanford.edu |
| Cambridge, Corpus Christi College, 44 | s. xi^med; Christ Church, Canterbury | *Parker Library on the web*, http://parkerweb.stanford.edu |
| London, British Library, Add. 57337 ('Anderson Pontifical') | c. AD 1000: Christ Church Canterbury | |
| London, British Library, Cotton Vitellius A.vii (fols. 1–112) | ?Ramsey / ?Exeter; seems to have belonged to Leofric, Bishop of Crediton (1046) and Exeter (1050) | |
| Paris, Bibliothèque nationale, 943 ('Dunstan Pontifical' or 'Sherborne Pontifical') | AD 960 x ?973; probably Christ Church, Canterbury | |
| Rouen, Bibliothèque municipale, 368 ('Lanalet Pontifical') | s. xi^in; St Germans / Wells | Doble, *Pontificale Lanaletense* |
| *Other books* | | |
| Cambridge, Corpus Christi College, 391 ('St Wulfstan's Portiforium'); a collectar and private prayer book | s. xi^2, or ?perhaps after 1070; Worcester (based on a Winchester exemplar)[3] | Hughes, *The Portiforium of St Wulstan*; *Parker Library on the web*, http://parkerweb.stanford.edu |
| Cambridge, Corpus Christi College, 422 ('Red Book of Darley'); a sacramentary, collectar, and 'manual'-type book | s. xi^med; perhaps written at Winchester for use at Sherborne[4] | *Parker Library on the web*, http://parkerweb.stanford.edu |
| Durham, Cathedral Library, A.IV.9 ('Durham Collectar' or 'Durham Ritual')[5] a collectar with rituals including benedictions; additional material for the offices, votive masses, benedictions | s. ix^ex / x^in, southern England, based on a continental exemplar additional material: before c.970; Chester-le-Street[6] | Corrêa, *The Durham Collectar*; Lindelöf, *Rituale ecclesiae Dunelmensis*; Brown, *The Durham Ritual* |

*Notes:* [1] See further Keefer, 'Manuals', 108–9; Keefer, '*Ut in omnibus*', 245–6; in addition to the editions given for specific manuscripts, some of these ordeal rituals are also printed (rather uncomfortably) in Liebermann, *Gesetze*, I.401–29. [2] For dating and other information about these pontificals see J.L. Nelson and R.W. Pfaff, 'Pontificals and Benedictionals', in Pfaff (ed.), *The Liturgical Books of Anglo-Saxon England*, 87–98; R. W. Pfaff, *The Liturgy in Medieval England: A History* (Cambridge, 2009); Hamilton, 'The Early Pontificals', 411–15, and nn. 7–9. [3] Corrêa, 'Daily Office Books', 57–8; Rushforth, *Saints in English Kalendars*, 44–5. [4] Corrêa, 'Daily Office Books', 56–7; Keefer, 'Manuals'; Gittos, 'Is there any Evidence for the Liturgy of Parish Churches'; S. Keynes, 'Wulfsige. Monk of Glastonbury, Abbot of Westminster (c 990–3), and Bishop of Sherborne (c 993–1002)', in K. Barker, D.A. Hinton and A. Hunt (eds) *St Wulfsige and Sherborne: Essays to Celebrate the Millennium of the Benedictine Abbey: 998–1998* (Oxford, 2005), 53–94, at 75–6; Rushforth, *Saints in English Kalendars*, 41–2. [5] Corrêa, 'Daily Office Books', 48–9; Keefer, '*Donne se cirlisca man*', 362–3. [6] See Alicia Corrêa, *The Durham Collectar*, Henry Bradshaw Society 107 (London, 1992), 76–88, for information about the dating and provenance of the manuscript.

While those who failed oaths might have to undergo ordeals, it is the treatment of those who failed ordeals which is most significant for identifying unease in Anglo-Saxon responses to ordeals as part of the system of justice, and in this context II Æthelstan is particularly interesting. In contrast to the apparently unified or general process for exculpation through oaths or ordeals in Æthelred's early law codes, II Æthelstan mentions the ordeal in two different types of contexts. These are firstly in the process of ascertaining truth in the case of specific offences, and secondly in the description of regulations for ordeals.[160] In most cases, the punishment for those who failed the ordeal was the same as if the accused had simply admitted guilt. For example, the penalty for a moneyer who issued coins falsely or incorrectly was that his hand should be struck off and fastened above the mint: this penalty was to be applied whether the moneyer simply admitted guilt (or if there was evidence to prove his guilt), or whether he took an ordeal in an attempt to clear himself, and failed it.[161] In the same way, someone accused of breaking into churches was required to pay compensation according to the written law if he attempted and failed to clear himself by undergoing an ordeal.[162]

But, significantly, there are also offences for which different penalties are prescribed for those who admit guilt and for those who attempt to clear themselves by an ordeal but fail it. If someone was accused of causing death through witchcraft or sorcery and was unable to deny it, presumably because sufficient evidence was adduced in support of the accusation, then the accused individual was to be condemned to death.[163] If he denied it and tried to take an ordeal to clear himself but failed, he was to be put in prison for 120 days: after his imprisonment, his relatives were to guarantee that he would not offend in the same way again, and to pay a fine of 120 shillings to the king and the appropriate wergeld to the dead man's kinsmen.[164] This procedure was also to be used in the cases of arsonists and those who avenged a thief, and since all these are usually treated more harshly than church-breaking or false coining it does not appear to be the specific offences which resulted in more lenient treatment for those who failed ordeals. But even understanding what failing an ordeal really meant at any point in Anglo-Saxon England is extremely complicated, especially since the vocabulary for describing the passing or failing of an ordeal is itself not clear-cut.

Usually, those who failed ordeals are described in Old English as 'ful', a word which means literally 'foul' or 'unclean', and by extension can also mean 'guilty'

[160]   II Æthelstan 4–7, 14–14.2, 19, 21, 23–4, ed. Liebermann, *Gesetze*, I.152–5, 158–9, 160–1, 162–5.
[161]   II Æthelstan 14.1, ed. Liebermann, *Gesetze*, I.158–9.
[162]   II Æthelstan 5, ed. Liebermann, *Gesetze*, I.152–3: 'bete be þam þe sio domboc secge'.
[163]   II Æthelstan 6, ed. Liebermann, *Gesetze*, I.152–3.
[164]   II Æthelstan 6.1, ed. Liebermann, *Gesetze*, I.154–5.

or 'sinful'.[165] In the one instance in Anglo-Saxon law codes where reference is made to the possibility that someone might pass an ordeal, the person who passes is referred to as 'clæne' (the opposite of 'ful'), which means 'clean' or 'pure' and so by extension also 'innocent' or 'sinless'.[166] Although it looks on the face of it as if legislators distinguished between the 'guilty' people who failed ordeals and the 'innocent' people who did not, there are complications with interpreting these words in this way. A text known as *Ordal*, usually dated roughly contemporaneously with Æthelstan's reign, provides instructions for ordeals of hot iron and hot water and refers to the process of wrapping up the hand and inspecting it after three days.[167] According to this text, the *hand* is to be inspected to see whether it is 'ful' or 'clean'. Here it is certain that the hand and not the person is meant, both because a feminine pronoun is used ('hand' is feminine in Old English), and because the text refers to the inspection 'within the seal', indicating that the 'ful' and 'clæn' refer to what is under the wrappings.[168] The use of these terms in their more literal sense to refer to the hand of the proband suggests that this choice of vocabulary for ordeals may at some point have been transferred from the hand specifically to the person more generally, especially since in the law codes 'ful' is used almost exclusively to refer to those who have failed ordeals. However, it is still not clear what precisely 'ful' and 'clæn' signify, except that one designates failure at, and one designates the passing of, an ordeal.

There is no evidence from Anglo-Saxon England which states clearly and unambiguously what lawmakers, judges, or anyone else expected to see on unwrapping the bandages, and this has led to uncertainty and confusion in scholarship over whether passing an ordeal required the proband's hand to be unburned, or simply that it should be healing rather than festering.[169] Ascertaining whether someone had passed or failed was presumably dependent on local circumstances to a great extent, as probably also was the treatment of those who had passed or failed.[170] Robert Bartlett argues

---

[165]    Cameron, Crandell Amos and diPaolo Healey, *Dictionary of Old English: A to G online*, see definitions 1, 2 and 4, esp. 4.c.: 'technical, in laws, of persons: guilty (of a charge or accusation)'.

[166]    Cameron, Crandell Amos and diPaolo Healey, *Dictionary of Old English: A to G online*, see definitions 1 and 6, esp. 6.d.: 'specifically: innocent of a crime or sinful act; in law: guiltless of a charge or accusation'.

[167]    *Ordal*, ed. Liebermann, *Gesetze*, I.386–7; Wormald, *Making of English Law*, 373–4.

[168]    Ordal, ed. Liebermann, *Gesetze*, I.386–7.

[169]    These two possibilities are found variously and sometimes even in the same work: for example, Bartlett states first that after trial by hot iron a man's hand would be examined and 'if it was "clean" – that is, healing without suppuration or discoloration – he was innocent or vindicated; if the wound was unclean, he was guilty'; but almost immediately afterwards he also states that ordeals 'required that the natural elements behave in an unusual way, hot iron or water not burning the innocent' (Bartlett, *Trial by Fire and Water*, 1, 2).

[170]    See P. Brown, 'Society and the supernatural: A medieval change', *Daedalus* 104:2 (1975): 133–51.

that the fact of having to take an ordeal stained the character of the accused, so that even if the accused person passed he was not necessarily considered innocent, and he also suggests that failure at an ordeal was not considered to be quite the same as a confession of guilt, adducing in support of this the decrees of II Æthelstan about those who cause death by sorcery.[171] This is problematic though, since in at least one case a decree associated with Æthelstan seems to say that failure at an ordeal is precisely the same as a confession of guilt: according to IV Æthelstan, someone repeatedly accused of theft should be killed 'if it is known certainly, that is if he does not deny it, or if he is guilty in the ordeal, or if it is known in any other way'.[172] But since this part of the code only survives in a later Latin translation, comparison with the Old English terminology is difficult: it seems likely that in Old English the phrase 'if he is guilty in the ordeal' was probably something like 'if he is 'ful' in the ordeal', but it is not clear whether this phrase was originally in the Old English text.

The situation is no clearer in other law codes associated with Æthelstan's reign, such as the decrees issued by the bishops and reeves of London (VI Æthelstan). These include a provision 'about thieves whom one cannot find out quickly [that he is] 'fule', and one finds out afterwards 'þæt he ful bið ⁊ scildig'' (that he is 'ful' and guilty), adding that such a person can be freed from prison on the same terms as one who was 'ful' at ordeal.[173] This in turn suggests that such a person's '"ful' and guilty' status was not ascertained through an ordeal, and raises questions about the circumstances in which it first was not, and later was, possible to ascertain this 'ful' status. It is also possible that the 'scildig' in the sentence indicates that a word has dropped out at an earlier stage: 'scyldig' does mean guilty, especially in the sense of 'sinful', but in the law codes it almost never refers to proven guilt in a legal sense.[174] Instead it usually appears in the phrase 'feores scyldig', 'guilty of his life', meaning that the offender should be condemned to death.[175] This decree may therefore be intended to refer specifically to those condemned to death as a result of a conviction for theft (i.e., those who are 'feores scildig'), and the possibility of their liberation. These decrees also seem to distinguish between thieves who cannot deny their offence and are thus immediately condemned to death,[176] and those accused of

---

[171]   Bartlett, *Trial by Fire and Water*, 67–9.

[172]   IV Æthelstan 6, ed. Liebermann, *Gesetze*, I.172: 'si pro certo sciatur – id est si uerbum non dixerit, ut andsaca sit – uel in ordalio reus sit (appareat) uel per aliud aliquid (culpabilis) innotescat'.

[173]   VI Æthelstan 9, ed. Liebermann, *Gesetze*, I.181.

[174]   See Cameron, Crandell Amos and diPaolo Healey, *Dictionary of Old English: A to G online*: 'feorh', definition 1.c; also established by searching A. diPaolo Healey, J.P. Wilkin and X. Xiang, *Dictionary of Old English Corpus on the World Wide Web* (2009), http://www.doe.utoronto.ca/index.html.

[175]   e.g. II Æthelstan 4, 6; III Æthelred 16; II Cnut 57, ed. Liebermann, *Gesetze*, I.152–3, 232–3, 348–9.

[176]   VI Æthelstan 1.4, ed. Liebermann, *Gesetze*, I.174.

theft who fail an ordeal and get a second chance, only receiving the death penalty if they fail an ordeal for theft a second time.[177]

The law codes associated with Æthelstan's reign therefore offer some variation in precisely how ordeals might be used, suggesting that the treatment of those who were subject to ordeals was not uniform even within Æthelstan's kingdom, especially in the case of those who failed. Despite this variation, it is noteworthy that the application of the same penalty both for those who failed ordeals and for those who admitted guilt is the exception rather than the rule. No Anglo-Saxon texts explain directly why this should be the case, but it is probably significant that Æthelstan's reign saw increased attention to the process of ordeals and a contemporaneous upsurge in regulations about ordeals, perhaps suggesting that ordeals had become a matter of concern in a way that they had not been previously, and in particular that following the correct process was considered to be extremely important. II Æthelstan contains a number of decrees which specifically articulate the process for ordeals and regulations about the elements to be used in them, including the involvement of a priest and religious ritual, and this is particularly interesting because this code is the earliest significant evidence for the working of ordeals in Anglo-Saxon England. The instructions for the process here state that the proband should fast and attend mass daily for three days before the ordeal is to take place, and that he should make an offering and receive communion on the day of the ordeal, as well as swearing an oath that he is innocent of the accusation according to 'folcryht', meaning public or customary law.[178] *Ordal* also gives clear instructions about fasting before an ordeal as well as the use of holy water, Christ's cross and a book (probably a gospel-book), and describes that ordeals should take place in a church.[179]

The appearance of these instructions early in the tenth century, and the survival of liturgical rituals for ordeals from the mid to late tenth century, suggests that there was a perceived need to regulate and to control ordeals, perhaps because something about their use or interpretation had changed, or because there was concern over them, or both. A similar phenomenon is found in the consecration of cemeteries, again visible in legal texts from the early tenth century and in liturgical texts from the latter part of the century, and here too it seems that the emergence of these references is linked to a comparatively recent development in rites and rituals.[180] While ordeals are clearly older than the tenth century, it is probable that the sudden appearance of information about them is linked with contemporary thought or practice, and perhaps changes in, or concern over, the ways that they were used. Both *Ordal* and II Æthelstan

---

[177]    VI Æthelstan 1, ed. Liebermann, *Gesetze*, I.173.

[178]    II Æthelstan 23–3.2, ed. Liebermann, *Gesetze*, I.162–5; see also Cameron, Crandell Amos and diPaolo Healey, *Dictionary of Old English: A to G online*: 'folc-riht', n.

[179]    *Ordal*, ed. Liebermann, *Gesetze*, I.386–7.

[180]    For information about consecrated cemeteries, see H. Gittos, 'Creating the Sacred: Anglo-Saxon Rites for Consecrating Cemeteries', in S. Lucy and A.J. Reynolds (eds), *Burial in Early Medieval England and Wales* (London, 2002), 195–208; and below, 273–8.

mention the possibility of invalidating an ordeal (and in *Ordal* a high fine is payable in this case), and both texts describe the processes in a way which shows that there was clearly some concern to make sure that the rituals were performed correctly, indicating that the proper functioning of the ordeal was perceived to be tightly linked to its correct performance according to set religious rites.[181] This concern seems to have been driven at least partly by those in high ecclesiastical office: *Ordal* refers at the beginning to 'the commands of God and the archbishop and all the bishops', and II Æthelstan's instructions for ordeals likewise note that these are made 'according to the command of God and of the archbishop'.[182]

What is not clear is whether this perceived need for regulation and the adjustment of penalties for those who fail ordeals is connected more with ideas about ordeals themselves or with ideas about the penalties that they might occasion. The possibility of invalidating an ordeal was evidently a real concern, suggesting that there may have been some uncertainty over the reliability of the ordeal verdict in all cases. With only a very few exceptions, the adjustment of the penalty for those who failed an ordeal was made in those cases where admitting guilt occasioned the death penalty, suggesting that the penalty as well as the method of ascertaining the truth might have been considered problematic.[183] If there was concern over false convictions, these would be particularly prominent in the case of offences which usually required the death penalty, given its finality. This may be why the penalty of amputation for false coining was considered to be an acceptable punishment both for those who admitted guilt and for those who failed ordeals, but the death penalty was not demanded for those who were convicted through the ordeal of causing death by sorcery, even though this was arguably a more serious offence. Although the moneyer might lose his hand and livelihood through a false conviction, he would at least be alive, and neither his soul nor the soul of the judge or executioner would be irretrievably imperilled. The remission of the death penalty for those who failed ordeals is particularly striking in the context of Æthelstan's laws, where judicial execution was stipulated far more frequently than in earlier legislation. And in Æthelstan's laws as in so many other Anglo-Saxon contexts, at least some of the impetus for this seems to have been ecclesiastically and theologically driven.

Similar concern seems to be evident in the only recorded account of an ordeal from Anglo-Saxon England, which appears in the late tenth-century accounts of the miracles of St Swithun. The ordeal in question probably took place in late 971 or 972 (assuming that a genuine event is described), and it was recorded in the *Translatio S. Swithuni*, written by Lantfred probably some time between 972 and 974.[184] Another

---

[181]   II Æthelstan 23.2, ed. Liebermann, *Gesetze*, I.162–5.

[182]   *Ordal*; II Æthelstan 23.2, ed. Liebermann, *Gesetze*, I.162–5, 386–7.

[183]   Some offences, such as treachery, occasioned the death penalty whether guilt was admitted directly or ascertained through an ordeal verdict, but as noted above, 149–50, treachery seems to have been one crime for which mercy was not expected or granted; see also Wormald, *Making of English Law*, 283–4; Pratt, *Political Thought*, 233–4.

[184]   Lapidge, *Cult of St Swithun*, 236–7, 308, n. 229.

version of the story also occurs in Wulfstan of Winchester's *Narratio metrica de S. Swithuno*, based on Lantfred's account and probably written between 994 and 996.[185] According to Lantfred, a slave belonging to a merchant named Flodoald was detained by the king's reeve, who ordered the slave to undergo ordeal by hot iron. Flodoald begged the reeve to waive the ordeal, offering instead to give him the slave and a pound of silver, while the kinsmen of the reeve also offered to give gifts to the reeve if he would let the slave go. The reeve refused and the slave was forced to undergo the ordeal, but a miracle occurred after Flodoald begged the help of St Swithun and promised the slave to the saint if his life could be saved. Although Flodoald and the slave's kinsmen saw the slave's hand burned and blistered, the hand appeared to the reeve and his men as if it had never been burned: the slave was thus saved from death and became a servant of St Swithun.[186]

As a record of the practice of ordeals, this account is extremely problematic for a number of reasons, and especially as a test case for the comparison of written law to the process of justice on the ground. There is no indication of the slave's supposed crime, and it is not clear which are the relevant laws for comparison in this case, so it is impossible to determine whether this case illustrates the application of written law or not. The ecclesiastical authors who recorded and reworked this story clearly position the merciful and sympathetic St Swithun (and by implication the Church and its officials too) against the grasping and merciless reeve, but as this opposition is placed in the context of St Swithun's miracle it is difficult to know precisely which aspects of the reeve's actions were perceived to be most unfair. Flodoald and the slave's kinsmen were apparently desperate to save him from harm, and their efforts to change the reeve's mind by offering him gifts seem to have been aimed both at ensuring that the slave did not have to undergo the ordeal, and thus in turn ensuring that the slave would not be killed. Lantfred related that Flodoald saw the slave on the second day and found him 'condemned and guilty' ('dampnatum et culpabilem'), but this is confusing in its theoretical impossibility, because the judgement on the verdict of the ordeal should only have been possible from the third day and when the bandages were unwrapped.

The miracle is also rather confusing, and surrounds the interpretation of the ordeal's verdict rather than its outcome *per se*. Here too the question of what people expected to see when the bandaged hand was unbound is an important one, if still not precisely answerable. Both Lantfred and Wulfstan describe the searing burn which filled the slave's hand as he picked up the iron, indicating that the slave was not treated to miraculous preservation from harm, a trope which

---

[185]   Ibid., 336.

[186]   Lantfred, *Translatio*, 25, ed. and trans. Lapidge, *Cult of St Swithun*, 308–11. This episode is discussed in D. Whitelock, 'Wulfstan Cantor and Anglo-Saxon Law', in A.H. Orrick (ed.), *Nordica et Anglica: Studies in Honour of Stefan Einarsson*, Janua Linguarum: Series Maior 22 (Paris, 1968), 83–92, at 87–92; Hyams, 'Trial by Ordeal'; K.O.B. O'Keeffe, 'Body and law in late Anglo-Saxon England', *Anglo-Saxon England* 27 (1998): 209–32, at 223–5.

appears in some other medieval miracle stories concerning ordeals.[187] When the hand was unwrapped, the bloodthirsty reeve was unable to see the burn on the slave's hand and so let him go, although the burn was visible to Flodoald and to the slave's kinsman. Lantfred seems to have assumed that the slave was guilty and was yet miraculously saved from death, since he relates that the slave's master 'considered him to be worthy of punishment' ('quem dominus ipse cernebat suppliciis dignum').[188] In the end, therefore, St Swithun thwarted the reeve's 'unfair judgement' ('iniquum … iudicium'), probably meaning the reeve's insistence on the death penalty in the event of the slave's failure, since as presented, the reeve is merciless in demanding this punishment, apparently without good reason.[189]

The retelling by Wulfstan of Winchester is interesting because of the slight adaptations which he made, although the general outline of the story is of course the same:[190] like Lantfred, Wulfstan explains that Flodoald found the slave condemned to death on the second day. However, Wulfstan describes the slave as 'fidelis', and while it is possible that this owes something to his use of poetic metre, it may be more significant than this. 'Fidelis' is roughly equivalent to the Old English 'getrywe', which described those who were of good reputation and so allowed to swear oaths: later translators of Anglo-Saxon laws rendered 'getrywe' as 'fidelis', but so too did contemporary Anglo-Saxon authors gloss 'fidelis' with 'getrywe'.[191] According to contemporary law codes, it is those who were *not* 'fidelis' or 'getrywe' ('trustworthy') who had to undergo ordeals. Although this is in itself a small point, it is noteworthy because Wulfstan, unlike Lantfred, never states unequivocally that the slave was guilty, simply explaining instead that 'the reeve was not able to proclaim, as he wanted to, that the man was guilty of the offence'.[192] This suggests that Wulfstan may not himself have been certain about the slave's guilt.

---

[187]    See for example a legend associated with St Swithun in the late twelfth-century *Annales de Wintonia*, in which Emma walked over hot ploughshares but remained unburned, ed. and trans. Lapidge, *Cult of St Swithun*, 149–53 and discussed in P. Stafford, *Queen Emma and Queen Edith: Queenship and Women's Power in Eleventh-Century England* (Oxford, 1997), 18–22; or the ordeal-like episode in Wulfstan of Winchester's *Life of Æthelwold*, discussed below, 171; see also Bartlett, *Trial by Fire and Water*, 86–90.

[188]    Lantfred, *Translatio*, 25, ll. 32–3, ed. Lapidge, *Cult of St Swithun*, 310.

[189]    Lantfred, *Translatio*, 25, l. 13, ed. Lapidge, *Cult of St Swithun*, 310; see also Whitelock, 'Wulfstan Cantor', 87–92, although with reference to Wulfstan's version only.

[190]    Wulfstan, *Narratio metrica*, II.viii, ed. and trans. Lapidge, *Cult of St Swithun*, 508–15.

[191]    For example, the (Norman) author of the *Instituta Cnuti* consistently translates 'fidelis' as 'getrywe' (e.g. II Cnut 22–3, ed. Liebermann, *Gesetze*, I.324–7); but Anglo-Saxon authors also glossed 'fidelis' this way (for example Ælfric, *Glossary*, ed. J. Zupitza, *Grammatik und Glossar, 1. Abt., Text und Varianten, Sammlung Englischer Denkmäler in kritischen Ausgaben* 1 (Berlin, 1880), 303, l. 5–6 ('*fidelis* getrywe oððe geleaffull. *infidelis* ungetreowe'); and *Hom.* XVI, ll. 210–12, ed. Pope, *Homilies of Ælfric*, I.555–6).

[192]    Wulfstan, *Narratio Metrica*, ii.viii, ll. 417–19, ed. Lapidge, *Cult of St Swithun*, 512.

Moreover, Wulfstan rather unexpectedly inserts a passage explaining that all of nature is subject to the commands of Christ, so that with a command from Christ nature will abandon its usual laws and change according to his direction. This is peculiar in the context of this miracle, because the nature of the hot iron did not change, and the man's hand was neither miraculously healed nor kept unharmed. This contrasts strongly with another miraculous event which Wulfstan related in his *Life of Æthelwold*, in which the monk Ælfstan was ordered by his abbot to remove a piece of food from the bottom of a cauldron of boiling water: Ælfstan was 'a straightforward and very obedient man' ('simplex et magnae obedientiae uir') who did what he was told, and apparently he did not even feel the heat of the boiling water.[193] This miracle does not relate to a judicial ordeal but it clearly alludes to the process of hot water ordeals, although it is not complicated by the prospect of the death penalty in the event of failure.[194] But this episode is significant here, both because this shows the more usual outcome expected in an account of a miracle connected with an ordeal, and because Wulfstan's statement about Christ's command over nature would be convincing in a case like this. In contrast, discussing Christ's command over nature in the story about Swithun's intervention in the ordeal is incongruous, and suggests that Wulfstan too did not quite know what to make of the miracle which saved Flodoald's slave.

Wulfstan concludes his narrative of the miracle performed in the ordeal by observing that since the reeve did not of his own accord relinquish the 'iniquum iudicium', he went home in disgrace without either the silver or the slave – and it seems likely that while Wulfstan frowned upon the reeve's demand for the slave's death, he meant by the 'iniquum iudicium' not the 'unfair judgement', but the 'unfair *ordeal*', especially given his description of the slave as 'fidelis'.[195] Wulfstan's reporting of the miracle suggests discomfort with the use of the procedure, and once again especially where death was demanded in the event of failure, but without specific comment that makes it easy to identify exactly what made him uneasy about the episode. Ultimately, and perhaps unsurprisingly, this miracle reveals less about the use of ordeals and how precisely they were performed in Anglo-Saxon England, and much more about the attitudes of authors towards the saints they glorified and to the events they described. It is clear, however, that where ordeals were used the interpretation of specific cases must have varied significantly, as in the miracle described by Lantfred and Wulfstan.

This problem seems to be recognised in the liturgical rituals, which advert to the possibility that the result may not be easily or clearly read and ask God to ensure

---

[193]    *Vita S. Æthelwoldi*, 14, ed. and trans. Lapidge and Winterbottom, *Wulfstan of Winchester: The Life of St Æthelwold*, 28/9.

[194]    Several of the details of this miracle too are rather problematic: it is not entirely clear why this is included in the *Life of Æthelwold* (since the miracle appears to show Ælfstan's virtue rather than Æthelwold's), or who Ælfstan's abbot was and why he thought it was a good idea to test Ælfstan this way.

[195]    Wulfstan, *Narratio metrica*, II.viii, ll. 420–3, ed. Lapidge, *Cult of St Swithun*, 512–14.

that demonic influence does not prevent the true working of the ordeal, as well as blessing and exorcising the elements before the ordeal to ensure that all demons were banished.[196] Such difficulties are probably one of the key factors in unease or uncertainty over ordeals in early medieval England as elsewhere, and even without clear discussions there are traces of discomfort: Nicholas Brooks suggests that Archbishop Dunstan's involvement in the case of Ecgferth, whose drowning may have occurred in the course of an ordeal, might reflect the archbishop's lack of confidence in the ordeal's verdict.[197] Although the evidence offers only hints, rather than the clear discussions of Agobard and Hincmar, the cumulative weight of evidence does suggest concern over ordeals, especially where the outcome might have been capital punishment. Given the roles of ecclesiastical officials in the production of legal texts, and that the procedures for ordeals were regulated increasingly in both liturgical and legal contexts, it seems likely that ecclesiastical agents were significant here. This shows the early stages of the slow process which culminated in IV Lateran's rejection of judicial ordeals in 1215, based in part on the discussions and objections of theologians working in the later eleventh and twelfth centuries, but it is also clear that in the early eleventh century both capital punishment and ordeals continued to be subject to serious scrutiny.

### Archbishop Wulfstan of York

Archbishop Wulfstan had a clear vision for a 'holy society' which followed God's commandments and obeyed secular law, and which would only maintain its relationship with God by doing so.[198] He is treated here on his own because the surviving corpus of his work is so extensive that both the opinions he held on the range of issues considered in this chapter and the links between them are much clearer than the scattered references of earlier periods. Like other Anglo-Saxon ecclesiastics, Wulfstan advised mercy in judgement, and once again seems to have been reluctant to use ordeals where alternative options were available: in both of these areas as in so many others, Wulfstan often stated his opinions much more clearly and more

---

[196] See for example a blessing for iron from CCCC 391, pp. 568–9: 'Benedic domine deus omnipotens per inuocationem sanctissimi nominis tui hoc genus metalli, ad manifestandum uerum iudicium tuum, ut omni demonum falsitate procul remota, ueritas ueri iudicii tui fidelibus tuis manifesta fiat' ('Almighty Lord God, bless this species of metal through the invocation of your most holy name, in order to reveal your true judgement, so that when all the fraudulence of demons has been removed far away, the truth of your true judgement may be made manifest to your faithful').

[197] S 1447; Brooks, *The Early History of the Church of Canterbury*, 248–9; see also below, 310.

[198] P. Wormald, 'Archbishop Wulfstan and the Holiness of Society', in D.A.E. Pelteret (ed.), *Anglo-Saxon History: Basic Readings* (New York, 1999), 191–224; J.T. Lionarons, *The Homiletic Writings of Archbishop Wulfstan: A Critical Study* (Cambridge, 2010), 3–8, 159–68, 175.

categorically than almost any of his Anglo-Saxon contemporaries and predecessors. As a bishop, Wulfstan played a key role in both secular and ecclesiastical affairs, and used his position of power to incorporate theology into legal judgements and process, just as he also sought to integrate the institutional Church and its officials more closely into the secular systems of discipline, and to give them a greater role. A number of manuscripts are associated with him, containing both his own writings and texts which he collected to help him in his duties, and these allow a glimpse into the process through which he came to his conclusions and worked out his thoughts (see Table 3.2). And it is in Wulfstan's works that the relationship between law and penance in Anglo-Saxon England really culminates, since he seems to have considered them as two complementary means to the same aim, that of ordering earthly society so as to be pleasing to God in the heavenly kingdom.

Wulfstan incorporated ideas from penitential texts into law codes much more thoroughly than any of his predecessors had done, and in the concept of merciful judgement it is possible to see him applying the theological principles of ecclesiastical judgements in penance to the secular judgements in legislation. Like earlier law codes, Wulfstan's laws for Æthelred and Cnut include decrees demanding that offenders should perform penance, but Wulfstan also ordered that judgements and sentences should be passed mercifully, and that all punishments should be moderated so that they were fair in the eyes both of God and of the world.[199] And like Alfred, Wulfstan repeatedly encouraged judgement according to the values of the pater noster, so that in judging other people, judges were instructed to consider how they themselves would like to be judged.[200] But more importantly, Wulfstan also incorporated injunctions that judgements should be made by distinguishing carefully between different types of people, between misdeeds committed deliberately or unintentionally, and according to the status of the individuals in question, since those in positions of power or authority can and should bear a greater burden of recompense.[201] Borrowed directly from penitential texts which survive in Wulfstan's own collections alongside his legal writings, this last idea appears frequently too in Wulfstan's legal and political writings.[202]

---

[199]   VI Æthelred 10.2; II Cnut 2, ed. Liebermann, *Gesetze*, I.250, 308–9.

[200]   E.g. II Cnut 2a, ed. Liebermann, *Gesetze*, I.308–9.

[201]   E.g. VI Æthelred 52–3; VIII Æthelred 5.2; II Cnut 38.1, 68–8.3, ed. Liebermann, *Gesetze*, I.258–9, 264, 338–9, 354–5.

[202]   See for example the *Old English Introduction*, 32.01.01–32.03.01, ed. Frantzen, *The Anglo-Saxon Penitentials: A Cultural Database*: 'Ðæt gedafenað ælcum sacerde þonne he mannum fæsten scrifeð þæt he wite hwýlc se man sig·trum þe untrum. welig. þe þearfa. hu geong he sig·oþþe hu eald·hwæðer he sig gehadod þe læwede. & hwýlce hreowe he hæbbe·& hwæþer he sig hægsteald. þe þe hæmedceorl; On eallum mannum behofað gesceadwisnýsse þeah þe hi gelice fýrene ne fremmen; Ricum mannum man sceal strangor deman þonne þam heanum·æfter canones dome;' ('It is fitting that whenever a priest assigns a fast to someone, he should know whether the man is sick or well, wealthy or needy, how young or how hold he is, and whether he is in orders or lay, and how remorseful he is, and whether he is a married man or not. It is appropriate

Table 3.2     Manuscripts containing material collected by and associated with Archbishop Wulfstan of York, and works written by him (many of these are often referred to as the manuscripts of his 'commonplace book')[1]

| Shelfmark | Date and provenance | Facsimile |
|---|---|---|
| Brussels, Bibliothèque royale, 8558–63, fols. 80–131 and 132–53 | fols. 80–131: s. $x^{med}$ fols. 132–53, s. $xi^1$ and s.xii[1] | |
| Cambridge, Corpus Christi College, 190 | s. $xi^1$; Worcester; Exeter | *Parker Library on the web* http://parkerweb.stanford.edu |
| Cambridge, Corpus Christi College, 201 | s. $xi^{med}$; Winchester provenance? | *Parker Library on the web* http://parkerweb.stanford.edu |
| Cambridge, Corpus Christi College, 265, pp. 1–268 | s. $xi^{med}$; Worcester | *Parker Library on the web* http://parkerweb.stanford.edu |
| Copenhagen, Kongelige Bibliotek, Gl. Kgl. 1595 | s. $xi^{1/4}$ (*c.*1002–1023); Worcester? York? | Cross, *The Copenhagen Wulfstan Collection* |
| London, British Library, Cotton Nero A.i | s. $xi^{in}$; Worcester? York? | Loyn, *A Wulfstan Manuscript* |
| London, British Library, Cotton Vespasian A.xiv, fols. 70–177[2] | s. $xi^{in}$; Worcester or York | |
| Oxford, Bodleian Library, Barlow 37 | s. $xii^{ex}$ or s. $xiii^{in}$; Worcester | |
| Oxford, Bodleian Library, Bodley 718 | s. $xi^1$; S England (Exeter?) | |
| Oxford, Bodleian Library, Junius 121 | s. $xi^{3/4}$; Worcester | |
| Paris, Bibliothèque nationale, lat. 3182 | s. $x^1$ or $x^2$; Brittany | |
| Rouen, Bibliothèque municipale, 1382, fols. 184r–198v | s. $xi^1$; England | |

*Notes*: [1] On this see in particular M. Bateson, 'A Worcester Cathedral Book of ecclesiastical collections, made c. 1000 AD', *English Historical Review* 10 (1895): 712–31; D. Bethurum, 'Archbishop Wulfstan's Commonplace Book', *Publications of the Modern Languages Association* 57 (1942): 916–29; J.E. Cross, 'A newly identified manuscript of Wulfstan's "Commonplace Book", Rouen, Bibliothèque Municipale, MS 1382 (U.109), fols 173r–198v', *Journal of Medieval Latin* 2 (1992): 63–83; H. Sauer, 'The Transmission and Structure of Archbishop Wulfstan's 'Commonplace Book'', in P.E. Szarmach (ed.), *Old English Prose: Basic Readings* Basic Readings in Anglo-Saxon England 5 (New York, 2000), 339–93. Three contain entries in Wulfstan's handwriting: these are Nero A.i, Vespasian A.xiv, and the Copenhagen manuscript (see Ker, 'The handwriting of Archbishop Wulfstan'). [2] See G. Mann, 'The Development of Wulfstan's Alcuin Manuscript', in M. Townend (ed.), *Wulfstan, Archbishop of York: The Proceedings of the Second Alcuin Conference*, Studies in the Early Middle Ages 10 (Turnhout, 2004), 235–78.

to distinguish between all men, even if they might commit similar offences. Rich men must be judged more severely than the poor, according to the judgement of the canon').

Although Alfred encouraged mercy and fairness in judgement, he seems to have been thinking of the making of the laws, and his discourse on merciful judging seems to have applied more to himself as lawgiver than to his judges as the enforcers of law. There is no clear indication in Alfred's laws that he intended his judges to vary their decisions according to individual cases. Instead, in Alfred's laws as in earlier legislation, variation in judgement usually occurs in relation to the victim's status rather than to the offender's: rape, for example, might occasion different penalties according to whether the woman was married, virgin or consecrated, free or unfree – and in this last case, the rank of her owner might also be taken into account.[203] In fact, Alfred's injunction to treat rich and poor alike suggests strongly that the letter of the law was to be the guideline for judges rather than independent thought (or bribery and corruption). In contrast, Wulfstan's statement indicates precisely the opposite, that the principle of judging according to circumstances should be applied by those who used and consulted the written laws in making specific judgements on individual cases. Some recognition of the transfer in approach from penance to law may perhaps be found in his statement that this principle should be applied to both ecclesiastical and secular judgements, even though ecclesiastical and secular reparation were to be made according to the prescriptions of each system.[204] Under Wulfstan's guiding hand, the importance of merciful judgement according to the circumstances of the offender was the duty of all judges, whether ecclesiastical or secular, as well as the duty of the Christian king who gave out the law.

The laws written by Wulfstan are famously homiletic in approach, containing exhortations alongside prescriptions and restrictions,[205] and this is connected with the recommendation in secular law of an approach found more usually in penitential texts. Wulfstan's incorporation of the Christian principle of mercy in judgement required secular and ecclesiastical judges to use their own initiative and careful assessment of each case before pronouncing sentence, and seen in this light, the exhortations in Wulfstanian law codes are much more understandable: judges were supposed to use the law as a guide, rather than handing down sentences according to written law with no adjustment for the status or situation of the offender. Comparison with continental evidence indicates that Wulfstan was by no means the first to suggest this: Alice Rio argues that in Francia, 'written law was understood more as a guide to be customised than as a rule to be enforced'.[206] The use of written texts as guides rather than rules is clear too in the work of Burchard, Bishop of Worms, an almost exact contemporary of Wulfstan's who, like him, played key roles in both ecclesiastical

---

[203]    See for example, Æthelberht 16–16.2, 21–1.2, 31, 77–7.2, ed. Oliver, *The Beginnings of English Law*, 64–9, 78–9; Alfred 8, 10, 11–11.5, 18, 25–5.1, 29, ed. Liebermann, *Gesetze*, I.54–9, 62–7.

[204]    VI Æthelred 52.1; II Cnut 38.2, ed. Liebermann, *Gesetze*, I.258–9, 338–9.

[205]    Wormald, *Making of English Law*, 196.

[206]    Rio, *Legal Practice*, 207.

and secular arenas. In writing his *Decretum*, a penitential handbook, Burchard seems in many cases to have tried to outline principles for judging rather than attempting to provide a specific penance for every sin.[207] These similar impulses in Wulfstan's and Burchard's writings may be indicative of wider changes in thought in the early eleventh century, but Wulfstan's relocation of penitential principles to a secular legal context is significant in extending theology from the realm of ecclesiastical discipline to the wider world, and in so doing, setting out guidelines rather than precise stipulations for the working of justice. This may have been how written law was intended to be used in England even before the eleventh century, but Wulfstan seems to be the first English writer to justify this approach on the basis of theology and penitential practice.

Wulfstan's interest in penitential practices and his concerns for the necessity of repentance and penance come through strongly throughout his works. Significantly, these concerns and interests informed his thinking on a wide range of matters, including the treatment of those who offended against secular law. Both in his own writings and in the material which he collected as sources there are numerous statements about the merciful treatment of offenders and specifically against the death penalty, making Wulfstan perhaps the most famous (and on the basis of the surviving evidence, the most vociferous) Anglo-Saxon advocate for alternatives to judicial execution.[208] In his laws for Æthelred and Cnut, Wulfstan insisted that Christians should not be condemned to death for small offences, but that they should be punished in other ways, noting that the destruction of what God has made should be avoided.[209] Wulfstan clearly did not seek to eradicate the death penalty entirely, and it is specified for a number of crimes in the laws which he wrote for Æthelred and Cnut, but the contexts for some of these stipulations are general statements demanding death or exile for particular offences or types of offenders, tempered with clauses revoking the sentence of execution if the individuals concerned cease from their wicked deeds and perform penance.[210] For other major offences such as treachery, the death penalty apparently remained the only appropriate response and no alternative was suggested.[211] Even here, it is probably worth bearing in mind Wulfstan's instructions to judges to be merciful, although the possibility of mercy for those who had offended against the person of the king seems rather unlikely.

---

[207]   Austin, *Shaping Church Law*, 138–40.

[208]   D. Whitelock, 'Wulfstan and the laws of Cnut', *English Historical Review* 63:249 (1948): 433–52, at 449; Thompson, *Dying and Death*, 182–4; N. Marafioti, 'Punishing bodies and saving souls: Capital and corporal punishment in late Anglo-Saxon England', *Haskins Society Journal: Studies in Medieval History* 20 (2009): 39–57.

[209]   V Æthelred 3, VI Æthelred 10–10.2; II Cnut 2.1, ed. Liebermann, *Gesetze*, I.238–9, 250–1, 308–11.

[210]   e.g. II Cnut 3–7, ed. Liebermann, *Gesetze*, I.310–13.

[211]   II Cnut 26, 64, ed. Liebermann, *Gesetze*, I.328–9, 352–3.

Wulfstan's thoughts on the death penalty were formed over a period of years, through the reading and collecting of theological and canonical material on the subject, and through discussion with his older monastic colleague, Ælfric of Eynsham.[212] The occasion for this discussion was the *Pastoral Letters* which Ælfric wrote for Wulfstan, probably shortly after 1002, apparently to be delivered to a group of priests and therefore in the voice of the bishop: these contain instructions and prescriptions on a whole range of topics from the anointing of the sick, to clerical celibacy, to the question of the role of ecclesiastics in secular judgements.[213] Ælfric wrote two letters in Latin which he later translated into English at Wulfstan's request, but a 'private' letter from Ælfric to Wulfstan also survives, and this reveals more fully some of the origins of the disagreement between the two clergymen. Wulfstan's letters to Ælfric are no longer extant, but his position can be understood both from Ælfric's objections and from his other works. The crucial difference between Wulfstan and Ælfric originates in the reasoning behind the limitation of the death penalty, and as both Victoria Thompson and Nicole Marafioti point out, the contexts from which each author wrote are significant in understanding their respective positions, since Ælfric's role as head of a monastery required him to deal much more with abstract problems than did Wulfstan's role as a reforming bishop who was active in both ecclesiastical and secular circles.[214] Both authors used abstract theological reasoning to inform their approaches, and both authors seem to have opposed judicial execution where possible, but with quite different results. Wulfstan's position is close to the Augustinian theology which sought to preserve God's creation and to allow offenders to repent and to save their souls through penance. In contrast, Ælfric's approach has two key aspects. The first is the importance of preserving life, drawn from Scripture and based on theology similar to that discernible in Wulfstan's works. The second is based on another aspect of the subject discussed in patristic writings, and that was the necessity of clerical purity and by extension, the prohibition of any clerical role in passing sentences of death.

In the first Latin Letter which Ælfric wrote for Wulfstan, he states that the 'authority of the canons' forbids clergy giving their assent to the death of any man, whether thief, robber, or murderer.[215] It is not clear precisely which canons Ælfric

---

[212]    For the relations between Wulfstan and Ælfric see P. Clemoes, 'The Old English Benedictine office, Corpus Christi College, Cambridge MS 190, and the relations between Ælfric and Wulfstan: A reconsideration', *Anglia* 78 (1960): 265–83; M. Godden, 'The Relations of Wulfstan and Ælfric', in Townend (ed.), *Wulfstan, Archbishop of York*, 353–74.

[213]    These letters are edited by Fehr, *Die Hirtenbriefe Ælfrics*. See Hill, 'Monastic Reform'; Godden, 'The Relations of Wulfstan and Ælfric', 354–62; J. Hill, 'Authorial Adaptation: Ælfric, Wulfstan and the Pastoral Letters', in O. Akio, F. Jacek and J. Scahill (eds), *Text and Language in Medieval English Prose* (Frankfurt am Main, 2005), 63–75.

[214]    Thompson, *Dying and Death*, 180–1; Marafioti, 'Punishing bodies', 50–1, 56–7.

[215]    2.191: 'et canonum auctoritas prohibet, ne quis episcopus aut clericus assensum praebeat in morte cuiuslibet hominis, siue latronis, siue furis, seu homicide, ne innocentem perdat', ed. Fehr, *Die Hirtenbriefe Ælfrics*, 56.

may have been thinking of, or whether he had identified specific canons at all, because in fact Ælfric's phrasing comes not from a canon collection, but directly from Abbo of Fleury's *Life of Edmund*, where Abbo describes Bishop Theodred's mistake in sentencing to death those who stole from the saint.[216] In Abbo's text, the 'authority of the canons' is the second reason given for why Theodred's actions were problematic;[217] the first was that Theodred did not remember God's command to try to redeem those who were condemned to death.[218] Ælfric's translation of the *Life* preserves both of these statements more or less intact, but in the *Pastoral Letter* he did not make any comment on attempting to redeem men condemned to death.[219] In the context of the *Pastoral Letters*, Ælfric was far more concerned with the issue of clerical involvement in secular judgements, and Ælfric's second Latin Letter for Wulfstan instructs that priests should not be judges in the condemnation of any man.[220] Ælfric followed this injunction with a long justification appealing to the authority of the gospels and the words of Christ himself, warning that those who do involve themselves in judgements may regret it if they hear Christ saying to them at the Last Judgement, 'Who made you to be a judge of thieves and robbers?'[221] Instead, Ælfric instructs that priests should be like innocent lambs, and notes that those who are judges or killers of men cannot be reckoned thus.[222] And in this letter too, Ælfric insists that the canons forbid clerical judgement in secular matters, perhaps again referring to the canons mentioned by Abbo.[223]

---

[216]    Abbo, *Passio S. Eadmundi*, XV, ed. Winterbottom, *Three Lives*, 83–5; see also XVI, ed. Arnold, *Memorials*, I.20–22.

[217]    Abbo, *Passio S. Eadmundi*, XV, ll. 45–8, ed. Winterbottom, *Three Lives*, 84: 'Unde canonum auctoritas prohibet ne quis episcopus aut quilibet de clero delatoris fungatur officio, quoniam satis dedecet ministros uitae caelestis assensum prebere in mortem cuiuslibet hominis'. See also XVI, ed. Arnold, *Memorials*, I.20–22.

[218]    Abbo, *Passio S. Eadmundi*, XV, ll. 38–9, ed. Winterbottom, *Three Lives*, 84: 'Eos qui ducuntur ad mortem eruere ne cesses'. See also Pr 24.11; IV Kgs 6.18ff; and XVI, ed. Arnold, *Memorials*, I.20–22.

[219]    *LS* XXXII, ll. 216–24, ed. Skeat, *Lives of Saints*, II.330: 'Ac he næs na gemyndig hu se mild-heorta god clypode þurh his witegan þas word þe hér standað. Eos qui ducutnur ad mortem eruere ne cesses. Þa þe man læt to deaðe alys hí ut symble. and eac þa halgan canones gehadodum forbeodað ge bisceopum ge preostum. to beonne embe þeofas. for-þan-þe hit ne gebyraþ þam þe beoð gecorene gode to þegnigenne þæt hi geþwærlæcan sceolon. on æniges mannes deaðe. gif hi beoð drihtnes þenas' ('But he did not remember how merciful God spoke these words through his prophet: *Eos qui ducuntur ad mortem eruere ne cesses*, 'those who are led to death, deliver them always'. And also, the holy canons forbid men in orders, both bishops and priests, to be occupied with thieves, because it is not fitting for them, who are chosen to serve God, that they should assent to any man's death, if they are the Lord's servants').

[220]    3.80–1, ed. Fehr, *Die Hirtenbriefe Ælfrics*, 66.

[221]    3.82–5, ed. Fehr, *Die Hirtenbriefe Ælfrics*, 66.

[222]    3.86, ed. Fehr, *Die Hirtenbriefe Ælfrics*, 67.

[223]    3.87, ed. Fehr, *Die Hirtenbriefe Ælfrics*, 67.

Most strikingly, Ælfric also enumerated his thoughts on these matters to Wulfstan in a 'private' letter, which seems to have been written before the public *Pastoral Letters*, and on which the second Latin Letter appears to be based.[224] Ælfric's condemnation of ecclesiastics who sit in judgement over secular matters is severe in both the public and the 'private' letters, but when writing to Wulfstan rather than for him Ælfric's approach can only really be described as a personal attack on Wulfstan and a direct criticism of his actions and thoughts. In this 'private' letter, Ælfric argues that it is not permitted for a *bishop* to be a judge of thieves and robbers, based on Abbo's discussion of Bishop Theodred; but he also claims the authority of the gospels, saying, 'if you don't believe me, listen to the words of Christ'.[225] In the *Pastoral Letters* Ælfric's words have rhetorical effect, since he wrote in the voice of a bishop addressing a number of priests,[226] but in the 'private' letter, where his justification of his position is more detailed in any case, his words are much more pointed and personal. Ælfric's choice to borrow the biblical simile that priests should be like 'lambs among wolves' was either targeted or unfortunate, since he was writing to Lupus himself; but Ælfric was not a stupid man and the former seems more likely.[227]

The information in the *Pastoral Letters* suggests that Wulfstan asked for information about a range of matters connected with ecclesiastical discipline and church custom, and it may be that Ælfric's outrage over ecclesiastical interference in secular judgement was in response to an expression of support by Wulfstan for the role of the bishop in this secular context. Ælfric clearly believed that putting people to death was problematic, but unlike Wulfstan, his major concern was for the souls of ecclesiastics who sat in judgement rather than for the souls of the offenders, similar to the position taken by the translator of the Old English *Boethius*.[228] However, Ælfric's irritation with Wulfstan's propensity to meddle in secular affairs apparently had little effect: in fact, Wulfstan seems to have had a marvellous tendency to cherry-pick interesting statements and to quote them out of context so that they supported his ideas rather than countered them. Even if Wulfstan ignored Ælfric's main message, his reuse of writings by Ælfric and others shows the development of his thought on the death penalty clearly.

In this context, an important body of material is the collection of canons and related texts found in some of the manuscripts associated with Wulfstan (see Table 3.1 at 163). This collection used to be known as the

---

[224]    *Councils and Synods*, I.i.255–60. This letter is 'private' in the sense that it was not intended primarily for public delivery as the *Pastoral Letters* were, but this does not mean that no one except Wulfstan was intended to read it: see Godden, 'The Relations of Wulfstan and Ælfric', 357–8.

[225]    2a.xv, ed. Fehr, *Die Hirtenbriefe Ælfrics*, 226–7.

[226]    Strangely, even in the public letters the singular 'credis' is used again rather than the plural form 'credite', suggesting that Ælfric may still have been having a dig at Wulfstan.

[227]    2a.xv, ed. Fehr, *Die Hirtenbriefe Ælfrics*, 226–7.

[228]    See above, 145–6.

*Excerptiones Pseudo-Ecgberhti*, but in the most recent edition it is entitled 'Wulfstan's *Canon Law Collection*'.[229] This is a highly complex body of material and at present the precise nature and extent of Wulfstan's role in its compilation is not immediately obvious. It exists in two different recensions, a shorter and probably earlier version (Recension A);[230] and a longer and probably later version (Recension B).[231] It is also important to note that the longer recension incorporates the *First Capitulary* of Bishop Ghaerbald of Liège (d.809) as a preface to the collection while retaining it as a distinct text: Michael Elliot suggests that this addition was perhaps made by Wulfstan himself, or someone working for him.[232] The collection of canons comprises material from councils, earlier selections of canon law, and a number of statements which appear also in works by Ælfric, but there has been some debate over the precise textual relationships between these canons and the works of Ælfric and Wulfstan. Patrick Wormald, as well as the most recent editors of the collection, J.E. Cross and Andrew Hamer, argued that the collection draws on statements in Ælfric's letters rather than the canons being the sources for the letters.[233] This suggests in turn that the collection can be dated no earlier than 1005, and no later than 1008, when they were used in the compilation of one of Æthelred's law codes.[234]

As a whole, this collection of canon law is most strongly associated with Wulfstan because it survives now in manuscripts which are closely connected with him. Even if it is not clear whether he should be regarded as an 'author' of the collection, the later recension (B) in particular seems to show his influence and was a significant source for his *Canons of Edgar*.[235] This is significant in considering how Ælfric's statements were reused beyond their immediate context in the *Pastoral Letters*. The earlier recension (A) includes Ælfric's statement that

---

[229]   The edition is Cross and Hamer, *Wulfstan's Canon Law Collection*.

[230]   Recension A is preserved in Cambridge, Corpus Christi College, 265; Oxford, Bodleian Library, Barlow 37; and Rouen, Bibliothèque municipale, 1382: see Table 3.1; and Cross and Hamer, *Wulfstan's Canon Law Collection*, 6–7.

[231]   Recension B is preserved in Cambridge, Corpus Christi College, 190; and London, British Library, Cotton Nero A.i: see Table 3.1; and Cross and Hamer, *Wulfstan's Canon Law Collection*, 8–12.

[232]   M. Elliot, 'Ghaerbald's first capitulary, the excerptiones pseudo-Ecgberhti, and the sources of Wulfstan's Canons of Edgar', *Notes and Queries* 57:2 (2010): 161–5, at 162–3.

[233]   Cross, J.E. and A. Hamer, 'Ælfric's *Letters* and the *Excerptiones Ecgberhti*', in J.A. Roberts, J.L. Nelson, M. Godden and J. Bately (eds), *Alfred the Wise: Studies in Honour of Janet Bately on the Occasion of her Sixty-Fifth Birthday* (Cambridge: D.S. Brewer, 1997), 5–13; Cross and Hamer, *Wulfstan's Canon Law Collection*, 17–32; Wormald, 'Archbishop Wulfstan and the Holiness of Society'; cf. M. Godden, 'Anglo-Saxons on the Mind', in M. Lapidge and H. Gneuss (eds), *Learning and Literature in Anglo-Saxon England: Studies Presented to Peter Clemoes on the Occasion of his Sixty-Fifth Birthday* (Cambridge, 1985), 271–98, at 282–3 and Godden, 'The Relations of Wulfstan and Ælfric', 364–5.

[234]   Wormald, *Making of English Law*, 202, 332–5, 353–4.

[235]   See Elliot, 'Ghaerbald's first capitulary'.

the canons prohibit any bishop or cleric from assenting to the death of any man.[236] This statement is also included in Recension B, but there it lacks the final clause explaining that priests should not be judges in case they lose their innocence (an issue which will be discussed in detail below); and it is preceded by Ælfric's warning that priests should take care not to be judges in the condemnation of any man, although here 'priests' was altered to 'clerics'.[237] Thus adjusted and relocated to their new context, these statements actually support the idea that ecclesiastics should take care to prevent the death penalty where possible, and there is barely a trace of Ælfric's specific objection to ecclesiastical involvement in secular judgements.

Ælfric's message in the English translations of the letters may also have been adjusted by Wulfstan, since the manuscripts which preserve these are associated primarily with Wulfstan rather than with Ælfric.[238] In Ælfric's preface to the English letters for Wulfstan, he states that 'by these [letters] we hope to be of use in correcting some people, although we realise that this has little pleased others. But it does not seem appropriate for us always to remain silent and not to reveal divine utterances to those below us, because if the messenger stays quiet, who will announce the judge who is to come?'[239] This too may have been aimed at Wulfstan and may suggest that Ælfric was told to exclude certain passages from his translation: it is notable that the diatribe of the second Latin Letter finds no place in its Old English translation, although it is not clear whether Wulfstan instructed Ælfric to omit this or whether it was simply removed when the letters were recopied (or both). It is also interesting that the section in the first Latin Letter about the canons' prohibition of clerical judgement is expanded slightly, and its emphasis adjusted, in two of the surviving copies of the first Old English letter:

---

[236]   Rec A. 79, Rec B. 161, ed. Cross and Hamer, *Wulfstan's Canon Law Collection*, 99, 168; *Pastoral Letter* 2.191, ed. Fehr, *Die Hirtenbriefe Ælfrics*, 56. For discussion of the collection see Cross and Hamer, 'Ælfric's *Letters* and the *Excerptiones Ecgberhti*'; Elliot, 'Ghaerbald's first capitulary' and Cross and Hamer, *Wulfstan's Canon Law Collection*, 3–61.

[237]   Rec B. 160, ed. Cross and Hamer, *Wulfstan's Canon Law Collection*; 3.80, ed. Fehr, *Die Hirtenbriefe Ælfrics*, 66.

[238]   For discussion of the manuscripts of the *Pastoral Letters*, see Fehr, *Die Hirtenbriefe Ælfrics*, liv–lxiv, and P. Clemoes, 'Supplementary Introduction', in Fehr (ed.), *Die Hirtenbriefe Ælfrics*; and Hill, 'Monastic Reform', 111–15.

[239]   II.1, ed. Fehr, *Die Hirtenbriefe Ælfrics*, 68–9: 'quibus speramus nos quibusdam prodesse ad correctionem, quamuis sciamus aliis minime placuisse. Sed non est nobis consultum semper silere et non aperire subiectis eloquia diuina, quia si preco tacet, quis iudicem uenturum nuntiet?'. I follow Malcolm Godden in taking 'quibus' to refer to the letters themselves, rather than Jonathan Wilcox's interpretation that this refers to Ælfric's comments on his chosen style of translation: see Godden, 'The Relations of Wulfstan and Ælfric', 360 and J. Wilcox, *Aelfric's Prefaces*, Durham Medieval Texts 9 (Durham, 1994), 134.

> We may not be occupied with any man's death: even if he is a homicide or a
> murderer or a great thief, we still must not assign death to him, and we may not
> judge about that. But let laymen assign life or death to him, so that we do not
> lose our meek innocence.[240]

Once again, this begins to look more like a prohibition of clerical involvement in
the death penalty rather than the prohibition of clerical judgement itself, although
Ælfric's concern is still visible here, and this passage too may be one that Ælfric
was asked to tone down in translation. But Cambridge, Corpus Christi College, 201,
part 1, a mid eleventh-century manuscript with a probable Winchester provenance,
contains a copy of the letter which seems to be a version that was rewritten by
Wulfstan himself: in this version, the passage has been removed completely and
replaced instead with instructions that priests should avoid worldly pursuits such
as war and woman, suggesting that Wulfstan was not entirely happy the passage
as he received it from Ælfric.[241]

The transmission of the Latin behind this passage is rather confusing, both in its
original context in the first Latin Letter and as excerpted in the canon law collection.
The first Old English letter refers to priestly loss of innocence ('unscæþþignysse')
for ecclesiastics who are involved with the death penalty, and is almost a direct
translation of the first Latin letter's 'ne innocentiam perdat', as it is preserved in an
early eleventh-century manuscript, now Copenhagen, Kongelige Bibliotek, Gl. Kgl.
Sam. 1595 (on fol. 74r). However, the other two manuscripts of the first Latin Letter
(Cambridge, Corpus Christi College, 190 and 265), preserve a different reading, 'ne
innocentem perdat'.[242] The result is that in the letters in CCCC 190 and CCCC 265
the reason given for why men in orders should not be judges is *not* 'so that we do not
lose our innocence', but instead something more like 'so that we do not destroy an
innocent man'.[243] Versions of these sentences also appear in the canon law collection:
Recension A (i.e., the shorter and probably earlier version) contains the sentence
from the Copenhagen manuscript (i.e., with the reading 'ne innocentiam perdat'),
while Recension B contains the first part of the sentence condemning ecclesiastical

---

[240] II.201, ed. Fehr, *Die Hirtenbriefe Ælfrics*, 140–1: 'We ne moton beon ymbe
mannes deað. Þeah-þe he manslaga beo oþþe morð gefremede oþþe mycel þeof-man, swa-
þeah we ne scylan him deað getæcan. Na we ne motan deman ymbe þæt. Ac tæcea þa
læwedan men him lif oþþe deað, þæt wé ne forleasan þa líþan unscæþþignysse'.

[241] II.200a–c, ed. Fehr, *Die Hirtenbriefe Ælfrics*, 140; see also Hill, 'Monastic
Reform', 113; Godden, 'The Relations of Wulfstan and Ælfric', 360–2.

[242] CCCC 190, p. 201; CCCC 265, p. 173.

[243] Rather than the abstract noun 'innocentia' ('innocence') the alternative reading
uses the adjective 'innocens' ('innocent'), but in this phrase it works substantively to mean
'an innocent person'.

involvement in the death penalty, but lacks the final clause about innocence (or an innocent man) altogether.[244]

This variation is interesting because it seems to reflect one of the differences in the positions expressed by Ælfric and Wulfstan: while Ælfric did not want clergy to lose their innocence, Wulfstan was concerned with justice and the saving of souls. The Copenhagen manuscript is a composite book and it seems that this copy of the letter may be closest to Ælfric's authorial text: Clemoes suggested that 'it may have been the manuscript which Ælfric himself sent to Wulfstan, as subsequently modified in Wulfstan's possession, or, perhaps, a copy of that manuscript'.[245] If the Copenhagen text stands closer to Ælfric, it may be that the version in the Latin letters in CCCC 201 and CCCC 265 was a deliberate change by Wulfstan in response to a passage with which he disagreed, reflected also in the omission of the whole passage from the first Old English letter in CCCC 201.

Ælfric's letters to and for Wulfstan give the impression that the two clergymen were rather talking at cross-purposes, and the end result seems to have been extreme irritation on Ælfric's part, while Wulfstan apparently determined to ignore Ælfric. Both authors were pastorally oriented, but Ælfric's knowledge and skill seem most often in a pastoral context to have been put towards providing material for priests to use so that they could teach their congregations.[246] Ælfric also seems to have been more concerned than Wulfstan to make sure that priests realised that if they failed to teach their congregations properly, they should not expect a favourable response at the Last Judgement: Ælfric apparently felt that the responsibility for souls fell much more heavily on priests than on individual lay people.[247] Wulfstan of course provided material for priests too, but in contrast to Ælfric, seems to have had much more of a direct pastoral concern for individual lay souls (and perhaps also their ultimate fates) than did Ælfric.[248] These differences in approach seem to have led

---

[244]    A.79, B.161, ed. Cross and Hamer, *Wulfstan's Canon Law Collection*, 99, 168. This means in fact that CCCC 190 preserves both readings, 'ne innocentem perdat' in the *Pastoral Letter* (CCCC 190, p. 201), and 'ne innocentiam perdat' in the excerpted statement in the canon law material (CCCC 190, p. 137).

[245]    Clemoes, 'Supplementary Introduction', cxxxv–cxxxix; see also the discussion in the introduction to J.E. Cross and J.M. Tunberg, *The Copenhagen Wulfstan Collection: Copenhagen Kongelige Bibliotek Gl. Kgl. Sam.1595*, Early English Manuscripts in Facsimile 25 (Copenhagen, 1993).

[246]    M. Clayton, 'Homiliaries and preaching in Anglo-Saxon England', *Peritia* 4 (1985): 207–42, at 231–2; Wilcox, 'Ælfric in Dorset', 53–4.

[247]    See for example Ælfric, *CH* II.3, ll. 238–42, ed. Godden, *Catholic Homilies*, 26; *Pastoral Letter* II.174–5, ed. Fehr, *Die Hirtenbriefe Ælfrics*, 130–1. Wulfstan did note this, for example in *Polity*, 104–44, ed. K. Jost, *Die 'Institutes of Polity, Civil and Ecclesiastical'*, Schweizer anglistische Arbeiten 47 (1959), 84–108, but the theme is more prominent in Ælfric's works.

[248]    Whitelock, 'Wulfstan and the laws of Cnut', 449.

to Wulfstan doing precisely what Ælfric had told him not to, since Wulfstan's writings show that he specifically encouraged ecclesiastical interference in secular judgement, especially if the ecclesiastics involved were bishops who could ensure that judgements were carried out appropriately in the sight of God.

Wulfstan's most developed ideas about Christian society are found in his (so-called) *Institutes of Polity*, and here he stated that bishops should forbid injustice, and work with secular officials and judges to prevent bad judgements in secular law.[249] Information on the duties of bishops in passing judgement is also found in *Episcopus*, a short text attributed to Wulfstan which discusses the responsibilities and powers of bishops.[250] This text survives in only one copy: it was incorporated into a version of *Polity* in Oxford, Bodleian Library, Junius 121, a manuscript written in Worcester in the third quarter of the eleventh century which draws heavily on an earlier collection of Wulfstanian material.[251] In *Episcopus*, Wulfstan encourages a strong episcopal role in all kinds of judgements, both ecclesiastical and secular.[252] He advises that bishops should settle disputes and dictate judgements along with secular judges, and that priests should help men to obtain right and seek to prevent the oppression of lesser men by greater.[253] A passage from Cnut's letter of 1020 advocates similar ideas and likewise seems to show Wulfstan's influence: Cnut calls for his reeves to make just judgements which they are to pronounce with the bishop's witness, and mercy according to the bishop's approval, so that the offender is able to endure the punishment.[254] Interestingly, Wulfstan was inclined to refer judgement to the bishop even in cases which traditionally would have required secular judgement: one such example is the stipulation in II Cnut that in the cases of those accused of homicide, and women accused of adultery, those who failed to clear themselves were to be sent to the bishop for judgement rather than to a secular authority.[255]

[249]  *Polity*, 41–64, ed. Jost, *Polity*, 62–9. Wulfstan also wrote about corrupt judges in one of his Latin sermons, *Contra iniquos iudices et falsos testes*, ed. T.N. Hall, 'Wulfstan's Latin Sermons', in Townend (ed.), *Wulfstan, Archbishop of York*, 93–139, at 120–1.

[250]  *Episcopus, Councils and Synods*, I.i, no. 56.

[251]  N.R. Ker, *Catalogue of Manuscripts Containing Anglo-Saxon* (Oxford, 1957), no. 338.

[252]  *Episcopus*, 1, *Councils and Synods*, I.i, no. 56.

[253]  *Episcopus*, 4, 9, *Councils and Synods*, I.i, no. 56.

[254]  *Letter of 1020*, 11, ed. Liebermann, *Gesetze*, I.274–5. For Wulfstan's role in the production or adaptation of this letter, see D. Whitelock, 'Wulfstan's authorship of Cnut's laws', *English Historical Review* 70 (1955): 72–85, at 83–4; A.G. Kennedy, 'Cnut's law code of 1018', *Anglo-Saxon England* 11 (1983): 57–81, at 62–4; Kennedy, 'Cnut's law code of 1018'; S. Keynes, 'The Additions in Old English', in J.J.G. Alexander and N. Barker (eds), *The York Gospels: A Facsimile with Introductory Essays by Jonathan Alexander* [et al.] (London, 1986), 81–99, at 95–6; Wormald, *Making of English Law*, 347.

[255]  II Cnut 53.1, 56.1, ed. Liebermann, *Gesetze*, I.348–9.

As in other cases, this decision seems to link concern over the death penalty and concern over ordeals. Homicide and adultery were the kinds of crimes where there was often little evidence, and which might therefore have been tried by ordeal: those who were guilty would have been sentenced to death, according to Æthelred's early legislation.[256] By sending those in this situation to the bishop, Wulfstan presumably hoped that these offenders would not be sentenced to death. This is significant, both because Wulfstan's most developed and detailed statements against the death penalty also come in the context of ordeals, and because Wulfstan seems to have been almost as concerned about the use and abuse of ordeals as about the use and abuse of judicial execution. Wulfstan's most famous recommendations for alternatives to the death penalty were made in the laws of Cnut. At the beginning of II Cnut, the 'secular' section of a two-part code, Wulfstan advocated justifiable punishments even for serious offences, and encouraged judgement according to the rule outlined in the pater noster.[257] In some cases in the law code, Wulfstan specifically substituted more lenient penalties where previous decrees had demanded death, but Wulfstan also outlined a theory of punishment which advocated mutilation for repeat offenders, so that the soul could be saved at the expense of the body. For those who were 'extremely untrustworthy' and who failed at ordeal for a second time, Wulfstan stipulated as punishment the amputation of hands and feet, or other body parts; and, once again taking into account the circumstances of offence and of offender, those guilty of greater crimes were to be subjected to more severe mutilations.[258]

Wulfstan's inspiration for mercy in judgement and for limitation of the use of the death penalty (or alternatives to it) is found in some of the texts in the manuscripts which represent his collections. Two related Latin passages discuss the practice of judging and how punishments should be implemented, one in CCCC 265, and the other in CCCC 190 and Cotton Nero A.i, this last a book which Wulfstan himself owned and annotated.[259] These passages are interesting in terms of considering how Wulfstan or others close to him may have reworked material. The opening sentences of the two different versions are the same, and they share some of the same information but not in the same order. The end result of this is that the two different versions present two different messages. Both versions include a complaint that secular judges condemn men to death for trivial offences and do not heed the apostle's warning to chastise but not to condemn: instead, men should be chastised and not killed, because they can be saved through punishments, so that the souls for which the Lord suffered are not consigned to eternal punishment. A list of punishments which can be used as alternatives to

---

[256]    I Æthelred 1–1.2; III Æthelred 4–4.2, ed. Liebermann, *Gesetze*, I.216–17, 228–31; Bartlett, *Trial by Fire and Water*, 19, 26–33.

[257]    II Cnut 2, 2a, 2.1, ed. Liebermann, *Gesetze*, I.308–11.

[258]    II Cnut 30.4–5, ed. Liebermann, *Gesetze*, I.332–3.

[259]    CCCC 265, pp. 108–9; CCCC 190, p. 242; Cotton Nero A.i, fols. 157r–157v. For the manuscripts, see Table 3.1.

execution also appears in both versions, and this list advocates amputation (of eyes or nose or hands or feet or other limbs) as a penalty, as Wulfstan does in II Cnut.[260]

The passage in CCCC 265 is much more concerned with judges and judgements than with specific instructions for the treatment of offenders. This version instructs the reader to set aside 'punishments', apparently meaning 'eternal punishments': the author warns that judges forget that they will be judged as they have judged, and quotes from the letter of James that 'those who judge without mercy will not be shown mercy themselves'.[261] This passage in CCCC 265 is included in the middle of a rather miscellaneous collection of material rubricated 'Exempla saxonica a[d] castigationem hominum' ('Saxon examples for punishing men'), which describes a range of different measures for punishment and penances, and includes information about ordeals of hot iron, treading over nine hot ploughshares, and an ordeal of burial (which required the buried person to breathe through a straw), as well as more general material about penance and the judgement of men in orders.[262] The passage about judges appears in the midst of this material without a separate rubric,[263] and is followed (again without rubrication) by information about the imposition of penance, before a new section which includes formulae for penitential letters, some of which are in the name of 'Lupus, bishop of London', and others of which are in the name of Pope John, and addressed to one 'Wulfstan'.[264] The association of this material with Wulfstan is therefore strong, even though the origins of the material and the purposes of this section in CCCC 265 are not entirely certain.

The related passage in CCCC 190 and Cotton Nero A.i prioritises different themes. In these manuscripts, the passage is headed 'De improuiso iudicio secularium' ('About the incautious judgements of seculars'). In CCCC 190 it comes in the middle of a penitential and liturgical compilation which includes information pertinent to the liturgical celebrations of Pentecost and Easter as well

---

[260]    Dorothy Whitelock cited the passage in CCCC 265 as the source for Wulfstan's statement in II Cnut, but it is difficult to account for her assertion that this passage does not expressly mention mutilation, since it clearly does (Whitelock, 'Wulfstan and the laws of Cnut', 449): 'Diversis itaque modis rei puniendi sunt. et non statim necandi. sed per penas saluandi. ne in eternas incidant alii ut diximus. catenis et flagellis. alii fame uel frigore constringendi sunt. Alii pellem et pilos simul perdentes. turpiter obprobia sustineant. et alii adhuc acrius constringantur. id est. membrum perdant. oculum uidelicet uel nasum. manum uel pedem. seu aliud aliquid membrum'.

[261]    CCCC 265, p. 109.

[262]    CCCC 265, pp. 105–8. Cotton Nero A.i (fols. 172v–173r) and CCCC 190 (pp. 12–13) include passages headed 'QVALITER APVD ORIENTALES PROVINCIES GERMANIE ATQUE SAXONIE PRO DIVERSIS CRIMINIBUS PENITENTIE. OBSERVATVR MODVS' but these do not seem to be related to this section in CCCC 265.

[263]    The passage is on pp. 108–9; a space seems to have been left for a rubric, but only a short one (perhaps 'ITEM').

[264]    M. Bateson, 'A Worcester Cathedral book of ecclesiastical collections, made c. 1000 AD', *English Historical Review* 10 (1895): 712–31, at 727–30.

as for the reconciliation of penitents. The passage is placed after sections which discuss different types of penance and sin as well as excommunication; and it is followed by another section on excommunication and the more practical and liturgical aspects of confession and penance, drawn at least partly from one of the confessional *ordines*.[265] The version of the passage in CCCC 190 and Cotton Nero A.i is less concerned with judges and how they make their judgements, and more with the death penalty and how it was enacted or avoided. Here, the statement about mutilation is followed by Jerome's statement from his commentary on Jeremiah that the punishment of murderers and those who commit sacrilege is not a pouring out of blood, but the ministry of the law; and that he who spares wicked men injures good ones.[266] The passage then concludes with a sentence which advocates allowing time for the offender to live and perform penance so that he may not suffer eternal pains afterwards (that is, after death).

Jerome's statement about the pouring out of blood is included in the canon law collection but only in (the later) Recension B, which is also preserved in both CCCC 190 and Cotton Nero A.i. The sequence of canons in Recension B thus presents this statement about the punishment of murderers following two other sentences concerning punishment and the killing of offenders, one of which is also by Jerome, and the other of which is (incorrectly) attributed to him in Cotton Nero A.i.[267] This is particularly important because the first two 'Jeromian' sentences in the sequence are also found in (the earlier) Recension A, while the statement about the pouring out of blood is not, suggesting that this was an addition to Recension B.[268] This is highly significant: Jerome's statement about the pouring out of blood is found only in the manuscripts containing the later Recension of the canon law collection; the version of the passage about judges which contains that statement is also only found in manuscripts which contain this later Recension. In turn, this may therefore suggest that the passage found in CCCC 190 and Nero A.i is a later, revised version of the passage in CCCC 265. It is possible, if not currently provable, that Wulfstan himself revised the passage in order to incorporate Jerome's statement about the pouring out of blood, as well as the idea that punishment must allow for penance in order to benefit the soul. This possibility is strengthened by the fact that Nero A.i is a book which Wulfstan owned and used himself.

---

[265] The liturgical texts are discussed and printed in C.A. Jones, 'Two composite texts from Archbishop Wulfstan's "Commonplace Book": The *De ecclesiastica consuetudine* and the *Institutio beati Amalarii de ecclesiasticis officiis'*, *Anglo-Saxon England* 27 (1998): 233–71; Fehr printed much of this material as an appendix to the pastoral letters (*Die Hirtenbriefe Ælfrics*, 234–49).

[266] CCCC 190, p. 242; Nero A.i, fol. 157r; Jerome, *Comm. in Hierem.* IV.35, ed. Reiter, *S. Hieronymi presbyteri opera, pars I. Opera exegetica, 3: In Hieremiam libri VI*, 201. See above, 139–40.

[267] See Rec A.50–1, Rec B.88–9, ed. Cross and Hamer, *Wulfstan's Canon Law Collection*, 88–9, 137.

[268] In Barlow 37, A.50 also contains the incorrect attribution to Jerome.

Jerome's statement about the pouring out of blood is particularly important in the way that it was juxtaposed with sentences about mutilation, because the effect is to suggest a much more literal interpretation than Jerome intended. Instead of exonerating those who were involved in judicial killing, it is the pouring out of blood occasioned by the amputation of limbs which is now to be reckoned as the administration of the law.[269] Whether Wulfstan was the author or compiler of this passage, or whether he simply used it, the evidence suggests that this more literal interpretation is crucial in understanding his attitude to capital punishment: even statements that could have been used in favour of the death penalty were turned to mean something quite different. It is clear too that it is the version of the passage in CCCC 190 and Nero A.i which was the driving force behind the mutilations prescribed for repeat offenders in II Cnut, where the importance of applying punishment in such a way as to preserve the soul is clearly stated. Here again, Wulfstan effectively established a way of linking ecclesiastical and secular forms of discipline so that all judgements were carried out in ways that satisfied both God's law and royal legislation: if death was avoided, then a lengthy penance was a possibility.

Wulfstan's prescriptions for mutilation were stipulated specifically for those who failed ordeals more than once, rather than as punishment for repeat offenders more generally, and this suggests that perhaps the link between ordeals and the passage in CCCC 265 may have retained its significance in Wulfstan's mind, even though it is the content of the revised version in CCCC 190 and Cotton Nero A.i which lies behind the prescriptions in II Cnut. This is important too given the changes which Wulfstan introduced into the way that ordeals were carried out. The process for exculpation set out in the laws of Cnut was adapted by Wulfstan from a series of decrees in the early legislation of Æthelred,[270] and broadly speaking, there are two changes that he made which are particularly significant here. The first is the removal of the death penalty in the event of failure at an ordeal. According to I Æthelred, the punishment for failure at ordeal was to be pecuniary in the first instance, and death on the second (and last) occasion; in contrast III Æthelred simply stipulated capital punishment for those who failed ordeals.[271] Wulfstan's revision eliminated capital punishment, and even the mutilations which he demanded were only to be applied in the event of a second failure at ordeal. Since

---

[269]   CCCC 190, p. 242: 'Castigandi enim sent rei diuersisque modis, arguendi et non statim necandi, sed per penas saluandi, ne anime pro quibus ipse dominus passus est, in eterna pena dispereant. Alii uinculis et flagris; alii autem fame uel frigore constrigendi sunt; alii quoque pellem, capillos et barbam simul perdentes turpiter obprobria sustineant; alii adhuc acrius constringantur, id est membrum perdant, oculum uidelicet uel nasum, manum uel pedem seu aliud aliquid membrum. Hieronimus dicit: Homicidas et sacrilegos punire non est effusio sanguinis, sed legum ministerium; Nocet itaque bonis. qui parcet malis;'.

[270]   Primarily I Æthelred, i.e. not the law codes written by Wulfstan for Æthelred.

[271]   I Æthelred 1.5–1.6; III Æthelred 4–4.2; cf. II Cnut, 30.4–30.5, ed. Liebermann, *Gesetze*, I.218–19, 228–31, 332–5.

Wulfstan clearly opposed capital punishment, this might seem more connected with issues of life and death than with the ordeal. But the second change that Wulfstan made was a substantial limitation of the types of people who would be made to undergo ordeals, such that theoretically ordeals would have been used far less frequently than before.

The process for exculpation in Æthelred's early legislation (I and III Æthelred) is quite complicated, but in outline, someone accused of an offence would have to undergo a threefold ordeal if he was considered to be 'tyhtbysig', of bad reputation – apparently because he would not have been considered to have the right to swear an oath.[272] Someone accused of an offence who was not 'tyhtbysig', but whose preliminary oath failed, might also have to undergo a threefold ordeal.[273] For the purposes of ordeals, the general population therefore seems (according to I and III Æthelred) to have been divided into those who were of good reputation, and those who were not. Wulfstan modified this so that those who were forced to undergo ordeals were people whose reputation was not merely bad, but absolutely terrible. Much of the process outlined in I Æthelred was retained quite closely in II Cnut; but crucially, Wulfstan changed the stipulations so that those who were required to undergo threefold ordeals were 'extremely untrustworthy', someone who was 'so untrustworthy in the hundred and of such bad reputation that he is accused by three men together'.[274] In contrast, those who were 'getreowe' ('trustworthy') and who had not failed an oath or an ordeal was allowed to swear an oath; those who were not trustworthy were (if possible) asked to swear a 'more difficult' oath, one where the compurgators were chosen for the accused.[275]

Wulfstan therefore re-divided the population into those who were trustworthy, those who were untrustworthy, and those who were extremely untrustworthy, and only stipulated that ordeals be required of this last, extremely untrustworthy, group of people. It is consequently all the more striking that his substitution of mutilation instead of execution was inserted in this context, since the process that he outlined apparently applied only to the most troublesome people in society. The amputation of limbs would evidently have been fairly effective in preventing such people from re-offending beyond their second failure at ordeal, and this may be one reason that Wulfstan felt confident in instituting alternatives to the death penalty, but it is also worth considering whether uncertainty over ordeals was another driving factor here. Wulfstan seems to have taken particular care over the outcome of ordeals, for

---

[272]    I Æthelred 1.1; III Æthelred 3.4–4.2, ed. Liebermann, *Gesetze*, I.216–17, 228–31. I and III Æthelred seem to have been intended as parallel codes in some respects: see P. Wormald, 'Æthelred the Lawmaker', in D. Hill (ed.), *Ethelred the Unready: Papers from the Millenary Conference* (Oxford, 1978), 47–80, at 61–2. The crucial difference between them with regard to ordeals is that III Æthelred seems to allow the possibility of offering payment instead of undergoing an ordeal at almost every stage of the process of exculpation.

[273]    I Æthelred 1.4, ed. Liebermann, *Gesetze*, I.218–19.

[274]    II Cnut 30, ed. Liebermann, *Gesetze*, I.330–1.

[275]    II Cnut 22–2.3, ed. Liebermann, *Gesetze*, I.324–7.

example in reserving to bishops the judgement of those who were accused of murder, and women who were accused of adultery, and who had failed in their attempt to clear themselves, presumably through oath or ordeal.[276] It is also significant that his writings contain a number of objections to ordeals (and sometimes to oaths too), although as in earlier texts there is never any clear stated reason for this, and it is therefore difficult to work out whether it was ordeals or something else (such as the possibility of execution) which was considered problematic.

In almost all the legal texts that Wulfstan wrote, he instructed that both oaths and ordeals should be prohibited on fast and feast days, and in seasons of fasting and feasting. This occurs in the 'Laws of Edward and Guthrum', probably the earliest surviving legal text that Wulfstan wrote, and then in the *Canons of Edgar*, in Æthelred's law codes, and in I Cnut.[277] This injunction is also linked with a statement that on fasts and feasts there should be no strife between Christians, and this seems ostensibly to be the reason behind Wulfstan's prohibition of these practices.[278] Wulfstan seems to have based his injunctions on sections of the *Capitula* of Theodulf, Carolingian regulatory texts which circulated in England both in their original Latin and in an Old English translation, and which state that there should be no strife and that no quarrel should be heard on such days.[279] However, the interpretation of this to include oaths and ordeals seems to be entirely Wulfstan's own, since it is apparently unparalleled in contemporary legal texts, Anglo-Saxon or otherwise. Moreover, the practical effect of this statement would have seriously limited the use of ordeals (and perhaps also oaths) in judicial practice, as shown by the example in Table 3.3: if this restriction was followed, oaths and ordeals would have been disallowed for more than one third of the year, and often for periods of more than a month at a time.

---

[276]  II Cnut 53.1, 56.1, ed. Liebermann, *Gesetze*, I.348–9.

[277]  Edward and Guthrum, 9; V Æthelred 18; VI Æthelred 25; I Cnut 17, ed. Liebermann, *Gesetze*, I.132–3, 242–3, 252–3, 296–7; *Canons of Edgar*, 24, ed. R. Fowler, *Wulfstan's 'Canons of Edgar'*, EETS, OS 266 (London, 1972), 6–7. The sentiment also appears in homilies which incorporate Wulfstanian material, although probably not written by him (*Hom.* 23, ed. A.S. Napier, *Wulfstan: Sammlung der ihm zugeschriebenen homilien nebst Untersuchungen über ihre Echtheit, Sammlung englisher Denkmäler in kritischen Ausgaben* 4 (Berlin, 1883), 117, l. 14 – 118, l. 1; and *Hom.* 43, ed. Napier, *Wulfstan*, 208, ll. 20–24). On the basis of the statement in Edward and Guthrum, Keefer suggests that 'trial by ordeal was customary in both Danish and English regions with the establishment of the Danelaw in the 880s' (Keefer, 'Đonne se cirlisca man', 360), but in fact this text has long been recognised as being a product of Wulfstan's authorship (see D. Whitelock, 'Wulfstan and the so-called Laws of Edward and Guthrum', *English Historical Review* 56:221 (1941): 1–21 and Wormald, *Making of English Law*, 389–91).

[278]  e.g. V Æthelred 19; VI Æthelred 25.1, ed. Liebermann, *Gesetze*, I.242–3, 252–3 (and *Hom.* 23, ed. Napier, *Wulfstan*, 118, ll. 1–3).

[279]  Theodulf, *Capitula*, xxiiii and xlii, ed. H. Sauer, *Theodulfi Capitula in England: die altenglischen Übersetzungen, zusammen mit dem lateinischen Text*, Texte und Untersuchungen zur englischen Philologie 8 (Munich, 1978), 336–7, 394–5.

Table 3.3      The effects of Wulfstan's injunctions forbidding oaths and ordeals on days and seasons of feasting and fasting (I Cnut 16–17), as applied to the year 1020 (in this year Easter fell on 17 April)

**January**

| Su | Mo | Tu | We | Th | Fr | Sa |
|----|----|----|----|----|----|----|
|    |    |    |    |    | 1  | 2  |
| 3  | 4  | 5  | 6  | 7  | 8  | 9  |
| 10 | 11 | 12 | 13 | 14 | 15 | 16 |
| 17 | 18 | 19 | 20 | 21 | 22 | 23 |
| 24 | 25 | 26 | 27 | 28 | 29 | 30 |
| 31 |    |    |    |    |    |    |

**February**

| Su | Mo | Tu | We | Th | Fr | Sa |
|----|----|----|----|----|----|----|
|    | 1  | 2  | 3  | 4  | 5  | 6  |
| 7  | 8  | 9  | 10 | 11 | 12 | 13 |
| 14 | 15 | 16 | 17 | 18 | 19 | 20 |
| 21 | 22 | 23 | 24 | 25 | 26 | 27 |
| 28 | 29 |    |    |    |    |    |

**March**

| Su | Mo | Tu | We | Th | Fr | Sa |
|----|----|----|----|----|----|----|
|    |    | 1  | 2  | 3  | 4  | 5  |
| 6  | 7  | 8  | 9  | 10 | 11 | 12 |
| 13 | 14 | 15 | 16 | 17 | 18 | 19 |
| 20 | 21 | 22 | 23 | 24 | 25 | 26 |
| 27 | 28 | 29 | 30 | 31 |    |    |

**April**

| Su | Mo | Tu | We | Th | Fr | Sa |
|----|----|----|----|----|----|----|
|    |    |    |    |    | 1  | 2  |
| 3  | 4  | 5  | 6  | 7  | 8  | 9  |
| 10 | 11 | 12 | 13 | 14 | 15 | 16 |
| 17 | 18 | 19 | 20 | 21 | 22 | 23 |
| 24 | 25 | 26 | 27 | 28 | 29 | 30 |

**May**

| Su | Mo | Tu | We | Th | Fr | Sa |
|----|----|----|----|----|----|----|
| 1  | 2  | 3  | 4  | 5  | 6  | 7  |
| 8  | 9  | 10 | 11 | 12 | 13 | 14 |
| 15 | 16 | 17 | 18 | 19 | 20 | 21 |
| 22 | 23 | 24 | 25 | 26 | 27 | 28 |
| 29 | 30 | 31 |    |    |    |    |

**June**

| Su | Mo | Tu | We | Th | Fr | Sa |
|----|----|----|----|----|----|----|
|    |    |    | 1  | 2  | 3  | 4  |
| 5  | 6  | 7  | 8  | 9  | 10 | 11 |
| 12 | 13 | 14 | 15 | 16 | 17 | 18 |
| 19 | 20 | 21 | 22 | 23 | 24 | 25 |
| 26 | 27 | 28 | 29 | 30 |    |    |

**July**

| Su | Mo | Tu | We | Th | Fr | Sa |
|----|----|----|----|----|----|----|
|    |    |    |    |    | 1  | 2  |
| 3  | 4  | 5  | 6  | 7  | 8  | 9  |
| 10 | 11 | 12 | 13 | 14 | 15 | 16 |
| 17 | 18 | 19 | 20 | 21 | 22 | 23 |
| 24 | 25 | 26 | 27 | 28 | 29 | 30 |
| 31 |    |    |    |    |    |    |

**August**

| Su | Mo | Tu | We | Th | Fr | Sa |
|----|----|----|----|----|----|----|
|    | 1  | 2  | 3  | 4  | 5  | 6  |
| 7  | 8  | 9  | 10 | 11 | 12 | 13 |
| 14 | 15 | 16 | 17 | 18 | 19 | 20 |
| 21 | 22 | 23 | 24 | 25 | 26 | 27 |
| 28 | 29 | 30 | 31 |    |    |    |

**September**

| Su | Mo | Tu | We | Th | Fr | Sa |
|----|----|----|----|----|----|----|
|    |    |    |    |    | 1  | 2  | 3 |
| 4  | 5  | 6  | 7  | 8  | 9  | 10 |
| 11 | 12 | 13 | 14 | 15 | 16 | 17 |
| 18 | 19 | 20 | 21 | 22 | 23 | 24 |
| 25 | 26 | 27 | 28 | 29 | 30 |    |

**October**

| Su | Mo | Tu | We | Th | Fr | Sa |
|----|----|----|----|----|----|----|
|    |    |    |    |    |    | 1  |
| 2  | 3  | 4  | 5  | 6  | 7  | 8  |
| 9  | 10 | 11 | 12 | 13 | 14 | 15 |
| 16 | 17 | 18 | 19 | 20 | 21 | 22 |
| 23 | 24 | 25 | 26 | 27 | 28 | 29 |
| 30 | 31 |    |    |    |    |    |

**November**

| Su | Mo | Tu | We | Th | Fr | Sa |
|----|----|----|----|----|----|----|
|    | 1  | 2  | 3  | 4  | 5  |    |
| 6  | 7  | 8  | 9  | 10 | 11 | 12 |
| 13 | 14 | 15 | 16 | 17 | 18 | 19 |
| 20 | 21 | 22 | 23 | 24 | 25 | 26 |
| 27 | 28 | 29 | 30 |    |    |    |

**December**

| Su | Mo | Tu | We | Th | Fr | Sa |
|----|----|----|----|----|----|----|
|    |    |    |    | 1  | 2  | 3  |
| 4  | 5  | 6  | 7  | 8  | 9  | 10 |
| 11 | 12 | 13 | 14 | 15 | 16 | 17 |
| 18 | 19 | 20 | 21 | 22 | 23 | 24 |
| 25 | 26 | 27 | 28 | 29 | 30 | 31 |

*Note*: The days shaded in grey are those on which oaths and ordeals were theoretically forbidden.

However, it is not clear what precisely what was meant by these limits placed on swearing oaths, not least because distinguishing between different types of oaths is difficult, as in earlier periods. In the laws which Wulfstan wrote for Æthelred and Cnut, people are encouraged to keep their oaths and pledges (as in Alfred's code),[280] but in the *Canons of Edgar*, Wulfstan stated that priests should guard themselves against oaths – and also forbid them.[281] The oaths and pledges that people were supposed to keep are presumably promissory, but it is not clear which type of oaths Wulfstan forbids in the *Canons of Edgar*: the statement is derived from Ghaerbald's first capitulary, which is included at the beginning of Recension B of the canon law collection associated

---

[280]   e.g. V Æthelred 22.2; cf. Alfred 1, ed. Liebermann, *Gesetze*, I.242–3, and 46–7.

[281]   *Canons of Edgar*, 60, ed. Fowler, *Canons of Edgar*, 14–15.

with Wulfstan, but it is difficult to see precisely how Wulfstan might have interpreted this in the context of late Anglo-Saxon England.[282] Surviving evidence from other records, such as the *Libellus Æthelwoldi*, suggests that particularly for civil cases the swearing of oaths could lead to lasting disharmony between the parties, and that where possible, amicable agreements were sought; it is possible that Wulfstan's limitation on oaths was made with such cases in mind.[283] But Wulfstan's prohibitions of ordeals and oaths may also have been connected with uncertainty about their reliability. The possibility of invalidating an ordeal is clear in laws from the time of Æthelstan, and the risk is mentioned too in the *Northumbrian Priests' Law*, a text probably not written by Wulfstan but perhaps showing his influence: here the priest is ordered to pay compensation if he conducts the ordeal incorrectly.[284]

The increased regulation of ordeals in the legislation associated with Æthelstan is paralleled by Wulfstan's efforts to provide more instructions for the performance of ordeals, when he did not simply attempt to limit or prevent their use. This is clear in his regulations concerning another type of ordeal described as 'corsnæd', which means something like 'chosen morsel' and which, according to liturgical rituals, apparently required the proband to swallow a piece of bread and cheese without choking or vomiting it up.[285] Wulfstan discusses this type of ordeal in VIII Æthelred and in I Cnut, two codes concerned with ecclesiastical issues and personnel, and which seem to have been intended as counterparts to secular codes.[286] The decrees about 'corsnæd' set out how clergy could exculpate themselves using this type of ordeal if they were unable to use other methods (such as swearing over the Host, or swearing with compurgators), and to some extent this seems to have been modelled on, and paralleled by, the process set out for laity (for example in II Cnut).[287] Outside of these law codes, Anglo-Saxon references to the 'corsnæd' ordeal are found only in liturgical rituals (though they do not use the Old English term 'corsnæd'): the rituals explain how the ordeal might be passed or failed, but give no precise information about how it was used in a legal context, or who might have been required to undergo this type of ordeal. This means that Wulfstan's regulations about 'corsnæd' are in fact the only surviving explanation of how, and for whom, this procedure was supposed to be used.

Liturgical rituals for ordeal by bread and cheese, and blessings for consecrating the elements, are found with rituals for other types of ordeals in eight English

---

[282]   Ghaerbald of Liège, *Capitula*, I.19, ed. P. Brommer et al., *Capitula episcoporum*, MGH (3 vols, Hannover, 1984–1995), I.21 (and Rec B.20, ed. Cross and Hamer, *Wulfstan's Canon Law Collection*, 120); see Elliot, 'Ghaerbald's First Capitulary'.

[283]   e.g. S 1454 and S 1460; Kennedy, 'Law and litigation in the Libellus Æthelwoldi episcopi', 170–1.

[284]   *Northumbrian Priests' Law*, 39, *Councils and Synods*, I.i, no. 63; Wormald, *Making of English Law*, 208; see also above, 167–8.

[285]   See Keefer, '*Ut in omnibus*', 241–2; and cf. Niles, 'Trial by Ordeal in Anglo-Saxon England: What's the Problem with Barley?'.

[286]   See Wormald, 'Æthelred the Lawmaker'.

[287]   VIII Æthelred, 19–27; I Cnut 5–5.4, ed. Liebermann, *Gesetze*, I.265–6, 284–9.

manuscripts dating from the late tenth and eleventh centuries.[288] This type of ordeal seems to be a later innovation than the others, and since the rituals first appear not much earlier than Wulfstan's earliest references to 'corsnæd', it may be that he was concerned to regulate something which was a comparatively recent institution and where there was little consensus about how the procedure should be used. The 'corsnæd' ordeal is quite strictly limited by Wulfstan, who instructed that it should only be used for priests who were unable to clear themselves in any other way; or for men in holy orders ('gehadod') who had been charged with vendetta and murder, and no kin or fellow-ecclesiastics to act as oath-helpers.[289] In this last case in I Cnut, the possibility of the 'corsnæd' ordeal is introduced as the final resort, to be undertaken only 'if he must' ('gif he þæt þurfe').[290] As with the other types of ordeal, Wulfstan ensured that the number of people who might ever undergo 'corsnæd' was actually very small, suggesting that he may not have been entirely comfortable with its use at all.

Wulfstan surely did not introduce the 'corsnæd' ordeal, but the fact that the only non-liturgical references to 'corsnæd' ordeals are found in his works poses a problem for modern scholars seeking to understand precisely how this procedure was used in Anglo-Saxon England. Since the stipulation that 'corsnæd' was to be used only for men in holy orders is not mentioned in the rituals themselves, it is not clear whether this is a regulation introduced by Wulfstan or his observation from the use of 'corsnæd' in practice. Given the questions over the relationship between legal texts and law in practice, it is not even clear whether the 'corsnæd' ordeal was used only for men in holy orders either before or after Wulfstan's stipulations. However, the inclusion of the procedures for clerical exculpation in ecclesiastical codes highlights Wulfstan's belief that clerical discipline was in some respects detached from the processes of secular justice, as indicated also by the decrees in II Cnut which treat men in orders separately from laity, and reserve their judgement to the bishop.[291] In light of Wulfstan's treatment of other types of ordeal, it is also significant that in the law codes which he wrote the death penalty seems not to have been stipulated for any offence committed by those in holy orders and thus failure at the 'corsnæd' ordeal could not (in theory) have resulted in capital punishment.[292] This suggests that Wulfstan's limitations of all types of ordeals may not have been driven only by his concern to avoid the death penalty, even though that too was clearly a major concern in other contexts.

---

[288]   Keefer, '*Ut in omnibus*', 245–6: Keefer notes that these are found in CCCC 44; CCCC 146; CCCC 391; CCCC 422; London, BL, Add. 57337; Cotton Vitellius A.vii; Paris, BN, 943; Rouen, BM, 368 (see Table 3.1).

[289]   VIII Æthelred 22, 24; I Cnut 5.2a, c, ed. Liebermann, *Gesetze*, I.266, 286–7.

[290]   I Cnut 5.2c, ed. Liebermann, *Gesetze*, I.286–7.

[291]   II Cnut 43, ed. Liebermann, *Gesetze*, I.342–3.

[292]   See for example II Cnut 41, 42, ed. Liebermann, *Gesetze*, I.340–3.

**Conclusion**

The hints of unease in Anglo-Saxon texts over the use of judicial ordeals and execution are only traces of what must have been a much fuller discussion which occurred as part of the lawmaking process. The surviving traces of this discussion do not permit a precise explanation for why Anglo-Saxon authors expressed their unease in this way, as they also do not exactly explain why, especially in the case of judicial ordeals, they were not forbidden more conclusively or the difficulties outlined more explicitly. Wulfstan's prohibitions in his legal writings come closest to preventing ordeals, since he forbade them for a considerable proportion of the year by stating that they should not take place at feasts and fasts; but Wulfstan too limited rather than forbade outright, and in England as elsewhere in Europe, ordeals were not officially forbidden by the Church until the rulings of Fourth Lateran Council in 1215. Domesday Book confirms the rights of certain administrative units or institutions to hold ordeals as they had before the reign of William I,[293] although it is more difficult to establish how far the attempts to lay claim to land through oaths and ordeals as recorded in the Domesday inquisitions represent pre-Conquest English practice:[294] before the Norman Conquest there is no evidence for the use of ordeals in civil cases such as property disputes in England (just as there is also no evidence for trial by battle).[295] While the death penalty of course persisted much longer than did ordeals, capital punishment continued to be discussed and scrutinised by ecclesiastics: in the latter part of the eleventh century English ecclesiastical councils forbade clerical involvement in the death penalty as well as in the amputation of limbs (although not these penalties themselves).[296]

This is interesting because of the way that attitudes to capital punishment and to the use of ordeals are entangled with one another in the surviving Anglo-Saxon texts which mention or discuss them, and because this seems to have continued to be the case for quite some time. In the thirteenth century this connection seems also to have been made by those who produced the canons of the Fourth Lateran Council, because the section which prohibited clerical participation in ordeals began by instructing that no cleric should hand down or carry out death sentences,

---

[293] e.g. Fleming, *Domesday Book and the Law*, no. 1354 (Taunton, Somerset); Great Domesday Book, fol. 87v, ed. Thorn and Thorn, *Domesday Book: 8, Somerset*, no. 2.4; and Erskine (ed.), *Great Domesday: a facsimile* (London, 1986–1992).

[294] See Fleming, *Domesday Book and the Law*, nos. 2230, 2399 (Norfolk) and 2834, 2839, 2868 (Suffolk) for those cases where the claimant appears to be English and to have been connected with the land in the time of King Edward.

[295] Hyams, 'Trial by Ordeal', 111–12; Bartlett, *Trial by Fire and Water*, 104.

[296] e.g. Council at London, (25 December 1074 x 28 August 1075), 9, *Councils and Synods*, I.i, no. 92: 'ut nullus episcopus vel abbas seu quilibet ex clero hominem occidendum vel menbris truncandum iudicet, vel iudicantibus suę auctoritatis favorem commodet' ('that no bishop, abbot, or any clergymen shall sentence a man to death or to have his limbs amputated, or give his authority to those judging').

or be present at executions. Finbarr McAuley argues that this statute aimed to deal with spiritual pollution occasioned by the shedding of blood, and thus covered clerical participation in any activity which involved blood-shed including capital punishment and ordeals as well as surgery that required burning or cutting; and he suggests that this statute does not reflect concern for the souls of clerics who were involved in death sentences, since there were theological arguments which exonerated the souls of those who passed, enforced or carried out death sentences.[297] But as the evidence discussed in this chapter demonstrates, it is clear that there was long-standing concern over the souls of those involved with death sentences despite the statements in theological texts which should have exonerated them.

Nevertheless, both ordeals and the death penalty continued to be prescribed, presumably because in some cases it was difficult to know what else to do. A number of scholars have suggested that the value of ordeals as a method of determining guilt or innocence may often have been in their use as a psychological weapon rather than what was revealed in or after the ritual: in many cases, the threat of pain may have been enough to secure an admission of guilt from the accused, without an ordeal actually taking place.[298] The fuller records of legal cases in continental sources also indicate that ordeals might be threatened and then withdrawn from at some point in the proceedings, so that they were used as a tactical approach to suggest the (in)validity of a particular claim, as Stephen White has shown.[299] It is worth remembering too that Domesday records often only note the intention to use oaths and ordeals, and not whether these proposed oaths or ordeals were actually enacted.[300] Clearly sometimes they were used, as is evident for example from a dispute between Bishop Gandulf of Rochester and Picot the Sheriff which occurred probably between 1077 and 1082, and which was recorded in the *Textus Roffensis*.[301] But in some cases it is also possible that the threat – or promise – of oath or ordeal was enough for the parties to come to an arrangement without recourse to divine judgement. Such a threat might sometimes have been effective, but White has demonstrated that this was a difficult game to play and that the opponents needed to proceed with some care, since withdrawal at a later stage might not always be possible.[302] Caution may have been needed on both sides: a few Anglo-Saxon decrees provide for situations in which the accuser

---

[297]   McAuley, 'Canon Law and the End of the Ordeal', 500–7.

[298]   Bartlett, *Trial by Fire and Water*, 111; White, 'Proposing the ordeal'.

[299]   White, 'Proposing the Ordeal'.

[300]   See Fleming, *Domesday Book and the Law*, for example nos. 622 (Hampshire), 966, 1190 (Lincolnshire), 2164, 2230, 2255, 2301, 2326, 2343, 2356, 2403, 2447, 2458, 2685, 2723, 2724 (Norfolk), 2834, 2839, 2868 (Suffolk).

[301]   Rochester, Cathedral Library, A.3.5 ('Textus Roffensis'), fols. 170v–171r; R. Fleming, *Kings and Lords in Conquest England* (Cambridge, 1991), 86, n. 139; Fleming, *Domesday Book and the Law*, 18–19.

[302]   White, 'Proposing the Ordeal'.

failed to attend an ordeal which had been arranged to take place, perhaps alluding to the possibility of fear that his accusation had been made falsely.[303]

This implies that beyond a certain point it was impossible for either side to back out, and this may be the significance of the decree in II Cnut which states that no fore-oath will ever be 'forgyfen', perhaps suggesting that after this had been sworn the engagement had been made and an ordeal could not be prevented.[304] This decree is unparalleled in earlier codes, and it is possible that it was intended by Archbishop Wulfstan to encourage the settling cases without recourse to oaths and ordeals, whether for theological or more practical reasons. On the other hand, it is not entirely clear how frequently ordeals actually took place in Anglo-Saxon England: the absence of records of ordeals could be because they occurred frequently enough that they were not considered interesting enough to record, or because they did not in fact take place particularly frequently, or simply because records of all kinds of legal cases from Anglo-Saxon England are so scarce. The one surviving record of a judicial ordeal, preserved in the Swithun material, does not inspire confidence either, since both Lantfred and Wulfstan of Winchester write as if they expect the audience to understand the procedure, and yet at the same time the miracle was evidently confusing, certainly to Wulfstan and perhaps also to Lantfred.

The insistence in the law codes on the necessity of proceeding with an ordeal once it had been arranged stands in direct contrast to the picture presented by the liturgical rituals, which encouraged the proband to admit guilt rather than proceed to oath, ordeal, or the mass which proceeded the ordeal itself. The importance of this is shown by the fact that a number of these adjurations were translated from Latin into Old English, so that they might actually have some effect in their vivid desriptions of the consequences of failing to confess or admit guilt.[305] One of the adjurations to be read before a cold water ordeal asks Christ to reveal if the man is guilty by not allowing the water to receive him when he is thrown in;[306] another invokes all the powers of heaven and warns the proband that magic will not help him to avoid God's judgement if he is truly guilty or if he knows anything about the offence, threatening that the water will not receive him and he will be condemned.[307] As with other liturgical rituals such as baptism, it seems likely that the process (and its effects) would have been explained beforehand, so that the formal ritual adjuration preserved in the liturgical manuscripts may not have been the only moment at which the proband was threatened with dire consequences. All the same, the drama of the moment (and the effectiveness of the adjuration)

---

[303]    e.g. III Æthelred 4.2, ed. Liebermann, *Gesetze*, I.230; according to this decree, the ordeal was supposed to take place whether or not the accuser attended.

[304]    II Cnut 22.3, ed. Liebermann, *Gesetze*, I.326–7.

[305]    It is not clear whether both Latin and English would have been read to the proband, or only English.

[306]    CCCC 146, p. 302.

[307]    CCCC 422, pp. 330–1.

was presumably intensified when the proband was faced with the immediately visible threat of a river or a deep pit of cold water, burning iron or boiling water, or hearing the sizzle of holy water landing on hot iron.

The admission of guilt in the context of an ordeal is connected with the formal confession which seems also to have been part of the ritual. If the proband was supposed to confess his sins in the context of the ordeal rituals, then theoretically this was another moment even before the adjuration at which he could admit guilt and back out.[308] Both legal texts and liturgical rituals mention a period of fasting prior to the performance of an ordeal as well as the mass which formed part of the ritual, and this is important because from a very early period communion and confession were linked, so that an individual was only supposed to receive the Eucharist if he had first confessed his sins.[309] Ordeal rituals remind the individual of his baptism and God's judgement and their significance, and since these issues appear also in the rituals for confession it is likely that in many cases this would already have been discussed with the proband before the adjuration.[310] It is significant too that these adjurations seem to have come before communion, and that the proband was encouraged not to go to the Eucharist or to the ordeal if he was guilty of the offence of which he had been accused, or even if he knew who had done it: if the man knew himself to be guilty in any way, even by implication through his knowledge of what had actually happened, the priest urged him to soften his heart and confess what he knew about the matter.[311] For the priest's threats to be effective, the proband needed to understand and believe the spiritual danger that he placed himself in by receiving communion or undergoing the ordeal if he knew the truth of the matter, just as the potential perjurer needed to understand and believe what would happen if he swore an oath falsely.

In urging confession and conversion to a more appropriate way of life, the liturgical rituals for ordeals seem to echo the thoughts of some of the Anglo-Saxon

---

[308]   Bartlett, *Trial by Fire and Water*, 79–80.

[309]   Wulfstan, *De conuersione et penitentia et communione*, ed. Hall, 'Wulfstan's Latin Sermons', 129–30; Meens, 'Frequency and Nature', 38; Hamilton, *Practice of Penance*, 58–60.

[310]   See for example the adjuration in CCCC 146, p. 302–3: 'adiuro te ... per baptismum et Christianismum, quod tu percepisti, ut non audeas hanc eucharistiam percipere, nisi innocens sis huius rei, cuius culpabilis detineris', 'Ic halsige þe ... þurh þæne fulluht ⁊ Cristendom, þe þu underfangen hæfst, þæt þu na geþristlæce, þæt þu þises husles onbyrige, buton þu si unscyldig þæs þinges, þe þu nu betigen eart'; see also 161.

[311]   CCCC 146, p. 308: 'Si tu reus sis, emollias cor tuum et confitearis quicquid in hoc scias'; 'gyf þu scyldig si, þænne ahnexa þu þine heortan ⁊ geandet, swa hwætt swa þu þar onwite'; or CCCC 146, p. 304: Ic halsige þe þurh þæne fæder ⁊ sunu ⁊ þæne halegan gast ⁊ þurh þine cristennysse, þe þu underfenge, ⁊ þurh þæne ancennedan sunu godes ⁊ þurh þa halegan þrynysse ⁊ þurh þæt halige godes spell ⁊ þurh þa halgan laua, þe innan þisre cyricean synt, ⁊ þurh þæne fulluht, þe se mæssepreost þe of geedcende, þæt þu na geþristlæce natestohwi to þisum husle to ganne ne furþon to þisum weofude to genealæcenne, gif þu þis dydest, þæt we embe synt, oþþe gif þu þarto geþwærudest oþþe wistest, hwa hyt dyde'.

ecclesiastics who sought to offer mercy instead of judgement and condemnation, and who therefore wove penance and confession into the secular judicial system. In the case of ordeals this is particularly important because it has been argued that ordeals and confession were effectively in competition with one another, since although the former was concentrated primarily on the body and the latter on the soul, both were intended to deal with criminal or sinful behaviour.[312] Again IV Lateran is significant here, because this council mandated annual confession for all adult Christians – and also refused Christian burial to those who would not make annual confession – and IV Lateran's decree has been seen as marking a new direction in penitential practice.[313] There is a danger with this interpretation of viewing ordeals as the final outcome rather than the means of proof, and thus as a type of punishment or torture, although since one of the effects of the rejection of ordeals was the more widespread use of judicial torture, this may not be entirely inaccurate. Certainly, the proband who did not fear the spiritual consequences and thus undertook to swear oaths or to undergo an ordeal despite knowing his guilt, must still have been concerned about drowning, or about the pain of searing iron or boiling water.

And perhaps more importantly, it is also clear that the requirement of annual confession in 1215 was, in a sense, nothing new: frequent confession had been recommended for centuries, and authors urged that if possible people should make confessions more frequently than only once a year. Wulfstan introduced requirements for confession into national legislation, the ecclesiastical decrees of the council at Enham in 1008 demanding that 'every Christian man shall go to confession frequently and confess his sins'.[314] These decrees also state that everyone should prepare himself to receive communion at least three times in the year, suggesting that ideally, confession too should occur at least three times yearly.[315] This is really where the concerns of ecclesiastical and secular authorities collide on a massive scale: if preachers and teachers could convince their congregations of the necessity of confession and penance, and remind them frequently of the horror of the eternal punishments for capital sins such as perjury, theft and murder, then secular law and order would theoretically also be reinforced. In this regard it is significant that several texts associated with Ælfric and Wulfstan mention the 'rihtscriftscir' ('proper

---

[312] Baldwin, 'From the Ordeal to Confession', 205; cf. O'Keeffe, 'Body and law in late Anglo-Saxon England'.

[313] IV Lateran, 21, ed. and trans. N.P. Tanner, *Decrees of the Ecumenical Councils* (2 vols, London, 1990), I.245; see also B. Poschmann, *Penance and the Anointing of the Sick*, trans. F. Courtney (Freiburg, 1964), 138ff; A. Murray, 'Confession before 1215', *Transactions of the Royal Historical Society*, 6th series 3 (1993): 51–81; Baldwin, 'From the Ordeal to Confession'.

[314] VI Æthelred 27, ed. Liebermann, *Gesetze*, I.254–5; Meens, 'Frequency and Nature'.

[315] VI Æthelred 27.1, ed. Liebermann, *Gesetze*, I.254–5; see also Meens, 'Frequency and Nature', 37–8; Hamilton, *Practice of Penance*, 5, 58–60.

confession area'), or 'scriftscir' ('confession area'), suggesting that a church's jurisdictional area or community was defined at least in part by consideration of those for whom the priest was responsible for hearing confessions and imposing penance.[316] Confession was significant as one of the major opportunities for priests to educate their parishioners, especially about topics such as the afterlife and the fate of sinners at the Last Judgement; but penitential and homiletic texts alike also warn priests that they should not hesitate to instruct people in their required penances if they desire their own protection on Judgement Day, and explain that the priest will lead to God for judgement the people for whom he was responsible in life.[317]

It is clear that ecclesiastical and secular systems of regulation and justice were intended to work together like this: Archbishop Wulfstan encouraged priests to inform the bishop in a 'synod' if they knew of any man in their 'scriftscir' who had fallen into serious sin, and he seems to mean here the 'capital sins' such as murder and perjury which by the tenth century had required the performance of public penance for their atonement.[318] This is particularly significant because where the law codes demand penance it is often to be performed 'according to the bishop's instruction', perhaps suggesting that public penance was required, and presumably alluding to the role of the bishop in local courts. More importantly, it is clear that Christian belief had permeated legal thought to such an extent that the system itself was based on the assumption of shared beliefs, without which it would be both ineffective and incomprehensible. Unless would-be perjurers had a basic understanding of the repercussions of swearing false oaths, the implicit (and perhaps also explicit) threat of divine wrath may have meant little. At least in theory, the necessity of pastoral care which was so frequently emphasised by Wulfstan and his predecessors had implications which stretched far beyond the boundaries of the Church or churches; but it was not until Wulfstan that both ecclesiastical and secular systems of discipline were called upon to work so closely to regulate the behaviour of society.

Rather than being directly in competition, ordeals and confession were both intended to reveal the truth in situations where it was hidden.[319] Offences against human laws were presumably committed then as now by those who imagined

---

[316]  Thompson, *Dying and Death*, 58; F. Tinti, 'The "Costs" of Pastoral Care: Church Dues in late Anglo-Saxon England', in Tinti (ed.), *Pastoral Care in late Anglo-Saxon England*, 27–51, at 34: the '(riht)scriftscir' may have been concerned more with the community for whom the priest was responsible than with the specific area of land.

[317]  *Old English Penitential*, SXY 43.15.01, ed. Frantzen, *The Anglo-Saxon Penitentials: A Cultural Database*; V. Thompson, 'The Pastoral Contract in Late Anglo-Saxon England: Priest and Parishioner in Oxford, Bodleian Library, MS Laud Miscellaneous 482', in Tinti (ed.), *Pastoral Care in late Anglo-Saxon England*, 106–20.

[318]  *Canons of Edgar*, 6, ed. Fowler, *Canons of Edgar*, 2–3.

[319]  See *Ordal* 4.3, ed. Liebermann, *Gesetze*, I.387: 'ne sy þær nan oðer spæc inne, buton þæt hig biddan God Ælmihtig georne, þæt he soðeste geswytelie' ('and no other word shall be spoken in the church, except that God be earnestly prayed to make clear the whole truth').

that they would not get caught. Since ordeals and oaths relied to a great extent on Christian understanding of, and belief in, the spiritual effects of these procedures, confession worked not primarily in competition with ordeals but rather in tandem with them, existing both alongside them and as part of the process. While the pain of an ordeal threatened, confession might be presented as an easier way of resolving the situation. And where ordeals resulted in a conviction, whether through the interpretation of God's judgement or through the admission of guilt in the process, Wulfstan's advocation of mutilations focused the punishment on the body only in order to preserve the soul, echoing the ordeal rituals which asked God to reveal guilt in the body so that the soul may be saved.[320] This focus on the soul is indicative of real concerns in contemporary thought, and perhaps also of gradually changing beliefs about the effects of confession in the ritual of penance, beliefs which would have significant effects in centuries to come, and some of which led to the pronouncements of IV Lateran in 1215.[321] The canons of IV Lateran may have marked a new direction, but they must also be seen as the end point of a long period of development, of which traces can be seen in Anglo-Saxon texts.

As for mercy in judgement, the archaeological evidence for execution cemeteries illustrates clearly that this was not always forthcoming. At least from the tenth century, the exclusion of offenders from communal and consecrated burial grounds was itself used as a threat and a penalty, demonstrating once again how tightly Christian theology had been bound up with royal legislation.[322] But although ideas about the Last Judgement infiltrated the legal system, this was not the only concern about the afterlife which emerged from theological discussion and into other contexts. The final chapter explores how the fate of the soul might be affected by the treatment of the bodies of the dead, as well as the treatment of the living by the dead; but the focus of the next chapter is purgatory, the interim between death and the Last Judgement, and the immediate post-mortem fate of souls. Once again, confession and penance as well as the theology behind them were extremely important: those who had the means did their best to wipe away their sins, attempting to limit their post-mortem punishment and to ensure that heaven was their ultimate destination. This in itself is an indicator that despite the evidential difficulties in using law codes and penitentials as records of practice, the messages they proclaimed had not entirely fallen on deaf ears.

---

[320] e.g. II Cnut 30.5, ed. Liebermann, *Gesetze*, I.332–5; Portiforium of St Wulfstan, CCCC 391, p. 566, ed. A. Hughes, *The Portiforium of St Wulstan: Corpus Christi College, Cambridge, MS. 391*, Henry Bradshaw Society 89–90 (2 vols, Leighton Buzzard, 1958–60), II.166. See also O'Brien O'Keefe, 'Body and law'.

[321] See Frantzen, *Literature of Penance*, 118–19; Hamilton, *Practice of Penance*, 15; H. Foxhall Forbes, 'The Development of the Notions of Penance, Purgatory and the Afterlife in Anglo-Saxon England', PhD thesis, University of Cambridge, 2009, 103–7.

[322] See below, 294–313.

# Chapter 4
# The Communion of Saints and the Forgiveness of Sins

O God, who prepare different dwelling-places for the souls of the faithful according to the quality of their merits, grant that your servant may rest in a dwelling-place of a sort in which he may evade all tribulation and find eternal consolation, and arise happy and purged [from sin] on the day of resurrection.[1]

## Introduction

The Last Judgement looms so large in Anglo-Saxon religious texts that it threatens to overshadow other ideas about the fate of the soul, and the terror of the final day was given as the reason for the constant exhortations to penance and confession. In order to be included in the good and to join the communion of saints, clergymen warned, it was imperative to avoid sin; and if anyone committed sin, it was necessary that he had recourse to proper penance and confession before death, so that at the final and awful tribunal, his soul would not be found stained with sin and sent into the punishments of hell for all eternity. But the soul also faced an individual judgement immediately upon leaving the body, and this was only a foretaste of the fate to come after the Last Judgement: between death and the Last Judgement there was a space of time, an interim while the soul waited until the final day of resurrection, as suggested by the prayer quoted above from the personal prayer book of Ælfwine, dean and later abbot of the New Minster, Winchester in the second quarter of the eleventh century.[2] What might happen to the soul in this interim space of time was much less clear than what would happen at the Last

---

[1]    Prayer from the prayer book of Ælfwine, dean of the New Minster, Winchester: London, British Library, Cotton Titus D.xxvi, fols. 75r–v, ed. B. Günzel, *Ælfwine's Prayerbook (London, British Library, Cotton Titus D.xxvi + xxvii)*, HBS 108 (London, 1993), no. 76.66: 'Deus, qui fidelium animabus pro meritorum qualitate diuersas preparas mansiones, presta ut anima famuli/e tui/e .N. tali mansione requiescat, in qua et omnes tribulationes euadat et consolationes sempiternas inueniat, atque in die resurrectionis laetus et purgatus resurgat'.

[2]    B. Daley, *The Hope of the Early Church: A Handbook of Patristic Eschatology* (Cambridge, 1991), 220. For information about Ælfwine and his prayer book see Günzel (ed.), *Ælfwine's Prayerbook*, 1–6; S. Keynes (ed.), *The Liber Vitae of the New Minster and Hyde Abbey, Winchester: British Library Stowe 944: Together with Leaves from British Library Cotton Vespasian A. VIII and British Library Cotton Titus D. XXVII*, EEMF 26 (Copenhagen, 1996), 37–41, 64–9.

Judgement, which was outlined in the Bible, even if interpretations of the details varied. In contrast, the fate of the soul between death and the Last Judgement is never fully discussed or outlined in Scripture: purgatory ultimately filled this gap, but it would become one of the most controversial theological topics as it became increasingly significant. Early discussions of post-mortem purgation are tentative and often difficult to interpret, perhaps indicating uncertainty over an idea which was not yet fully crystallised in the minds of those who discussed it; purgatory was an issue over which Catholics and Protestants fought bitterly at the Reformation, over which Catholic and Orthodox Christians are still not in absolute agreement, and which continues to be reinterpreted and to cause controversy in modern scholarship.[3]

For the most part, Anglo-Saxon authors do not seem to have felt a need to discuss the interim in any great detail, and there are only a very few Anglo-Saxon texts which explore purgatory and the interim as significant topics in their own right. However, there are frequent references to the fate of the soul in the interim and to the purging of sins after death, even if these were not discussed in so much detail (or so obsessively) as was the Last Judgement. It is clear too that the post-mortem fates of souls were a significant concern to both lay and religious men and women. The efforts of those who could afford to make spiritual provision for their souls after death, and the content of the documents which record these efforts, show clearly that although the Last Judgement was a major concern it was not perceived to be the only fear or struggle which followed death. While homiletic and penitential texts underline the finality of death, and so the importance of completing penance and confession before there was no longer an opportunity for forgiveness of sins in this life, other texts witness to the high value of prayers and offerings made on behalf of the dead. The relationships between members of a family and members of a monastic community remained, and the obligations to those people also remained even in death. This is particularly significant in considering the interim, because purgatory is much more closely connected with earthly society than are heaven and hell, and therefore much more receptive to changes in the perception of society, both the living and the dead.

---

[3]    See for example W. Allen, *A defense and declaration of the Catholike Churchies doctrine, touching purgatory, and prayers for the soules departed* ([Antwerp], 1565); W. Fulke, W. Allen and J.d. Albin de Valsergues, *Tvvo treatises written against the papistes: the one being an answere of the Christian Protestant to the proud challenge of a popish Catholicke: the other a confutation of the popish churches doctrine touching purgatory & prayers for the dead: by William Fulke Doctor in diuinitie* (London, 1577); and R. Ombres, 'Latins and Greeks in debate over purgatory, 1230–1439', *Journal of Ecclesiastical History* 35:1 (1984): 1–14; J. Jorgenson, 'The debate over the patristic texts on purgatory at the Council of Ferrara-Florence, 1438', *St Vladimir's Theological Quarterly* 30:4 (1986): 309–34; C. Burgess, '"A fond thing vainly invented": An Essay on Purgatory and Pious Motive in Late Medieval England', in S.J. Wright (ed.), *Parish, Church and People: Local Studies in Lay Religion 1350–1750* (London, 1988), 56–84.

## Defining Purgatory

The existence of purgatory before the later Middle Ages has been called into question by Jacques Le Goff, who asserted that purgatory was only 'born' towards the end of the twelfth century, when it received a name in Latin ('purgatorium') and was conceptualised as a place rather than a state.[4] Le Goff's work on this topic is significant, because his study was the first to trace in such detail the history of purgatory from ancient Indo-European beliefs to the late Middle Ages.[5] But many of his contentions and approaches have been vigorously challenged on the basis that his criteria are too strict or inappropriate;[6] and one of the greatest problems with Le Goff's key arguments is that by defining purgatory as it occurs in the context of twelfth-century thought, he finds (unsurprisingly) that it is only in the twelfth-century that authors discuss the interim in a way which corresponds to his definition. Scholars of the early medieval and late antique worlds have often rejected Le Goff's conclusions, either in whole or in part: Andreas Merkt suggests that there was a third place in the beyond as early as the third century and that many of the characteristics of Le Goff's purgatory are visible from much earlier, while Isabel Moreira stresses that although there was variety of belief in early centuries, post-mortem purgation or purgatory was not a 'novelty' for medieval authors.[7]

Purgatory has been seen in the writings of Bede and in the works of Gregory of Tours, amongst others; and above all, the writings of Augustine and the *Dialogues* of Gregory the Great have been examined as proof of early belief in purgatory.[8]

---

[4]    J. Le Goff, *La naissance du Purgatoire*, *Bibliothèque des histoires* (Paris, 1981); cited throughout in English translation: J. Le Goff, *The Birth of Purgatory*, trans. A. Goldhammer (Chicago, 1984).

[5]    The most extensive study prior to this was the entry for purgatory in the *Dictionnaire Théologie Catholique* (A. Michel, 'Purgatoire', in A. Vacant and E. Mangenot (eds), *Dictionnaire de théologie catholique, contenant l'exposé des doctrines de la théologie catholique: leurs preuves et leur histoire* (Paris, 1915), 1163–326), in fact an extended essay but more limited in scope than Le Goff's work.

[6]    e.g. R.E. Lerner, 'La naissance du Purgatoire', *The American Historical Review* 87:5 (1982): 1374–5; A.H. Bredero, 'Le Moyen Age et le Purgatoire', *Revue d'histoire ecclesiastique* 78:2 (1983): 429–52; A.E. Bernstein, 'La naissance du purgatoire', *Speculum: A Journal of Medieval Studies* 59:1 (1984): 179–83.

[7]    A. Merkt, *Das Fegefeuer. Entstehung und Funktion einer Idee* (Darmstadt, 2005), *passim*, esp. 65–90; I. Moreira, *Heaven's Purge: Purgatory in Late Antiquity* (Oxford, 2010), *passim*, esp. 15–37. For extended discussion see also H. Foxhall Forbes, 'The Development of the Notions of Penance, Purgatory and the Afterlife in Anglo-Saxon England', PhD thesis, University of Cambridge, 2009.

[8]    See, for example, M.M. Gatch, *Death: Meaning and Mortality in Christian Thought and Contemporary Culture* (New York, 1969); P. Jay, 'Saint Augustin et la doctrine du Purgatoire', *Recherches de théologie ancienne et médiévale* 36 (1969): 17–30; R.R. Atwell, 'From Augustine to Gregory the Great: An evaluation of the emergence of the doctrine of

Nevertheless, this remains an important issue because among some scholars, especially (although not exclusively) those of the later Middle Ages and beyond, Le Goff's thesis has received greater acceptance even when some of his methods or aspects of his conclusions have been questioned.[9] This is not the place for a detailed analysis of purgatory or its development, but it is useful here to outline the features which will be considered here as pointing to Anglo-Saxon beliefs about purgatory and the interim state, and how these in turn affected other aspects of life and practice in Anglo-Saxon England. The details of purgatory, such as the fire or whether purgatory was believed to be a place or state, have been continually reinterpreted or given greater or lesser importance depending on the context of discussion or purposes of the author.[10] In contrast, the purging and purifying function which is purgatory's defining characteristic has remained the same. The main ambiguity concerning the interim from at least the second century is not whether purging occurred after death, but rather when and how this purification took place, at the Last Judgement or immediately after death.[11]

This is tightly connected with the individual judgement, as noted already, and with other theological questions including prayer for the dead and mortal and venial sin, which again cannot be treated in significant detail here but must be mentioned

purgatory', *Journal of Ecclesiastical History* 38:2 (1987): 173–86; Daley, *Eschatology*; A.E. Bernstein, *The Formation of Hell: Death and Retribution in the Ancient and Early Christian Worlds* (Ithaca, NY, 1993); C. Carozzi, *Le voyage de l'âme dans l'au-delà, d'après la littérature latine: V<sup>e</sup>–XIII<sup>e</sup> siècle*, Collection de l'École française de Rome, 189 (Roma, 1994); J.P. Marmion, 'Purgatory Revisited', *Downside Review* 112 (1994): 121–41; B. Mondin, *Gli abitanti del cielo: trattato di ecclesiologia celeste e di escatologia*, Nuovo corso di teologia dogmatica 5 (Bologna, 1994); P. Brown, 'Vers la naissance du purgatoire. Amnistie et pénitence dans le christianisme occidental de l'Antiquité tardive au Haut Moyen Age', *Annales Histoire, Sciences Sociales* 52:6 (1997): 1247–61; C. Carozzi, *Apocalypse et salut dans le christianisme ancien et médiéval*, Collection historique (Paris, 1999); M. Dunn, 'Gregory the Great, the vision of Fursey, and the origins of purgatory', *Peritia* 14 (2000): 238–54; M. Smyth, 'The origins of purgatory through the lens of seventh-century Irish eschatology', *Traditio: Studies in Ancient and Medieval History, Thought, and Religion* 57 (2003): 91–132; H. Foxhall Forbes, '"Diuiduntur in quattuor": The interim and judgement in Anglo-Saxon England', *Journal of Theological Studies* 61:2 (2010): 659–84.

[9] See for example M. McLaughlin, *Consorting with Saints: Prayer for the Dead in Early Medieval France* (Ithaca, NY, 1994), 17–19; P. Binski, *Medieval Death: Ritual and Representation* (London, 2001); A. Wareham, 'The transformation of kinship and the family in late Anglo-Saxon England', *Early Medieval Europe* 10:3 (2001): 375–99; V. Thompson, 'Constructing Salvation: A Homiletic and Penitential Context for Late Anglo-Saxon Burial Practice', in S. Lucy and A.J. Reynolds (eds), *Burial in Early Medieval England and Wales* (London, 2002), 229–40, 240; J. Arnold, *Belief and Unbelief in Medieval Europe* (London, 2005), 163–9.

[10] See further Foxhall Forbes, 'Penance, Purgatory and the Afterlife', 18–19, 21, 28–30.

[11] For more detail, see Foxhall Forbes, 'Penance, Purgatory and the Afterlife', 10, 13–30; Moreira, *Heaven's Purge: Purgatory in Late Antiquity*, 17–24.

because of their importance for interpreting the surviving evidence.[12] The issue of prayer for the dead has been somewhat hijacked by the pervading influence of the debates of the Reformation, which were split between those who saw prayer for the dead as confirmation that purgatory had always existed, and those who saw such prayers as part of a Catholic invention of purgatory.[13] Prayer for the dead is found in early Jewish and Christian thought, perhaps without connection to the interim, but it still looks to a future time and is bound up with a desire for the forgiveness of sin.[14] Early perceptions of the afterlife placed souls in some kind of sleep until their awakening for the resurrection and Last Judgement, and since the fires of the Last Judgement themselves might purge souls, in some contexts prayers offered for the dead were expected to be efficacious at the Last Judgement but not before.[15] In itself, therefore, prayer for the dead does not indicate that the souls for whom prayer is offered are understood to await the judgement in a state of interim purgation.

But if prayer for the dead is understood to affect the fate of the souls at the moment that prayers are offered for them, those souls do not sleep, but await the judgement in an interim which progresses simultaneously with the lives of those on earth. This is the importance of the individual judgement, which grew in importance from about the second century onwards: if souls are judged individually before the universal and final judgement, their interim fate anticipates, or is related to, their fate at that Last Judgement.[16] A belief in a purgatorial interim in which souls can be helped by the prayers of the living as those prayers are offered, and from which souls will enter heaven after purification, is thus reliant on the individual judgement. Another important conceptual point tangled up with prayer for the dead is the nature of different types of sins, and specifically what would in the later Middle Ages be described as mortal and venial sins. These are once again viewed by Le Goff as a late development: he argues that the distinction between mortal and venial sin was only worked out in conjunction with the emergence of purgatory, although he concedes that it was founded on early discussions by Augustine and Gregory the Great; and in fact some distinction is evident as early as

---

[12]   See further Le Goff, *Purgatory*, 5, 148–9, 152, 165–6, 216–20.

[13]   As for example the *Thirty-Nine Articles* of the Church of England (1563), which state at Article XXII that 'purgatory ... is a fond thing, vainly invented, and grounded upon no warranty of Scripture': see the discussion and exposition in G. Burnet, *An Exposition of the Thirty-Nine Articles of the Church of England* (Dublin, 1721), 282–330. See also McLaughlin, *Consorting*, 10–15.

[14]   G. Tellenbach, 'Die historische Dimension der liturgischen Commemoratio im Mittelalter', in K. Schmid and J. Wollasch (eds), *Memoria: der geschichtliche Zeugniswert des liturgischen Gedenkens im Mittelalter*, Münstersche Mittelalter-Schriften 48 (Munich, 1984), 200–14, at 203.

[15]   C. McDannell and B. Lang, *Heaven: A History* (New Haven, 1988), 33; Marmion, 'Purgatory Revisited', 125.

[16]   Daley, *Eschatology*, 220.

the New Testament.[17] Early medieval authors might not have wrestled specifically with what made a mortal sin mortal and a venial sin venial, as later scholastic theologians would, but they understood precisely the effects of those sins: more serious sins lead to eternal death, whereas smaller sins can be purged away, even after the death of the body.[18]

By the seventh century, authors such as Isidore of Seville (d.636) were able to speak of the post-mortem purgation of sin in the interim between death and the Last Judgement as 'catholic' belief, in the sense that it was held universally.[19] Anglo-Saxon texts may not discuss 'purgatorium', but they frequently mention or allude to souls in the interim who can be helped immediately by the offerings of the living, and explain that these souls are purged of small sins. It is also clear from Anglo-Saxon texts that this interim condition runs concurrently with earthly time and is temporary, so that these souls will be released at the Last Judgement if not before. Before the intricate scholastic debates of the twelfth century and later, the crucial question is whether Anglo-Saxons looked only towards heaven and hell after death, or towards purgatory and the hope of interim purgation. While the ultimate desire was to achieve forgiveness of sin and join the communion of saints immediately – and the ultimate fear was to be excluded from the communion of saints forever on account of sins – it is clear that many lay and religious men and women believed that the immediate destination for the soul after death was somewhere in between these two possibilities. As they considered the fate of the soul after death, they sought to provide for themselves and for their loved ones in the interim as well as at the final judgement.

### Anglo-Saxon Theological Discussions of Purgatory and the Interim

The paradox in Anglo-Saxon religious writing is that the Last Judgement is so often the focus of discussion that the interim is almost completely eclipsed by it, and yet the fate of the soul in the interim is mentioned in passing in a way which suggests it was commonly accepted that sins could be purged after death. The writings of Augustine of Hippo (d.430) were particularly influential in this context, and many statements are based on Augustine's ideas of how offerings affected the souls of the departed. Augustine explained that 'for the very good, masses are an offering of thanks; for those who are not very good, they are propitiatory; and for the very

---

[17]    Le Goff, *Purgatory*, 216–17. See 1 Jn 5:16; P. Galtier, *Aux origines du sacrement de pénitence* (Rome, 1951), 70.

[18]    e.g. Aquinas, *Summa Theologiae*, 1a2ae.72, 5, ed. J. Fearon, *Summa theologiae* (London, 1969), XXV.41–5. See also Augustine's clear distinctions between which sins are 'grave' and which are less so: *Enchiridion*, XXI.78–80, ed. E. Evans, *Aurelii Augustini Opera Pars XIII, 2*, CCSL 46 (Turnhout, 1969), 92–4.

[19]    Isidore, *De ecclesiasticis officiis*, I.xviii.11–12, ed. C.M. Lawson, *Sancti Isidori Episcopi Hispalensis: De ecclesiasticis officiis*, CCSL 113 (Turnhout, 1989), 22–3.

bad they are at least of some comfort to the living, even if they cannot help the souls of the dead'. Those souls in the middle, who were 'not very good' in life, can nonetheless be helped after death by the prayers and offerings of the living.[20] In only one instance does an Anglo-Saxon author seem to exclude the possibility of interim purgation: at the beginning of one of his sermons, Archbishop Wulfstan of York (d.1023) instructed his audience that everyone needed to know where he came from and where he would go, noting further that after death souls will receive eternal punishment or eternal happiness according to what they did in life. One later reader asserted (rather hopefully) that 'here Archbishop Wulfstan denies the third place after this life';[21] but Wulfstan's tendency was to refer to the Last Judgement and he was one of the Anglo-Saxon authors who seems to have been most affected by millennial fears of impending doom, so it seems likely that he simply refers to the Judgement here rather than excluding the interim in his theology.[22]

There are really only two extensive theological discussions of the interim from Anglo-Saxon England, and these are found in the works of Bede (d.735) and Ælfric (d.1009/1010), both of whom described how certain categories of souls in the afterlife would suffer torment.[23] In the vision of Dryhthelm recorded in his *Historia Ecclesiastica*, and in his homily for the second Sunday in Advent, Bede describes a place or state where souls will be purged and cleansed, those who were neither truly good nor truly wicked and who died with some small sins remaining, so that at the final judgement they will be considered worthy to join the company of the elect.[24] In the late tenth century, Ælfric translated Bede's account of Dryhthelm's vision in one of his *Catholic Homilies*, but also produced his own extensive discussion of the fate of the soul after death in another homily which is in fact rather more like a treatise.[25] Like Bede, he describes the purgatorial interim,

[20]   *Enchiridion* XXIX.110, ll. 24–9, ed. Evans, *Enchiridon*, 108–9: 'Cum ergo sacrificia, siue altarius siue quarumcumque eleemosynarum, pro baptizatis defunctis omnibus offeruntur, pro ualde bonis gratiarum actiones sunt, pro non ualde bonis propitiationes sunt, pro ualde malis etiam si nulla sint adiumenta mortuorum qualescumque uiuorum consolationes sunt'.

[21]   *Hom.* XIII, ll. 8–11, with marginal note in Cambridge, Corpus Christi College, 201, p. 20 (ed. D. Bethurum, *The Homilies of Wulfstan* (Oxford, 1957), 225, 339, see also 25): 'Hic Archiepiscopus Wulfstanus diserte negat tertium locum post hanc vitam'.

[22]   M. Godden, 'The Millennium, Time, and History for the Anglo-Saxons', in R. Landes, A. Gow and D.C. Van Meter (eds), *The Apocalyptic Year 1000: Religious Expectation and Social Change, 950–1050* (Oxford, 2003), 155–80, 167–75.

[23]   Only the essential points are given here: for full discussion see Foxhall Forbes, 'Diuiduntur in quattuor'.

[24]   Bede, *HE* V.12, ed. M. Lapidge, P. Monat and P. Robin, *Histoire ecclésiastique du peuple anglais = Historia ecclesiastica gentis Anglorum*, Sources chrétiennes 489–91 (3 vols Paris, 2005), III.68–84.

[25]   Ælfric, *CH* II.21, ed. M. Godden, Ælfric's Catholic Homilies: The Second Series Text, EETS, SS 5 (Oxford, 1979), 199–205; *Hom.* XI, ed. J.C. Pope, *Homilies of Ælfric: A*

distinguishing between the eternity of hell for some souls and the temporary punishments for others, and again noting that only little sins can be cleansed in these temporary punishments.[26] Both Bede and Ælfric emphasise that souls in this purgatorial interim can be aided and indeed released from suffering by the almsgiving and especially by the masses offered for them by the living, and this aspect of the interim state which related the souls of the departed to the actions of the living is one of the most significant in understanding how ideas about purgatory developed and travelled through popular consciousness.

The interim fate of the soul is frequently mentioned in contexts which sound anecdotal, such as another story recorded by Bede in his *Historia Ecclesiastica*, about a thegn named Imma who was captured in battle. When Imma did not return from battle, his brother, who was a priest, thought that he was dead and offered masses on his behalf. The result of this was that Imma's chains were miraculously loosed, and as the brothers discovered when they met after Imma's release, this loosing had taken place at exactly the time that the masses had been offered.[27] Bede comments that many people who learned of this were inspired to have masses offered on their behalf, not least because Imma himself apparently explained to his captors that if he were in the otherworld, the masses would have released his soul from torments.[28] Other anecdotal accounts, especially of visions, similarly record the power of masses to release: one of the letters included in the Bonifatian correspondence records how a visionary saw a woman released from torment at exactly the moment when a mass was offered on her behalf.[29] The more famous vision of the brother of Wenlock, discussed in some detail above, includes an account of a man who was suffering because his brother had refused to release a slave – another practice held to benefit the soul in the beyond – in direct contravention of the agreement that they had made before death.[30] The brother of Wenlock's vision also includes a description of places which, in some of the details, suggest the possibility of purgation in the interim: souls are purged of their sins and will ultimately reach the joy of heaven, some at the Last Judgement and some before.[31]

---

*Supplementary Collection*, EETS, OS 259–60 (2 vols, London, 1967–8), I.415–47, and see also I.407–10; M.M. Gatch, *Preaching and Theology in Anglo-Saxon England: Aelfric and Wulfstan* (Toronto, 1977), 101–4.

[26]    Ælfric, *Hom.* XI, esp. ll. 220–8, ed. Pope, *Homilies of Ælfric*, I.426–7.

[27]    Bede, *HE*, IV.22, ed. Lapidge, Monat and Robin, *Histoire ecclésiastique*, II.310–16; the story of Imma was also translated by Ælfric and is included at the end of *CH* II.21, ed. Godden, *Catholic Homilies*, 204–5.

[28]    Bede, *HE*, IV.22.5, ed. Lapidge, Monat and Robin, *Histoire ecclésiastique*, II.316.

[29]    *Epistola* 115, ed. M. Tangl, *Die Briefe des Heiligen Bonifatius und Lullus*, MGH, Epistolae Selectae 1 (Berlin, 1916), 247–50, at 248, ll. 5–7.

[30]    *Epistola* 10, ed. Tangl, *Die Briefe*, 13, ll. 28–36; see also above, 75–7.

[31]    *Epistola* 10, ed. Tangl, *Die Briefe*, 11, l. 3 – 12, l. 9. For more detailed discussion of the theological significance of these parts of the brother of Wenlock's vision, see S. Foot,

These concerns are visible too even in the penitential texts which focus primarily on the sins of the living, although here there is an interesting distinction between the earlier and later texts which is not found so clearly in homiletic and exegetical works. Penitential texts are concerned with how to achieve the remission of sin in life, but occasionally mention the practice of prayer for the dead. The late seventh- and early eighth-century versions of the material associated with the teachings of Archbishop Theodore of Canterbury (d.690) contain a number of instructions on the masses allowed for the dead, and also note rather inconclusively that while someone who fasts for a dead man will benefit himself, it is not clear what the effect is for the dead person.[32] Versions of this statement are repeated in later vernacular penitentials, such as the *Old English Canons of Theodore* and *Old English Scriftboc*, both of which probably date to the tenth century, and perhaps fairly early in the century.[33] In contrast, the tenth-century *Old English Introduction* explains the effectiveness of offerings for the dead quite clearly in a list of different ways of remitting sins, noting that 'the eighth forgiveness of sin is when someone goes from this life to punishments, and his friend then in this life can release him, and earn him forgiveness from God with divine service and with his worldly possessions'.[34] Penitentials are conservative books, and as already noted, it is difficult to establish how widely, or even precisely how, they were used; other evidence suggests that the belief expressed by the *Introduction* was much more common by the tenth century.[35]

Brief comments on the difference between 'deadly' or 'serious' and 'small' or 'less serious' sins demonstrate a belief in post-mortem purgation, and different fates for different types of sinners. The Anglo-Saxon abbot of Tours, Alcuin (d.804),

---

'Anglo-Saxon "Purgatory"', in P.D. Clarke and T. Claydon (eds), *The Church, the Afterlife and the Fate of the Soul: Papers Read at the 2007 Summer Meeting and the 2008 Winter Meeting of the Ecclesiastical History Society*, Studies in Church History 45 (Woodbridge, 2009), 87–96, at 93–5; Foxhall Forbes, 'Diuiduntur in quattuor', 673–4.

[32]   e.g. D 113, U II.XIV.2, ed. P.W. Finsterwalder, *Die Canones Theodori Cantuariensis und ihre Überlieferungsformen* (Weimar, 1929), 248, 332; see T.M. Charles-Edwards, 'The Penitential of Theodore and the "Iudicia Theodori"', in M. Lapidge (ed.), *Archbishop Theodore: Commemorative Studies on his Life and Influence* (Cambridge, 1995), 141–74; R. Flechner, 'The making of the Canons of Theodore', *Peritia* 17/18 (2004): 121–43.

[33]   21.08.01, 78.06.02, ed. A.J. Frantzen, *The Anglo-Saxon Penitentials: A Cultural Database* (2008), http://www.anglo-saxon.net/penance, accessed November 2012.

[34]   34.08.91, ed. Frantzen, *The Anglo-Saxon Penitentials: A Cultural Database*, quoted here from Laud misc. 482: 'Seo eahtoþe forgyfenys ys þæt se man of þis life fare to wíte. & his frynd þonne þe on þis life beoð hine magon alysan. & him forgyfennysse æt gode geearnigan mid godcundum þeowdome·& mid hyra world æhton'.

[35]   Given that some manuscripts contain both texts and therefore both statements, it is not clear either how the different provisions would have been read (see for example Oxford, Bodleian Library, Laud misc. 482 and Junius 121; and Cambridge, Corpus Christi College, 190; Frantzen, *The Anglo-Saxon Penitentials: A Cultural Database*). See also above, 50–1, 134–5.

advised Bishop Arno of Salzburg that after the potential penitent has learned of
the immortality of the soul and eternal life, he can learn which sins condemn the
soul to eternal punishment.[36] In his commentary on the psalms Alcuin noted that
those who are without mortal sins ('sine mortali crimine') are those who walk
in the way of the Lord, explaining that since we cannot be without small sins
('minuta'), we ought not to fall into greater sins ('maiora').[37] Similar ideas are
found in tenth-century Anglo-Saxon homilies too: a warning in the third Blickling
homily to keep from serious sins on the grounds that anyone who dies with these
on their conscience will be condemned to everlasting punishment tacitly implies
an interim state which does permit the release of souls, an idea repeated in the fifth
Blickling homily, and both possibly drawing on Alcuin's commentary.[38] Similarly,
Ælfric warns that the 'capital sins' such as murder and witchcraft will not be
purged in the 'punishing' fire, but will send those who commit them and who are
unrepentant to the eternal punishments of hell: he advises further that it is better
to confess and repent both smaller and greater sins, so that the soul experiences
neither the 'sharp burning' nor indeed eternal damnation, but rather eternal life.[39]
There is a clear distinction between the smaller sins which can be removed in the
cleansing punishments of purgatory, and the greater sins which will send the soul
to the unending torment of hell.

There are also references to the purgatorial interim which sound anecdotal, and
this, combined with the complete absence of any explanation about what purgatory
was or how it worked, suggests strongly that the concept was widely understood.
One such story is about a man who was spoken to by the bones of his departed
friend, and urged to turn to a more righteous life: following this advice, the man
earned the grace of the Holy Spirit (i.e., saved himself) and freed his friend's soul
from torments.[40] The fourth Blickling homily instructs that bishops and priests
who serve God correctly must sing mass weekly for all Christian people who have
ever been born, from the beginning of the world, and notes that the offering of the
mass is the greatest cause of irritation to devils, 'because they have many souls
in their power to whom God will yet show mercy on account of their powerful
supplications, and on account of the prayers of earthly men, and of all saints, and
for his great mercy'.[41] Almsgiving is imbued with a similar power in the third
Vercelli homily: the author notes, apparently following Augustine, that 'it looses

[36]   Alcuin, *Epistola* 110, ed. E.L. Dümmler, *Epistolae Karolini aevi*, MGH, Epistolae
Karolini aevi II (Berlin, 1895), 158–9.

[37]   *Expositio in psalmum* CXVIII, 1, *PL* 100.597C–598A.

[38]   *Hom*. III, ed. R. Morris, *The Blickling Homilies of the 10th Century: From the
Marquis of Lothian's Unique MS. A.D.971*, EETS, OS 58 (London, 1874), 36; *Hom*. V, ed.
Morris, *Blickling Homilies*, 62.

[39]   *CH* II.40, ll. 223–93, ed. Godden, *Catholic Homilies*, 342–4; see also *Hom*. XI, ll.
220–35, ed. Pope, *Homilies of Ælfric*, I.426–7.

[40]   *Hom*. X, ed. Morris, *Blickling Homilies*, 113.

[41]   *Hom*. IV, ed. Morris, *Blickling Homilies*, 45–7.

men from death and from torments'.[42] Pinning down the audience and even the origins of many of these homilies is notoriously difficult, as can be the localisation of the manuscripts.[43] But especially in the case of the tenth-century Blickling book, it is clear that eschatology was a major concern of the compiler, and although these homilies are often very close to their sources, the fact that he did not feel the need to expand or explain passages which allude to the interim is significant.[44]

Concern about the fate of the soul after death is clear too from the letters which passed between men and women in religious life, asking for masses or prayers to be said for each other or – more importantly in this context – for their dead friends and relatives. A number of the letters in the correspondence of Boniface and his contemporaries refer to the practice of exchanging names so that communities and individuals could pray for each other, and to the practice of offering masses or prayers for the dead.[45] Boniface also received more personal requests to offer prayers or masses: Leoba asked Boniface to pray for her mother, who was unwell, and her father, who was dead;[46] Bugga asked Boniface to offer masses for the soul of her kinsman who was dear to her above all others.[47] In the same way, Alcuin's letters frequently make reference to the power of prayer after death, and he states that even if someone died in his sins, divine mercy will make him live: Alcuin even notes that the one who dies before his friend is better off, 'since he has someone to intercede for him every day with brotherly love and to wash away the errors of his earlier life with tears'.[48] These must be seen in the context of the culture of prayer and memorial for the dead which saw the living and dead as part

---

[42]    *Hom.* III, ll. 144–51, ed. D.G. Scragg, *The Vercelli Homilies and Related Texts*, EETS, OS 300 (London, 1992), 82.

[43]    D.G. Scragg, 'The Homilies of the Blickling Manuscript', in M. Lapidge and H. Gneuss (eds), *Learning and Literature in Anglo-Saxon England: Studies Presented to Peter Clemoes on the Occasion of his Sixty-Fifth Birthday* (Cambridge, 1985), 299–316, at 315–16; M.M. Gatch, 'The unknowable audience of the Blickling Homilies', *Anglo-Saxon England* 18 (1989): 99–115, at 114–15; Scragg, *Vercelli Homilies*, xix–lxxix; E.M. Treharne, 'The Form and Function of the Vercelli Book', in A.J. Minnis and J. Roberts (eds), *Text, Image, Interpretation: Studies in Anglo-Saxon Literature and its Insular Context in Honour of Éamonn Ó Carragáin* (Turnhout, 2007), 253–66.

[44]    M.M. Gatch, 'Eschatology in the anonymous Old English homilies', *Traditio: Studies in Ancient and Medieval History, Thought, and Religion* 21 (1965): 117–65, at 124, 134–5.

[45]    e.g. *Epistolae* 38, 81, 106, 111, 114, ed. Tangl, *Die Briefe*, 63, 181–2, 231–2, 239–43, 246–7.

[46]    *Epistola* 29, ed. Tangl, *Die Briefe*, 52, l. 17 – 53, l. 2.

[47]    *Epistola* 15, ed. Tangl, *Die Briefe*, 27, l. 28 – 28 l. 1.

[48]    Alcuin, *Epistola* 105, ed. Dümmler, *Epistolae*, 151–2: 'Forte in peccatis suis mortuus est; sed in misericordia potest fieri, ut vivat, divina … Si duo sunt amici, felicior est mors praecedentis quam subsequetis; habet enim, qui fraterno amore pro se cotidie intercedat et lacrimis lavet pristinae errores vitae … Larga est et inestimabilis pietas domini nostri Iesu Christi, qui vult omnes homines salvos fieri et neminem perire'.

of one Christian community, and which became part of the way of life for religious communities in the early Middle Ages.


## Prayer and Memorials for the Dead

By the early Middle Ages, communal commemoration and prayer for the dead were an important part of life in religious communities, and the amount of time and effort dedicated to prayer for and remembrance of the dead – and the significance laid upon these – seems to have increased through the period. Information about the commemoration of the dead at monastic houses is recorded in the liturgical customaries which sought to regulate Benedictine monastic life in early medieval England, such as the *Regularis Concordia*, drawn up in Winchester in *c*.970, and Ælfric's expansion and reworking of the *Concordia*, known as his *Letter to the Monks of Eynsham*, written in the late tenth or early eleventh century;[49] and for the latter part of the eleventh century the *Constitutions* of Archbishop Lanfranc of Canterbury (d.1089).[50] These instruct extensive commemoration for those who were members of the community, requiring a substantial investment of time and energy in the form of special prayers, masses and almsgiving for those who had recently died, but they also describe the ongoing regular commemoration of the dead members of the community.[51] From the ninth century the use of the Office of the Dead became gradually more important as part of the commemoration and remembrance of the dead, and this was especially significant because it was said communally: by the end of the ninth century in some places, and more generally in the tenth and eleventh centuries, the Office of the Dead was recited every day regardless of whether there had been a recent death, thus incorporating all the dead members of a community into its regular prayers.[52]

---

[49]    T. Symons (ed.), *Regularis Concordia: The Monastic Agreement of the Monks and Nuns of the English Nation* (London, 1953); Ælfric, *Letter to the Monks of Eynsham*, ed. C.A. Jones, Ælfric's Letter to the Monks of Eynsham, Cambridge Studies in Anglo-Saxon England 24 (Cambridge, 1998): see 5–17 for information about the uncertain dating of this text.

[50]    D. Knowles and C.N.L. Brooke (eds), *The Monastic Constitutions of Lanfranc* (Oxford, 2002); for discussion of date and monasteries where these were used, see xxviii–xxxix.

[51]    *RC*, 65–8, ed. Symons, *Regularis Concordia*, 64–8; *LME*, 65–9, ed. Jones, Ælfric's Letter, 140–4.

[52]    L. Eisenhofer and J. Lechner, *The Liturgy of the Roman Rite* (Freiburg, 1961), 474–5; A.A. Häußling, *Mönchskonvent und Eucharistiefeier: einer Studie über die Messe in der abendländischen Klosterliturgie des frühen Mittelalters und zur Geschichte der Messhäufigkeit*, Liturgiewissenschaftliche Quellen und Forschungen 58 (Münster, Westfalen, 1973), 321; McLaughlin, *Consorting*, 40–1, 72–3.

It seems to have been common custom for early medieval religious communities to record the names of their living and dead members, a practice which had originated in the early centuries of Christianity, when the names of living and dead Christians were recorded on diptychs; in the early Middle Ages it was usual to write the names on blank pages in books, or to add sheets with lists into other books, and entire books known as *libri memoriales* (memorial books) or *libri vitae* (books of life) were custom-made for communities to remember their dead.[53] From at least the early sixth century, the names of the departed were read out in weekday masses and requiem masses: Roman and Gallican customs varied, but the *Memento* for the dead which is found in early Gallican books was ultimately incorporated into the Roman canon of the mass, perhaps attributable to the influence of Alcuin's liturgical writings.[54] There is comparatively little liturgical evidence from England before about the ninth century but what there is seems to contain elements of both Gallican and Roman tradition, so it is difficult to know what was practiced in the early centuries of Christianity in England.[55]

It is clear, however, that names were collected and kept, because *libri vitae* and other lists of names survive from England, primarily from monastic houses, though there appears to be no Old English term for these books, and it is possible that this reflects their predominantly monastic provenance.[56] There are also scattered references to these books and requests to be included in them, such as Bede's request in his Prologue to the prose version of his *Life of Cuthbert* to be remembered in masses and to have his name inscribed in the book of the Lindisfarne community.[57]

---

[53]   K. Schmid and J. Wollasch, 'Die Gemeinschaft der Lebenden und Verstorbenen in Zeugnissen des Mittelalters', *Frühmittelalterliche Studien* 1 (1967): 365–405, at 368–9; McLaughlin, *Consorting*, 91; Keynes, *Liber Vitae of the New Minster*, 49–50.

[54]   M. Andrieu, 'L'Insertion du "Memento" des morts au canon romain de la messe', *Revue des Sciences Religieuses* 1 (1921): 151–4, at 153; B. Botte and C. Mohrmann, *L'Ordinaire de la messe. Texte critique, traduction et études*, Études liturgiques 2 (Paris, 1953), 24; G. Ellard, 'An example of Alcuin's influence on the liturgy', *Manuscripta* 4:1 (1960): 23–8; G.G. Willis, *Essays in Early Roman Liturgy*, Alcuin Club Collections 46 (London, 1964), 36; G.G. Willis, *A History of Early Roman Liturgy: To the Death of Pope Gregory the Great* (London, 1994), 38–9. It has been suggested that memorial books originated in England: see A. Angenendt, 'Missa specialis: Zugleich ein Beitrag zur Entstehung der Privatmessen', *Frühmittelalterliche Studien* 17 (1983): 153–221, at 203.

[55]   B. Botte, *Le canon de la messe romain. Edition critique*, Textes et études liturgiques 2 (Louvain, 1935), 15–17; G.G. Willis, *Further Essays in Early Roman Liturgy* (London, 1968), 37, 192–7.

[56]   H. Gneuss, 'Liturgical Books in Anglo-Saxon England and their Old English Terminology', in Lapidge and Gneuss (eds), *Learning and Literature in Anglo-Saxon England*, 91–141, at 140–1; J. Gerchow, *Die Gedenküberlieferung der Angelsachsen: mit einem Katalog der libri vitae und Necrologien*, Arbeiten zur Frühmittelalterforschung 20 (Berlin, 1988).

[57]   Bede, *Vita S. Cuthberti prosa*, Prologue, ed. B. Colgrave, *Two Lives of Saint Cuthbert: A Life by an Anonymous Monk of Lindisfarne and Bede's Prose Life* (Cambridge,

The *libri vitae* of religious houses on the continent reveal traces of personal connections established across Europe, made in the course of pilgrimages and journeys for business: Anglo-Saxon names are found in the *libri vitae* of Brescia, St Gallen, Reichenau and Pfäfers, for example.[58] The earliest surviving English memorial book is the Durham *Liber Vitae* (now London, British Library, Cotton Domitian A.vii), which contains at its core what appears to be a 'fair copy' of a list from the mid ninth century written at Lindisfarne or Wearmouth-Jarrow, but the book was frequently added to and seems to have been in continuous use until the sixteenth century.[59] Perhaps the most famous of the Anglo-Saxon memorial books is the *Liber Vitae* of the New Minster, Winchester (now London, British Library, Stowe 944), which contains a core of names dating probably from the 970s, although the book itself was made in the 1030s while Ælfwine was abbot.[60] This book is a lavish production: it contains an image of King Cnut and Queen Emma placing a golden cross on the altar of the New Minster, with Christ in Majesty and SS Mary and Peter above, apparently representing the real donation of such a cross to the abbey.[61]

The New Minster's *Liber Vitae* includes a preface to the list of names which is informative in understanding the use of the book, explaining that every day in the mass, the names are to be read out if there is time, and afterwards to be placed on the altar at the right hand of the celebrant.[62] Some votive masses refer to the reading of names, such as Alcuin's liturgy for the living and the departed which

1985 [orig. pub. 1940]), 146: '... et nomen meum inter uestra scibere dignemini. Nam et tu sanctissime antiestes hoc te mihi promisisse iam retines. In cuius etiam testimonium futurae conscriptionis religioso fratri nostro Gudfrido mansionario praecepisti, ut in albo uestrae sanctae congregationis meum nunc quoque nomen apponeret'. See also Alcuin, *Epistolae* 67, 284, 286, ed. Dümmler, *Epistolae*, 110, ll. 30–3, 442–3, 444–5.

58   S. Keynes, 'Anglo-Saxon Entries in the Liber Vitae of Brescia', in J.A. Roberts et al. (eds), *Alfred the Wise: Studies in Honour of Janet Bately on the Occasion of her Sixty-Fifth Birthday* (Cambridge, 1997), 99–119, at 110–12: Keynes suggests that the names at St Gallen and Reichenau were entered in connection with the journey of Cenwald to Germany in about 929, and in Pfäfers perhaps in connection with an English visit in the early 940s.

59   L. Rollason, 'The *Liber Vitae* of Durham and Lay Association with Durham Cathedral Priory in the Later Middle Ages', in B. Thompson (ed.), *Monasteries and Society in Medieval Britain: Proceedings of the 1994 Harlaxton Symposium*, Harlaxton Medieval Studies, n.s. 6 (Stamford, 1999), 277–95, at 277–8. The book is now available as a digital facsimile: see D.W. Rollason et al., *Durham Liber vitae: London, British Library, MS Cotton Domitian A.VII: Edition and Digital Facsimile with Introduction, Codicological, Prosopographical and Linguistic Commentary, and Indexes* (London, 2007), and see 23–4 for information about the date of the writing of the original core and the subsequent Anglo-Saxon additions.

60   Keynes, *Liber Vitae of the New Minster*, 31–2, 37, 39. This is the same Ælfwine whose prayer book has already been discussed: see above, 201.

61   Stowe 944, fol. 6r; Keynes, *Liber Vitae of the New Minster*, 35–7.

62   Stowe 944, fols. 13r–v.

asks for the health of those whose bodies lie in the *monasterium*, or whose names are read before the altar, and for a refreshment to be granted to those souls.[63] Memorial books may also have been used in the Liturgy of the Hours as well as at the mass.[64] The numbers of names in books such as this increased quite rapidly, so that commemoration was also made more generally without recitation by simply placing the book on the altar, as the New Minster's preface also makes clear.[65] This is significant in considering the form of commemoration and what it meant for people to have their names included in memorial books. Those whose names were recorded in the New Minster's *Liber Vitae* were instructed to 'rejoice, for your names are written in heaven'.[66] Inclusion in the earthly *liber vitae* was symbolically comparable to inclusion in the heavenly *liber vitae* mentioned several times in Scripture, a book containing the names of the righteous who will be saved, and communities consciously used the biblical imagery of the book of life.[67]

Other kinds of memorial records included necrologies or obituaries, lists of names which were organised according to the calendar and could therefore be used to mark the anniversaries of individuals on particular days, rather than the more general commemoration afforded to those whose names were recorded in *libri vitae*.[68] The kalendars found in liturgical books might also be used to note obits, sometimes those of personal importance, as for example the names of the family members of Ælfwine or St Wulfstan, in their own private prayer books.[69] The remembrance of these aniversaries was important in incorporating the dead into personal and communal prayers, and like the general remembrance of names, was also intended to be beneficial after death and before the Last Judgement. One of the clearest statements about the purpose of remembering anniversaries was made by the Carolingian writer, Amalarius of Metz (d.c.850), in his liturgical

---

[63]    *Missa pro salute uiuorum et mortuorum*, ed. J. Deshusses, 'Les messes d'Alcuin', *Archiv für Liturgiewissenschaft* 14 (1972): 7–41, at 27–8.

[64]    Schmid and Wollasch, 'Gemeinschaft der Lebenden und Verstorbenen', 367.

[65]    J. Wollasch, 'Toten- und Armensorge', in K. Schmid and J. Wollasch (eds), *Gedächtnis, das Gemeinschaft Stiftet*, Schriftenreihe der Katholischen Akademie der Erzdiözese Freiburg (Munich, 1985), 9–38, at 18; McLaughlin, *Consorting*, 92.

[66]    Keynes, *Liber Vitae of the New Minster*, 82–3.

[67]    Schmid and Wollasch, 'Gemeinschaft der Lebenden und Verstorbenen', 365. The 'book of life' is referred to in Ps. 68:29; Philippians 4:3; Revelation 3:5; 13:8; 17.8; 20:12, 15; 21:27 and implicitly in Daniel 12.

[68]    K. Schmid and J. Wollasch, 'Societas et Fraternitas: Begründung eines kommentierten Quellenwerkes zur Erforschung der Personen und Personengruppen des Mittelalters', *Frühmittelalterliche Studien* 9 (1975): 1–48, at 34–5; McLaughlin, *Consorting*, 93–6.

[69]    For Ælfwine's prayer book see Günzel, *Ælfwine's Prayerbook*, 1; Keynes, *Liber Vitae of the New Minster*, 40–1; and above, 201. St Wulfstan's personal prayer book is now Cambridge, Corpus Christi College, 391: see A. Hughes, *The Portiforium of St Wulstan: Corpus Christi College, Cambridge, MS. 391*, HBS 89–90 (2 vols Leighton Buzzard, 1958–60).

treatise known as the *Liber officialis* (or *De ecclesiasticis officiis*).[70] Amalarius discussed anniversaries in the context of masses offered for the dead, noting when they should be offered, and quoting Augustine's comments on the people for whom masses could be valuable.[71] Crucially, Amalarius explains why keeping anniversaries is important for the dead, and he contrasts this with the reason for remembering the anniversaries of the saints:

> For this reason anniversary days are kept for the dead, because we do not know what their situation is in the other life: so just as the anniversary days in honour of the saints are brought to our memory for our benefit, so those of the dead are performed for their benefit and for our devotion, and we believe that they will come to the company of saints at some future time.[72]

The *Liber officialis* seems to have reached England in the early tenth century, although the textual history of this work is complicated: Amalarius himself produced three different editions, and the text that seems to have been available in England before about the middle of the eleventh century was an edited and epitomised version of the third edition, made some time after Amalarius' death, and known now as the *Retractio prima*.[73] In this version several passages about offerings for the dead have been rearranged from their original context so that they are collected together, and this extract about anniversaries is included here.[74] This is significant because the evidence of manuscripts and the citation and influence of Amalarius in Anglo-Saxon texts shows that this version of the *Liber officialis* was reasonably well known in later Anglo-Saxon England.[75] Given the importance

---

[70] *Liber officialis*, ed. J.M. Hanssens, *Amalarii episcopi opera liturgica omnia* (3 vols Vatican City, 1948), II.

[71] III.44, ed. Hanssens, *Amalarii episcopi opera liturgica omnia*, 381–6.

[72] Amalarius of Metz, *Liber officialis*, III.44.16, ed. Hanssens, *Amalarii episcopi opera liturgica omnia*, II.385–6: 'Anniversaria dies ideo repetitur pro defunctis, quoniam nescimus qualiter eorum causa habeatur in alia vita. Sicut sanctorum anniversaria dies in eorum honore ad memoriam nobis reduciter super utilitate nostra, ita defunctorum, ad utilitatem illorum et nostram devotionem implendam, credendo eos aliquando venturos ad consortium sanctorum'.

[73] See the discussion in Hanssens, *Amalarii episcopi opera liturgica omnia*, I.133–69; M.M. Gatch, 'The Office in Late Anglo-Saxon Monasticism', in Lapidge and Gneuss (eds), *Learning and Literature in Anglo Saxon England*, 341–62, at 349; Jones, Ælfric's Letter, 60–3; S. Ambrose, 'The *Collectio Canonum Hibernensis* and the literature of the Anglo-Saxon Benedictine reform', *Viator* 36 (2005): 107–18.

[74] Detailed information about the selection and arrangement of chapters in the *Retractatio prima* is in Hanssens, *Amalarii episcopi opera liturgica omnia*, I.163–8, see esp. 167.

[75] Jones, Ælfric's Letter, 62–5; C.A. Jones, 'The book of the liturgy in Anglo-Saxon England', *Speculum: A Journal of Medieval Studies* 73 (1998): 659–702, at 676–7; and also C.A. Jones, 'Ælfric's exemplar of Amalarius: An additional witness', *American Notes and*

of commemoration for the dead by this time, it seems likely that even in religious houses where a copy of the *Liber officialis* was not available, an interpretation of their value like that given by Amalarius would have been understood. Interestingly, despite the extensive use of Amalarius in his customary, Ælfric did not cite this passage explaining the purpose of anniversaries, perhaps because by the time he was writing this was considered to be utterly self-evident: the prayers which were offered for the dead beg God to grant mercy to the souls of the departed so that they are not tormented, so that their sins are wiped away, and so that they will come to heaven and join the communion of saints.[76]

The importance of commemoration and prayer for the dead is also clear from the confraternity arrangements made between religious houses to pray for one another, and especially for the dead members of the communities. When a member of a religious house died, a messenger would bring news of the death to other communities, sometimes with a special mortuary roll which could be used to inscribe prayers or the names of other individuals to be recorded in the *liber memorialis*, whether as an individual anniversary in a necrology, or more generally in a *liber vitae*.[77] The process is described in the Anglo-Saxon liturgical customaries, which emphasise that those who were part of a confraternity could expect to be treated as if they were one of the community's own, and thus prayers, masses and almsgiving would be offered on their behalf.[78] The value of prayer, masses and almsgiving for the dead is also clear in other types of mutual agreement, as for example in the early eleventh-century record of a bishops' synod, where it was agreed that if one of the bishops died, each of the others was to make offerings for his soul including masses and Offices of the Dead, almsgiving, manumission, and the washing of paupers.[79]

Like the texts which discuss purgatory, the evidence for the culture of prayer and commemoration is strongly bound up with religious houses, especially monastic foundations. It is clear nonetheless that the concerns which lay behind prayer for the dead, and the desire to be commemorated at religious houses, were not limited to those in religious life, and that the importance of prayer and offerings for the

---

*Queries* 13:2 (2000): 6–14; C.A. Jones, *A Lost Work by Amalarius of Metz: Interpolations in Salisbury, Cathedral Library MS 154*, HBS, Subsidia 2 (Woodbridge, 2001).

[76]  See for example the prayers *in agenda mortuorum* in Oxford, Bodleian Library, Bodley 579 ('Leofric Missal'), fols. 246r–253r, ed. N. Orchard, *The Leofric Missal*, HBS 113–14 (2 vols, London, 2002), nos. 2198–2241; or Rouen, Bibliothèque municipale, 274 ('Missal of Robert of Jumièges'), fols. 213v–218r, ed. H.A. Wilson, *The Missal of Robert of Jumièges*, HBS 11 (London, 1896), 297–303; for information about the manuscripts see below, 286 and Table 5.1.

[77]  Keynes, *Liber Vitae of the New Minster*, 49–50.

[78]  Ælfric, *LME*, 67–9, ed. Jones, *Ælfric's Letter*, 142–4; see also J.E. Burton, 'Confraternities in the Durham *Liber vitae*', in Rollason et al. (eds), *Durham Liber Vitae*, I.73–5.

[79]  *Decisions at a Bishops' Synod, Councils and Synods*, I.i, no. 53.

dead was understood far beyond the confines of monastic communities. Homilists warned their congregations not to rely on offerings made for their souls after death, implying that the idea of the purgatorial interim was very well understood, so much so that homilists had to work hard to ensure that their congregations confessed and performed penance for their own souls, rather than relying on the help of their friends. In the eighth Blickling homily, the author warns that no man may be released from punishments if he will not turn to repentance himself, because he must merit what his friends will do for him afterwards.[80] The fourteenth Vercelli homily explains that 'the sacrifice [of the mass] truly releases the soul from torments', and yet warns that 'no man can truly release another after death, if earlier, while in the world, he neglects the salvation of his soul', noting that each man is better off doing for himself what he hopes that his friends will do for him afterwards.[81] Ælfric also warned that 'we ask forgiveness for our sins in this world, and not in that which is to come: the man who does not want to repent of his sins in his life will not receive forgiveness in the next'.[82] Even if in some cases these sentiments are drawn from earlier writings, as for example Vercelli XIV draws on the *Dialogues* of Gregory the Great, it does not mean that this was no longer a contemporary issue.[83]

These kinds of comments, especially when set alongside the anecdotal references which do not explain purgatory in detail, suggest that the concept of the purgatorial interim, as well as the concomitant belief in the effects of masses and offerings for the dead, was quite widely understood. It is significant too that accounts of visions and even anecdotal stories found in homilies do seem to have circulated more widely, as already discussed, so that these kinds of accounts were probably better known and understood than detailed discussions on some other aspects of theology.[84] In this context, Bede's comment that Imma's story inspired people to have masses offered on behalf of their friends is striking in its implication that a thegn like Imma was well aware of the power of the mass in releasing souls in the interim, although it should not be forgotten that since Imma's brother was a priest he may have been more knowledgeable about such topics than many others. Interestingly, the account of Imma is one of the 'memorable events' from Bede's *Historia Ecclesiastica* which Alcuin selected as most worthy of retelling in his poem on the bishops, kings and saints of York: once again the power of the mass for the soul is very clearly highlighted and Alcuin notes that he thinks this event 'will be valuable to many readers', although he then qualifies this by wondering

---

[80]  *Hom.* VIII, ed. Morris, *Blickling Homilies*, 101.

[81]  *Hom.* XIV, ll. 45–53, 62–77, ed. Scragg, *Vercelli Homilies*, 242–3.

[82]  *CH* I.19, ll. 203–6, ed. P. Clemoes, Ælfric's Catholic Homilies: The First Series, EETS, SS 17 (Oxford, 1997), 332: 'On þyssere worulde we biddað ure synna forgyfenyssæ. ꝺ na on þære toweardan; Se man þe nele his synna behreowsian on his life. ne begyt he nane forgyfennysse on þam toweardan'.

[83]  Scragg, *Vercelli Homilies*, 237–8.

[84]  See above, 120–5.

(probably with false modesty) whether anyone will consider his work worthy of reading in any case.[85]

However, accounts which sound anecdotal are not always all they seem on the surface, even if they did circulate orally. Bede's story of Imma is very similar to one recorded in Gregory's *Dialogues*, and evidently related to it, and it is difficult to know how far such episodes really represent popular stories in any case: Bede's retelling of Dryhthelm's otherworld experience likewise purports to be an accurate record of a vision, but the alignment of the afterlife in this account with the information in Bede's homily for the Second Sunday in Advent indicates that much has been adapted and reworked.[86] Purgatory is a difficult topic because it is not included in the credal statements which may represent the basis for catechetical teaching in Anglo-Saxon England, and as already noted, it is uncertain how frequently people attended church, or how attentively they listened to homilies.[87] More fruitfully, it is possible to explore ideas about purgatory and the interim by examining documents which were produced in response to the concerns of lay and religious men and women who sought to provide for their souls in the afterlife, and for the souls of their friends and relatives. Lay men and women could not themselves offer masses for their dead friends and relatives, nor commemorate them in the full Offices of the Dead; but perhaps more importantly, if they wanted to arrange for these services for their own souls, then self-evidently they were dependent on other people, whether individuals or religious communities. By associating themselves with religious houses, lay men and women arranged prayers and masses for themselves, had their names written in *libri memoriales*, and thereby attempted to ensure that after their deaths their souls would not languish in purgatorial suffering, unaided and unremembered.

## Donating to the Saints and their Servants

The records of property and wealth donated to religious houses (and sometimes to religious individuals) by lay and religious men and women present a body of evidence for strong and specific concern about the fate of the soul after death, and these donations often record that they were made in return for offerings to be made for the donors' souls, or for their friends or relatives. Sometimes these donations are bequests in wills, where the benefactor set out how all of his property was to be distributed after his death; at other times donations were transferred before

---

[85] Alcuin, *Versus de patribus regibus et sanctis euboricensis ecclesiae*, ll. 786–835, ed. P. Godman, *Alcuin: The Bishops, Kings and Saints of York* (Oxford, 1982), 66–8.

[86] *Dialogues*, IV.57.8–14, ed. A. de Vogüé and P. Antin, *Dialogues de Grégoire le Grand: Livre IV, texte critique et notes*, Sources chrétiennes 265 (Paris, 1980), III.188–92; for discussion of the relationship between Dryhthelm's vision and Bede's homily, see Foxhall Forbes, 'Diuiduntur in quattuor', 660–73.

[87] See above, 47–8.

death, and perhaps prompted by an event which was not always recorded in the surviving document.[88] Gifts such as these had multivalent meanings, depending on both social and theological contexts for their significance, but in many cases there was a clear and overriding concern to ensure the forgiveness of sins which would ultimately allow donors – or their dead friends and relatives on whose behalf the gifts were offered – to join the communion of saints.[89] These gifts were beneficial for the soul both because they were a form of almsgiving and because through them it was possible to arrange for other sorts of memorial and prayer. Donors seem also to have wanted to associate themselves with the saints, the patrons whom religious communities served. The surviving records of lay dealings with churches reveal that there was a strong lay desire to be associated with and commemorated by religious foundations, and that members of the secular clergy might also wish for connections with monastic communities.

In considering this body of evidence, it is important to take account of how these documents were produced.[90] A large number of the documents considered here are charters, which are formal and relatively formulaic: they usually include an introductory statement (the proem), which may contain a religious statement on (for example) the transitory nature of life, the importance of committing records to writing, or the spiritual value of almsgiving; a dispositive section which includes

---

[88]   S. Keynes, *The Diplomas of King Æthelred 'the Unready' 978–1016: A Study in their Use as Historical Evidence*, Cambridge Studies in Medieval Life and Thought, 3rd series, 13 (Cambridge, 1980), 6–8, 35–42; McLaughlin, *Consorting*, 134–6; L. Tollerton, *Wills and Will-Making in Anglo-Saxon England* (Woodbridge, 2011), 56–79.

[89]   For discussion, see for example Schmid and Wollasch, 'Gemeinschaft der Lebenden und Verstorbenen'; J. Wollasch, 'Die mittelalterliche Lebensform der Verbrüderung', in Schmid and Wollasch (eds), *Memoria*, 215–32; S.D. White, *Custom, Kinship, and Gifts to Saints: The laudatio parentum in Western France, 1050–1150*, Studies in Legal History (Chapel Hill, NC, 1988); B.H. Rosenwein, *To Be the Neighbor of Saint Peter: The Social Meaning of Cluny's Property, 909–1049* (Ithaca, NY, 1989); McLaughlin, *Consorting*; see also the essays in W. Davies and P. Fouracre, *The Languages of Gift in the Early Middle Ages* (Cambridge, 2010).

[90]   This is a complex topic and what is given here is just a summary: for detailed discussion see P. Chaplais, 'The origin and authenticity of the royal Anglo-Saxon diploma', *Journal of the Society of Archivists* 3:2 (1965): 48–61; P. Chaplais, 'The Anglo-Saxon chancery: From the diploma to the writ', *Journal of the Society of Archivists* 3:4 (1966): 160–76; P. Chaplais, 'Some early Anglo-Saxon diplomas on single sheets: Originals or copies?', *Journal of the Society of Archivists* 3:7 (1968): 315–36; Keynes, *Diplomas*; S.E. Kelly, 'Anglo-Saxon Lay Society and the Written Word', in R. McKitterick (ed.), *The Uses of Literacy in Early Mediaeval Europe* (Cambridge, 1990), 36–62; and see also N. Brooks, 'Anglo-Saxon Charters: A Review of Work 1953–73, with a Postscript on the Period 1973–98', in N. Brooks (ed.), *Anglo-Saxon Myths: State and Church, 400–1066* (London, 2000), 181–215; S. Keynes, 'Anglo-Saxon Charters: Lost and Found', in J. Barrow and A. Wareham (eds), *Myth, Rulership, Church and Charters: Essays in Honour of Nicholas Brooks* (Aldershot, 2008), 45–66.

information about what the donor intends to give the beneficiary; some information about the bounds of the land given; a sanction clause warning of the ecclesiastical or spiritual penalties which will befall anyone who contravenes the terms of the grant; and a list of the witnesses to the transaction.[91] Initially charters were written entirely in Latin, but from the ninth century the boundaries of the land granted were more routinely recorded in English; from this time the vernacular was also used for a range of other types of agreements, administrative documents and bequests or wills, although sometimes these are written in a mixture of both Latin and English.[92] Towards the end of the Anglo-Saxon period records of donations also survive in the form of writs, vernacular documents which are much shorter than charters and which are a kind of 'administrative letter' that was used for many different purposes: it seems likely that these were used earlier as well, even though surviving writs date only from the late tenth or early eleventh century.[93]

Anglo-Saxon charters in particular are striking for the religious sentiment which they express, especially when compared to their contemporary continental counterparts, and this is perhaps a reflection of their ecclesiastical origin.[94] The sanction clauses found in continental charters usually order a fine to be paid by anyone who infringed the terms of the documents, while in contrast Anglo-Saxon sanction clauses threaten divine punishment after death, and sometimes excommunication during life as well.[95] Potential infringers were often warned that

[91]    Keynes, *Diplomas*, xiv, 30–1.

[92]    Kelly, 'Anglo-Saxon Lay Society and the Written Word', 46; S. Keynes, 'Royal Government and the Written Word in Late Anglo-Saxon England', in McKitterick (ed.), *Uses of Literacy in Early Mediaeval Europe*, 226–57, at 233–4; K.A. Lowe, 'The development of the Anglo-Saxon boundary clause', *Nomina* 21 (1998): 63–100; P.J. Geary, 'Land, language and memory in Europe 700–1100', *Transactions of the Royal Historical Society* 6th series,9 (1999): 169–84, at 176–83; M.T. Clanchy, *From Memory to Written Record: England 1066–1307* (Oxford, 2013), 30–35.

[93]    Keynes, *Diplomas*, 134–45; S. Keynes, 'Regenbald the Chancellor (sic)', *Anglo-Norman Studies* 10 (1987): 185–222, at 217–21; F.E. Harmer, *Anglo-Saxon Writs* (Stamford, 1989), 1–38; Keynes, 'Royal Government', 248; C. Insley, 'Where did all the charters go? Anglo-Saxon charters and the new politics of the eleventh century', *Anglo-Norman Studies* 24 (2001): 109–27; R. Sharpe, 'The use of writs in the eleventh century', *Anglo-Saxon England* 32 (2003): 247–91; see also J. Barrow, 'What Happened to Ecclesiastical Charters in England 1066–c.1100?', in Barrow and Wareham (eds), *Myth, Rulership, Church and Charters*, 229–48.

[94]    See further discussion in P. Chaplais, 'Who introduced charters into England? The case for Augustine', *Journal of the Society of Archivists* 3:10 (1969): 526–42; S.E. Kelly, *Charters of St Augustine's Abbey, Canterbury and Minster-in-Thanet*, Anglo-Saxon Charters 4 (Oxford, 1995), lxxiii–lxxv; R.H. Bremmer, 'The Final Countdown: Apocalyptic Expectations in Anglo-Saxon Charters', in G. Jaritz and G. Moreno-Riano (eds), *Time and Eternity: The Medieval Discourse* (Turnhout, 2000), 501–14, at 506–10.

[95]    Chaplais, 'Some early Anglo-Saxon diplomas on single sheets: Originals or copies?', 320–3; Keynes, *Diplomas*, 29, 31; Kelly, 'Anglo-Saxon Lay Society and the

they would have to account for their deeds at judgement, as in the grant made in 860 by King Æthelbald of Wessex to his minister, Osmund, which admonished that 'if anyone dares to infringe or change this, let him know that he will have to give account for it before the tribunal of the eternal judge on the day of judgement, in the presence of Christ and all his saints, unless before this he makes amends with reparation'.[96] The introductory proems also contain a wide variety of religious sentiments, often noting that pious giving is to be encouraged, or that those who give will receive in turn.[97] This is especially frequent in grants of land, portable wealth or privileges to religious institutions, who were 'poor in spirit', allowing the donors to transform their wealth into eternal riches through almsgiving, although this sentiment also appears in grants to laity.[98]

Before about the late ninth or early tenth century charters were regularly drawn up by scribes at religious houses, often those which were the beneficiaries of the grant.[99] Eventually the responsibility for drafting royal (and some other) diplomas seems to have been handed over for the most part to scribes in a royal writing office, a transfer which appears to have taken place in the early tenth century, but it can be assumed that even most royal scribes were trained initially in religious contexts, and some documents were still produced by scribes at religious houses.[100] Royal writs likewise seem primarily to have been produced in a royal writing office,

---

Written Word', 43; see also L.K. Little, 'Anger in Monastic Curses', in B.H. Rosenwein (ed.), *Anger's Past: The Social Uses of an Emotion in the Middle Ages* (Ithaca, NY, 1998), 9–35, at 10–14.

[96]   S 326 (*Shaft* no. 3): 'Si uero quis infringere uel mutare presumpserit, noscat se ante tribunal eterni iudicis in die iudicii coram Christo et omnibus sanctis racionem redditurum esse, nisi prius satisfaccione emendauerit'.

[97]   e.g. S 48 (*Sel* 41–2, no. 9): 'scimus retributorem operum nostrorum'. Cf. Rosenwein, *Neighbor of St Peter*, 138; see also Insley, 'Where did all the charters go?', 109–10.

[98]   A. Angenendt, 'Buße und liturgisches Gedenken', in Schmid and Wollasch (eds), *Gedächtnis, das Gemeinschaft Stiftet*, 39–50, at 41–4; see also S. Foot, *Monastic Life in Anglo-Saxon England, c. 600–900* (Cambridge, 2006), 318–21.

[99]   N. Brooks, *The Early History of the Church of Canterbury: Christ Church from 597 to 1066*, Studies in the early history of Britain (Leicester, 1984), 164–74, 327–30; Kelly, 'Anglo-Saxon Lay Society and the Written Word', 42–4; S. Keynes, 'The West Saxon charters of King Æthelwulf and his sons', *English Historical Review* 109 (1994): 1109–49, at 1109, 1146–7.

[100]   To some extent this is a contested issue: see Keynes, *Diplomas*, 14–82; P. Chaplais, 'The Royal Anglo-Saxon "Chancery" of the Tenth Century Revisited', in H. Mayr-Harting and R.I. Moore (eds), *Studies in Medieval History Presented to R.H.C. Davis* (London, 1985), 41–51; C. Insley, 'Charters and episcopal scriptoria in the Anglo-Saxon south-west', *Early Medieval Europe* 7 (1998): 173–97, at 179–84; Insley, 'Where did all the charters go?', 112–13; see also D.N. Dumville, 'English square minuscule script: The background and earliest phases', *Anglo-Saxon England* 16 (1987): 147–79; D.N. Dumville, 'English square minuscule script: The mid-century phases', *Anglo-Saxon England* 23 (1994): 133–64.

while writs in the name of ecclesiastics and others, as well as wills and other types of agreements (including charters) which were made directly between religious houses and non-royal laity, may instead have been drawn up by ecclesiastical scribes.[101] Those responsible for drafting charters and writs relied on formulae, often derived from or based upon earlier documents, and so charters drawn up at particular religious houses, or by specific individual draftsmen, may share common features even if they record grants of land from a number of different individuals or to a range of different beneficiaries.[102]

This has a bearing on the appearance of the saints in these documents, as patrons or beneficiaries. For example, Ecgberht, king of the West Saxons, granted land in 836 to Ciaba, a cleric of St Peter's, Canterbury, 'where the body of our holy father St Augustine rests'; after his day it was to revert to the minster, which would ultimately become known as St Augustine's, because his relics lay there.[103] In time, some grants were made directly to saints, rather than to individuals or communities worshipping in saints' churches. Depending on the perspective from which it is approached, this phenomenon may be both remarkable or unremarkable. Susan Kelly warns that in ascertaining the authenticity of Anglo-Saxon charters, those that record donations to laymen and eventually found their way into the archives of a religious house may be more reliable than those which record a grant to the community or to the saint.[104] On the other hand, McLaughlin finds that in early medieval France, most of the grants to religious houses were actually made directly to a saint rather than to the community.[105] Kelly's caution is useful but there are contemporary documents which record gifts made directly to saints, such as the agreement transferring the see of Crediton to Exeter in 1050, which granted the land 'to God and to St Peter and to the community of canons there'.[106] Such phrasing is also included in documents which, although not original, are copies made not long after the gift took place: some of these date from quite early in the period, such as the grant made by King Wihtred of Kent in 700 or 715 which

---

[101]   D. Whitelock, *Anglo-Saxon Wills*, Cambridge Studies in English Legal History (Cambridge, 1930); K.A. Lowe, 'The nature and effect of the Anglo-Saxon vernacular will', *Journal of Legal History* 19 (1998): 23–61; K.A. Lowe, 'Latin versions of Old English wills', *Journal of Legal History* 20 (1999): 1–23; Sharpe, 'The use of writs in the eleventh century', 252–3; Tollerton, *Wills and Will-Making in Anglo-Saxon England*, 11–50, 61–2.

[102]   See for example S. Keynes, 'The "Dunstan B" charters', *Anglo-Saxon England* 23 (1994): 165–93, esp. 172–93; Keynes, 'The West Saxon charters of King Æthelwulf and his sons', esp. 1131–47; cf. also S.E. Kelly, *Charters of Abingdon Abbey, Part I*, Anglo-Saxon Charters 7 (Oxford, 2000), cxv–cxxxi.

[103]   S 279 (*CantStA* no. 18): 'ubi pausat corpus sancti patris nostri Augustini'; see also S 297.

[104]   Kelly, *Charters of St Augustine's*, lxii–lxiii, cvii–cviii.

[105]   McLaughlin, *Consorting*, 152.

[106]   S 1021 (*Councils and Synods*, I.i, no. 71): 'deo sanctoque Petro fratribusque canonicis ibi famulantibus'.

states 'I also grant part of that land to Mary, mother of God, likewise to be held in perpetuity', and which survives as an eighth-century single sheet.[107]

Saints reappear also in the sanction clauses of wills and grants: some refer to the company of saints, threatening exclusion from this blessed community for those who sought to overturn the provisions of the document, just as those who donated hoped to achieve fellowship of the company of saints.[108] Some of the grants which are made directly to a particular saint name him or her in the sanction clause, and the potential malefactor is warned that he will have to account to these saints: in the late tenth or eleventh century Sifflæd granted land to St Edmund, and asked that he be guardian over the free property; in the sanction clause, she invoked St Edmund once more as protector, asking that those who alter the will should be excommunicated from God, from all the saints, and from St Edmund.[109] Similarly, Archbishop Eadsige's grant of land to St Augustine's, Canterbury, made some time between 1042 and 1050, warns anyone who is tempted to infringe the terms of the grant that if he does, he will be separated from the community of the holy church of God, and to him will be judged anathema by the holy virgin of virgins, Mary, by Peter, who bears the keys of heaven, by St Augustine, and by all the saints.[110] It is difficult to know how far these sentiments reflect the wishes of donors, although other practices such as burial *ad sanctos*, near saints' relics, suggest that the desire to be associated with saints was widespread.[111] But saints were powerful intercessors: some texts show a belief that souls in purgatorial punishment, or even judged as damned, could be released through the intercession of the saints, and so it was spiritually valuable to make connections with saints by donating to them or to their servants in religious foundations.[112]

Records of lay dealings with religious houses show one way that laity might come into contact with the written word, although of course only the richest

---

[107] S 21 (K 47): 'Terrulae quoque partem eiusdem Dei genetrici beatae Mariae similiter inperpetuum possidendam perdono'. The manuscript is now London, British Library, Cotton Augustus ii. 88.

[108] e.g. S 173 (BCS 343): 'Si quis vero regum vel principium seu prefectum hunc libertatem meam infringere aut minuere voluerit sciat se separatum esse in die judicii a consortio sanctorum'.

[109] S 1525 (Whitelock, *Wills*, no. 37): 'into seynt Eadmune' ... 'be seynt Eadmund mund þer ouer þene freschot'; 'Se þe þise cuide wille awenden be he amansid from god almichtin ꝺ from alle hise halegen ꝺ fram sancte Eadmunde'.

[110] S 1401 (*CantStA* no. 37): 'a consortio sancte Dei ecclesie separetur et anathema a sancta uirginum uirgine Maria et a sancto Petro celestis regni clauigero et a sancto Augustino et ab omnibus sanctis iudicetur'. The charter was apparently placed on the tomb of St Augustine, symbolising that the grant was made to the saint himself: see Kelly, *Charters of St Augustine's*, 132.

[111] See below, 266–8.

[112] See M. Clayton, 'Delivering the damned: A motif in Old English homiletic prose', *Medium Ævum* 55 (1986): 92–102.

(and noble or aristocratic) laity would be able to donate large amounts of land or significant wealth to religious houses.[113] They also show how the technology and power of writing could be used even by laity, whether or not they could read, as for example in the account of the dispute between Eadgifu and Goda, contained in a document dating to *c*.959: this records that Eadgifu placed her charters on the altar and entrusted the lands to Christ Church, Canterbury for the 'rest' of her soul, and she is also reported to have said that Christ and his heavenly host would curse anyone who changed or reduced her gift.[114] The documents themselves held a symbolic and material value in representing proof of ownership, and in this sense the content might be seen as less significant than the existence of a charter itself, especially given the formulaic nature of the texts: it might be assumed that the phrasing and religious sentiments in charters are simply derivative, or represent the choices of the draftsmen rather than reflecting the exact wishes or preferences of the donors.[115] In some cases this may be so, and perhaps too the general sentiments found in charters may indeed have been what were most important to donors. However, even where formulae are used it does not mean that the statements were insincere, as is clear (for example) from the sanction clauses contained in some wills, which exempt the testator from the punishment threatened to those who dared to alter the will: Bishop Ælfsige, who drew up his will somewhere between 955 and 958, concluded by asking his friend Ælfheah not to permit any changes to the will, and warning that 'if anyone does so, may God destroy him in soul and in body, here and in the future, unless I change it myself'.[116]

But in fact, it is not the formulae found in the proem or sanction clause which allow the greatest insight into the donor's wishes. Instead, the most revealing parts of these records are often the motivations or intentions expressed by the donor, and in some documents the specific arrangements – such as liturgical commemoration – which were made as part of the transaction.[117] Some grants record a generally

---

[113]  Kelly, 'Anglo-Saxon Lay Society and the Written Word'.

[114]  S 1211 (A. Rabin, 'Anglo-Saxon women before the law: A student edition of five Old English lawsuits', *Old English Newsletter* 41:3 (2008): 33–56, no. 1): 'Þa nam Eadgifu, be þæs cynincges leafe ꝺ gewitnesse ꝺ ealra his bisceopa, þa bec ꝺ land betæhte in to Cristes cyrcean mid hire agenum handum upon þone altare lede þan hyrede on ecnesse to are ꝺ hire sawle to reste. ꝺ cwæþ *þæt* Crist sylf mid eallum heofonlicum mægne þane awyrgde on ecnesse þe þas gife æfre awende oþþe gewanude'; see also Kelly, 'Anglo-Saxon Lay Society and the Written Word', 44.

[115]  Kelly, 'Anglo-Saxon Lay Society and the Written Word', 45–6.

[116]  S 1491 (*WinchNM*, no. 18): 'Gif hit þonne hwa do, God hine fordo ge mid sawle ge mid lichoman ge her ge on þam toweardan, butan ic hit self on oþer wænde'; S. Foot, 'Reading Anglo-Saxon Charters: Memory, Record, or Story?', in E.M. Tyler and R. Balzaretti (eds), *Narrative and History in the Early Medieval West* (Turnhout, 2006), 39–65, at 53.

[117]  See also Keynes, *Diplomas*, 121–6, for discussion of some diplomas which seem to have been drawn up with input from the beneficiaries.

pious motive for donation, such as 'for the love of God almighty', or 'for the honour of God almighty',[118] but many others stress that the donation is intended for the good of the soul, and for the expiation or absolution of the sin of the donor(s). There are copious examples of donations made for the forgiveness of sins,[119] including grants of rights or privileges as well as land: Æthelbald, king of Mercia, granted remission of tolls to Worcester, probably between 743 and 745, 'for the remedy of his soul' and 'for his sins'.[120] There is no denying that many of these too are formulaic, but it is worth noting that the range of intentions and motivations expressed is large, and usually varies according to the type of beneficiary: gifts made to laity usually record that the grant was made (for example) because of the friendship or faithfulness of that individual, or express no reason for the gift, thereby distinguishing such gifts from almsgiving to religious houses.[121] Sometimes these different types of gifts are distinguished in the charters themselves, for example in the grant made in 732 by Æthelberht II, king of Kent: he granted land 'not for some money to a secular, but only for the remedy of my soul, to you [Dunn, priest and abbot] and to the church of blessed Mary'.[122]

Even sentiments which are frequently used, as encapsulated in phrases like 'for the remedy of my soul', in fact have numerous variations: it seems likely that even when formulae were used, the desire to safeguard the soul was usually genuine rather than an empty expression dependent only on the reproduction of formulae.[123] Any gift to a religious institution was spiritually valuable because it

---

[118]   e.g. S 168 (BCS 335): 'pro honore Dei omnipotentis'; S 279 (CantStA, 74–7, no. 18): 'pro Dei omnipotentis amore'.

[119]   e.g. S 96 (BCS 181): 'pro redemptione animae meae. et pro expiatione facinorum meorum'; S 129 (Roch, no. 12): 'pro remedio et salute anime mee'; S 316 (BCS 467): 'pro expiatione piaculorum meorum et obsolutione criminum meorum'; S 340 (BCS 520): 'pro remedio animae meae'; S 979 (K 1324): 'pro redemptione animae meae et criminum meorum absolutione'; S 1169 (BCS 65): 'pro remedio animæ meæ et indulgentia commissorum criminum'; S 1264 (Fleming, 'Christ Church', 83–55, no. 17): 'pro expiatione piaculorum meorum'.

[120]   S 98 (BCS 171): 'for minre sawle læcedome', 'for minum synnum'.

[121]   e.g. S 461, 524, 937, 961; although some grants do use the language of almsgiving even when donating to a layman if land or money referred to in the charter is to be used for pious purposes, such as S 58; or S 287 (BCS 426), a grant of land from King Æthelwulf of Wessex to a layman in Kent in 839 'for the expiation of my sins, and for the hope of eternal remuneration, and for the agreed sum which I have received' ('pro expiatione piaculorum meorum proque spe remunerationis æterne necnon et conpetenti pecunia quam accepi').

[122]   S 23 (BCS 148): 'non pro pecunia aliqua sæculari sed pro remedio tantum animae meae tibi et ecclesiae beatae Mariae'. It is not entirely clear whether the distinction here is to be made between secular and monastic clergy, or those in religious and secular life: in any case, the point is that the land is not sold for financial return, but given to a religious house for spiritual return.

[123]   e.g. S 1184 (Sel no. 11): 'pro remedio anime meae'; Foot, Monastic Life, 80; Foot, 'Reading Anglo-Saxon Charters: Memory, Record, or Story?'.

could be considered as almsgiving, and in a sense there was therefore no need for a draftsman to insert expressions reflecting the piety which had motivated the gift, or to emphasise the forgiveness of sins and spiritual benefit which the giver would receive: while in some cases such expressions may represent the formulaic nature of the drafting process, in others they may have been prompted by the donors, even if these were then recorded using established formulae. It is noteworthy too that these sentiments are also expressed in writs, even though they lacked the charter's formal proem and more wordy pious statements, as for example the writ of 1020 in which King Cnut granted rights to Archbishop Æthelnoth 'for the eternal salvation of my soul';[124] Thored's grant land of land to the community of Christ Church, Canterbury, made in 1036, was likewise offered 'for my soul'.[125]

In some cases gifts are specifically described as almsgiving, as in Edward the Confessor's writ announcing his grant (1060 x 1066) of a church at Axminster (Devon) to the church of York,[126] or as in the sanction clause in the record of the restitution of land to Heahberht, bishop of Worcester, made in 840 by of King Berhtwulf of Mercia, which warned that 'if anyone, king or prince or a man of any other rank is deceived through diabolical greed so that he is tempted to infringe or diminish this our almsgiving and liberty, let him know that he will be separated from the company of all the saints of God on the great day of judgement before the tribunal of Christ – unless he makes amends to God and men with worthy satisfaction'.[127] The possible benefits of pious benefactions extended to contemporary concerns as well as to the state of the donor's soul, as revealed in a grant made in 840 by Æthelwulf, king of Wessex, to Eadberht the deacon 'for the redemption of my own soul, and the remission of my sins, and for the stability of my kingdom ... in eternal almsgiving'.[128] But as donations were made 'for the redemption of our souls and for the hope of eternal salvation',[129] or 'for the love of the heavenly kingdom and for the redemption of my soul',[130] or more simply 'for the eternal salvation of my soul',[131] the grantors were evidently concerned not

---

[124]   S 986 (Harmer, *Anglo-Saxon Writs*, no. 28): 'ic hæbbe Criste þas gerihta forgyfen minre sawle to ecere alysendnesse'.

[125]   S 1222 (Fleming, 'Christ Church', no. 68): 'Ic Þored geann þæt land æt Horslege þam hirede æt Cristes cyrcean for mine sawle swa full ꟻ swa forð swa ic sylf hit ahte'.

[126]   S 1161 (*North*, no. 10): 'to almesse'.

[127]   e.g. S 192 (BCS 430): 'Si quis vero rex aut princeps vel alicujus gradus homo hanc nostram elemosinam et libertatem per diabolicam avaritiam deceptus sit. ut frangere vel minuere temptaverit sciat se separatum a consortio omnium sanctorum Dei in die magni judici ante tribunal Christi nisi hic Deo et hominibus cum bona satisfactione emendaverit'.

[128]   S 290 (*Sher*, no. 3): 'pro unicę animę meę redemptione. et criminum meorum remissione – et pro stabilitate regni mei ... in elemosinam sempiternam'.

[129]   e.g. S 210 (BCS 509): 'pro redemptione animee nostre et pro spe eterne salutis'.

[130]   e.g. S 92 (BCS 140): 'pro amore cælestis patriæ. et pro redemptione animae meae'.

[131]   e.g. S 11 (*CantStA*, no. 41): 'pro eterna salute anime mee'; S 155 (Fleming, 'Christ Church', no. 15), 'pro perpetua salute [anime] mee'.

only about their present life: their actions (and indeed in some cases their words) show them 'providing for myself in the future'[132] or 'thinking about my soul in the beyond',[133] or 'knowing [my donation] to be useful to me in the future'.[134]

Most significantly in this context, some documents state that grants were made not only for the health of the donor's soul, but also (or instead) for the departed souls of their relatives or friends, such as King Edmund's grant to the New Minster in 940, made 'for the remission of my father's sins'.[135] Such cases indicate both that the donor must have made this intention clear so that it was recorded, and that he or she was aware of the power of almsgiving to help the souls of the dead as well as the living. These grants are therefore a witness to a general understanding among the lay and religious individuals who granted land that penitential works performed during life – such as almsgiving – could play an important role in salvation. One of the reasons that almsgiving was frequently advocated as a means for the forgiveness of sin was that the prayers of those who received alms (whether the genuine poor, or the religious 'poor in spirit') were believed to be very valuable, and so the connection between almsgiving and penance is very strong.[136] As always, it is more difficult to gauge how widely this belief had filtered through to other sections of society, but the existence of donations made for the souls of the departed shows both that some people understood the importance of this, and that these record the specific demands of the donor, even if they might be expressed formulaically.[137]

In addition to the fact of the grant itself, made for the good of the soul, some documents recording donations also include information about arrangements for liturgical commemorations for the benefactors or for their friends or relatives (sometimes living, sometimes deceased). The liturgical services requested and offered most frequently in Anglo-Saxon documents were prayers, psalms, masses and almsgiving, those services which were identified by homilists and others as the most effective for the forgiveness of sins and so also for souls in the interim. In the analysis of these requests it is worth noting that it is difficult to identify precise numbers of documents, partly because authenticity is not always certain: in some cases the surviving records of charters are judged to be 'partially' or 'substantially' authentic, and although the liturgical burden placed on a house might seem unlikely to be part of a forgery, it is not always possible to tell with certainty.[138] Information about liturgical commemoration from surviving records of Anglo-

---

[132]     S 19 (Fleming, 'Christ Church', no. 6): 'prouidens mihi in futuro'.

[133]     S 20 (*CantStA*, no. 10): 'consulens anime meae in posterum'.

[134]     S 45 (*Sel*, no. 2): 'sciens mihi in futuro prodisse'.

[135]     S 470 (*WinchNM*, no. 12): 'pro redemptione piaculorum patris mei'; King Æthelstan, Edmund's father, had died in 939.

[136]     Angenendt, 'Buße', 41–4.

[137]     See further below, 238–48.

[138]     e.g. S 183, which seems to have been based on a ninth-century original but not to be entirely authentic in its present form, and which contains instructions for masses and

Saxon donations of course reflects the peculiarities of the surviving evidence, so there is more information from southern England in the tenth and eleventh centuries than for other areas and periods. The form of the documents is also significant, because writs do not tend to contain information about liturgical commemoration in the way that charters and wills might. It is worth noting, however, that requests and arrangements for liturgical commemoration are found throughout the period and, significantly, each one of these is usually distinctive, and the way in which the liturgical obligations are framed not completely dependent on formulae.[139] It should of course be kept in mind that since the surviving record is incomplete and patchy, there might in theory have been more similarities originally than are now apparent.

However, the variety in what was formally arranged in writing suggests that each record represents a particular process of negotiation, often connected with what a particular house might be able or willing to offer: these are personal arrangements made according to the wishes of the donor(s) and through a discussion with the beneficiaries. Thus in the mid ninth century, Ealhburg arranged for food renders to be given to St Augustine's, Canterbury and in return they were to sing Psalm 20 every day on her behalf;[140] the roughly contemporary grant of render from Lulle, also to St Augustine's, records that in return for her gift the community should go to church on the day it was given and sing the psalter, and each priest was to offer a mass, and they should say their pater noster every day.[141] The priest Werhard, who gave land to Christ Church, Canterbury in the early 830s, requested that every day a mass should be offered for his soul and the souls of others who had helped Christ Church, and that alms should

---

psalms to be offered: see Kelly, *Charters of Abingdon 1*, 42–5). In other cases liturgical obligations are mentioned in documents which are obviously forged, e.g. S 414.

[139] See for example S 16, 71 (late seventh century); S 28, 31, 87, 103b, 149, 153, 1180 (eighth century); S 197, 223, 294, 294a/b, 302–305, 307–8, 323, 1188, 1198, 1204a, 1239, 1268, 1414 (ninth century); S 365, 418–19, 422 (and 423), 876, 1497, 1501, 1533 (tenth century); 899, 903, 975, 1523, 1532, 1516 (eleventh century). This list is not exhaustive but it is worth noting that with the exception of the charters associated with King Æthelwulf of Mercia (d.858) and his decimations (S 294, 294a/b, 302–305 and 307–308; see S.E. Kelly, 'King Æthelwulf's decimations', *Anglo-Saxon* 1 (2007): 285–317), the liturgical requests in each document are framed differently.

[140] S 1198 (*CantStA*, no. 24): 'Swylc man se þæt land hebbe þas ðinge agyfe for Ealdredes saule ⁊ for Ealhburge ; ⁊ þa hiwan asingan ælce dæge æfter hyra ferse þæne sealm for hia Exaudiat te Dominus'; see also D. Pratt, *The Political Thought of King Alfred the Great*, Cambridge Studies in Medieval Life and Thought, 4th series 67 (Cambridge, 2007), 244.

[141] S 1239 (*CantStA*, no. 25): 'Ðonne is þis þara gode lean, þæt þa hiwen don scealon þat hi agan ealle to cyrican ⁊ gesingan hore psaltere sealme elce dage þe hia þa god wicgen ⁊ ælce messe prest ane messe ⁊ ælce dage hire pater noster'.

be given, including gifts of food and money to paupers on his anniversary.[142] Ealdorman Alfred and his wife Wærburh rescued a gospel-book from Viking raiders for a large sum of money, probably in the latter part of the ninth century, and donated them to Christ Church: they asked that the gospels should be read every month for them and for their daughter Alhthryth, and recorded the request and their donation in the gospel-book itself.[143] Away from Canterbury, King Beorhtwulf of Mercia (d.852) granted privileges to the community at *Breodune* (probably Breedon on the Hill, Leicestershire) in 848, and in addition to the land and money which he received, he requested that he should be remembered in their prayers, by day and by night.[144] Although this is a small selection, it is evident that in each of these cases what was arranged depended on individual circumstances and was a personal arrangement in return for what the donors offered, and this is clear too from the many other records which survive, as the following discussion will show.

Like the donations themselves, liturgical services requested from religious communities could be valuable for a range of purposes and not only after death: in times of need, for example, masses could be offered as a way to entreat divine aid, a tactic employed by Charlemagne at least twice in response to contemporary concerns.[145] The troubles of King Æthelred's reign caused him to stipulate a heavy burden in return for a grant which he made to the monastery of St Peter at Westminster in 1002, asking for intercession and making his gift 'on condition that they should offer three hundred oblations of masses for me and go through the whole psalter in the month'.[146] This monthly psalter recitation was presumably intended to be additional to (and separate from) the weekly recitation of the whole psalter which formed part of the Benedictine Office and the Roman Office, used in

---

[142] S 1414 (Fleming, 'Christ Church', no. 31): 'In quo etiam scripto constituit elemosinam quam cotidie fieri precepit in illis terris quas ipse adquisiuit pro anima sua et pro animabus omnium illorum qui ecclesie Christi aliquid auxilii impendissent ... Cotidie quoque precepit missam celebrari pro anima sua et pro animabus supra memoratorum. In anniuersario suo precepit dari mille.cc. pauperibus ad manducandum, cuique panem .i. et caseum aut lardum et denarium .i.'.

[143] S 1204a (BCS 634): 'to ðæm gerade ðæt heo mon arede eghwelce monaðe for Aelfred ꝼ for Werburge ꝼ for Alhðryðe heora saulum to ecum lecedome. ða hwile ðe God gesegen haebbe ðæt fulwiht æt ðeosse stowe beon mote'. The book is now Stockholm, Kungliga Biblioteket, A.135, known as the 'Codex Aureus': it is written in gold letters on purple parchment, and was clearly considered to be extremely valuable. The donation is recorded on fol. 11r.

[144] S 197 (*Pet*, no. 8): 'ut memoria regis Beorhtuulfi ... in eorum sacris orationibus diebus ac noctibus memoretur ...'.

[145] Häußling, *Mönchskonvent*, 276.

[146] S 903 (J.A. Robinson, *Gilbert Crispin, Abbot of Westminster: A Study of the Abbey under Norman Rule*, Notes and documents relating to Westminster Abbey 3 (Cambridge, 1911), 167–8): 'interposita condicione ut trescentas pro me missarum oblaciones offerant, totidemque Dauitici cursus modulationes pro me mente deuota persoluant'.

this period by monastic and secular clerical communities respectively.[147] Æthelred's grant states that he made the donation 'for the good of his soul' ('pro anime mee remedio'), but he also received 100 mancuses of gold in this transaction. Simon Keynes notes that payment for land is not in itself remarkable, and that whether or not this was recorded was a matter of preference, although this is among the first recorded in Æthelred's reign.[148] It is interesting nonetheless that in the context of this kind of transaction, the condition of prayers could be laid upon the monastery in addition to the payment required, especially given that by this time English tradition required specific psalms to be said for the king, queen and benefactors in any case.[149]

The exchange of liturgical commemoration for land or money (or both) almost gives the impression that prayers were regarded as a type of commodity. In her analysis of grants to religious houses in early medieval France, McLaughlin suggests instead that understanding these as gift exchange may be more appropriate than a commercial interpretation, especially in societies where gift exchange may have been widely understood alongside commercial exchange:[150] the sense of contractual agreement between donors and God, and donors and religious communities, created a situation where the giving of a gift necessitated a return-gift, and benefactors expected to receive something in reward for their generosity.[151] The importance of countergifts in early medieval cultures should not be underestimated, but the social status that might be acquired from a generous donation can hardly have been insubstantial, and in any case almsgiving itself brought spiritual gifts and rewards for the soul. The fact that prayers and masses were felt to be necessary over and above the spiritual benefits of almsgiving indicates the perceived significance of arranging liturgical commemoration if possible, and so also the concomitant consciousness of an afterlife in which those prayers would be most effective.

---

[147]  J. Black, 'The Divine Office and Private Devotion in the Latin West', in T.J. Heffernan and E.A. Matter (eds), *The Liturgy of the Medieval Church* (Kalamazoo, MI, 2001), 45–71, at 57–9; J.D. Billett, 'The Divine Office and the Secular Clergy in Later Anglo-Saxon England', in C. Leyser, D.W. Rollason and H. Williams (eds), *England and the Continent in the Tenth Century: Studies in Honour of Wilhelm Levison (1876–1947)* (Turnhout, 2011), 429–71.

[148]  Keynes, *Diplomas*, 107–8.

[149]  *RC*, 19–20, ed. Symons, *Regularis Concordia*, 14–16.

[150]  McLaughlin, *Consorting*, 138–53; see also T.M. Charles-Edwards, 'The Distinction between Land and Moveable Wealth in Anglo-Saxon England', in P.H. Sawyer (ed.), *English Medieval Settlement* (1979), 97–104, at 97–8.

[151]  Angenendt, 'Buße', 44–5, 47; Rosenwein, *Neighbor of St Peter*, 137–8; McLaughlin, *Consorting*, 144–5; W. Davies, 'When Gift is Sale: Reciprocities and Commodities in Tenth-Century Christian Iberia', in W. Davies and P. Fouracre (eds), *The Languages of Gift in the Early Middle Ages* (Cambridge, 2010), 217–37.

This is particularly important when looking at the phrasing of the Anglo-Saxon donations which request liturgical services from their beneficiaries, since these are frequently phrased not as gift and countergift, but as a gift with conditions imposed, as in Æthelred's grant to Westminster. That is, property is explicitly donated on the condition that certain services are performed, and there is a contractual obligation to continue this, the sense being that if the services are no longer performed, the beneficiary is no longer entitled to the gift. In the late seventh or early eighth century, King Wihtred of Kent and his wife Æthelburh granted land to St Peter's minster (later to become St Augustine's, Canterbury), 'on the condition that they have the memory of us as much in the solemnities of masses as in their prayers, incessantly asking mercy for us from God'.[152] The underlying implication here is that, should the recipients of such gifts fail to keep their side of the bargain, they are no longer entitled to what was given them so generously. The sanction clause, which here warns that 'whoever presumes to go against this donation of our generosity, he should know that he will be alienated from participation of the body and blood of our Lord Jesus Christ, and separated from the company of the faithful',[153] presumably applied as much to the liturgical arrangements as to the land. Almsgiving on these terms, therefore, is the 'gift that keeps on giving', since perpetual possession of the donation requires perpetual commemoration for the donor. Although Wihtred's grant does not specifically state that the commemoration he seeks should be perpetual, there is no indication of when the prayers should end, and this in itself identifies it as the unending commemoration asked for in other documents which underline the intended perpetuity of both gift and services. The donation of land by 'book', that is in charters, meant that the land itself was also granted in perpetuity, and so the time frame for the ownership of the land matched the conditions for commemoration which were laid upon the land's recipients.[154]

The representation in the written record of these careful individual arrangements for liturgical commemoration is striking in comparing requests made by the same person, the most unusual perhaps in a series of related documents issued by King Æthelstan in December 932 and January 933. On 24 December, Æthelstan granted land to the nuns of Shaftesbury Abbey on the condition that the community and their successors should celebrate the morning mass 'for the excesses of his soul', and sing 50 psalms for him after prime, and this was to continue until the day

---

[152]   S 16 (*CantStA*, no. 9; AD 696 or 711): 'conditione interposita ut nostri memoriam habeatis tam in missarum solemniis quam in orationibus uestris, incessanter nobis misericordiam a Domino postulantes'.

[153]   S 16 (*CantStA*, no. 9): 'Quisquis uero contra hanc largitatis nostre donationem quolibet tempore contraire presumpserit, nouerit se quisquis ille sit a participatione corporis et sanguinis Domini nostri Iesu Christi alienum et a consortio fidelium segregandum'.

[154]   Keynes, *Diplomas*, 31–3; S. Reynolds, 'Bookland, folkland and fiefs', *Anglo-Norman Studies* 14 (1991): 211–27, esp. 216–17.

of judgement.[155] On the same day, Æthelstan also granted land to his minister, Alfred, and – quite unusually in a grant to a layman – asked for almsgiving, laying upon Alfred the condition that every day until the day of judgement, he and his successors should feed 120 paupers according to the example of the gospel – a significant burden in exchange for the twelve hides of land.[156] Around a month later, on 26 January, Æthelstan granted land to the community of clerics at Sherborne, on the condition that every year on All Saints' Day, each of the clerics should sing the whole psalter 'for the excesses of his soul', and he should be remembered tirelessly in masses and prayers.[157] The heavy burdens that Æthelstan laid upon all of his beneficiaries at this time suggest a troubled soul; but whatever prompted this, the charters as a group illustrate clearly how the formulaic demands of such documents were adapted according to the specific circumstances of the beneficiaries.[158]

These charters were drafted by 'Æthelstan A', a scribe of the royal writing office noted for his extraordinary Latin, and all begin with the 'Flebilia fortiter' proem, have similar sanction clauses, and include the phrase 'for the excesses of

[155] S 419 (*Shaft*, no. 8): 'ea interiacente condicione, ut omni die usque magne discrecionis iudicii anno illa successoresque eius cotidie post primam quinquaginta decantent psalmos, anime pro excessibus mee, horaque mediante tercia missam percelebrent, ut diuinam consequi plenissime ualeam misericordiam tribuo'. Cf. S 422, 423; and V Æthelstan 3, ed. F. Liebermann, *Die Gesetze der Angelsachsen* (3 vols, Halle, 1903–1916), I.168; S.E. Kelly, *Charters of Shaftesbury Abbey*, Anglo-Saxon Charters 5 (Oxford, 1996), 33. Interestingly, the commemoration of the king at the morrow mass also matches the provisions of the *Regularis Concordia*, produced some thirty years after Æthelstan's death: see *RC*, 20, 27, ed. Symons, *Regularis Concordia*, 16, 23–4.

[156] S 418 (*WinchNM*, no. 10): 'ea interiacente conditione, ut omni die usque magne districtionis iudicii anno ille successoresque eius centum uiginti ewangelici paradigmatis pauperes semel pane cum pulmento dulcifero haustuque potifero pascere, anime pro excessibus mee sub sorte ullius contradictionis non obliuiscantur, familie quoque aet Stanham pastum semper conferre electissimum diuinam ut consequi plenissime ualeam misericordiam non pigrescant'.

[157] S 422 (*Sher*, no. 7) and S 423 (*Sher*, no. 8) both purport to date from 26 January 933, and both include similar information about liturgical commemoration. S 422 appears to be genuine, but it is difficult to be certain that S 423 was not adapted from it at some later date; see the discussion in M.A. O'Donovan, *Charters of Sherborne*, Anglo-Saxon Charters 3 (Oxford, 1988), 29–33. S 422: 'eo tamen interposito tenore – ut unusquisque predicta ex familia. omni anno in cunctorum festiuitate sanctorum – que semper fit in kalendis Nouembris an\i/me pro excessibus mee. integrum exceptis aliis orationum obsecrationibus – decantet psalterium; adiectis insuper missarum celebrationibus indefessis'; S 423 also mentions Beorhtwulf: 'ea tamen interiacente condicione. ut omni anno in kalendis Nouembris unusquisque ex familia – exceptis missarum orationumque celebrationibus. quas ut indesinenter horis canonicis peragat fas est. integrum pro anime mee excessibus quoque anime Beorhtulfi comitis. spiritu et mente decantet'. S 379 (*WinchNM*, no. 8) is very like these and must depend on a charter similar to them, but the date has been changed to 921 and the donor to Edward the Elder; see also Kelly, *Charters of Shaftesbury*, 33.

[158] See further below, 238–48.

my soul' ('anime pro excessibus mee').[159] But while these aspects of the charters repeat formulae, the specific arrangements for commemoration and almsgiving which were required of the beneficiaries do not, and this is at least partly because of the different types of beneficiaries. Both psalms and masses are requested from the communities at Sherborne and Shaftesbury, but the women's house at Shaftesbury was only able to offer commemoration in the communal mass. In contrast, the grant to Sherborne emphasises that 'each one of the community' should offer masses and prayers for Æthelstan, implying that these were to be said privately by each man rather than being part of the communal liturgical celebration which was identified in the Shaftesbury grant: a female community would not have been able to fulfil a request for private masses. Alfred, who was a layman and unable to offer masses at all, was required to give alms instead. Even in such closely related charters as these, the specific arrangements – as they must be – are entirely dependent on what could be agreed with the beneficiaries according to their means and abilities.[160] Each grant represents a different process of negotiation between the giver and the beneficiary which was concluded before the charter was written, and only formalised in the symbolic recording of the transaction in writing.

This process of negotiation in the context of donations to religious houses is another moment at which lay donors could be brought into contact with Christian learning and theological discussions. In many cases, laity who wished to donate land to religious houses, either as a gift granted immediately or as a bequest in a will, must have come to discuss the transaction with the religious communities, and to make the precise arrangements (such as liturgical commemoration) that they desired. In turn, this must have been a useful opportunity for the proposed beneficiaries to emphasise the benefit to the soul of perpetual commemoration, and how the prayers, masses or alms agreed on and recorded in writing would aid the souls of the donors once they had passed over to the interim. Behind the records of grants of lands, therefore, lies the unspoken witness to one of the ways in which those with means to donate to religious communities could learn about the interim, and how to ensure the release of souls from purgatorial punishments. Commemoration of the dead was particularly important in monastic communities because it was written into the rules and customaries which prescribed monastic life, so that the dead remained part of the community and their commemoration

---

[159]    For 'Æthelstan A' see Keynes, *Diplomas*, 44; S. Keynes, *An Atlas of Attestations in Anglo-Saxon Charters, c.670–1066* (Cambridge, 2002), no. XXVII; D.A. Woodman, "Æthelstan A' and the rhetoric of rule', *Anglo-Saxon England* 42 (forthcoming). I am grateful to David Woodman for allowing me to see a copy of his article prior to publication. See also M. Lapidge, 'The hermeneutic style in tenth-century Anglo-Latin literature', *Anglo-Saxon England* 4 (1975): 67–111, at 99–101.

[160]    It should also be noted that there are other charters with the 'Flebilia fortiter' proem which include no request for alms or liturgical commemoration (e.g. S 416, dated 931, to a minister named Wulfgar): see further Keynes, *An Atlas of Attestations in Anglo-Saxon Charters, c.670–1066*, no. XXVII.

was part of the daily round of life and prayers.[161] But communicating the importance and value of offerings for the dead to laity was also in the interests of religious communities, if it meant that this would persuade potential donors to give larger gifts.

It is also important to consider the liturgical services which were offered and requested, and why, especially in the context of different types of masses which would or could be offered by different communities. During the early Middle Ages, private masses (also-called 'special' or 'votive') of the type requested by Æthelstan from Sherborne became increasingly popular and appeared with growing frequency in missals and sacramentaries.[162] New mass liturgies were composed to meet this demand, such as Alcuin's masses for the days of the week or for particular intentions.[163] Based mostly on the evidence from continental religious houses, there has been considerable discussion of the value of individual commemoration in private masses compared to general commemoration in communities' regular masses, and of how these masses were understood by those who requested or offered them. One line of argument holds that even when masses were performed privately, they were understood as constituent parts of the liturgy which united the community, and merely elaborated the liturgy which the community already performed: by being remembered at a community's mass, either privately, or in the regular offering, the individual was tied to and took part in the liturgical offerings of that community.[164] In contrast, it has been suggested that masses offered especially for individuals were believed to be more effective than the general masses in which their commemoration might simply be implied, and therefore the accumulation of large numbers of *missae speciales* was felt to be particularly valuable: it has been argued too that as the importance of private masses increased, female communities were placed at a disadvantage in this respect.[165] Linking the effects of votive masses very closely to tariff-penance,

---

[161]    Schmid and Wollasch, 'Gemeinschaft der Lebenden und Verstorbenen'; Häußling, *Mönchskonvent*, 321.

[162]    J.A. Jungmann, 'Von der "Eucharistia" zur "Messe"', *Zeitschrift für katholische Theologie* 89 (1967): 29–40, at 36–7; C. Vogel, 'Une Mutation culturelle inexpliquée: Le passage de l'Eucharistie communautaire à la messe privée', *Revue des Sciences Religieuses* 54 (1980): 231–50; C. Vogel, 'Deux conséquences de l'eschatologie grégorienne: la multiplication des messes privées et les moines-prêtres', in J. Fontaine, R. Gillet and S. Pellistrandi (eds), *Grégoire le Grand: Chantilly, Centre culturel Les Fontaines, 15–19 septembre 1982: actes* (Paris, 1986), 267–76.

[163]    Deshusses, 'Messes d'Alcuin'.

[164]    Häußling, *Mönchskonvent*, 250–60, 314–29.

[165]    Angenendt, 'Missa specialis', 178–80, 212–13; P. Halpin, 'Women religious in late Anglo-Saxon England', *Haskins Society Journal: Studies in Medieval History* 6 (1994): 97–110, at 99–100; B. Yorke, *Nunneries and the Anglo-Saxon Royal Houses* (London, 2003), 107–8.

Arnold Angenendt argues that the release of souls in the interim could only occur when the sin-burden had been fully expiated.[166]

Accounts from vision literature confirm a belief that souls were released from their punishments in the interim when they were fully cleansed of their sin and that this could be achieved through the offering of masses, but the idea that individual masses were more effective in achieving this than communal masses is not borne out by the Anglo-Saxon evidence.[167] Requests for masses and other offerings vary significantly between documents, depending apparently on local circumstances, what was being granted, and what the beneficiaries would or could agree too. In the case of the group of documents issued by Æthelstan in the winter of 932–3, commemoration was requested in both private and communal masses, but in most cases in Anglo-Saxon documents the type of mass requested for commemoration – private or communal – is simply not specified.[168] This may indicate no more than that this part of the arrangement was made orally, so that the donor knew what he or she expected to receive, but it might also indicate that donors were comparatively uninterested in the type of mass that they would receive, and that other factors were more influential in affecting the arrangements they made. This is comparable to the evidence from early medieval France, where some charters refer to commemoration in masses without specifying whether these were to be special or regular, and others suggest that benefactors were seeking commemoration in the regular celebration of mass in the community.[169] McLaughlin concludes that for early medieval French donors, their treatment as members of a community was ultimately more important than the particular type of masses they received, although they were naturally not uninterested in special masses, psalms and prayers that might be performed on their behalf, some of which might be acquired along with other privileges such as burial in the monastic cemetery.[170]

It is worth noting that from the surviving evidence it is difficult to quantify or evaluate the prayers and masses requested in any meaningful way, suggesting that donors did not attempt to calculate or quantify the sin-burden for which they needed to atone, as a sample comparison of two documents shows. In the late tenth century, Æthelgifu granted land and freedom to her priest Eadwine on condition that he offered three masses a week and intercession on her behalf and on behalf of her lord, and requested psalters from three young women whom she freed;

---

[166]     Angenendt, 'Missa specialis', 134–5, 147–9.

[167]     For example, see *Epistola* 115 in the Bonifatian collection, ed. Tangl, *Die Briefe*, 247–50; see further Foxhall Forbes, 'Diuiduntur in quattuor'.

[168]     Sarah Foot, *Monastic Life*, 207, suggests that masses offered for commemorative purposes in England may have been public rather than private, because of the role that liturgical commemoration played in an institutions sense of communal identity; but it is often quite difficult to tell what donors thought they wanted, especially because the range of different types of requests varies so much. See also Häußling, *Mönchskonvent*, 251.

[169]     McLaughlin, *Consorting*, 154–5.

[170]     Ibid., 155, 158. See also below, 278–94.

she also requested 30 masses and 30 psalters every year for her soul and for her lord's soul from St Alban's, where her body was to be buried, and 30 masses a year from the communities at Braughing and Welwynn.[171] In contrast, in the mid eleventh century, Wulfric and Eadwine made and recorded their agreement to give land to Bury St Edmund's, and one mass was to be said for their souls every day, apparently at the abbey.[172] In neither case is it clear whether the masses requested were to be part of the regular cycle of masses or whether they were special masses for the donors; it is just possible though that Æthelgifu's request for psalters as well suggests that all of these were to be additional to the regular cycle of prayers, and therefore that she also wanted additional (i.e., special) masses.

Æthelgifu's grant sounds much more impressive, but Wulfric and Eadwine actually have a larger total of masses offered on their behalf, and in theory it is possible to 'calculate' how these might affect sin. Instructions for the commutation of penance are found in some of the late Anglo-Saxon penitentials, and describe the kinds of penitential deeds (such as almsgiving, releasing slaves, or taking cold baths) which can be performed instead of the fasts prescribed by the penitentials. In some cases these commutations relate precise numbers of psalms or masses to periods of fasting, as in the late tenth- or early eleventh-century *Old English Handbook*: this penitential instructs that one mass will commute twelve days of fasting, ten masses will commute four months of fasting, and 30 masses can redeem a twelve-month fast.[173] Again, in theory this could then be compared with the provisions in the two wills: Wulfric and Eadwine have 365 (or 366) masses offered for them every year by Bury St Edmund's, or – according to the *Handbook* – the equivalent of just over twelve years of fasting. To put this in perspective, seven years of fasting is prescribed by the *Handbook* for adultery committed by lay people.[174] Æthelgifu's arrangement gives her 90 masses each year from the religious communities (equivalent to three years of fasting) and 156 offered by Eadwine, her priest (equivalent to just over five years of fasting), but the masses offered by Eadwine could not be perpetual since he would eventually die. Æthelgifu had also arranged for more than 90 psalters to be offered each year, but these were not as valuable as masses for redeeming fasts, so the 'total' is still lower.[175] And in either case what was needed would depend on the specific sins committed by the individuals, and the (unknowable) guilt remaining to be purged at their deaths.

[171]    S 1497 (*StAlb*, no. 7). See also D. Whitelock, *The Will of Aethelgifu: A Tenth Century Anglo-Saxon Manuscript* (Oxford, 1968).

[172]    S 1516 (Whitelock, *Wills*, no. 3).

[173]    55.19.01, ed. Frantzen, *The Anglo-Saxon Penitentials: A Cultural Database*; on the date and for the argument that this text is connected with Wulfstan, see R. Fowler, 'A late Old English handbook for the use of a confessor', *Anglia* 83 (1965): 1–34, at 7–12.

[174]    54.14.01; 54.17.02, ed. Frantzen, *The Anglo-Saxon Penitentials: A Cultural Database*.

[175]    See 55.19.01, ed. Frantzen, *The Anglo-Saxon Penitentials: A Cultural Database*.

This sort of comparison is clearly ludicrous. It seems extremely unlikely that Anglo-Saxons drawing up their wills made such precise calculations, or attempted to reckon the correspondence between the sin-burden and the mass as they arranged for liturgical commemoration, not least because it would be impossible to know how many sins would need to be expiated. The numbers of masses requested are more symbolic than arithmetic, and some numbers had particular value or credence from biblical precedents to explain when, or how many, masses should be offered.[176] In the context of the mass, 30 was a particularly important number, not least because of a story in the *Dialogues* of Gregory in which the monk Justus was supposed to have been released from torment after mass was offered for him for 30 days.[177] Large numbers of masses might have been perceived as more beneficial because they were more likely to appease the debt of sin, but probably not because people imagined the sin-burden in a numerical way: trying to quantify the effectiveness of prayer is a hopeless exercise. Even in a context where the influence of tariffed penance was felt strongly, it is not numbers themselves but rather the frequency, regularity and most of all, perpetuity of the commemoration which was significant, as well as the prestige and social status gained from making such donations and from the association with religious communities.[178]

### Associations with the Saints and their Servants

All sorts of masses and offerings were valuable, whether requested from communities or individuals, and the possibility that donors would be incorporated into the liturgy of a religious foundation or be treated as a member of a community was not the only factor driving a desire for liturgical commemoration. But the importance of religious communities is that they did not die, as individuals did, and perpetual commemoration is clearly significant in ensuring that the souls of the donors were provided for in death as well as in life, and therefore that the soul would continue to receive help in the interim and before it faced the Last Judgement. There are occasional references in charters to differing provisions for donors in life and death, such as the grant of rights to St Peter's, Worcester

---

[176]  e.g. D 60, U II.V.5–6, ed. Finsterwalder, *Canones Theodori*, 244, 318–19; Amalarius, *Liber officialis*, III.44.3–6, ed. Hanssens, *Amalarii episcopi opera liturgica omnia*, 382–4.

[177]  *Dialogues*, IV.57.8–14, ed. de Vogüé and Antin, *Dialogues, Livre IV*, III.188–92; Angenendt, 'Buße', 44; McLaughlin, *Consorting*, 242.

[178]  See C. Senecal, 'Keeping up with the Godwinesons: In pursuit of aristocratic status in late Anglo-Saxon England', *Anglo-Norman Studies* 23 (2000): 251–66, at 258–61; R. Fleming, 'The new wealth, the new rich and the new political style in late Anglo-Saxon England', *Anglo-Norman Studies* 23 (2001): 1–22, at 12–15, 20–1; M.F. Smith, P. Halpin and R. Fleming, 'Court and piety in late Anglo-Saxon England', *Catholic Historical Review* 87:4 (2001): 569–602, at 581–602.

(AD 884 x 901) made by Æthelræd and Æthelflæd, rulers of Mercia.[179] At Matins, Terce and Vespers, 'De profundis' was to be said during their lives, and 'Laudate Dominum' after their deaths; and both during their lives and afterwards a mass was to be said every Saturday and 30 psalms sung on their behalf.[180] But more usually the strongest impression received from the evidence of charters and wills is a deep desire to ensure commemoration in death, and to ensure that the memory of the donor, or the person on behalf of whom the donation is made, was not forgotten. This is evident for example in King Æthelwulf's confirmation of a grant of land to Christ Church, Canterbury some time between 833 and 839: he stated that the land was to be held freely in perpetuity for the expiation of his crimes, so that 'the praise of God will be raised up every day by the community in that place, for our souls and for the souls of all our friends', unceasingly, as long as Christianity remains there.[181] Both land and prayers were intended to continue for the duration of earthly time. Similarly, King Offa of Mercia (d.796) granted land to the church at Woking, stating that this was for the expiation of his sins, and so that the memory of his name should endure perpetually at the same church.[182]

Even if there was little attempt in bequests and charters to distinguish between private and regular masses, there is evidence that other sorts of personal and individual commemoration were considered valuable, and here too the emphasis on perpetuity remained important. Some charters make reference to the keeping of anniversaries, and in some cases outline what should happen on those anniversaries, indicating that lay patrons of religious houses wanted to be incorporated into the more general forms of commemoration which were afforded to the members of religious communities. In this context, the charters associated with Earl Oswulf and his wife Beornthryth are particularly remarkable for the extensive commemoration which they record. Oswulf granted land to Lyminge, probably in the early years of the ninth century, 'for the perpetual redemption and health of my soul, and of my wife Beornthryth', on the condition that as long

---

[179]    S 223 (BCS 579).

[180]    S 223 (BCS 579): 'On[d] Wærferð biscop ꝥ se heored habbað gesetted þæs godcundnesse beforan ðære þe him mon dæghwamlice deð, ge be heora life ge æfter heora life: þæt ðonne æt eolcum uhtsonge ꝥ æt ælcum æfensonge ꝥ æt eolcum undernsonge 'De profundis' ðone sealme, ða hwile þe heo lifgeon, ꝥ æfter heora life 'Laudate Dominum'; ꝥ ælce Sæternesdæge on Sancte Petres cyrcean ðrittig sealma ꝥ heora mæssan, ægðer ge for heo lifgende ge eac forðgeleorde'. 'De profundis' is Ps. 129, one of the penitential psalms; 'Laudate Dominum' is probably Ps. 148, but might also be Ps. 116 or 150.

[181]    S 323 (BCS 407): 'ut laus Dei a congregatione illa intercessioque animarum nostrarum omniumque amicorum nostrorum in illo loco incessanter, quamdiu Christiana fides permaneat, cotidie erigatur'. For information about the date, see Brooks, *The Early History of the Church of Canterbury*, 354 n. 54.

[182]    S 144 (*Pet*, no. 6): '... et pro expiatione piaculorum meorum Domino deuote largitus sum, et ut memoria nominis mei apud eandem ęcclesiam pro Domino perpetualier perseueret'.

as the Catholic faith continues among the English their anniversary should be celebrated every year, 'with fasts and in the divine offices and in psalters and in the celebrations of masses, and also in the refection of the brothers, in food and drink'; and the community was to give alms on the anniversary as well.[183]

Another charter in Oswulf's name, this time recording the donation of land to Christ Church, Canterbury, asks in return that Oswulf and Beornthryth might be in the fellowship of all those there who serve God, who were lords, and who were benefactors, and that their anniversary be celebrated with offices and the distribution of alms as those lords' and benefactors' anniversaries were.[184] This charter continues with the confirmation of this grant by Wulfred, Archbishop of Canterbury, who commanded that both of their anniversaries should be celebrated together on one day, with offices, almsgiving and a feast for the community; then follows a long list of the provisions to be paid from the estate, at least some of which were presumably destined for the feast. Bread was to be given from the communal provisions as almsgiving, and wax to the church (for candles); the liturgical offices were specified as two masses for each of them from priests, or two Passions from deacons, or for those not in priestly orders, two sets of 50 psalms, all for the benefit of their souls. Wulfred asks, almost as a postscript, that he be remembered on the same anniversary as seems fitting.[185] This is a difficult document because the earliest (ninth-century) copy is written in a peculiar script, and the wording of Wulfred's 'confirmation' seems to imply that Oswulf was not involved at the time of its writing. It has therefore been suggested that this charter may not be genuine but might instead have been based on the earlier grant to Lyminge: Oswulf may in fact have died before the second document was written.[186] However, it is plausible that what now survives represents some kind of a re-expression of an earlier agreement made between Christ Church and Oswulf,

[183]   S 153 (BCS 289): 'Hac uero condicione interposita. ut unicuique anno post.xii. mensibus migrationis nostrae tempus ab illa familia æt Limingge cælebretur quamdiu fides catholica in gente Anglorum perseueret. cum ieiunio diuinisque orationibus in psalmodiis et missarum caelebrationibus. seu etiam in refectione fratrum in cibo et potu. iuxta quod fraternitati uestrae uidetur quod producere poteritis et in uestra bonitate confidimus. Una \que/ panis cum cibo uernaculo uel paupere illius monasterii die illa tradatur. Hocque in posterum successoribus uestris praecipere praecamus'. For discussion see J.C. Crick, 'Church, land and local nobility in early ninth-century Kent: The case of Ealdorman Oswulf', *Historical Research* 61:146 (1988): 251–69; C. Cubitt, *Anglo-Saxon Church Councils, c.650–c.850*, Studies in the early history of Britain (London, 1995), 277.

[184]   S 1188 (BCS 330): 'Ond mid micelre eaðmodnisse biddað ðæt wit moten bion on ðem gemanon ðe ðaer Godes ðiowas siondan ꝺ ða menn ða ðaer hlafordas wæron ꝺ ðara monna ðe hiora lond to ðaere cirican saldon; ond ðættæ mon unce tide ymb tuælf monað mon geweorðiæ on godcundum godum ꝺ æc on aelmessan suæ mon hiora doeð'.

[185]   S 1188 (BCS 330): 'suilce iow cynlic ðynce'.

[186]   Crick, 'Church, land and local nobility', 252–5, 263–7.

written in the 830s or 840s, and perhaps reflecting Christ Church's interpretation of an oral arrangement which had not been formalised in writing.[187]

It is also worth bearing in mind that the written records of Oswulf's late eighth-century donations survive in copies which were probably written within 50 years of the transactions, perhaps in the early or mid ninth century. This means that even if the terms of the grants are not precisely what Oswulf and Beornthryth had originally had in mind, it is quite probable that at least parts of the documents record what was usual practice in this area, or what might be convincing, either for the late eighth century or for the early to mid ninth (or perhaps for both). Even if these documents represent a later reworking of Oswulf's and Beornthryth's arrangements, it is difficult otherwise to account for why their commemoration is likened to 'what is done on the anniversaries of lords', and it is also difficult to see how such an elaborate description of their commemoration would have been specifically helpful to Christ Church if the forgery were intended to strengthen their claim to land.[188] These charters suggest at the least that ninth-century landowners could demand significant privileges from the beneficiaries of their gifts, including the commemoration of their anniversaries. The surviving records of obits and anniversaries from Christ Church, Canterbury contain the names of individuals who lived in the ninth, tenth and eleventh centuries; and they do not include Oswulf's name, perhaps because of a complete loss of records and archives at the end of the eighth century, but clearly the recording and commemoration of anniversaries was felt to be significant at least from the ninth century, if not before.[189]

Several of the requests for anniversaries include provision for funding an annual memorial or celebration on the anniversary of the donor's death, although perhaps not as elaborate as the commemoration described in Oswulf's grants. In the 930s, Wulfgar bequeathed land to his wife which was to revert to the New Minster: she was instructed to pay the monks three days rent, and give the priest five pence on his commemoration day, presumably so that a mass would be said for him.[190] Other fleeting references are also suggestive: the will of Æthelric, made probably between 961 and 964, gave land at Rayne to St Paul's, London for the spreading of Christendom and the provision of lights, perhaps for an anniversary celebration, or

---

[187]    Ibid., 262, 267–8.

[188]    S 1188 (BCS 330): 'suae mon aet hlaforda tidum doeð'.

[189]    Brooks, *The Early History of the Church of Canterbury*, 121; R. Fleming, 'Christchurch's Sisters and Brothers: An Edition and Discussion of Canterbury Obituary Lists', in M.A. Meyer (ed.), *The Culture of Christendom: Essays in Medieval History in Commemoration of Denis L.T. Bethell* (London, 1993), 115–53, at 115–16.

[190]    S 1533 (BCS 678): 'Ic Wulfgar an þæs landes æt Collingaburnan ofer minne dæg Æffan hiere dæg ] heo tilige uncer begea sawla þearfe gemænelice ðæron. ] feormige þrie dagas þa Godes þeowas þær min lic reste 'on þone gemynddæg' ] selle þam mæssepreoste fif peningas …'.

for a saint's altar, so that he could benefit from the prayers of the saints.[191] Annual commemorations might also include a feast (as Oswulf's supposedly did), and this might be mentioned almost tangentially, or the grants might include specific information about the provision of a food-render, or a donation of food, perhaps in time for the anniversary.[192] King Edmund's donation to the New Minster in 940, made 'for the redemption of the sins of my father', instructed that the grant was primarily for clothing the brothers and should not be used for food 'except only on the anniversary-day of my father'.[193]

At some point during the reign of King Æthelred (978–1016), Ærnketel and his wife, Wulfrun, bequeathed land at Hickling and Kinoulton (Nottinghamshire) to St Benedict's, Ramsey (Cambridgeshire): if Wulfrun lived longer than Ærnketel, she was to give a substantial food-rent to the abbey each year on St Benedict's summer feast-day (6 July).[194] Although this must at least have contributed to a feast in honour of the abbey's patron, it seems likely that Ærnketel's intention was that he would be also be remembered on this occasion as a major benefactor. Some donations were made specifically to a community's refectory, suggesting the intention of an annual feast even if this was not specified. In 852, Wulfred leased land from Abbot Ceolred and the community at *Medeshamstede* (later Peterborough), and paid yearly food renders to the community; after his death, 20 hides of land were to be given to the community for the refectory.[195] At the beginning of the tenth century, a woman named Ceolwynn bequeathed land to Old Minster, Winchester for the refectory, on condition that they remember her and the soul of Osmod, who was probably her husband: no feast is mentioned, but the date of Osmod's anniversary is included as 'seven days before Rogation' and the intention was presumably that the anniversary should be commemorated.[196] In the 1050s Earl Leofric and his wife, Godgifu, granted estates to the refectory of the

---

[191] S 1501 (Whitelock, *Wills,* no. 16 [1]): '⁊ ic geann þæs landes æt Roægene be westan. into sancte Paule þam bisceope to to geleohtenne. ⁊ þar on Godes folce cristendom to dælenne'; see also information about the provision of lights in the material associated with Theodore: D 47, G 165, Co 63, U II.I.8, ed. Finsterwalder, *Canones Theodori,* 244, 267, 275, 312; and McLaughlin, *Consorting,* 153.

[192] See McLaughlin, *Consorting,* 150–1.

[193] S 470 (*WinchNM,* no. 12): 'Non tribuo ad pastum corporalis refectionis esui. nisi tantum anniuersarium mei patris diem minime in obliuione habeant sed omnino impleant quod condictum est'.

[194] S 1493 (K 971): 'Ego autem Wlfrun singulis annis uitae meae ad festum sancti Benedicti quod est in aestate .X. mittas de brasio, et .V. de grut, et .X. mittas farinae triticeae, et .VIII. pernas, et .XVI. caseos, et duas uaccas pingues de terra mea Hikelinge pro respectu decerno eidem aecclesiae procurari, in capite uero quadragesimae .VIII. isicios'.

[195] S 1440 (*Pet,* no. 9).

[196] S 1513 (BCS 566): 'into hære beddarn æt ðam bisceopstole mid swelcan yrfe swelcan hi ðenne to gehagað on ða gerað ðe hi on ða gerað ðe hi gemunen hi ⁊ Osmodes saulæ swa him rihtlic ⁊ cynlic þince to his gemunde dege ðæt beoð seofan nihtan ær gangdagan'.

monastery of St Mary at Worcester, on condition that the brothers interceded for their souls.[197] Whether or not a feast was intended from these lands, the fact that the lands were associated with the benefactors would perhaps also have encouraged memory and prayer for the benefactors when income or produce from those lands came into the monastery. Domesday Book specifically records that some lands were set aside for the refectories of communities, and it would seem that once established, this link was maintained at least in some cases.[198]

The surviving memorial books and documents describing donations to religious houses often record only one event or instant in a process of establishing and building up relationships which individuals and families worked hard to maintain, and which could last decades.[199] In some cases it is possible to take a longer view, when there is more evidence for continuing and developing relationships. One example is Alfred and Wærburh, whose donation of a gospel-book to Christ Church, Canterbury, after they had ransomed it from Viking raiders, has already been mentioned; but this was not the only moment at which Alfred and his family came into contact with the community at Christ Church.[200] Another gift of land to Christ Church, and the provisions of Alfred's will, record other events in a relationship lasting probably several decades, and ultimately Alfred and his wife and daughter were incorporated into Christ Church's anniversary lists.[201] This is particularly significant because the surviving documents associated with this family do not mention anniversaries or commemoration in the memorial books, even though they requested the gospels to be read for them in life and in death, and even though Alfred's will mentions a yearly gift to Christ Church of 100 pence in alms, which may have been connected with an anniversary. Robin Fleming has suggested that the remembrance of benefactors may have been as much about celebration of a religious community's lands as it was about commemoration and prayer: even so, their donations still ensured the perpetual prayer for the benefactor's soul which seems to have been eagerly sought.[202]

---

[197]    S 1232 (K 766), dated 1052 x 1057.

[198]    See for example Great Domesday Book, fol. 41r, land at Freefolk, ed. J. Munby, *Domesday Book: 4, Hampshire* (Chichester, 1982). no. 3.5: '… Frigefolc. ] fuit de uictu monachorum'; or fol. 59v, land at Sotwell, ed. P. Morgan, *Domesday Book: 5, Berkshire* (Chichester, 1979), no. 10.2: 'in dominio de uictu monachorum'; see R.W.H. Erskine (ed.), *Great Domesday: a facsimile* (London, 1986–1992).

[199]    Schmid and Wollasch, 'Societas et Fraternitas', 37–8; White, *Custom*; Rosenwein, *Neighbor of St Peter*; C.B. Bouchard, *Holy Entrepreneurs: Cistercians, Knights, and Economic Exchange in Twelfth-Century Burgundy* (Ithaca, NY, 1991); McLaughlin, *Consorting*, 134–5.

[200]    S 1204a (BCS 634); see also above, 230.

[201]    Fleming, 'Christchurch's sisters and brothers', 120–1.

[202]    R. Fleming, 'History and liturgy at pre-Conquest Christ Church', *Haskins Society Journal: Studies in Medieval History* 6 (1995): 67–83, at 80–1.

It seems likely that many grants to religious houses must similarly have resulted in commemoration and inclusion in *libri memoriales* even when this was not specified or recorded, in the same way that the decision to record various other details (such as whether or not payment was made for land) was a matter of preference. Many of the names listed in the New Minster's *Liber Vitae* are grouped under the heading 'familiarior uel benefactor', but it is often not possible to match the benefactor to a specific donation: perhaps in some cases these were smaller or more portable gifts which did not require formal diplomas; but in others the decision to include the donor's name in the book for commemoration may not have been recorded in writing except in the book itself.[203] This is important as a reminder both of the (often quite extensive) process of negotiation and discussion which presumably preceded most gifts to religious houses, and that what is recorded now is only an echo of that process, rather than the full details. It is also worth remembering that at least some of those whose names were recorded in memorial books may have been considered to be in a formal relationship of confraternity with that religious house. Like commemoration on anniversaries, entry into confraternity could be arranged through the donation of land, and it seems to have been considered to be a valuable spiritual privilege: one example here is the record of an arrangement made some time between 1053 and 1066, by which Oswulf and his wife Æthelgyth granted money and land to St Albans in return for admission into confraternity with the abbey.[204]

In this context the New Minster's decision to list people under the label 'familiarior' is interesting too because it suggests that those who had this status were perceived to be closely associated with the community and to have some kind of special relationship like that of confraternity.[205] The *Regularis Concordia* uses the word 'familiaris' to describe a religious house joined to the community in confraternity, while Ælfwine's prayer book includes a prayer for 'the souls of all the faithful, who have commended themselves to our prayers, and from whom we have received alms, and also those who are joined to us by 'familiarity' or by affinity of the flesh', perhaps also referring to those in confraternity with the community.[206] All those whose names were listed in a memorial book could at least expect to receive general commemoration in the mass, but it is worth noting that the names of other religious communities (such as Abingdon and Ely) were also listed in the book, suggesting perhaps that both religious and lay were understood

[203]   Stowe 944, fols. 25r–v.

[204]   S 1235 (*StAlb*, no. 17): 'Ðis is seo forpeard þe Ospulf ] ÆgeliÞ his pif geporhton piÞ þone abbod Leofstan ] piÞ þæne hired æt Albanes stope. Ðæt is ærest þ hig geafan an pund þam abbode Leofstane ] eallum gebroþrum to karitate þa þa hig eodon þær on broÞorræddene …'.

[205]   See McLaughlin, *Consorting*, 77–82, 91; it is possible that this is also what was meant by those listed as 'frater laicus': see Keynes, *Liber Vitae of the New Minster*, 96.

[206]   *RC*, 68, ed. Symons, *Regularis Concordia*, 67; Cotton Titus D.xxvi, fols. 64v–65r, ed. Günzel, *Ælfwine's Prayerbook*, no. 76.42.

to be formally in confraternity with the New Minster.[207] Lanfranc's *Constitutiones* describe the formal process by which individuals or entire monastic houses might enter into confraternity with a community, which involved coming to the chapter office and lying prostrate to make the petition.[208] It is difficult to ascertain whether this ritual reflects continental or English custom (or how far the two were different at this stage), but it is clear that this was an occasion of some solemnity. Although it apparently did not enjoin any particular mode of life upon the individuals as the later medieval Tertiary Orders did, confraternity must have been viewed in some ways as a similar connection to monastic life, and once admitted, those in confraternity with a community would be commemorated as if one of their own.

Many of those who were recorded in the books of religious communities, especially if they had donated significant quantities of lands or money for the privilege, must have belonged to the higher echelons of society, and indeed the names of kings and nobles are often among the most prominent, and sometimes listed separately, in these books.[209] Not all such patronage originated from the highest ranks of the nobility, however. The efforts of the lesser nobility to associate themselves with churches, by building them or donating to them, may not be as prominent in the surviving evidence, but is visible nonetheless. Sometimes inscriptions identify these sorts of pious acts, such as three which survive now in Yorkshire. St Mary's Castlegate in York contains an inscription recording the construction and consecration of a church by Grim and Æse, probably dating from the late tenth or early eleventh century;[210] an inscription on a sundial in Aldborough which is probably of a similar date records that someone called Ulf had the church constructed for Gunwaru's soul, and for himself.[211] A thegn named Orm, the son of Gamul, recorded on another sundial that he had bought and rebuilt St Gregory's minster in Kirkdale after it had fallen into a state of disrepair, in the time of King Edward and Earl Tostig (1055 x 1065).[212] None of these mentions

[207]   Stowe 944, fols. 26v–27r (Abingdon), fols. 27r–v (Ely).

[208]   Lanfranc, *Constitutiones*, 108, ed. Knowles and Brooke, *The Monastic Constitutions of Lanfranc*, 108–10.

[209]   See for example Stowe 944, fols. 14r–v, 17r–v; Cotton Domitian A.vii, fols. 15r–17r, ed. Rollason et al., *Durham Liber Vitae*, 91–4.

[210]   E. Okasha, *Hand-List of Anglo-Saxon Non-Runic Inscriptions* (Cambridge, 1971), no. 146; Senecal, 'Keeping up with the Godwinesons', 260. The inscription also contains another name which is no longer legible. It is not clear whether the church referred to in the inscription was on the site of St Mary's Castlegate. 'M[I]NSTER SET[TON ... ]ARD ˥ GRIM ˥ ÆSE : O[N NA]MAN DRIHTNES HÆ[LGES] CRISTES [˥] SCA MA[RI. ˥ SC]E [:] MARTINI : ˥ SCE C[ ... ]TI ˥ OMNIVM SCŌR[VM CONS]ECRATA : EST : AN[ ... ]VIS IN : VITA: ET[ ... ]'.

[211]   Okasha, *Hand-List of Anglo-Saxon Non-Runic Inscriptions*, no. 1: 'VLF [HE]T ARŒRAN CYRICE FOR H[A]NVM ˥ FOR GVN[ÞARA] SAVLA'.

[212]   Okasha, *Hand-List of Anglo-Saxon Non-Runic Inscriptions*, no. 64; J.T. Lang, *Corpus of Anglo-Saxon Stone Sculpture: Vol. 3, York and Eastern Yorkshire* (Oxford, 1991),

prayers or commemoration, but the monumental nature of the inscriptions and the acts of piety which they record suggest that these benefactors hoped to be commemorated in the churches which they built or rebuilt.

There are also numerous surviving pieces of stone sculpture which do ask for prayers or rest for the soul. Many of these are identifiable with religious communities, such as the memorial stones found at (for example) Lindisfarne, Monkwearmouth and Jarrow, Hackness, Hartlepool, Hexham, and Whitby,[213] while an inscribed cross-shaft from Yarm (Yorkshire), probably dating to the first half of the ninth century, records that a priest set up a monument in memory of his brother.[214] In other cases it is more difficult to identify whether the people commemorated, or those who commissioned such monuments, were lay or religious, although some of them seem likely to have been laity. An inscription probably dating to the eleventh century, on what looks like a gravestone or grave-cover now in the parish church at Stratfield Mortimer (Berkshire), records that 'on 24 September, Æthelweard son of Kypping was put in this place: may the man who prays for his soul be blessed'.[215] The Domesday Book records that thegns named 'Cheping' and 'Eduuinus' were recorded as holding a church at Stratfield manor in the time of King Edward, and the correspondence between Cheping and

---

163–6; C.E. Karkov, *The Art of Anglo-Saxon England* (Woodbridge, 2011), 259–60. 'ORM : GAMAL | SUNA : BOHTE : SCS | GREGORIUS : MIN | STER | ÐONNEHI | T : ÞESÆL : TOBRO | CAN: ꝢTOFALAN: ꝢH/E | HITLET [:] MACAN[:] NEÞAN: FROM | GRVNDEXÞE: Ꝣ /SCS/ GREGORI | VS : IN : EADÞARD : DAGVM : CŃG | ꝢNTOS*TI* [:] DAGVM : EORL |'.

[213]   For discussion of these see C.E. Karkov, 'Whitby, Jarrow and the Commemoration of Death in Northumbria', in J. Hawkes and S. Mills (eds), *Northumbria's Golden Age* (Stroud, 1999), 126–35; J.T. Lang and D. Craig, *Corpus of Anglo-Saxon Stone Sculpture: Vol. 6, Northern Yorkshire* (Oxford, 2001), 52–3; E. Okasha, 'Memorial Stones or Grave-Stones?', in P. Cavill (ed.), *The Christian Tradition in Anglo-Saxon England: Approaches to Current Scholarship and Teaching* (Woodbridge, 2004), 91–101; for the sculpture see R. Cramp, *Corpus of Anglo-Saxon Stone Sculpture: Vol. 1, County Durham and Northumberland* (Oxford, 1984), I.194–208 (Lindisfarne); I.106–22, 122–34 (Jarrow and Monkwearmouth); I.97–105 (Hartlepool); I.174–93 (Hexham) and illustrations in vol. II; Lang, *Corpus of Anglo-Saxon Stone Sculpture: Vol. 3, York and Eastern Yorkshire*, 135–42 (Hackness); Lang and Craig, *Corpus of Anglo-Saxon Stone Sculpture: Vol. 6, Northern Yorkshire*, 231–66 (Whitby).

[214]   Okasha, *Hand-list of Anglo-Saxon non-runic inscriptions*, no. 145; Lang and Craig, *Corpus of Anglo-Saxon stone sculpture: Vol. 6, Northern Yorkshire*, 274–6: '[ ... M] BEREHCT SĀC ALLA SIGNUM AEFTER HIS BREODER A[S]SETAE'.

[215]   Okasha, *Hand-List of Anglo-Saxon Non-Runic Inscriptions*, no. 111; D. Tweddle, M. Biddle and B. Kjølbye-Biddle, *Corpus of Anglo-Saxon Stone Sculpture: Vol. 4, South-East England* (Oxford, 1995), 335–7: 'VIII : KL : OCTB : FVIT : POSITVS : ÆGELÞA[R] DVS : FILIVS : KYPPINGVS : IN ISTO LOVO : BEATVS : SIT OMO : QVI : ORAT : PRO ANI[MA] : EIVS : TOKI : ME : SCRIPSIT:'. It is not clear whether the inscription is pre- or post-Conquest.

Kypping suggests that these individuals may have belonged to the same family, and that perhaps this stone and inscription should be seen in this family context.[216]

The records of guilds formed in various places in tenth- and eleventh-century England likewise show a concern to provide for the soul, and for burial. These guilds seem to have been connected with thegns, although perhaps not always the super-rich. The guild at Abbotsbury is a particularly interesting example. It was founded by Urk (or Orc) and his wife (Tola), who established a monastery in Abbotsbury and endowed it.[217] The guild was founded in memory of Urk and Tola and functioned alongside the monastery, for the benefit both of the church and the guild-brothers, and ultimately the anniversaries of Urk and Tola were also commemorated at Abbotsbury.[218] One of their chief purposes of the guild at Abbotsbury, as also for guilds in Exeter, in Bedwyn and in Cambridge, appears to have been the provision of spiritual benefits akin to those of confraternity. All the guild regulations contain information about what should be done in the event of the death of one of the members, and with the exception of the regulations from Cambridge, all outline the burial arrangements for the body of a dead guild-member, and the masses which are to be offered for his soul.[219] It is significant too that these are found at the beginning of the statues, indicating their importance to the guild, and that these offerings are the only religious obligations which all the statutes have in common.[220]

By way of example, the statutes of one of the Exeter guilds record that at each meeting, two masses were to be sung, one for the living and one for the departed, and if a guild-member died each member was to pay for six masses or full psalters to be said. In addition, each guild-member was required to say two psalters, one for the living and one for the departed. The rules for those who failed to perform their duties require the offender to pay for three masses to be said on the first occasion, five on the second, and on the third he was not allowed to clear himself (unless for sickness or for his lord's needs), and presumably would have been

---

[216] See Great Domesday Book, fol. 62v, ed. Morgan, *Domesday Book: 5, Berkshire*, no. 46.3; Erskine (ed.), *Great Domesday: a facsimile*; and Okasha, *Hand-List of Anglo-Saxon Non-Runic Inscriptions*, no. 11.

[217] For the text, see *Councils and Synods*, I.i, no. 67.

[218] The anniversaries are recorded in a late thirteenth-century manuscript, now London, British Library, Cotton Cleopatra B.ix, at fols. 57r and 59v (and the dedication of the church is noted on fol. 59r): see S. Keynes, 'The lost cartulary of Abbotsbury', *Anglo-Saxon England* 18 (1989): 207–43, at 208–9, and n. 14.

[219] For the texts, see *Councils and Synods*, I.i, nos. 16, 67; and B. Thorpe, *Diplomatarium Anglicum aevi Saxonici: A Collection of English Charters from the Reign of King Aethelberht of Kent, A.D. 605 to that of William the Conqueror* (London, 1865), 605–17.

[220] V. Thompson, *Dying and Death in Later Anglo-Saxon England* (Woodbridge, 2004), 112–13.

required to leave the guild.[221] The Devon guilds may have focused collectively on the cathedral minster at Exeter because of the possibilities for masses and other offerings as they and the minster gave and received mutual support, and Elaine Treharne has recently suggested that the 'manumissions' that were written into a gospel-book (now Cambridge, University Library Ii.2.11) in Exeter are in fact records of entry into guild-membership, so that the gospel-book itself became a guild book.[222] The guilds are striking for their spiritual focus, especially since the impetus to found them was apparently driven by the laity even when the guilds were centred on a church; and once again, these are quite personal arrangements, even if they then became institutionalised, and do not seem to be dependent on the empty reproductions of formulae.[223] Prayers and masses were clearly desired by the people who set up and belonged to these later Anglo-Saxon guilds.

This demonstrates once again that the concern for the fate of the soul was not confined to theologians and scholars, or even only to monastic communities, but that the message had filtered through at least as far as the people who came together to form the guilds, perhaps the middling and lower sorts of thegns. This is significant too because in some cases there may have been little difference between wealthy freemen and minor thegns.[224] The guild statutes illustrate the possibilities for the laity to influence and involve themselves in religious life: perhaps, like confraternal relationships, the guilds were in some sense similar to (although less demanding than) later medieval Tertiary Orders.[225] Guild statutes suggest a desire for inclusion in social groups and the emulation of those who had the means to donate large quantities of land to religious communities. But perhaps the most significant aspect of the guilds' practices is the clear assumption that the duties of one member to another did not end at death, but rather continued and even increased, mirroring the perspective of religious houses which linked living and dead members together as continual members of their community. This long view, particularly important in the context of provision for the soul, is clear too in the obligations to living and departed family members, and the long-lasting nature of family relationships, especially visible in wills and charters where the donor mentions the souls of his ancestors and those to whom the property will be passed.

---

[221]   *The Exeter Guild Statutes*, 3, *Councils and Synods*, I.i, no. 16.

[222]   J. Blair, *The Church in Anglo-Saxon Society* (Oxford, 2005), 340, 403–4 and esp. 453–5; E. Treharne, 'The Conners of Exeter, 1070–1150', *Festschrift for Patrick Conner* (forthcoming). I am grateful to Elaine Treharne for allowing me to see this before publication.

[223]   G. Rosser, 'The Anglo-Saxon Gilds', in J. Blair (ed.), *Minsters and Parish Churches: The Local Church in Transition, 950–1200* (Oxford, 1988), 31–43, at 31.

[224]   Senecal, 'Keeping up with the Godwinesons', 258.

[225]   See also Rosser, 'Gilds', 32–3.

**Obligations and Relationships**

Commemoration and remembrance after death are tightly bound up with the
personal relationships established in life between individuals and their families
on the one hand, and religious houses and/or corporate groups such as the guilds
on the other. The ways in which relationships were built and established, and
with whom such links were created, underlie the ways in which Christians in
Anglo-Saxon England remembered their dead and sought to provide for their
own commemoration in turn: understanding how individuals perceived their
personal relationships with their families and with religious communities, and
the mutual obligations which were attendant on these relationships, is crucial to
understanding the ritualised almsgiving of charters and wills, and how and for
whom such donations were made. As property passed through a family from one
generation to another and from one individual to another, each heir inherited a
debt to the ancestors who had acquired the property, especially if this property
was alienable and could therefore be given as alms to benefit the souls of the heir
and his family.[226] To borrow an example from early medieval France, the *Liber
manualis*, an instructional text written in the ninth century by the noblewoman
Dhuoda for her son William, directs that William should pray for the relatives who
obtained property and bequeathed it through the family line.[227] Such generosity
might be recorded specifically in the formal documents which arranged for
bequests for religious houses, such as in the late tenth-century will of Æthelric,
who bequeathed land to Christ Church, Canterbury for his soul and his wife's, and
for the soul of his father who obtained it.[228]

   As people drew up their bequests and arranged for such donations, the
exhortations of the homilists may have been ringing in their ears. As already noted,
some homilists warned their congregations that they needed to focus on atoning
for sin in this life, rather than relying on the offerings of others in the next.[229] Even
more strikingly, one of the Blickling homilies warns that people should ensure
that they arrange almsgiving for their own souls, since wealth is transitory and
our relatives die. Significantly, the author also notes that 'it often happens that
after death, property comes into the power of those whom he liked worst in this

---

[226]   White, *Custom*, 121; P.J. Geary, *Living with the Dead in the Middle Ages* (Ithaca,
NY, 1994), 80–1; J.C. Crick, 'Posthumous Obligation and Family Identity', in W.O. Frazer
and A. Tyrrell (eds), *Social Identity in Early Medieval Britain* (London, 2000), 193–208,
at 199–201.

[227]   *Liber manualis* 8.14, ed. M. Thiébaux, *Dhuoda, Handbook for her Warrior Son:
Liber Manualis*, Cambridge Medieval Classics 8 (Cambridge, 1998), 204. Dhuoda's text
is interesting for its apparently clear indication that an educated laywoman could have
considerable knowledge of purgatory and the effects of offerings for the dead, especially
masses, in the afterlife: see Geary, *Living with the Dead in the Middle Ages*, 79–87.

[228]   S 1501 (*c.* 960 x 994).

[229]   See above, 130, 201–2.

life, sometimes into the wife's power, sometimes into the husband's. And then the person will not distribute anything profitable for his soul, of his gold, silver, or earthly riches, if he will not distribute the best portion to God for himself while he is alive here'.[230] Although this is reminiscent of many exhortations to almsgiving and the donation of earthly wealth, the specific focus on the difficulty of controlling property after death is striking in the context of the wills and charters which sought to make provision for the afterlife. These concerns are noted elsewhere too, as in the case of the man seen in the brother of Wenlock's vision whose brother had refused to release a slave on his behalf when he had died.[231] It is also clear that the homilist is not far wrong: sometimes property did end up in the 'wrong' hands, and sometimes intended bequests were not seen through to fulfilment, as the will of King Eadred (d.955), which seems never to have been implemented.[232]

The perceived damage to souls when bequests or donations had been subverted is also clear from a record of a late ninth- or early tenth-century case in which the instructions of the original benefactor, Eanbald, had not been heeded. Eanbald had made an arrangement with Bishop Milred of Worcester about an estate at Sodbury: the agreement was that as long as someone in Eanbald's family was in holy orders they could retain the estate; but if not, the land was to revert to the Worcester bishopric, 'for all their souls'.[233] Eanbald had in turn given the land to Eastmund, but after Eastmund's death neither condition was fulfilled and the family apparently held the estate without anyone being in holy orders. The bishop of Worcester, by this time Wærferth, was keen to reclaim the land for the bishopric, but it was not only the bishops of Worcester who were perceived to have suffered: the document explaining the resolution of the dispute notes that 'after Eastmund's death, his kin robbed both the spirits of the dead men and the bishop and the church at Worcester of this land'.[234] This theft from the dead is significant, as Victoria Thompson notes, because it is not simply the land which was at stake, since the souls of the dead men should have been prayed for, either by the men in holy orders who held the estate, or at the cathedral if the estate had reverted to them.[235] It is also significant that by this time the Eanbald and Eastmund must have

---

[230]   *Hom.* XVI, ed. Morris, *Blickling Homilies*, 195; this fragment numbered XVI by Morris has now been identified as part of the homily that he numbered IV: see R. Willard (ed.), *The Blickling Homilies*, EEMF 10 (Copenhagen, 1960), 38–40.

[231]   *Epistola* 10, ed. Tangl, *Die Briefe*, 13, ll. 28–36.

[232]   See Keynes, *Liber Vitae of the New Minster*, 23–4; S. Foot, *Veiled Women: 1. The Disappearance of Nuns from Anglo-Saxon England; 2. Female Religious Communities in England, 871–1066* (Aldershot, 2000), 250; S. Miller, *Charters of the New Minster, Winchester*, Anglo-Saxon Charters 9 (Oxford, 2001), 78–80.

[233]   S 1446 (BCS 582): 'for heora ealra saule'.

[234]   S 1446 (BCS 582): 'þa æfter Eastmundes forðsiðe bereafode seo mægð þæs ilcan londes ge þa gastas þara forðgewitenra manna ge þone bisceop ⁊ þa ciricean æt Wigeornaceastre'.

[235]   Thompson, *Dying and Death*, 22–3.

been dead for quite some time: nothing more is known of them, but Bishop Milred died in around 774 or 775, at least 100 years before this dispute was recorded.[236] Even if the bishop's interest in land for Worcester outweighed his concern for the donors' souls, the ultimate result was to the benefit of those souls.

In part, this kind of problem may explain another phenomenon: property was sometimes given away to a family member only on the condition that the recipient later transferred it to a religious institution on his or her death. This also enabled the testator to give the same piece of land both to his descendants for use in their lifetimes, and to a religious community as almsgiving. In the eleventh century, for example, Thurketel bequeathed land to his daughter Ælfwyn only on the condition that she could not freely give it away, and that after her death it was to go to the community at Holme, for his soul and for hers.[237] Julia Crick argues that many of the recorded bequests which survive to the present day may represent such continuations of earlier agreements rather than donations made by individuals in their own right, especially when those bequeathing land were women who may have inherited it from their husbands.[238] It is notable that in some such cases, those who passed on the land might not mention the previous benefactor even while they offered land for their own and other souls. Ketel Alder donated land at Sisted to Christ Church, Canterbury, on behalf of the souls of his father and Sæflæd (who may have been his wife), but did not apparently wish to record that he gave it on behalf of his mother, Wulfgyth, even though the survival of her will reveals that in fact she had also donated the land to Christ Church and Ketel held only it during his lifetime.[239]

Three related wills, those of Ælfgar and his two daughters, Ælfflæd and Æthelflæd,[240] provide a particularly clear example of the intricate and complex circumstances that surviving wills represent, including the way in which land was bequeathed to religious institutions via other family members, the ongoing

---

[236]   Ibid., 23.

[237]   S 1528.

[238]   J.C. Crick, 'Women, posthumous benefaction, and family strategy in pre-conquest England', *Journal of British Studies* 38 (1999): 399–422; see also Crick, 'Posthumous Obligation and Family Identity'; J.C. Crick, 'Women, Wills and Movable Wealth in pre-Conquest England', in M. Donald and L. Hurcombe (eds), *Gender and Material Culture in Historical Perspective* (London, 2000), 17–37.

[239]   Crick, 'Women, posthumous benefaction, and family strategy', 402–3. S 1519 (Whitelock, *Wills*, no. 34): 'Her is on þis write Keteles quide þat is þat ic an Stistede after mine tyme for mine fader soule and for Sefledan into Cristes kirke'; and S 1535 (K.A. Lowe, 'A new edition of the will of Wulfgyth', *Notes and Queries* 36, ns (1989): 295–8, at 297): 'ic yan þet land at Stistede. a Godes ywitnesse and mine vrenden. into Xpes cherecke. þa muneken. to vostre. on þan yrede þet Elfkitel. and Kytel mine bea'r'n. bruke þas londes. hyre dey. and seþþen gange. þet land into Xpes cherecke buten ecchere aȝentale vor mine saule and vor Elfwines mines hlouerdes. and vor alre mine bierne'. See also R. Fleming, *Kings and Lords in Conquest England* (Cambridge, 1991), 141–3.

[240]   S 1483 (Ælfgar); S 1486 (Ælfflæd); S 1494 (Æthelflæd).

concern for the souls of the family's ancestors, and the way that personal, familial and institutional relationships were all significant in the disposal of property and arrangements for commemoration. Ælfgar granted various lands to Stoke for his soul, some of which were first granted to one or both of his daughters. Stoke was a community with which Ælfgar's family had apparently long maintained a relationship and where the bodies of his ancestors were buried; one of the conditions placed upon Æthelflæd was that she was to hold the land while she did what she could for the community of Stoke, for the sake of Ælfgar's soul and of their ancestors' souls.[241] Ælfgar also granted land to St Mary's, Barking, for the good of their ancestors' souls – but it was only to go to Barking when (or if) it had already gone to both daughters and neither of them had had children, a condition of other lands which were eventually to come to Stoke.[242] A certain Ælfwold was also a beneficiary of Ælfgar's will, receiving land on condition that he paid an annual food-rent to the community of St Paul's for the souls of their ancestors, perhaps intended to provide an anniversary feast.[243] It seems that Ælfgar may have been worried about Æthelflæd's dedication to the causes that he was supporting, since he mentions twice that she is to hold lands on condition that she does what she can for the souls of her family, named as Ælfgar himself, her mother and her brother, and her ancestors more generally.[244]

But Ælfgar's concerns seem to have been unfounded for the most part: in Æthelflæd's will, the lands granted to her by Ælfgar are duly passed on to the various communities or to her sister as he requested, although she gave some lands to her sister for her lifetime which were supposed to have gone directly to religious beneficiaries; she also arranged for offerings for the souls of others with whom she had connections, such as King Edmund and King Edgar.[245] She granted land

[241]   S 1483 (Whitelock, *Wills*, no. 2): 'And ic an þat Athelfled bruke þe lond þer wile þe hire lef beth one raða heo it on riht helde. and on þe red þat heo do þan hirde so wel so heo best may into Stoke for mine soule and for ure aldre'; see also S 1486 (Whitelock, *Wills*, no. 15): 'þa halgan stowæ et Stocæ þæ mine yldran on restaþ' ('the holy place at Stoke where my ancestors are buried').

[242]   S 1483 (Whitelock, *Wills*, no. 2): 'and ic an þat lond at Babingþirne Atelflede mine douhter. And after hire day; min other douhter hire day. And ouer here bothre day; mine douhter berne gif he bern habbe. And gif he bern ne habbe; þanne go it into sancte Marie Stowe at Berkynge for vre aldre soule'.

[243]   S 1483 (Whitelock, *Wills*, no. 2): 'And ic an þat lond at Tidwoldingtone Alfwold ouer mine day þe he formige ilke ihere þen hird at Paulesbiri for vre aldre soule'.

[244]   S 1483 (Whitelock, *Wills*, no. 2): 'And ic an Athelflede mine douhter þe lond at Cokefeld. and at Dittone. and þat at Lauenham. ouer min day. on þe red þat heo be þe bet for mine soule. and hire moder soule ꝺ for hire brother soule. ꝺ for hire seluen. And þanne ouer vre aldre day ic an þat lond at Cokefeld into Beodricheswrthe to seynt Eadmundes stowe'; 'And ic an þat Athelfled bruke þe lond þer wile þe hire lef beth one raða heo it on riht helde. and on þe red þat heo do þan hirde so wel so heo best may into Stoke for mine soule and for ure aldre'.

[245]   Crick, 'Women, posthumous benefaction, and family strategy', 402.

to Æthelmær, her priest, after her death, presumably so that he would pray for her (and perhaps also for her family) and requested that half of her men in every village be freed for her soul, and half of her stock in every village be distributed for her soul.[246] Ælfflæd's will also shows her passing on the property bequeathed to her by her sister and her father, so that it went to religious communities as they had requested. She granted her property 'as her ancestors had granted it', continuing the line of transmission which had been initiated in Ælfgar's will; and she also gave land to Ealdorman Æthelmær on the condition that he be a true friend and advocate of the foundation at Stoke, her ancestral resting place.[247] Ælfflæd was married to Byrhtnoth (of Maldon fame), and so she granted land to Ely, where Byrhtnoth's body was buried; and she and Byrhtnoth were also remembered in the obituaries at Canterbury because of her gifts.[248]

These three wills illustrate neatly the links and relationships which were established and strengthened by individuals, and which are dependent on both familial and personal relationships. Thus while Ælfflæd retains the connection with Stoke and St Mary's, Barking from her family, she is also associated with the foundations at Ely through her marriage to Byrhtnoth, and commemorated with him – but without the rest of her family – at Canterbury. All three of the individuals disposing property here were concerned, as they distributed it, with their own souls and what they could do for them by donation. They were also concerned with the souls of their ancestors, especially those ancestors from whom their property was received, since it was these earlier individuals who had made the pious benefactions possible. These three wills also provide a rare insight into the way that relationships between communities and families could extend over many years: more usually wills survive alone, without such related documents, and therefore the extent of the relationship is not clear. It seems likely that other surviving documents should be considered as representing similar situations, so that in many cases what seems to be a straightforward relationship between a

---

[246]   S 1494 (Whitelock, *Wills*, no. 14): '⁊ ic gean Æþælmære minum præoste twægra hida on Dunninglandæ ofæ[r] minne dæg'; '⁊ ic wille þæt man frigæ hæalue mine men on elcum tune for mine sawlæ. ⁊ þæt man dele æal healf þæt yrue þæt ic hæbbæ on ælcum tune for mire sawle'.

[247]   S 1486 (Whitelock, *Wills*, no. 15): 'ic gean æalswa mine yldran his 'er' gæuþan'; '⁊ ic gean Æðelm[æ]re æaldorman þes landes æt Lellinge ofer mine deg mid mete. ⁊ mid mannum. æalswa hit stent on þet gerad þæt he beo on minum life min fulla freod. ⁊ forespreca. ⁊ mira manna. ⁊ efter minum dege beo þara halgan stowe. ⁊ þeræ are ful freod. ⁊ forespeca æt Stocæ þe mine yldran on restaþ'.

[248]   S 1486 (Whitelock, *Wills*, no. 15): '⁊ ic gean into Ælig sanctæ Petre. ⁊ sanctæ Æþældryþe. ⁊ sancte Wihtburhe. ⁊ sanctæ Sexburhe. ⁊ sancte Æormenhilde þer mines hlafordes lichoma rest þara þreo landa þe wit buta geheotan gode. ⁊ his halga[n]. þæt is æt Rettendune þe wes min morgangyfu. ⁊ æt Sægham. ⁊ æt Dictune ealswa min hlaford. ⁊ min swæstar his er geuþan. ⁊ þaræ anre hide æt Cæafle þe min swystar begeat. ⁊ þes bæahges gemacan þe man sæalde minum hlaforde to sawlescæatte'; see MS G, 3 Ides August, ed. Fleming, 'Christchurch's sisters and brothers', 128.

religious house and an individual is much more complicated, incorporating also connections between other members of a family, and perhaps also others who had previously held estates, even if these are not always visible in the surviving documents.[249]

The moments recorded in the sources show that the transactions which brought individuals into contact with religious houses were part of a continuous process of maintaining contacts, whether by handing on property on the conditions by which it had been granted, or by initiating new relationships.[250] In this context, it is particularly interesting to note that even when a gift was made in return for a sum of money, the desire for the spiritual benefits of almsgiving often found expression in the terms of the charter, suggesting perhaps that the donor (or 'vendor'?) might have offered a reduced price for the land in question, or that a transaction might be both gift and sale.[251] In 811, Coenwulf granted land in Kent to Archbishop Wulfred, donating 'for the honour of Almighty God and for the expiation of his sins, and for the most reverent love of Archbishop Wulfred, as well as for his generous remuneration of money'.[252] Granting privileges to Bishop Heahberht of Worcester in 841, King Berhtwulf of Mercia's charter states that this was done 'for the redemption of my soul and for his money'.[253] The act of negotiating such a transaction was therefore beneficial even if it was not technically almsgiving in the most generous sense.

Leases are also interesting in this context, since unlike donations (even those which are both gift and sale), they are not so obviously a type of almsgiving, but they could nevertheless be spiritually valuable to the lessee. The usual practice was to lease the land for a number of 'lives', normally three; that is, the original lessee, and two further individuals, before the land returned to the leasing institution.[254] Leasing land from a monastery might be enough of a connection to have one's body buried there, a privilege which was perceived to be extremely valuable.[255] The rent paid on a lease might also be understood in the terms of gift exchange, and since some of the agreements resulted in large amounts of food or money being paid to the monastery, there may also have been a sense of almsgiving attached to these. Rents ranged from money, to food, to livestock: 20 mancuses of

---

[249]    Crick, 'Women, posthumous benefaction, and family strategy', 402–3; Crick, 'Posthumous obligation and family identity', 202–5.

[250]    McLaughlin, *Consorting*, 134–6.

[251]    Davies, 'When gift is sale'.

[252]    S 168 (BCS 335): 'Pro honore Dei omnipotentis ac pro expiatione piaculorum ejus. atque pro reverentissima dilectione Uulfredi archiepiscopi. seu etiam pro ejus larga pecuniarum remuneratione'.

[253]    S 194 (BCS 436): 'pro redemptione anime meae et pro ejus peccunia placabile'.

[254]    Crick, 'Women, posthumous benefaction, and family strategy', 413–15.

[255]    McLaughlin, *Consorting*, 155, 158; S. Hamilton, *The Practice of Penance, 900–1050* (Woodbridge, 2001), 98 and see below, 278–9.

gold,[256] 60 mancuses of gold;[257] two pounds of silver and livestock;[258] church-scot and the produce of one acre;[259] an annual food-render;[260] four pounds of silver and an annual food-render;[261] for 1,000 shillings and a night's hospitality every year;[262] and one lease was given in exchange for the lease of a larger piece of land, which would then revert to the bishopric.[263] The will of Ealdorman Æthelwold of Wessex, made probably in 946 or 947, asks that a distribution of the property that he held on lease be made for the good of his soul, showing that even non-alienable property could be valuable for almsgiving.[264]

Saints also appear in the sanction clauses of leases, suggesting another way in which these transactions may have been spiritually beneficial. A considerable number of leases survive from Worcester, many of which were issued by St Oswald, Bishop of Worcester (d.992).[265] Those made by Oswald in the tenth century sometimes contain a statement invoking the protection of St Mary, St Michael and St Peter, which relates to the churches in the cathedral precinct in Worcester at the time.[266] The tenants of Bishop Oswald were therefore in a sense also the tenants of St Mary, St Michael and St Peter, to whom the churches were dedicated and to whom the land properly belonged. In the eleventh century, St Oswald and St Mary are invoked in the sanction clause of a grant made by Leofric and his wife Godgifu to the refectory of St Mary's, Worcester, suggesting that eleventh-century tenants, like their tenth-century predecessors, may also have been viewed as tenants of St Oswald.[267] The continuity of the relationships between the living and the dead which were encouraged by religious communities thus also enabled continuity of patronage and protection.

In the case of the leases of St Oswald, Vanessa King observes that although most of the leases are to laymen, the lay tenants seem to have been a small group of individuals linked personally to the bishop: one Eadric leased six times from Oswald, for example.[268] Of the 78 leases made by St Oswald, 45 record the names

---

[256]    S 1278 (AD 872).

[257]    S 660 (AD 959).

[258]    S 1362 (AD 990).

[259]    S 1354 (AD 987).

[260]    S 385 (c. AD 909).

[261]    S 1465 (AD 1032 or 1035).

[262]    S 1412 (AD 786 x 796).

[263]    S 1355 (AD 988).

[264]    S 1504.

[265]    For discussion of these, see V. King, 'St Oswald's Tenants', in N. Brooks and C. Cubitt (eds), *St Oswald of Worcester: Life and Influence* (London, 1996), 100–16.

[266]    e.g. S 1312; J. Barrow, 'The Community of Worcester, 961–c.1100', in Brooks and Cubitt (eds), *St Oswald of Worcester*, 84–99, at 89–90.

[267]    S 1232.

[268]    King, 'Oswald's Tenants', 103; 'Eadric 21', *Prosopography of Anglo-Saxon England*, http://www.pase.ac.uk, accessed October 2012. See also A. Wareham, 'St

of those who subsequently received the lease after the death of the original lessee,[269] but many of these individuals are mentioned only once, with no indication of their relationship to the lessee, or to Oswald. King suggests that bishops may have leased land to family and close retainers because of potential problems with recovering land at the end of the third life, when the lease expired.[270] However, it is clear that relationships with the institution rather than with the individual figure of the bishop were also maintained: there were leases to tenants in St Oswald's time who leased land under Cenwald, the previous bishop.[271] And it was possible, if both parties wished, for the lease to be renewed, ensuring that the relationship between family and institution was maintained.[272] A trace of the renewal of a lease is found in the record that Tova, widow of Wihtric gave three gold marks to the abbot of St Albans, probably in around 1050, to ensure the lifetime use of an estate for herself and her son, after which time it would revert to the abbey.[273] This suggests that on a lessee's death the new lessee might also come into contact with the religious community, whether or not this was always recorded formally.

Since the lease was for 'lives', rather than for a fixed period of years, it would logically have been in the interests of the lessee, if he wished to keep the land in his family for as long as possible, to pass the lease on to the youngest member of his family, who in turn at his death could also pass it to the youngest member. In many cases it is difficult to establish the relationships (and the ages) of the subsequent heirs to the lease, and so generalisation about practices is difficult, since arrangements must have varied hugely according to individual circumstances, and the policies of different institutions may have affected the forms of documents and the types of individuals to whom land was leased. But from across the period and from different houses, where the names of the subsequent heirs are included in the original lease, they seem to be most often the wives, siblings and children of the original lessee.[274] This means that although a lease might be for three lives, it would normally last for only one or two generations, so the connection made with a monastery by leasing was not as long-lasting as might be imagined (although the possibility of renewal might extend this connection). Leases were made, for example, to couples;[275] to brothers;[276] to a father and child;[277] to a man

---

Oswald's Family and Kin', in Brooks and Cubitt (eds), *St Oswald of Worcester*, 46–63.

[269]    King, 'Oswald's Tenants', 102.

[270]    Ibid., 110.

[271]    S 1325, 1336, 1343; King, 'Oswald's Tenants', 104.

[272]    e.g. S 1287, from Winchester.

[273]    S 1425 (*StAlb*, no. 15); Crick, 'Women, posthumous benefaction, and family strategy', 414.

[274]    Crick, 'Women, posthumous benefaction, and family strategy', 415.

[275]    Æthelwulf and his wife, Wulfthryth, S 1273; Wulfmær and his wife, S 1420; Cuthred and his wife Wulfthryth and one person of their choice, S 1275.

[276]    e.g. Beornheah and Beorhstan, S 1363.

[277]    e.g. Æthelweard and his daughter, Eadgifu, S 1319.

and his mother.[278] A more complex arrangement is seen in the lease by Oswald to his brother, Oswulf, which was to revert to his wife (Eadleofu) if there were no surviving children, and then to two of her brothers.[279] This may indicate that the lease had originally been granted to her family, rather than Oswulf's.[280] Even in this case, Oswulf does not ask that the lease pass to a child and then a grandchild, and so its scope is limited to only two generations.

This limit on the number of generations included in the lease is comparable to the patterns found in wills and charters: donations made on behalf of the souls of others only rarely refer back as far as the grandparental generation, and are usually restricted to parents.[281] In 1002, King Æthelred donated land to Abbess Heanflæd and Wherwell abbey for the remedy of the souls of his father, Edgar, and his mother, Ælfthryth;[282] the grant made by King Edmund in 940 for the soul of his father, Æthelstan, has already been mentioned.[283] The will of Wulfgar, probably written between 933 and 939, shows him bequeathing land to his wife, Æffe, with a quarter of the crops to go to the monks at Kintbury for the souls of his father and grandfather;[284] the ætheling Æthelstan, when he drew up his will in 1014, bequeathed land for the soul of his father Æthelred (who was still alive at the time), and for the soul of his grandmother Ælfthryth (who wasn't).[285] Land was also granted or bequeathed for the souls of the family in general, the ancestors: in 1062, King Edward the Confessor granted land for his memory, his wife Edith's, his father's and mother's, and all, both dead and alive, who were joined to them by blood;[286] and elsewhere more simply for the health of his soul and for his ancestors;[287] in the late eighth century, Headda granted land to his descendants, ultimately reverting to Worcester, for the health of his soul and of the soul of his kinsman, Haðeredi, along with all the members of his family.[288]

And as in leases, grants or bequests which look forward likewise do not usually look beyond the children or possibly the grandchildren.[289] In some cases this is clearly because they have not yet been born, but the documents do not usually name future generations *in potentia*, nor allude to any expectation that such future generations will exist. Ælfgifu's will makes provision for her sister and two

---

[278]   Ælfwald and his mother, S 1298.

[279]   S 1326.

[280]   King, 'Oswald's Tenants', 108.

[281]   See also Crick, 'Women, posthumous benefaction, and family strategy'; Crick, 'Posthumous Obligation and Family Identity'.

[282]   S 904.

[283]   See above, 228, 242; S 470.

[284]   S 1533.

[285]   S 1533.

[286]   S 1036.

[287]   S 1036, (K 774); 'pro meae animae salute et parentum meorum'.

[288]   S 1413.

[289]   See also Crick, 'Posthumous Obligation and Family Identity', 201.

individuals who appear to be her brothers, but is apparently unconcerned for any children they may have, since the land is to pass to the Old Minster for her soul after their deaths; similarly, she asks for intercession for her mother but is apparently unconcerned about her family stretching further back.[290] Ælfgar, disposing of his property, only once allocates a piece of land to continue through his family line to his children's children: more often, he arranged for land to pass from sister to sister and then to a monastery, rather than to their children.[291] Since neither of his daughters seems to have had children, this may have been a wise decision, as it meant that he retained control over the property even after death, and ensured that it was given as almsgiving for his soul. However, it also illustrates an apparent lack of concern for provision for his family line, in the same way as do the leases which provide for a man's wife and child, but no further than that. Even more so does the document recording that Brihtmær made an agreement with Archbishop Stigand and the community of Christ Church, Canterbury (probably in the mid eleventh century) that after the death of his wife, Eadgifu, and his children, Eadmær and Æthelwine, the homestead where he lives and the church there would be given to the community for the redemption of their souls.[292] Brihtmær's children were clearly already born, since they were named, but he was still prepared to give away a family home, knowing that his children's children would not own it.

Naturally it is not the case that there was no concern at all that property should remain in the family, but the documents which record grants and bequests are silent on this issue much more frequently than they mention it. This is at least partly because other land would have been automatically inherited through the family, and so these records tend to mention only land which could be bequeathed freely by the testator.[293] Perpetual inheritance of land by kin is specified very rarely but did happen, as for example in the mid eleventh-century will of Eadwine of Caddington, who stated that the various property which is to be made over to nephews in the case of his son's misfortune is to remain forever in the family, passing through the male line.[294] There are a few recorded instances of other sorts of arrangements: in the ninth century, Alfred, who donated to Canterbury the gospel-books which he had rescued from the Vikings, bequeathed land to his wife and then to his children but stated that if there were no children, his paternal kinsmen were to be allowed to buy it at half-price.[295] And efforts were certainly made to ensure that leased land was passed through kin, as in the case of a lease made by Oswald to Gardulf, a kinsman, but who seems to have been kin

[290]   S 1484; 'Ælfgifu 4' bequeathed land to 'Ælfweard 12', 'Æthelweard 25' and 'Ælfwaru 2', *Prosopography of Anglo-Saxon England*.

[291]   S 1483.

[292]   S 1234.

[293]   S. Keynes, 'A lost cartulary of St Albans Abbey', *Anglo-Saxon England* 22 (1993): 253–79, at 277–8.

[294]   S 1517.

[295]   S 1508.

by marriage: the lease was to be inherited through Leofflæd, Gardulf's wife, rather than by Gardulf's own kin.[296] This seems also to be the case in one of Oswald's leases to his brother, Oswulf, already discussed above.[297] Since land transferred by 'book' was alienable, it may only rarely have been considered necessary to mention in written documents that alienation was possible; instead, it is where the grantor wishes that something else should occur, such as reversion to a monastery, that this must be specified.

It seems that Anglo-Saxon landowners were not uninterested in future generations, but as with past generations, these future heirs simply did not impinge greatly on their consciousness. Anthropological scholarship has frequently assumed that familial memory extends beyond the grandparental generation to a common ancestry, but recent ethnographic work by has demonstrated that this is not always the case: for example, when individuals in a twentieth-century Greek community in Methana (a peninsula in the Peloponnese) were questioned as to their family background, they could frequently remember back to their grandparents but no further.[298] In this community, individuals could recognise relationships between members of the family who were dependent on common ancestors prior to grandparents, such as second cousins (descended from shared great-grandparents), even when they had no information about the identity of the common ancestor, not even the name.[299] Other ancient societies also seem to have had a 'limit' of three generations of familial awareness, but comparison with the Methana community is interesting because in this context as in Anglo-Saxon England, it was important for individuals to know those people to whom they were related, and in which degree of consanguinity, in order to abide by the (quite complex) regulations about marriage. Crucially, it was relationships between individuals, and not the identity of the common ancestors, which were important in both cases.[300]

In Anglo-Saxon England, kinship seems to have been strongly bilateral: that is, men and women had strong ties both to their paternal and to their maternal

---

[296]   S 1345; King, 'Oswald's Tenants', 110; Wareham, 'St Oswald's family and kin'.

[297]   S 1326.

[298]   H.A. Forbes, *Meaning and Identity in a Greek landscape: An Archaeological Ethnography* (New York, 2007), 134–41.

[299]   Forbes, *Meaning and Identity*, 135.

[300]   See for example R.P. Saller and B.D. Shaw, 'Tombstones and Roman family relations in the principate: Civilians, soldiers and slaves', *The Journal of Roman Studies* 74 (1984): 124–56, at 133–5; L. Foxhall, 'Monumental Ambitions: The Significance of Posterity in Ancient Greece', in N. Spencer (ed.), *Time, Tradition, and Society in Greek Archaeology: Bridging the 'Great Divide'* (London, 1995), 132–49; see also M.G. Peletz, 'Kinship studies in late twentieth-century anthropology', *Annual Review of Anthropology* 24 (1995): 343–72, at 350–1; D.W. Read, 'Kinship Theory: A Paradigm Shift', *Ethnology* 46–4 (2007): 329–64.

families, and married women retained a strong connection to their natal family.[301] This has a number of implications which are significant for understanding how people conceptualised their families, and how they considered the familial religious duties and obligations – both for whom they should make offerings, and who would make offerings on their behalf. The importance of connections to both maternal and paternal lines meant that very rapidly, the number of relatives (e.g. cousins and first cousins) would become so large that it would have been incredibly difficult to keep track of them, which probably explains why information about ancestors beyond the grandparental generation is lacking in most cases. Bilateral kin groupings also meant that any one person would not necessarily have the same kin connections as another even if they were quite close relatives, for example first cousins or even sisters: the links to Stoke from Ælfflæd's natal family are shared with her sister Æthelflæd, but Ælfflæd's links to Ely through her husband Byrhtnoth were not.[302]

Those who donated land in the Anglo-Saxon period were noble and often must have married within relatively small social circles, but unless they were royal or closely connected with the royal line, it seems unlikely that extensive information about lineage and patronage was kept orally or in writing on a regular basis. There is evidence that some records were kept orally, and clearly this could be an important part of family history, but only in rare cases did information extend back further than a few generations.[303] The *Chronicle of Æthelweard*, written in response to a request from his cousin Matilda in Essen, indicates that Matilda could identify her cousin but herself had little information about other ancestors.[304] Æthelweard's closeness to the royal court and his proximity to other surviving members of the family presumably gave him access to more information, since he traces the family over six generations and incorporated the written traditions of the *Anglo-Saxon Chronicle*, but it is clear from this case and others that even those of noble birth could quickly lose track of their origins or relatives: Æthelweard himself admitted that he had no information about some of the women who were married off to husbands abroad.[305]

In contrast, to return briefly to early medieval France once again, Dhuoda gave her son William a list of people for whom he should pray which extended back no further than his grandfather, and which included both men and women

---

[301]    J. Goody, *The Development of the Family and Marriage in Europe* (Cambridge, 1983), 18–19; Wareham, 'The transformation of kinship and the family in late Anglo-Saxon England', 375: Wareham argues for a change towards the end of the period towards agnatic kinship (i.e. patrilinear).

[302]    See above, 252–3; S 1486.

[303]    E.M.C. van Houts, *Memory and Gender in Medieval Europe, 900–1200*, Explorations in Medieval Culture and Society (Basingstoke, 1999), 65–92.

[304]    *Prologue*, ed. A. Campbell, *The Chronicle of Æthelweard* (London, 1962), 1–2.

[305]    *Prologue*, ed. A. Campbell, *The Chronicle of Æthelweard* (London, 1962), 1–2; van Houts, *Memory and Gender in Medieval Europe, 900–1200*, 69–70, 79–80.

although they seem to have been mainly connected with his father's line.[306] Medieval historians and chroniclers themselves seem to have considered that three generations, or 100 years, was about the maximum length of time for which oral testimony could be considered valid.[307] The comparatively limited duration of family awareness or 'memory' is perhaps at least partly the reason that Anglo-Saxon donors did not name ancestors earlier than their grandparents. The children to whom land was bequeathed could provide for their own grandchildren, or their own souls, if the land was freely alienable: but that was their responsibility, and not the responsibility of their parents. On the other hand, past and future relatives were part of a network of relationships which tied together the living and the dead, religious communities and the saints they served, and also individuals with whom other sorts of relationships had been established. A number of documents mention the obligations laid by donors on future owners of lands, whether or not they were directly related: often these were in the form of yearly payments or food-rents, such as the food-rent which was to be paid for the souls of Ealdred and Ealhburg by whomever held the land which they had granted.[308]

Individuals were also tied together through the offering of prayers, as in the case of Theodred, bishop of London, who recorded in his will (942 x c.951) his intention to distribute property for his soul and for his ancestors' souls, but also for the souls of the men for whom he intercedes, for the souls of those from whom he has received alms, and for those for whom he ought to pray.[309] A prayer from Ælfwine's prayer book reveals how widely the ties of obligation might extend, asking for the forgiveness of sins of all of God's monastic servants (male and female), and for 'our' brothers and sisters and parents (perhaps also meaning ancestors more generally) and friends, for all those (male and female) whose bodies lie in the cemeteries, and finally for all those from whom alms have been received.[310] The 'friends' in this prayer may genuinely be personal, since other instances of this prayer ask forgiveness only for the monastic *familia*, and not for family, friends and benefactors: given the sense of personality that is revealed in this prayer book, and that it seems to have been produced specifically for Ælfwine, it is not impossible that these additions were Ælfwine's own.[311]

In the context of communities in which the living and the dead were tied together, and in which the living had a familial awareness which was relatively limited in its time-depth, religious foundations played a crucial part in memorialising the dead.

---

[306]    Dhuoda, *Liber Manualis*, 10.5, ed. Thiébaux, *Dhuoda, Handbook for her Warrior Son: Liber Manualis*, 226–7 and discussion of the individuals for whom prayer was requested at 272–3, n. 23.

[307]    van Houts, *Memory and Gender in Medieval Europe, 900–1200*, 36–7.

[308]    S 1190 (*CantStA*, no. 4).

[309]    S 1526.

[310]    Cotton Titus D.xvi, fols. 64r–v, ed. Günzel, *Ælfwine's Prayerbook*, 76.39.

[311]    See Bodley 579, fols. 244r, 263r–v, ed. Orchard, *Leofric Missal*, nos. 2184, 2280; and Günzel, *Ælfwine's Prayerbook*, 2–3.

They offered perpetual commemoration and played a role in recording the people who participated in these communities, even seeking justice on behalf of the dead from whom land or intercession had been stolen. *Libri memoriales*, like the lands donated to religious houses, were intended to be used in perpetuity. This meant that individuals could ensure that their memory did not disappear within two or three generations, and that commemoration, even if general and collective rather than personal, would continue. Some charters ask specifically for the memory of the donors to be kept alive, and even more note the enduring nature of the written word as a motive for recording the donation in writing.[312] It is precisely this which made commemoration in religious communities so attractive: communities and the saints they served outlived the individuals and even the families with whom relationships were established, and could guarantee continual remembrance and offerings on their behalf in a way that families could not.[313]

The spiritual obligation of religious houses to those who bestowed gifts upon them continued at least as long as the communities continued to hold and use the gifts, repaid primarily by liturgical celebrations and commemoration: the services provided by religious communities went beyond what could be offered by families themselves, even if familial ties and obligations were important in securing them. But the sense of family, or more properly, 'familiarity', was still significant and still remained, in that the confraternal relationship brought individuals into the folds of the monastic family. As McLaughlin notes, in many cases the greatest desire of the men and women who associated themselves with religious houses was that they should be treated as a brother or a sister, and that the community could be relied on to look out for them as a family member.[314] By offering prayers and masses for their *familiores* as for the members of the *familia* proper, religious communities ensured that departed members did not languish in purgatorial suffering in the beyond.

## Conclusion

The names of the men and women in the memorial books of early medieval English religious houses are a testament to the strong desire for commemoration by, and incorporation into the liturgical life of, communities which offered continual prayer for their souls. The offerings which were so carefully planned by individuals during their lifetimes attest clearly to the perceived need to prepare as far as possible for the fate of the soul after death; and those which were made by relatives, friends and confratres on behalf of those who had died indicate accepted obligations to the dead and concern over the fate of the soul. At least in part, this

---

[312]   Foot, 'Reading Anglo-Saxon Charters: Memory, Record, or Story?', 47; see for example S 13, S 367a, S 1034, S 1280.

[313]   Wollasch, 'Toten- und Armensorge', 18–19.

[314]   McLaughlin, *Consorting*, 89–90, 157–60, 177.

is a response to the sentiments which underlie the repeated exhortations of the homilists, who were always looking to the afterlife, and paradoxically, the absence of extended discussion of the interim may in fact indicate how far it was taken for granted: certainly the occasional references which are scattered throughout Anglo-Saxon texts suggest that the purgatorial interim as a destination for the souls of the 'ordinary' dead was very widely accepted. Vision literature and anecdotal stories may also have helped to reinforce the power of almsgiving and especially liturgical commemoration – linked in any case, since arrangements for the mass were often arranged through almsgiving – as the primary way of aiding those who had passed from this world to the next.

Such offerings ensured also that the memory of departed individuals did not fade, which was crucial in guaranteeing the perpetual commemoration which was so important for the soul, in the absence of more certain knowledge of any individual's fate. But the requests for these memorials also served to establish the links with religious and especially monastic institutions that many laity evidently so desired. Particularly in cases where more formal links of confraternity were created, there was an institutional obligation towards the dead which was comparable to familial duty. Anniversary celebrations and other more personal commemoration such as votive masses might have added an individualised aspect to the memorial of the dead, but even if commemoration were general, the association with a religious house resulted in the incorporation of the benefactor – whether living or dead – into the community's liturgical life. It is naturally only those at the higher end of society who had the means to make such donations, but it is significant all the same that the value of almsgiving for the soul, or for the souls of relatives, friends and ancestors, was understood so clearly by this section of the lay population, and not confined to those in religious life. Given the processes which must have taken place before the grant was recorded in writing, it seems likely that there was further opportunity for those in religious life to impress upon potential benefactors the spiritual effects of their donations as their souls waited to be received into the communion of saints. The language of the charters suggests that the spiritual benefit was at the forefront of the minds of those on both sides who were involved in such transactions, and the desire of benefactors to have prayers said on their behalf in perpetuity, or to foster a connection which would entitle them to special privileges at their deaths, indicates that this was an extremely significant consideration.

The association with religious and especially monastic communities is particularly important given that it is from these institutions that many of the texts discussing the afterlife and interim were propagated and disseminated. It is difficult to determine how far down the social and religious scale such ideas were clearly understood, but the accumulated evidence suggests that these beliefs were not utterly confined to aristocratic and monastic circles. Moreover, the power of conventions and aspirations to drive social practice must have been significant in ensuring that people were actively interested in establishing relationships with religious communities, allowing further opportunity for clarification of their spiritual reasons and benefits. While those further down the social hierarchy might not have made donations which left their imprint in writing, it seems unlikely that they did not understand the reasons that donations and prayers were important. The fact that the guilds sought to arrange for prayer for the dead collectively, most likely because their members could not afford the more elaborate and personal arrangements made by the highest levels of the aristocracy, is a clear indicator of the high value of this prayer. The promise of a share in the company of saints, achieved by inclusion in a *liber memorialis* or by association with a religious community, was evidently also valuable. Family memory would fade, and friends and relatives would join their loved ones beyond the grave and so be unable to make offerings on their behalf, but the communities which offered continual praise to God and which kept memories alive in their masses and prayers ensured that their names would not be wiped out of the book of life, but inscribed with the just. Even if these souls were temporarily delayed in the interim while their sins were washed away, they would ultimately find a place with the elect who stand at Christ's right hand, and join the communion of saints.

# Chapter 5

# The Resurrection of the Body and the Life Everlasting

The land is given to the minster on these terms: that at our end-day someone will fetch us with the minster's resources and provide for us a burial place such as is necessary for us before God, and appropriate before the world.[1]

## Introduction

At the moment of death, the person who once kept the company of the living becomes instead body and soul: the two distinct entities that were once united to make up a living, breathing individual are unentangled and unentwined so that the body is inanimate, and lifeless. While the immortal and invisible soul begins its journey in the next world, the mortal and visible body remains behind on earth until after the Last Judgement, when the bodies of all humankind will be resurrected and reunited with their souls, in preparation for eternal life in heaven or eternal torment in hell. Patristic writers had explored whether the treatment of the body after death might have theological implications for the soul, and one example given was that of the martyrs, whose bodies had been disfigured and sometimes destroyed, but whose souls were generally accepted to have reached heaven immediately. Here one of the most influential authors was Augustine of Hippo (d.430), who concluded that the treatment of the body did not in itself affect the fate of the soul in the world to come.[2] Augustine's was not the only opinion though, and it is quite clear both from surviving texts and from the archaeological record that there was deep concern over the treatment of the body in death and about the place of burial, throughout the early Middle Ages just as also beforehand and afterwards. The passage from the grant of land quoted above, made in the tenth century by Ordnoth and his wife to the Old Minster, Winchester, illustrates precisely this concern, and emphasises the importance of burial place both according to what was required before God, and what was appropriate in the context of worldly society. This highlights how far practices which were both driven and justified by theological considerations were tied up with social context.

---

[1]   S 1524 (K 943): 'on ða gereðnesse is þæt land geseld to þam mynstre þæt man unc gefecce. æt uncrum ændedege mid þes mynstres crafte ꝺ unc swylce legerstowe forescewian swylc unc for gode þearflice sy. ꝺ for weorulde gerysenlic'.

[2]   See C.W. Bynum, *The Resurrection of the Body in Western Christianity, 200–1336*, Lectures on the History of Religions (New York, 1995), 94–114.

While the surviving written record contains the clearest articulation of belief, archaeological remains shed the most light on the variety of practice through which belief was played out. This tension between textual and material evidence means that it is sometimes difficult to understand precisely why certain rites, places, or other features of burials were used, desired or rejected. Textual evidence about burials in Anglo-Saxon England tends to ignore the mundane, focusing only on burials which were exceptional (in both good and bad senses); or it may be normative, and therefore illustrate what ought to have happened but provide no confirmation that it did happen, or that it usually happened in quite the way outlined in the texts. In contrast, archaeological evidence provides information about burials which actually happened, but is notoriously difficult to interpret. One of the problems with burial evidence is that it is not always easy to determine whether it represents the wishes of the buriers or the person whose body lies in the grave, or to what extent a combination of the two; but there is also significant variation in burials across the period, and it is extremely difficult to know how to interpret some practices, especially when they occur in Christian contexts but do not appear to be closely matchable to any surviving information about Christian belief as it is articulated in the surviving texts.[3] On the other hand, material remains can provide information which corroborates, expands or complicates normative textual evidence, as (for example) recent work on execution cemeteries has shown.[4]

The practice of burial *ad sanctos* is one example of an enduring belief which is discussed in the surviving textual sources, and which is also clearly visible in the archaeological record. From an early period in Christian history, it was widely believed that burial near to the bodily remains of the saints (especially the martyrs) would be valuable to the soul of the deceased.[5] Early medieval English examples of this practice include the clustering of graves around the tomb of St Swithun in the cemetery at Winchester, and this is perhaps also how the cemetery at Nazeing (Essex) should be interpreted, where graves clustered around what may have been

---

[3]    M. Parker Pearson, *The Archaeology of Death and Burial* (Stroud, 1999), 3; S. Tarlow, *Bereavement and Commemoration: An Archaeology of Mortality*, Social Archaeology (Oxford, 1999), 2–4, 11–12.

[4]    e.g. A.J. Reynolds, *Anglo-Saxon Deviant Burial Customs* (Oxford, 2009); for the dialogue (or lack of it) between disciplines see also A. Woolf, 'A Dialogue of the Deaf and the Dumb: Archaeology, History and Philology', in Z. Devlin and C.N.J. Holas-Clark (eds), *Approaching Interdisciplinarity: Archaeology, History and the Study of Early Medieval Britain, c.400–1100* (Oxford, 2009), 3–9.

[5]    M. McLaughlin, *Consorting with Saints: Prayer for the Dead in Early Medieval France* (Ithaca, NY, 1994), 30–1; B. Effros, *Caring for Body and Soul: Burial and the Afterlife in the Merovingian World* (University Park, PA, 2002), 75–8. The practice was extremely long-lived: see for example J. Schmid, *Et pro remedio animae et pro memoria: bürgerliche repraesentatio in der Cappella Tornabuoni in S. Maria Novella*, I Mandorli 2 (Munich, 2002), 25.

the burials of the founders.[6] In the tenth and eleventh centuries, when burial was more closely controlled, ecclesiastical regulations discuss who might receive the privilege of being buried in a church: this suggests that there was some concern over who might be considered worthy to receive such a privilege, and points also to the continuing desire to be buried inside churches and close to saints' relics.[7] But establishing how exactly those who sought burial *ad sanctos* believed it would help them is rather more complex, and it should not be forgotten that the practice was connected with social status and display as well as the desire to provide for the soul in the afterlife.

In the early fifth century, Augustine had considered this issue in response to a letter from Paulinus, bishop of Nola (d.431), who had asked whether burial of the body at the tombs of saints was beneficial to the soul after death.[8] Augustine began his discussion by re-iterating his earlier statements on the importance of behaviour in this life for the fate of the soul after death, and emphasised that commemoration of and prayers for the dead affected souls according to how they had lived in life.[9] In considering the treatment of the body specifically, he concluded that the examples of the martyrs and the treatment of their bodies illustrate that nothing that is done to the body can harm the soul, and that care of the body, burial and obsequies are of more comfort to the living than they are of benefit to the dead.[10] Augustine did accept that the bodies of the Christian dead should not be despised, and he stated too that burying friends or relatives near the saints was a mark of affection – but therefore only an office of humanity, and not any kind of help for salvation.[11] He argued that the only benefit for the person buried was that in recalling the location of the body near to a saint, friends and

---

[6]    P.J. Huggins, 'Excavation of Belgic and Romano-British farm with Middle Saxon cemetery and churches at Nazeingbury, Essex, 1975–6', *Essex Archaeology and History* 10 (1978): 29–117, at 51; B. Kjølbye-Biddle, 'Dispersal or Concentration: The Disposal of the Winchester Dead over 2000 Years', in S.R. Bassett (ed.), *Death in Towns: Urban Responses to the Dying and the Dead, 100–1600* (Leicester, 1992), 210–47, at 223–4, 227–9.

[7]    See for example Wulfstan, *Canons of Edgar*, 29, ed. R. Fowler, *Wulfstan's 'Canons of Edgar'*, EETS, OS 266 (London, 1972), 8–9.

[8]    *De cura mortuis*, I.1, ed. J. Zycha, *Sancti Aureli Augustini, De fide et symbolo; De fide et operibus; De agone christiano; De continentia; De bono coniugali; De Sancta virginitate; De bono viduitatis; De adulterinis coniugiis lib. II; De mendacio; Contra mendacium; De opere monachorum; De divinatione daemonum; De cura pro mortuis gerenda; De patientia*, CSEL 41 (Vienna, 1900), 621–2.

[9]    *De cura mortuis*, I.2, ed. Zycha, *Sancti Aureli Augustini, De fide et symbolo, etc.*, 622–3; see also above, 206–11.

[10]    *De cura mortuis*, I.3–II.4, VI.8, ed. Zycha, *Sancti Aureli Augustini, De fide et symbolo, etc.*, 623–7, 633–4; see also *DCD*, XX.20, ll. 76–95, ed. B. Dombert and A. Kalb (eds), *Sancti Aurelii Augustini. De civitate dei*, CCSL 47–8 (2 vols Turnhout, 1955), II.735–6.

[11]    XVIII.22, ll. 19–21, ed. Zycha, *Sancti Aureli Augustini, De fide et symbolo, etc.*, 658: 'corpori autem humando quidquid inpenditur, non est praesidium salutis, sed humanitatis officium secundum affectum, quo nemo umquam carnem suam odio habet'.

relatives might offer prayers commending the person to that saint, who could then act as patron and help them by interceding for them with God; and he stressed too that this prayer and commendation could take place whether or not the person was buried near a saint, the saint's memorial being useful primarily for the jogging of human memory.[12] Augustine also stated clearly that it is prayer and supplication which helps the souls of the dead, and that without this, even burial of the body in holy places could not help the soul.[13]

Augustine's *De cura mortuis* seems to have had a relatively limited circulation in early medieval England, but the passages which explain that the final resting place of the body was ultimately unimportant in determining the fate of the soul were quoted by later writers, as in the *Prognosticon futuri saeculi* of Julian of Toledo (d.690), and were thus more widely available to Anglo-Saxon authors.[14] Moreover, Augustine incorporated a considerable portion of the *De cura mortuis* into his *De civitate dei*, which was very widely known, copied and cited: it was therefore available to Anglo-Saxon authors either directly, or indirectly through quotations in other authors.[15] The possibility of indirect knowledge is especially significant because even some very well-read authors may not have had direct access to the work: Ælfric, for example, seems not to have used *De civitate dei* as a source for his homilies, but the passages from it which are relevant here were quoted in the version of the *Liber officialis* of Amalarius of Metz which Ælfric knew and used.[16] More generally, Anglo-Saxon knowledge of Augustine's writings on this topic is important because there are comparatively few Anglo-Saxon theological discussions of how burial and the location or treatment of the body might or might not have affected the soul, even though archaeological and other textual evidence shows that this was clearly a topic of great significance. The occasional references that do exist confirm the influence of Augustinian theology, as for example in one of the tenth-century Blickling homilies, which

---

[12]   *De cura mortuis*, IIII.6, ed. Zycha, *Sancti Aureli Augustini, De fide et symbolo, etc.*, 629–31.

[13]   *De cura mortuis*, IIII.6, ed. Zycha, *Sancti Aureli Augustini, De fide et symbolo, etc.*, 631: 'si autem deessent istae supplicationes, quae fiunt recta fide ac pietate pro mortuis, puto, quod nihil prodesset spiritibus eorum, quamlibet locis sanctis exanima corpora ponerentur'.

[14]   Julian of Toledo, *Prognosticon futuri saeculi*, I.19–20, ed. J.N. Hillgarth, *Sancti Iuliani sedis episcopis opera*, CCSL (Turnhout, 1976), 36–8; M. Lapidge, *The Anglo-Saxon Library* (Oxford, 2006), 284, 317–18.

[15]   Lapidge, *Anglo-Saxon Library*, 284.

[16]   Amalarius, *Liber officialis*, IV.40.7–12, ed. J.M. Hanssens, *Amalarii episcopi opera liturgica omnia* (3 vols, Vatican City, 1948), II.533–4; M. Godden, *Ælfric's Catholic Homilies: Introduction, Commentary and Glossary*, EETS, SS 18 (Oxford, 2000), xlvii–xlviii; M. Clayton, 'Suicide in the works of Ælfric', *Review of English Studies* n.s. 60: 245 (2009): 339–70, at 343; see also above, 215–17.

warns that no one should think that the body can affect the sin-burden in the grave, where it will simply rot and await judgement.[17]

However, the relationship between body and soul is complex, and Augustine's writings were not the only discussion of the matter. Here a particularly important text is the *Dialogues* of Gregory the Great (d.604), which circulated widely in Latin and was also translated into English in the late ninth century by Wærferth, bishop of Worcester.[18] Peter the Deacon, Gregory's interlocutor in the *Dialogues*, asks directly whether burial in church should be considered of benefit to the souls of the dead, and Gregory explains that those who are not weighed down by heavy sins do indeed benefit from being buried in church, because their friends and relatives see the burial place and pray for them.[19] Although Gregory's response accords with Augustinian thought, it is framed in a way which is unambiguously positive about burial in church, without Augustine's complex and qualified discussion. Gregory also underlines more closely the continuing connection between body and soul after death: he explains that those who were burdened by heavy sins and who therefore did not deserve church-burial might incur worse condemnation as a result, giving a number of examples in support of this, such as that of an unworthy nun who was buried in a church.[20] The sacristan of the church had a vision in which he saw her led to the altar and cut in two before she was burned by fire, and Gregory notes that the floor in front of the altar was indeed found burned.[21] Gregory also gives two examples of bodies which were unworthily buried inside a church and subsequently evicted from their graves, one which simply vanished and the other which was dragged out by wicked spirits, and he warns that church-burial will not help the wicked but will add further to their condemnation.[22]

This emphasis on the continuing connection between body and soul is important because although both Augustine and Gregory emphasised that the burial place of a body did not in itself help the soul, Gregory's *exempla* in particular show a clear belief that the fate of the soul might be revealed in the body. This belief of course underpins the theology of the cults of saints, which held that the merits of those who were very holy, the 'very special dead', might be revealed through

---

[17]    *Hom.* X, ed. R. Morris, *The Blickling Homilies of the 10th Century: From the Marquis of Lothian's Unique MS. A.D.971*, EETS, OS 58 (London, 1874), 109.

[18]    See M. Godden, 'Wærferth and King Alfred: The Fate of the Old English *Dialogues*', in J.A. Roberts et al. (eds), *Alfred the Wise: Studies in Honour of Janet Bately on the Occasion of her Sixty-Fifth Birthday* (Cambridge, 1997), 35–51; D.F. Johnson, 'Why Ditch the Dialogues? Reclaiming an invisible text', in C.D. Wright, F.M. Biggs and T.N. Hall (eds), *Source of Wisdom* (Toronto, 2007), 201–16.

[19]    Gregory, *Dialogues*, IV.52, ll. 1–9, ed. A. de Vogüé and P. Antin, *Dialogues de Grégoire le Grand: Livre IV, texte critique et notes, Sources chrétiennes* (Paris, 1980), 176.

[20]    Gregory, *Dialogues*, IV.52–3.1, ed. de Vogüé and Antin, *Dialogues, Livre IV*, 176–8.

[21]    Gregory, *Dialogues*, IV.53.2–3, ed. de Vogüé and Antin, *Dialogues, Livre IV*, 178.

[22]    Gregory, *Dialogues*, IV.54–6, ed. de Vogüé and Antin, *Dialogues, Livre IV*, 178–84.

their bodies after they had died, or at the site of their burial.[23] While the souls of the saints went straight to heaven, their holiness was demonstrated by miracles enacted through their bodily remains, which sometimes also remained incorrupt, as (for example) did the body of Æthelthryth of Ely.[24] The stories in the *Dialogues* which present the fate of the wicked soul being enacted through the body show a logical development of the idea that the continuing connection between body and soul might be visible in the body, even if the location or treatment of the body itself did not affect the soul. In some cases, the site of burial itself might also be affected by the soul's punishment: Gregory gives the example of a courtier who had committed a wicked sin, and whose grave was consumed by fire and sank several inches into the ground. According to Gregory, this demonstrated the punishment which the man's soul faced in the afterlife, visibly revealed on the body which was buried in the earth.[25]

Both Augustine and Gregory stressed that prayers and offerings for the dead, especially the mass, were the most significant ways that departed souls could be helped; and both argued that this was only possible in any case if those souls deserved this help through their actions in life.[26] Augustine reports that his mother told her sons that she did not care where her body was buried, and asked only to be remembered at the altar, in the mass,[27] while in the *Dialogues* there are a number of *exempla* demonstrating the power of the mass to release departed souls from suffering.[28] As the previous chapter has shown, the documents from Anglo-Saxon England which record requests for prayers and especially masses after death indicate that providing for the soul in the afterlife was a significant concern in England in the early Middle Ages as it was elsewhere in Europe and as it had been in the Mediterranean in late antiquity. But the evidence both of written sources and of material culture also attests to concerns about arrangements for

---

[23]    P. Brown, *The Cult of the Saints: Its Rise and Function in Latin Christianity* (Chicago, 1981), 69–85; see also M. Dal Santo, 'Philosophy, Hagiology and the Early Byzantine Origins of Purgatory', in P.D. Clarke and T. Claydon (eds), *The Church, the Afterlife, and the Fate of the Soul* (Woodbridge, 2009), 41–51; and Bynum, *The Resurrection of the Body in Western Christianity*.

[24]    Bede, *HE*, IV.17, ed. M. Lapidge, P. Monat and P. Robin, *Histoire ecclésiastique du peuple anglais = Historia ecclesiastica gentis Anglorum, Sources chrétiennes* 489–91 (3 vols Paris, 2005), II.292–302.

[25]    Gregory, *Dialogues*, IV.33, ed. de Vogüé and Antin, *Dialogues, Livre IV*, 108–12.

[26]    Augustine *De cura mortuis*, I.2, ed. Zycha, *Sancti Aureli Augustini, De fide et symbolo, etc.*, 622–3; *DCD*, XXI.26, ed. Dombert and Kalb, *De civitate dei*, II.796–9; *Enchiridion*, XXIX.110, ll. 24–9, ed. E. Evans, *Aurelii Augustini Opera Pars XIII, 2*, CCSL 46 (Turnhout, 1969), 108–9; Gregory, *Dialogues*, IV.59.6, ed. de Vogüé and Antin, *Dialogues, Livre IV*, 198–200.

[27]    *Confessiones*, IX.xi.27, ed. L. Verheijen, *Sancti Augustini Confessionum Libri XIII*, CCSL 27 (Turnhout, 1981), 149.

[28]    *Dialogues*, IV.57–9, ed. de Vogüé and Antin, *Dialogues, Livre IV*, 184–200.

burial, especially how, where and by whom the body would be laid to rest. These are not entirely disentangleable from concern over offerings for the soul, since the place and arrangements for burial might also be connected with commemoration. Anglo-Saxon evidence gives the impression that despite the considerable influence of Augustine and Gregory on the theology of the afterlife, the rejection of the importance of the place of burial by Augustine in particular was either not accepted or not understood, even though his insistent assertion that the state of the soul at death was the only significant factor in salvation was repeated frequently, especially by the later Anglo-Saxon homilists.[29]

Concern for the body and for the resting places of the dead is found frequently in Anglo-Saxon narrative sources: with the possible exception of those who were martyred, the bodies of saints are almost always described as being treated with great reverence, and buried in places of honour, and the bodies of some nobles too seem to have received similar treatment.[30] Although they may not have enjoyed such elaborate rites, rituals or resting places, the archaeological evidence suggests that the bodies of the ordinary dead who were buried in churchyard cemeteries were usually placed in the ground with some care, and some of the practices visible in the grave seem to have been connected with the careful presentation of the body, or to support it, such as the placement of stones under or around the head.[31] The idea of quiet and peace recurs frequently, appearing in funerary liturgies and in the rites for the consecration of cemeteries as well as in narrative texts: in the early twelfth century, William of Malmesbury (d. in or after 1142) recorded that in the time of Dunstan (d.988) the cemetery at Glastonbury was enclosed so that there was no sound of footsteps, and the bodies of the saints resting there were buried in peace.[32] The sought-for peace and

---

[29]    e.g. Alcuin, *Epistola* 295, ed. E.L. Dümmler, *Epistolae Karolini aevi*, MGH, Epistolae Karolini aevi II (Berlin, 1895), 453; Ælfric, *Lives of Saints*, XII, ll. 152–77, ed. W.W. Skeat, *Aelfric's Lives of Saints, Being a Set of Sermons on Saints' Days Formerly Observed by the English Church*, EETS 76, 82 (vol. 1), 94, 114 (vol. 2) (4 vols in 2, London, 1881–1900), I.272–4.

[30]    e.g. Stephen of Ripon, *Vita S. Wilfridi*, lxvi, ed. B. Colgrave, *The Life of Bishop Wilfrid by Eddius Stephanus* (Cambridge, 1985 [orig. pub. 1927]), 142–4; Wulfstan of Winchester, *Vita S. Æthelwoldi*, 41–3, ed. M. Lapidge and M. Winterbottom, *Wulfstan of Winchester: The Life of St Æthelwold* (Oxford, 1991), 62–6; and the description of the funeral of Ealdorman Æthelwine, in *Vita S. Oswaldi*, 21, ed. and trans. M. Lapidge, *The Lives of St Oswald and St Ecgwine* (Oxford, 2009), 198–201.

[31]    V. Thompson, *Dying and Death in Later Anglo-Saxon England* (Woodbridge, 2004), 122–6; D.M. Hadley and J. Buckberry, 'Caring for the Dead in late Anglo-Saxon England', in F. Tinti (ed.), *Pastoral Care in Late Anglo-Saxon England*, Anglo-Saxon Studies 6 (Woodbridge, 2005), 121–47; see also for example the cemetery at Raunds Furnells (Northants), A. Boddington, G. Cadman and J. Evans, *Raunds Furnells: The Anglo-Saxon Church and Churchyard* (London, 1996).

[32]    William of Malmesbury, *Vita S. Dunstani*, i.16.2, ed. M. Winterbottom and R.M. Thomson, *William of Malmesbury: Saints' Lives. Lives of SS. Wulfstan, Dunstan, Patrick, Benignus and Indract* (Oxford, 2002), 204–6; see also (for example) Paris, Bibliothèque

quiet may not always have been a reality though, since William also recorded that St Wulfstan of Worcester (d.1095) apparently tried to prevent people riding horses through cemeteries, saying that 'reverence is due to the many bodies of the saints who lie there, whose souls are with God'.[33] The possible evidence for paths in some excavated cemeteries, as at Nazeing, suggests too that people wanted to walk around, rather than over, the bodies of the dead, whether to visit the graves or simply to pass through the cemeteries.[34]

In contrast, the 'dishonourable' treatment of bodies is clear from the archaeological evidence of cemeteries in which offenders were interred, where heads and bodies may be buried separately, bodies might be thrown rather than placed into the grave, or multiple bodies might be put in one grave.[35] While this might apply to those who were executed according to the law, shameful treatment of the body is also recorded as a means of humiliation or vengeance, such as the report that Harthacnut had the body of his half-brother Harold dug up and thrown into a fen.[36] The importance of careful burial of the whole body is also visible in William of Malmesbury's description of Dunstan's unintentional 'curse' of a man named Ælfwold: irritated by the man, Dunstan is supposed to have said 'let foxes eat him'.[37] After he died, when his body was being carried to Glastonbury, foxes duly appeared, prompting the bearers of the corpse to set down the body and chase them away, but the foxes returned and ate the body so that there was little left: William warns darkly that this was 'a terrifying judgement of God, that a man who had provoked the benign Mother of God should leave little or nothing for the earth to receive to its tranquil bosom'.[38]

---

nationale, Lat. 10575 (s. x2 or AD *c.*1000, Sherborne or west country,'Egbert Pontifical'), fols. 75v–76r, ed. H.M.J. Banting, *Two Anglo-Saxon Pontificals (the Egbert and Sidney Sussex Pontificals)*, HBS 104 (London, 1989), 59: 'Omnipotens sempiternę deus annue quesumus precibus nostris ea que poscimus. et dona omnibus quorum hic corpora requiescunt refrigerii sedem quietis beatitudinem luminis claritatem ut qui peccatorum suorum pondere pregrauantur eos supplicatio commendet aeclesie'.

[33]   William of Malmesbury, *Vita S. Wulfstani*, iii.11.1, ed. Winterbottom and Thomson, *William of Malmesbury: Saints' Lives*, 124: 'Multa ibi sanctorum iacere corpora, quorum animabus quae apud Deum sunt debeatur reuerentia'.

[34]   Huggins, 'Excavation of Belgic and Romano-British farm', 51.

[35]   See for example J.L. Buckberry and D.M. Hadley, 'An Anglo-Saxon execution cemetery at Walkington Wold, Yorkshire', *Oxford Journal of Archaeology* 26:3 (2007): 309–29; Reynolds, *Anglo-Saxon Deviant Burial Customs*, 34–60.

[36]   *ASC* (CD), *s.a.* 1040, ed. K.O'B. O'Keeffe, *The Anglo-Saxon Chronicle: A Collaborative Edition: Vol. 5, MS C: A Semi-Diplomatic Edition with Introduction and Indices* (Cambridge, 2001), 107; and G.P. Cubbin (ed.), *The Anglo-Saxon Chronicle: A Collaborative Edition: Vol. 6, MS D: A Semi-Diplomatic Edition with Introduction and Indices* (Cambridge, 1996), 66; see also the significance of the fens, above, 90–3.

[37]   *Vita S. Dunstani*, ii.25.3, ed. and trans. Winterbottom and Thomson, *William of Malmesbury: Saints' Lives*, 280–1: 'illum comedant uulpes'.

[38]   *Vita S. Dunstani*, ii.25.4, ed. and trans. Winterbottom and Thomson, *William of Malmesbury: Saints' Lives*, 280–3: 'tremendo Deo iuditio, ut parum aut nichil de illo in

This warning stands in contrast to the received wisdom that at the Last Judgement all the bodies of the dead will be raised up, whether they were buried, drowned, eaten by wild animals or fish, or destroyed in any other way.[39] It is clearly important that even after the soul had departed, the lifeless body could not be separated from what was once a living person, a body animated by its soul. Even once a person is dead the body retains its personal, cultural and social identities or some aspects of them, and disentangling someone's wickedness or sanctity from the body which only made up part of that person was inevitably difficult.[40] Anglo-Saxon writers themselves noted that sometimes 'anima' ('soul') could be used instead of 'corpus' ('body') or 'flesh' ('caro'), or the other way around, or that one of these could stand for the whole person.[41] The complexity of the continuing relationship between body and soul is evident in the treatment of the body after death and attitudes to different practices, and these practices were themselves driven by a wide range of beliefs which were often internally inconsistent or less than fully coherent: in some cases, actual or reported burial practices were evidently considered odd or incomprehensible even by those who followed not long afterwards.[42] The intertwining of social, personal, cultural and theological factors and the mutual effects of these upon each other find their focus in the dead body, now only the semblance of the person it had once been, but still needing to be dealt with appropriately, and urgently.

## The Concept of Christian Burial

Burials and burial rituals have traditionally been viewed as one area in which it is possible to see the impact of belief on, or perhaps better in, the ground. In the period before widespread conversion, practices of both inhumation and cremation seem to have been reasonably common, whereas a high proportion of

---

placiditatem sinus sui terra susciperet qui Dei matris benignitatem irritasset'.

[39] *Hom.* VII, ed. Morris, *Blickling Homilies*, 95; see also Jer 41.9, Ps 78.2.

[40] S. Tarlow, *Ritual, Belief, and the Dead Body in Early Modern Britain and Ireland* (Cambridge, 2010), 10.

[41] Bede, *In Genesim*, III.xii.5, ll. 1045–50, ed. C.W. Jones, *Bedae venerabilis opera, pars II: Opera exegetica, 1. Libri quattor in principium Genesis usque ad nativitatem Isaac et eiectionem Ismahelis adnotationum*, CCSL 118A (Turnhout, 1967), 171: 'Solet enim in scripturis homo aliquando "animae" solius, aliquando "carnis" nomine solius, indicari: animae sicut dictum est, anima quae peccauerit ipsa morietur; carnis ut in psalmo, at te omnis caro ueniet, cum neque caro sine anima ad deum uenire neque sine carne possit anima peccare, sed propter unam partem totus homo signetur'; see also the glosses on Byrhtferth's *Life of Ecgwine*, probably written by Byrhtferth himself, ed. Lapidge, *The Lives of St Oswald and St Ecgwine*, 313: 'corporibus: sepe corpus pro anima ponitur et anima pro corpore. Sicut euuangelia dicunt: "qui odit animam suamque corpus suum custodit eam"'.

[42] See below, 325–7.

Anglo-Saxon burials from the seventh century and later are supine inhumations, usually unaccompanied by grave-goods, and often aligned west-east, although there is still significant variety in the finer details of burial practice.[43] Grave-goods do not seem to have been forbidden by ecclesiastical authorities, but it is accepted that Christianisation did ultimately have an impact on the way that people buried their dead and thought about the burial of the dead, though this was clearly a complex process and not as straightforward as was once thought.[44] By the end of the Anglo-Saxon period, there was a fairly well-defined concept of Christian burial which included not only the burial of the body itself in consecrated ground, but also the performance of liturgical rites both during the burial itself and afterwards, in the perpetual commemoration of the dead.[45] In later Anglo-Saxon England, wealthy and well-connected people recorded their preferences for the place of their burial, and sometimes also for the rituals which might accompany their burial and commemorate them. Ostensibly these arrangements were made for the fate of the soul, but in arranging for the soul's need there is a clear concern for the fate of the body too. The most elaborate versions of Christian burial in later Anglo-Saxon England included liturgical rituals as the person lay dying, especially for the inhabitants of monastic houses and in some cases for laity who sought the privilege of dying in a monastery.[46]

Some of these elements are visible too in early sources: the late seventh- and early eighth-century material associated with the teachings of Theodore instructs that priests who deny confession to the dying bear responsibility for those souls.[47] In the eighth century, Bede mentions the rites for the dying and the funeral liturgies which accompanied burials, as well as ongoing commemoration, but he usually refers to these in monastic contexts, and in Bede's time it seems that these were privileges reserved for the inhabitants of monastic communities and their benefactors or dependents, and perhaps also some high-ranking lay individuals,

---

[43]    Hadley and Buckberry, 'Caring', 132–43; Z. Devlin, *Remembering the Dead in Anglo-Saxon England: Memory Theory in Archaeology and History* (Oxford, 2007), 53.

[44]    See for example H. Geake, 'Invisible kingdoms: The use of grave-goods in seventh-century England', *Anglo-Saxon Studies in Archaeology and History* 10 (1999): 203–15; H. Geake, 'The Control of Burial Practice in Anglo-Saxon England', in M. Carver (ed.), *The Cross Goes North* (Woodbridge, 2003), 259–69; Devlin, *Remembering the Dead in Anglo-Saxon England*, 79.

[45]    See above, 238–48.

[46]    F.S. Paxton, *Christianizing Death: The Creation of a Ritual Process in Early Medieval Europe* (Ithaca, NY, 1990), 126–7, 196–9; Thompson, *Dying and Death*, 67–81; V. Thompson, 'The Pastoral Contract in Late Anglo-Saxon England: Priest and Parishioner in Oxford, Bodleian Library, MS Laud Miscellaneous 482', in Tinti (ed.), *Pastoral Care in Late Anglo-Saxon England*, 106–20, at 109–19.

[47]    G 37, U I.viii.5, ed. P.W. Finsterwalder, *Die Canones Theodori Cantuariensis und ihre Überlieferungsformen* (Weimar, 1929), 256, 300.

especially where monastic communities were isolated from lay settlements.[48] Before about the tenth century, burial in a churchyard seems to have been primarily a monastic privilege: religious communities had their own cemeteries where they buried their dead with care and respect, even if the ground was not formally and liturgically consecrated in the way that it would be in later centuries.[49] In some cases the location of the cemetery itself was clearly considered to be of some significance, as for example when the sisters at Barking had had to choose a new place for their cemetery, they were supposed to have been guided by a bright light which miraculously hovered over the southern part of the monastery, to the west of the oratory: according to Bede, this indicated the place where their bodies were to rest and wait for the day of resurrection.[50] The evidence of excavations suggests that in some cases laity may have been buried in the cemeteries of religious communities, but that lay and monastic dead might be separated from one another.[51] This suggests that both social and theological significance was attached to the precise places where the dead were buried, even if the exact meaning cannot always be recovered.

Where settlements were located within easy reach of religious communities, churchyard burial might perhaps have been more easily available to laity in the early Anglo-Saxon period, but here the developments in ecclesiastical institutions and ministry had a significant effect on the ways that burials occurred, and how they were understood. Bede's description of the ministry of wandering priests relates that they performed baptisms and masses for those in the villages that they visited, but burial is not listed as one of the services offered to the laity.[52] There is of course a very good, and very obvious, reason for this: the burial of the dead could not be delayed for long, especially in warm weather, and in communities where access to a priest was limited, burial accompanied by Christian rites would simply have been impractical for those without means or resources to move the body, even assuming that such rites were desired or considered important in those communities. There seems to have been no organised ecclesiastical push to encourage laity to seek burial in churches' cemeteries at this period: rather,

---

[48]    H. Gittos, 'Creating the Sacred: Anglo-Saxon Rites for Consecrating Cemeteries', in S. Lucy and A.J. Reynolds (eds), *Burial in Early Medieval England and Wales* (London, 2002), 195–208, at 202.

[49]    D.A. Bullough, 'Burial, Community and Belief in the Early Medieval West', in P. Wormald et al. (eds), *Ideal and Reality in Frankish and Anglo-Saxon Society: Studies Presented to J.M. Wallace-Hadrill* (Oxford, 1983), 177–201, at 179–81; J. Blair, *The Church in Anglo-Saxon Society* (Oxford, 2005), 241–5, 466–71; S. Foot, *Monastic Life in Anglo-Saxon England, c. 600–900* (Cambridge, 2006), 312–18.

[50]    Bede, *HE*, IV.7.2, ed. Lapidge, Monat and Robin, *Histoire ecclésiastique*, II.236.

[51]    R. Cramp, *Wearmouth and Jarrow Monastic Sites* (2 vols, Swindon, 2005), I.86–90; Kjølbye-Biddle, 'Dispersal', 222–7.

[52]    See Council of *Clofesho* (747), 8–11, ed. A.W. Haddan and W. Stubbs, *Councils and Ecclesiastical Documents Relating to Great Britain and Ireland* (3 vols, Oxford, 1869), 365–6.

where concerns about burial are expressed, these were often connected with other types of issues, such as the regulations in the material associated with Theodore's teaching which prohibit the consecration of an altar in a church where bodies (in some versions specified as bodies of unbelievers) are buried, or which instruct that the bodies of unbelievers should be ejected from holy places.[53] This suggests that in this period, while many of those in religious life (as presumably also some laity) considered burial at or in churches a valuable privilege, there was little ecclesiastical concern over controlling or being involved with most lay burials, and perhaps little interest. As a result, there is substantial variation in the location of burial sites before about the tenth century.[54]

A significant change seems to have occurred in the late ninth or early tenth century with the introduction of consecrated cemeteries, which provided an enclosed sacred space in which the bodies of the dead could rest until the Last Judgement.[55] While the earliest liturgical rituals for consecrating cemeteries survive only in books from the latter part of the tenth century, Helen Gittos notes that the uniformity of the rites at this stage suggests that by this time they were fairly well established, and there is also reference to the practice of burial in consecrated ground, or rather, exclusion from it, in one of Æthelstan's law codes.[56] References to exclusion from consecrated ground as a penalty appear again in later tenth-century lawcodes as well as those from the eleventh century, and similar references in the *Northumbrian Priests' Law* give some indication that the geographic spread of the practice was not limited to southern England, or at least not by the second quarter of the eleventh century.[57] All the same, it is not clear how quickly the practice spread, or whether the land around all churches was consecrated using these rites: some churches do not seem to have had churchyards, and older churches which were already considered sanctified might not have been reconsecrated if the rite was usually performed following the consecration of a church.[58] Although it is difficult to verify the accuracy of the account, William of Malmesbury's statement

---

[53]  See D 59, G 149–50, U II.1.4–5, ed. P.W. Finsterwalder, *Die Canones Theodori Cantuariensis und ihre Überlieferungsformen, Penitential* (Weimar, 1929), 244, 267, 312; see also Synod of Aachen (809), *Concilium incerti loci (post a.614)*, 6, ed. C. de Clercq, *Concilia Galliae, A.511 – A.695*, CCSL 148A (Turnhout, 1963), 287.

[54]  S. Lucy and A.J. Reynolds, 'Burial in Early Medieval England and Wales: Past, Present and Future', in Lucy and Reynolds (eds), *Burial in Early Medieval England and Wales*, 1–23, at 20–1; Blair, *The Church*, 228–45.

[55]  The manuscripts containing the rites for the consecration of cemeteries are outlined in Gittos, 'Consecrating Cemeteries', 195–9.

[56]  II Æthelstan 26, ed. F. Liebermann, *Die Gesetze der Angelsachsen* (3 vols, Halle, 1903–1916), I.164–5; Gittos, 'Consecrating Cemeteries', 201–2.

[57]  *Northumbrian Priests' Law*, 62, 64, *Councils and Synods*, I.i, no. 63.

[58]  Gittos, 'Consecrating Cemeteries', 204; see also B.H. Rosenwein, *Negotiating Space: Power, Restraint, and Privileges of Immunity in Early Medieval Europe* (Manchester, 1999), 178–80.

that Dunstan enclosed the monks' cemetery at Glastonbury may be an example of a case where an older church had its cemetery reconsecrated, here apparently in the context of rebuilding work at Glastonbury.[59]

It is difficult to identify how quickly the importance of burial in consecrated ground filtered from its monastic and episcopal contexts into wider public consciousness, and this is significant in considering the appearance of references to consecrated ground in legal texts. If the rite (and indeed, the concept) of consecrated burial grounds was only introduced in the later ninth century, it is difficult to understand precisely how effective a penalty or threat Æthelstan's prohibitions of burial in consecrated ground might have been, assuming that the written text was applied more or less as recorded.[60] In the same way, it is not clear whether Archbishop Wulfstan's instructions that those who did not want to learn and understand the pater noster and creed should be included from consecrated ground reflects a genuine problem of poorly catechised or 'unChristian' individuals seeking inclusion in Christian burial grounds, or whether this is simply another example of Wulfstan attempting to regulate a 'Holy Society'.[61] Practices of exclusion are visible in written sources and in the archaeological record, but ascertaining precisely what the effects of that exclusion were believed to be is much more complicated than has sometimes been assumed, and is a problem which will be explored in due course.[62] What is immediately clear is that in burial rites and rituals, there is a very close link between the necessity of spiritual inclusion, which was informed by theological considerations and which aimed at the ultimate inclusion of each of the Christian dead in the company of saints, and the necessity of social inclusion, which reflected practices and ideas connected with religious belief, and which may have initially operated independently of theology but which came to be bound up with it.

For the vast majority of 'ordinary' people in Anglo-Saxon England, there is no surviving information about what they desired or feared as they approached death and considered their burial. The shift from field cemeteries to churchyard burial over the period is revealing, but it is worth bearing in mind too that especially in urban areas with cathedrals, the range of possible options for burial even in later centuries may have been relatively limited for those who could not afford the privilege of being buried in the cemetery of their choosing.[63] These 'ordinary' burials stand in contrast to the desires and requests expressed by

---

[59]  *Vita S. Dunstani*, i.16.2, ed. Winterbottom and Thomson, *William of Malmesbury: Saints' Lives*, 204–6.

[60]  For information on the relationship between written legal text and law in practice, see above, 135–7.

[61]  P. Wormald, 'Archbishop Wulfstan and the Holiness of Society', in D.A.E. Pelteret (ed.), *Anglo-Saxon History: Basic Readings* (New York, 1999), 191–224, at 206–7.

[62]  See below, 294–313.

[63]  M.J. Franklin, 'The Cathedral as Parish Church: The Case of Southern England', in D. Abulafia, M.J. Franklin and M. Rubin (eds), *Church and City, 1000–1500: Essays in Honour of Christopher Brooke* (Cambridge, 1992), 173–98, at 174–5.

wealthy and well-connected Anglo-Saxons, and to the offenders and miscreants who were excluded from consecrated ground and whose bodies were disposed of in a way which was almost certainly not how they would have wished. Although in a sense the bodies of the 'ordinary' dead might be said to represent 'ordinary' belief, as Sarah Tarlow suggests,[64] it remains difficult to ascertain how far these 'ordinary' burials were constrained by lack of choice, because of ecclesiastical regulations, lack of resources (financial or otherwise), or other factors. This means that although they are in many ways unrepresentative, the extremes of what was desired in burial, or what people wanted to avoid, cast some light on which aspects of burial practice or the treatment of the body were believed to be particularly significant. These kinds of burials are also those where social factors are more likely to play a greater role in different practices. While unpicking theological ideas from their social context is not always easy, the range of approaches to burial reflects the spread of theological ideas from the page to the wider world, and shows how theology became entangled with practices which also served significant social functions.

### Desires and Requests

Burial in holy places was evidently believed to be important, whether the places were hallowed by rites which demarcated the appropriate resting places of the dead, or hallowed by association with the bodily remains of the saints.[65] While the desire for burial as close to saints' bodies as possible is clearly visible in the archaeological record, more general requests for burial in the cemeteries of large churches and religious communities illustrate their perceived value as resting places, probably both because of the relics which sanctified the churches and their cemeteries, and because of the prayers which could be offered for them. Religious communities were considered to be an attractive place for the body to await the final judgement from early on, and some institutions were specifically founded with the intention that they would also serve as mausolea, such as the minster at Lastingham, which Oethelwald asked Bishop Cedd (d.664) to establish so that he could benefit from the prayers that were offered there.[66] There is some evidence that burial in monastic communities was held to be especially valuable, and at least in the early period, this can be seen from the desire of some bishops to be buried in monasteries rather than in their cathedral churches, such as Boniface and Willibrord.[67] While most lower status lay Christians were probably not buried

---

[64]    Tarlow, *Ritual, Belief, and the Dead Body*, 104–9.

[65]    See R.A. Markus, 'How on earth could places become holy? Origins of the Christian idea of holy places', *Journal of Early Christian Studies* 2:3 (1994): 257–71.

[66]    Bede, *HE*, III.23, ed. Lapidge, Monat and Robin, *Histoire ecclésiastique*, II.128–32; Foot, *Monastic Life*, 314–15.

[67]    N. Ohler, *Sterben und Tod im Mittelalter* (Munich, 1990), 38.

in the cemeteries of religious communities in the early period, it is possible that tenants of religious foundations were entitled to burial in their cemeteries, secured through the link made by leasing the land.[68]

The perceived value of burial at religious institutions did not fade, but seems rather to have continued and multiplied, as witnessed in the numerous grants and wills which request burial at particular institutions, and the substantial donations which were made to secure the privilege. At least from the ninth century this was apparently formalised as 'soul-scot', a payment which seems to have been made in return for the various funerary and pre-funerary rites, including confession and anointing of the sick, although in some cases it may have been viewed as payment for a grave-plot.[69] There are also texts which seem to treat soul-scot as pious bequests to several churches rather than one payment for burial, suggesting that its meaning may not have always been clear-cut.[70] The tenth- and eleventh-century guild statutes which provide for the burial of members at a minster indicate how a collective could be formed as a means of obtaining this benefit.[71] In other cases personal connections as well as donation were significant in securing the privilege of burial in major churches: as in earlier centuries, founders might be buried in the churches that they had established, such as Ealdorman Æthelwine in the tenth century, who had founded Ramsey.[72] Close connections of other sorts were also valuable, as the late tenth-century *Life of Dunstan* shows in the account of the burial of Dunstan's brother Wulfric, who had been appointed to manage affairs outside the monastery: when Wulfric died, the monks went off to fetch his body and brought it back with prayers and some ceremony to the place where it was to be buried.[73]

Some charters highlight the physical presence of the saints in the churches to which land is granted, such as the grant made in 836 by King Ecgberht of Wessex to Ciaba, a cleric of St Peter's, Canterbury, 'where the body of our holy father Augustine rests', or the grant made in 788 by King Offa to St Andrew's, Rochester, 'where blessed Paulinus rests'.[74] This also points to the awareness and importance of those saints in the

---

[68]    B. Yorke, *The Conversion of Britain: Religion, Politics and Society in Britain, c.600–800* (Harlow, 2006), 217.

[69]    Blair, *The Church*, 437–8; F. Tinti, 'The "Costs" of Pastoral Care: Church Dues in Late Anglo-Saxon England', in Tinti (ed.), *Pastoral Care in Late Anglo-Saxon England*, 27–51, at 34, 36.

[70]    See, for example, the will of Wynflæd, S 1539; Blair, *The Church*, 446.

[71]    See for example the Exeter and Abbotsbury guild statutes: *Councils and Synods*, I.i, nos. 16, 67; and above, 247–8.

[72]    *Vita S. Oswaldi*, 21, ed. and trans. Lapidge, *The Lives of St Oswald and St Ecgwine*, 198–201.

[73]    B, *Vita S. Dunstani*, 18.1–3, ed. M. Winterbottom and M. Lapidge, *The Early Lives of St Dunstan* (Oxford, 2012), 58.

[74]    S 279 (*CantStA*, no. 18): 'ubi pausat corpus sancti patris nostri Augustini'; S 129, ed. A. Campbell, *Charters of Rochester*, Anglo-Saxon Charters 1 (Oxford, 1973), no. 12:

minds of those granting property for their souls, as in turn for those who were buried in the cemeteries of these communities. As with requests for prayer and other liturgical services, connection with the community was important, and people might be buried at churches where they had made associations through previous instances of ritualised gift-giving. Æthelberht II, king of Kent (d.762), made two recorded benefactions to St Mary's, Lyminge, for the remedy of his soul, and there is one surviving recorded transaction with SS Peter and Paul, Canterbury, exchanging the half-use of a mill in return for pasture rights.[75] Another grant, made after Æthelberht's death by his minister, Dunwald, indicates that Æthelberht's body was buried at SS Peter and Paul, evidently arranged as part of the ongoing relationship between Æthelberht and the community which included the one surviving grant now visible in the historical record.[76]

The visibility of specific requests for burial increases throughout the period, and in charters and wills these requests are often placed first, or close to the beginning, indicating their significance. When one Æthelwold drew up his will and arranged for the division of his property, some time after 987, he first allocated his soul-scot of 20 mancuses of gold and a cup to the New Minster, Winchester, probably indicating his desire to be buried there, before recording how the rest of his property was to be distributed.[77] In about 1050, a man named Wulf recorded that he bequeathed land to 'the holy place at St Albans where I wish to be buried', before noting that various other portable goods including a chalice, mass-book and dorsal were to be given to St Albans so that two masses could be celebrated every week for his soul.[78] Family connections were significant in burial arrangements in churches, and in some cases several generations of a family were buried in one centre which was the major focus of their patronage, as the wills of Ælfgar, Æthelflæd and Ælflæd demonstrate in their frequent references to Stoke, where their ancestors lay buried.[79] Both the family and the community would presumably wish to maintain such a custom, since both would benefit, either from the donations or from the privilege of burial.

The memories of those who donated land to monasteries and were buried there were often preserved in multiple and connected ways, in the records of the lands they had given as well as in the resting-places of their bodies, which might be identified by memorial markers. According to a late eleventh-century Worcester cartulary written (at least partly) by the scribe Hemming, the enlargement of the cathedral church at Worcester in the middle of the eleventh century had led to the destruction of a gravestone commemorating Wiferd and Alta, erected some

---

'ubi beatus Paulinus pausat'. See also above, 223.

[75]   S 23, 24, 25.

[76]   S 1182. See also above, 226.

[77]   S 1505 (*WinchNM*, no. 29): 'þæt is ærest þæt he gean for his sawle .xx. mancusas goldes into niwan menstre ꝺ ane cuppan him to sawelsceatte'.

[78]   S 1532.

[79]   S 1483, 1486, 1494; see also above, 251–4.

time in the ninth century.[80] Hemming notes that this was made of stone with a cross, and was built as a memorial of their generosity and as a monument to their souls, but his discussion of the gravestone appears in conjunction with the record of their donation of 15 hides of land to the monastery in the late eighth century, indicating how much the memory of patrons was bound up with the memory of lands.[81] It is significant too that the land was granted 'to the church of St Peter, where the bodies of our ancestors rest', highlighting the sense of continuity in a relationship between a family and a religious community.[82] This also illustrates how the burial practices of one generation could both influence the burial practices of another, and in turn be commemorated through them and their deeds, since by implication it is not only the actions of Wiferd and Alta which were remembered several centuries later but also those of their ancestors.

This gravestone seems to have been very prominent, as Francesca Tinti notes, since it was used by Oswald as a place to preach when the cathedral (St Peter's) became too small to house the congregation, and this as well as the burial location next to the cathedral indicates the value of the patronage and the high status of this couple.[83] Other aspects of high-status burial might include practices which involved significant investment, and in the case of crafted goods this is particularly important since that investment could not be easily recovered once it was buried in the grave. Coffins made of wood and especially stone are frequently used to identify burials believed to be high status, but other practices which are less well understood are also often associated with high-status burials.[84] One

---

[80] S 1185 (T. Hearne, *Hemingi Chartularium Ecclesiæ Wigorniensis* (Oxford, 1723), II.341–3): 'Qua de re ego Wiferd, et conjunx mea, Alta nomine, Christo Domino concessimus, et omnibus sanctis in celis, quamdiu fides catholica et baptismum Christi in Brittannua servetur, aliquas agellicas portiones, pro remedio anime nostre, ad ecclesiam beatissimi apostolorum principis Sancti Petri, ubi corpora parentum nostrorum quiescunt [ … ]. Post finem autem vite illorum, lapidum structura, more antiquorum, super sepulchrm eorum, opere artificioso, cum cruce dominica, ob monumentum largitatis et monimentum animarum ipsorum, composita est. Juxta quem lapidem beatus pater Oswaldus, propter loci planiciem, sermonem facere ad populum sepius solebat, eo quod ecclesia sedis episcopalis in honore Sancti Petri, apostolorum principis, dedicata, admodum stricta multitudinem concurrentis populi capere nequibat, nec dum scilicet constructo honorabili monasterio beate Dei genitricis Marie, quod ipse beatus pater ad sedem episcopalem laudabiliter incepit, laudabiliusque consummavit. Perduravit igitur hec lapidum structura usque ad tempora Eadwardi regis, quo regnante Alricus, frater Berhteachi episcopi, presbiterium supradicte beate Petri ecclesie ampliare studuit, ipsamque lapidum congeriem destructam operi immiscuit'. F. Tinti, *Sustaining Belief: The Church of Worcester from c. 870 to c. 1100* (Farnham, 2010), 314.

[81] See also R. Fleming, 'History and liturgy at pre-Conquest Christ Church', *Haskins Society Journal: Studies in Medieval History* 6 (1995): 67–83, at 81–2.

[82] This charter only survives in the cartulary and not as a single sheet: it may have been adjusted when or before it was copied into the cartulary, and perhaps quite significantly, but the detail about the resting place of the ancestors of Wiferd and Alta seems likely to be not to be an interpolation.

[83] Tinti, *Sustaining Belief*, 314.

[84] See for example D.M. Hadley, 'Burying the Socially and Physically Distinctive in Later Anglo-Saxon England', in J. Buckberry and A.K. Cherryson (eds), *Burial in Later*

of the most interesting of these is charcoal burial, which has been suggested to have penitential overtones on the basis of the perceived similarity between charcoal and ash.[85] In fact, charcoal requires much more effort in production than ash does, since charcoal is very difficult to make accidentally whereas ash is simply a by-product of burning.[86] Often it is difficult to understand whether such practices were intended to be imbued with religious or theological meaning or had another function. Augustine notes that charcoal was placed under boundary posts since it remained visible in the ground, but he also explains that this is because of its incorruptibility, and either of these (whether known from Augustine or observed from real life) might have been important in its use in the context of burial.[87]

Some indication of how the specific place for burial might be chosen is given by an account in the late tenth-century *Life of Dunstan*. The author describes that Æthelflæd's priest came to the monastery asking to choose a place where he might be buried after his death, and pointed out the specific location in the cemetery which he had chosen for his burial.[88] In the context of the miracle this event was foretold by Wulfred, a former monk of Glastonbury, who had appeared to Dunstan in a vision: Wulfred had identified a place that the priest would choose in the southern part of the cemetery, and Dunstan had marked it with a stone so that he could confirm the veracity of Wulfred's account when the priest arrived to choose his burial place.[89] Since the miracle was Dunstan's foreknowledge and not the fact that the priest had chosen his burial place, this may indeed represent something of the specificity with which some individuals could choose the places where their body would rest, especially if they were well-connected: Æthelflæd is described in the same text as the niece of King Æthelstan, and so presumably could have arranged such a privilege for her priests.[90]

---

*Anglo-Saxon England, c.650–1100 AD* (Oxford, 2010), 103–15; E. Craig-Atkins, 'Chest burial: A middle Anglo-Saxon funerary rite from northern England', *Oxford Journal of Archaeology* 31:3 (2012): 317–37.

[85]   V. Thompson, 'Constructing Salvation: A Homiletic and Penitential Context for Late Anglo-Saxon Burial Practice', in Lucy and Reynolds (eds), *Burial in Early Medieval England and Wales*, 229–40, at 238–40; Thompson, *Dying and Death*, 118–22.

[86]   See also J. Holloway, 'Material Symbolism and Death: Charcoal Burial in Later Anglo-Saxon England', in Buckberry and Cherryson (eds), *Burial in Later Anglo-Saxon England*, 83–92; and K. Jonsson, 'Burial rods and charcoal graves: new light on old burial practices', *Viking and Medieval Scandinavia* 3 (2007): 43–73.

[87]   Augustine, *DCD*, 21.4, ll. 38–44, ed. Dombert and Kalb, *De civitate Dei*, II.762: 'quid, in carbonibus nonne miranda est et tanta infirmitas, ut ictu leuissimo frangantur, pressu facillimo conterantur, et tanta firmitas, ut nullo umore corrumpantur, nulla aetate uincantur, usque adeo ut eos substernere soleant, qui limites figunt, ad conuincendum litigatorem, quisquis post quantalibet tempora extiterit fixum que lapidem limitem non esse contenderit?'.

[88]   B, *Vita S. Dunstani*, 9, ed. Winterbottom and Lapidge, *Early Lives*, 30–4.

[89]   B, *Vita S. Dunstani*, 9.3, ed. Winterbottom and Lapidge, *Early Lives*, 32.

[90]   B, *Vita S. Dunstani*, 10.3, ed. Winterbottom and Lapidge, *Early Lives*, 34.

Bequests to religious foundations in return for burial are a form of ritualised almsgiving and they were often of very high value and, as in Wulf's case, request liturgical offerings as well as burial.[91] In the late tenth century, Æthelgifu bequeathed substantial amounts of land, money and livestock to the monks of St Albans in return for the burial of her body, and in addition to this she gave silver cups, horns, a book, a wall-hanging and a seat-cover for the good of her soul and of her lord's, and requested both masses and psalms to be said for her soul and for her lord's.[92] In the late tenth or early eleventh century, Ærnketel and his wife Wulfrun recorded their intention to bequeath land to St Benedict's, Ramsey, and requested that their bodies be buried there.[93] Ærnketel stated that 'for the price of burial and for the salvation of my soul', he would give 15 pounds in silver and gold as well as the chattels he possess at the time of his death, and Wulfrun was to give land and chattels; she also promised that while she lived, she would give a substantial annual donation of food, including hams, cheese, malt, wheat and two fat cows in the summer for the feast of St Benedict, and eight salmon in Lent.[94] This may have been intended to provide for an anniversary meal which was to commemorate Ærnketel and Wulfrun, as well as to celebrate the feast of St Benedict.[95]

The liturgical services which might be offered after burial were clearly considered important by those with the means and status to arrange for them, and it seems likely too that the desire for burial in the cemeteries of large churches was connected not only with concern about the place where the body would rest, but also about how the body was committed to the ground, as the development of the payment of soul-scot also suggests. Funerary rites, including rituals for burial as well as for commemoration after burial, survive in a number of manuscripts from later Anglo-Saxon England (see Table 5.1). However, before about the tenth century, when churchyard burial started to become more usual practice, it seems unlikely that burial away from churches and their cemeteries was accompanied by extensive Christian rites, and may have been much more of a family affair.[96] From the late ninth century there were increasing numbers of local churches, some of which had or came to have graveyards: this not only provided a location for the bodies of the Christian dead which was an alternative to minsters or field cemeteries, but may also have served to strengthen the idea in local communities that burial in or near a church, and according to Christian rites, was important.[97]

---

[91]   See also above, 238–48.

[92]   S 1497.

[93]   S 1493.

[94]   S 1493 (K 971): 'in pretium sepulturae meae et animae salutem'.

[95]   For information on anniversaries see above, 239–47.

[96]   Bullough, 'Burial', 198–9; Blair, *The Church*, 243–5; see also A.K. Cherryson, '"Such a Resting-Place as is Necessary for Us in God's Sight and Fitting in the Eyes of the World": Saxon Southampton and the Development of Churchyard Burial', in Buckberry and Cherryson (eds), *Burial in Later Anglo-Saxon England*, 54–72.

[97]   Blair, *The Church*, 463–71.

Table 5.1 Anglo-Saxon manuscripts containing funerary rites and rituals for the dead[1]

| Shelfmark | Date and Provenance | Edition/facsimile |
|---|---|---|
| Cambridge, Corpus Christi College, 163 [Office of the Dead only] | s. $xi^2$, probably s. $x^{4/4}$. Worcester, or Old Minster, Winchester, perhaps for the Nunnaminster?[2] | *Parker Library on the web*, http://parkerweb.stanford.edu |
| Cambridge, Corpus Christi College, 422 ('Red Book of Darley'); a sacramentary, collectar, and 'manual'-type book | s. $xi^{med}$, perhaps written at Winchester for use at Sherborne[3] | *Parker Library on the web*, http://parkerweb.stanford.edu;[4] partially ed. Fehr, 'Altenglische Ritualtexte' |
| Orléans, Bibliothèque municipale, 105 (127) ('Winchcombe Sacramentary') | s. $x^{ex}$; England, but probably taken to Fleury within a few decades of its production[5] | Davril, *The Winchcombe Sacramentary* |
| Oxford, Bodleian Library, Bodley 579 ('Leofric Missal')[6] | 'Leofric A': s. $x^{1/4}$;?perhaps written for Plegmund (Archbishop of Canterbury, 890–923)[7] 'Leofric B': additions made probably at Canterbury between the second quarter of the tenth century and the end of the century.[8] 'Leofric C': additions made during the book's ownership by Leofric (d.1072; Bishop of Crediton (1046) and Exeter (1050))[9] | Orchard, *The Leofric Missal Early Manuscripts at Oxford University*, http://image.ox.ac.uk |
| Oxford, Bodleian Library, Laud misc. 482 [the final pages of this manuscript are missing and only the beginning of the funerary rites now survive] | s. $xi^{med}$; Worcester[10] | partially ed. Fehr, 'Altenglische Ritualtexte' |
| Rouen, Bibliothèque municipale, 274 (Y.6) ('Missal of Robert of Jumièges') | s. $xi^1$; probably written at Ely or Peterborough[11] | Wilson, *Missal of Robert of Jumièges* Fehr, 'Altenglische Ritualtexte' |
| Worcester, Cathedral Library, F. 173 | s. xi; written for use at Old Minster, Winchester;?later Worcester provenance[12] | |

Table 5.1    Continued

| Shelfmark | Date and Provenance | Edition/facsimile |
|---|---|---|
| London, British Library, Cotton Vitellius E.xii [Office of the Dead only] | s. xi$^{med}$ | |
| Cambridge, Corpus Christi College, 391 (St Wulfstan's *Portiforium*) [Office of the Dead only] | s. xi$^2$, or?perhaps after 1070; Worcester (based on a Winchester exemplar)[13] | Hughes, *The Portiforium of St Wulstan*, Parker Library on the web, http://parkerweb.stanford.edu |

*Notes:* [1] See further Keefer, 'Manuals', 105–6. [2] See M. Lapidge, 'The origin of CCCC 163', *Transactions of the Cambridge Bibliographical Society* 8 (1981), 18–28; M. Budny, *Insular, Anglo-Saxon and Early Anglo-Norman Manuscript Art at Corpus Christi College. Cambridge: An Illustrated Catalogue* (2 vols. Kalamazoo, MI, 1997), I.593–98. [3] A. Corrêa, 'Daily Office Books: Collectars and Breviaries', in R.W. Pfaff (ed.), *The Liturgical Books of Anglo-Saxon England*, Old English Newsletter, Subsidia 23 (Kalamazoo, MI, 1995), 45–60, at 56–7; S.L. Keefer, 'Manuals', in Pfaff (ed.), *The Liturgical Books of Anglo-Saxon England*, 99–109; H. Gittos, 'Is there any Evidence for the Liturgy of Parish Churches in Late Anglo-Saxon England? The Red Book of Darley and the Status of Old English', in Tinti (ed.), *Pastoral Care in Late Anglo-Saxon England*, 63–82; S. Keynes, 'Wulfsige, Monk of Glastonbury, Abbot of Westminster (*c* 990–3), and Bishop of Sherborne (*c* 993–1002)', in K. Barker, D.A. Hinton and A. Hunt (eds), *St Wulfsige and Sherborne: Essays to Celebrate the Millennium of the Benedictine Abbey, 998–1998* (Oxford, 2005), 53–94, at 75–6; Rushforth, *Saints in English Kalendars*, 41–2. [4] The liturgical rubrics are also printed in R.I. Page, 'Old English Liturgical directions in Corpus Christi College, Cambridge, MS 422', *Anglia* 96 (1978): 149–58; T. Graham, 'The Old English liturgical directions in Corpus Christi College, Cambridge, MS 422', *Anglia* 111 (1993): 439–46. [5] R.W. Pfaff, 'Massbooks: Sacramentaries and Missals', in Pfaff (ed.), *The Liturgical Books of Anglo-Saxon England*, 7–34, at 14–15. [6] This is a very complex, composite book and what is provided here is only the briefest summary. For detailed discussion see N. Orchard, *The Leofric Missal*, HBS 113–14 (2 vols, London, 2002); Pfaff, *The Liturgy in Medieval England: A history*, 72–7, 136–8. [7] See Orchard, *Leofric Missal*, I.23–131; Pfaff, *The Liturgy in Medieval England*, 72–5. [8] Orchard, *Leofric Missal*, I.132–205; Pfaff, *The Liturgy in Medieval England*, 75–7. [9] Orchard, *Leofric Missal*, I.206–33; Pfaff, *The Liturgy in Medieval England*, 136–8. [10] For detailed discussion of this manuscript and its uses, see Thompson, *Dying and Death*, 57–91. [11] Pfaff, 'Massbooks: Sacramentaries and Missals', 15–19; Pfaff, *The Liturgy in Medieval England*, 88–91. [12] Pfaff, 'Massbooks', 25–6. [13] Corrêa, 'Daily Office Books', 57–8; Rushforth, *Saints in English Kalendars*, 44–5.

Late Anglo-Saxon royal and ecclesiastical legislation grants particular rites to different types of churches, based at least partly on the presence or absence of graveyards and the pastoral services which churches seem to have provided. The concept of the 'rihtscriftscir', the proper confession area, is found in texts associated with Ælfric and Wulfstan and is significant in the context of burial because it defined an area or community for which a minster was pastorally responsible in life and in death.[98] The laws of Æthelred and Cnut, for example, note that if someone was buried outside his 'rihtscriftscir', his soul-scot should be paid to the minster which was responsible for him in life.[99] This is usually interpreted in the context of rising numbers of smaller churches with graveyards, on the assumption that these were beginning to compete with the cemeteries at minster communities, which wanted to retain the soul-scot for themselves.[100] However, it is possible that in this context, what is meant by 'mynstre' in the law codes is in fact a church more generally, rather than a religious community specifically: the desire to be buried in the cemeteries of large religious houses suggests that not all individuals would have attempted to be buried at local churches, even if they had founded them.[101] Contemporary continental examples of people paying sepulture to a parish church but seeking burial in the cemetery of a religious community suggests that this interpretation deserves further study.[102] In any case, on this issue practice must have varied quite widely according to local context.

Even when the concepts of consecrated cemeteries and Christian burial were more fully developed, the possibilities for funerary rites and rituals must have varied significantly between the small, local churches staffed by one priest and the large minsters housing religious communities, from which the surviving manuscripts originate. This can be shown at one extreme by an eleventh-century funeral ritual designed for use in Winchester (and surviving now in Worcester, Cathedral Library, F. 173), which involved carrying the body around various chapels and churches in Winchester's monastic precinct, and offering prayers to the different saints whose relics were present in each place, or to whom the churches or chapels were dedicated.[103] In contrast, churches connected to small settlements may have had a priest who was able to offer some funerary rituals, but even these might have been fairly limited in scope, depending on the abilities of the priest and the availability of resources.[104] Funerary rituals became increasingly important across the period, but they were only one aspect

---

[98]   Thompson, *Dying and Death*, 58; Blair, *The Church*, 429–30.

[99]   V Æthelred 12.1, I Cnut 13.1, ed. Liebermann, *Gesetze*, I.240–1, 294–5.

[100]   See for example Blair, *The Church*, 444.

[101]   For the use of minster in this sense, see R. Morris, *Churches in the Landscape* (London, 1989), 128–31.

[102]   McLaughlin, *Consorting*, 122–3.

[103]   This text is partially ed. C.H. Turner, 'The churches at Winchester in the early eleventh century', *Journal of Theological Studies* 17 (1916): 65–8.

[104]   Gittos, 'Is there any Evidence for the Liturgy of Parish Churches', 68–70.

of a concept of a Christian death which presented dying and death together as a process accompanied by ritual and drama. The rites for the dying were designed to ease the passing of the soul into the next world, and incorporate confession and absolution in the hope of directing the soul towards rest, rather than torment, after death.[105]

The reception of communion immediately before death was also considered to be a significant help in the preparation of the soul, and had been since at least the fourth century, when the First Council of Nicaea determined that even those who had not completed penance should not be denied this viaticum if they were in danger of death, a provision repeated in later texts such as the tenth-century *Old English Penitential*.[106] Similarly, in the early 730s, Pope Gregory III instructed Boniface that those who had killed family members should be denied communion their whole lives – except at the time of death, when it was to be allowed as viaticum.[107] Liturgical *ordines* for the dying instruct that the sick man must be given the viaticum even if he has already eaten that day, in contradiction to the usual stipulation that the Eucharist must be received after fasting, because the viaticum will be the defender and helper in the resurrection of the just, and it will resuscitate him.[108] Ælfric's instruction that the host should be given while the person is still sick, rather than when he had already died, illustrates how important the viaticum was held to be, and perhaps also the confusion that may have existed in the minds of some priests about how it actually worked.[109] Another measure

---

[105]    Paxton, *Christianizing Death*, 88–91, 102–27; see also above, 111–16, and Table 2.1.

[106]    First Council of Nicaea (325), 13, ed. and trans. N.P. Tanner, *Decrees of the Ecumenical Councils* (2 vols, London, 1990), I.12; *Old English Penitential*, 41.03.01, ed. A.J. Frantzen, *The Anglo-Saxon Penitentials: A Cultural Database* (2008), http://www.anglo-saxon.net/penance, accessed November 2012; Paxton, *Christianizing Death*, 35–6.

[107]    *Epistola* 28, ed. M. Tangl, *Die Briefe des Heiligen Bonifatius und Lullus*, MGH, Epistolae Selectae 1 (Berlin, 1916), 51, ll. 12–14: 'De his vero dicimus, qui patrem matrem fratrem aut sororem occiderint, ut toto vitae suae tempore corpus non suscipiat dominicum nisi sui temporis exitu pro viatico'; and see also *Epistola* 64, ed. Tangl, *Die Briefe*, 134, ll. 1–4.

[108]    See for example Bodley 579, fol. 246r, ed. N. Orchard, *The Leofric Missal*, HBS 113–14 (2 vols London, 2002), no. 2198: 'Mox autem ut cum uiderint ad exitum propinquare, communicandus est de sacrificio sancto, etiamsi comedisset ipsa die, quia communio erit ei defensor et adiutor in resurrectione iustorum, et ipsa eum resuscitabit' ('But as soon as they see that death is near, he should be given communion, even if he has already eaten that day, because in the resurrection of the just, communion will be a defender and a helper for him, and it will raise him up again'); see also Laud misc. 482, fol. 68r, ed. B. Fehr, 'Altenglische Ritualtexte für Krankenbesuch, heilige Ölung und Begräbnis', in H. Boehmer (ed.), *Texte und Forschungen zur englischen Kulturgeschichte: Festgabe für Felix Liebermann zum 20. Juli 1921* (Halle, 1921), 20–67, at 65.

[109]    *Pastoral Letter* III.11–13, ed. B. Fehr, *Die Hirtenbriefe Ælfrics in altenglischer und lateinischer Fassung*, Bibliothek der angelsächsischen Prosa 9 (Darmstadt:

of how important the rites for the dying were believed to be is found in the *Old English Penitential*, which claims that if someone receives these rites, his soul is as clean after death as the soul of a child after baptism, although the *Penitential* stops short of assuring such souls a place in heaven.[110]

On the other hand, it is not immediately obvious how readily available these rites were to laity, or whether the most that could be expected for many lay Christians in Anglo-Saxon England was burial with some Christian rites or prayers. Even in the late seventh century deathbed confession seems to have been considered to be ideal, although it is impossible to know how often it was actually offered in practice.[111] Some liturgical books and penitential texts include directions for the performance of the rites for the sick in houses rather than in churches,[112] and priests were instructed to keep to hand the oils used for anointing in baptism or in the rites of the sick, as well as the Eucharist, to ensure that those in danger of death could be provided with the necessary rites to ease their souls' passing.[113] One of the collections of canons in the group of manuscripts associated with Wulfstan includes a statement that a priest should always have the Eucharist prepared for the sick, so that they do not die without communion, and another which declares that priests are to give the viaticum to all the sick before they depart this life.[114] Instructional texts aimed at priests emphasise the importance of the performance of the rites for the sick and dying, and the need for priests to be prepared to perform these offices in times of urgency, apparently assuming that this could be expected of all priests.[115] Penitential texts also warn priests that if they simply refused to perform the rites for the sick and dying for someone in need, they must bear responsibility for that soul on Judgement Day.[116]

There is some evidence that wealthy and powerful laity received the last rites, and sometimes from high-ranking ecclesiastics. Towards the end of the tenth century, Byrhtferth recorded in his *Life of Oswald* that the founder of Ramsey abbey, Ealdorman Æthelwine, died after making his confession, being anointed with holy

---

Wissenschaftliche Buchgesellschaft, 1966, reprinted with supplementary introduction by P. Clemoes [orig. pub. 1914]), 150–1.

[110]    41.15.02, ed. Frantzen, *The Anglo-Saxon Penitentials: A Cultural Database*.

[111]    G 37, U I.viii.5, ed. Finsterwalder, *Canones Theodori*, 256, 300; Foot, *Monastic Life*, 316.

[112]    See above, 112.

[113]    See for example Ælfric, *Pastoral Letter* I.85, ed. Fehr, *Die Hirtenbriefe Ælfrics*, 19; Wulfstan, *Canons of Edgar*, 69, ed. Fowler, *Canons of Edgar*, 18–19.

[114]    Rec B.21, 23, ed. and trans. J.E. Cross and A. Hamer, *Wulfstan's Canon Law Collection* (Cambridge, 1999), 120–1.

[115]    See for example *Pastoral Letter* I.84–92, ed. Fehr, *Die Hirtenbriefe Ælfrics*, 19–21; *Old English Penitential* 41.03.01, 41.15.01–02, ed. Frantzen, *The Anglo-Saxon Penitentials: A Cultural Database*.

[116]    BY 77.02.03, ed. Frantzen, *The Anglo-Saxon Penitentials: A Cultural Database*.

oil, and finally receiving communion: he chanted psalms with those around him until he died, and he was apparently accompanied by Ælfheah, bishop of Winchester, as well as Germanus, abbot of Winchcombe, and their monks.[117] It seems that Æthelwine did not die in the monastery at Ramsey, since his body was apparently carried there with ceremony and met by a procession of the Ramsey monks.[118] In the eleventh century, Earl Godwine seems to have been attended by Bishop Wulfstan and others from Worcester. In addition to performing the last rites and anointing him with oil, their concern was to reclaim land belonging to Worcester which he had claimed inappropriately: according to the account in Hemming's cartulary, Godwine performed penance for this, seemingly on his deathbed, although in due course his son disregarded this.[119] Neither of these accounts is without difficulty, but it seems likely that affluent individuals in particular might have been attended on their deathbeds by representatives of major churches hoping to encourage them to donate for the good of their souls.[120] Indeed, the rituals for the sick and dying encourage the dying man to bequeath his property, while one of the Blickling homilies encourages priests not to be too eager for the wealth of dead men.[121]

Such bequests are visible too in the *Libellus Æthelwoldi*, a collection of tenth-century material embedded in the later history of Ely known as the *Liber Eliensis*, including the account of how, when Siferth of Downham felt that his last hour was approaching, he summoned Abbot Byrhtnoth and the Ely community, and arranged to draw up his will.[122] Siferth seems to have lived some time longer, since his will was apparently sent to Ealdorman Æthelwine, who sent back a message asking

[117] *Vita S. Oswaldi*, 21, ed. and trans. Lapidge, *The Lives of St Oswald and St Ecgwine*, 199–201.

[118] *Vita S. Oswaldi*, 21, ed. and trans. Lapidge, *The Lives of St Oswald and St Ecgwine*, 199–201.

[119] Hearne, *Hemingi Chartularium*, I.259–60: 'Nam Godwinus quidam, frater Leofrici comitis, ejusdem villule possessor, infirmitate tactus, cum ad extrema ductus esset, a pie memorie Wulfstano, tunc temporis monacho et decano, postea vero episcopo, et a venerabili Wilstano, qui postea abbas Gloeceastre claruit, oleo unctus est, penitentia que sibi injuncta, de terra illa ab ipsis calumniatus est. Qui statim eam de jure ecclesie esse recognovit, eamque bono animo eis tradidit in jus ecclesiasticum possidendam, penitentiam agens, quod tam diu eam retinuit. Post mortem autem ejus, filius ejus, nomine Agelwinus, qui a Danis obses manibus truncatus est, testamentum patris sui irritum faciens, adjutorio patrui sui, comitis videlicet jam dicti Leofrici, eandem terram monasterio auferens, suo juri addixit. Nec multum post ea, justo Dei judicio, ipsam, et omnia, que habebat, cum vita sua perdidit, morteque ignominiosa in casa bovarii sui vitam finiens, vix duorum servorum ministerio sepulture traditus est'; Tinti, *Sustaining Belief*, 4, 308.

[120] This is also suggested by the eighth-century *Dialogues of Ecgberht*, Responsio II, ed. Haddan and Stubbs, *Councils*, III.404; Foot, *Monastic Life*, 316.

[121] e.g. Laud misc. 482, fol. 50v, and CCCC 422, p. 401, both ed. Fehr, 'Altenglische Ritualtexte', 50 and discussed above, 112–16; *Hom.* IV, ed. Morris, *Blickling Homilies*, 43; Tinti, *Sustaining Belief*, 308.

[122] II.11, ed. E.O. Blake, *Liber Eliensis* (London, 1962), 84–8.

about precisely what was wanted, and the conditions under which his property was distributed: it appears that Siferth was able to reply to this message as well. The account also records that Siferth had previously visited Ely and asked to be buried there,[123] and that he had visited on a second occasion and asked to be taken to the burial place of Goding of Gretton, a friend of his. On this second occasion, when he was in the churchyard, Siferth seems to have identified his own preferred place of burial more precisely, perhaps like the priest in the *Life of Dunstan*.[124] The interest of the *Libellus* is in the land at least as much as in its patrons, and the author does not record whether Siferth was attended in his final hours by anyone from Ely, or by a priest at all, but the care with which he apparently made arrangements for his death suggests that he might have been expected to have sought this out. These cases are clearly exceptional, but the expectation of the use of these rites in instructional literature suggests that at least towards the end of the period, the rites for the dying in some form were probably available to people who lived in settlements with a church and a priest, although in some cases what was offered may have been very simple.

In contrast, the rites for those who died in monasteries may often have been much more complex, as with the provision of funerary rites for the body. Death in a monastery was a communal occasion, the dead person surrounded by the living as the entire community gathered to share in the liturgy, as death is communal in that it is shared by the wider church.[125] The liturgical rituals outlined in the late tenth-century *Regularis Concordia*, and in Ælfric's *Letter to the Monks of Eynsham* (which draws on the *Regularis Concordia*) instruct that when a sick brother is approaching death, everyone should come together to assist his passing, and they are to sing the prayers which commend the soul to God.[126] Other liturgical *ordines* state that after the dying person has received his last communion, he is to be read the Passion until his soul finally leaves his body, at which point the seven penitential psalms should be sung, and a litany performed, followed by prayers requesting that angels come to guide the

---

[123]   II.11, ed. E.O. Blake, *Liber Eliensis* (London, 1962), 86: '… dixit se sortitum esse locum sepulture sue rogavitque omnes qui aderant, ut super hac re sibi testificarentur'.

[124]   II.11, ed. E.O. Blake, *Liber Eliensis* (London, 1962), 86–7: 'Alio quoque tempore, post mortem scilicet Godingi de Gretune, venit secundo idem vir ad Hely, ubi noverat illum esse sepultum, rogavitque fratres, ut eum ad sepulturam illius ducerent. Nam erat ei familiarissimus. Quo cum venissent, vocavit ad se abbatem et Ædricum et Leovricum de Berle et Levingum de Trumpentune innotuitque eis, quod sui karissimi et fidelissimi amici ibi essent sepulti et quod ipse nimia infirmitate depressus morti appropinquasset, 'ideoque', inquid, 'o karissimi mei, volo ut conventio mea coram vobis renovetur, videlicet quomodo hic elegi mihi locum sepulture mee …'.

[125]   A.G. Martimort, 'Comment meurt un chrétien', *La Maison-Dieu* 44 (1955): 5–28, at 20; C. Cubitt, 'Monastic Memory and Identity in Early Anglo-Saxon England', in W.O. Frazer and A. Tyrrell (eds), *Social Identity in Early Medieval Britain* (London, 2000), 252–76, at 268–71.

[126]   RC, 67, ed. T. Symons, *Regularis Concordia: The Monastic Agreement of the Monks and Nuns of the English Nation* (London, 1953), 65.

soul.[127] Monastic rituals in particular highlight the care of the body, describing how the body should be washed and dressed in appropriate vestments, and instructing that brothers should stay by the body chanting psalms until the burial.[128]

These more complex and extensive rituals were probably usually employed almost exclusively by and for those in religious communities and those of high rank who were associated with them, and even in many religious communities these precise rituals may not have been the norm, since both the *Regularis Concordia* and Ælfric have strong Winchester connections. It is not clear whether those who arranged for burial in minster cemeteries also wanted their bodies to be prepared for burial at the community, or whether those at the minster simply identified the burial place and committed the body to the ground. It is just possible that some individuals wished not only to be buried in a monastery but also to die there, and so to take advantage of the more extensive rituals offered to monastic inhabitants. There are several recorded instances of individuals entering a monastery towards the end of their lives, notable among them being some of the kings in the early Anglo-Saxon period who abdicated in favour of ending their lives in a monastery.[129] A different phenomenon is discussed by Megan McLaughlin, who notes that in early medieval Francia some individuals became full members of monastic communities on their deathbeds, thus entitling them to privileges otherwise granted only to monastic inhabitants.[130] There are hints of this practice in Anglo-Saxon England too, although it is not clear how accurate the information is: according to the C and D versions of the *Anglo-Saxon Chronicle*, Earl Odda (also known as Æthelwine) was consecrated a monk shortly before his death in 1056; and William of Malmesbury records that in Dunstan's time, one Ælfwold sought to become a monk on his deathbed.[131]

---

[127] e.g. Bodley 579, fol. 246r, ed. Orchard, *Leofric Missal*, no. 2198–9; Rouen, BM, 274, fols. 213v–214v, ed. H.A. Wilson, *The Missal of Robert of Jumièges*, HBS 11 (London, 1896), 297–8; also Orléans, BM, 105, pp. 336–40, ed. A. Davril, *The Winchcombe Sacramentary: Orléans, Bibliothèque municipale, 127 (105)*, HBS 105 (London, 1995), nos. 1840e–1846; Worcester, F. 173, fols. 16r–18r; see also CCCC 422, pp. 430–1, partially edited by Fehr, 'Altenglische Ritualtexte', 66.

[128] *RC*, 67, ed. Symons, *Regularis Concordia*, 65.

[129] For discussion see C. Stancliffe, 'Kings Who Opted Out', in D. Bullough, R. Collins and P. Wormald (eds), *Ideal and Reality in Frankish and Anglo-Saxon Society: Studies Presented to John Michael Wallace-Hadrill* (Oxford, 1983), 154–76; S.J. Ridyard, 'Monk-kings and the Anglo-Saxon hagiographic tradition', *Haskins Society Journal: Studies in Medieval History* 6 (1995): 13–27. In some cases the decision of a king or nobleman to retire to a monastery may have been taken because of political circumstances: see C. Cubitt, 'Ælfric's Lay Patrons', in H. Magennis and M. Swan (eds), *A Companion to Ælfric* (Leiden, 2009), 165–92, at 175–6, for example.

[130] McLaughlin, *Consorting*, 168–9.

[131] *ASC* (CD), s. a. 1056, ed. O'Keeffe, *The Anglo-Saxon Chronicle: A Collaborative Edition: Vol. 5, MS C*, 116–17; and Cubbin (ed.), *The Anglo–Saxon Chronicle: A Collaborative Edition: Vol. 6, MS D*, 75; William of Malmesbury, *Vita S. Dunstani*, ii.25.1, ed. and trans. Winterbottom and Thomson, *William of Malmesbury: Saints' Lives*, 280–1.

Earlier sources too seem to suggest the perceived value of dying in a monastery as well as burial there, and in this context, the grant made by Ordnoth and his wife is particularly interesting.[132] Ordnoth and his wife granted their property to the Old Minster on the condition that the Minster had a responsibility to fetch them on their last day, but they do not specify whether it was their dead bodies which were to be fetched, or whether they wanted to spend their last hours in the monastery. The involvement of Ordnoth's wife might call the latter interpretation into question, since the preparation of a woman's body for death by the Old Minster monks might have been considered to be problematic, although archaeological evidence confirms that both men and women were buried in the Old Minster's lay cemetery.[133] Similarly, the eleventh-century Abbotsbury guild statutes instruct that 15 men should fetch a guild-brother who falls ill within 60 miles, and 30 should fetch him if he has died, and they are to bring him to the place which he desired in life; while if someone died in the local area as many guild-brothers as possible were to attend the body and bring it to the minster, as well as offering prayers for his soul.[134] The guild statutes do not identify who was responsible for preparing the body for burial, or whether an ill but living guild-brother would be taken to the minster while dying so that he could receive the rites for the sick there, but it may be that these were desired just as burial at the minster was.

Burial in the cemeteries of major churches brought with it inclusion in the prayers of the community, and the masses and prayers offered for their souls illustrate the importance of the final resting place in this context. Alcuin's mass for the living and the dead asks God to show mercy on those who have given alms and those who are joined to the community in familiarity, and to deem worthy to add to the company of the elect those whose bodies rest in the *monasterium* or whose names are read out before the altar, and for refreshment to be granted to those souls.[135] Similarly, a prayer from the personal prayer book of Ælfwine, dean of the New Minster, Winchester in the early eleventh century, asks for forgiveness of sins for all those whose bodies lie in the cemeteries, and also for all those from whom alms have been received.[136] The bodies of those who had arranged for their burials in the cemeteries of religious houses were a perpetual reminder of the duty of those communities to pray for their souls, highlighting that as with the bodies and souls of the saints, it was difficult to separate them conceptually even when they were visibly separated and the body laid to rest.

---

[132]    S 1524.

[133]    Kjølbye-Biddle, 'Dispersal', 218–33.

[134]    Abbotsbury guild statutes, *Councils and Synods*, I.i, no. 67.

[135]    Alcuin, *Missa pro salute uiuorum et mortuorum*, ed. J. Deshusses, 'Les messes d'Alcuin', *Archiv für Liturgiewissenschaft* 14 (1972): 7–41, at 27–8.

[136]    London, British Library, Cotton Titus D.xxvi, fols. 64r–v, ed. B. Günzel, *Ælfwine's Prayerbook (London, British Library, Cotton Titus D.xxvi + xxvii)*, HBS 108 (London, 1993), no. 76.39.

Another significant aspect of the funerary rituals for the body is the concern shown over the struggle for the soul which was believed to take place between angels and demons immediately following death.[137] The viaticum was believed to be important in the context of this struggle, because it was understood as a necessary preparation for the journey faced by the soul, including the assaults of devils, where it could act as a shield against the demonic attacks that would beset the soul as it left the body.[138] Funerary rituals contain requests for the help of angels to keep these demons away from the soul and to lead the soul into a place of rest, and often call on St Michael in particular, as his power in defeating demons and leading souls to rest was believed to be very great.[139] Here the continual prayer and the continual watch over the body until it was buried were significant in keeping these demons at bay. For those who were not considered to be saintly, this process may have been considered to take some time, especially if there was a prolonged struggle between angels and devils, and a belief that the soul might linger near the body for some time may also have contributed to the desire to offer prayers to dispel the demons, both for the benefit of the soul and for the benefit of those who kept watch over the body.[140]

Just as people hoped that their souls would find a place of rest after death, they were also concerned to arrange a suitable place where their bodies would rest in peace until they were resurrected. The provisions that were made for the body were often intended to affect the soul as well, whether directly or indirectly: souls would benefit from the prayers offered for those whose bodies lay in the cemeteries of religious communities, where memorials might also prompt more prayers; the careful treatment of the body in the hours before, during and after death and especially the rituals for the sick and dying were primarily designed for the soul even though they were enacted on the body. Those who requested such services evidently understood that these were believed to have a significant effect in the afterlife, but people also wanted burial places which reflected their status, or which allowed them to await the final judgement near their friends or relatives. Societal, cultural and theological concerns were melded together and sometimes it is not easy to disentangle the driving factors: Ealdorman Æthelwine undoubtedly wanted to be buried

---

[137]   See above, 111–16, and below, 318–23.

[138]   G. Grabka, 'Christian Viaticum: A Study of its Cultural Background', *Traditio: Studies in Ancient and Medieval History, Thought, and Religion* 9 (1953): 1–43; D. Sicard, 'Christian Death', in A.G. Martimort (ed.), *The Church at Prayer: Vol. 3, The Sacraments* (Collegeville, MN, 1988), 221–40, at 226.

[139]   See for example Bodley 579, fols. 246r–250v, ed. Orchard, *Leofric Missal*, nos. 2199–2228; CCCC 422, pp. 429–35, ed. Fehr, 'Altenglische Ritualtexte', 65–7; Rouen, BM, 274, fols. 214r–v, ed. Wilson, *Jumièges*, 297–8; D. Keck, *Angels and Angelology in the Middle Ages* (Oxford, 1998), 204–5; and above, 115–18.

[140]   For this belief in a later context, see E.A.R. Brown, 'Death and the human body in the later Middle Ages: The legislation of Boniface VIII on the division of the corpse', *Viator* 12 (1981): 221–70, esp. 223 and n. 3; see also below, 318–23.

in the monastery at Ramsey because of the implications of social status that this brought with it, but the rites for body and soul which preceded his burial were enacted as part of his association with the Ramsey community, and they brought him into closer contact with that community even as he left the world of the living in which it operated.

## Exclusion

Consecrated ground is mentioned infrequently in requests for burial, presumably because once the practice was widely established it was simply taken for granted. While it may have been some time before formal consecrations of earlier cemeteries took place, the larger churches and communities which are most visible in the historical record were evidently considered attractive as places of rest for such a range of reasons that burial in their cemeteries was probably considered akin to burial in consecrated ground even if the cemeteries themselves had not been formally and liturgically consecrated. The focus of consecrated cemeteries is the inclusion of the Christian dead as part of the company of believers who will be resurrected to eternal life, but naturally the demarcation of places of inclusion highlights also the possibility of exclusion, whether deliberate or accidental. The time and effort invested in securing burial places or rituals which resulted in inclusion in the cemeteries of religious communities or commemoration in their prayers is indicative of its importance, and it follows that people who believed in the value of these prayers and places of burial would not want to be excluded. Once again theological factors are of course bound up with social and cultural values, since even those who were sceptical or ignorant of the finer points of Christian belief might wish to be buried near friends or relatives, and not be treated as an outcast either in life or death. This is particularly important since it is clear that inclusion and exclusion in burial were significant even before consecrated burial grounds existed in the sense of spaces defined, marked out and hallowed by liturgical rites. Moreover, the concept of consecrated ground does not explain clearly how, or why, the treatment of the mortal body was believed to affect the immortal soul.

These complexities are illustrated neatly by Bede's description in his *Historia Ecclesiastica* of a brother he had known personally, who had been retained in his monastery despite his bad behaviour and drunkenness on the grounds that he was a good craftsman whose skills were useful to the other monks.[141] At the point of death, this brother had a vision: he was shown hell with a place reserved for him alongside Satan and Caiphas, and although the other brothers urged him to repent while he was still alive, he was thrown into despair and died without receiving viaticum. Bede notes that the brother's body was buried in the remotest places of the monastery, and that no one presumed (or dared?) to pray for him.[142]

---

[141]	*HE*, V.14, ed. Lapidge, Monat and Robin, *Histoire ecclésiastique*, III.90–4.

[142]	*HE*, V.14.2, ll. 1–4, ed. Lapidge, Monat and Robin, *Histoire ecclésiastique*, III.92: 'Talia dicens sine uiatico salutis obiit, et corpus eius in ultimis est monasterii locis humatum,

Excavated seventh- and eighth-century Northumbrian monastic cemeteries indicate the communal burial places where monastic inhabitants expected to rest, and the deliberate decision to treat this brother's body differently is therefore highly significant.[143] This point was not lost in later centuries: one manuscript of the Old English translation of Bede's history seems to advert to its unhappy end with the image of a small figure, its legs entangled with rings, as the initial I at the beginning of this chapter (see Figure 5.1).[144] It is especially interesting that Bede begins his account by noting that if it would have done any good, he could have mentioned the brother's name: the deeds of the unnamed brother are remembered as a warning to others to choose a different (and less damning) path while there is still time, but his name was not preserved in the written record. Unlike those who wanted so desperately to be remembered and prayed for, this brother ensured his absence from the communal record except as an example for others to avoid.

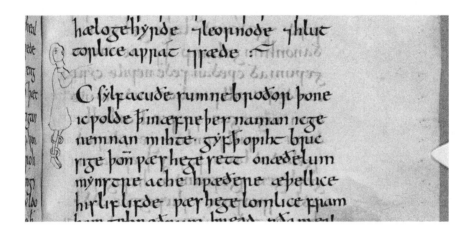

Figure 5.1    Cambridge, Corpus Christi College, 41, p. 433, detail

*Note*: By kind permission of The Master and Fellows of Corpus Christi College, Cambridge.

---

neque aliquis pro eo uel missas facere uel psalmos cantare uel saltim orare praesumebat'. This is strikingly similar to the story of Justus in the *Dialogues* of Gregory the Great, IV.57.8–14, ed. de Vogüé and Antin, *Dialogues, Livre IV*, III.188–92.

[143]    e.g. Cramp, *Wearmouth and Jarrow Monastic Sites*, 76–90, 173–86; R.A. Hall and M. Whyman, 'Settlement and monasticism at Ripon, North Yorkshire, from the 7th to 11th centuries A.D', *Medieval Archaeology: Journal of the Society for Medieval Archaeology* 40 (1996): 62–150, at 73–99, 120–4.

[144]    Cambridge, Corpus Christi College, 41, p. 433. For discussion of this manuscript see above, 83 and n. 104. The Old English text in this manuscript notes that ultimately 'his lichama wæs bebyrged on ðam ytemestem stowum þæs mynstres ] nænig mann ne dorste for hine sealmas ne mæssan singan ne furðon for hine gebiddan' (CCCC 41, p. 435).

What is deeply puzzling in this account is precisely why the brother's body was treated differently, a point which Bede does not explain. It is clear from Bede's narrative that the brother's soul was held to be in significant peril, as the brother himself reported that he was damned, and his death without repentance and without viaticum surely did not help him in this matter. The effects of prayer for different groups in the afterlife as outlined by Augustine held that prayers for the wicked were at least some consolation to the living, even if they could not actually help the dead souls, but this seems to be in the context of the uncertainty of the fate of the soul, where people offered prayers in the hope of helping their departed friends and relatives in the beyond. Where the soul was known (or believed) to be damned, as in this case, the situation might be different: Augustine's views are repeated in the collections of Theodore's teachings, but they are presented alongside the statement that the one who offers masses for a wicked man blasphemes against God; and these statements were ultimately incorporated into the tenth-century *Old English Scriftboc*.[145] It is not clear whether Augustine's views were intended to modify or to complement the statement about blasphemy against God, but clearly a distinction was drawn between cases of certain damnation like this one, and the more general uncertainty that attended the deaths of all but the 'very special dead'. This distinction seems to reappear in the later penitentials which forbid funerary mass and psalm-singing for those who died either by their own hand, or as a result of judicial execution.[146]

Although there seems to be a theological basis for denying prayers for the brother who saw his own damnation, there is no such obvious explanation for the exclusion of the body. Bede might have been expected to follow Augustine's interpretation of the relationship between body and soul and to have concluded that the body was unimportant. But perhaps here Gregory's warnings about what might happen to the bodies of the wicked were more influential: fear of alarming occurrences at the grave, such as the body being thrown or dragged out of its grave, might have made it seem expedient to bury the body of the wicked monk as far away as was feasible. In considering why the bodies of certain types of offenders were excluded from consecrated ground, some of whom had been executed probably as a result of the workings of the judicial system, there are similar difficulties in interpretation. In particular, it is not immediately obvious which way around the spiritual effects of exclusion were understood to work, or whether there was even consistency of thought on the matter. The 'damned' status of the brother in Bede's account was confirmed independently of the location of his body, so that the location followed from this condemnation and not the other way around; in contrast, the texts which refer to the exclusion of bodies from consecrated ground never explain whether the bodies of offenders were excluded

---

[145]   D 83–4, U II.V.8–9, ed. Finsterwalder, *Canones Theodori*, 246, 319; *Scriftboc*, 21.06.01–21.07.01, ed. Frantzen, *The Anglo-Saxon Penitentials: A Cultural Database*.

[146]   e.g. *Old English Penitential*, 42.05.01–02; *Old English Handbook* 54.13.01–02, ed. Frantzen, *The Anglo-Saxon Penitentials: A Cultural Database*; see also below, 303.

because they were believed to be damned, or whether they were believed to be damned because they were excluded; nor yet whether damnation was a necessary condition either of executed offenders or of those whose bodies were excluded from consecrated ground.

These differences are small but significant: the questions that they raise are not easy to answer and there may have been considerable variety in belief, but it is crucial to remember that the overwhelming impression from so many of the written sources is that the fate of specific individual souls after death is uncertain, especially in complex and difficult cases. The offences which might result in exclusion from consecrated ground, such as perjury, were also those which were believed to send those who committed them to hell with no hope of reprieve, if they died unrepentant.[147] Homilists warned their audiences, with little qualification or adjustment for circumstances, that committing these serious sins endangered the immortal soul.[148] But despite this, the messages from penitential literature more generally illustrate uncertainty about all types of souls. Even though penitential texts emphasise that the rites for the dying brought extraordinary benefits to the soul, they are not prepared to state that the rites guarantee automatic entry into heaven; likewise, they observe that in the case of someone performing penance who was forbidden the Eucharist and who died without it, the fate of this soul is unknown except to God, with whom the soul's judgement rests.[149] The poetic list of truisms in the Old English *Maxims II* includes a statement that offenders must hang because of the offences they commit, followed immediately by a comment that no one knows where that soul will go after death, nor any souls, all of whom await judgement by God.[150]

This uncertainty is particularly important in the light of assertions in some recent scholarship that certain burial practices may be a 'sign' of damnation, that those excluded from consecrated ground were automatically damned, or that exclusion from consecrated ground was a deliberate attempt to bring about

---

[147] II Æthelstan 26; III Æthelred 7; II Cnut 33.1, 54.1, ed. Liebermann, *Gesetze*, 164–5, 230–1, 336–7, 348–9; *Old English Penitential* 42.05.01–02; *Old English Handbook* 54.13.01–02, ed. Frantzen, *The Anglo-Saxon Penitentials: A Cultural Database*; see also above, 157–8, 198–9.

[148] e.g. *Hom.* V, ed. Morris, *Blickling Homilies*, 61; Ælfric, *De auguriis*, XVII, ll. 23–9, ed. Skeat, *Lives of Saints*, I.364–6.

[149] *Old English Penitential*, 41.13.01, ed. Frantzen, *The Anglo-Saxon Penitentials: A Cultural Database*. In the same way, if a woman takes the brother of her first husband as a second husband and the couple only repent when close to death, the rites are to be performed for them but only if they promise that they will repent for a long time if they live; if they die in this condition, the fate of their souls is left to God's judgement: *Old English Penitential*, 42.11.02, ed. Frantzen, *The Anglo-Saxon Penitentials: A Cultural Database*.

[150] *Maxims II*, ll. 55–61, ed. E.V.K. Dobbie, *The Anglo-Saxon Minor Poems*, Anglo-Saxon Poetic Records 6 (London, 1942), 57: '... wearh hangian, fægere ongildan þæt he ær facen dyde mann cynne. Meotod ana wat hwyder seo sawul sceal syððan hweorfan, and ealle þa gastas þe for gode hweorfað æfter deaðdæge, domes bidað on fæder fæðme'.

damnation.[151] The fate of each individual soul was dependent on the actions of each individual person, and it is made clear in both penitential and homiletic texts that repentance right up until the moment of death was both allowable and desirable. The *Old English Penitential* notes that whenever genuine conversion takes place, even on the day of death, it should be accepted, and that God's mercy is so great as to be unrecountable.[152] The fifth Blickling homily, a Lenten homily which takes as its theme the imminence of death and the necessity of preparation for it, warns that hell is filled with thieves, evil judges, murderers and others, before noting that good judges are those who punish the wicked severely, including thieves and those who swear false oaths.[153] But it is clear that even offenders of this nature are not necessarily doomed to hell: the homilist also states that if someone commits murder and realises the severity of the offence and turns to penance, 'there is no doubt that the Lord will grant forgiveness to those who seek to deserve it'.[154]

While Ælfric warned in one of his homilies that many types of offence would result in damnation if the perpetrators did not repent before death, elsewhere he gave a rather more concrete example, based on the 'Good Thief' who was crucified with Christ and who repented immediately before his death: he insisted that unrepentant thieves would be led to hell after they were executed, but he also instructed that thieves awaiting death should repent while they still had time.[155] Ælfric also explained in his letter for Bishop Wulfsige of Sherborne (d.1002) that confession and penance even in the last hour would allow men to come to God's mercy rather than to be condemned to hell,[156] and although this instruction was aimed at priests responsible for performing the ritual of anointing, he explored the same idea elsewhere in his homilies, stating that if a man turns from his sins, he will be saved even if he dies very soon afterwards.[157] Crucially, Ælfric also warned that even if someone appears to be wicked, his friends should not despair of him, because no one knows the extent of God's mercy.[158] This uncertainty and

---

[151]  Thompson, *Dying and Death*, 171–5; Hadley, 'Burying the Socially and Physically Distinctive in Later Anglo-Saxon England', 112.

[152]  *Old English Penitential*, 41.02.01, 41.09.02, ed. Frantzen, *The Anglo-Saxon Penitentials: A Cultural Database*; see also G 37, U I.viii.5, ed. Finsterwalder, *Canones Theodori*, 256, 300.

[153]  *Hom.* V, ed. Morris, *Blickling Homilies*, 62.

[154]  *Hom.* V, ed. Morris, *Blickling Homilies*, 64.

[155]  Ælfric, *Passio S. Albani* [*Acitofel et Absalon*], *LS* XIX, ll. 154–9, ed. Skeat, *Lives of Saints*, I.424–6; N. Marafioti, 'Punishing bodies and saving souls: Capital and corporal punishment in late Anglo-Saxon England', *Haskins Society Journal: Studies in Medieval History* 20 (2009): 39–57, at 46–8.

[156]  Ælfric, *Pastoral Letter for Wulfsige*, I.92, ed. Fehr, *Die Hirtenbriefe Ælfrics*, 21.

[157]  *Hom.* XV, l. 52–4, ed. J.C. Pope, *Homilies of Ælfric: A Supplementary Collection*, EETS, OS 259–60 (2 vols London, 1967–8), 531.

[158]  *CH* I.35, ll. 208–18, ed. P. Clemoes, *Ælfric's Catholic Homilies: The First Series*, EETS, SS 17 (Oxford, 1997), 482–3.

reluctance to pronounce on the fate of the soul, even about those who seem to be wicked, is extremely important in considering the perception of those who were judicially killed.

The importance of confession before execution was ultimately incorporated into legal texts too, when Wulfstan included in royal legislation the provision that condemned men who desired confession should be never be refused their request, and demanded that compensation should be made if such a request was refused.[159] It is not clear whether Wulfstan instituted this or merely enshrined in law an existing practice that was perhaps infrequently applied: Ælfric seems to assume that a confessor might be available to condemned men, but it is also possible, as Nicole Marafioti argues, that in such cases Ælfric considered that the usual requirement of confession to a priest should be waived.[160] Wulfstan also instructed that condemned men were not to be executed during the feast-time of Sunday, and it is therefore possible that this too may have allowed a window of opportunity for confession to take place before execution; and although he stops short of forbidding executions during seasons of feasting and fasting more generally, as he had forbidden oaths and ordeals (and marriages), it is possible that this may have been intended.[161] Wulfstan's approach to the use of judicial execution was informed by penitential theology, so that he attempted to allow offenders the opportunity of repentance and penance by focusing punishment on the body in order to preserve the soul, and this same penitential theology lies behind his insistence of the availability of confession for condemned men.[162]

Law and penance might have worked together here: those who had confessed their sins and genuinely repented should not, according to ecclesiastical teaching and tradition, have been believed to be damned even if they were executed, and even if their bodies might still be buried in unconsecrated ground. Wulfstan's efforts to prevent the damnation of souls if at all possible warn that the exclusion of bodies from consecrated ground in the legislation which he wrote, at least, should not be interpreted as a deliberate effort on his part to punish by attempting to bring about damnation. Moreover, the issue of good judges and fair judgements was evidently of some concern to Anglo-Saxon ecclesiastics and legislators, and the frequent warnings about the importance of good and appropriate judgements in life suggest that those who attempted to pre-judge souls, or to use a burial location to 'force' the judgement of God – whose own mercy and just judgement would determine whether or not a soul was damned or saved – would probably endanger their own souls in the attempt.[163] This would also run directly contrary to the message of penitential theology, which is that repentance should always

---

[159]    II Cnut 44–4.1, ed. Liebermann, *Gesetze*, I.342–3.
[160]    Marafioti, 'Punishing bodies', 48–9.
[161]    II Cnut 45, ed. Liebermann, *Gesetze*, I.342–3.
[162]    See above, 198–9.
[163]    See above, 143–7, 175–7.

be encouraged, in the same way that it is inconceivable that penance could ever involve execution.

Confession and its effects are of course not directly visible in the archaeological record, and it is therefore just as impossible to confirm whether any of the individuals buried in execution cemeteries had made confession as it is to say with any certainty that they were considered to be damned because of their location of burial. In fact, it is questionable whether any practice in the ground is indicative of damnation *per se*, since damnation is, in the first instance, a condition of the soul and not of the body. This is not to say that unusual burial practices were not significant, that they did not indicate concern about the body, that some people did not worry about either the souls or the bodies of those buried outside consecrated ground, or that there were not unorthodox beliefs about the nature of executed or other dead bodies. Some practices may have been thought to have a range of effects: William of Malmesbury notes with some surprise that Ælfheah's body remained incorrupt despite his decapitation, which was apparently usually thought to be impossible, although it is possible too that this was a dig at Bury St Edmunds, where the body of St Edmund was held to be incorrupt (and the head and body joined together) despite Edmund having been decapitated.[164] It is of course also important to recognise that there may have been multiple interpretations of burial in unconsecrated ground or of particular treatments of the body, and some perhaps tied up more with the fear of societal repercussions and social exclusion than with exclusion in the afterlife. Burial outside consecrated ground was a penalty which may have been held by some people to have spiritual consequences, but its meaning was probably both more varied, and more complex and sophisticated, than a straightforward and very general equation with damnation.

Another indication of the complexity of interpreting the apparently rigid condemnation of certain types of offences is evident in the context of suicides, another group of problematic souls who were equated in some circumstances with executed offenders. Suicide was condemned in both homiletic and penitential texts, as it had been condemned by patristic writers such as Jerome and Augustine, because it contravened the law on killing and because suicide naturally allowed no opportunity for repentance, confession and penance, unless the act was not fully completed immediately.[165] Despite occasional references in ecclesiastical writings, suicide is not mentioned in Anglo-Saxon secular legislation, and finding clear evidence for suicide in Anglo-Saxon England is difficult: even if there was apparently no legal penalty, it is reasonable to assume that there must have been significant social stigma attached to suicide. As Alexander Murray has shown, actual cases of suicide seem often to have been covered up or were presumably

---

[164]   William of Malmesbury, *Vita Dunstani*, II.34.3, ed. Winterbottom and Thomson, *William of Malmesbury: Saints' Lives*, 296. I am grateful to Elisabeth van Houts for the suggestion of the possible connection with Bury St Edmund's.

[165]   A. Murray, *Suicide in the Middle Ages: 2, The Curse on Self-Murder* (Oxford, 2000), 90–190; Clayton, 'Suicide in the works of Ælfric', 342–4.

simply not recorded precisely because it was considered to be so problematic, since it seems inconceivable that suicide was never a reality in the Middle Ages.[166] It is of course also difficult to identify suicide clearly in the archaeological record: many methods of suicide may have left no clear trace on the skeleton and in some cases covering up a suicide might have meant that the body was not treated differently from others.

It is possible that those who were believed to have brought about their own deaths might have been buried in or near execution cemeteries, or in locations on boundaries where other problematic bodies were buried.[167] There are some possible candidates for suicides known from archaeological excavations, and it may be that the practice of burying suicides at crossroads, attested in later sources and lasting at least into the nineteenth century, had some currency in early medieval England too. In this context, Andrew Reynolds notes the body of a woman discovered at the crossroads between the Pilgrim's Way and the Roman road heading south from Rochester, dating probably from some time between the late seventh and late tenth centuries, a find made during the excavations which took place prior to the construction of part of the Channel Tunnel Rail Link.[168] Another possible candidate for a suicide is the crossroads burial discovered near Broad Town (Wiltshire), dating probably to the sixth or seventh century.[169] Both of these discoveries were unexpected, chance finds: since early medieval crossroads are not normally excavated on their own merits, it is not easy to test how frequently crossroad-burial might have taken place in the early Middle Ages. Where isolated burials are found, perhaps especially those on boundaries, these might be possible candidates for the burials of suicides, but once again it is often difficult or impossible to identify from the body whether suicide or some other perceived problem resulted in the burial of these individuals away from communal and consecrated cemeteries.[170]

The textual information about suicide from late seventh- and early eighth-century England is complex. Although most authors condemned suicide, Jerome had considered it acceptable in extreme cases where virginity was threatened: Aldhelm followed this line in his treatise on virginity, but noted that usually

---

[166]   A. Murray, *Suicide in the Middle Ages: 1, The Violent against Themselves* (Oxford, 1998), 21–30, 120–60.

[167]   Reynolds, *Anglo-Saxon Deviant Burial Customs*, 216–17.

[168]   Ibid., 212: the date was established through C14 analysis, which returned a date of AD 680–980 at 68% confidence (GU–9013).

[169]   B. Clarke, 'An early Anglo-Saxon cross-roads burial from Broad Town, north Wiltshire', *Wiltshire Archaeological and Natural History Magazine* 97 (2004): 89–94.

[170]   See for example Reynolds, *Anglo-Saxon Deviant Burial Customs*, 216–17; J. Buckberry, 'Cemetery Diversity in the Mid to Late Anglo-Saxon Period in Lincolnshire and Yorkshire', in Buckberry and Cherryson (eds), *Burial in Later Anglo-Saxon England*, 1–25, at 14–16.

suicides were considered to be outside the society of the Church.[171] The various versions of the material which seems to represent Theodore's penitential and canonical teachings contain a range of instructions about suicides, primarily about what priests should do in response to suicides and what can be done for the bodies or souls of those who took their own lives.[172] The earliest version of this material, known now as the *Iudicia Theodori* and probably written by an Irish student of Theodore's, instructs that masses should not be said for those who kill themselves of their own will, but that some people do offer masses for Christians who kill themselves because they have gone out of their mind through sudden temptation or through insanity.[173] A version which circulated under the heading *Canones Gregorii*, and which is less easy to date, instructs that prayers can be offered for a suicide only if he killed himself because he was afflicted by the devil and if he was a religious; in contrast, those who kill themselves because of despair, fear, or other unknown reasons (or who were laity), are to be left to the judgement of God and prayers are not to be offered for them.[174]

Both of these texts were available to a compiler known as the 'Disciple of the Northumbrians', who probably worked in the first half of the eighth century, and who tried to reconcile the various versions of Theodore's teaching from the conflicting accounts which he found, and by asking Theodore's students.[175] This version incorporated both of the earlier prescriptions with a couple of small additions which do not entirely aid clarification, ultimately creating a set of conflicting and ambiguous instructions. The compiler repeats both of the statements from the *Canones Gregorii* but adds that 'we do not dare to pray' for those who killed themselves from despair or fear.[176] He then also repeated the statements from the *Iudicia*, noting that masses should not be offered for those who kill themselves but

[171]   Aldhelm, *Prosa de virginitate*, XXXI, ed. R. Ehwald, *Aldhelmi opera*, MGH, Scriptores, Auctores Antiquissimi 15 (Berlin, 1919), 270, l. 1: 'extraneus ab ecclesiae societate inter biothanatos reputabiter'; Murray, *Suicide in the Middle Ages: 2, The Curse on Self-Murder*, 99–102; Clayton, 'Suicide in the works of Ælfric', 343.

[172]   For discussion of this material see in particular Clayton, 'Suicide in the works of Ælfric', 344–7, where she corrects the analysis of Murray, *Suicide in the Middle Ages: 2, The Curse on Self-Murder*, 252–63.

[173]   D.92–3, ed.Finsterwalder, *Canones Theodori*, 246; T.M. Charles-Edwards, 'The Penitential of Theodore and the "Iudicia Theodori"', in M. Lapidge (ed.), *Archbishop Theodore: Commemorative Studies on his Life and Influence* (Cambridge, 1995), 141–74, at 151; Clayton, 'Suicide in the works of Ælfric', 345.

[174]   G 152, ed. Finsterwalder, *Canones Theodori*, 267–8; Charles-Edwards, 'The Penitential of Theodore and the "Iudicia Theodori"', 157; Clayton, 'Suicide in the works of Ælfric', 346.

[175]   Charles-Edwards, 'The Penitential of Theodore and the "Iudicia Theodori"', 148–55, 158; R. Flechner, 'The making of the Canons of Theodore', *Peritia* 17/18 (2004): 121–43, at 126–30.

[176]   U II.10.1–2, ed. Finsterwalder, *Canones Theodori*, 324; Clayton, 'Suicide in the works of Ælfric', 346–7.

adding that prayer and alms may be offered for these souls, and noting that some people do say masses for Christians who killed themselves because of insanity.[177] In all of these rulings, the permissibility of masses or other offerings is rather ambiguous, and dependent on the status of the suicide (religious or lay), or on motivations which are not always easy to identify.

It is noteworthy that these prescriptions are rather different from the regulations set down in a canon of a council held in Braga in 561, which Murray identifies as one of the most significant and pervasive influences on the treatment of suicides.[178] This canon instructed that suicides and those who were judicially killed should not be commemorated at all, that they should not be remembered in the offering, and that their bodies should not be buried with psalm-singing.[179] While the instructions in the material associated with Theodore indicate that both the bodies and souls of suicides were considered to be highly problematic, it seems that rather more leeway was allowed here than it may have been elsewhere in Europe. By the late tenth century, however, the Braga canon had been incorporated into Anglo-Saxon penitential texts: the *Old English Penitential* instructs that if someone commits suicide with a weapon or at the devil's instigation, no one should sing mass or commit the body to earth with psalms, and the same treatment is specified for those who are executed as a result of their offences.[180] The *Old English Handbook*, an early eleventh-century penitential text which may be connected with Archbishop Wulfstan, repeats these prescriptions but adds that the bodies of suicides and executed offenders should not be buried in consecrated ground.[181] In contrast to the prescriptions in the material associated with Theodore, the Old English penitential texts are apparently unconcerned with the motivation behind the deed and whether the perpetrator was lay or religious, or how these might affect the body or soul of a suicide. In all of these statements, however, there is no explicit indication of what was believed about the fates of these souls, just as no explicit judgement is made about the souls of executed offenders.

This is significant because other texts suggest strongly that suicides were believed to have earned their damnation. The most notorious biblical example was Judas, who is said to have killed himself according to the narrative in Matthew's gospel.[182] An echo of this is found in the sanction clause of the will of Æthelgifu, which threatens that if anyone tries to contravene the terms of the will, 'may he

---

[177]    U II.10.3–4, ed. Finsterwalder, *Canones Theodori*, 324; Clayton, 'Suicide in the works of Ælfric', 346–7.

[178]    Murray, *Suicide in the Middle Ages: 1, The Violent against Themselves*, 363; Murray, *Suicide in the Middle Ages: 2, The Curse on Self-Murder*, 183.

[179]    I Braga (561), 16, ed. J. Vives, T. Marín Martínez and G. Martínez Díez, *Concilios visigóticos e hispano-romanos, España cristiana: Testo v 1* (Barcelona, 1963), 10.

[180]    42.05.01–02, ed. Frantzen, *The Anglo-Saxon Penitentials: A Cultural Database.*

[181]    54.13.01–02, ed. Frantzen, *The Anglo-Saxon Penitentials: A Cultural Database.*

[182]    Mt 27:3–5. The narrative in Acts 1:18 gives a different account: see Murray, *Suicide in the Middle Ages: 2, The Curse on Self-Murder*, 95.

be as hateful to God as was Judas, who hanged himself'.[183] More authoritative information comes from Ælfric's writings, which reveal clearly that he believed that the fate of suicides was to be punished in hell for all eternity, as Mary Clayton has shown.[184] In discussing the suicide of Judas, who was already damned because he had betrayed Christ, Ælfric added that Judas had sinned 'against Christ, and even more against himself, because a suicide will suffer in eternity', a comment not found in any of his sources.[185] His discussion elsewhere was no more forgiving: in the same homily in which he urged that thieves should repent even immediately before death, he concluded that 'everyone who kills himself will be condemned, and every suicide will suffer forever in eternity'.[186] While commenting on characters from the Bible, Ælfric extended his condemnation of their acts to apply to all suicides, and where he mentioned two cases of suicide occasioned by madness or demonic instigation he was no more sympathetic, just as he seems also have condemned those who became irrational through excessive fasting and thus took their own lives.[187]

Whether or not Ælfric had encountered cases of real suicide, his approach in the context of the pulpit seems to show no mercy or understanding for the mental states of suicides, since he condemned it in the harshest terms. This may be because the official line on suicide and the responses by people who actually had to deal with real cases were quite different, as Murray suggests, and a glimpse of this is visible in Anglo-Saxon England too. The only possible case of suicide that Murray was able to find from Anglo-Saxon England is rather uncertain, as it is only recorded in later sources whose reliability may be dubious, but it is worth exploring this briefly. Both the *Historia regum* of Symeon of Durham (*fl. c.*1090–*c.*1128) and William of Malmesbury record that Æthelstan was responsible for his brother Eadwine's death at sea: William states that Æthelstan commanded that Eadwine

---

[183]  S 1497, ed. D. Whitelock, *The Will of Æthelgifu: A Tenth Century Anglo-Saxon Manuscript* (Oxford, 1968): 'Heo ne anbit na hyre cynehlaforde ne hire hlæfdian ac gif hpa bidde þ[æt] ðes cpide standan ne mote purðe he aporpen on þa pynstran hand þonne se hælend his dom deme ] he pdeme gode spa lað spa Iudas þæs þy hyne selfne aheng buton hio hit get self apende ] þa ne lybben þe hit nu becpeden ys' ('She does not expect it of her lord or her lady; but if any one ask that this will may not be allowed to stand, may he be cast on the left hand when the Saviour pronounces his judgement and may he be as hateful to God as was Judas, who hanged himself, unless she herself change it hereafter, and those be not alive to whom it is now bequeathed').
[184]  Clayton, 'Suicide in the works of Ælfric'.
[185]  Ælfric, *CH* II.14, ll. 160–2, ed. M. Godden, *Ælfric's Catholic Homilies: The Second Series Text*, EETS, SS 5 (Oxford, 1979), 143: 'On criste hé syngode. and swiðor on him sylfum. for ðan þe agenslaga. on ecnysse ðrowað'; Clayton, 'Suicide in the works of Ælfric', 351.
[186]  *Passio S. Albani [Acitofel et Absalon]*, *LS* XIX, ll. 229–30, ed. Skeat, *Lives of Saints*, I.428: 'Ælc man bið eac fordemed þe hine sylfne adyt. and ælc agen-slaga á on ecnysse ðrowað'; Clayton, 'Suicide in the works of Ælfric', 353.
[187]  For detailed discussion see Clayton, 'Suicide in the works of Ælfric', 351–65.

should be put in a ship with no oars or rudder, and as a result Eadwine sought his own death by throwing himself into the sea, although he prefaces this with the warning that he learned this from 'cantilenae' ('songs', or perhaps 'popular report') rather than from history books.[188] William also records that Æthelstan did penance for seven years, and elsewhere, stated that he founded religious houses at Milton and Muchelney as a result of his remorse.[189] Eadwine's death is not recorded in contemporary versions of the Anglo-Saxon Chronicle but it appears in the year 933 in the E version of the Chronicle, a copy made at Peterborough in the eleventh and twelfth centuries which draws on earlier Northumbrian Latin annals like those used by Symeon of Durham, and which reveals at least as much about the perceptions of its time of production as it does about the events of earlier centuries.[190] Eadwine's death was also recorded by Folcuin the deacon, who completed his cartulary-chronicle of St Bertin in 961–2: he states that in 933 when Eadwine's body was washed ashore after he had drowned, he was buried at St Bertin, and Æthelstan sent gifts and alms to the monastery in return.[191]

The precise relationship between all of these accounts is not easy to pin down: the information in the *Historia Regum* and the Peterborough Chronicle may be connected, but William of Malmesbury's account may have come from a different source, and it is not immediately certain where Folcuin's information came from. Whether or not the account of suicide is entirely legendary is more difficult to establish, but it is worth considering whether there might be some connection with the penitential charters granted by Æthelstan at Christmas in 932 and early January 933, in which Æthelstan displays an extraordinary and apparently sudden concern 'for the excesses of his soul', asking for numerous masses, psalms and alms to be offered on his behalf.[192] At first sight the dates are problematic, but it is just possible that the year of Eadwine's death recorded as in the *Anglo-Saxon Chronicle* and subsequently in later histories might have been given as 933 because the year was reckoned from the autumn (of 932) rather than

---

[188] Symeon, *Historia regum*, 107, ed. T. Arnold, *Symeonis monachi opera omnia: Vol. 2, Historia regum*, Rolls Series (London, 1885), 124; William, *Gesta regum*, ii.138–40, ed. R.A.B. Mynors, R.M. Thomson and M. Winterbottom, *Gesta regum anglorum: The History of the English Kings* (Oxford, 1998), 224–8.

[189] *Gesta pontificum*, ii.85, 93, ed. M. Winterbottom and R.M. Thomson, *William of Malmesbury: Gesta pontificum Anglorum* (Oxford, 2007), I.292, 312.

[190] S. Irvine, *The Sources of the Anglo-Saxon Chronicle (E)* (2002), http://fontes. english.ox.ac.uk, accessed October 2012; S. Irvine, *The Anglo-Saxon Chronicle: A Collaborative Edition: Vol. 7, MS E: A Semi-Diplomatic Edition with Introduction and Indices* (Cambridge, 2004), lviii.

[191] Folcuin, *Gesta abbatum*, 107, ed. O. Holder-Egger, 'Gesta Abbatum S. Bertini Sithiensium', *Supplementa tomorum I–XII, pars I*, MGH, Scriptores in Folio 13 (1881), 600–35, at 629, ll. 10–19.

[192] S 418, 419, 422, 423; see also above, 232–4.

from 1 January (933).[193] None of the sources state when in the year Eadwine was supposed to have drowned, and if he had in fact died during December 932 then Æthelstan's penitential donations would have followed very shortly afterwards. Eadwine is not mentioned in the charters, although arguably if he had committed suicide, it might have been considered problematic to name him or to ask prayers for him; in theory, the omission of his death from the contemporary versions of the *Chronicle* might also be connected with the manner of his end, perhaps itself connected with political unrest.[194] Ultimately this must remain speculation since the evidence is mostly so late and its reliability uncertain, but the coincidence is interesting if no more.

There are in fact two other accounts of suicide from Anglo-Saxon England, one more straightforward than the other. The first is contained in the A version of the Anglo-Saxon Chronicle, which records that in the year 962, King Sigferth killed himself ('fell upon himself'), and his body lies at Wimborne.[195] It is interesting (although perhaps coincidence) that this is followed by a statement that during that year there was a great pestilence, given that in other contexts the burial of suicides in 'inappropriate' places (such as churchyards) seems to have been believed to have led to chaotic weather or sickness.[196] The other, less straightforward, account which seems to record a suicide in Anglo-Saxon England, found in Byrhtferth of Ramsey's *Life of Oswald*, written some time between 997 and 1002, and therefore within a decade of Oswald's death.[197] In this account there is in fact no explicit statement that a suicide took place, but the peculiarity of the circumstances described suggest that the episode was rather more problematic than presented.

Byrhtferth explains that while Oswald was at Ramsey, a messenger came from Ely to inform them of a sudden death: a monk had fallen from the walls of the church and had died from the fall.[198] Hagiography is surprisingly full of instances where people fell off high towers or walls, but usually the authors explain why the individual concerned had any business being up so high (such as building work), and significantly, the inclusion of the account in a saint's life is normally to

[193]    See K. Harrison, 'The beginning of the year in England, c.500–900', *Anglo-Saxon England* 2 (1973): 51–70, at 66–9.

[194]    S. Foot, *Æthelstan: The First king of England* (Yale, 2011), 40–3.

[195]    *ASC* (A), s.a. 962, ed. J. Bately, *The Anglo-Saxon Chronicle: A Collaborative Edition: Vol. 3, MS A: A Semi-Diplomatic Edition with Introduction and Indices* (Cambridge, 1986), 75: 'ꝺ Sigferð cyning hine offeoll ꝺ his lic ligð æt Wimburnan. ꝺ þa on geare wæs swiðe micel mancwealm ... '. I am grateful to Alex Woolf for bringing this reference to my attention.

[196]    Murray, *Suicide in the Middle Ages: 1, The Violent against Themselves*, 110–112; Murray, *Suicide in the Middle Ages: 2, The Curse on Self-Murder*, 342–3, 447–8.

[197]    Lapidge, *The lives of St Oswald and St Ecgwine*, xxxvii–xxxviii.

[198]    Byrhtferth, *Vita S. Oswaldi*, V.2, ed. Lapidge, *The Lives of St Oswald and St Ecgwine*, 148.

demonstrate that the saint had worked a miracle in saving the person who fell.[199] In this case, not only had the monk died, but Byrhtferth also records that he had been 'led to punishment'.[200] This is a remarkable statement because it ought to have been impossible for anyone to have known his fate in the afterlife, and Byrhtferth himself had already noted in the previous chapter that in this life 'we do not know who are the elect and who are the wicked'.[201] This suggests that the fall from the church walls was much more problematic than Byrhtferth was prepared to indicate explicitly, and that it was probably a case of suicide.[202]

Oswald's response to this news is also revealing. Byrhtferth records that when he heard about the monk's death, the 'merciful bishop' became sad, and asked some of the monks of Ramsey to say mass and vigils for the monk for 30 days, while Oswald himself set out for York.[203] The monk appeared to Oswald when he was in York to thank him for the prayers that had been offered on behalf of his soul, explaining that 'yesterday my soul received the refreshment of eternal salvation'.[204] On his return to Ramsey, Oswald reported to the monks there what had happened, telling them that God had freed the monk through their prayers, but Byrhtferth notes that the soul's release had in fact been achieved through Oswald's prayers, because 'the prayer of a just man availeth much'.[205] This is extremely significant because it is a large claim to Oswald's sanctity: if Oswald could rescue souls from punishment, even deeply problematic souls such as this one, then he clearly had great power. Although Byrhtferth was reticent about giving the full circumstances of the monk's death, the educated reader is presumably supposed to understand that the situation is more complex than is revealed here, because this simply adds to Oswald's power. Byrhtferth's characterisation of Oswald here as 'merciful' is important too, because it seems

---

[199]  See for example: *Vita S. Wilfridi*, xxiii, ed. and trans. Colgrave, *Life of Bishop Wilfrid*, 46–7; Wulfstan of Winchester, *Vita S. Æthelwoldi*, 34, ed. and trans. Lapidge and Winterbottom, *Wulfstan of Winchester: The Life of St Æthelwold*, 52–3.

[200]  Byrhtferth, *Vita S. Oswaldi*, V.2, ed. Lapidge, *The Lives of St Oswald and St Ecgwine*, 148: 'ad poenam perductus'.

[201]  Byrhtferth, *Vita S. Oswaldi*, V.1, ed. Lapidge, *The Lives of St Oswald and St Ecgwine*, 146: 'ignoramus qui sint electi quique reprobi'.

[202]  There are roughly contemporary examples from elsewhere in Europe of 'problematic falls' which should probably be interpreted as suicides: see Murray, *Suicide in the Middle Ages: 1, The Violent against Themselves*, 340–3.

[203]  This was a standard period of commemoration, as in the account of Justus in the *Dialogues* of Gregory the Great, IV.57.14, ed. de Vogüé and Antin, *Dialogues, Livre IV*, III.192; see also D 60, U II.V.5–6, ed. Finsterwalder, *Canones Theodori*, 244, 318–19, and Amalarius, *Liber officialis*, III.44.3–11, ed. Hanssens, *Amalarii episcopi opera liturgica omnia*, 382–4; and above, 238.

[204]  Byrhtferth, *Vita S. Oswaldi*, V.2, ed. Lapidge, *The Lives of St Oswald and St Ecgwine*, 148: 'hesterno die sumpsit anima mea refrigerium aeterne salutis'.

[205]  Byrhtferth, *Vita S. Oswaldi*, V.2, ed. Lapidge, *The Lives of St Oswald and St Ecgwine*, 150.

to relate to his decision to offer masses for someone who might otherwise have been forbidden them. Although the burial of this monk is not discussed, this account is a reminder that those to whom certain rites were supposedly denied might receive them all the same, and that might extend to burial (as in the case of Sigeferth) as well as to post-mortem prayer.

What constituted an 'enemy' or a wicked person for Augustine, writing in the early fifth century, or for Gregory, writing in late sixth-century Rome, might have been rather different from the way this was interpreted in early medieval England, but their statements seem to lie behind the justification for the exclusion of certain types of people from prayer and remembrance. The body of the peasant who mocked St Ecgwine (and was punished by cutting his head off with his own scythe) is reported to have been thrown off Ecgwine's land and buried in dirty soil with no funerary rites.[206] Similarly, the brother described by Bede, who had assured the other monks that he was certainly damned, thereby excluded himself from prayer on the grounds that the Church did not pray for the damned: it is the 'faithful departed' who are the beneficiaries of her prayers, not those who lived in such a way that they did not deserve mercy.[207] Those who had been executed, or had cut themselves off from God by committing suicide, could therefore not be grouped among the faithful departed and so were not permitted to receive prayers. As Augustine says, 'the Church will not, and does not now, pray for the ungodly or unbelieving'.[208] Pope Gregory III echoed this in response to Boniface's questions on prayer for the dead, advising him that this was appropriate for the Christian dead, 'but not for the wicked, even if they were Christians'.[209]

But it is crucial to remember that a lack of such offerings did not in itself mean damnation, because prayer for the dead simply eased or quickened the punishments of those who could benefit from them, and the souls who could benefit from prayers or masses would all enter heaven after the Last Judgement even if these were not offered in the meantime. In the same way, prayers and masses might have reduced the amount of time spent in purgatorial punishments, but could not in themselves prevent damnation if that was what the soul had earned. This is particularly important in an Anglo-Saxon context because of the implications for those who were denied prayers or masses after death along with

---

[206] *Vita S. Ecgwini*, iv.10, ed. and trans. Lapidge, *The Lives of St Oswald and St Ecgwine*, 290–7; see above, 26–7.

[207] See Isidore, *De ecclesiasticis officiis*, I.xviii.11, ed. C.M. Lawson, *Sancti Isidori Episcopi Hispalensis: De ecclesiasticis officiis*, CCSL 113 (Turnhout, 1989), 22.

[208] *DCD*, XXI.24, ll. 46–7, Dombert and Kalb, *De civitate dei*, 790: '... quamuis pro hominibus, tamen iam nec nunc oretur pro infidelibus impiisque defunctis'.

[209] *Epistola* 28, ed. Tangl, *Die Briefe*, 50–1: 'Pro oboeuntibus quippe consoluisse dinosceris, si liceat oblationes offerre. Sancta sic tenet ęcclesia, ut quisque pro suis mortuis vere christianis offerat oblationes atque presbiter eorum faciat memoriam. Et quamvis omnes peccatis sub iaceamus, congruit, ut sacerdos pro mortuis catholicis memoriam faciat et intercedat. Non tamen pro impiis, quamvis christiani fuerint, tale quid agere licebit'.

the penalty of execution for their offences. For the souls of those who had recourse to confession, or were repentant just before death, the effect would be to ensure that even if these souls would ultimately reach heaven, purgatorial punishment really did continue until the Last Judgement, without the prior remission which could have been effected through prayers or masses. This seems to show an attempt to extend punishment for offences against human and divine law from this world into the next, so that even after death correction could continue: here too the decision seems to have been handed over to God as to whether this punishment was vindictive or purgative, and thus whether the soul would ultimately reach heaven or not.

This can be seen for example in an instruction in Ælfric's first Old English *Pastoral Letter* for Wulfstan that priests killed while fighting can be buried, but should not have masses offered for them; in one manuscript Wulfstan adjusted this statement to say that they could be buried in consecrated ground, but everything else should be left to God's judgement.[210] This suggests strongly that the fate of such priests hung very much in the balance: perhaps they would be saved, and perhaps they would not be, but this was for God to decide, and not for men. Understanding the more subtle effects of the denial of prayers and masses is also important because of the implications for those who were incorrectly or inappropriately denied prayer, for example innocent people executed as offenders, or those whose bodies were treated mercilessly by their enemies. Although this is clearly a special case, the treatment of the body of Edward Martyr is interesting here. According to Byrhtferth, after Edward was killed his body was taken without chant or funerary rites to the house of a ceorl, and buried in a rather undignified manner.[211] When he was exhumed a year later, the body was discovered to be incorrupt, at which point it was transported in a coffin with some ceremony and then reburied honourably, and masses and prayers were offered for his soul.[212] In this case, neither the place of burial nor the lack of offerings seems to have made any difference, and neither to Edward's body nor to his soul.[213]

---

[210]     II.189, ed. Fehr, *Die Hirtenbriefe Ælfrics*, 134–5; CCCC 201 (D) contains the change; CCCC 190 (O) and Oxford, Bodleian Library, Bodley 343 (Oz) contain the alternative.

[211]     *Vita S. Oswaldi*, iv.18–19, ed. Lapidge, *The Lives of St Oswald and St Ecgwine*, 136–43. See also William of Malmesbury's *Vita S. Dunstani*, ii.20.2–3, ed. Winterbottom and Thomson, *William of Malmesbury: Saints' Lives*, 272–3, for the additional note that he was not buried in church ground.

[212]     *Vita S. Oswaldi*, iv.19, ed. Lapidge, *The lives of St Oswald and St Ecgwine*, 140–2.

[213]     See also Simeon, *Historia regum*, 5, ed. Arnold, *Symeonis monachi opera omnia: Vol. 2, Historia regum*, 8–9. This is a description of the bodies of the murdered princes Æthelberht and Æthelred, probably attributable to Byrhtferth: see M. Lapidge, 'Byrhtferth of Ramsey and the early sections of the Historia Regum attributed to Symeon of Durham', *Anglo-Saxon England* 10 (1982): 97–122.

Two isolated references in tenth-century charters indicate how the inappropriate denial or allowance of consecrated burial might be perceived by families and others, and the possible responses of ecclesiastical and judicial officials in such cases. The first of these dates from somewhere between 950 and 968 and refers to one Ecgfrith, who had apparently entrusted his estate and charters to Archbishop Dunstan with the request that Dunstan should act as guardian for his wife and child.[214] After Ecgfrith had died, Dunstan approached King Edgar about the matter and was told that Ecgfrith's property was forfeit 'through the sword which hung on his hip when he drowned'.[215] The precise meaning of this has been debated and it may be that Ecgfrith drowned in the course of undergoing ordeal by cold water;[216] it is clear nonetheless that Ecgfrith had committed some significant offence. When Dunstan offered Ecgfrith's wergeld to the king he was told that while the payment might help in obtaining burial in consecrated ground for Ecgfrith, the whole case was now in the hands of Ealdorman Ælfheah, to whom Edgar had given the land after the forfeiture.[217] Ecgfrith's burial, whether in consecrated ground or outside it, does not seem to have bothered the king: it is even more striking that Dunstan, who (as archbishop of Canterbury) might have been expected to have the final say in whether it was permissible to include such a man in a church's burial grounds, was essentially told to contact Ealdorman Ælfheah to discuss the matter of Ecgfrith's burial and whether his burial in consecrated ground would be possible.[218]

The second reference is no less enigmatic, and even more complicated. This charter records that in 995, King Æthelred granted land in Oxfordshire to his thegn, Æthelwig, and it details the history of the land and how it had come to be given away.[219] A man named Leofric stole a bridle and when this was discovered, the people from whom the bridle had been stolen fought with three brothers named Ælfnoth, Ælfric and Æthelwine, who were Leofric's masters. In the course of this fight, Ælfnoth and Ælfric were killed, while Leofric and Æthelwine managed to escape and claim sanctuary. What happened next is rather confusing in the details: the charter notes that when this was known, Æthelwig (the reeve in Buckhingham, and ultimately the recipient of the land) and Wynsige (the reeve in Oxford) 'buried the brothers with Christians'.[220] Ealdorman Leofsige of Essex came to Æthelred to object about this, on the grounds that 'the brothers were not rightly buried

---

[214]   S 1447 (Robertson, *Anglo-Saxon Charters*, no. 44).

[215]   S 1447 (Robertson, *Anglo-Saxon Charters*, no. 44 [92, ll. 6–7]): 'þurh þæt swyrd þe him ón hype hangode þá hé adranc'.

[216]   N. Brooks, *The Early History of the Church of Canterbury: Christ Church from 597 to 1066*, Studies in the early history of Britain (Leicester, 1984), 249.

[217]   See also S 702, which records the grant of land from Edgar to Ælfheah.

[218]   To some extent this may be a reflection of the relationship between Dunstan and Edgar in the context of the law: see Brooks, *The Early History of the Church of Canterbury*, 249.

[219]   S 883 (*Abing*, no. 125).

[220]   S 886 (*Abing*, no. 125): 'inter Christianos predictos sepelierunt fratres'.

with Christians', but King Æthelred did not want to upset Æthelwig, so he both permitted the brothers 'to rest with Christians' and gave Æthelwig the land which the brothers had forfeited.[221]

This account raises significant questions, not least of which is why Leofsige was so worried about the brothers' burial 'with Christians', when Æthelred evidently was not; and whether Æthelwig arranged for Christian burial for some particular reason or simply made a mistake in not excluding them from consecrated ground. Since Leofsige was Ealdorman of Essex his interest in this legal case in Oxfordshire is odd in any case;[222] it is possible that Leofsige had an interest in land which Æthelwig also had designs on, and therefore attempted to use the details of inappropriate Christian burial to claim it for himself. In due course, Leofsige was apparently driven out of the kingdom after killing someone, and other members of his family seem also to have caused problems for Æthelred in their attempts to thwart justice.[223] The idea that the reeves were responsible for the bodies of the dead brothers is itself significant, acting as a reminder that dealing with corpses was part of the 'job' of justice. Once again the ecclesiastical role in burial is simply not mentioned at all, and apparently there was no objection from ecclesiastical officials to laying the brothers to rest in consecrated ground, only from Leofsige. The effect of burial 'with Christians' on the brothers' souls or bodies is never explicitly considered, and yet the charter concludes with a fairly standard anathema informing those who break its terms that they will be 'separated from the company of Christians', as indeed it might be supposed that the two brothers should have been.

Overall, it is difficult to know what to make of this, especially if Leofsige's objection was simply a pretext to claim the land for himself rather than a genuine concern about burial: the events recounted here almost suggest that there was no real concern about the inclusion of offenders in consecrated ground, either from judicial or ecclesiastical officials, or from the king. The only one of Æthelred's decrees which apparently refers to consecrated ground specifically seems to explain how someone can clear a kinsman buried as a thief in unconsecrated ground, and so bury him elsewhere.[224] This suggests that some people were indeed concerned about the resting places of the bodies of their relatives (as Ecgferth's wife was), but it is of course not certain how often anyone had recourse to this procedure.

---

[221]  S 886 (*Abing*, no. 125): '... peremptis fratribus non recte inter Christianos sepultis'; '... sepultos cum Christianis requiscere permisi'.

[222]  J. Blair, *Anglo-Saxon Oxfordshire* (Stroud, 1994), 194; S.E. Kelly, *Charters of Abingdon Abbey: Part 2*, Anglo-Saxon Charters 8 (Oxford, 2001), 488.

[223]  See *ASC* (CDE) s.a. 1002 for Leofsige's exile: O'Keeffe, *The Anglo-Saxon Chronicle: A Collaborative Edition: Vol. 5, MS C*, 89; Cubbin, *The Anglo-Saxon Chronicle: A Collaborative Edition: Vol. 6, MS D*, 51; Irvine, *The Anglo-Saxon Chronicle: A Collaborative Edition: Vol. 7, MS E*, 64. S 926 (*Roch*, no. 33) records the seizure of land from Leofsige's sister, Æthelflæd, because she had helped her brother who was in exile.

[224]  III Æthelred 7, ed. Liebermann, *Gesetze*, 230–1.

This decree is found in III Æthelred but not I Æthelred, and so it is theoretically possible that this was a provision used in the Danelaw but not in southern England, where this case occurred.[225] Even so, that Leofsige made an objection which was taken seriously enough to be recorded in writing gives the impression that the practice of excluding certain types of offenders from consecrated ground was reasonably widely known (and perhaps also followed) by this time. On the other hand, the disinterest with which these two cases are discussed seems to call into question the effectiveness and purpose of exclusion from consecrated ground as a legal penalty, while the apparent inability of ecclesiastical officials to play any role in the place of burial is also perplexing.

In the case of the two brothers, the terminology is confusing too. It is not immediately obvious what the opposite of burial 'with Christians' was understood to be, whether 'with non-Christians', or 'not with Christians', or how significant that distinction might be. Some English sources dating from after the Anglo-Saxon period refer to exclusion from consecrated ground as burial 'with the damned' or 'with thieves',[226] although of course even burial 'with the damned' does not necessarily mean that all of those buried there were damned, or even that some of them were, if 'the damned' in fact refers to the wicked spirits who were believed to inhabit some of the places where offenders' bodies were buried. These subtleties and shades of belief are almost impossible to pick up in the archaeological record, even when there are recorded or actual practices which suggest considerable unease or even fear about the body placed in the ground, whether that unease applied literally to the inanimate body itself or more generally to the person whose body was being buried. Bodies buried face down or with stones on top of them might suggest that some problem with these bodies (or with the people who owned them) was perceived at burial or before, but they may not reveal precisely what that problem was.[227] It is interesting here to note the record of the burial of one Thunor 'under a heap of stones' in the part of Symeon of Durham's *Historia regum* which may be attributable to Byrhtferth of Ramsey, especially given that Thunor's soul is explicitly stated to be in hell, although it is not immediately clear what relationship this account bears to any real event or practice.[228]

[225]     P. Wormald, 'Æthelred the Lawmaker', in D. Hill (ed.), *Ethelred the Unready: Papers from the Millenary Conference* (Oxford, 1978), 47–80, at 61–2.

[226]     Thompson, *Dying and Death*, 176–7.

[227]     Reynolds, *Anglo-Saxon Deviant Burial Customs*, 68–71, 160–1; see for example burial G41 at Sewerby (E. Yorkshire), discussed in S.M. Hirst, *An Anglo-Saxon Inhumation Cemetery at Sewerby, East Yorkshire* (York, 1985), 38–43; S.M. Hirst, 'Death and the Archaeologist', in M.O.H. Carver (ed.), *In Search of Cult: Essays in Honour of Philip Rahtz* (Woodbridge, 1993), 41–4; C. Knüsel, R. Janaway and S. King, 'Death, decay and ritual reconstruction: Archaeological evidence of cadaveric spasm', *Oxford Journal of Archaeology* 15 (1996): 121–8.

[228]     *Historia regum*, 8, ed. Arnold, *Symeonis monachi opera omnia: Vol. 2, Historia regum*, 11; Lapidge, 'Byrhtferth of Ramsey and the early sections of the Historia Regum

In considering the differential treatment of bodies and exclusion from Christian burial practices as these changed across the period, what seems to be most important is that there were grades of exclusion and subtle differences between the possible ways of treating the body. The precise effects of any of these were probably not outlined because they were often held to be impossible to determine without other incontrovertible evidence from beyond the grave. While some bodies were supposed to be included in consecrated cemeteries but their souls denied prayers or masses, others were excluded from both and yet may have made their confessions or have repented inwardly before their deaths. Still others may have been buried in consecrated ground but have had unrevealed sins on their conscience which, if known, would have been believed to have ensured their damnation. Prayers or masses may have been denied to certain people precisely because it was believed that this would ensure that the soul suffered longer in purgative punishments in the beyond, if this was what it deserved, and so that offerings would not be made for the damned if this was indeed that individual's fate, so that punishment and justice were both handed over to God. The subtleties of these distinctions were almost certainly lost on some people, who may have worried or feared that their loved ones were damned if they did not receive burial in consecrated ground. However, those who made the rules probably did understand these distinctions, and even if this was a rather shadowy area in which the details were not always clear, it seems unlikely that there was any organised and deliberate attempt from ecclesiastical officials to try to damn specific souls: the warnings that priests would stand with their own congregations at the Last Judgement originate from the same clergymen who restricted or allowed burial in hallowed ground.

## Body and Soul

Byrhtferth's story of the monk from Ely and the account of the two brothers given Christian burial incorrectly suggest that (perhaps unsurprisingly) the strict injunctions set out in penitential, homiletic and legal texts may not always have been closely followed. On the other hand, it may be that these episodes receive attention in the sources precisely because they were unusual. In understanding the perceived relationship between souls and bodies, as in these cases, Augustine's writings are once again informative and interesting. In the *De cura mortuis*, Augustine discussed whether the dead had any knowledge of the deeds of the living as they occurred, connecting this issue with the appearance of the dead in dreams or visions, especially in cases where dead men appeared asking for their bodies to be buried.[229] His conclusions are telling: he dismissed the idea that the dead had any knowledge of the deeds of the living, and attributed the appearance of the

---

attributed to Symeon of Durham'.

[229] *De cura mortuis*, XII.15–XV.18, ed. Zycha, *Sancti Aureli Augustini, De fide et symbolo, etc.*, 644–52.

dead in dreams to factors such as angelic interference, as he also conceded that the dead might learn some information about events in the world from angels; but he seems to have been responding to concerns and opinions expressed by other people, especially as he went to some length to respond to different questions arising from the theological arguments that he presented.

Augustine concluded that it was not in the power of the dead who so wished to have any interest in worldly affairs, but he made an exception for the 'very special dead', stating that where this did happen, it was attributable to divine power.[230] He evidently found it more difficult to explain how the saints could help people on earth, although emphasising that it was certain that they did so: on this issue he decided that 'the question overcomes the strength of my understanding', that it was a matter too complicated for him to understand, and that he therefore would not dare to pose a definitive solution.[231] He did suggest two possibilities though, either that the saints could be present simultaneously both in the afterlife where they rest, and in the places where their memorials were; or that they were in a place of rest and removed from contact with earth, but that they prayed generally for those who requested their help, and these prayers were answered by God.[232] In the *Dialogues*, Gregory also addressed this question to some degree, explaining that the miracles enacted through the bodies of the saints revealed clearly what sort of experience their souls had where they live now.[233] Gregory also included a number of miracles demonstrating that the dead did indeed have knowledge of the deeds of the living, focused in particular on the idea that the dead might ask the living to make offerings on their behalf.[234]

The idea that the fate of the soul was visible at the tomb or in the body is a central part of the concept of the cult of saints. The inscription at the tomb of

---

[230] *De cura mortuis*, XVI.19, ed. Zycha, *Sancti Aureli Augustini, De fide et symbolo, etc.*, 652–3.

[231] XVI.20, ed. Zycha, *Sancti Aureli Augustini, De fide et symbolo, etc.*, 653, ll. 16–18: 'quamquam ista quaestio uires intellegentiae meae uincit, quemadmodum opitulentur martyres his, quos per eos certum est adiuuari'.

[232] XVI.20, ed. Zycha, *Sancti Aureli Augustini, De fide et symbolo, etc.*, 653, l. 18 – 654, l. 12: 'utrum ipsi per se ipsos adsint uno tempore tam diuersis locis et tanta inter se longinquitate discretis, siue ubi sunt eorum memoria siue praeter suas memorias, ubicumque adesse sentiuntur, an ipsis in loco suis meritis congruo ab omni mortalium conuersatione remotis et tamen generaliter orantibus pro indigentia supplicantum – sicut nos oramus pro mortuis, quibus utique non praesentamur nec ubi sint uel quid agant scimus – deus omnipotens, qui est ubique praesens nec concretus nobis nec remotus a nobis, exaudiens martyrum preces, per angelica ministeria usquequaque diffusa praebeat hominibus ista solacia, quibus in huius uitae miseria iudicat esse praebenda, et suorum martyrum merita ubi uult, quando uult, quomodo uult, maxime que per eorum memorias, quoniam hoc nouit expedire nobis ad aedificandam fidem christi, pro cuius illi confessione sunt passi, mirabili atque ineffabili potestate ac bonitate commendet'.

[233] IV.6, ed. de Vogüé and Antin, *Dialogues, Livre IV*, 38–40.

[234] IV.49, 57, ed. de Vogüé and Antin, *Dialogues, Livre IV*, 168–72, 184–94.

St Martin of Tours clearly illustrates this 'real presence', stating that 'here lies Bishop Martin of holy memory, whose soul is in the hand of God, but he is fully present here, manifest in miracles of all kinds'.[235] There is no evidence that Anglo-Saxon writers agonised as Augustine had over whether the soul could exist both in heaven and in a physical location on earth. In fact, the evidence from early medieval England (and elsewhere) suggests rather that many people believed that the dead were aware of the deeds of the living: allusions and direct references to a spiritual existence both in the otherworld and near the body appear in many different contexts, for saints and, less clearly articulated, for the problematic dead. The beliefs expressed in early medieval sources seem to depend on a tacit assumption that the soul could be present in multiple places, but Augustine's uncertainties are not articulated in these accounts. One especially clear example of the importance of multiple presences for both soul and body is found in the late eleventh century account of the miracles of Mildreth by Goscelin of St Bertin, who notes that 'by a sign it was revealed that Mildreth should be understood to be present always in both her former and current dwelling-place' (i.e., in the tomb and in heaven).[236] The sign in question was that Mildreth slapped a brother in the face when he fell asleep before her shrine, and although the slap occurred in a vision, the brother said that 'when he was now completely awake, with open eyes, he saw her go back down into her tomb', illustrating that Mildreth's presence was at least as much physical and bodily as spiritual.[237]

At the other extreme, the dead who did not rest in peace, the spiritual fate of the soul might also be revealed through the body, as illustrated by the examples from Gregory's *Dialogues* noted above.[238] An account from the ninth-century *Life of Leoba* by Rudolf is close to one of Gregory's: he describes a nun at Wimbourne who was over-zealous in her enforcement of discipline and strict observance and thereby managed to irritate many of the younger members of the community; and who refused to ask forgiveness even at death.[239] After she was buried, earth was

---

[235]    E.F. Le Blant, *Inscriptions chrétiennes de la Gaule antérieures au VIIIe siècle* (2 vols Paris, 1856), I.240: 'hic conditus est sanctae memoriae Martinus episcopus cuius anima in manu Dei est, sed hic totus est praesens manifestus omni gratia virtutum'; Brown, *The Cult of the Saints: Its Rise and Function in Latin Christianity*, 4.

[236]    *Translatio S. Mildrethe uirginis*, 20, ed. D. Rollason, 'Goscelin of Canterbury's account of the translation and miracles of St Mildrith (BHL 5961/4): An edition with notes', *Mediaeval Studies* 48 (1986): 139–210, at 180–1.

[237]    *Translatio S. Mildrethe uirginis*, 20, ed. D. Rollason, 'Goscelin of Canterbury's account': 'prorsus isdem nun luminibus apertis et aperte uigilans conspicit redeuntem tumbamque suam subeuntem'.

[238]    See above, 269–70.

[239]    Rudolf, *Vita Leobae*, 4, ed. G. Waitz, 'Vita Leobae abbatissae Biscofesheimensis auct. Rudolfo Fuldensi', *Supplementa tomorum I–XII, pars III*, MGH, Scriptores in Folio 15.1 (Hannover, 1887), 118–31, at 123–4. For information about the text, see above, 28–9.

heaped over her and a tomb was placed over her grave. The young nuns, still angry, climbed on her tomb and made as if to stamp on her corpse, uttering curses over her body. The abbess, Tetta, was understandably disturbed by this and rebuked and corrected the young nuns, but when she went to visit the grave she was shocked: the earth over the grave had sunk and lay well below the surface of the nearby ground. Some readers might have assumed that this sinking was the result of rather vigorous stamping on the tomb, but for Tetta, another interpretation was clear, 'for she understood the punishment of the woman who had been buried from the collapsing of the earth and weighed the severity of the just judgement of God from the sinking of the grave'.[240] Urging the other nuns to Christian forgiveness and reconciliation, she ordered that for the next three days they would all fast, and offer prayer and psalms for the nun's soul. At the final offerings made on the third day, the earth rose up again, so that 'by this it was revealed that since the grave had visibly returned to its former state, through the prayers of the holy virgin, divine power had invisibly absolved the soul of the dead woman'.[241]

This miracle is included to demonstrate the sanctity of Tetta, who was Leoba's teacher, but it also illustrates clearly the perceived effect that the fate of the soul might have on a person's mortal remains, and it is possible that it was this or similar concern which resulted in the exclusion of the damned monk from the community cemetery, as described by Bede. One of the Blickling homilies includes a story about a man who visited the grave of a friend who had been a rich man, and records that the bones of the friend called out to him, saying that in the tomb was just dust and dry bones, and urging the man to pray and turn to God. Following this advice, the man not only earned the grace of the Holy Spirit, but he also delivered his friend's soul from punishment and torments.[242] The awareness of the deeds of the living by the departed, and the consequences of the actions of the living for the dead, is also revealed in other contexts, away from the tomb: Boniface's account of the vision of the monk of Wenlock includes a description of a man suffering in the afterlife because his brother had refused to fulfil the promise to release a slave on his behalf.[243] As already noted, these kinds of stories are indicative of the currency of belief in purgatorial punishments after death which could be relieved by the prayers of friends, relatives, and especially those in religious life. They also illustrate that although the link between the living and the dead was significant in a range of contexts, it might often (though not always) find its focus at the tomb,

---

[240] Rudolf, *Vita Leobae*, 4, ed. G. Waitz, 'Vita Leobae abbatissae', 123, ll. 39–40: 'Intellexit enim ex defectu terrae poenam sepultae et severitatem iusti iudicii Dei perpendit ex detrimento sepulchri'.

[241] Rudolf, *Vita Leobae*, 4, ed. G. Waitz, 'Vita Leobae abbatissae', 124, ll. 5–6: 'Qua ex re manifeste ostenditur, quod, cum monumentum visibiliter ad priorem statum rediit, per orationes sanctae virginis defunctae animam virtus divina invisibiliter absolvit'.

[242] *Hom.* X, ed. Morris, *Blickling Homilies*, 112.

[243] *Epistola* 10, ed. Tangl, *Die Briefe*; see also above, 208.

where the fates both of saintly souls who rested, and of those who suffered, could be revealed.

Another interesting belief, or (perhaps better) a fear, which appears sporadically in early medieval texts is that the bodies of those who were especially wicked might not stay in the ground.[244] In some cases the body is recorded as having been simply thrown out of the ground as if the earth refused to receive it. Goscelin's account of St Kenelm relates that he was killed by his sister Cwoenthryth, and after her death, Cwoenthryth's body could not be kept buried in the church, in the cemetery or in an open field.[245] The idea that the ground might reject the body is particularly interesting in the context of consecrated ground, and in considering the parallel with the ordeal of cold water, in which the consecrated water was believed to reject the guilty body so that it floated.[246] While Cwoenthryth's body was clearly so problematic that no ground could hold it, the idea that holy places would reject unholy souls or bodies is visible too in a number of other contexts. The *Dialogues* contain a number of stories which illustrate this belief: in addition to those already cited, a particularly interesting example is that of the body of a young monk which would not stay in its grave until the Eucharist was placed on top of him (a practice which, if repeated in later centuries, would of course not be visible archaeologically).[247] Gregory's comments on the possible consequences of burying unworthy bodies in churches shed an interesting light on the statement in Wulfstan's *Canons of Edgar* that burial in a church should only be granted to those who are known in life to have been holy enough to deserve it: while this surely reflects concern with privileges and rights, it may also be connected with the fear of what would happen if unholy bodies were placed in holy ground.[248]

There are also stories, dating mostly from after the Conquest, of bodies which were not simply thrown out of the ground but which got up and walked around of their own accord, sometimes causing trouble to those in settlements around them. These were inevitably bodies that had belonged to problematic people in life, but the immediate reason for their movements might not be the problematic soul or body *per se*: instead, the cause of walking corpses seems sometimes to have been believed to be the reanimation of the body by a demonic spirit. This is the interpretation given by Hermann of Bury (*fl.*1070–1100) in a case which

---

[244] This seems almost to be what Ælfric suggests of Judas after he had hanged himself, in *CH* II.1, ll. 164–6, ed. Godden, *Catholic Homilies*, 143. See also J. Blair, 'The Dangerous Dead in Early Medieval England', in S.D. Baxter et al. (eds), *Early Medieval Studies in Memory of Patrick Wormald* (Farnham, Surrey, 2009), 539–59.

[245] Goscelin, *Vita et miracula S. Kenelmi*, 16, ed. and trans. R.C. Love, *Three Eleventh-Century Anglo-Latin Saints' Lives: Vita S. Birini, Vita et miracula S. Kenelmi, and Vita S. Rumwoldi* (Oxford, 1996), 70–2; Blair, 'The Dangerous Dead in early medieval England', 550.

[246] See above, 159–60.

[247] *Dialogues*, II.24, ed. de Vogüé and Antin, *Dialogues, Livre IV*, II.210–12.

[248] See above, 269–70.

was supposed to have occurred in about the year 1000 in Suffolk: the body of a sheriff was moved by demons so that it began to walk after his death, and this was connected with the fact that in life, he had invaded the sanctuary of St Edmund.[249] Despite surviving only in a later account, it seems that the ultimate source for this may date from Æthelred's reign, although whether the interpretation of the corpse as demonically animated belonged to the original source or was introduced by Hermann is not clear.[250] Demonic animation is mentioned too in Ælfric's objection to practices of witchcraft, where he complains that witches go to crossroads and to heathen burial places to call upon the devil, who appears in the body of the person buried, as if risen from death.[251]

Even where the dead are miraculously returned to life in hagiographical accounts it is quite clear that this could be rather a shock for those who attended the body.[252] The significant cases are those in which the dead appear to have returned to life unexpectedly, rather than being healed by a saint on the request of grieving friends and relatives. Bede relates the account of Dryhthelm, a seventh-century Northumbrian layman, who was returned to his body after being shown a vision of the afterlife: when he unexpectedly sat up from death everyone who was weeping over the body ran away, except for his wife, who apparently stayed because she loved him more, but Bede emphasises that she was 'trembling and fearful'.[253] Byrhtferth of Ramsey also provides a vivid glimpse into what might happen when a dead man came back to life in his account of the death of Foldbriht, abbot of Pershore. Byrhtferth recounts that when Foldbriht became ill, he sent for Abbot Germanus of Winchcombe, and Abbot Ælfheah (perhaps of Deerhurst).[254] The account of Foldbriht's death follows all the usual customs: he made his confession

---

[249]   Hermann, *Liber de miraculis S. Eadmundi*, 2, ed. T. Arnold, *Memorials of St Edmund's Abbey* (London, 1890), 30–2; Blair, 'The Dangerous Dead in Early Medieval England', 540.

[250]   A. Gransden, 'The composition and authorship of the De miraculis Sancti Eadmundi attributed to "Hermann the Archdeacon"', *Journal of Medieval Latin* 5 (1995): 1–52, at 26–7; Blair, 'The Dangerous Dead in Early Medieval England', 540.

[251]   Ælfric, *Hom.* XXIX, ll. 118–23, ed. Pope, *Homilies of Ælfric*, II.796.

[252]   See also the case of Eardwulf, recorded for the year 790, in Symeon of Durham, *Historia regum*, 55, ed. Arnold, *Symeonis monachi opera omnia: Vol. 2, Historia regum*, 52: 'Eardulf dux captus est et ad Ripun perductus, ibique occidi jussus extra portam monasterii a rege prefato [Osredo]. Cujus corpus fratres cum Gregorianis concentibus ad ecclesiam portantes, et in tentorio foris ponentes, post mediam noctem vivus est in ecclesia inventus' ('Ealdorman Eardwulf was captured and taken to Ripon and there he was ordered to be killed outside the gate of the monastery, by the aforementioned king [Osred]. The brothers carried his body into the church with Gregorian chant and placed it outside in a tent: after midnight he was found living, inside the church').

[253]   Bede, *HE*, V.12.1, ll. 8–13, ed. Lapidge, Monat and Robin, *Histoire ecclésiastique*, III.68.

[254]   Byhtferth, *Vita S. Oswaldi*, IV.8, ed. Lapidge, *The Lives of St Oswald and St Ecgwine*, 112 and 113 n.77.

and he was anointed, after he had died his body was placed in the middle of the house with a cross placed upon it, and the monks stood around chanting psalms for his soul. Byrhtferth also adds, tellingly, that the two abbots wanted to have a mass said for the redemption of his soul, wanting to defend it so that the wicked one (i.e., the devil) could not snatch it.[255]

Byrhtferth then relates that as the monks continued to chant psalms, they watched in terror as first the man's heart began to beat and to shake off the cross, and then he sat up 'quickly in anger'.[256] The monks were terrified and immediately ran away, apparently thinking that the man was following them, although Byrhtferth is careful to add that he was not. One of the monks managed to reach Abbot Germanus, who had just finished saying mass, telling him that 'Abbot Foldbriht lives again' and the response of the two abbots seems realistic, though comic.[257] Byrhtferth reports that Abbot Germanus did not want to go to Foldbriht without taking someone else with him, so he sent for Ælfheah in case Foldbriht attacked them, but on hearing this Ælfheah was rather disturbed and backed off. There then seems to have been an argument about which one of them should go into the room and face Foldbriht first, until Germanus decided to be brave and went in with Ælfheah following, both of them very frightened. Foldbriht ordered them to come over to him, and then to have the servants lift him into bed, which they did; but Foldbriht's instructions that they should all go away apparently 'did not please Germanus'.[258] The rest of the story is a rather less exciting account of the vision which Foldbriht had while out of the body, in which he had seen Jesus and been forgiven all of his sins, and had been guided by St Benedict; Foldbriht is reported to have died peacefully half a day later.

Byrhtferth's account is really striking in his description of how the other monks behaved in response to what clearly seemed to them to be a walking corpse. This is particularly interesting given that he began the account by warning that although Foldbriht had seemed to be a hard man to those who did not know how to examine the secret places which are in a man, he only seemed this way to people who judge according to appearance – people who, Byrhtferth notes, usually complain about the evil they see in men but do not mention the good.[259] These comments suggest that Foldbriht may not have been well liked, and there is an interesting parallel here with the severe nun of Wimbourne whose grave was jumped up and down on by the younger members of the community. Perhaps Foldbriht was someone who was considered in life to be difficult enough that his corpse might be susceptible to reanimation by demonic spirits. It

---

[255]   Byhtferth, *Vita S. Oswaldi*, IV.8, ed. Lapidge, *The Lives of St Oswald and St Ecgwine*, 114; see also *RC*, 65–6, ed. Symons, *Regularis Concordia*, 64–5.

[256]   Byhtferth, *Vita S. Oswaldi*, IV.8, ed. Lapidge, *The Lives of St Oswald and St Ecgwine*, 114: 'uelociter cum ira'.

[257]   Byhtferth, *Vita S. Oswaldi*, IV.8: 'Abbas Foldbrihtus uiuit iterum'.

[258]   Byhtferth, *Vita S. Oswaldi*, IV.8, 116: 'Germano non grata hec erant'.

[259]   Byhtferth, *Vita S. Oswaldi*, IV.8, 112.

is also probably significant here that Foldbriht's body came back to life while the monks were standing nearby and chanting psalms for his soul, and just as mass was being offered in an attempt to prevent the devil taking it.

Although the idea of the angelic and demonic struggle for the soul is well-attested, quite how that was played out is more complex.[260] For those who were especially blessed, visions of their souls being led directly and immediately to heaven by angels suggest that the soul was not believed to wait around for long and that the struggle was therefore not arduous: Bede records that at the precise moment that Sigefrith's soul passed from his body, the brothers who were with him had reached Psalm 82, which is concerned with the physical and spiritual enemies of the Church and their attempt to destroy souls, and concludes that these enemies will themselves perish for all eternity. For Bede, this had great significance, since it demonstrated that with the help of God the enemies could not harm Sigefrith, and that his soul had not been hindered or delayed by the evil spirits.[261] In contrast, wicked souls were often seen in visions being dragged off by demons to hell.[262] This is in effect the individual judgement which determined whether souls would be punished, purged, or at rest until the Last Judgement, and the psalms, prayers and masses offered for departing souls highlight the importance of these in this struggle.

What is not clear is precisely how the journey and entry of the soul into its allotted place in the afterlife relate to the soul's continuing proximity to the body. A story in the *Dialogues* suggests the possibility that the spirits of the dead remain close to their bodies: the spirits of two nuns who had been excommunicated and yet were buried in a church were seen to get up and leave every time the mass was offered.[263] It may be that some people believed that the soul might linger near the corpse, or continue some kind of existence near it, until the body had been buried and the flesh had decomposed.[264] An account of a miracle in the eighth-century *Life of Wilfrid*, by Stephen of Ripon, seems to suggest that the soul was believed to remain near the body after death: Wilfrid is reported to have asked God to 'send the soul of a boy back into his body, that he might live', suggesting perhaps that the boy's soul was not far away.[265] The idea of the lingering soul is particularly interesting in considering the incorrupt bodies of saints and their physical presence in the churches where they lay: the anonymous *Life of Cuthbert* is noteworthy in

---

[260]   See above, 111–16.

[261]   *Historia abbatum*, 14, ed. C. Plummer, *Venerabilis Baedae Historiam ecclesiasticam gentis Anglorum: Historiam abbatum, Epistolam ad Ecgberctum, una cum Historia abbatum auctore anonymo, ad fidem codicum manuscriptorum denuo recognovit, Epistola ad Ecgberctum* (2 vols, Oxford, 1896), 377–9.

[262]   e.g. Bede, *HE*, V.12.3, ed. Lapidge, Monat and Robin, *Histoire ecclésiastique*, III.72–4.

[263]   *Dialogues*, II.23.2–5, ed. de Vogüé and Antin, *Dialogues, Livre IV*, II.206–8.

[264]   Brown, 'Death', 223 and n. 3.

[265]   Stephen, *Vita S. Wilfridi*, 23, ed. and trans. Colgrave, *Life of Bishop Wilfrid*, 46–7.

its description of miracles omitted from the text, including the enigmatic reference to 'how, when present, he healed some with only a word'.[266]

There are also references to the idea that the soul might move about and visit its body, as in the later Anglo-Saxon 'soul and body' motif which appears in both homiletic and poetic contexts. This motif presents good and bad souls addressing their bodies (also good and bad, respectively), explaining that the soul visits the body at intervals between their separation at death and their reunification after the Last Judgement.[267] The key message of this motif is of course that the deeds of the body in life have a powerful effect on the fate of the soul, but the idea that the soul might visit its body is significant for understanding the treatment of dead bodies and the perceived relationship between body and soul. Narrative accounts also suggest similar ideas: the late seventh- or early eighth-century *Life of Gregory the Great*, written perhaps at Whitby, records the story of a priest instructed by a vision to rescue the bones of King Edwin from the battlefield where he had been killed, and where his body still lay. Almost as an aside, the author of the *Life* notes that afterwards, the priest lived for some time at the site where Edwin had first been buried, and that he had seen the spirits of four of those who had been killed coming to visit their bodies, and that they had certainly been baptized.[268] Similarly, Dunstan is said to have been praying in the church of St Mary, where the bodies of St Augustine of Canterbury and the other archbishops were buried, when he heard the sound of singing – and Byrhtferth adds the detail, not found in the earlier *Life of Dunstan*, that this was a hymn which 'the holy souls of those whose bodies were buried in the church were singing'.[269]

This is one area where an attempt to find unified coherency of belief would be rather pointless: the logical implications of the sources include simultaneous multiple existences of the soul of precisely the kind that Augustine had worried about, and although continuing relationships between bodies and souls were clearly understood to exist these were evidently extremely complex, dependent on many factors, and their details not always precisely worked out. This is clear

[266] *Vita S. Cuthberti*, xviii, ed. B. Colgrave, *Two Lives of Saint Cuthbert: A Life by an Anonymous Monk of Lindisfarne and Bede's Prose Life* (Cambridge, 1985 [orig. pub. 1940]), 138: 'quomodo praesens uerbo tantum alios sanauit'.

[267] For discussion of this motif see R. Willard, 'The address of the soul to the body', *Publications of the Modern Languages Association* 50 (1935): 957–83; A.J. Frantzen, 'The Body in *Soul and Body I*', *Chaucer Review: A Journal of Medieval Studies and Literary Criticism* 17 (1982–3): 76–88; C.D. Wright, '*Docet deus, docet diabolus*: A Hiberno-Latin theme in an Old English body-and-soul homily', *Notes and Queries* 232 (1987): 451–3; D. Moffat, *The Old English Soul and Body* (Woodbridge, 1990); Thompson, *Dying and Death*, 138–44.

[268] *Vita S. Gregorii*, 19, ed. B. Colgrave, *The Earliest Life of Gregory the Great* (Cambridge, 1985 [orig. pub. 1968]), 104–5.

[269] Byrhtferth, *Vita S. Oswaldi*, V.7, ed. Lapidge, *The Lives of St Oswald and St Ecgwine*, 162.

not only in the comparison of sources but also within the same source and even in the same story. The *Life of Wilfrid* relates that at the moment of Wilfrid's last breath, a sound of approaching birds was heard: on another day, when abbots had come to the monastery to wash and care for the holy body, the noise of birds was heard again as the body was carried to the place where it would rest, and this was interpreted as Michael and his angels coming to take the soul away.[270] If the second part of the story had not been added, most readers would have assumed that the appearance of the angels at the moment of Wilfrid's death indicated that they had come to take his soul, but it is not clear what Wilfrid's soul was supposed to be doing in the time between his death and the burial of his body, and whether it had reached heaven as well as or instead of waiting near the body, especially given the more usual assumption that saints' souls entered heaven immediately, with no delay. The precise chronology seems to have been as unclear to the author as it is now to the account's readers.

While some angels and demons were always present in the air, this account and others indicate that more spirits were believed to come to the dying soul, and it seems that demons in particular may have been thought to be specifically attracted to dead and dying bodies. Cuthbert is supposed to have said that he had been more persecuted by 'adversaries' while he was sick and dying on Lindisfarne than in the whole of the rest of the time that he had been on the island, and while this may be representative of Bede's belief rather than Cuthbert's actual words, it is significant nonetheless.[271] It is unclear whether the ongoing commemoration of the dead in the days and weeks after the funeral was intended to assist in a struggle which was also ongoing because of the continued presence of the soul near the body: given the uncertainty over precisely how the soul existed after death, perhaps both of these were accepted, and they are in any case related concepts.

Keeping demons away from dying and dead bodies was not only important in the attempt to prevent them from snatching the soul, but also in case they tried to enter the body and re-animate the soul, which seems to have been the fear in Foldbriht's case. It seems that the attraction of demons to wicked people and angels to good people, described so clearly in the brother of Wenlock's vision of the otherworld, extended to the bodies of the dead as well as to the whole living person. As the stories of bodies re-animated by devils demonstrate, the bodies which were attractive to wicked spirits were inevitably those which had been inhabited in life by problematic souls, and it is this in particular which makes Byrhtferth's description of Foldbriht so interesting. The inclusion of prayers requesting that God keep wicked or unclean spirits away from enclosed cemeteries in the rites used to consecrate them may be another reflection of concerns that these spirits might seek out bodies or be attracted to them: several rites contain a prayer asking God to allow the bodies of his servants to rest in quiet in the cemetery without the incursion of wicked spirits, and another to be said in the western part

---

[270]   Stephen, *Vita S. Wilfridi*, lxv–lxvi, ed. Colgrave, *Life of Bishop Wilfrid*, 140–5.

[271]   Bede, *Vita S. Cuthberti prosa*, xxxvii, ed. Colgrave, *Two Lives of Cuthbert*, 277.

of the cemetery asking God to guard the cemetery of the saints from the filth of unclean spirits.[272] In some cases there are also prayers asking God that in addition to blessing and consecrating the cemetery, he strengthen it against the designs of invisible enemies, as long as the bodies rest there, and the mass offered in the cemetery asks that an angel guard the souls of those who rest in the cemetery.[273]

Angels were apparently believed to remain near the bodies of the blessed as well leading their souls to rest, as the consecration rites suggest, and angelic presence near the resting place of holy bodies has biblical precedent in the angels surrounding the tomb of Christ.[274] The anonymous (and probably roughly contemporary) account of the life and death of Ceolfrith (d.716) records that the night after Ceolfrith had been buried, a wonderful smell and a light filled the church, and the light eventually rose to the roof of the church before rising up to the sky. To those watching around the tomb, 'it was understood clearly that ministers of eternal light and perpetual sweetness had been there, who by their visit had consecrated the resting-place of the holy body': in other words, angels had visited Ceolfrith's final resting place.[275] An episode in the *Life of Wilfrid* suggests that angels might also be attracted to places where saints had breathed their last: when a marauding band set fire to the monastery at Oundle, the room where Wilfrid had died remained miraculously untouched, and when one man tried to go into the room to set it alight, he found a young man, dressed in white and holding a golden cross, whom he immediately identified as an angel protecting the place.[276] The presence of angels around the bodies of the holy dead is another reminder of the extent to which the body retained the identity and attributes of the person it had once been, even once its animating force had gone.

## Conclusion

Christian funerary liturgies request peace, light and refreshment for the soul, and ask God that the time between death and the Last Judgement should be one of quiet

---

[272]    See for example Paris, Bibliothèque nationale, lat. 10575 ('Egbert Pontifical'), fol. 74, ed. Banting, *Two Anglo-Saxon Pontificals*, 58; or Cambridge, Corpus Christi College, 146 ('Samson Pontifical'), p. 92; for detailed discussion of the rites see Gittos, 'Consecrating Cemeteries', 195–9.

[273]    CCCC 146, p. 93.

[274]    Mt 28:1–4; Lk 24:1–8; Jn 20:12.

[275]    *Historia Abbatum auctore Anonymo*, 40, ed. Plummer, *Venerabilis Baedae Historiam ecclesiasticam*, I.403–4: '... ut palam daretur intelligi ministros aeternae lucis et perpetuae suauitatis adfuisse, qui sedem sancti corporis sua uisitatione consecrauerint'. See I.N. Wood, 'The foundation of Bede's Wearmouth-Jarrow', in S. DeGregorio (ed.), *The Cambridge Companion to Bede* (Cambridge, 2010), 84–96, at 84–7 and esp. 86, where a date of 'some point later than the spring of 717' is suggested.

[276]    Stephen, *Vita S. Wilfridi*, 67, ed. and trans. Colgrave, *Life of Bishop Wilfrid*, 144–7.

and rest. Overwhelmingly, rest and quiet was sought for the body as well: bodies were said to sleep in the grave until they would awake at the Last Judgement and cemeteries are described as places of rest, and the rites for consecrating cemeteries echo funerary liturgies in their requests for peace and quiet. The incorrupt bodies of saints were often described as looking as if they were sleeping rather than being dead, an image which emphasises both the continuing 'life' of the saint in heaven and the rest of the saint's bodily remains on earth. And yet despite the emphasis on rest, there are frequent reminders of the corruptibility of the body and the fact that all normal bodies will rot, a fact which modern sanitised audiences usually prefer to put from their minds.[277] The author of the tenth Blickling homily warns his audience that no one should think that while in the grave he could affect the burden of sin he had built up, but instead his body will rot and await the Last Judgement, when the Almighty will come with a sword and pierce the bodies through.[278] In part this was intended to encourage contemplation of the soul's deeds rather than the body's, but it is clear that it was also simply anticipated as a fact of life and death and was not necessarily connected with the fate of the soul. Not even all saints' bodies remained incorrupt, and when saints were translated it seems that clean bones were not necessarily expected; it is also clear from both textual and archaeological evidence that bodily remains of the ordinary dead were found when new graves cut through old ones.[279]

This is a reminder too that the bodies of the dead continued to affect burial practices in the present, in multiple ways. In addition to burial *ad sanctos* or the placement of bodies in or near earlier burial mounds, more prosaic considerations such as earlier graves affected the treatment of the bodies of the dead. At Barton on Humber (Lincolnshire), the construction of the late Saxon church resulted in the careful 'translation' of a group of 29 early burials.[280] In other cases earlier burials might simply be reincorporated into the newly dug graves, as for example in Addingham (Yorkshire), where burials from the western part of the cemetery seem to have been dug up and reinterred in new graves in the eastern part of the cemetery instead.[281] Sometimes when cemeteries became full bones might be collected up and placed in a charnel house, as Bede describes for Barking, or as

---

[277]    Although see http://seemerot.com [accessed November 2012], a website whose purpose is to stream live video from inside coffins.

[278]    The homilist may draw here on Augustine, *DCD*, XX.21, ll. 95–106, ed. Dombert and Kalb, *De civitate dei*, II. 738–9.

[279]    Bede, *HE*, IV.28, ed. Lapidge, Monat and Robin, *Histoire ecclésiastique*, II.374–6; *Hom.* XIV, ll. 27–9, 33–5, 40–2, ed. B. Assmann, *Angelsächsische Homilien und Heiligenleben*, Bibliothek der angelsächsischen Prosa 3 (Darmstadt, 1964), 165.

[280]    W. Rodwell, C. Atkins and T. Waldron, *St Peter's, Barton-upon-Humber, Lincolnshire: A Parish Church and its Community* (3 vols, Oxford, 2007), I.30.

[281]    M. Adams, 'Excavation of a pre-Conquest cemetery at Addingham, West Yorkshire', *Medieval Archaeology: Journal of the Society for Medieval Archaeology* 40 (1996): 151–91, at 182–4.

strikingly demonstrated at the 'lost' church of St Peter's in Leicester: here, the stone walls of the charnel house were later robbed for building material but the bones themselves were left apparently untouched.[282]

The choice of burial spot in the cemetery might otherwise simply have been determined according to how many other graves filled the space, how (or if) they were marked, and whether the cemetery was enclosed or could be expanded further in one direction. It is interesting that occasionally the chosen place is designated as being in the southern part of the cemetery, or in the case of the sisters at Barking that the cemetery itself was in the southern part of the monastery: it may be that the light requested in funeral liturgies was perhaps desired for the body's resting place as well.[283] In his interpretation of Genesis, Bede notes that mystically the south is connected with divine light and love, and since the south is nearer to the light and heat of the sun, on the moral level of allegory it often signifies the life of the faithful.[284] Whether the allegorical and mystical significance of the south was important in burial practice, or whether people simply preferred the sunnier parts of the cemetery is unclear: there is no clear evidence from Anglo-Saxon cemeteries to suggest that the south was necessarily the better part of the cemetery, although sometimes in medieval cemeteries the southern areas are more favoured, or the northern areas are more sparsely filled.[285]

It is worth noting too that sometimes changing perceptions, beliefs and values seem to have rendered earlier burial practices enigmatic or difficult to understand even by those who stood much closer in time and space to these practices than modern scholars do, and this warns against assuming that practices or beliefs as found in the ground or in textual descriptions are necessarily comprehensible now.

---

[282] See T. Gnanaratnam, 'Revealing a lost community', *British Archaeology* 91 (2006): 20–1; T. Gnanaratnam, 'An urban medieval population from St Peter's, Leicester', *The Archaeologist* 60 (2006): 26–7.

[283] B, *Vita S. Dunstani*, 9.3, ed. Winterbottom and Lapidge, *Early Lives*, 32; Bede, *HE*, IV.7.2, ed. Lapidge, Monat and Robin, *Histoire ecclésiastique*, II.236.

[284] Bede, *In principium Genesis*, III.13.2, ll. 1219–23; IV.20.1, ll. 1331–3, ed. Jones, *Bedae venerabilis opera, pars II: opera exegetica, 1. Libri quattor in principium Genesis usque ad nativitatem Isaac et eiectionem Ismahelis adnotationum*, 176, 231: 'Hoc est enim mystice ascendentes de egypto ad australem plagam uenire expletis nos carnis necessariis, supernae lucis et caritatis profectum a domino sedula intentione postulare. Tali namque uoto ac proposito mentis ad celestem nos patriam iter facere non dubium est'; 'Terra quippe australis, quae luci et ardori solis uicinior est, illam saepe uitam fidelium iuxta mortales sensus indicat, quae, discusso torpore concupiscentiae mundalis, interna luce supernae dilectionis magis magisque cotidie solebat innouari'.

[285] See for example Rivenhall (Essex): W. Rodwell and K.A. Rodwell, *Rivenhall: Investigations of a Villa, Church, and Village, 1950–1977*, Chelmsford Archaeological Trust Report 4 (London, 1985), 101; the 'lost' church of St Peter's in Leicester also has fewer burials to the north than to the east and west, but the southern part of the cemetery was not excavated. I am grateful to Richard Buckley for allowing me access to the grey literature on this site.

Symeon of Durham's *Historia regum* records that Bishop Acca of Hexham was buried in 740, and translated about three hundred years later. At the time of his eleventh-century translation, a tablet made of wood was found on his chest in the form of an altar, and with the inscription 'Almae Trinitati, Agiae Sophiae, Sanctae Mariae': Symeon remarks that 'it is not known whether relics were placed in it, or why it was placed in the earth with him, but it is believed that it was not buried with his holy body, in honour of highest veneration, without some cause of sensible devotion'.[286] For Symeon as for modern scholars, it is not possible to recover the specific beliefs which prompted this practice in any detailed sense, but broadly speaking it seems to have been intended to display devotion and reverence.

In other cases differences of opinion may also have made earlier beliefs seem redundant or peculiar. The author of the anonymous *Life of Cuthbert* records that Cuthbert was buried with his shoes, 'in readiness to meet Christ'.[287] While this may have an echo in the Anglo-Saxon rituals for the dying which instruct that the gloves and socks placed on a sick man must be left on him if he dies within the week, it is difficult to find any sensible explanation for gloves, socks or shoes in the grave, or how or why they might have been considered to have any useful purpose.[288] Patristic theology might suggest that the clothes that people wore in death were irrelevant, but evidently it was not always seen this way: the account of Wilfrid's death and burial notes that some people wanted to ensure that the body was decently clothed; in the late ninth century, Bishop Wærferth of Worcester seems to have been perfectly comfortable with the idea that bodies might be dressed in clothes or wrapped in shrouds;[289] and one of the Blickling homilies presents the Blessed Virgin Mary choosing with some care the clothes that her body would wear in death.[290] Returning to Cuthbert, it seems that Bede also did not understand why Cuthbert would need his shoes to meet Christ since he omitted this detail in his version, although he wrote his account only about 20 years after the anonymous *Life* and drew on it for much of his information.[291] For Bede, Cuthbert's virtuous deeds had prepared him

---

[286]   Symeon, *Historia regum*, 36, ed. Arnold, *Symeonis monachi opera omnia: Vol. 2, Historia regum*, 33: 'Utrum vero reliquiae in ea positae fuerint, vel qua de causa cum eo in terra posita sit, ignoratur. Attamen absque rationabili devotionis causa, summae venerationis cultu cum sancto ejus corpore nequaquam esse condita creditur'. Or, as some archaeologists might suggest, it must have had ritual significance.

[287]   *Vita S. Cuthberti*, 13, ed. and trans. Colgrave, *Two Lives of Cuthbert*, 130–1.

[288]   Amalarius clearly also found this deeply confusing, to judge from his comments in the *Liber officialis*, IV.41.1–6, ed. Hanssens, *Amalarii episcopi opera liturgica omnia*, 531–3.

[289]   Thompson, *Dying and Death*, 20–1; see also above, 322.

[290]   *Hom.* XIII, ed. Morris, *Blickling Homilies*, 143.

[291]   Colgrave, *Two Lives of Cuthbert*, 13–16. In his retelling of the story of a boy who was cured by wearing Cuthbert's shoes, Bede emphasised that the shoes in question were those worn by Cuthbert in the grave before he was translated. The earlier *Life* describes the

well for the moment when his soul and body would be reunited before Christ, shoeless or otherwise.

In some cases and perhaps especially in the early period, medieval monastic burial may have involved an unmarked grave, in contrast to the showy monuments which were later used to encourage memorial and remembrance, but burial at a monastery was an expression of community identity which was desired and sought out by those of wealth and status, and the prayers and offerings made for the community's dead were probably at least as significant as the body's final resting place.[292] Christian belief was an important prerequisite for Christian burial, as noted by Wulfstan and also by funerary rituals, which recall that while all are sinful, belief ensures salvation: one prayer asks God for mercy, pleading that 'although it is acknowledged that he sinned, yet he did not deny the Father and the Son and the Holy Spirit but believed'.[293] Yet at the same time the complexities of beliefs surrounding both body and soul are far greater than the simple credal statements of belief in one God and his creation of the visible and invisible worlds, the Last Judgement or the forgiveness of sins, or the resurrection of the body and the life everlasting. People knew what was desirable in burial, and people also knew what was best avoided, and as in the modern world, ordinary people in Anglo-Saxon England presumably did not usually consider which aspects of burial were important for which types of reasons, whether social, cultural, personal or theological.

As with the beliefs surrounding purgatory, it is not always easy to determine whether beliefs about the body and soul and their continued relationship are official or orthodox, or unofficial or unorthodox. Augustine is a useful benchmark for canonical belief simply because he was so influential, but his uncertainty on such matters illustrates precisely how difficult it is to delineate official or orthodox belief in this context. Gregory's greater certainty may have been significant in providing authority for the acceptance of many of these ideas, but it is still not easy to find a clear official line. The difference between practice and justification

---

same miracle but does not clarify this (although presumably Cuthbert only had one pair of shoes?), suggesting that the reason for wearing shoes 'to meet Christ' may not even have been clear to the author of the earlier *Life* or to any of his contemporaries. It is worth noting too that Amalarius of Metz, who seems to have thought that the anonymous *Life* was by Bede and thus carried his authority, got in a real tangle over why the shoes might have been important, and this led him to discuss a whole range of occasions from Scripture when people were clothed or naked and why clothing for burial might be significant: see *Liber Officialis*, IV.40, ed. Hanssens, *Amalarii episcopi opera liturgica omnia*, II.531–5.

[292] N. Rogers, 'Monuments to Monks and Monastic Servants', in B. Thompson (ed.), *Monasteries and Society in Medieval Britain: Proceedings of the 1994 Harlaxton Symposium*, Harlaxton Medieval Studies, n.s. 6 (Stamford, 1999), 262–76, at 262; see also Schmid, *Pro remedio animae*, 153–4, 162.

[293] Bodley 579, fol. 246v, ed. Orchard, *Leofric Missal*, no. 2201: 'Licet enim peccauit, tamen patrum et filium et spiritum sanctum non negauit sed credidit, et zelum dei habuit, et deum qui omnia fecit adorauit'.

(and sometimes, by implication, belief) is important too: even if Bede objected to the reason given for putting shoes on Cuthbert's body, he probably did not object to the wearing of shoes in the grave in itself. The discovery of amulets or other objects in excavated graves suggests that their inclusion with the body was desired by some people, whether the buriers or the buried; others (like Ælfric) might have objected to such practices; and still others may simply not have worried, cared or thought much about it.[294]

There was evidently more ecclesiastical control over burial practices by the end of the Anglo-Saxon period, but as far as the evidence allows such conclusions to be drawn, it does not seem to be the case that unwilling populations had Christian burial forced upon them. Rather, at least some aspects of the theological ideas which informed practices such as burial in consecrated ground or the rites for the sick and dying seem to have been communicated to and accepted by the laity, although perhaps as much out of a desire for social inclusion as out of religious belief. The credal declaration that the body would rise again meant that it could never be unimportant even if the body's fate was determined by the soul and not by the body itself. Depending on the person who had owned it a body might be repulsive or attractive, but the body retained power both as an object and, in a Christian context, as the enduring sign and remaining physical manifestation of that person's belief.

---

[294]  See for example R. Gilchrist, 'Magic for the dead? The archaeology of magic in later medieval burials', *Medieval Archaeology: Journal of the Society for Medieval Archaeology* 52 (2008): 119–59.

# Epilogue

On [Maundy] Thursday, which is called the Lord's Supper, the Night Office shall be performed according to what is set down in the Antiphonary. We have also learned that in the churches of some religious men, a practice has begun to be performed which is an outward sign of an inner spiritual matter, for the compunction of souls ... This practice of religious compunction was created by Catholic men, as I think, so that the terror of the darkness which hit the tripartite world with unaccustomed fear at our Lord's Passion, and the consolation of apostolic preaching, which revealed Christ to the entire world, obedient to his Father even to death for the salvation of humankind, might be clearly indicated.[1]

These instructions for the performance of part of the liturgy for Maundy Thursday come from the *Regularis Concordia*, a liturgical customary for monastic life drawn up in Winchester in about 970.[2] This passage is notable for its use of the first person in the interpretation of a liturgical custom, and it has been attributed to Æthelwold, Bishop of Winchester (d.984), who was explaining continental customs which he was introducing into English liturgical use.[3] The practice referred to here required that with the candles extinguished and the church in darkness, two children should sing 'Kyrie eleison' ('Lord have mercy') from the right-hand side of the choir, answered by two more from the left-hand side with 'Christe eleison' ('Christ have mercy'), so that these prayers were sung and answered across the church. Then from the west (i.e., towards the back of the church, away from the altar), two more

---

[1]    *RC*, 37, ed. T. Symons, *Regularis Concordia: The Monastic Agreement of the Monks and Nuns of the English Nation* (London, 1953), 36–7: 'Quinta feria, quae et Cena Domini dicitur, nocturnale officium agatur secundum quod in Antiphonario habetur. Comperimus etiam in quorundam reli<gi>osorum ecclesiis quiddam fieri quod ad animarum compunctionem spiritualis rei indicium exorsum est ... Qui, ut reor, ecclesiasticae compunctionis usus a catholicis ideo repertus est ut tenebrarum terror, qui tripertitum mundum dominica passione timore perculit insolito, ac apostolicae praedicationis consolatio, quae [uniuerso mundo] Christum Patri usque ad mortem pro generis humani salute oboedientem reuelauerat, manifestissime designetur'.
[2]    Symons, *Regularis Concordia*, xxiii–xxiv; L. Kornexl, 'The Regularis Concordia and its Old English gloss', *Anglo-Saxon England* 24 (1995): 95–130, at 96–101.
[3]    Kornexl, 'The Regularis Concordia and its Old English gloss', 100–1. Helen Gittos notes a similar example of the first person being used to interpret a liturgical ritual in the 'Dunstan Pontifical' (now Paris, Bibliothèque nationale, lat. 943; Christ Church, Canterbury, s. x²), in the rite for the consecration of a church: see H. Gittos, 'Introduction', in H. Gittos and M.B. Bedingfield (eds), *The Liturgy of the Late Anglo-Saxon Church*, HBS, Subsidia 5 (London, 2005), 1–11, at 6 and n. 12.

children should sing 'Domine miserere nobis' ('Lord have mercy upon us'), and then the whole choir should reply 'Christus dominus factus est oboediens usque ad mortem' ('Christ the Lord was made obedient even unto death'). This sequence was to be repeated twice more, so that it was sung through three times in total. Afterwards, the brothers were to say prayers kneeling in silence as usual; and this whole process was to be repeated for three nights. Æthelwold explains that it seemed appropriate to insert this information in case anyone wanted to know about it, but he is careful to add that no one should be compelled to perform this against his will.[4]

Holy Week marks the culmination of the Christian liturgical calendar, and its liturgy is some of the most dramatic and most moving.[5] On Maundy Thursday the events of the Last Supper and the betrayal of Jesus which followed it are commemorated and re-enacted: liturgical customaries provide instructions for foot-washing, the stripping of the altars, and, as above, the plunge into darkness from which children's voices are heard begging the Lord for mercy.[6] On Good Friday Christ's Passion was commemorated, again with dramatic ritual including the reading of the passion and the adoration and deposition of the cross; while the symbolic change from the darkness of death to the light of Christ began with the Blessing of the New Fire at the Easter Vigil, on the evening before Easter Sunday itself.[7] These liturgies were performed year after year and recall events which, by the time the *Regularis Concordia* was written down, had occurred nearly one thousand years previously. But, as the passage from the *Regularis Concordia* shows, these liturgies were not unchanging and nor were the ways that old and new customs were considered, understood and interpreted. Liturgy is remarkably conservative, but even here it is possible to see innovation and change, and with those changes come new theological interpretations.[8]

Æthelwold's comments seem to show his own personal response to a practice which he felt added to the drama and the momentousness of the occasion commemorated. Some of the services offered in the Old Minster while Æthelwold was bishop might have been attended by people living in Winchester (though probably not the Night Office, which is the context for the 'Kyrie eleison' ritual); but their responses to, and their own interpretations of, the liturgies enacted at Holy Week or throughout the Christian year can never be known. And yet these are the people whose bodies were buried in the lay cemetery at the Old Minster,

---

[4]   *RC*, 37, ed. Symons, *Regularis Concordia*, 36–7; Kornexl, 'The Regularis Concordia and its Old English gloss', 96–101.

[5]   For a detailed discussion see M.B. Bedingfield, *The Dramatic Liturgy of Anglo-Saxon England* (Woodbridge, 2002), 114–70.

[6]   Symons, *Regularis Concordia*; Bedingfield, *The Dramatic Liturgy of Anglo-Saxon England*, 115–22.

[7]   Symons, *Regularis Concordia*; Bedingfield, *The Dramatic Liturgy of Anglo-Saxon England*, 123–39.

[8]   See further Gittos, 'Introduction'.

and who may have been baptised there, since although there were other churches in Winchester by the late tenth century the cathedral seems to have held almost exclusive rights to burials and baptisms for Winchester's citizens.[9] They may have heard homilies there, including perhaps both the more rigorously canonical and the less orthodox; they may have attended masses or made their confessions there, or in Winchester's smaller churches. The townspeople of Winchester also populate the accounts of the miracles of St Swithun, who was 'discovered' while Æthelwold was bishop: while some appear to have come into, or been brought into, the cathedral when seeking a cure, at other times they were presumably as frustrated as were some of the monks by Æthelwold's insistence that the bell should be rung as soon as a miracle was discovered, whatever time of day or night it was.[10]

Churches and religious houses clearly played a major role in society and in daily life, but the effects and impact of 'the Church' as an institution are not the whole story. Issues such as control of the laity, the acquisition of wealth, or negotiating changing political circumstances may have been one aspect of the complex business which went on at religious houses and churches, but another major aspect was theology, and the production and interpretation of theological texts. While it is possible, if rare, to hear Æthelwold speaking about his own theological interpretation of a custom which he evidently felt to be a useful introduction to liturgical practice of his own day, the opinions and interpretations of almost all of those for whom Æthelwold was responsible as bishop remain unrecorded. But theology could be significant as the driving force behind the decisions and actions of bishops, who, as political players and advisers, could thus ensure that theology was influential in contexts where it would have a far-reaching impact even on the lives of those who might not be able to read it for themselves. One of the most striking examples of this is in the context of the law. The complexities of theological discussion over the death penalty or how

---

[9]    The only exceptions seem to have been Winchester's other two religious houses, the New Minster and the Nunnaminster, which were enclosed in the same precinct and seem likewise to have held rights of burial and perhaps also baptism. See M. Biddle and D. Keene, 'Winchester in the Eleventh and Twelfth Centuries', in M. Biddle (ed.), *Winchester in the Early Middle Ages: An Edition and Discussion of the Winton Domesday* (Oxford, 1976), 241–448, at 312, 314, 330–5; D. Keene and A.R. Rumble, *Survey of Medieval Winchester*, Winchester Studies 2 (Oxford, 1985), I.108–9; M.J. Franklin, 'The Cathedral as Parish Church: The Case of Southern England', in D. Abulafia, M.J. Franklin and M. Rubin (eds), *Church and City, 1000–1500: Essays in Honour of Christopher Brooke* (Cambridge, 1992), 173–98, at 174–5; B. Kjølbye-Biddle, 'Dispersal or Concentration: The Disposal of the Winchester Dead over 2000 years', in S.R. Bassett (ed.), *Death in Towns: Urban Responses to the Dying and the Dead, 100–1600* (Leicester, 1992), 210–47, at 224–6; see also H. Foxhall Forbes, 'Squabbling siblings: Gender and monastic life in late Anglo-Saxon Winchester', *Gender & History* 23:3 (2011): 653–84, at 666–7.

[10]    Lantfred, *Translatio S. Swithuni*, 10, ed. M. Lapidge, *The Cult of St Swithun*, Winchester Studies 4.ii (Oxford, 2003), 292–6.

judgements were to be reached may have been unknown to most people in later Anglo-Saxon England, but the application of the law touched people in life and death, determining punishment in life and in some cases affecting where their bodies could rest in death (Chapter 3).

On the other hand, the effectiveness of sanctions such as burial in unconsecrated ground depended, at least to some extent, on those same people understanding the value of burial in consecrated ground, and the value of the prayers for the dead which were offered for those whose bodies lay in hallowed cemeteries. On the basis of the surviving evidence, the importance of offerings for the dead seems initially to have been felt more by those in religious houses, but it is clear that by the later Anglo-Saxon period (if not before) there was significant lay interest in ensuring the provision of liturgical commemoration (Chapter 4). At the same time, it is clear that there was quite a wide variety of beliefs about dead bodies and the fate of the soul, many of which were inconsistent or contradictory, and which were often bound up with ideas about social inclusion or social status as much as they were connected with theological discussion (Chapter 5). Some of the beliefs which supported these ideas, especially those about the roles that angels and devils played in life and death, seem to have been inculcated, discussed or reinforced at particular occasions throughout the year, and to have spread quite widely, so that they appear in the context of the landscape, or seem to have travelled by popular report (Chapter 2).

It is also important to note that it is possible to see theology changing and developing in Anglo-Saxon England, in contrast to the traditional representation of early medieval theology as static and derivative (Chapter 1). Theology in the early Middle Ages was not undertaken in the same way as it would be from the twelfth century onwards, and changes in institutional ecclesiastical structures and purpose were also significant in transforming how theology was used and what it was for, as well as the way in which it was carried out. Nonetheless, it is striking that a number of the issues discussed at the Fourth Lateran Council in 1215 were evidently a matter of concern in the early Middle Ages, especially since this was one of the most important medieval ecclesiastical councils and is usually seen as marking a decisive turning-point, particularly for issues such as ordeals or confession. While Lateran IV was certainly significant, it is worth remembering that a good number of the topics discussed there, and many of the provisions that were made in response to those discussions, had a substantial prehistory. Lateran IV is also interesting in this context for its statement that a 'theologian' could be the person designated to instruct priests in Scripture, especially in those things which pertain to pastoral care.[11] This suggests that even by the early thirteenth century, the speculative examination of abstract concepts or issues in complete isolation from their practical application was not necessarily seen to be a useful exercise, and the importance of pastoral theology then comes to the fore.

---

[11]    IV Lateran (1215), 11, ed. and trans. N.P. Tanner, *Decrees of the Ecumenical Councils* (2 vols, London, 1990), I.240.

As Æthelwold's statement about the liturgy for Maundy Thursday shows, theology may be used to explain, interpret or provide justification for new or existing practices or beliefs. Theology therefore responds to changing beliefs and ideas as much as it may help to drive changes in society or in social practice, as in the case of the law. This is the importance of theology – especially pastoral theology – in its social context, because it cannot be detached from the world in which it operates. At the same time, so much of the surviving evidence for early medieval Christian societies like those in Anglo-Saxon England originated in contexts where theology played a major role that arguably, if the importance of theology is not taken into consideration, the subtleties of the evidence itself cannot be understood in the detail they deserve. The relationship between theology and its social context has been discussed in detail through the case studies explored in this book, with the aim of highlighting the importance of understanding theology in interpreting the surviving Anglo-Saxon evidence, as well as in understanding the societies and individuals from whom they originate. Written theological discussion may have been abstract and remote from many people in Anglo-Saxon England but it was still significant in shaping practices, just as beliefs which may have initially owed more to social or cultural factors came to be incorporated into religious contexts and given theological interpretations or justification.

The meeting-points between these are just visible in the surviving textual and material evidence, even if it remains impossible to access personal interiority for the vast majority of Anglo-Saxon Christians, and this sheds light on the mutual relationship between the academic world of theology and the broader social contexts in which it existed. The beliefs, and above all the faith, of individuals and communities connect these and act as a pivot-point around which they centre and focus. Like beliefs which did not derive so clearly from a learned or theological tradition, theology was also flexible and subject to debate; and the possibility of variability of belief both horizontally and vertically in society warns against the search for static and unchanging ideas either within learned and literate contexts or outside them. The early Middle Ages may not be an age of faith in the sense of a period marked entirely by superstition and incredulity, as once imagined, but nonetheless faith and theology permeate the surviving evidence just as they clearly permeated many Anglo-Saxon social contexts. For Christians in Anglo-Saxon England, theology could explore and explain the relationship between God and his creation and, in so doing, it served to narrow the gap between heaven and earth.

# Bibliography

**Primary Sources**

Alcuin, *Expositio in psalmum CXVIII*, PL 100.597C–598A.
Alcuin, *De animae ratione liber ad Eulaliam virginem*, PL 101.639–47.
Alcuin, *De virtutibus et vitiis*, 20, PL 128.628C–629B.
Alexander, J.J.G. and N. Barker (eds.), *The York Gospels: A Facsimile with Introductory Essays by Jonathan Alexander [et al.]* (London: Roxburghe Club, 1986).
Allen, W., *A defense and declaration of the Catholike Churchies doctrine, touching purgatory, and prayers for the soules departed* ([Antwerp]: [I. Latius], 1565).
Anlezark, D. (ed.), *The Old English Dialogues of Solomon and Saturn* (Woodbridge: Boydell & Brewer, 2009).
Arnold, T. (ed.), *Symeonis monachi opera omnia: Vol. 2, Historia regum*, Rolls Series (London: Longmans & Co, 1885).
Arnold, T. (ed.), *Memorials of St. Edmund's Abbey* (London: HMSO, 1890).
Assmann, B. (ed.), *Angelsächsische Homilien und Heiligenleben*, Bibliothek der angelsächsischen Prosa 3 (Darmstadt: Wissenschaftliche Buchgesellschaft, 1964).
Baker, P.S. and M. Lapidge (eds), *Byrhtferth's Enchiridion*, EETS, SS 15 (Oxford: Published for EETS by Oxford University Press, 1995).
Banting, H.M.J. (ed.), *Two Anglo-Saxon Pontificals (the Egbert and Sidney Sussex Pontificals)*, HBS 104 (London: Henry Bradshaw Society, 1989).
Bately, J. (ed.), *The Anglo-Saxon Chronicle: A Collaborative Edition: Vol. 3, MS A: A Semi-Diplomatic Edition with Introduction and Indices* (Cambridge: Brewer, 1986).
Bazire, J. and J.E. Cross (eds), *Eleven Old English Rogationtide Homilies*, Toronto Old English Series 7 (Toronto: Published in association with The Centre for Medieval Studies, University of Toronto, by University of Toronto Press, 1982).
Bethurum, D. (ed.), *The Homilies of Wulfstan* (Oxford: Oxford University Press, 1957).
Bieler, L. and D.A. Binchy (eds), *The Irish Penitentials*, Scriptores Latini Hiberniae 5 (Dublin: Dublin Institute for Advanced Studies, 1963).
Blake, E.O. (ed.), *Liber Eliensis* (London: Royal Historical Society, 1962).
Böhringer, L. (ed.), *Hinkmar von Reims, De divortio Lotharii regis et Theutbergae reginae*, MGH, Concilia IV, Supplementum 1 (Hannover: Hahn, 1992).

Botte, B. (ed.), *Le canon de la messe romain. Édition critique*, Textes et études liturgiques 2 (Louvain: Abbaye du Mont Cesar, 1935).

Botte, B. and C. Mohrmann (eds), *L'Ordinaire de la messe. Texte critique, traduction et études*, *Études liturgiques* 2 (Paris: Editions de Cerf, 1953).

Boyer, B.B. and R. McKeon (eds), *Sic et Non: A Critical Edition* (Chicago: University of Chicago Press, 1977).

Brommer, P., R. Pokorny, M. Stratmann and W.-D. Runge (eds), *Capitula episcoporum*, MGH (3 vols, Hannover: Hahnsche Buchhandlung, 1984–1995).

Burnet, G., *An Exposition of the Thirty-Nine Articles of the Church of England* (Dublin: printed by Elizabeth Sadleir in School-House-Lane, near High-Street, 1721 [3rd ed., corr.]).

Campbell, A. (ed.), *The Chronicle of Æthelweard* (London: Nelson, 1962).

Campbell, A. (ed.), *Charters of Rochester*, Anglo-Saxon Charters 1 (Oxford: published for the British Academy by Oxford University Press, 1973).

*Catechism of the Catholic Church: Popular and Definitive Edition* (London: Continuum, 2000).

Chibnall, M. (ed.), *The Ecclesiastical History of Orderic Vitalis* (6 vols, Oxford: Clarendon Press, 1969–1980).

Clemoes, P. (ed.), *Ælfric's Catholic Homilies: The First Series*, EETS, SS 17 (Oxford: Oxford University Press for EETS, 1997).

Clercq, C. de (ed.), *Concilia Galliae, A.511 – A.695*, CCSL 148A (Turnhout: Brepols, 1963).

Cockayne, O. (ed.), *Leechdoms, wortcunning and starcraft of early England: Being a collection of documents, for the most part never before printed, illustrating the history of science in this country before the Norman Conquest* (3 vols, 1864).

Colgrave, B. (ed.), *The Life of Bishop Wilfrid by Eddius Stephanus* (Cambridge: Cambridge University Press, 1985 [orig. pub. 1927]).

Colgrave, B. (ed.), *Two Lives of Saint Cuthbert: A Life by an Anonymous Monk of Lindisfarne and Bede's Prose Life* (Cambridge: Cambridge University Press, 1985 [orig. pub. 1940]).

Colgrave, B. (ed.), *Felix's Life of Saint Guthlac: Introduction, Text, Translation and Notes* (Cambridge: Cambridge University Press, 1985 [orig. pub. 1956]).

Colgrave, B. (ed.), *The Earliest Life of Gregory the Great* (Cambridge: Cambridge University Press, 1985 [orig. pub. 1968]).

Corrêa, A. (ed.), *The Durham Collectar*, HBS 107 (London: Henry Bradshaw Society, 1992).

Crick, J. (ed.), *Charters of St Albans*, Anglo-Saxon Charters 12 (Oxford: Published for the British Academy by Oxford University Press, 2007).

Cross, J.E. and A. Hamer (eds), *Wulfstan's Canon Law Collection* (Cambridge: D.S. Brewer, 1999).

Cross, J.E. and J.M. Tunberg (eds), *The Copenhagen Wulfstan Collection: Copenhagen Kongelige Bibliotek Gl. Kgl. Sam.1595*, EEMF 25 (Copenhagen: Rosenkilde and Bagger, 1993).

Cubbin, G.P. (ed.), *The Anglo-Saxon Chronicle: A Collaborative Edition: Vol. 6, MS D: A Semi-Diplomatic Edition with Introduction and Indices* (Cambridge: D.S. Brewer, 1996).

Dalrymple, W., *From the Holy Mountain: A Journey in the Shadow of Byzantium* (London: Harper Collins, 1997).

Danforth, J.N., *Gleanings and Groupings from a Pastor's Portfolio* (New York: A.S. Barnes & Co., 1852).

Davril, A. (ed.), *The Winchcombe Sacramentary: Orléans, Bibliothèque municipale, 127 (105)*, HBS 105 (London: Boydell Press, 1995).

de Vogüé, A. and P. Antin (eds), *Dialogues de Grégoire le Grand: Livre IV, texte critique et notes*, Sources chrétiennes 265 (Paris: Cerf, 1980).

Dekkers, E. and I. Fraipont (eds), *Sancti Aurelii Augustini enarrationes in Psalmos*, CCSL 38–40 (3 vols, Turnhout: Brepols, 1956).

Demeulenaere, R. (ed.), 'Vincentius Lerinensis, Commonitorium', in R. Demeulenaere and J. Mulders (eds), *Foebadius, Victricius, Leporius, Vincentius Lerinensis, Evagrius, Ruricius: Liber contra Arrianos; De laude sanctorum; Libellus emendationis; Epistulae; Commonitorium. Excerpta ex operibus S. Augustini; Altercatio legis inter Simonem Iudaeum et Theophilum christianum*, CCSL 64 (Turnhout: Brepols, 1985), 127–95.

Deshusses, J., 'Les messes d'Alcuin', *Archiv für Liturgiewissenschaft* 14 (1972): 7–41.

diPaolo Healey, A. (ed.), *The Old English Vision of St. Paul*, Speculum Anniversary Monographs 2 (Cambridge, MA: Mediaeval Academy of America, 1978).

Doane, A.N. (ed.), *Genesis A: A New Edition* (Madison: University of Wisconsin Press, 1978).

Dobbie, E.V.K. (ed.), *The Anglo-Saxon Minor Poems*, Anglo-Saxon Poetic Records 6 (London: Routledge, 1942).

Doble, G.H. (ed.), *Pontificale lanaletense: (Bibliothèque de la Ville de Rouen A. 27. Cat. 368.) A Pontifical Formerly in Use at St. Germans, Cornwall*, HBS 74 (London: Henry Bradshaw Society, 1937).

Dodwell, C.R. and P. Clemoes (eds), *The Old English Illustrated Hexateuch: British Museum Cotton Claudius B. IV*, EEMF 18 (Copenhagen: Rosenkilde and Bagger, 1974).

Dombert, B. and A. Kalb (eds), *Sancti Aurelii Augustini. De civitate Dei*, CCSL 47–8 (2 vols, Turnhout: Brepols, 1955).

Dümmler, E.L. (ed.), *Epistolae Karolini aevi*, MGH, Epistolae Karolini aevi II (Berlin: Weidmann, 1895).

*Early Manuscripts at Oxford University*, http://image.ox.ac.uk, accessed November 2012.

Ehwald, R. (ed.), *Aldhelmi opera*, MGH, Scriptores, Auctores Antiquissimi 15 (Berlin: Weidmann, 1919).

Erskine, R.W.H. (ed.), *Great Domesday: a facsimile* (London: Alecto Historical Editions, 1986–1992).

Evans, E. (ed.), *Aurelii Augustini Opera Pars XIII, 2*, CCSL 46 (Turnhout: Brepols, 1969).

Fadda, A.M.L. (ed.), *Nuove omelie anglosassoni della rinascenza benedettina*, Filologia germanica, testi e studi 1 (Florence: F. Le Monnier, 1977).

Fearon, J. (ed.), *Thomas Aquinas, Summa theologiae* (London: Blackfriars, 1969).

Fehr, B. (ed.), 'Altenglische Ritualtexte für Krankenbesuch, heilige Ölung und Begräbnis', in H. Boehmer (ed.), *Texte und Forschungen zur englischen Kulturgeschichte: Festgabe für Felix Liebermann zum 20. Juli 1921* (Halle: M. Niemeyer, 1921), 20–67.

Fehr, B. (ed.), *Die Hirtenbriefe Ælfrics in altenglischer und lateinischer Fassung*, Bibliothek der angelsächsischen Prosa 9 (Darmstadt: Wissenschaftliche Buchgesellschaft, 1966, reprinted with supplementary introduction by P. Clemoes [orig. pub. 1914]).

Finsterwalder, P.W. (ed.), *Die Canones Theodori Cantuariensis und ihre Überlieferungsformen* (Weimar: H. Böhlaus, 1929).

Fowler, R. (ed.), *Wulfstan's 'Canons of Edgar'*, EETS, OS 266 (London: Oxford University Press for EETS, 1972).

Fraipont, J. and D. de Bruyne (eds), *Quaestionum in Heptateuchum, libri VII; Locutionum in Heptateuchum, libri VII; De octo quaestionibus ex Veteri Testamento*, CCSL 33 (Turnhout: Brepols, 1958).

Frantzen, A.J. (ed.), *The Anglo-Saxon Penitentials: A Cultural Database* (2008), http://www.anglo-saxon.net/penance, accessed November 2012.

Fulke, W., W. Allen and J. de Albin de Valsergues, *Tvvo treatises written against the papistes: The one being an answere of the Christian Protestant to the proud challenge of a popish Catholicke: The other a confutation of the popish churches doctrine touching purgatory & prayers for the dead: by William Fulke Doctor in diuinitie* (London: Thomas Vautrollier dwelling in the Blacke friers, 1577).

Fulk, R.D., R.E. Bjork, J.D. Niles and F. Klaeber (eds), *Klaeber's Beowulf and the Fight at Finnsburg*, Toronto Old English Series 21 (Toronto: University of Toronto Press, 2008).

Gerchow, J. (ed.), *Die Gedenküberlieferung der Angelsachsen: mit einem Katalog der libri vitae und Necrologien*, Arbeiten zur Frühmittelalterforschung 20 (Berlin: de Gruyter, 1988).

Glorie, F. (ed.), *Commentariorum in Hiezechielem libri XIV*, CCSL 75 (Turnhout: Brepols, 1964).

Godden, M. (ed.), *Ælfric's Catholic Homilies: The Second Series Text*, EETS, SS 5 (Oxford: Oxford University Press for EETS, 1979).

Godden, M. and S. Irvine (eds), *The Old English Boethius: An Edition of the Old English Versions of Boethius's 'De consolatione philosophiae'* (2 vols, Oxford: Oxford University Press, 2009).

Godman, P. (ed.), *Alcuin: The Bishops, Kings and Saints of York* (Oxford: Clarendon Press, 1982).

Goldbacher, A. (ed.), *S. Aureli Augustini Hipponiensis episcopi epistulae, pars III, ep. CXXIV–CLXXXIV A*, CSEL 44 (Vienna: F. Tempsky, 1894).

Günzel, B. (ed.), *Ælfwine's Prayerbook (London, British Library, Cotton Titus D.xxvi + xxvii)*, HBS 108 (London: Boydell Press for the Henry Bradshaw Society, 1993).

Haddan, A.W. and W. Stubbs (eds), *Councils and Ecclesiastical Documents Relating to Great Britain and Ireland* (3 vols, Oxford: Clarendon Press, 1869).

Hall, T.N., 'Wulfstan's Latin Sermons', in M. Townend (ed.), *Wulfstan, Archbishop of York: The Proceedings of the Second Alcuin Conference*, Studies in the Early Middle Ages 10 (Turnhout: Brepols, 2004), 93–139.

Hanssens, J.M. (ed.), *Amalarii episcopi opera liturgica omnia* (3 vols, Vatican City: Biblioteca Apostolica Vaticana, 1948).

Harmer, F.E. (ed.), *Anglo-Saxon Writs* (Stamford: Shaun Tyas, 1989).

Hearne, T. (ed.), *Hemingi chartularium ecclesiæ Wigorniensis* (Oxford: Sheldonian Theatre, 1723).

Hecht, H. (ed.), *Bischofs Waerferth von Worcester Übersetzung der Dialoge Gregors des Grossen über das Leben und die Wunderthaten italienischer Väter und über die Unsterblichkeit der Seelen*, Bibliothek der angelsächsischen Prosa 5 (Leipzig: G.H. Wigland, 1900).

Hillgarth, J.N. (ed.), *Sancti Iuliani sedis episcopis opera*, CCSL 115 (Turnhout: Brepols, 1976).

Holder-Egger, O. (ed.), 'Gesta Abbatum S. Bertini Sithiensium', *Supplementa tomorum I–XII, pars I*, MGH, Scriptores in Folio 13 (1881), 600–35.

Hughes, A. (ed.), *The Portiforium of St Wulstan: Corpus Christi College, Cambridge, MS. 391*, HBS 89–90 (2 vols, Leighton Buzzard: Henry Bradshaw Society, 1958–60).

Hurst, D. (ed.), *Bedae venerabilis opera, pars III: opera homiletica*, CCSL 112 (Turnhout: Brepols, 1955).

Irvine, S. (ed.), *The Anglo-Saxon Chronicle: A Collaborative Edition: Vol. 7, MS E: A Semi-Diplomatic Edition with Introduction and Indices* (Cambridge: D.S. Brewer, 2004).

Jones, C.W. (ed.), *The Saint Nicholas Liturgy and its Literary Relationships: Ninth to Twelfth Centuries by C.W. Jones; With an Essay on the Music by G. Reaney*, University of California Publications, English Studies 27 (Berkeley: University of California Press, 1963).

Jones, C.W. (ed.), *Bedae venerabilis opera, pars II: Opera exegetica, 1. Libri quattor in principium Genesis usque ad nativitatem Isaac et eiectionem Ismahelis adnotationum*, CCSL 118A (Turnhout: Brepols, 1967).

Jones, C.W. (ed.), *Opera didascalia, 2. de temporum ratione*, CCSL 123B (Turnhout: Brepols, 1977).

Jones, C.W. (ed.), C.B. Kendall, M.H. King and F. Lipp, *Opera didascalia, 1. De orthographia; De arte metrica et de schematibus et tropis; De natura rerum*, CCSL 123A (Turnhout: Brepols, 1975).

Jones, C.A., 'Two composite texts from Archbishop Wulfstan's "Commonplace Book": The *De ecclesiastica consuetudine* and the *Institutio beati Amalarii de ecclesiasticis officiis*', *Anglo-Saxon England* 27 (1998): 233–71.

Jones, C.A. (ed.), *Ælfric's Letter to the Monks of Eynsham*, Cambridge Studies in Anglo–Saxon England 24 (Cambridge: Cambridge University Press, 1998).

Jones, C.A. (ed.), *Old English Shorter Poems: Vol. 1, Religious and Didactic* (Cambridge, MA: Harvard University Press, 2012).

Jost, K. (ed.), *Die 'Institutes of Polity, Civil and Ecclesiastical'*, Schweizer anglistische Arbeiten 47 (1959).

Kelly, S.E. (ed.), *Charters of St Augustine's Abbey, Canterbury and Minster-in-Thanet*, Anglo-Saxon Charters 4 (Oxford: Published for the British Academy by Oxford University Press, 1995).

Kelly, S.E. (ed.), *Charters of Shaftesbury Abbey*, Anglo-Saxon Charters 5 (Oxford: Published for the British Academy by Oxford University Press, 1996).

Kelly, S.E., *Charters of Selsey Abbey*, Anglo-Saxon Charters 6 (Oxford: Published for the British Academy by Oxford University Press, 1998).

Kelly, S.E. (ed.), *Charters of Abingdon Abbey, Part 1*, Anglo-Saxon Charters 7 (Oxford: Published for the British Academy by Oxford University Press, 2000).

Kelly, S.E. (ed.), *Charters of Abingdon Abbey, Part 2*, Anglo-Saxon Charters 8 (Oxford: Published for the British Academy by Oxford University Press, 2001).

Kelly, S.E. (ed.), *Charters of Malmesbury Abbey*, Anglo-Saxon Charters 11 (Oxford: Published for the British Academy by Oxford University Press, 2006).

Kelly, S.E. (ed.), *Charters of Bath and Wells*, Anglo-Saxon Charters 13 (Oxford: Published for the British Academy by Oxford University Press, 2007).

Kelly, S.E. (ed.), *Charters of Peterborough Abbey*, Anglo-Saxon Charters 14 (Oxford: Published for the British Academy by Oxford University Press, 2009).

Kemble, J.M. (ed.), *Codex diplomaticus aevi Saxonici* (6 vols, London: Sumptibus Societatis, 1839–48).

Keynes, S. (ed.), *The Liber Vitae of the New Minster and Hyde Abbey, Winchester: British Library Stowe 944: Together with Leaves from British Library Cotton Vespasian A. VIII and British Library Cotton Titus D. XXVII*, EEMF 26 (Copenhagen: Rosenkilde and Bagger, 1996).

Knowles, D. and C.N.L. Brooke (eds), *The Monastic Constitutions of Lanfranc* (Oxford: Oxford University Press, 2002).

Krapp, G.P. (ed.), *The Vercelli Book*, Anglo-Saxon Poetic Records 2 (New York: Columbia University Press, 1932).

Lapidge, M. (ed.), *Anglo-Saxon Litanies of the Saints*, HBS 106 (Woodbridge: Published for the Henry Bradshaw Society by Boydell Press, 1991).

Lapidge, M. (ed.), *The Cult of St Swithun*, Winchester Studies 4.ii (Oxford: Clarendon Press, 2003).

Lapidge, M. (ed.), *The Lives of St Oswald and St Ecgwine* (Oxford: Clarendon Press, 2009).

Lapidge, M. and M. Winterbottom (eds), *Wulfstan of Winchester: The Life of St Æthelwold* (Oxford: Clarendon Press, 1991).

Lapidge, M., P. Monat and P. Robin (eds and trans.), *Histoire ecclésiastique du peuple anglais = Historia ecclesiastica gentis Anglorum*, Sources chrétiennes 489–91 (3 vols, Paris: Cerf, 2005).

Lawson, C.M. (ed.), *Sancti Isidori Episcopi Hispalensis: De ecclesiasticis officiis*, CCSL 113 (Turnhout: Brepols, 1989).

Le Blant, E.F. (ed.), *Inscriptions chrétiennes de la Gaule antérieures au VIIIe siècle* (2 vols, Paris: l'Imprimerie impériale, 1856).

Liebermann, F. (ed.), *Die Gesetze der Angelsachsen* (3 vols, Halle: Niemeyer, 1903–1916).

Lindelöf, U. (ed.), *Rituale ecclesiae Dunelmensis: The Durham collectar; A New and Revised Edition of the Latin Text with the Interlinear Anglo-Saxon Version*, Surtees Society Publications 140 (Durham: Andrews, for the Surtees Society, 1923).

Love, R.C. (ed.), *Three Eleventh-Century Anglo-Latin Saints' Lives: Vita S. Birini, Vita et Miracula S. Kenelmi, and Vita S. Rumwoldi* (Oxford: Oxford University Press, 1996).

Lowe, K.A., 'A new edition of the will of Wulfgyth', *Notes and Queries* 36, ns (1989): 295–8.

Loyn, H.R. (ed.), *A Wulfstan Manuscript Containing Institutes, Laws and Homilies: British Museum Cotton Nero A.i*, EEMF 27 (Copenhagen: Rosenkilde and Bagger, 1971).

Mac Lean, G.E., 'Ælfric's version of Alcuini Interrogationes Sigeuuulfi in Genesin', *Anglia* 7 (1884): 1–59.

Marsden, R. (ed.), *The Old English Heptateuch and Aelfric's Libellus de Veteri Testamento et Novo: Vol. 1, Introduction and Text*, EETS, OS 330 (Oxford: Oxford University Press for the EETS, 2008).

Miller, S. (ed.), *Charters of the New Minster, Winchester*, Anglo-Saxon Charters 9 (Oxford: Published for the British Academy by Oxford University Press, 2001).

Moffat, D. (ed.), *The Old English Soul and Body* (Woodbridge: Brewer, 1990).

Morgan, P. (ed.), *Domesday Book: 5, Berkshire* (Chichester: Phillimore, 1979).

Morin, G. (ed.), *Caesarius Arelatensis opera pars I, 2, Sermones*, CCSL 103–4 (2 vols, Turnhout: Brepols, 1953).

Morris, R. (ed.), *The Blickling Homilies of the 10th Century: From the Marquis of Lothian's Unique MS. A.D. 971*, EETS, OS 58 (London: Trübner for EETS, 1874).

Mountain, W.J. and F. Glorie (eds), *Sancti Aurelii Augustini de Trinitate libri XV*, CCSL 50–50A (2 vols, Turnhout: Brepols, 1968).

Muir, B.J. (ed.), *The Exeter Anthology of Old English Poetry: An Edition of Exeter, Dean and Chapter MS 3501*, Exeter Medieval English Texts and Studies (2 vols, Exeter: University of Exeter Press, 2000).

Munby, J. (ed.), *Domesday Book: 4, Hampshire* (Chichester: Phillimore, 1982).

Mynors, R.A.B., R.M. Thomson and M. Winterbottom (eds), *Gesta regum anglorum: The History of the English Kings* (Oxford: Clarendon Press, 1998).

Napier, A.S. (ed.), *Wulfstan: Sammlung der ihm zugeschriebenen homilien nebst Untersuchungen über ihre Echtheit*, Sammlung englischer Denkmäler in kritischen Ausgaben 4 (Berlin: Weidmann, 1883).

Neufville, J. and A. de Vogüé (eds), *La règle de Saint Benoît*, Sources chrétiennes 181–6 (6 vols, Paris: Editions du Cerf, 1971).

O'Brien O'Keeffe, K. (ed.), *The Anglo-Saxon Chronicle: A Collaborative Edition: Vol. 5, MS C: A Semi-Diplomatic Edition with Introduction and Indices* (Cambridge: D.S. Brewer, 2001).

O'Donovan, M.A. (ed.), *Charters of Sherborne*, Anglo-Saxon Charters 3 (Oxford: Published for the British Academy by Oxford University Press, 1988).

Ohlgren, T.H., *Anglo-Saxon Textual Illustration: Photographs of Sixteen Manuscripts with Descriptions and Index* (Kalamazoo, MI: Medieval Institute Publications Western Michigan University, 1992).

Oliver, L. (ed.), *The Beginnings of English Law* (Toronto: University of Toronto Press, 2002).

Orchard, N. (ed), *The Leofric Missal*, HBS 113–14 (2 vols, London: Henry Bradshaw Society, 2002).

*Parker Library on the web*, http://parkerweb.stanford.edu, accessed November 2012.

Pettit, E., *Anglo-Saxon Remedies, Charms, and Prayers from British Library Ms Harley 585: The Lacnunga, Mellen Critical Editions and Translations* 6a–b (2 vols, Lewiston, NY: Edwin Mellen Press, 2001).

Plummer, C. (ed.), *Venerabilis Baedae Historiam ecclesiasticam gentis Anglorum: Historiam abbatum, Epistolam ad Ecgberctum, una cum Historia abbatum auctore anonymo, ad fidem codicum manuscriptorum denuo recognovit, Epistola ad Ecgberctum* (2 vols, Oxford: Clarendon Press, 1896).

Pokorny, R. (ed.) *Capitula episcoporum*, MGH (4 vols, Hannover: Hahnsche Buchhandlung, 1995).

Pope, J.C. (ed.), *Homilies of Ælfric: A Supplementary Collection*, EETS, OS 259–60 (2 vols, London: Oxford University Press for EETS, 1967–8).

Pseudo-Alcuin, *De divinis officiis*, PL 101.1173–1286.

Rabin, A., 'Anglo-Saxon women before the law: A student edition of five Old English lawsuits', *Old English Newsletter* 41:3 (2008): 33–56.

Rau, R. (ed.), *Briefe des Bonifatius; Willibalds Leben des Bonifatius, nebst einigen zeitgenössischen Dokumenten* (Darmstadt: Wissenschaftliche Buchgesellschaft, 1968).

Reiter, S. (ed.), *S. Hieronymi presbyteri opera, pars I. Opera exegetica, 3: In Hieremiam libri VI*, CCSL 74 (Turnhout: Brepols, 1960).

Richter, M. and T.J. Brown (eds), *Canterbury Professions* (Torquay: Devonshire Press, 1973).

Robinson, J.A. (ed.), *Gilbert Crispin, Abbot of Westminster: A Study of the Abbey under Norman Rule*, Notes and documents relating to Westminster Abbey 3 (Cambridge: Cambridge University Press, 1911).

Rollason, D.W. (ed.), *The Mildrith Legend: A Study in Early Medieval Hagiography in England* (Leicester: Leicester University Press, 1982).

Rollason, D., 'Goscelin of Canterbury's account of the translation and miracles of St. Mildrith (BHL 5961/4): An edition with notes', *Mediaeval Studies* 48 (1986): 139–210.

Rollason, D.W., L. Rollason, E. Briggs and A.J. Piper (eds), *Durham Liber Vitae: London, British Library, MS Cotton Domitian A.VII: Edition and Digital Facsimile with Introduction, Codicological, Prosopographical and Linguistic Commentary, and Indexes* (London: British Library, 2007).

Sauer, H. (ed.), *Theodulfi Capitula in England: die altenglischen Übersetzungen, zusammen mit dem lateinischen Text*, Texte und Untersuchungen zur englischen Philologie 8 (Munich: Fink, 1978).

Sawyer, P.H. (ed.), *Charters of Burton Abbey*, Anglo-Saxon Charters 2 (Oxford: Published for the British Academy by Oxford University Press, 1979).

Schmidt, P.G. (ed.), *Otloh von St. Emmeram: Liber visionum*, MGH, Quellen zur Geistesgeschichte des Mittelalters 13 (Weimar: Hermann Böhlaus Nachfolger, 1989).

Schmitt, F.S. (ed.), *S. Anselmi Cantuariensis Archiepiscopi, opera omnia* (Edinburgh: Thomas Nelson, 1946–61).

Scholz, B.W., 'Eadmer's Life of Bregwine, Archbishop of Canterbury, 761–764', *Traditio* 22 (1966), 124–48

Scragg, D.G. (ed.), 'The Battle of Maldon', in D.G. Scragg (ed.), *The Battle of Maldon, AD 991* (Oxford: 1991), 1–36.

Scragg, D.G. (ed.), *The Vercelli Homilies and Related Texts*, EETS, OS 300 (London: Oxford University Press for EETS, 1992).

Searle, W.G. (ed.), *Ingulf and the Historia Croylandensis*, Cambridge Antiquarian Society Octavo Publications 27 (Cambridge: Cambridge Antiquarian Society, 1894).

Sisam, K., 'An Old English translation of a letter from Wynfrith to Eadburga (A.D. 716–17) in Cotton MS. Otho C.1', *Modern Language Review* 18 (1923): 253–72.

Skeat, W.W. (ed.), *Aelfric's Lives of Saints, Being a Set of Sermons on Saints' Days Formerly Observed by the English Church*, EETS 76, 82 (vol. 1), 94, 114 (vol. 2) (4 vols in 2, London: Kegan Paul, Trench, Trübner & Co. for EETS, 1881–1900).

Smith, J., *The Book of Mormon: An Account Written by the Hand of Mormon upon Plates Taken from the Plates of Nephi* (Liverpool: F.D. Richards, 1854).

Stevenson, W.H. (ed.), *Asser's Life of King Alfred together with the Annals of Saint Neots, Erroneously Ascribed to Asser* (Oxford: Clarendon Press, 1904).

Symons, T. (ed.), *Regularis Concordia: The Monastic Agreement of the Monks and Nuns of the English Nation* (London: Thomas Nelson and Sons Ltd, 1953).

Tangl, M. (ed.), *Die Briefe des Heiligen Bonifatius und Lullus*, MGH, Epistolae Selectae 1 (Berlin: Weidmannsche, 1916).

Tanner, N.P. (ed.), *Decrees of the Ecumenical Councils* (2 vols, London: Sheed & Ward, 1990).

Thiébaux, M. (ed.), *Dhuoda, Handbook for her Warrior Son: Liber Manualis*, Cambridge Medieval Classics 8 (Cambridge: Cambridge University Press, 1998).

Thorn, C. and Thorn. F. (eds), *Domesday Book: 8, Somerset* (Chichester, 1980).

Thorpe, B. (ed.), *Diplomatarium Anglicum aevi Saxonici. A Collection of English Charters from the Reign of King Aethelberht of Kent, A.D. 605 to that of William the Conqueror* (London: Macmillan, 1865).

Torkar, R. (ed.), *Eine altenglische Übersetzung von Alcuins 'De virtutibus et vitiis', Kap. 20 (Liebermanns Judex): Untersuchungen und Textausgabe*, Texte und Untersuchungen zur englischen Philologie 7 (Munich: Fink, 1981).

Treharne, E.M. (ed.), *The Old English Life of St Nicholas with the Old English Life of St Giles*, Leeds Texts and Monographs, n.s. 15 (Leeds: University of Leeds School of English, 1997).

Turner, C.H., 'The churches at Winchester in the early eleventh century', *Journal of Theological Studies* 17 (1916): 65–8.

Verheijen, L. (ed.), *Sancti Augustini confessionum Libri XIII*, CCSL 27 (Turnhout: Brepols, 1981).

Vives, J., T. Marín Martínez and G. Martínez Díez (eds), *Concilios visigóticos e hispano-romanos, España cristiana: Testo v 1* (Barcelona: Consejo Superior de Investigaciones Científicas, Instituto Enrique Flórez, 1963).

Waitz, G. (ed.), 'Vita Leobae abbatissae Biscofesheimensis auct. Rudolfo Fuldensi', *Supplementa tomorum I–XII, pars III*, MGH, Scriptores in Folio (Hannover: Impensis Bibliopolii Hahniani, 1887), 118–31.

Whitelock, D. (ed.), *Anglo-Saxon Wills*, Cambridge Studies in English Legal History (Cambridge: University Press, 1930).

Whitelock, D., *The Will of Æthelgifu: A Tenth Century Anglo-Saxon Manuscript* (Oxford: Oxford University Press for members of the Roxburghe Club, 1968).

Whitelock, D., M. Brett and C.N.L. Brooke (eds), *Councils and Synods with Other Documents Relating to the English Church. 1, pt. 1: A.D. 871–1066; 1, pt. 2: 1066–1204* (Oxford: Clarendon Press, 1981).

Wilcox, J. (ed.), *Aelfric's Prefaces*, Durham Medieval Texts 9 (Durham: Durham Medieval Texts, 1994).

Willard, R. (ed.), *The Blickling Homilies*, EEMF 10 (Copenhagen: Rosenkilde and Bagger, 1960).

Willems, R. (ed.), *Sancti Aurelii Augustini in Iohannis Euangelium tractatus CXXIV*, CCSL 36 (Turnhout: Brepols, 1954).

Wilmart, A., 'La légende de Ste Edithe en prose et vers par le moine Goscelin', *Analecta Bollandiana* 56 (1938): 5–101 and 265–307.

Wilson, H.A. (ed.), *The Missal of Robert of Jumièges*, HBS 11 (London: Henry Bradshaw Society, 1896).

Winterbottom, M. (ed.), *Three Lives of English Saints* (Toronto: Published for the Centre for Medieval Studies by the Pontifical Institute of Mediaeval Studies, 1972).

Winterbottom, M. and M. Lapidge (ed.), *The Early Lives of St Dunstan* (Oxford: Clarendon Press, 2012).

Winterbottom, M. and R.M. Thomson (eds), *William of Malmesbury: Saints' Lives. Lives of SS. Wulfstan, Dunstan, Patrick, Benignus and Indract* (Oxford: Oxford University Press, 2002).

Winterbottom, M. and R.M. Thomson (ed.), *William of Malmesbury: Gesta pontificum Anglorum* (2 vols, Oxford: Clarendon Press, 2007).

Woodman, D.A. (ed.), *Charters of Northern Houses*, Anglo-Saxon Charters 16 (Oxford: Oxford University Press for the British Academy, 2012).

Wright, C.E. (ed.), *Bald's Leechbook: British Museum Royal Manuscript 12 D.xvii*, EEMF 5 (Copenhagen: Rosenkilde and Bagger, 1955).

Zupitza, J. (ed.), *Grammatik und Glossar, 1. Abt., Text und Varianten*, Sammlung englischer Denkmäler in kritischen Ausgaben 1 (Berlin: Weidmann, 1880).

Zycha, J. (ed.), *Sancti Aureli Augustini de Genesi ad litteram libri duodecim eiusdem libri capitula; De Genesi ad litteram imperfectus liber; Locutionum in Heptateuchum libri septem*, CCSL 28 (Vienna: F. Tempsky, 1894).

Zycha, J., *Sancti Aureli Augustini, De fide et symbolo; De fide et operibus; De agone christiano; De continentia; De bono coniugali; De Sancta virginitate; De bono viduitatis; De adulterinis coniugiis lib. II; De mendacio; Contra mendacium; De opere monachorum; De divinatione daemonum; De cura pro mortuis gerenda; De patientia*, CSEL 41 (Vienna: F. Tempsky, 1900).

**Secondary Scholarship**

Abram, C., 'New light on the illumination of Grendel's mere', *Journal of English and Germanic Philology* 109:2 (2010): 198–216.

Adams, J.N. and M. Deegan, 'Bald's leechbook and the *Physica Plinii*', *Anglo-Saxon England* 21 (1992): 87–114.

Adams, M., 'Excavation of a pre-Conquest cemetery at Addingham, West Yorkshire', *Medieval Archaeology: Journal of the Society for Medieval Archaeology* 40 (1996): 151–91.

Ambrose, S., 'The *Collectio Canonum Hibernensis* and the literature of the Anglo-Saxon Benedictine reform', *Viator: Medieval and Renaissance Studies* 36 (2005): 107–18.

Ammon, M., 'Pledges and Agreements in Old English: A Semantic Field Study', PhD thesis, University of Cambridge, 2010.

Andrieu, M., 'L'Insertion du "Memento" des morts au canon romain de la messe', *Revue des sciences religieuses* 1 (1921): 151–4.

Angenendt, A., 'Missa specialis: Zugleich ein Beitrag zur Entstehung der Privatmessen', *Frühmittelalterliche Studien* 17 (1983): 153–221.

Angenendt, A., 'Buße und liturgisches Gedenken', in K. Schmid and J. Wollasch (eds), *Gedächtnis, das Gemeinschaft Stiftet* (Munich: Verlag Schnell & Steiner, 1985), 39–50.

Anlezark, D., 'The Fall of the Angels in Solomon and Saturn II', in K. Powell and D.G. Scragg (eds), *Apocryphal Texts and Traditions in Anglo-Saxon England* (Woodbridge: Boydell & Brewer, 2003), 121–33.

Argyriou, A., 'Angéologie et démonologie à Byzance: formulations théologiques et représentations populaires', *Cuadernos del CEMYR* 11 (2003): 157–84.

Arnold, J., *Belief and Unbelief in Medieval Europe* (London: Hodder Arnold, 2005).

Ashley, S., 'The Lay Intellectual in Anglo-Saxon England: Ealdorman Æthelweard and the Politics of History', in J.L. Nelson and P. Wormald (eds), *Lay Intellectuals in the Carolingian World* (Cambridge: Cambridge University Press, 2007), 218–45.

Astill, G.G., 'Overview: Trade, Exchange, and Urbanization', in S. Crawford, H. Hamerow and D.A. Hinton (eds), *The Oxford Handbook of Anglo-Saxon Archaeology* (Oxford: Oxford University Press, 2011), 503–14.

Atwell, R.R., 'From Augustine to Gregory the Great: An evaluation of the emergence of the doctrine of purgatory', *Journal of Ecclesiastical History* 38:2 (1987): 173–86.

Austin, G., *Shaping Church Law around the Year 1000: The Decretum of Burchard of Worms* (Farnham: Ashgate, 2009).

Bailey, R.N., 'The Winwick Cross and a Suspended Sentence', in A.J. Minnis and J. Roberts (eds), *Text, Image, Interpretation: Studies in Anglo-Saxon Literature and its Insular Context in Honour of Éamonn Ó Carragáin* (Turnhout: Brepols, 2007), 449–72.

Baldwin, J.W., 'The crisis of the ordeal: Literature, law, and religion around 1200', *Journal of Medieval and Renaissance Studies* 24:3 (1994): 327–53.

Baldwin, J.W., 'From the Ordeal to Confession: In Search of Lay Religion in Early Thirteenth-Century France', in P. Biller and A.J. Minnis (eds), *Handling Sin: Confession in the Middle Ages* (Woodbridge: York Medieval Press, 1998), 191–209.

Barlow, F., *The English Church 1000–1066: A History of the Later Anglo-Saxon Church* (London: Longman, 1978).

Barrow, J., 'The Community of Worcester, 961–c.1100', in N. Brooks and C. Cubitt (eds), *St Oswald of Worcester: Life and Influence* (London: Leicester University Press, 1996), 84–99.

Barrow, J., 'Churches, Education and Literacy in Towns 600–1300', in D.M. Palliser (ed.), *The Cambridge Urban History of Britain: Vol. 1, 600–1540* (Cambridge: Cambridge University Press, 2000), 127–52.

Barrow, J., 'The Clergy in English Dioceses c. 900–c. 1066', in F. Tinti (ed.), *Pastoral Care in Late Anglo-Saxon England*, Anglo-Saxon Studies 6 (Woodbridge: Boydell and Brewer, 2005), 17–26.

Barrow, J., 'What Happened to Ecclesiastical Charters in England 1066–c.1100?', in J. Barrow and A. Wareham (eds), *Myth, Rulership, Church and Charters: Essays in Honour of Nicholas Brooks* (Aldershot: Ashgate, 2008), 229–48.

Bartlett, R., *Trial by Fire and Water: The Medieval Judicial Ordeal* (Oxford: Clarendon Press, 1986).

Bartlett, R., *The Natural and the Supernatural in the Middle Ages: The Wiles Lectures given at the Queen's University of Belfast, 2006*, The Wiles Lectures (Cambridge: Cambridge University Press, 2008).

Bassett, S., 'Boundaries of Knowledge: Mapping the Land Units of Late Anglo-Saxon and Norman England', in W. Davies, G. Halsall and A.J. Reynolds (eds), *People and Space in the Middle Ages, 300–1300* (Turnhout: Brepols, 2006), 115–42.

Bateson, M., 'A Worcester Cathedral book of ecclesiastical collections, made c. 1000 AD', *English Historical Review* 10 (1895): 712–31.

Bayless, M., 'Humour and the Comic in Anglo-Saxon England', in M.H. Sandra and H. Paul (eds), *Medieval English Comedy* (Turnhout: Brepols, 2007), 13–30.

Bedingfield, M.B., *The Dramatic Liturgy of Anglo-Saxon England*, Anglo-Saxon Studies 1 (Woodbridge: Boydell Press, 2002).

Bernstein, A.E., 'La naissance du purgatoire', *Speculum: A Journal of Medieval Studies* 59:1 (1984): 179–83.

Bernstein, A.E., *The Formation of Hell: Death and Retribution in the Ancient and Early Christian Worlds* (Ithaca, NY: Cornell University Press, 1993).

Bernstein, D., 'The blinding of Harold and the meaning of the Bayeux Tapestry', *Anglo-Norman Studies* 5 (1982): 40–64.

Bethurum, D., 'Archbishop Wulfstan's Commonplace Book', *Publications of the Modern Languages Association* 57 (1942): 916–29.

Biddle, M., 'Excavations at Winchester 1968: Seventh Interim Report', *Antiquaries Journal* 49 (1969): 295–329.

Biddle, M. and D. Keene, 'Winchester in the Eleventh and Twelfth Centuries', in M. Biddle (ed.), *Winchester in the Early Middle Ages: An Edition and Discussion of the Winton Domesday* (Oxford: 1976), 241–448.

Billett, J.D., 'The Divine Office and the Secular Clergy in Later Anglo-Saxon England', in C. Leyser, D.W. Rollason and H. Williams (eds), *England and the Continent in the Tenth Century: Studies in Honour of Wilhelm Levison (1876–1947)* (Turnhout: Brepols, 2011), 429–71.

Binski, P., *Medieval Death: Ritual and Representation* (London: British Museum Press, 2001).

Bishop, T.A.M., 'Notes on Cambridge Manuscripts, Part VI', *Transactions of the Cambridge Bibliographical Society* 3 (1959–63): 412–23.

Black, J., 'The Divine Office and Private Devotion in the Latin West', in T.J. Heffernan and E.A. Matter (eds), *The Liturgy of the Medieval Church* (Kalamazoo, MI: Medieval Institute Publications, 2001), 45–71.

Blair, J., *Anglo-Saxon Oxfordshire* (Stroud: Sutton, 1994).

Blair, J., 'A Saint for Every Minster? Local Cults in Anglo-Saxon England', in A. Thacker and R. Sharpe (eds), *Local Saints and Local Churches in the Early Medieval West* (Oxford: Oxford University Press, 2002), 455–94.

Blair, J., *The Church in Anglo-Saxon Society* (Oxford: Oxford University Press, 2005).

Blair, J., 'The Dangerous Dead in Early Medieval England', in S.D. Baxter, C.E. Karkov, J.L. Nelson and D.A.E. Pelteret (eds), *Early Medieval Studies in Memory of Patrick Wormald* (Farnham, Surrey: Ashgate, 2009), 539–59.

Blair, J., 'The Prehistory of English Fonts', in M. Henig and N. Ramsay (eds), *Intersections: The Archaeology and History of Christianity in England, 400–1200: Papers in Honour of Martin Biddle and Birthe Kjølbye-Biddle* (Oxford: Archaeopress, 2010), 149–77.

Boddington, A., G. Cadman and J. Evans, *Raunds Furnells: The Anglo-Saxon Church and Churchyard* (London: English Heritage, 1996).

Bosworth, J. and T.N. Toller, *An Anglo-Saxon Dictionary, Based on the Manuscript Collections of the Late Joseph Bosworth* (Oxford: The Clarendon Press, 1898).

Bouchard, C.B., *Holy Entrepreneurs: Cistercians, Knights, and Economic Exchange in Twelfth-Century Burgundy* (Ithaca, NY: Cornell University Press, 1991).

Boyer, P., *The Naturalness of Religious Ideas: A Cognitive Theory of Religion* (Berkeley: University of California Press, 1994).

Brakke, D., *Demons and the Making of the Monk: Spiritual Combat in Early Christianity* (Cambridge, MA: Harvard University Press, 2006).

Bredehoft, T.A., 'Filling the margins of CCC 41: Textual space and a developing archive', *Review of English Studies* 57:232 (2006): 721–32.

Bredehoft, T.A., 'Old Saxon Influence on Old English Verse: Four New Cases', in H. Sauer, J. Story and G. Waxenberger (eds), *Anglo-Saxon England and the Continent* (Tempe, AZ: Arizona Center for Medieval and Renaissance Studies, 2011), 83–111.

Bredero, A.H., 'Le Moyen Age et le Purgatoire', *Revue d'histoire ecclésiastique* 78:2 (1983): 429–52.

Bremmer, R.H., 'The Final Countdown: Apocalyptic Expectations in Anglo-Saxon Charters', in G. Jaritz and G. Moreno-Riano (eds), *Time and Eternity: The Medieval Discourse* (Turnhout: Brepols, 2000), 501–14.

Brooks, N., *The Early History of the Church of Canterbury: Christ Church from 597 to 1066*, Studies in the early history of Britain (Leicester: Leicester University Press, 1984).

Brooks, N., 'Anglo-Saxon Charters: A Review of Work 1953–73, with a Postscript on the Period 1973–98', in N. Brooks (ed.), *Anglo-Saxon Myths: State and Church, 400–1066* (London: Hambledon, 2000), 181–215.

Brooks, N., 'The Fonthill Letter, Ealdorman Ordlaf and Anglo-Saxon Law in Practice', in S.D. Baxter, C.E. Karkov, J.L. Nelson and D.A.E. Pelteret (eds), *Early Medieval Studies in Memory of Patrick Wormald* (Farnham, Surrey: Ashgate, 2009), 301–17.

Brown, E.A.R., 'Death and the human body in the later Middle Ages: The legislation of Boniface VIII on the division of the corpse', *Viator: Medieval and Renaissance Studies* 12 (1981): 221–70.

Brown, G.H., *A Companion to Bede* (Woodbridge: Boydell & Brewer, 2009).

Brown, M.P., 'The Lichfield angel and the manuscript context: Lichfield as a centre of insular art', *Journal of the British Archaeological Association* 160 (2007): 8–19.

Brown, P., 'Society and the supernatural: A medieval change', *Daedalus* 104:2 (1975): 133–51.

Brown, P., *The Cult of the Saints: Its Rise and Function in Latin Christianity* (Chicago: University of Chicago Press, 1981).

Brown, P., 'Vers la naissance du purgatoire. Amnistie et pénitence dans le christianisme occidental de l'Antiquité tardive au Haut Moyen Age', *Annales Histoire, Sciences Sociales* 52:6 (1997): 1247–61.

Brown, P., *The Rise of Western Christendom: Triumph and Diversity, AD 200– 1000* (Oxford: Blackwell, 2003).

Buckberry, J., 'Cemetery Diversity in the Mid to Late Anglo-Saxon Period in Lincolnshire and Yorkshire', in J. Buckberry and A.K. Cherryson (eds), *Burial in Later Anglo-Saxon England, c.650–1100 AD* (Oxford: Oxbow Books, 2010), 1–25.

Buckberry, J.L. and D.M. Hadley, 'An Anglo-Saxon execution cemetery at Walkington Wold, Yorkshire', *Oxford Journal of Archaeology* 26:3 (2007): 309–29.

Budny, M., *Insular, Anglo-Saxon and Early Anglo-Norman Manuscript Art at Corpus Christi College, Cambridge: An Illustrated Catalogue* (2 vols, Kalamazoo, MI: Medieval Institute Publications, Western Michigan University in association with Research Group on Manuscript Evidence, the Parker Library, Corpus Christi College, Cambridge, 1997).

Bullough, D.A., 'Burial, Community and Belief in the Early Medieval West', in P. Wormald, D.A. Bullough, R. Collins and J.M. Wallace-Hadrill (eds), *Ideal and Reality in Frankish and Anglo-Saxon Society: Studies Presented to J.M. Wallace-Hadrill* (Oxford: Blackwell, 1983), 177–201.

Burgess, C., '"A fond thing vainly invented": An Essay on Purgatory and Pious Motive in Late Medieval England', in S.J. Wright (ed.), *Parish, Church and People: Local Studies in Lay Religion 1350–1750* (London: Hutchinson, 1988), 56–84.

Burke, P., 'History and folklore: A historiographical survey', *Folk-Lore* 115:2 (2004): 133–9.

Burton, J.E., 'Confraternities in the Durham *Liber Vitae*', in D.W. Rollason, L. Rollason, E. Briggs and A.J. Piper (eds), *Durham Liber Vitae: London, British Library, MS Cotton Domitian A.VII: Edition and Digital Facsimile with Introduction, Codicological, Prosopographical and Linguistic Commentary, and Indexes* (London: British Library, 2007), I.73–5.

Butts, R., 'The analogical mere: Landscape and terror in *Beowulf*', *English Studies* 68 (1987): 113–21.

Bynum, C.W., *The Resurrection of the Body in Western Christianity, 200–1336*, Lectures on the History of Religions (New York: Columbia University Press, 1995).

Cambridge, E., 'The early Church in County Durham: A reassessment', *Journal of the British Archaeological Association* 137 (1984): 65–85.

Cambridge, E. and D.W. Rollason, 'Debate: The pastoral organization of the Anglo-Saxon Church: A review of the "Minster hypothesis"', *Early Medieval Europe* 4 (1995): 87–104.

Cameron, A., A. Crandell Amos and A. diPaolo Healey, *Dictionary of Old English: A to G online* (2007), http://tapor.library.utoronto.ca/doe/index.html, accessed July 2012.

Cameron, M.L., 'Anglo-Saxon medicine and magic', *Anglo-Saxon England* 17 (1988): 191–215.

Cameron, M.L., 'Bald's leechbook and cultural interactions in Anglo-Saxon England', *Anglo-Saxon England* 19 (1990): 5–12.

Cameron, M.L., 'The Visions of Saints Anthony and Guthlac', in S. Campbell and D.N. Klausner (eds), *Health, Disease and Healing in Medieval Culture* (Basingstoke: Macmillan, 1992), 152–8.

Cameron, M.L., *Anglo-Saxon Medicine*, Cambridge Studies in Anglo-Saxon England 7 (Cambridge: Cambridge University Press, 1993).

Capelle, B., 'Valeurs spirituelles de la liturgie des défunts', *Questions liturgiques et paroissiales* 38 (1957): 191–6.

Carey, J., 'Varieties of Supernatural Contact in the Life of Adomnán', in J. Carey, M. Herbert and P. Ó Riain (eds), *Studies in Irish Hagiography: Saints and Scholars* (Dublin: Four Courts Press, 2001), 49–62.

Carozzi, C., *Eschatologie et au-delà: recherches sur l'Apocalypse de Paul* (Aix-en-Provence: Université de Provence, Service des publications, 1994).

Carozzi, C., *Le voyage de l'âme dans l'au-delà, d'après la littérature latine: Vᵉ–XIIIᵉ siècle*, Collection de l'École française de Rome, 189 (Roma: École française de Rome, 1994).

Carozzi, C., *Apocalypse et salut dans le christianisme ancien et médiéval*, Collection historique (Paris: Aubier, 1999).

Carver, M.O.H., *Sutton Hoo: A Seventh-Century Princely Burial Ground and its Context*, Reports of the Research Committee of the Society of Antiquaries of London 69 (London: British Museum Press, 2005).

Carver, M.O.H., *The Birth of a Borough: An Archaeological Study of Anglo-Saxon Stafford* (Woodbridge: Boydell, 2010).

Caseau, B., 'Crossing the Impenetrable Frontier between Earth and Heaven', in R.W. Mathisen and H. Sivan (eds), *Shifting Frontiers in Late Antiquity: Papers from the First Interdisciplinary Conferences on Late Antiquity, the University of Kansas, March, 1995* (Aldershot: Variorum, 1996), 333–43.

Chaplais, P., 'The origin and authenticity of the royal Anglo-Saxon diploma', *Journal of the Society of Archivists* 3:2 (1965): 48–61.

Chaplais, P., 'The Anglo-Saxon chancery: From the diploma to the writ', *Journal of the Society of Archivists* 3:4 (1966): 160–76.

Chaplais, P., 'Some early Anglo-Saxon diplomas on single sheets: Originals or copies?', *Journal of the Society of Archivists* 3:7 (1968): 315–36.

Chaplais, P., 'Who introduced charters into England? The case for Augustine', *Journal of the Society of Archivists* 3:10 (1969): 526–42.

Chaplais, P., 'The Royal Anglo-Saxon "Chancery" of the Tenth Century Revisited', in H. Mayr-Harting and R.I. Moore (eds), *Studies in Medieval History Presented to R.H.C. Davis* (London: Hambledon, 1985), 41–51.

Charles-Edwards, T.M., 'The Distinction between Land and Moveable Wealth in Anglo-Saxon England', in P.H. Sawyer (ed.), *English Medieval Settlement* (1979), 97–104.

Charles-Edwards, T.M., 'The Penitential of Theodore and the "Iudicia Theodori"', in M. Lapidge (ed.), *Archbishop Theodore: Commemorative Studies on his Life and Influence* (Cambridge: Cambridge University Press, 1995), 141–74.

Chazelle, C., 'Exegesis in the Ninth-Century Eucharist Controversy', in C. Chazelle and B.v.N. Edwards (eds), *The Study of the Bible in the Carolingian Era* (Turnhout: Brepols, 2003), 167–87.

Cherryson, A.K., '"Such a Resting-Place as is Necessary for Us in God's Sight and Fitting in the Eyes of the World": Saxon Southampton and the Development of Churchyard Burial', in J. Buckberry and A.K. Cherryson (eds), *Burial in Later Anglo-Saxon England, c.650–1100 AD* (Oxford: Oxbow Books, 2010), 54–72.

Ciccarese, M.P., 'Alle origini della letteratura delle Visioni: il contributo di Gregorio di Tours', *Studi storicoreligiosi* 5:2 (1981): 251–66.

Clanchy, M.T., *From Memory to Written Record: England 1066–1307* (Oxford: Basil Blackwell, 2013).

Clarke, B., 'An early Anglo-Saxon cross-roads burial from Broad Town, north Wiltshire', *Wiltshire Archaeological and Natural History Magazine* 97 (2004): 89–94.

Clay, J.-H., *In the Shadow of Death: Saint Boniface and the Conversion of Hessia, 721–54*, Cultural encounters in Late Antiquity and the Middle Ages 11 (Turnhout: Brepols, 2010).

Clayton, M., 'Homiliaries and preaching in Anglo-Saxon England', *Peritia* 4 (1985): 207–42.

Clayton, M., 'Delivering the damned: A motif in Old English homiletic prose', *Medium Ævum* 55 (1986): 92–102.

Clayton, M., *The Cult of the Virgin Mary in Anglo-Saxon England*, Cambridge Studies in Anglo-Saxon England 2 (Cambridge: Cambridge University Press, 1990).

Clayton, M., 'The Old English promissio regis', *Anglo-Saxon England* 37 (2008): 91–150.

Clayton, M., 'Suicide in the works of Ælfric', *Review of English Studies* n.s. 60:245 (2009): 339–70.

Clemoes, P., 'The Chronology of Ælfric's Works', in P. Clemoes (ed.), *The Anglo-Saxons: Studies in Some Aspects of their History and Culture Presented to Bruce Dickins* (London: Bowes & Bowes, 1959), 213–47.

Clemoes, P., 'The Old English Benedictine Office, Corpus Christi College, Cambridge MS 190, and the relations between Ælfric and Wulfstan: A reconsideration', *Anglia* 78 (1960): 265–83.

Clemoes, P., 'Supplementary Introduction', in B. Fehr (ed.), *Die Hirtenbriefe Ælfrics in altenglischer und lateinischer Fassung* (Darmstadt: Wissenschaftliche Buchgesellschaft, 1966 [orig. pub. Hamburg 1914]), cxxvii–cxlviii.

Coatsworth, E. and J. Higgitt, *Corpus of Anglo-Saxon Stone Sculpture: Vol. 8, Western Yorkshire* (Oxford: Published for the British Academy by Oxford University Press, 2008).Cole, A., 'The distribution and use of mere as a generic in place-names', *Journal of the English Place-Name Society* 25 (1992–3): 51–2.

Colish, M.L., 'Carolingian debates over nihil and tenebrae: A study in theological method', *Speculum: A Journal of Medieval Studies* 59:4 (1984): 757–95.

Colish, M.L., 'The Early Scholastics and the Reform of Doctrine and Practice', in M.B. Christopher and I.H. Louis (eds), *Reforming Church before Modernity* (Aldershot: Ashgate, 2005), 61–8.

Colman, R.V., 'Reason and unreason in early medieval law', *Journal of Interdisciplinary History* 4:4 (1974): 571–91.

Conner, P.W., *Anglo-Saxon Exeter: A Tenth-Century Cultural History* (Woodbridge: Boydell, 1993).

Corrêa, A., 'Daily Office Books: Collectars and Breviaries', in R.W. Pfaff (ed.), *The Liturgical Books of Anglo-Saxon England*, Old English Newsletter, Subsidia 23 (Kalamazoo, MI: The Medieval Institute Western Michigan University, 1995), 45–60.

Cowdrey, H.E.J., *Pope Gregory VII, 1073–1085* (Oxford: Clarendon Press, 1998).

Cownie, E., *Religious Patronage in Anglo-Norman England, 1066–1135* (Woodbridge: Boydell for the Royal Historical Society, 1998).

Craig-Atkins, E., 'Chest burial: A middle Anglo-Saxon funerary rite from northern England', *Oxford Journal of Archaeology* 31:3 (2012): 317–37.

Cramer, P., *Baptism and Change in the Early Middle Ages, c. 200 – c. 1150* (Cambridge: Cambridge University Press, 1993).

Cramp, R., *Corpus of Anglo-Saxon Stone Sculpture: Vol.1, County Durham and Northumberland* (Oxford: Oxford University Press for the British Academy, 1984).

Cramp, R., *Wearmouth and Jarrow Monastic Sites* (2 vols, Swindon: English Heritage, 2005).

Cramp, R. and C.R. Bristow, *Corpus of Anglo-Saxon Stone Sculpture: Vol. 7, South-West England* (Oxford: Oxford University Press, for the British Academy, 2006).

Crick, J.C., 'Church, land and local nobility in early ninth-century Kent: The case of Ealdorman Oswulf', *Historical Research* 61:146 (1988): 251–69.

Crick, J.C., 'Women, posthumous benefaction, and family strategy in pre-conquest England', *Journal of British Studies* 38 (1999): 399–422.

Crick, J.C., 'Posthumous Obligation and Family Identity', in W.O. Frazer and A. Tyrrell (eds), *Social Identity in Early Medieval Britain* (London: Leicester University Press, 2000), 193–208.

Crick, J.C., 'Women, Wills and Movable Wealth in Pre-Conquest England', in M. Donald and L. Hurcombe (eds), *Gender and Material Culture in Historical Perspective* (London: Macmillan, 2000), 17–37.

Cross, J.E., 'Oswald and Byrhtnoth: A Christian saint and a hero who is Christian', *English Studies* 46 (1965): 93–109.

Cross, J.E., '"Legimus in ecclesiasticis historiis": A sermon for All Saints and its use in Old English prose', *Traditio: Studies in Ancient and Medieval History, Thought, and Religion* 33 (1977): 101–35.

Cross, J.E., 'A newly-identified manuscript of Wulfstan's "Commonplace Book", Rouen, Bibliothèque Municipale, MS 1382 (U.109), fols 173r–198v', *Journal of Medieval Latin* 2 (1992): 63–83.

Cross, J.E. and A. Hamer, 'Ælfric's *Letters* and the *Excerptiones Ecgberhti*', in J.A. Roberts, J.L. Nelson, M. Godden and J. Bately (eds), *Alfred the Wise: Studies in Honour of Janet Bately on the Occasion of her Sixty-Fifth Birthday* (Cambridge: D.S. Brewer, 1997), 5–13.Cubitt, C., *Anglo-Saxon Church Councils, c.650–c.850,* Studies in the early history of Britain (London: Leicester University Press, 1995).

Cubitt, C., 'Monastic Memory and Identity in Early Anglo-Saxon England', in W.O. Frazer and A. Tyrrell (eds), *Social Identity in Early Medieval Britain* (London: Leicester University Press, 2000), 252–76.

Cubitt, C., 'Sites and sanctity: Revisiting the cult of murdered and martyred Anglo-Saxon royal saints', *Early Medieval Europe* 9 (2000): 53–83.

Cubitt, C., 'Memory and Narrative in the Cult of Early Anglo-Saxon Saints', in Y. Hen and M. Innes (eds), *The Uses of the Past in the Early Middle Ages* (Cambridge: Cambridge University Press, 2000), 29–66.

Cubitt, C., 'Images of St Peter: The Clergy and the Religious Life in Anglo-Saxon England', in P. Cavill (ed.), *The Christian Tradition in Anglo-Saxon England: Approaches to Current Scholarship and Teaching* (Woodbridge: Boydell and Brewer, 2004), 41–54.

Cubitt, C., 'The clergy in early Anglo-Saxon England', *Historical Research* 78:201 (2005): 273–87.

Cubitt, C., 'Bishops, priests and penance in late Saxon England', *Early Medieval Europe* 14:1 (2006): 41–63.

Cubitt, C., 'Folklore and Historiography: Oral Stories and the Writing of Anglo-Saxon History', in R. Balzaretti and E.M. Tyler (eds), *Narrative and History in the Early Medieval West* (Turnhout: Brepols, 2006), 189–223.

Cubitt, C., 'Bishops and Councils in Late Saxon England: The Intersection of Secular and Ecclesiastical Law', in A. Grabowsky and W. Hartmann (eds), *Recht und Gericht in Kirche und Welt um 900* (München: Oldenbourg, 2007), 151–68.

Cubitt, C., 'Pastoral Care and Religious Belief', in P. Stafford (ed.), *A Companion to the early Middle Ages: Britain and Ireland c.500–1100* (Oxford: Wiley-Blackwell, 2009), 395–413.

Cubitt, C., '"As the lawbook teaches": Reeves, lawbooks and urban life in the anonymous old English legend of the seven sleepers', *English Historical Review* 124:510 (2009): 1021–49.

Cubitt, C., 'Ælfric's Lay Patrons', in H. Magennis and M. Swan (eds), *A Companion to Ælfric* (Leiden: Brill, 2009), 165–92.

Cubitt, C., 'The Institutional Church', in P. Stafford (ed.), *A Companion to the Early Middle Ages: Britain and Ireland c.500–1100* (Oxford: Wiley-Blackwell, 2009), 376–94.

Cushing, K.G., *Reform and the Papacy in the Eleventh Century: Spirituality and Social Change*, Manchester Medieval Studies (Manchester: Manchester University Press, 2005).

Da Rold, O., 'Homilies and Lives of Saints: Cambridge, University Library, Ii.1.33', in O. Da Rold, T. Kato, M. Swan and E. Treharne (eds), *The Production and Use of English Manuscripts 1060 to 1220* (Leicester, 2010), available at http://www.le.ac.uk/english/em1060to1220/mss/EM.CUL.Ii.1.33. htm, accessed November 2012.

Dal Santo, M., 'Philosophy, Hagiology and the Early Byzantine Origins of Purgatory', in P.D. Clarke and T. Claydon (eds), *The Church, the Afterlife, and the Fate of the Soul* (Woodbridge: Boydell & Brewer for the Ecclesiastical History Society, 2009), 41–51.

Daley, B., *The Hope of the Early Church: A Handbook of Patristic Eschatology* (Cambridge: Cambridge University Press, 1991).Daniélou, J., *Les anges et leur mission: d'après les Pères de l'Eglise*, Collection Irenikon, n.s. 5 (Paris: Chevotogne, 1953).

D'Aronco, M.A., 'How 'English' is Anglo-Saxon Medicine? The Latin Sources for Anglo-Saxon Medical Texts', in C.S.F. Burnett and N. Mann (eds), *Britannia Latina: Latin in the Culture of Great Britain from the Middle Ages to the Twentieth Century* (London: Warburg Institute, 2005), 27–41.

Davies, W., 'When Gift is Sale: Reciprocities and Commodities in Tenth-Century Christian Iberia', in W. Davies and P. Fouracre (eds), *The Languages of Gift in the Early Middle Ages* (Cambridge: Cambridge University Press, 2010), 217–37.

Davies, W. and P. Fouracre, *The Languages of Gift in the Early Middle Ages* (Cambridge: Cambridge University Press, 2010).

de Jong, M., 'Growing up in a Carolingian monastery: Magister Hildemar and his oblates', *Journal of Medieval History* 9:2 (1983): 99–128.

de Letter, P., 'Revelations, Private', *New Catholic Encyclopedia* (Washington, DC: Gale in association with the Catholic University of America, 2003), 202.

DeGregorio, S. (ed.), *Innovation and Tradition in the Writings of the Venerable Bede* (Morgantown: West Virginia University Press, 2006).

DeGregorio, S. (ed.), *The Cambridge Companion to Bede* (Cambridge: Cambridge University Press, 2011).

Delumeau, J., *Le catholicisme entre Luther et Voltaire, Nouvelle Clio* (Paris: Presses universitaires de France, 1971).

Devlin, Z., *Remembering the Dead in Anglo-Saxon England: Memory Theory in Archaeology and History* (Oxford: Archaeopress, 2007).

Di Pilla, A., 'Cosmologia e uso delle fonti nel *De natura rerum* di Beda', *Romanobarbarica* 11 (1992): 129–47.

Diem, A., 'Encounters between Monks and Demons in Latin Texts of Late Antiquity and the Early Middle Ages', in K.E. Olsen, A. Harbus and T. Hofstra (eds), *Miracles and the Miraculous in Medieval Germanic and Latin Literature* (Leuven: Peeters, 2004), 51–67.

diPaolo Healey, A., J.P. Wilkin and X. Xiang, *Dictionary of Old English Corpus on the World Wide Web* (2009), http://www.doe.utoronto.ca/index.html, accessed June 2012.Duffy, E., 'Elite and popular religion: The Book of Hours and lay piety in the later Middle Ages', in K. Cooper and J. Gregory (eds), *Elite and Popular Religion: papers read at the 2004 Summer Meeting and the 2005 Winter Meeting of the Ecclesiastical History*, Studies in Church History 42 (Woodbridge: Published for the Ecclesiastical History Society by the Boydell Press, 2006), 140–61.

Dumville, D.N., 'On the dating of the early Breton lawcodes', *Etudes celtiques* 21:1–2 (1984): 207–21.

Dumville, D.N., 'English square minuscule script: The background and earliest phases', *Anglo-Saxon England* 16 (1987): 147–79.Dumville, D.N., 'English square minuscule script: The mid-century phases', *Anglo-Saxon England* 23 (1994): 133–64.

Dunn, M., 'Gregory the Great, the vision of Fursey, and the origins of purgatory', *Peritia* 14 (2000): 238–54.Eckenrode, T.R., 'Venerable Bede as a scientist', *American Benedictine Review* 22:4 (1971): 486–507.

Eckenrode, T.R., 'The growth of a scientific mind: Bede's early and late scientific writings', *Downside Review* 94:316 (1976): 197–212.

Eco, U., 'Waiting for the Millennium', in R. Landes, A. Gow and D.C. Van Meter (eds), *The Apocalyptic Year 1000: Religious Expectation and Social Change, 950–1050* (Oxford: Oxford University Press, 2003), 121–35.

Effros, B., *Caring for Body and Soul: Burial and the Afterlife in the Merovingian World* (University Park, PA: Pennsylvania State University Press, 2002).

Eisenhofer, L. and J. Lechner, *The liturgy of the Roman Rite* (Freiburg: Herder, 1961).

Ellard, G., 'An example of Alcuin's influence on the liturgy', *Manuscripta* 4:1 (1960): 23–8.

Elliot, M., 'Ghaerbald's first capitulary, the excerptiones pseudo-Ecgberhti, and the sources of Wulfstan's Canons of Edgar', *Notes and Queries* 57:2 (2010): 161–5.

Farmer, H., 'A monk's vision of purgatory', *Studia Monastica* 1 (1959): 393–7.

Fell, C.E., 'Some Implications of the Boniface Correspondence', in H. Damico and A.H. Olsen (eds), *New Readings on Women in Old English Literature* (Bloomington, IN: Indiana University Press, 1990), 29–43.

Fell, C.E., 'Paganism in Beowulf: A Semantic Fairy-Tale', in T. Hofstra, L.A.J.R. Houwen and A.A. MacDonald (eds), *Pagans and Christians: The Interplay between Christian Latin and Traditional Germanic Cultures in Early Medieval Europe. Proceedings of the Second Germania Latina Conference held at the University of Groningen, May 1992* (Groningen: Egbert Forsten, 1995), 9–34.

Flechner, R., 'The making of the Canons of Theodore', *Peritia* 17/18 (2004): 121–43.

Fleming, R., *Kings and Lords in Conquest England* (Cambridge: Cambridge University Press, 1991).

Fleming, R., 'Christchurch's Sisters and Brothers: An Edition and Discussion of Canterbury Obituary Lists', in M.A. Meyer (ed.), *The Culture of Christendom: Essays in Medieval History in Commemoration of Denis L.T. Bethell* (London: Hambledon, 1993), 115–53.

Fleming, R., 'History and liturgy at pre-Conquest Christ Church', *Haskins Society Journal: Studies in Medieval History* 6 (1995): 67–83.

Fleming, R., 'Christ Church Canterbury's Anglo-Norman Cartulary', in C. Warren Hollister (ed.), *Anglo-Norman Political Culture and the Twelfth-Century Renaissance: Proceedings of the Borchard Conference on Anglo-Norman History, 1995* (Woodbridge: Boydell, 1997), 83–55.

Fleming, R., *Domesday Book and the Law: Society and Legal Custom in Early Medieval England* (Cambridge: Cambridge University Press, 1998).

Fleming, R., 'The new wealth, the new rich and the new political style in late Anglo-Saxon England', *Anglo-Norman Studies* 23 (2001): 1–22.

Flint, V.I.J., *The Rise of Magic in Early Medieval Europe* (Oxford: Clarendon Press, 1991).

Flint, V.I.J., 'The Saint and the Operation of the Law: Reflections upon the Miracles of St Thomas Cantilupe', in R. Gameson and H. Leyser (eds), *Belief and Culture in the Middle Ages: Studies Presented to Henry Mayr-Harting* (Oxford: Oxford University Press, 2001), 342–57.

Fontes Anglo-Saxonici Project, *Fontes Anglo-Saxonici: World Wide Web Register*, http://fontes.english.ox.ac.uk, accessed November 2012.

Foot, S., 'Parochial ministry in early Anglo-Saxon England: The role of monastic communities', in W.J. Sheils and D. Wood (eds), *The Ministry: Clerical and Lay: papers read at the 1988 Summer Meeting and the 1989 Winter Meeting of the Ecclesiastical History Society*, Studies in Church History 26 (Oxford: Published for the Ecclesiastical History Society by Basil Blackwell, 1989), 43–54.

Foot, S., '"By Water in the Spirit": The Administration of Baptism in Early Anglo-Saxon England', in J. Blair and R. Sharpe (eds), *Pastoral Care before the Parish* (Leicester: Leicester University Press, 1992), 171–92.

Foot, S., *Veiled Women: 1, The Disappearance of Nuns from Anglo-Saxon England; 2, Female Religious Communities in England, 871–1066* (Aldershot: Ashgate, 2000).

Foot, S., 'Reading Anglo-Saxon Charters: Memory, Record, or Story?', in E.M. Tyler and R. Balzaretti (eds), *Narrative and History in the Early Medieval West* (Turnhout: Brepols, 2006), 39–65.

Foot, S., *Monastic Life in Anglo-Saxon England, c. 600–900* (Cambridge: Cambridge University Press, 2006).

Foot, S., 'Anglo-Saxon "Purgatory"', in P.D. Clarke and T. Claydon (eds), *The Church, the Afterlife and the Fate of the Soul: Papers Read at the 2007 Summer Meeting and the 2008 Winter Meeting of the Ecclesiastical History Society*, Studies in Church History 45 (Woodbridge: Boydell & Brewer, 2009), 87–96.

Foot, S., *Æthelstan: The First King of England* (Yale: Yale University Press, 2011).

Forbes, H.A., *Meaning and Identity in a Greek Landscape: An Archaeological Ethnography* (New York: Cambridge University Press, 2007).

Fouracre, P., 'The Origins of the Carolingian Attempt to Regulate the Cult of Saints', in J. Howard-Johnston and P.A. Hayward (eds), *The Cult of Saints in Late Antiquity and the Middle Ages: Essays on the Contribution of Peter Brown* (Oxford: Oxford University Press, 1999), 143–65.

Fowler, R., 'A late Old English handbook for the use of a confessor', *Anglia* 83 (1965): 1–34.

Fox, M., 'Ælfric on the creation and fall of the angels', *Anglo-Saxon England* 31 (2002): 175–200.

Foxhall, L., 'Monumental Ambitions: The Significance of Posterity in Ancient Greece', in N. Spencer (ed.), *Time, Tradition, and Society in Greek Archaeology: Bridging the 'Great Divide'* (London: Routledge, 1995), 132–49.

Foxhall Forbes, H., 'The Development of the Notions of Penance, Purgatory and the Afterlife in Anglo-Saxon England', PhD thesis, University of Cambridge, 2009.

Foxhall Forbes, H., '"Diuiduntur in quattuor": The interim and judgement in Anglo-Saxon England', *Journal of Theological Studies* 61:2 (2010): 659–84.

Foxhall Forbes, H., 'Squabbling siblings: Gender and monastic life in late Anglo-Saxon Winchester', *Gender & History* 23:3 (2011): 653–84.

Foxhall Forbes, H., 'Making Books for Pastoral Care in Late Eleventh-Century Worcester: Oxford, Bodleian Library, Junius 121 and Hatton 113+114', in P.D. Clarke and S. James (eds), *Pastoral Care in the Middle Ages* (Farnham: Ashgate, forthcoming).

Foxhall Forbes, H., 'O domine libera anima mea! Visualizing Purgatory in Anglo-Saxon England', in J.D. Niles, S.S. Klein and J. Wilcox (eds), *Anglo-Saxon England and the Visual Imagination* (Tempe, AZ: Arizona Center for Medieval and Renaissance Studies, forthcoming).

Fraher, R.M., 'IV Lateran's Revolution in Criminal Procedure: The Birth of Inquisitio, the End of Ordeals, and Innocent III's Vision of Ecclesiastical Politics', in R.J. Castillo Lara (ed.), *Studia in honorem eminentissimi Cardinalis Alphonsi M. Stickler* (Rome: Libreria Ateneo Salesiano, 1992), 97–110.

Franklin, M.J., 'The Cathedral as Parish Church: The Case of Southern England', in D. Abulafia, M.J. Franklin and M. Rubin (eds), *Church and City, 1000–1500: Essays in Honour of Christopher Brooke* (Cambridge: Cambrige University Press, 1992), 173–98.

Frantzen, A.J., 'The significance of the Frankish penitentials', *Journal of Ecclesiastical History* 30 (1979): 409–21.

Frantzen, A.J., 'The body in *Soul and Body I*', *Chaucer Review: A Journal of Medieval Studies and Literary Criticism* 17 (1982–3): 76–88.

Frantzen, A.J., 'The tradition of penitentials in Anglo-Saxon England', *Anglo-Saxon England* 11 (1983): 23–56.

Frantzen, A.J., *The Literature of Penance in Anglo-Saxon England* (New Brunswick, NJ: Rutgers University Press, 1983).

Fredriksen, P., 'Apocalypse and redemption in early Christianity: From John of Patmos to Augustine of Hippo', *Vigiliae Christianae* 45 (1991): 151–83.

Freeman, C., *The Closing of the Western Mind: The Rise of Faith and the Fall of Reason* (New York: A.A. Knopf, 2003).

Galtier, P., *Aux origines du sacrement de pénitence* (Rome: Apud aedes Universitatis Gregorianae, 1951).

Gameson, R. (ed.), *St Augustine and the Conversion of England* (Stroud: Sutton, 1999).

Gatch, M.M., 'Eschatology in the anonymous old English homilies', *Traditio: Studies in Ancient and Medieval History, Thought, and Religion* 21 (1965): 117–65.

Gatch, M.M., *Death: Meaning and Mortality in Christian Thought and Contemporary Culture* (New York: Seabury Press, 1969).

Gatch, M.M., *Preaching and Theology in Anglo-Saxon England: Aelfric and Wulfstan* (Toronto: University of Toronto Press, 1977).

Gatch, M.M., 'The Achievement of Aelfric and his Colleagues in European perspective', in P.E. Szarmach and B.F. Huppe (eds), *Old English Homily and its Backgrounds* (Albany: State University of New York Press, 1978), 43–73.

Gatch, M.M., 'The harrowing of Hell: A liberation motif in medieval theology and devotional literature', *Union Seminary Quarterly Review* 36 Suppl. (1981): 75–88.

Gatch, M.M., 'The Office in Late Anglo-Saxon Monasticism', in M. Lapidge and H. Gneuss (eds), *Learning and Literature in Anglo Saxon England* (Cambridge: Cambridge University Press, 1985), 341–62.

Gatch, M.M., 'The unknowable audience of the Blickling Homilies', *Anglo-Saxon England* 18 (1989): 99–115.

Geake, H., 'Invisible kingdoms: The use of grave-goods in seventh-century England', *Anglo-Saxon Studies in Archaeology and History* 10 (1999): 203–15.

Geake, H., 'The Control of Burial Practice in Anglo-Saxon England', in M. Carver (ed.), *The Cross Goes North* (Woodbridge: York Medieval Press, 2003), 259–69.

Geary, P.J., *Furta sacra: Thefts of Relics in the Central Middle Ages* (Princeton, NJ: Princeton University Press, 1990).

Geary, P.J., *Living with the Dead in the Middle Ages* (Ithaca, NY: Cornell University Press, 1994).

Geary, P.J., 'Land, language and memory in Europe 700–1100', *Transactions of the Royal Historical Society*, 6th series, 9 (1999): 169–84.

Gelling, M., *Place-Names in the Landscape* (London: Dent, 1984).

Gelling, M., 'The landscape of *Beowulf*', *Anglo-Saxon England* 31 (2002): 7–11.

Gelling, M. and A. Cole, *The Landscape of Place-Names* (Stamford: Shaun Tyas, 2000).

Gilchrist, R., 'Magic for the dead? The archaeology of magic in later medieval burials', *Medieval Archaeology: Journal of the Society for Medieval Archaeology* 52 (2008): 119–59.

Gittos, H., 'Creating the Sacred: Anglo-Saxon Rites for Consecrating Cemeteries', in S. Lucy and A.J. Reynolds (eds), *Burial in Early Medieval England and Wales* (London: Society for Medieval Archaeology, 2002), 195–208.

Gittos, H., 'Introduction', in H. Gittos and M.B. Bedingfield (eds), *The Liturgy of the Late Anglo-Saxon Church* (London: The Boydell Press, 2005), 1–11.

Gittos, H., 'Is there any Evidence for the Liturgy of Parish Churches in Late Anglo-Saxon England? The Red Book of Darley and the Status of Old English', in F. Tinti (ed.), *Pastoral Care in Late Anglo-Saxon England*, Anglo-Saxon Studies 6 (Woodbridge: Boydell and Brewer, 2005), 63–82.

Gnanaratnam, T., 'An urban medieval population from St Peter's, Leicester', *The Archaeologist* 60 (2006): 26–7.

Gnanaratnam, T., 'Revealing a lost community', *British Archaeology* 91 (2006): 20–1.

Gneuss, H., 'Liturgical Books in Anglo-Saxon England and their Old English Terminology', in M. Lapidge and H. Gneuss (eds), *Learning and Literature in Anglo-Saxon England. Studies Presented to Peter Clemoes on the Occasion of his Sixty-Fifth Birthday* (Cambridge: Cambridge University Press, 1985), 91–141.

Gneuss, H., *Handlist of Anglo-Saxon Manuscripts: A List of Manuscripts and Manuscript Fragments Written or Owned in England up to 1100* (Tempe, AZ: Arizona Center for Medieval and Renaissance Studies, 2001).

Gneuss, H., 'Addenda and corrigenda to the handlist of Anglo-Saxon manuscripts', *Anglo-Saxon England* 32 (2003): 293–305.

Godden, M., 'Anglo-Saxons on the Mind', in M. Lapidge and H. Gneuss (eds), *Learning and Literature in Anglo-Saxon England: Studies Presented to Peter Clemoes on the Occasion of his Sixty-Fifth Birthday* (Cambridge: Cambridge University Press, 1985), 271–98.

Godden, M., 'Wærferth and King Alfred: The Fate of the Old English *Dialogues*', in J.A. Roberts, J.L. Nelson, M. Godden and J. Bately (eds), *Alfred the Wise: Studies in Honour of Janet Bately on the Occasion of her Sixty-Fifth Birthday* (Cambridge: D.S. Brewer, 1997), 35–51.

Godden, M., *Ælfric's Catholic Homilies: Introduction, Commentary and Glossary*, EETS, SS 18 (Oxford: Published for the EETS by the Oxford University Press, 2000).

Godden, M., 'The Millennium, Time, and History for the Anglo-Saxons', in R. Landes, A. Gow and D.C. Van Meter (eds), *The Apocalyptic Year 1000: Religious Expectation and Social Change, 950–1050* (Oxford: Oxford University Press, 2003), 155–80.

Godden, M., 'The Relations of Wulfstan and Ælfric', in M. Townend (ed.), *Wulfstan, Archbishop of York: The Proceedings of the Second Alcuin Conference* (Turnhout: Brepols, 2004), 353–74.

Goody, J., *The Development of the Family and Marriage in Europe* (Cambridge: Cambridge University Press, 1983).

Gordon, B. (ed.), *Protestant History and Identity in Sixteenth-Century Europe: Vol. 1, The Medieval Inheritance* (Aldershot: Scolar, 1996).

Grabka, G., 'Christian viaticum: A study of its cultural background', *Traditio: Studies in Ancient and Medieval History, Thought, and Religion* 9 (1953): 1–43.

Graham, T., 'The Old English liturgical directions in Corpus Christi College, Cambridge, MS 422', *Anglia* 111 (1993): 439–46.

Gransden, A., 'The composition and authorship of the *De miraculis Sancti Eadmundi* attributed to "Hermann the Archdeacon"', *Journal of Medieval Latin* 5 (1995): 1–52.

Grant, E., *God and Reason in the Middle Ages* (Cambridge: Cambridge University Press, 2001).

Green, W. and E. Treharne, 'Homilies: Cambridge, Corpus Christi College, 421', in O. Da Rold, T. Kato, M. Swan and E. Treharne (eds), *The Production and Use of English Manuscripts 1060 to 1220* (Leicester, 2010), available at http://www.le.ac.uk/english/em1060to1220/mss/EM.CCCC.421.htm, accessed October 2012.

Grundy, L., *Books and Grace: Ælfric's Theology*, King's College London Medieval Studies 6 (London: King's College London Centre for Late Antique and Medieval Studies, 1991).Gurevich, A., 'Popular and scholarly medieval cultural traditions: Notes in the margins of Jacques Le Goff's book', *Journal of Medieval History* 9:2 (1983): 71–90.Hadley, D.M., 'Burying the Socially and Physically Distinctive in Later Anglo-Saxon England', in J. Buckberry and A.K. Cherryson (eds), *Burial in Later Anglo-Saxon England, c.650–1100 AD* (Oxford: Oxbow Books, 2010), 103–15.

Hadley, D.M., 'Late Saxon Burial Practice', in S. Crawford, H. Hamerow and D.A. Hinton (eds), *The Oxford Handbook of Anglo-Saxon Archaeology* (Oxford: Oxford University Press, 2011), 288–314.

Hadley, D.M. and J. Buckberry, 'Caring for the Dead in Late Anglo-Saxon England', in F. Tinti (ed.), *Pastoral Care in Late Anglo-Saxon England*, Anglo-Saxon Studies 6 (Woodbridge: Boydell and Brewer, 2005), 121–47.

Hadley, D.M. and J.D. Richards, *Cultures in Contact: Scandinavian Settlement in England in the Ninth and Tenth Centuries*, Studies in the Early Middle Ages 2 (Turnhout: Brepols, 2000).

Hall, A., *Elves in Anglo-Saxon England: Matters of Belief, Health, Gender and Identity*, Anglo-Saxon Studies 8 (Woodbridge: Boydell Press, 2007).

Hall, R.A., 'Burhs and Boroughs: Defended Places, Trade, and Towns. Plans, Defences, Civic Features', in S. Crawford, H. Hamerow and D.A. Hinton (eds), *The Oxford Handbook of Anglo-Saxon Archaeology* (Oxford: Oxford University Press, 2011), 600–24.

Hall, R.A. and M. Whyman, 'Settlement and monasticism at Ripon, North Yorkshire, from the 7th to 11th centuries A.D', *Medieval Archaeology: Journal of the Society for Medieval Archaeology* 40 (1996): 62–150.

Halpin, P., 'Women religious in late Anglo-Saxon England', *Haskins Society Journal: Studies in Medieval History* 6 (1994): 97–110.

Hamerow, H., 'Settlement mobility and the middle Saxon shift: Rural settlements and patterns in Anglo-Saxon England', *Anglo-Saxon England* 20 (1991): 1–17.

Hamerow, H., 'The development of Anglo-Saxon settlement structure', *Landscape History* 31:1 (2010), 5–22.

Hamerow, H., 'Overview: Rural Settlement', in S. Crawford, H. Hamerow and D.A. Hinton (eds), *The Oxford Handbook of Anglo-Saxon Archaeology* (Oxford: Oxford University Press, 2011), 119–27.

Hamilton, S., *The Practice of Penance, 900–1050* (Woodbridge: Boydell & Brewer Ltd, 2001).

Hamilton, S., 'Remedies for "Great Transgressions": Penance and Excommunication in Late Anglo-Saxon England', in F. Tinti (ed.), *Pastoral Care in Late Anglo-Saxon England*, Anglo-Saxon Studies 6 (Woodbridge: Boydell and Brewer, 2005), 83–105.

Hamilton, S., 'Rites for Public Penance in Late Anglo-Saxon England', in H. Gittos and M.B. Bedingfield (eds), *The Liturgy of the Late Anglo-Saxon Church* (Woodbridge: Boydell Press, 2005), 65–103.

Hamilton, S., 'The Early Pontificals: The Anglo-Saxon Evidence Reconsidered from a Continental Perspective', in C. Leyser, D.W. Rollason and H. Williams (eds), *England and the Continent in the Tenth Century: Studies in Honour of Wilhelm Levison (1876–1947)* (Turnhout: Brepols, 2011), 411–28.

Hannah, D.D., *Michael and Christ: Michael Traditions and Angel Christology in Early Christianity*, Wissenschaftliche Untersuchungen zum Neuen Testament 2 (Tübingen: Mohr Siebeck, 1999).

Hardy, G., *Understanding the Book of Mormon: A Reader's Guide* (Oxford: Oxford University Press, 2010).Harris, S.J. and B.L. Grigsby, *Misconceptions about the Middle Ages* (London: Routledge, 2008).

Harrison, K., 'The beginning of the year in England, c.500–900', *Anglo-Saxon England* 2 (1973): 51–70.

Häußling, A.A., *Mönchskonvent und Eucharistiefeier: einer Studie über die Messe in der abendländischen Klosterliturgie des frühen Mittelalters und zur Geschichte der Messhäufigkeit*, Liturgiewissenschaftliche Quellen und Forschungen 58 (Münster, Westfalen: Aschendorff, 1973).

Hawkes, J., 'Gregory the Great and Angelic Mediation: The Anglo-Saxon Crosses of the Derbyshire Peaks', in A.J. Minnis and J. Roberts (eds), *Text, Image, Interpretation: Studies in Anglo-Saxon Literature and its Insular Context in Honour of Éamonn Ó Carragáin* (Turnhout: Brepols, 2007), 431–48.

Hayward, P.A., 'Translation-narratives in post-conquest hagiography and English resistance to the Norman Conqest', *Anglo-Norman Studies* 21 (1998): 67–93.

Heal, F., 'Appropriating History: Catholic and Protestant polemics and the national past', *Huntington Library Quarterly* 68:1/2 (2005): 109–32.

Heal, F., 'What can King Lucius do for you? The Reformation and the early British Church', *English Historical Review* 120:487 (2005): 593–614.

Heinz, A., 'Saint Michel dans le "monde germanique". Histoire – Culte – Liturgie', in P. Bouet, G. Otranto and A. Vauchez (eds), *Culto e santuari di san Michele nell'Europa medievale = Culte et sanctuaires de saint Michel dans l'Europe médiévale: atti del Congresso internazionale di studi, Bari, Monte Sant'Angelo, 5–8 aprile 2006* (Bari: 2007), 39–55.

Henderson, G., 'The Programme of Illustrations in Bodleian MS Junius XI', in G. Robertson and G. Henderson (eds), *Studies in Memory of David Talbot Rice* (Edinburgh: Edinburgh University Press, 1975), 113–45.

Henig, M., 'The Fate of Late Roman Towns', in S. Crawford, H. Hamerow and D.A. Hinton (eds), *The Oxford Handbook of Anglo-Saxon Archaeology* (Oxford: Oxford University Press, 2011), 515–33.

Higham, N.J., 'Harold Godwinesson: The Construction of Kingship', in G.R. Owen-Crocker (ed.), *King Harold II and the Bayeux Tapestry* (Woodbridge: Boydell Press, 2005), 19–34.

Highley, C., *Catholics Writing the Nation in Early Modern Britain and Ireland* (Oxford: Oxford University Press, 2008).

Hill, D., 'Athelstan's urban reforms', *Anglo-Saxon Studies in Archaeology & History* 11 (2000): 173–86.

Hill, D. and R. Cowie (eds), *Wics: The Early Medieval Trading Centres of Northern Europe* (Sheffield: Sheffield Academic Press, 2001).

Hill, J., 'Monastic Reform and the Secular Church: Ælfric's Pastoral Letters in Context', in C. Hicks (ed.), *England in the Eleventh Century: Proceedings of the 1990 Harlaxton Symposium*, Harlaxton Medieval Studies 2 (Stamford: Paul Watkins, 1992), 103–17.

Hill, J., 'Ælfric, Authorial Identity and the Changing Text', in D.G. Scragg and P.E. Szarmach (eds), *The Editing of Old English* (Cambridge: Brewer, 1994).

Hill, J., 'Archbishop Wulfstan: Reformer?', in M. Townend (ed.), *Wulfstan, Archbishop of York: The Proceedings of the Second Alcuin Conference*, Studies in the Early Middle Ages 10 (Turnhout: Brepols, 2004), 309–24.

Hill, J., 'Authorial Adaptation: Ælfric, Wulfstan and the Pastoral Letters', in O. Akio, F. Jacek and J. Scahill (eds), *Text and Language in Medieval English Prose* (Frankfurt am Main: Peter Lang, 2005), 63–75.

Hill, J., 'Ælfric: His Life and Works', in H. Magennis and M. Swan (eds), *A Companion to Ælfric* (Leiden: Brill, 2009), 35–66.

Hill, N.G., 'Excavations on Stockbridge Down, 1935–36', *Proceedings of the Hampshire Field Club & Archaeological Society* 13 (1937): 247–59.

Hill, T.D., 'The Fall of Angels and Man in the Old English Genesis B', in L.E. Nicholson and D.W. Frese (eds), *Anglo-Saxon Poetry: Essays in Appreciation for John C. McGalliard* (London: University of Notre Dame Press, 1975), 279–90.

Hill, T.D., 'When God blew Satan out of Heaven: The motif of exsufflation in Vercelli Homily XIX and later English literature', *Leeds Studies in English* n.s. 16 (1985): 132–41.

Hill, T.D., 'Imago Dei: genre, symbolism and Anglo-Saxon hagiography', in P.E. Szarmach (ed.), *Holy Men and Holy Women: Old English Prose Saints' Lives and their Contexts* (Albany, NY: State University of New York Press, 1996), 35–50.

Hirst, S.M., *An Anglo-Saxon Inhumation Cemetery at Sewerby, East Yorkshire* (York: York University Archaeological Publications, 1985).

Hirst, S.M., 'Death and the Archaeologist', in M.O.H. Carver (ed.), *In Search of Cult: Essays in Honour of Philip Rahtz* (Woodbridge: Boydell, 1993), 41–4.

Hollis, S.J., *Anglo-Saxon Women and the Church: Sharing a Common Fate* (Woodbridge: Boydell Press, 1992).

Holloway, J., 'Material Symbolism and Death: Charcoal Burial in Later Anglo-Saxon England', in J. Buckberry and A.K. Cherryson (eds), *Burial in Later Anglo-Saxon England, c.650–1100 AD* (Oxford: Oxbow Books, 2010), 83–92.

Hooke, D., *Trees in Anglo-Saxon England: Literature, Lore and Landscape*, Anglo-Saxon Studies 13 (Woodbridge: Boydell, 2010).

Hough, C., 'Penitential literature and secular law in Anglo-Saxon England', *Anglo-Saxon Studies in Archaeology & History* 11 (2000): 133–42.

Howe, N., 'Falling into Place: Dislocation in the Junius Book', in M.C. Amodio and K. O'Brien O'Keefe (eds), *Unlocking the Wordhord: Anglo-Saxon Studies in Memory of Edward B. Irving, Jr.* (Toronto: University of Toronto Press, 1998), 14–37.

Howe, N., *Writing the Map of Anglo-Saxon England: Essays in Cultural Geography* (New Haven, CT.: Yale University Press, 2008).

Huggins, P.J., 'Excavation of Belgic and Romano-British farm with Middle Saxon cemetery and churches at Nazeingbury, Essex, 1975–6', *Essex Archaeology and History* 10 (1978): 29–117.

Hyams, P.R., 'Trial by Ordeal: The Key to Proof in the Early Common Law', in M.S. Arnold, T.A. Green, S.A. Scully and S.D. White (eds), *On the Laws and Customs of England: Essays in Honor of Samuel E. Thorne* (Chapel Hill: University of North Carolina Press, 1981), 90–126.

Insley, C., 'Charters and episcopal scriptoria in the Anglo-Saxon south-west', *Early Medieval Europe* 7 (1998): 173–97.

Insley, C., 'Where did all the charters go? Anglo-Saxon charters and the new politics of the eleventh century', *Anglo-Norman Studies* 24 (2001): 109–27.

Irvine, S., 'The Compilation and Use of Manuscripts Containing Old English in the Twelfth Century', in M. Swan and E. Treharne (eds), *Rewriting Old English in the Twelfth Century*, Cambridge Studies in Anglo-Saxon England 30 (Cambridge: Cambridge University Press, 2000), 41–61.

Irvine, S., *The Sources of the Anglo-Saxon Chronicle (E)* (2002), http://fontes. english.ox.ac.uk/, accessed November 2012.

Jacobsson, M., *Wells, Meres, and Pools: Hydronymic Terms in the Anglo-Saxon Landscape*, Acta Universitatis Upsaliensis, Studia Anglistica Upsaliensia 98 (Uppsala: Uppsala University Press, 1997).

Jaeger, C.S., *The Envy of Angels: Cathedral Schools and Social Ideals in Medieval Europe, 950–1200*, Middle Ages Series (Philadelphia: University of Pennsylvania Press, 1994).

James, M.R., 'Names of angels in Anglo-Saxon and other documents', *Journal of Theological Studies* 11 (1909–10): 569–71.

Jay, P., 'Saint Augustin et la doctrine du Purgatoire', *Recherches de théologie ancienne et médiévale* 36 (1969): 17–30.

Johnson, D.F., 'The fall of Lucifer in Genesis A and two Anglo-Latin royal charters', *Journal of English and Germanic Philology* 97:4 (1998): 500–21.

Johnson, D.F., 'A Program of Illumination in the Old English Illustrated Hexateuch: "Visual Typology"?', in R. Barnhouse and B.C. Withers (eds), *The Old English Hexateuch: Aspects and Approaches* (Kalamazoo, MI: Medieval Institute Publications, 2000), 165–99.

Johnson, D.F., 'The Crux Usualis as Apotropaic Weapon in Anglo-Saxon England', in E.K. Catherine, K. Sarah Larratt and J. Karen Louise (eds), *The Place of the Cross in Anglo-Saxon England* (Woodbridge: The Boydell Press, 2006), 80–95.

Johnson, D.F., 'Why Ditch the Dialogues? Reclaiming an Invisible Text', in C.D. Wright, F.M. Biggs and T.N. Hall (eds), *Source of Wisdom* (Toronto: University of Toronto Press, 2007), 201–16.

Johnson, D.F. and W. Rudolf, 'More notes by Coleman', *Medium Ævum* 79:1 (2010): 1–13.

Johnson, R.F., 'Archangel in the Margins: St. Michael in the Homilies of Cambridge, Corpus Christi College 41', *Traditio: Studies in Ancient and Medieval History, Thought, and Religion* 53 (1998): 63–91.

Johnson, R.F., *St Michael the Archangel in Medieval English Legend* (Woodbridge: Boydell and Brewer, 2005).

Jolly, K.L., *Popular Religion in Late Saxon England: Elf Charms in Context* (Chapel Hill, NC: University of North Carolina Press, 1996).

Jolly, K.L., 'Cross-Referencing Anglo-Saxon Liturgy and Remedies: The Sign of the Cross as Ritual Protection', in H. Gittos and M.B. Bedingfield (eds), *The Liturgy of the Late Anglo-Saxon Church* (Woodbridge: Boydell Press, 2005), 213–43.

Jolly, K.L., 'Prayers from the field: Practical protection and demonic defense in Anglo-Saxon England', *Traditio: Studies in Ancient and Medieval History, Thought, and Religion* 61 (2006): 95–147.

Jolly, K.L., 'Tapping the Power of the Cross: Who and for Whom?', in K.L. Jolly, C.E. Karkov and S.L. Keefer (eds), *The Place of the Cross in Anglo-Saxon England* (Woodbridge: Boydell Press, 2006), 58–79.

Jolly, K.L., C.E. Karkov and S.L. Keefer (eds), *Cross and Culture in Anglo-Saxon England: Studies in Honor of George Hardin Brown* (Morgantown, WV: West Virginia University Press, 2008).

Jones, C.A., 'The Book of the Liturgy in Anglo-Saxon England', *Speculum: A Journal of Medieval Studies* 73 (1998): 659–702.

Jones, C.A., 'Two composite texts from Archbishop Wulfstan's "Commonplace Book": The De ecclesiastica consuetudine and the Institutio beati Amalarii de ecclesiasticis officiis', *Anglo-Saxon England* 27 (1998): 233–71.

Jones, C.A., 'Ælfric's exemplar of Amalarius: An additional witness', *American Notes and Queries* 13:2 (2000): 6–14.

Jones, C.A., *A Lost Work by Amalarius of Metz: Interpolations in Salisbury, Cathedral Library MS 154*, HBS, Subsidia 2 (Woodbridge: Boydell & Brewer for the Henry Bradshaw Society, 2001).

Jones, C.W., 'Some introductory remarks on Bede's Commentary on Genesis', *Sacris Erudiri* 19 (1969–70): 115–98.

Jonsson, K., 'Burial rods and charcoal graves: New light on old burial practices', *Viking and Medieval Scandinavia* 3 (2007): 43–73.

Jorgenson, J., 'The debate over the patristic texts on purgatory at the Council of Ferrara-Florence, 1438', *St Vladimir's Theological Quarterly* 30:4 (1986): 309–34.

Jost, K., 'Einige Wulfstantexte und ihre Quellen', *Anglia* 56 (1932): 265–315.

Jungmann, J.A., 'Von der "Eucharistia" zur "Messe"', *Zeitschrift für katholische Theologie* 89 (1967): 29–40.

Karkov, C.E., 'Whitby, Jarrow and the Commemoration of Death in Northumbria', in J. Hawkes and S. Mills (eds), *Northumbria's Golden Age* (Stroud: Sutton, 1999), 126–35.

Karkov, C.E., 'The Anglo-Saxon Genesis: Text, Illustration, and Audience', in R. Barnhouse and B.C. Withers (eds), *The Old English Hexateuch: Aspects and Approaches* (Kalamazoo, MI: Medieval Institute Publications, 2000), 201–37.

Karkov, C.E., *Text and Picture in Anglo-Saxon England: Narrative Strategies in the Junius 11 Manuscript* (Cambridge: Cambridge University Press, 2001).

Karkov, C.E., S.L. Keefer and K.L. Jolly (eds), *The Place of the Cross in Anglo-Saxon England* (Woodbridge: Boydell Press, 2006).

Karkov, C.E., *The Art of Anglo-Saxon England* (Woodbridge: The Boydell Press, 2011).

Keck, D., *Angels and Angelology in the Middle Ages* (Oxford: Oxford University Press, 1998).

Keefe, S.A., *Water and the Word: Baptism and the Education of the Clergy in the Carolingian Empire*, Publications in Mediaeval Studies (Notre Dame, IN: University of Notre Dame Press, 2002).

Keefer, S.L., 'Manuals', in R.W. Pfaff (ed.), *The Liturgical Books of Anglo-Saxon England*, Old English Newsletter, Subsidia 23 (Kalamazoo, MI: The Medieval Institute Western Michigan University, 1995), 99–109.

Keefer, S.L., 'Margin as archive: The liturgical marginalia of a manuscript of the Old English Bede', *Traditio: Studies in Ancient and Medieval History, Thought, and Religion* 51 (1996): 147–77.

Keefer, S.L., '*Ut in omnibus honorificetur Deus:* The *corsnaed* Ordeal in Anglo-Saxon England', in J. Hill and M. Swan (eds), *The Community, the Family and the Saint: Patterns of Power in Early Medieval Europe: Selected Proceedings of the International Medieval Congress, University of Leeds, 4–7 July 1994, 10–13 July 1995* (Turnhout: Brepols, 1998), 237–64.

Keefer, S.L., 'Ðonne se cirlisca man ordales weddigeð: The Anglo-Saxon Lay Ordeal', in S.D. Baxter, C.E. Karkov, J.L. Nelson and D.A.E. Pelteret (eds), *Early Medieval Studies in Memory of Patrick Wormald* (Farnham: Ashgate, 2009), 353–67.

Keefer, S.L., K.L. Jolly and C.E. Karkov, *Cross and Cruciform in the Anglo-Saxon World: Studies to Honor the Memory of Timothy Reuter* (Morgantown: West Virginia University Press, 2010).

Keene, D. and A.R. Rumble, *Survey of Medieval Winchester*, Winchester Studies 2 (Oxford: Clarendon Press, 1985).

Kelly, H.A., *The Devil at Baptism: Ritual, Theology, and Drama* (Ithaca, NY: Cornell University Press, 1985).

Kelly, S.E., 'Anglo-Saxon Lay Society and the Written Word', in R. McKitterick (ed.), *The Uses of Literacy in Early Mediaeval Europe* (Cambridge: 1990), 36–62.

Kelly, S.E., 'King Æthelwulf's decimations', *Anglo-Saxon* 1 (2007): 285–317.

Kennedy, A.G., 'Cnut's law code of 1018', *Anglo-Saxon England* 11 (1983): 57–81.

Kennedy, A.G., 'Law and litigation in the Libellus Æthelwoldi episcopi', *Anglo-Saxon England* 24 (1995): 131–83.

Ker, N.R., 'Old English notes signed "Coleman"', *Medium Ævum* 18 (1949): 29–31.

Ker, N.R., *Catalogue of Manuscripts Containing Anglo-Saxon* (Oxford: Clarendon Press, 1957).

Ker, N.R., 'The Handwriting of Archbishop Wulfstan', in P. Clemoes and K. Hughes (eds), *England before the Conquest: Studies in Primary Sources*

*Presented to Dorothy Whitelock* (Cambridge: Cambridge Univ Press, 1971), 315–31.

Keynes, S., *The Diplomas of King Æthelred 'the Unready' 978–1016: A Study in their Use as Historical Evidence*, Cambridge Studies in Medieval Life and Thought, 3rd series, 13 (Cambridge: Cambridge University Press, 1980).

Keynes, S., 'King Æthelstan's Books', in M. Lapidge and H. Gneuss (eds), *Learning and Literature in Anglo-Saxon England: Studies Presented to Peter Clemoes on the Occasion of his Sixty-Fifth Birthday* (Cambridge: Cambridge University Press, 1985), 143–201.

Keynes, S., 'The Additions in Old English', in J.J.G. Alexander and N. Barker (eds), *The York Gospels: A Facsimile with Introductory Essays by Jonathan Alexander* [*et al.*] (London: Roxburghe Club, 1986), 81–99.

Keynes, S., 'Regenbald the Chancellor (sic)', *Anglo-Norman Studies* 10 (1987): 185–222.

Keynes, S., 'The lost cartulary of Abbotsbury', *Anglo-Saxon England* 18 (1989): 207–43.

Keynes, S., 'Royal Government and the Written Word in Late Anglo-Saxon England', in R. McKitterick (ed.), *Uses of Literacy in Early Mediaeval Europe* (Cambridge: Cambridge University Press, 1990), 226–57.

Keynes, S., 'The Æthelings in Normandy', *Anglo-Norman Studies* 13 (1991): 173–205.

Keynes, S., 'Raedwald the Bretwalda', in C.B. Kendall and P.S. Wells (eds), *Voyage to the Other World: The Legacy of Sutton Hoo* (Minneapolis, MN: 1992), 103–23.

Keynes, S., 'A lost cartulary of St Albans Abbey', *Anglo-Saxon England* 22 (1993): 253–79.

Keynes, S., 'Cnut's Earls', in A.R. Rumble (ed.), *The Reign of Cnut: King of England, Denmark and Norway* (London: Leicester University Press, 1994), 43–88.

Keynes, S., 'The "Dunstan B" charters', *Anglo-Saxon England* 23 (1994): 165–93.

Keynes, S., 'The West Saxon charters of King Æthelwulf and his sons', *English Historical Review* 109 (1994): 1109–49.Keynes, S., 'Anglo-Saxon Entries in the Liber Vitae of Brescia', in J.A. Roberts, J.L. Nelson, M. Godden and J. Bately (eds), *Alfred the Wise: Studies in Honour of Janet Bately on the Occasion of her Sixty-Fifth Birthday* (Cambridge: D.S. Brewer, 1997), 99–119.

Keynes, S., *An Atlas of Attestations in Anglo-Saxon charters, c.670–1066* (Cambridge: University of Cambridge, 2002).

Keynes, S., 'Wulfsige, Monk of Glastonbury, Abbot of Westminster (*c* 990–3), and Bishop of Sherborne (*c* 993–1002)', in K. Barker, D.A. Hinton and A. Hunt (eds), *St. Wulfsige and Sherborne: Essays to Celebrate the Millennium of the Benedictine Abbey, 998–1998* (Oxford: Oxbow Books, 2005), 53–94.

Keynes, S., 'An abbot, an archbishop, and the viking raids of 1006–7 and 1009–12', *Anglo-Saxon England* 36 (2006): 151–224.

Keynes, S., 'Anglo-Saxon Charters: Lost and Found', in J. Barrow and A. Wareham (eds), *Myth, Rulership, Church and Charters: Essays in Honour of Nicholas Brooks* (Aldershot: Ashgate, 2008), 45–66.

King, V., 'St Oswald's Tenants', in N. Brooks and C. Cubitt (eds), *St Oswald of Worcester: Life and Influence* (London: Continuum, 1996), 100–16.

Kjølbye-Biddle, B., 'Dispersal or Concentration: The Disposal of the Winchester Dead over 2000 Years', in S.R. Bassett (ed.), *Death in Towns: Urban Responses to the Dying and the Dead, 100–1600* (Leicester: Leicester University Press, 1992), 210–47.

Kleist, A.J., 'Anglo-Saxon Homiliaries in Tudor and Stuart England', in A.J. Kleist (ed.), *The Old English Homily: Precedent, Practice, and Appropriation* (Turnhout: Brepols, 2007), 445–92.

Knüsel, C., R. Janaway and S. King, 'Death, decay and ritual reconstruction: Archaeological evidence of cadaveric spasm', *Oxford Journal of Archaeology* 15 (1996): 121–8.

Kopar, L., *Gods and Settlers: The Iconography of Norse Mythology in Anglo-Scandinavian Sculpture* (Turnhout: Brepols, 2012).

Kornexl, L., 'The Regularis Concordia and its Old English gloss', *Anglo-Saxon England* 24 (1995): 95–130.

Lang, J.T., *Corpus of Anglo-Saxon Stone Sculpture: Vol. 3, York and Eastern Yorkshire* (Oxford: Published for the British Academy by Oxford University Press, 1991).

Lang, J.T. and D. Craig, *Corpus of Anglo-Saxon Stone Sculpture: Vol. 6, Northern Yorkshire* (Oxford: Published for the British Academy by Oxford University Press, 2001).

Lapidge, M., 'The hermeneutic style in tenth-century Anglo-Latin literature', *Anglo-Saxon England* 4 (1975): 67–111.

Lapidge, M., 'The origin of CCCC 163', *Transactions of the Cambridge Bibliographical Society* 8 (1981), 18–28

Lapidge, M., 'Byrhtferth of Ramsey and the early sections of the Historia Regum attributed to Symeon of Durham', *Anglo-Saxon England* 10 (1982): 97–122.

Lapidge, M., 'Latin learning in ninth-century England', *Anglo-Latin Literature, 600–899* (London: Hambledon Press, 1996), 409–54.

Lapidge, M., 'Cynewulf and the Passio S. Iulianae', in M.C. Amodio and K. O'Brien O'Keefe (eds), *Unlocking the Wordhord: Anglo-Saxon Studies in Memory of Edward B. Irving, Jr.* (Toronto: University of Toronto Press, 1998), 147–71.

Lapidge, M., *The Anglo-Saxon Library* (Oxford: Oxford University Press, 2006).

Lariviere, R.W., 'Ordeals in Europe and in India', *Journal of the American Oriental Society* 101:3 (1981): 347–9.

Le Goff, J., *La naissance du Purgatoire*, Bibliothèque des histoires (Paris: Gallimard, 1981).

Le Goff, J., *The Birth of Purgatory*, trans. A. Goldhammer (Chicago: University of Chicago Press, 1984).

Le Goff, J., 'The Learned and Popular Dimensions of Journeys in the Otherworld in the Middle Ages', in S.L. Kaplan (ed.), *Understanding Popular Culture: Europe from the Middle Ages to the Nineteenth Century* (Berlin: Mouton, 1984), 19–37.

Le Goff, J., *The Medieval Imagination*, trans. A. Goldhammer (Chicago: University of Chicago Press, 1992).

Lea, H.C., *Superstition and Force: Essays on the Wager of Law – The Wager of Battle – The Ordeal – Torture* (Philadelphia: Henry C. Lea, 1870).

Lendinara, P., '"*frater non redimit, redimit homo...*": A Homiletic Motif and its Variants in Old English', in E. Treharne and S. Rosser (eds), *Early Medieval English Texts and Interpretations: Studies Presented to Donald G. Scragg* (Tempe, Arizona: Arizona Center for Medieval and Renaissance Studies, 2002), 67–80.

Lerner, R.E., 'La naissance du Purgatoire', *The American Historical Review* 87:5 (1982): 1374–5.

Lethaby, W.R., 'The perjury at Bayeux', in R. Gameson (ed.), *The Study of the Bayeux Tapestry* (Woodbridge: Boydell & Brewer, 1997), 19–20.

Leyser, C., 'Angels, Monks, and Demons in the Early Medieval West', in R. Gameson and H. Leyser (eds), *Belief and Culture in the Middle Ages: Studies Presented to Henry Mayr-Harting* (Oxford: Oxford University Press, 2001), 9–22.

Lifshitz, F., 'Beyond positivism and genre: "Hagiographical" texts as historical narrative', *Viator: Medieval and Renaissance Studies* 25 (1994): 95–113.

Lifshitz, F., *The Name of the Saint: The Martyrology of Jerome and Access to the Sacred in Francia, 627–827*, Publications in Medieval Studies (Notre Dame, IN: University of Notre Dame Press, 2006).

Lionarons, J.T., *The Homiletic Writings of Archbishop Wulfstan: A Critical Study* (Cambridge: D.S. Brewer, 2010).

Little, L.K., 'Anger in Monastic Curses', in B.H. Rosenwein (ed.), *Anger's Past: The Social Uses of an Emotion in the Middle Ages* (Ithaca, NY: Cornell University Press, 1998), 9–35.

Liuzza, R.M., 'Prayers and/or Charms Addressed to the Cross', in K.L. Jolly, C.E. Karkov and S.L. Keefer (eds), *Cross and Culture in Anglo-Saxon England: Studies in Honor of George Hardin Brown* (Morgantown, WV: West Virginia University Press, 2008), 276–320.

Love, R.C., 'Hagiography', in M. Lapidge, J. Blair, S. Keynes and D.G. Scragg (eds), *The Blackwell Encyclopaedia of Anglo-Saxon England* (Oxford: Blackwell, 1999), 226–8.

Lowe, K.A., 'The development of the Anglo-Saxon boundary clause', *Nomina* 21 (1998): 63–100.

Lowe, K.A., 'The nature and effect of the Anglo-Saxon vernacular will', *Journal of Legal History* 19 (1998): 23–61.

Lowe, K.A., 'Latin versions of Old English wills', *Journal of Legal History* 20 (1999): 1–23.Lucy, S. and A.J. Reynolds, 'Burial in Early Medieval England

and Wales: Past, Present and Future', in S. Lucy and A.J. Reynolds (eds), *Burial in Early Medieval England and Wales* (London: Society for Medieval Archaeology, 2002), 1–23.

Lynch, J.H., *Christianizing Kinship: Ritual Sponsorship in Anglo-Saxon England* (Ithaca, NY: Cornell University Press, 1998).

Magennis, H., 'Ælfric Scholarship', in H. Magennis and M. Swan (eds), *A Companion to Ælfric* (Leiden: Brill, 2009), 5–34.

Magennis, H. and M. Swan (eds), *A Companion to Ælfric* (Leiden: Brill, 2009).

Mango, C.A., 'The Invisible World of Good and Evil', in C.A. Mango (ed.), *Byzantium: The Empire of New Rome* (London: Weidenfeld and Nicolson, 1980), 151–65.

Mann, G., 'The Development of Wulfstan's Alcuin Manuscript', in M. Townend (ed.), *Wulfstan, Archbishop of York: The Proceedings of the Second Alcuin Conference* (Turnhout: Brepols, 2004), 235–78.

Marafioti, N., 'Punishing bodies and saving souls: Capital and corporal punishment in late Anglo-Saxon England', *Haskins Society Journal: Studies in Medieval History* 20 (2009): 39-57.

Marafioti, N., 'Spiritual Dangers and Earthly Consequences: Judging and Punishing in the Old English *Consolation of Philosophy*', in J. Gates and N. Marafioti (eds), *Capital and Corporal Punishment* (forthcoming).

Markus, R.A., 'From Caesarius to Boniface: Christianity and paganism in Gaul', in J. Fontaine and J.N. Hillgarth (eds), *Le Septième siècle: Changements et continuités. Actes du Colloque bilatéral franco-britannique tenu au Warburg Institute les 8–9 juillet 1988*, Studies of the Warburg Institute 42 (London: The Warburg Institute, University of London, 1992), 154–72.

Markus, R.A., 'How on earth could places become holy? Origins of the Christian idea of holy places', *Journal of Early Christian Studies* 2:3 (1994): 257–71.

Markus, R.A., 'Gregory the Great's Pagans', in R. Gameson and H. Leyser (eds), *Belief and Culture in the Middle Ages: Studies Presented to Henry Mayr-Harting* (Oxford: Oxford University Press, 2001), 23–34.

Markus, R.A., 'Living within Sight of the End', in C. Humphrey and W.M. Ormrod (eds), *Time in the Medieval World* (Woodbridge: York Medieval Press, 2001), 23–34.

Marmion, J.P., 'Purgatory revisited', *Downside Review* 112 (1994): 121–41.

Martimort, A.G., 'Comment meurt un chrétien', *La Maison-Dieu* 44 (1955): 5–28.

Martimort, A.G., 'Prayer for the Sick and Sacramental Anointing', in A.G. Martimort (ed.), *The Church at Prayer: Vol. 3, The Sacraments* (Collegeville, Minnesota: The Liturgical Press, 1988), 117–37.

Mayr-Harting, H., *The Coming of Christianity to Anglo-Saxon England* (London: Batsford, 1972).

Mayr-Harting, H., *Perceptions of Angels in History: An Inaugural Lecture Delivered in the University of Oxford on 14 November 1997* (Oxford: Clarendon Press, 1998).

McAuley, F., 'Canon law and the end of the ordeal', *Oxford Journal of Legal Studies* 26:3 (2006): 473–513.

McDannell, C. and B. Lang, *Heaven: A History* (New Haven: Yale University Press, 1988).

McKitterick, R., 'Some Carolingian Law-Books and Their Function', in B. Tierney and P. Linehan (eds), *Authority and Power: Studies on Medieval Law and Government Presented to Walter Ullman on his Seventieth Birthday* (Cambridge: Cambridge University Press, 1980), 13–27.

McKitterick, R., *The Carolingians and the Written Word* (Cambridge: Cambridge University Press, 1989).

McLaughlin, M., *Consorting with Saints: Prayer for the Dead in Early Medieval France* (Ithaca, NY: Cornell University Press, 1994).

McNulty, J.B., *The Narrative Art of the Bayeux Tapestry Master* (New York: AMS Press, 1989).

Meaney, A.L., 'Felix's life of St Guthlac: Hagiography and/or truth', *Proceedings of the Cambridge Antiquarian Society* 90 (2001): 29–48.

Meens, R., 'The Frequency and Nature of Early Medieval Penance', in P. Biller and A.J. Minnis (eds), *Handling Sin: Confession in the Middle Ages*, York Studies in Medieval Theology 2 (Woodbridge: Boydell & Brewer, 1998), 35–61.

Meens, R., 'Die Bußbücher und das Recht im 9. und 10. Jahrhundert: Kontinuität und Wandel', in A. Grabowsky and W. Hartmann (eds), *Recht und Gericht in Kirche und Welt um 900* (Munich: Oldenbourg, 2007), 217–34.

Menzer, M.J., 'The Preface as Admonition: Ælfric's Preface to Genesis', in R. Barnhouse and B.C. Withers (eds), *The Old English Hexateuch: Aspects and Approaches* (Kalamazoo, MI.: Medieval Institute Publications, 2000), 15–39.

Merkt, A., *Das Fegefeuer. Entstehung und Funktion einer Idee* (Darmstadt: Wissenschaftliche Buchgesellschaft, 2005).

Michel, A., 'Purgatoire', in A. Vacant and E. Mangenot (eds), *Dictionnaire de théologie catholique, contenant l'exposé des doctrines de la théologie catholique: leurs preuves et leur histoire* (Paris: Letouzey et Ané, 1915), 1163–326.

Mills, A.D., *A Dictionary of British Place-Names* (Oxford: Oxford University Press, 2003).

Mondin, B., *Gli abitanti del cielo: trattato di ecclesiologia celeste e di escatologia*, Nuovo corso di teologia dogmatica 5 (Bologna: Edizioni Studio Domenicano, 1994).

Moore, M.E.H., 'Demons and the battle for souls at Cluny', *Studies in Religion / Sciences religieuses* 32:4 (2003): 485–97.

Moore, R.I., *The Formation of a Persecuting Society: Authority and Deviance in Western Europe, 950–1250* (Oxford: Blackwell, 2007).

Moorhead, J., 'Bede on the papacy', *Journal of Ecclesiastical History* 60:2 (2009): 217–32.

Moreira, I., *Heaven's Purge: Purgatory in Late Antiquity* (Oxford: Oxford University Press, 2010).

Morris, R., *Churches in the Landscape* (London: Dent, 1989).

Morris, R.K., 'Baptismal Places: 600–800', in N. Lund and I.N. Wood (eds), *People and Places in Northern Europe, 500–1600: Essays in Honour of Peter Hayes Sawyer* (Woodbridge: 1991), 15–24.

Murray, A., 'Confession before 1215', *Transactions of the Royal Historical Society,* 6th series 3 (1993): 51–81.

Murray, A., *Suicide in the Middle Ages: 1, The Violent against Themselves* (Oxford: Oxford University Press, 1998).

Murray, A., *Suicide in the Middle: Ages 2, The Curse on Self-Murder* (Oxford: Oxford University Press, 2000).

Nelson, J.L., 'Wealth and Wisdom: The Politics of Alfred the Great', in J.T. Rosenthal (ed.), *Kings and Kingship* (Binghampton, NY: The Center for Medieval and Early Renaissance Studies, SUNY, 1986), 31–52.

Nelson, J.L. and R.W. Pfaff, 'Pontificals and Benedictionals', in R.W. Pfaff (ed.), *The Liturgical Books of Anglo-Saxon England,* Old English Newsletter, Subsidia 23 (Kalamazoo, MI: The Medieval Institute Western Michigan University, 1995), 87–98.

Neuman De Vegvar, C., 'Converting the Anglo-Saxon Landscape: Crosses and their Audiences', in A.J. Minnis and J. Roberts (eds), *Text, Image, Interpretation: Studies in Anglo-Saxon Literature and its Insular Context in Honour of Éamonn Ó Carragáin* (Turnhout: Brepols, 2007), 407–29.

Neville, J., *Representations of the Natural World in Old English Poetry,* Cambridge Studies in Anglo-Saxon England 27 (Cambridge: Cambridge University Press, 1999).

Niewöhner, F. and O. Pluta, *Atheismus im Mittelalter und in der Renaissance* (Wiesbaden: Harrassowitz in Kommission, 1999).

Niles, J.D., 'Trial by Ordeal in Anglo-Saxon England: What's the Problem with Barley?', in S.D. Baxter, C.E. Karkov, J.L. Nelson and D.A.E. Pelteret (eds), *Early Medieval Studies in Memory of Patrick Wormald* (Farnham: Ashgate, 2009), 369–82.

Noel, W., *The Harley Psalter,* Cambridge Studies in Palaeography and Codicology 4 (Cambridge: Cambridge University Press, 1995).

Nokes, R.S., 'The several compilers of Bald's leechbook', *Anglo-Saxon England* 33 (2004): 51–76.

Nussbaum, D., 'Reviling the Saints or Reforming the Calendar? John Foxe and his 'Kalendar' of Martyrs', in C.J. Litzenberger and S. Wabuda (eds), *Belief and Practice in Reformation England: A Tribute to Patrick Collinson from his Students* (Aldershot and Brookfield, VT: Ashgate, 1998), 113–36.

O'Brien O'Keeffe, K., 'Body and law in late Anglo-Saxon England', *Anglo-Saxon England* 27 (1998): 209–32.

O'Carroll, M., 'Apparitions', *Theotokos: A Theological Encyclopedia of the Blessed Virgin Mary* (Wilmington, DE: Michael Glazier, 1982), 47–8.

O'Sullivan, D., 'Space, Silence and Shortage on Lindisfarne: The Archaeology of Asceticism', in H. Hamerow and A. MacGregor (eds), *Image and Power in the*

*Archaeology of Early Medieval Britain: Essays in Honour of Rosemary Cramp* (Oxford: Oxbow Books, 2001), 33–52.

Oakley, T.P., *English Penitential Discipline and Anglo-Saxon Law in their Joint Influence* (New York: Columbia University Press, 1923).

Oakley, T.P., 'The cooperation of mediaeval penance and secular law', *Speculum: A Journal of Medieval Studies* 7:4 (1932): 515–24.

Ohler, N., *Sterben und Tod im Mittelalter* (Munich: Patmos Verlag GmbH, 1990).

Okasha, E., *Hand-List of Anglo-Saxon Non-Runic Inscriptions* (Cambridge: Cambridge University Press, 1971).

Okasha, E., 'Memorial Stones or Grave-Stones?', in P. Cavill (ed.), *The Christian Tradition in Anglo-Saxon England: Approaches to Current Scholarship and Teaching* (Woodbridge: Boydell and Brewer, 2004), 91–101.

Ombres, R., 'Latins and Greeks in debate over purgatory, 1230–1439', *Journal of Ecclesiastical History* 35:1 (1984): 1–14.

O'Neill, P.P., 'On the date, provenance and relationship of the Solomon and Saturn dialogues', *Anglo-Saxon England* 26 (1997): 139–68.

Openshaw, K.M., 'Weapons in the daily battle: Images of the conquest of evil in the early medieval psalter', *Art Bulletin* 75:1 (1993): 17–38.

Orchard, A., 'Old sources, new resources: Finding the right formula for Boniface', *Anglo-Saxon England* 30 (2001): 15–38.

Orchard, A., *A Critical Companion to Beowulf* (Cambridge: D.S. Brewer, 2003).

Orchard, A., 'Parallel lives: Wulfstan, William, Coleman and Christ', in J. Barrow and N. Brooks (eds), *St Wulfstan and his World* (Aldershot: Ashgate, 2005), 39–57.

Orme, N., 'St. Michael and his mount', *Journal of the Royal Institution of Cornwall* n.s. 10:1 (1986–7): 32–43.

Orme, N., 'Bishop Grandisson and popular religion', *Devonshire Association Report and Transactions* 124 (1992): 107–18.

Orme, N., *English Church Dedications: With a Survey of Cornwall and Devon* (Exeter: University of Exeter Press, 1996).

Orme, N., *The Saints of Cornwall* (Oxford: Oxford University Press, 2000).

Ortenberg, V., *The English Church and the Continent in the Tenth and Eleventh Centuries: Cultural, Spiritual, and Artistic Exchange* (Oxford: Oxford University Press, 1992).

Oxford English Dictionary, *perjury, n.*, http://www.oed.com/view/Entry/141131, accessed June 2012.

Page, R.I., 'Old English liturgical rubrics in Corpus Christi College, Cambridge, MS 422', *Anglia* 96 (1978): 149–58.

Page, R.I., 'Anglo-Saxon Paganism: The Evidence of Bede', in T. Hofstra, L.A.J.R. Houwen and A.A. MacDonald (eds), *Pagans and Christians: The Interplay between Christian Latin and Traditional Germanic Cultures in Early Medieval Europe. Proceedings of the Second Germania Latina Conference held at the University of Groningen, May 1992* (Groningen: Egbert Forsten, 1995), 99–129.

Palmer, J.T., 'Defining paganism in the Carolingian world', *Early Medieval Europe* 15:4 (2007): 402–25.

Palmer, J.T., *Anglo-Saxons in a Frankish world, 690 – 900*, Studies in the Early Middle Ages 19 (Turnhout: Brepols, 2009).Parker Pearson, M., 'The powerful dead: Archaeological relationships between the living and the dead', *Cambridge Archaeological Journal* 3:2 (1993): 203–29.

Parker Pearson, M., R. Van de Noort and A. Woolf, 'Three men and a boat: Sutton Hoo and the east Saxon kingdom', *Anglo-Saxon England* 22 (1993): 27–50.

Parker Pearson, M., *The Archaeology of Death and Burial* (Stroud: Sutton, 1999).

Parsons, D., 'A note on the Breedon angel', *Leicestershire Archaeological and Historical Society Transactions* 51 for 1975–1976 (1977): 40–2.

Paxton, F.S., *Christianizing Death: The Creation of a Ritual Process in Early Medieval Europe* (Ithaca, NY: Cornell University Press, 1990).

Paxton, F.S., 'Curing bodies-curing souls: Hrabanus Maurus, medical education, and the clergy in ninth-century Francia', *Journal of the History of Medicine and Allied Sciences* 50:2 (1995): 230–52.Peers, G., 'Hagiographic models of worship of images and angels', *Byzantion: Revue internationale des études byzantines* 67:2 (1997): 407–20.

Peletz, M.G., 'Kinship studies in late twentieth-century anthropology', *Annual Review of Anthropology* 24 (1995): 343–72.

Pelteret, D.A.E., *Slavery in Early Mediaeval England: From the Reign of Alfred until the Twelfth Century*, Studies in Anglo-Saxon History (Woodbridge: Boydell, 1995).

Pestell, T., 'Markets, Emporia, Wics, and "Productive" Sites: Pre-Viking Trade Centres in Anglo-Saxon England', in S. Crawford, H. Hamerow and D.A. Hinton (eds), *The Oxford Handbook of Anglo-Saxon Archaeology* (Oxford: Oxford University Press, 2011), 556–79.

Pestell, T. and K. Ulmschneider (eds), *Markets in Early Medieval Europe: Trading and Productive Sites, 650–850* (Macclesfield: Windgather, 2003).

Pettegree, A., *Reformation and the Culture of Persuasion* (Cambridge: Cambridge University Press, 2005).

Pfaff, R.W., *The Liturgical Books of Anglo-Saxon England*, Old English Newsletter, Subsidia 23 (Kalamazoo, MI: The Medieval Institute Western Michigan University, 1995).

Pfaff, R.W., 'Massbooks: Sacramentaries and Missals', in R.W. Pfaff (ed.), *The Liturgical Books of Anglo-Saxon England*, Old English Newsletter, Subsidia 23 (Kalamazoo, MI: The Medieval Institute Western Michigan University, 1995), 7–34.

Pfaff, R.W., *The Liturgy in Medieval England: A History* (Cambridge: Cambridge University Press, 2009).

Pickles, T., 'Angel veneration on Anglo-Saxon stone sculpture from Dewsbury (West Yorkshire), Otley (West Yorkshire) and Halton (Lancashire): Contemplative preachers and pastoral care', *Journal of the British Archaeological Association* 162 (2009): 1–28.

Pickles, T., 'Church Organization and Pastoral Care', in P. Stafford (ed.), *A Companion to the Early Middle Ages: Britain and Ireland c. 500–1100* (Oxford: Wiley-Blackwell, 2009), 160–76.

Pluta, O., 'Atheismus im Mittelalter', in K. Kahnert and B. Mojsisch (eds), *Umbrüche: Historische Wendepunkte der Philosophie von der Antike bis zur Gegenwart. Festschrift für Kurt Flasch zu seinem 70. Geburtstag* (Amsterdam: Grüner, 2001), 117–30.

Poschmann, B., *Penance and the Anointing of the Sick*, trans. F. Courtney (Freiburg: Herder, 1964).

Pratt, D., 'Persuasion and Invention at the Court of King Alfred the Great', in C. Cubitt (ed.), *Court Culture in the Early Middle Ages: The Proceedings of the First Alcuin Conference* (Turnhout: Brepols, 2003), 189–222.

Pratt, D., *The Political Thought of King Alfred the Great*, Cambridge Studies in Medieval Life and Thought, 4th series, 67 (Cambridge: Cambridge University Press, 2007).

Pratt, D., 'Written Law and the Communication of Authority in Tenth-Century England', in C. Leyser, D.W. Rollason and H. Williams (eds), *England and the Continent in the Tenth Century: Studies in Honour of Wilhelm Levison (1876–1947)* (Turnhout: Brepols, 2011), 331–50.

*Prosopography of Anglo-Saxon England*, http://www.pase.ac.uk/, accessed August 2012.

Rahner, K., 'Über Visionen und verwandte Erscheinungen', *Geist und Leben* 21 (1948): 179–213.

Raw, B.C., 'The probable derivation of most of the illustrations in Junius II from an illustrated Old Saxon Genesis', *Anglo-Saxon England* 5 (1976): 133–48.

Raw, B.C., *Trinity and Incarnation in Anglo-Saxon Art and Thought*, Cambridge Studies in Anglo-Saxon England 21 (Cambridge: Cambridge University Press, 1997).

Read, D.W., 'Kinship theory: A paradigm shift', *Ethnology* 46–4 (2007): 329–64.

Rebillard, É., *The Care of the Dead in Late Antiquity*, Cornell Studies in Classical Philology 59 (Ithaca, NY: Cornell University Press, 2009).

Reynolds, A.J., 'The Definition and Ideology of Anglo-Saxon Execution Sites and Cemeteries', in G. De Boe and F. Verhaege (eds), *Death and Burial in Medieval Europe: Papers of the 'Medieval Europe Brugge 1997' Conference*, 2 (Zelik: Instituut voor het Archeologisch Patrimonium, 1997), 33–41.

Reynolds, A.J., 'Burials, Boundaries and Charters', in S. Lucy and A.J. Reynolds (eds), *Burial in Early Medieval England and Wales* (London: Society for Medieval Archaeology, 2002), 71–94.

Reynolds, A.J., *Anglo-Saxon Deviant Burial Customs* (Oxford: Oxford University Press, 2009).

Reynolds, S., 'Bookland, folkland and fiefs', *Anglo-Norman Studies* 14 (1991): 211–27.

Reynolds, S., 'Social mentalities and the case of medieval scepticism', *Transactions of the Royal Historical Society*, 6th series, 1 (1991): 21–41.

Richards, J.D., 'What's so special about "productive sites"? Middle Saxon settlements in Northumbria', *Anglo-Saxon Studies in Archaeology & History* 10 (1999): 71–80.

Ridyard, S.J., 'Monk-kings and the Anglo-Saxon hagiographic tradition', *Haskins Society Journal: Studies in Medieval History* 6 (1995): 13–27.

Rio, A., *Legal Practice and the Written Word in the Early Middle Ages: Frankish Formulae, c. 500–1000*, Cambridge Studies in Medieval Life and Thought, 4th series, 75 (Cambridge: Cambridge University Press, 2009).

Rivard, D.A., *Blessing the World: Ritual and Lay Piety in Medieval Religion* (Washington, DC: Catholic University of America Press, 2009).

Robinson, B.S., 'John Foxe and the Anglo-Saxons', in C. Highley and J.N. King (eds), *John Foxe and his World* (Aldershot: Ashgate, 2002), 54–72.

Robinson, P.R., 'Self-contained units in composite manuscripts of the Anglo-Saxon period', *Anglo-Saxon England* 7 (1978): 231–8.

Rodwell, W., 'The Lichfield angel: A spectacular Anglo-Saxon painted sculpture', *Antiquaries' Journal* 88 (2008): 48–108.

Rodwell, W. and K.A. Rodwell, *Rivenhall: Investigations of a Villa, Church, and Village, 1950–1977*, Chelmsford Archaeological Trust Report 4 (London: Council for British Archaeology, 1985).

Rodwell, W., C. Atkins and T. Waldron, *St Peter's, Barton-upon-Humber, Lincolnshire: A Parish Church and its Community* (3 vols, Oxford: Oxbow, 2007).

Rogers, N., 'Monuments to Monks and Monastic Servants', in B. Thompson (ed.), *Monasteries and Society in Medieval Britain: Proceedings of the 1994 Harlaxton Symposium* (Stamford: Paul Watkins, 1999), 262–76.

Rollason, D.W., 'Lists of saints' resting-places in Anglo-Saxon England', *Anglo-Saxon England* 7 (1978): 61–94.

Rollason, D.W., 'Monasteries and Society in Early Medieval Northumbria', in B. Thompson (ed.), *Monasteries and Society in Medieval Britain: Proceedings of the 1994 Harlaxton Symposium*, Harlaxton Medieval Studies, n.s. 6 (Stamford: Paul Watkins, 1999), 59–74.

Rollason, L., 'The *Liber Vitae* of Durham and Lay Association with Durham Cathedral Priory in the Later Middle Ages', in B. Thompson (ed.), *Monasteries and Society in Medieval Britain: Proceedings of the 1994 Harlaxton Symposium* (Stamford: Paul Watkins, 1999), 277–95.

Rosenwein, B.H., *To Be the Neighbor of Saint Peter: The Social Meaning of Cluny's property, 909–1049* (Ithaca, NY: Cornell University Press, 1989).

Rosenwein, B.H., *Negotiating Space: Power, Restraint, and Privileges of Immunity in Early Medieval Europe* (Manchester: Manchester University Press, 1999).

Rose-Troup, F., 'The ancient monastery of St Mary and St Peter at Exeter': *Report and Transactions – The Devonshire Association for the Advancement of Science, Literature and Art* 2 (1931): 179–220.

Rosser, G., 'The Anglo-Saxon Gilds', in J. Blair (ed.), *Minsters and Parish Churches: The Local Church in Transition, 950–1200* (Oxford: Oxford University Committee for Archaeology, 1988), 31–43.

Rosser, G., 'Sanctuary and Social Negotiation in Medieval England', in J. Blair and B. Golding (eds), *The Cloister and the World: Essays in Medieval History in Honour of Barbara Harvey* (Oxford: Clarendon Press, 1996), 57–79.

Rowe, T., 'Blessings for Nature in the English Liturgy, c. 900–1200', PhD thesis, University of Exeter, 2010.

Rubin, M., *Corpus Christi: The Eucharist in Late Medieval Culture* (Cambridge: Cambridge University Press, 1991).

Rubin, S., 'The Anglo-Saxon Physician', in M. Deegan and D.G. Scragg (eds), *Medicine in Early Medieval England: Four Papers* (Manchester: Centre for Anglo-Saxon Studies, University of Manchester, 1989), 7–15.

Rushforth, R., *Saints in English Kalendars before AD 1100*, HBS 117 (Woodbridge: Boydell Press for the Henry Bradshaw Society, 2008).

Ryan, J.J., 'Pseudo-Alcuin's *Liber de divinis officiis* and the *Liber 'Dominus vobiscum'* of St. Peter Damiani', *Mediaeval Studies* 14 (1952): 159–63.

Saller, R.P. and B.D. Shaw, 'Tombstones and Roman family relations in the principate: Civilians, soldiers and slaves', *The Journal of Roman Studies* 74 (1984): 124–56.

Sandberg, A., 'Quantum Gravity Treatment of the Angel Density Problem', *Annals of Improbable Research* 7:3 (2001): http://improbable.com/airchives/paperair/volume7/v7i3/angels-7-3.htm, accessed November 2012.

Sauer, H. 'The Transmission and Structure of Archbishop Wulfstan's 'Commonplace Book'', in P.E. Szarmach (ed.), *Old English Prose: Basic Readings*, Basic Readings in Anglo-Saxon England 5 (New York: Routledge, 2000), 339–93.

Sawyer, P.H., *Anglo-Saxon Charters: An Annotated List and Bibliography* (London: Royal Historical Society, 1968).

Schmid, J., *Et pro remedio animae et pro memoria: bürgerliche repraesentatio in der Cappella Tornabuoni in S. Maria Novella, I Mandorli* 2 (München: Deutscher Kunstverlag, 2002).

Schmid, K. and J. Wollasch, 'Die Gemeinschaft der Lebenden und Verstorbenen in Zeugnissen des Mittelalters', *Frühmittelalterliche Studien* 1 (1967): 365–405.

Schmid, K. and J. Wollasch, 'Societas et Fraternitas: Begründung eines kommentierten Quellenwerkes zur Erforschung der Personen und Personengruppen des Mittelalters', *Frühmittelalterliche Studien* 9 (1975): 1–48.

Schmitt, J.-C., 'Au Moyen Age: culture folklorique, culture clandestine', *Revue du Vivarais* (1979): 143–8.

Schmitt, J.-C., 'Les traditions folkloriques dans la culture médiévale. Quelques réflexions de méthode', *Archives de sciences sociales des religions* 52:1 (1981): 5–20.

Schöpf, B., *Das Tötungsrecht bei den frühchristlichen Schriftstellern bis zur Zeit Konstantins*, Studien zur Geschichte der katholischen Moraltheologie 5 (Regensburg: F. Pustet, 1958).

Schwab, U., 'The Battle of Maldon: A Memorial Poem', in J. Cooper (ed.), *The Battle of Maldon: Fiction and Fact* (London: Hambledon, 1993), 63–85.

Scragg, D.G., 'Napier's "Wulfstan" Homily XXX: Its sources, its relationship to the Vercelli Book and its style', *Anglo-Saxon England* 6 (1977): 197–211.

Scragg, D.G., 'The corpus of vernacular homilies & prose saints' lives before Ælfric', *Anglo-Saxon England* 8 (1979): 223–77.

Scragg, D.G., 'The Homilies of the Blickling Manuscript', in M. Lapidge and H. Gneuss (eds), *Learning and Literature in Anglo-Saxon England: Studies Presented to Peter Clemoes on the Occasion of his Sixty-Fifth Birthday* (Cambridge: Cambridge University Press, 1985), 299–316.

Scribner, B., 'Is a history of popular culture possible?', *History of European Ideas* 10:2 (1989): 175–91.

Semple, S., 'A fear of the past: The place of the prehistoric burial mound in the ideology of middle and later Anglo-Saxon England', *World Archaeology* 30:1 (1998): 109–26.

Semple, S., 'Illustrations of damnation in late Anglo-Saxon manuscripts', *Anglo-Saxon England* 32 (2003): 231–45.

Senecal, C., 'Keeping up with the Godwinesons: In pursuit of aristocratic status in late Anglo-Saxon England', *Anglo-Norman Studies* 23 (2000): 251–66.

Sexton, J.P., 'Saint's law: Anglo-Saxon sanctuary protection in the *Translatio et Miracula S. Swithuni*', *Florilegium* 23:2 (2006): 61–80.

Sharpe, R., 'The use of writs in the eleventh century', *Anglo-Saxon England* 32 (2003): 247–91.

Shippey, T.A., 'Wealth and wisdom in King Alfred's preface to the Old English Pastoral Care', *English Historical Review* 94 (1979): 346–55.

Sicard, D., 'Christian Death', in A.G. Martimort (ed.), *The Church at Prayer: Vol. 3, The Sacraments* (Collegeville, MN: The Liturgical Press, 1988), 221–40.

Silverstein, T., 'The "Vision of Leofric" and Gregory's Dialogues', *Review of English Studies* 9 (1933): 186–8.

Sims-Williams, P., *Religion and Literature in Western England, 600–800*, Cambridge Studies in Anglo-Saxon England 3 (Cambridge: Cambridge University Press, 1990).

Sims-Williams, P., 'A Recension of Boniface's Letter to Eadburg about the Monk of Wenlock's Vision', in K. O'Brien O'Keeffe and A. Orchard (eds), *Latin Learning and English Lore*, I (Toronto: University of Toronto Press, 2005), 194–214.

Smith, M.F., P. Halpin and R. Fleming, 'Court and piety in late Anglo-Saxon England', *Catholic Historical Review* 87:4 (2001): 569–602.

Smyth, M., *Understanding the Universe in Seventh-Century Ireland*, Studies in Celtic History 15 (Woodbridge: Boydell, 1996).

Smyth, M., 'The origins of purgatory through the lens of seventh-century Irish eschatology', *Traditio: Studies in Ancient and Medieval History, Thought, and Religion* 57 (2003): 91–132.

Southern, R.W., *St Anselm: A Portrait in a Landscape* (Cambridge: Cambridge University Press, 1992)

Stafford, P., 'The laws of Cnut and the history of Anglo-Saxon royal promises', *Anglo-Saxon England* 10 (1982): 173–90.

Stafford, P., *Queen Emma and Queen Edith: Queenship and Women's Power in Eleventh-Century England* (Oxford: Blackwell, 1997).

Stancliffe, C., 'Kings Who Opted Out', in D. Bullough, R. Collins and P. Wormald (eds), *Ideal and Reality in Frankish and Anglo-Saxon Society: Studies Presented to John Michael Wallace-Hadrill* (Oxford: Blackwell, 1983), 154–76.

Stephenson, R., 'Byrhtferth's *Enchiridion*: The Effectiveness of Hermeneutic Latin', in E.M. Tyler (ed.), *Conceptualising Multilingualism in England, c. 800 – c. 1250* (Turnhout: Brepols, 2011), 121–43.

Stevens, W.O., *The Cross in the Life and Literature of the Anglo-Saxons* (New York: Henry Holt and Co., 1904).

Stoneman, W.P., 'Another Old English note signed "Coleman"', *Medium Ævum* 56:1 (1987): 78–82.

Swan, M. and H. Foxhall Forbes, 'St Wulfstan's Homiliary, part 1: Oxford, Bodleian Library, Hatton 113', in O. Da Rold, T. Kato, M. Swan and E. Treharne (eds), *The Production and Use of English Manuscripts 1060 to 1220* (Leicester, 2010), available at http://www.le.ac.uk/english/em1060to1220/mss/EM.Ox.Hatt.113.htm, accessed November 2012.

Tamburr, K., *The Harrowing of Hell in Medieval England* (Cambridge: Boydell & Brewer, 2007).

Tanner, N.P., *The Ages of Faith: Popular Religion in Late Medieval England and Western Europe* (London: I.B. Tauris, 2009).

Tarlow, S., *Bereavement and Commemoration: An Archaeology of Mortality*, Social Archaeology Series (Oxford: Blackwell, 1999).

Tarlow, S., *Ritual, Belief, and the Dead Body in Early Modern Britain and Ireland* (Cambridge: Cambridge University Press, 2010).

Taylor, H.M., 'Tenth Century Church Building in England and on the Continent', in D. Parsons (ed.), *Tenth-Century Studies: Essays in Commemoration of the Millennium of the Council of Winchester and Regularis Concordia* (London: Phillimore, 1975), 141–68, 237.

Tellenbach, G., 'Die historische Dimension der liturgischen Commemoratio im Mittelalter', in K. Schmid and J. Wollasch (eds), *Memoria: der geschichtliche Zeugniswert des liturgischen Gedenkens im Mittelalter* (Munich: Fink, 1984), 200–14.

Thacker, A., 'Monks, Preaching and Pastoral Care in Early Anglo-Saxon England', in J. Blair and R. Sharpe (eds), *Pastoral Care before the Parish* (Leicester: Leicester University Press, 1992), 137–70.

Thompson, V., 'Constructing Salvation: A Homiletic and Penitential Context for Late Anglo-Saxon Burial Practice', in S. Lucy and A.J. Reynolds (eds), *Burial in Early Medieval England and Wales* (London: Society for Medieval Archaeology, 2002), 229–40.

Thompson, V., *Dying and Death in Later Anglo-Saxon England*, Anglo-Saxon Studies 4 (Woodbridge: The Boydell Press, 2004).

Thompson, V., 'The Pastoral Contract in Late Anglo-Saxon England: Priest and Parishioner in Oxford, Bodleian Library, MS Laud Miscellaneous 482', in F. Tinti (ed.), *Pastoral Care in Late Anglo-Saxon England*, Anglo-Saxon Studies 6 (Woodbridge: Boydell and Brewer, 2005), 106–20.

Throness, L., *A Protestant Purgatory: Theological Origins of the Penitentiary Act, 1779* (Aldershot: Ashgate, 2008).

Tinti, F., 'The "costs" of Pastoral Care: Church Dues in Late Anglo-Saxon England', in F. Tinti (ed.), *Pastoral Care in Late Anglo-Saxon England*, Anglo-Saxon Studies 6 (Woodbridge: Boydell and Brewer, 2005), 27–51.

Tinti, F., *Sustaining Belief: The Church of Worcester from c. 870 to c. 1100* (Farnham: Ashgate, 2010).

Tinti, F., 'England and the Papacy in the Tenth Century', in C. Leyser, D.W. Rollason and H. Williams (eds), *England and the Continent in the Tenth Century: Studies in Honour of Wilhelm Levison (1876–1947)* (Turnhout: Brepols, 2011), 163–84.

Tkacz, C.B., 'Heaven and Fallen Angels in Old English', in A. Ferreiro (ed.), *The Devil, Heresy and Witchcraft in the Middle Ages: Essays in Honor of Jeffrey B. Russell* (Leiden: Brill, 1998), 327–44.

Tollerton, L., *Wills and Will-Making in Anglo-Saxon England* (Woodbridge: York Medieval Press in association with the Boydell Press, 2011).

Townend, M. (ed.), *Wulfstan, Archbishop of York: The Proceedings of the Second Alcuin Conference* (Turnhout: Brepols, 2004).

Treharne, E.M., 'A unique Old English formula for excommunication from Cambridge, Corpus Christi College 303', *Anglo-Saxon England* 24 (1995): 185–211.

Treharne, E.M., 'Ælfric's Account of St Swithun: Literature of Reform and Reward', in R. Balzaretti and E.M. Tyler (eds), *Narrative and History in the Early Medieval West* (Turnhout: Brepols, 2006), 167–88.

Treharne, E.M., 'The Form and Function of the Vercelli Book', in A.J. Minnis and J. Roberts (eds), *Text, Image, Interpretation: Studies in Anglo-Saxon Literature and its Insular Context in Honour of Éamonn Ó Carragáin* (Turnhout: Brepols, 2007), 253–66.

Treharne, E.M., 'Homilies: London, Lambeth Palace Library, 489', in O. Da Rold, T. Kato, M. Swan and E. Treharne (eds), *The Production and Use of English Manuscripts 1060 to 1220* (Leicester, 2010), available at http://www.le.ac.uk/english/em1060to1220/mss/EM.Lamb.489.htm, accessed October 2012.

Treharne, E.M., 'The Conners of Exeter, 1070–1150', *Festschrift for Patrick Conner* (forthcoming).

Treschow, M., 'The prologue to Alfred's law code: Instruction in the spirit of mercy', *Florilegium* 13 (1994): 79–110.

Tselos, D., 'English manuscript illumination and the Utrecht psalter', *The Art Bulletin* 41:2 (1959): 137–49.

Turner, S., *Making a Christian Landscape: The Countryside in Early Medieval Cornwall, Devon and Wessex* (Exeter: University of Exeter Press, 2006).

Tweddle, D., M. Biddle and B. Kjølbye-Biddle, *Corpus of Anglo-Saxon Stone Sculpture: Vol. 4, South-East England* (Oxford: Published for the British Academy by Oxford University Press, 1995).

van Arsdall, A., *Medieval Herbal Remedies: The Old English Herbarium and Anglo-Saxon Medicine* (London: Routledge, 2002).

van Houts, E.M.C., 'Women and the writing of history in the early middle ages: The case of Abbess Matilda of Essen and Æthelweard', *Early Medieval Europe* 1 (1992): 53–68.

van Houts, E.M.C., *Memory and Gender in Medieval Europe, 900–1200*, Explorations in Medieval Culture and Society (Basingstoke: Macmillan, 1999).

Vogel, C., 'Une Mutation culturelle inexpliquée: Le passage de l'Eucharistie communautaire à la messe privée', *Revue des sciences religieuses* 54 (1980): 231–50.

Vogel, C., 'Deux conséquences de l'eschatologie grégorienne: la multiplication des messes privées et les moines-prêtres', in J. Fontaine, R. Gillet and S. Pellistrandi (eds), *Grégoire le Grand: Chantilly, Centre culturel Les Fontaines, 15–19 septembre 1982: actes* (Paris: Editions du CNRS, 1986), 267–76.

Vollrath, H., 'Gesetzgebung und Schriftlichkeit. Das Beispiel der angelsächsischen Gesetze', *Historisches Jahrbuch* 99 (1979): 28–54.

Vollrath, H., 'Taufliturgie und Diözesaneinteilung in der frühen angelsächsischen Kirche', in P. Ní Chatháin and M. Richter (eds), *Irland und die Christenheit: Bibelstudien und Mission / Ireland and Christendom: The Bible and the Missions* (Stuttgart: Klett-Cotta, 1987), 377–86.

Vorgrimler, H., *Sacramental Theology* (Collegeville, MN: Liturgical Press, 1992).

Wallace-Hadrill, J.M., *The Frankish Church*, Oxford History of the Christian Church (Oxford: Clarendon Press, 1983).

Wallis, F., 'Si naturam quaeras: Reframing Bede's "Science"', in S. DeGregorio (ed.), *Innovation and Tradition in the Writings of the Venerable Bede* (Morgantown, WV: West Virginia University Press, 2006), 65–99.

Wallis, F., 'Bede and Science', in S. DeGregorio (ed.), *The Cambridge Companion to Bede* (Cambridge: Cambridge University Press, 2011), 113–26.

Walsham, A., 'Invisible helpers: Angelic intervention in post-Reformation England', *Past & Present* 208:1 (2010): 77–130.

Walsham, A., *The Reformation of the Landscape: Religion, Identity, and Memory in Early Modern Britain and Ireland* (Oxford: Oxford University Press, 2011).

Wareham, A., 'St Oswald's Family and Kin', in N. Brooks and C. Cubitt (eds), *St. Oswald of Worcester: Life and Influence* (Leicester and New York: Leicester University Press, 1996), 46–63.

Wareham, A., 'The transformation of kinship and the family in late Anglo-Saxon England', *Early Medieval Europe* 10:3 (2001): 375–99.

Watkins, C.S., 'Sin, penance and purgatory in the Anglo-Norman realm: The evidence of visions and ghost stories', *Past and Present* 175:1 (2002): 3–33.

Watkins, C.S., '"Folklore" and "popular religion" in Britain during the middle ages', *Folk-Lore* 115:2 (2004): 140–50.

Watkins, C.S., *History and the Supernatural in Medieval England* (Cambridge: Cambridge University Press, 2007).

Watts, V.E., J. Insley and M. Gelling, *The Cambridge Dictionary of English Place-Names: Based on the Collections of the English Place-Name Society* (Cambridge: Cambridge University Press, 2004).

Werckmeister, O.K., 'The political ideology of the Bayeux Tapestry', *Studi medievali* 17, 3rd series (1976): 535–95.

Whitbread, L., "The Old English poems of the Benedictine office and some related questions", *Anglia* 80 (1962): 37–49.

White, S.D., *Custom, Kinship, and Gifts to Saints: The laudatio parentum in Western France, 1050–1150*, Studies in Legal History (Chapel Hill, NC: University of North Carolina Press, 1988).

White, S.D., 'Proposing the Ordeal and Avoiding it: Strategy and Power in Western French Litigation, 1050–1100', in T. Bisson (ed.), *Cultures of Power: Lordship, Status and Process in Twelfth-Century Europe* (Philadelphia: University of Pennsylvania Press, 2005), 89–123.

Whitelock, D., 'Wulfstan and the so-called Laws of Edward and Guthrum', *English Historical Review* 56:221 (1941): 1–21.

Whitelock, D., 'Wulfstan and the laws of Cnut', *English Historical Review* 63:249 (1948): 433–52.

Whitelock, D., 'Wulfstan's authorship of Cnut's laws', *English Historical Review* 70 (1955): 72–85.

Whitelock, D., 'Wulfstan Cantor and Anglo-Saxon Law', in A.H. Orrick (ed.), *Nordica et Anglica: Studies in Honour of Stefan Einarsson* (Paris: Mouton, 1968), 83–92.Wilcox, J., 'The Dissemination of Wulfstan's Homilies: The Wulfstan Tradition in Eleventh-Century Vernacular Preaching', in C. Hicks (ed.), *England in the Eleventh Century: Proceedings of the 1990 Harlaxton Symposium*, Harlaxton Medieval Studies 2 (Stamford: Paul Watkins, 1992), 199–217.

Wilcox, J., '"Tell Me What I am": Old English Riddles', in D.F. Johnson and E. Treharne (eds), *Readings in Medieval Texts* (Oxford: Oxford University Press, 2005), 46–59.

Wilcox, J., 'Ælfric in Dorset and the Landscape of Pastoral Care', in F. Tinti (ed.), *Pastoral Care in Late Anglo-Saxon England*, Anglo-Saxon Studies 6 (Woodbridge: Boydell and Brewer, 2005), 52–62.

Wilcox, J., 'The Audience of Ælfric's *Lives of Saints* and the Face of Cotton Caligula A. xiv, fols. 93–130', in A.N. Doane and K. Wolf (eds), *Beatus Vir: Studies in Early English and Norse Manuscripts: In Memory of Phillip*

*Pulsiano* (Tempe, AZ: Arizona Center for Medieval and Renaissance Studies, 2006), 229–63.

Willard, R., 'The address of the soul to the body', *Publications of the Modern Languages Association* 50 (1935): 957–83.

Williams, H., 'Ancient landscapes and the dead: The reuse of prehistoric and Roman monuments as early Anglo-Saxon burial sites', *Medieval Archaeology: Journal of the Society for Medieval Archaeology* 41 (1997): 1–32.

Williams, H., 'Monuments and the past in early Anglo-Saxon England', *World Archaeology* 30:1 (1998): 90–108.

Williams, H., 'Death, Memory and Time: A Consideration of the Mortuary Practices at Sutton Hoo', in C. Humphrey and W.M. Ormrod (eds), *Time in the Medieval World* (York: York Medieval Press, 2001), 35–71.

Willis, G.G., *Essays in Early Roman Liturgy*, Alcuin Club Collections 46 (London: Published for the Alcuin Club by Society for the Promotion of Christian Knowledge, 1964).

Willis, G.G., *Further Essays in Early Roman Liturgy* (London: Published for the Alcuin Club by Society for the Promotion of Christian Knowledge, 1968).

Willis, G.G., *A History of Early Roman Liturgy: To the Death of Pope Gregory the Great* (London: Published for the Henry Bradshaw Society by Boydell Press, 1994).Withers, B.C., *The Illustrated Old English Hexateuch, Cotton Claudius B.iv: The Frontier of Seeing and Reading in Anglo-Saxon England* (London: The British Library, 2007).

Withers, B.C., 'Satan's Mandorla: Translation, Transformation and Interpretation in Late Anglo-Saxon England', in C. Hourihane (ed.), *Insular and Anglo-Saxon Art and Thought in the Early Medieval Period* (Princeton, NJ: Princeton University in association with Penn State University Press, 2011), 247–70.

Wollasch, J., 'Die mittelalterliche Lebensform der Verbrüderung', in K. Schmid and J. Wollasch (eds), *Memoria: der geschichtliche Zeugniswert des liturgischen Gedenkens im Mittelalter* (Munich: Fink, 1984), 215–32.

Wollasch, J., 'Toten- und Armensorge', in K. Schmid and J. Wollasch (eds), *Gedächtnis, das Gemeinschaft Stiftet* (Munich: Verlag Schnell & Steiner, 1985), 9–38.

Wood, I.N., 'Monasteries and the geography of power in the age of Bede', *Northern History* 45:1 (2008): 11–25.

Wood, I.N., 'The foundation of Bede's Wearmouth-Jarrow', in S. DeGregorio (ed.), *The Cambridge Companion to Bede* (Cambridge: Cambridge University Press, 2010), 84–96.

Wood, S., *The Proprietary Church in the Medieval West* (Oxford: Oxford University Press, 2006).

Woodman, D.A., "Æthelstan A' and the rhetoric of rule', *Anglo-Saxon England* 42 (forthcoming).

Woolf, A., 'A Dialogue of the Deaf and the Dumb: Archaeology, History and Philology', in Z. Devlin and C.N.J. Holas-Clark (eds), *Approaching*

*Interdisciplinarity: Archaeology, History and the Study of Early Medieval Britain, c.400–1100* (Oxford: Archaeopress, 2009), 3–9.

Wormald, P., 'Æthelred the Lawmaker', in D. Hill (ed.), *Ethelred the Unready: Papers from the Millenary Conference* (Oxford: 1978), 47–80.

Wormald, P., 'A handlist of Anglo-Saxon lawsuits', *Anglo-Saxon England* 17 (1988): 247–81.

Wormald, P., 'Domesday Lawsuits: A Provisional List and Preliminary Comment', in C. Hicks (ed.), *England in the Eleventh Century: Proceedings of the 1990 Harlaxton Symposium*, Harlaxton Medieval Studies 2 (Stamford: Paul Watkins, 1992), 61–102.

Wormald, P., 'Archbishop Wulfstan and the Holiness of Society', in D.A.E. Pelteret (ed.), *Anglo-Saxon History: Basic Readings* (New York: Routledge, 1999), 191–224.

Wormald, P., 'Frederic William Maitland and the Earliest English Law', *Legal Culture in the Early Medieval West: Law as Text, Image and Experience* (London: Hambledon Press, 1999), 45–69.

Wormald, P., 'Giving God and King their Due: Conflict and its Regulation in the Early English State', *Legal Culture in the Early Medieval West: Law as Text, Image and Experience* (London: Hambledon Press, 1999), 333–57.

Wormald, P., 'Lex Scripta and Verbum Regis: Legislation and Germanic Kingship from Euric to Cnut', *Legal Culture in the Early Medieval West: Law as Text, Image and Experience* (London: Hambledon Press, 1999), 1–44.

Wormald, P., *The Making of English Law: King Alfred to the Twelfth Century* (Oxford: Blackwell, 1999).

Wrenn, C.L., 'Some Aspects of Anglo-Saxon Theology', in E. Bagby Atwood and A.A. Hill (eds), *Studies in Language, Literature and Culture of the Middle Ages and Later* (Austin: University of Texas at Austin, 1969), 182–9.

Wright, C.D., '*Docet deus, docet diabolus*: A Hiberno-Latin theme in an Old English body-and-soul homily', *Notes and Queries* 232 (1987): 451–3.

Wright, C.D., *The Irish Tradition in Old English Literature*, Cambridge Studies in Anglo-Saxon England 6 (Cambridge: Cambridge University Press, 1992).

Wright, C.D., 'The Old English "Macarius" Homily, Vercelli Homily IV, and Ephrem Latinus, *De paenitentia*', in T.N. Hall (ed.), *Via Crucis: Essays on Early Medieval Sources and Ideas in Memory of J.E. Cross* (Morgantown, WV: West Virginia University Press, 2002), 210–34.

Yorke, B., *Nunneries and the Anglo-Saxon Royal Houses* (London: Continuum, 2003).

Yorke, B., *The Conversion of Britain: Religion, Politics and Society in Britain, c.600–800* (Harlow: Pearson Longman, 2006).

Zadora-Rio, E., 'The making of churchyards and parish territories in the early-medieval landscape of France and England in the 7th–12th centuries: A reconsideration', *Medieval Archaeology: Journal of the Society for Medieval Archaeology* 47 (2003): 1–19.

# Index

Abbo of Fleury 149, 178
Abbotsbury 247, 279n, 292
Abelard, Peter 16–17
Acca, Bishop of Hexham 326
Ælfheah, Bishop of Winchester,
    Archbishop of Canterbury and St
    (d.1012) 289, 300 (and ?318–19)
Ælfheah, Ealdorman 310
Ælfric of Eynsham 5, 6, 16–18, 19, 20,
    24, 26, 29, 30, 31, 40–2, 44, 46–9,
    57–8, 65–7, 71, 73, 75, 79, 81–3,
    86, 101–2, 106–9, 115–23, 125,
    127, 131, 149, 177–84, 198, 207–8,
    210, 212, 218, 268, 286–7, 290–1,
    298–9, 304, 309, 317n, 318, 328
Ælfwine, Abbot of the New Minster,
    Winchester 80, 82, 87, 125, 201,
    214, 215, 244, 261, 292
Æthelflæd, Lady of the Mercians 34, 239
Æthelred II, King of England (d.1016) 54,
    230–2, 242, 257, 318
    laws 131, 160–4, 173, 176, 180, 185,
    188–92, 286, 310–12
Æthelstan, ætheling (d.1014) 257
Æthelstan, King of England (d.939) 54,
    146, 149, 165, 167, 192, 232–6,
    257, 282, 304–6
    laws 131, 140, 142, 146–50, 154, 158,
    162, 164, 166–8, 192, 276–7
Æthelweard, Dux of the West Saxons 68, 260
Æthelwine, Ealdorman of East Anglia
    (d.992) 136, 271n, 279, 288–9, 293
Æthelwold, Bishop of the New Minster,
    Winchester, and St (d.984) 71, 73,
    171, 192, 329–31, 333
Alcuin, 5, 6, 47n, 71, 75n, 76n, 80n, 101,
    104, 144–5, 209–11, 213–15,
    218–19, 235, 271n, 292
Aldebert 21–2, 25, 31, 124

Aldhelm, Bishop of Sherborne (d.709/10)
    122, 301
Alfred, Ealdorman in Kent 230, 243, 258
Alfred, King of the Anglo-Saxons (d.899)
    4, 131, 140–6, 173, 175
    laws 43, 140–4, 149, 154, 175, 191
almsgiving 208, 210, 212, 217–18, 220,
    222, 226–9, 231–5, 237, 239–40,
    243–4, 249–51, 254–5, 258, 261,
    263–4, 292, 303, 305
altars 72, 152, 155, 156n, 214–15, 225,
    242, 269, 270, 276, 292, 326,
    329–30; *see also* relics
Amalarius of Metz 215–17, 268, 307n, 326n
angels 22, 27, 29–30, 60, 63–127, 290–1,
    293, 314, 320, 322–3, 332; *see also*
    Gabriel; Michael; Raphael
    creation 63–9
    fall 69–72
    guardian 66, 77, 108–9, 118, 125
    visual representation of 101–3
anniversaries 215–17, 230, 239–44, 247,
    252, 263, 283
Annunciation 64, 68
anointing; *see also* oil
    at baptism 288
    of the sick 52, 67, 86, 112, 161, 177,
    279, 288–9, 298, 319
Anselm of Canterbury 23–4
archaeology 8–10, 29, 34, 86, 200, 301
art 9, 69–70, 77–8, 95–6, 102–3
Ascension 46n, 107, 129
Ash Wednesday 52
Augustine of Hippo, St 3, 21, 48n, 63–4,
    117, 138–9, 145, 203, 205–6, 210,
    216, 265, 267–71, 282, 296, 300,
    308, 313–15, 321, 327
Augustine, Archbishop of Canterbury and
    St 223, 279, 321

baptism 2, 5, 10, 19–20, 22, 31, 32, 34, 37, 42–5, 48, 49, 50, 51, 52, 57, 60, 61, 67, 71, 78–9, 82, 101, 103–11, 118, 120, 127, 161, 196–7, 275, 288, 331; *see also* sacrament
    infant 43–44
barrows 93–4, 96–8
baths, cold 237
Bede, the Venerable, St 1–3, 5–6, 10, 12, 16–17, 37, 38, 41–2, 46–7, 49–50, 59, 63, 65–9, 71, 74, 76, 83, 87–8, 91, 109, 110n, 119, 121–3, 141, 203, 207–8, 213, 218–19, 274, 294–6, 308, 316, 318, 320, 322, 324, 325, 326, 327n, 328
belief 11–16, 20, 23, 29, 30, 31, 32, 33, 42–3, 60–1
bells 331
*Beowulf* 59, 88–9, 93
bequests *see* wills
Bible *see* Scripture
bishops 39–40, 52
Boniface, Archbishop of Mainz and St 6, 19–20, 21–2, 24–5, 31, 37, 50, 67n, 75–7, 81, 91, 99, 108, 122–4, 211, 278, 287, 308, 316
booklets 51–2, 58, 121, 137
books 6, 8, 9, 19, 38–9, 50–2, 58, 66, 77, 82, 85–6, 87n, 88, 102, 104, 108, 110, 112, 113, 115, 121, 122, 123, 132, 136–7, 144, 148, 152, 156n, 161, 167, 173, 209, 213–15, 230, 232, 243, 244, 245, 248, 258, 258, 262, 264, 276, 280, 283, 288, 305; *see also libri vitae; and individual shelfmarks in the* Index of Manuscripts (below)
boundaries 56, 90, 92, 93n, 97–8, 221, 282, 301
Breedon on the Hill, Leics. 36, 102, 230
Brittany 148
Burchard of Worms 156, 175–6
burial 2, 59–60, 266–313
    charcoal 282
    mounds 12, 93–6, 324
Byrhtferth of Ramsey, 26–9, 49, 50, 68–9, 79, 81, 82, 87, 118, 273n, 288, 306–7, 309, 312, 313, 318–20, 321, 322

Candlemas 53
candles 240–1, 242n, 329
canon law 1, 6–7, 133, 140, 147–9, 178, 180–91
Canterbury 79, 105, 109, 114, 148, 161, 163, 225, 227, 229–30, 239, 240, 241, 243, 249, 251, 253, 258, 279, 280, 284
    archbishops 39, 105, 114, 147, 284, 310; *see also individual names of archbishops*
    Christ Church 77, 114, 225, 227, 229–30, 239, 240–1, 243, 249, 251, 253, 258, 329n
    professions to archbishops 39–40
    St Augustine's 223, 224, 229, 232, 279, 280
cemeteries 2, 9, 52, 59–60, 86, 94, 96–8, 200, 236, 261, 266–7, 271–2, 275–83, 286, 291–5, 301, 313, 316–17, 322–5, 330, 332
    consecrated 1–2, 59, 97, 158, 167, 200, 274–8, 286, 294, 296–301, 303, 309–13, 317, 322–4, 328, 332; *see also* liturgy
    execution 94, 97–8, 200, 266, 272, 300–1
Ceolred, King of the Mercians 76–8, 123
charnel 324–5
charters 8, 10, 219–38
children 38–39, 43–5, 50, 64, 106–7, 111, 120, 147–9, 252, 256–8, 261, 288, 310, 320, 326n, 329–30; *see also* family; inheritance
    representation of soul as a child 96
church
    attendance at 47, 52, 54, 76, 106, 107, 110, 116, 124, 167, 219, 229, 330
churches 2, 8, 33–41, 47, 51–9, 66, 73, 76, 84, 99–102, 107, 116, 124–7, 131, 140–1, 152, 154, 156n, 157, 161–7, 199, 200n, 220–7, 239, 240, 245–8, 250, 255, 258, 267–71, 275–83, 286, 288–90, 292, 294, 306–7, 317, 318n, 320–5, 329, 331
    building of 34, 245, 277, 306
    mother 35
church-scot 255
churchyard *see cemeteries*

*Collectio Canonum Hibernensis* 147–8
commemoration 56, 212–52, 262–3, 267,
    271, 274, 280–3, 294, 303, 307n, 322
communion 5, 46, 47, 49, 107, 167, 197,
    198, 287–9, 290, 297; *see also*
    Eucharist; mass; viaticum
computus 49, 68, 79
confession 14, 21, 32, 34, 45–8, 51, 52, 61,
    77, 112, 134–5, 140, 145, 147, 151,
    166, 187, 196–202, 210, 218, 274,
    279, 286–8, 298–300, 309, 313,
    318, 331, 332; *see also* pastoral
    care; penance
confirmation 44–5, 52
confraternity 217, 244–5, 247, 263
consecrated ground *see* cemeteries
conversion 4, 57, 273
corsnæd *see* ordeals, bread and cheese
creation 10, 59, 63–9, 71–2, 74–5, 101,
    102, 139, 177, 327, 333
cross 152, 167, 214, 323
    adoration of 330
    consecrated 152, 156n, 167
    gift of 214
    pectoral 60, 319
    sign of the cross 56, 79, 80–2, 84–6,
        104, 281
    standing crosses 55–6, 100, 124, 246
Crucifixion 45, 53, 68, 80
Cuthbert, Bishop of Lindisfarne and St 60,
    73, 90–1, 141, 322, 326–8

Daniel, Bishop of Winchester 45
death 2, 8, 111–25, 265
death penalty *see* punishment, capital
demons *see* devils
devils 10, 27–9, 30, 60, 63–127, 172, 210,
    293, 304, 318–20, 322, 332
Dewsbury, Yorks. 102
Dhuoda 249, 260
Domesday Book 36, 151n, 161n, 194–5,
    243, 246
dragons 93–4, 98n, 100, 120
druids 62
Dunstan, Archbishop of Canterbury and St
    73–4, 82n, 163, 271, 272, 277, 279,
    282, 290, 310, 321

Easter 44, 46n, 48, 52–3, 107n, 110–11,
    120, 186, 191, 330
ecclesiastical councils 6–7, 16, 22, 41, 44,
    47, 67, 146–7, 180, 194, 198, 332
    Braga (561) 303
    *Clofesho* (747) 41, 43n, 47n, 58–9
    I Constantinople (381) 64n
    I Nicaea (325) 64n, 287
    IV Lateran (1215) 22–3, 46–7, 158,
        194–5, 198, 332
    London (25 December 1074 x 28
        August 1075) 23n
    Westminster (1102) 23
Edgar, King of England 136, 252, 257, 310
    laws 136–7
Edmund, King of the East Angles and St
    56, 149, 178, 224, 237, 300, 318
Edmund, King of England 228, 242, 252,
    257
Edward the Confessor, King of England
    99, 194n, 227, 245, 246, 257
Edward the Elder, King of Wessex 148
    laws 162
Edward the Martyr 309
Epiphany 5, 106
eschatology 2, 11, 111–22, 129, 201, 211
Etna, Mt. 95
Eucharist 1, 5, 18n, 20, 49, 78, 101, 197,
    287, 288, 297, 317; *see also* mass
*Excerpta libris romanorum et francorum*
    147–8
excommunication 47n, 132, 187, 221, 224,
    320
execution 23, 94–8, 130, 138–42, 146–50,
    168, 176–7, 185–6, 189–90, 194–5,
    200, 266, 272, 296–303, 308–9;
    *see also* cemeteries, execution;
    punishment, capital
Exeter 38, 54, 223, 247–8

family 259–62, 264
fasting 74, 134, 138, 167, 173n, 190, 191,
    194, 197, 209, 237, 240, 287, 299,
    304, 316
feasting 58–9, 77, 190–1, 194, 240–3, 252,
    283, 299; *see also* anniversaries
fens 91–2, 247, 272
footprints 55, 99

Fulda 28, 29, 91
Fursey 116, 118–19, 123–4

Gabriel, Archangel 119, 126
Gargano, Monte (Puglia) 98–9
Glastonbury 82n, 271, 272, 277, 282
Good Friday 53, 80n, 330
Goscelin of St-Bertin 315, 317
gospel-books 152, 167, 230, 243, 248, 258
grave-goods 275
gravestones 246, 280–1
graveyards *see* cemeteries
Gregory the Great, Pope and St 3, 7, 21,
       66, 143, 205, 218, 245, 269–71,
       296, 308, 314–15, 317, 321, 327
       *Dialogues* 79, 95, 116, 121, 123, 203,
       218–19, 238, 269, 321
Gregory of Tours 203
Gregory III, Pope 287, 308
guilds 8, 247–8, 249, 264, 279, 292
Guthlac, hermit and St 73–4, 91–4

heaven 18, 63–4, 65–8, 69, 70–1, 74, 78,
       87–8, 99–100, 109, 117, 119, 126,
       129, 173, 196, 202, 205, 206, 208,
       215, 217, 224, 225, 227, 265, 270,
       288, 297, 308–9, 315, 322, 324, 333
Heavenfield, battle-site of 55
hell 18, 21, 70, 74, 77, 89, 94–6, 109, 115,
       122, 124, 129, 201–2, 206, 208,
       210, 265, 294, 297–8, 304, 312, 320
       harrowing of hell 21–2
heresy 14, 19–22, 26, 64, 67
holy water 167, 197
homilies 81, 83,124–5, 218, 298
hundreds
       boundaries 97–8
       courts 136, 189
Ine
       laws 43, 140, 142, 155, 157, 160
Isidore of Seville 87, 206

Jarrow 33, 34, 36, 38, 214, 246
Jerome 21, 139, 140, 187, 188, 300, 301
judgement
       Last Judgement 2, 17, 111, 115, 129–31,
       138, 145, 151, 152, 155–8, 178,
       183, 199–208, 215, 238, 265, 273,
       276, 288, 308–9, 313, 320–4, 327
       individual judgement 111, 201, 204–5,
       320
       secular judgement 129–200

keys 28–9, 224

landscape 10, 21, 33–4, 36, 52, 55–6, 60,
       61, 65, 72, 75, 76, 88–101, 103,
       126, 332
Lanfranc, Archbishop of Canterbury 212
law ch 3 *passim*
law codes, 6, 135–7, 140, 142–4
*libri vitae* 213–15, 217, 244–5
Lichfield, Staffs. 102
Lindisfarne 34, 37, 214, 246
litanies 84, 113, 290
literacy 4, 20, 85, 88–9, 90, 95, 106, 123,
       127, 136–7, 220–1, 333
liturgical texts 7, 10, 20n, 22, 44, 48, 51–4,
       57, 67, 71, 79, 80n, 84, 86–7, 101,
       103–6, 108, 110, 111–16, 118, 124,
       131, 133, 137, 151, 159–62, 167,
       171–2, 186–7, 192, 196, 212–17,
       271
liturgy
       baptismal 43–5, 71, 82, 103–111
       blessings 53–4, 57, 61, 81, 85, 88
       books for 38, 42, 51, 82, 105, 161–2,
       186–7, 192–3, 196–7, 215–17,
       284–5, 288
       consecration of cemeteries 2, 7, 52,
       167, 271, 275–7, 322–4
       funerary 10, 67, 111, 115, 118, 161,
       271, 274, 279, 283–6, 290–1, 293,
       296, 308, 309, 323–5, 327; *see also*
       Office of the Dead
       for ordeals 192–3
       rites for the sick and dying 112–16,
       288–90; *see also* anointing
Liturgy of the Hours *see* Office, Divine
London Bridge 160n

magic 20n, 57–8, 67, 129, 196
manumission 217, 237, 248, 250, 316

manuscripts *see* books; *see also individual shelfmarks in the* Index of Manuscripts (below)
marriage 21, 54, 133, 173n, 175, 253, 259–60, 297n, 299
Mary, Blessed Virgin 25, 49, 64, 78, 115, 126, 214, 224, 226, 243, 245, 252–3, 255, 280, 321, 326
mass, sacrament of 19, 34, 37, 46, 47, 49, 51, 52, 54, 67, 84–5, 107, 110, 159, 161, 167, 196–7, 206, 212, 213, 214–17, 218, 228, 230–8, 244, 263–4, 270, 275, 292, 296, 302–3, 308–9, 313, 320, 331
liturgy for 82, 84, 113, 159, 161, 197, 213, 214, 235, 280, 292, 323
offered for people 13, 112–13, 206, 208, 209, 210, 211, 212, 214–17, 218, 219, 235, 247–8, 262, 296, 302–3, 307–8, 319–20
requests for 211, 213, 228, 229–30, 232–4, 236–8, 239–41, 247–8, 270, 280, 283, 305, 307–8
special 234–9, 263
Maundy Thursday 52–3, 329–30, 333
mausolea 278
medicine 83–7
Michael, Archangel 88, 94, 98–100, 115, 117–19, 255, 293, 322
minsters 34–7, 52, 223, 232, 245, 248, 265, 278–9, 283, 286, 291, 292
monks 1–2, 13, 26, 28–30, 37–8, 53, 95, 119–21, 122, 171, 238, 241, 257, 277, 279, 280, 283, 289, 291–2, 294, 296, 306–8, 313, 316–17, 319–20, 331
monsters 60, 88, 89, 92, 95, 101, 103, 126–7
Mont-Saint-Michel 99
murder 139, 157, 177, 182, 187, 190, 193, 198–9, 210, 298, 303

Nazeing, Essex 34, 36, 86, 266, 272
*Northumbrian Priests' Law* 161, 192, 276
nuns 23, 28–30, 79, 232, 269, 315–16, 319–20

oaths 11, 26–7, 158–9, 162, 164, 167, 170, 189–200, 298–9
of allegiance 153

coronation 134, 153
judicial 130–1, 133, 150–8, 162, 164, 167, 189–200, 298–9
of loyalty 149, 153
Odda, Earl (d.1056) 291
Office, Divine 81, 161, 163, 230, 240
Office of the Dead 212, 217, 219, 284, 329–30
oil 85, 288, 289; *see also* anointing
*Ordal* 165, 167–8, 199n
ordeals 7, 11, 27n, 130–1, 133, 150–2, 154, 158–72, 185–200, 299, 310, 317, 332
bread and cheese ('corsnæd') 192–3
burial 186
cold water 159–60, 197
hot iron 151, 159–60, 165, 169–71, 186, 197
hot ploughshares 170n, 186
hot water 151, 159–60, 165, 171
Orderic Vitalis 40–1
Oswald, Bishop of Worcester, Archbishop of York, and St 255–9, 281, 288, 306–8
Oswald, King of Northumbria and St 23, 55–6
Otley, Yorks. 102
Oundle 323

paganism 12, 14, 22, 54, 57–9, 97
Palm Sunday 5, 107
papacy 15–17
pastoral care 5, 32–53, 72, 80, 82, 87, 101, 120, 125, 134, 157–8, 183, 199, 286, 332
Patristic writings 21
penance, 6, 37, 45, 47n, 50, 52, 77, 111n, 119, 122, 130–8, 14–9, 151, 156–8, 173–7, 186–8, 198–210, 218, 228, 235–8, 282, 287–300, 305–6; *see also* confession; pastoral care; penitential handbooks
penitential handbooks 6–7, 43, 51, 111n, 132–8, 155–8, 173–6, 186–7, 199–200, 202, 209, 238, 287–8, 296–303, 313; *see also* confession; penance; pastoral care
Pentecost 44, 46n, 68, 107n, 110, 119, 186

perjury 133, 152n, 153, 155–8, 162, 197,
    198, 199, 297
Pershore 318–20
Peter, St 115
place-names 10, 56, 88–93, 98, 100
Pliny the Elder 87
'popular' religion 14, 22
prayer 76, 83–7
    for the dead 31, 96, 120, 127, 201–64,
        267–94, 300–20, 327–8
    private 80, 82, 87, 115, 124, 125, 162,
        201, 215, 244, 261
preaching 32, 47, 51, 80, 83, 100–1, 104,
    110, 120–4, 281
priests 13–14, 17, 19, 31, 32–52, 58, 68, 78,
    81, 82, 85, 103–4, 106–7, 110, 112,
    116, 121, 133–7, 139, 154, 167,
    173n, 177, 178, 178n, 179, 181–4,
    191–3, 197, 199, 208, 210, 218,
    226, 229, 236–7, 240, 241, 246,
    253, 274, 275, 282, 286, 287–9,
    290, 298–9, 302, 309, 313, 321, 332
processions 52–6, 61, 289
punishment 111, 119, 130, 133, 138–50,
    153, 158, 164, 168, 170, 172–90,
    193, 194, 195, 198, 200, 299, 309,
    313, 316, 332
    capital 131, 138–50, 164, 172, 177–90,
        193, 194, 195
purgatory 11, 17–18, 19, 96, 127, 200,
    202–19, 224, 234, 249n, 262, 263,
    308–9, 313, 316, 327

Rædwald, King of the East Angles 12
Ramsey 163, 242, 279, 283, 288–9, 294,
    306–8
Raphael, Archangel 83, 113, 115
Raunds, Northants. 37, 271n
Regularis Concordia 38, 212, 233n, 244,
    290, 329–30
relics 2, 21, 54, 55, 56, 133, 152, 154,
    156n, 157, 159, 223, 224, 267, 278,
    286, 326
resurrection 23n, 45, 201, 205, 265, 275,
    287, 293, 294, 327
rihtscriftscir 199, 286
Ripon, Yorks. 33, 318n
rites for the sick see liturgy

Rochester 195, 279, 301
Rogation 46n, 53, 56, 58–9, 61, 107n, 242
royal writing office 222, 233
Rule of Benedict 87

sacraments 2, 19, 37–8, 85, 103–4,
    108; see also baptism; mass;
    pastoral care; penance; theology,
    sacramental
St Albans 237, 244, 256, 280, 283
saints 2, 7–8, 24, 26, 31, 54–6, 140–1,
    219–38, 266; see also entries under
    specific names, e.g. Oswald
sanctuary 140–1, 310, 318
schools, cathedral 38
science 64, 69, 87
scriftscir see rihtscriftscir; see also
    confession; pastoral care
Scripture 3, 5, 21, 22, 24, 25, 40, 41, 63,
    64, 67, 87, 120, 138–9, 177, 202,
    215, 327n, 332
sculpture 8–9, 56, 66, 100, 102, 246
Shaftesbury 232–4
Sherborne 38, 49, 104–5, 114, 161, 163,
    233–5, 272n, 284, 298
sin 6, 21 69, 71, 76, 81, 97, 101, 103,
    110, 119–20, 126, 127, 130,
    133, 134, 135, 138–9, 151, 176,
    187, 197–200, 201–11, 217–18,
    226–8, 236–9, 249, 269, 270, 292,
    297–9, 313, 319, 324, 327; see also
    confession; penance
    angelic 71
    mortal (deadly, capital, or serious)
        52, 69, 157, 198–9, 204, 205–10,
        269–70, 297
    original 101–3, 110, 120, 138–9
    unforgivable 138n
    venial (slight, or small) 204, 205–10
slaves 14, 144, 169–71, 208, 237, 250, 316
soul 313–23
soul-scot 279, 280, 283, 286
suicide 300–8
Sutton Hoo 12, 94
Swithun, Bishop of Winchester and St 26,
    30, 31, 140–1, 168–9, 171, 196,
    266, 331
Symeon of Durham 304–5, 312, 318n, 326

synod 21, 199, 217

teaching 3, 5, 12, 32, 37, 40–52, 68, 80–1, 111, 127, 157, 183, 219
theft 134, 140, 142, 146–7, 149–50, 152, 157, 159n, 166–7, 198, 250; *see also* thieves
Theodore of Tarsus, Archbishop of Canterbury and St 6, 209, 242n, 274, 276, 296, 302–3
Theodred, Bishop of London 147, 149, 178–9, 261
theology, 2–3, 109–10, 129–31, 332 (and *passim*)
   sacramental 2, 19–20, 20n
thieves 28, 129, 134, 140–2, 147, 149, 164, 166, 177, 178, 179, 182, 298, 304, 311–12; see *also* theft
tithes 35
Trinity 45

Vercelli homilies 82, 109, 218
viaticum 287–8, 293, 294, 296; *see also* communion; Eucharist; mass
Vikings 124, 230, 243, 258
vision literature 117–18, 207–8, 236; *see also* Fursey
   *Visio S. Pauli* 89, 109, 116–18
visual culture 8, 66, 70–1, 102

wax 240; *see also* candles
Wearmouth 34, 214
wells 24, 54, 56–7, 162
Wihtred, King of Kent 223, 232
   laws 142n, 154–5
Wilfrid, Bishop of Ripon and St 320, 322–3, 326
William the Conqueror 152, 194
William of Malmsbury 39, 271–2, 291, 300, 304–5
wills 8, 219–57, 279–80
   Æthelgifu (S 1497) 13, 14, 236–7, 283, 303–4

Winchester 23, 34, 37–8, 39, 45, 53–4, 71, 80, 84, 104, 105, 108n, 114, 161, 162, 163, 169, 170, 174, 182, 196, 201, 212, 214–15, 241–2, 244, 265–6, 280, 284–5, 286, 289, 291, 292, 329–31
   New Minster 53–4, 80, 87, 201, 214–15, 228, 241, 242, 244, 280, 292, 331n
   Nunnaminster 105, 284, 331n
   Old Minster 53, 105, 162, 163, 242, 258, 265, 284, 292, 330
witchcraft 159, 164, 210, 318
witches 159, 160n, 318
women 4, 13, 27, 34, 74, 85–6, 124–5, 160n, 175, 182, 184, 190, 208, 211, 219, 234, 236–7, 242, 249, 251, 259–60, 292, 297n, 301, 316
Worcester 40, 42, 51, 58, 123, 161, 226, 243, 238–9, 250, 255
Wulfhelm, Archbishop of Canterbury 147–9
Wulfred, Archbishop of Canterbury 240, 254
Wulfsige, Bishop of Sherborne (d.1002) 38, 44, 49, 298
Wulfstan I, Bishop of Worcester (d.956) 289
Wulfstan II, Bishop of Worcester and Archbishop of York (d.1023) 1–2, 4–6, 18, 29, 40–2, 46, 48, 49, 57, 59, 71n, 78, 82–3, 104, 106–8, 110, 127, 131, 137, 148, 161, 172–94, 196, 198–200, 207, 277, 286, 288, 299, 303, 309, 317, 327
Wulfstan II, Bishop of Worcester and St (d.1095) 58, 162, 163, 215, 272, 285
Wulfstan of Winchester 169–71, 196

York 5, 34, 218, 227, 245, 307

Zacharius, Pope 19–21, 50, 91

# Index of Manuscripts

Brussels, Bibliothèque royale, MS 8558-63: 174

Cambridge, Corpus Christi College, 41: 83, 109, 295

Cambridge, Corpus Christi College, 44: 163, 193n

Cambridge, Corpus Christi College, 146 ('Samson Pontifical'): 193n, 196n, 197n, 323n

Cambridge, Corpus Christi College, 163: 103n, 105, 284

Cambridge, Corpus Christi College, 190: 174, 180n, 182–8, 209n, 309n

Cambridge, Corpus Christi College, 201, Part 1 (pp. 1–178): 18n, 42, 45, 49, 108, 120, 174, 182–3, 309n

Cambridge, Corpus Christi College, 201, Part 2 (pp. 179–202): 117n

Cambridge, Corpus Christi College, 265: 174, 180n, 182–8

Cambridge, Corpus Christi College, 279: 148

Cambridge, Corpus Christi College, 391 ('St Wulfstan's Portiforium'): 115n, 161, 163, 172n, 193n, 200n, 215n, 285

Cambridge, Corpus Christi College, 419: 109n

Cambridge, Corpus Christi College, 421: 79

Cambridge, Corpus Christi College, 422 ('Red Book of Darley'): 82, 103n, 104–5, 112, 113n, 114, 116, 159n, 161, 163, 184, 193n, 196n, 284, 289n, 291n, 293n

Cambridge, University Library, Gg.3.28: 42

Cambridge, University Library, Ii.1.33: 107n

Cambridge, University Library, Ii.2.11: 248

Copenhagen, Kongelige Bibliotek, Gl. Kgl. 1595: 174, 182–3

Durham, Cathedral Library, A.IV.9 ('Durham Collectar' or 'Durham Ritual'): 161, 163

Exeter, Cathedral Library, 3501 ('Exeter Book'): 42, 74

London, British Library, Additional 57337 ('Anderson Pontifical'): 163, 193n

London, British Library, Cotton Augustus ii.88: 224

London, British Library, Cotton Claudius B.iv (Old English Hexateuch): 9, 70, 160n

London, British Library, Cotton Cleopatra B.ix: 247

London, British Library, Cotton Domitian A.vii: 214, 245n

London, British Library, Cotton Nero A.i: 174, 180n, 185–8

London, British Library, Cotton Otho C.i: 123n

London, British Library, Cotton Otho E.xiii: 148

London, British Library, Royal 5. E.xiii: 148

London, British Library, Royal 12. D.xvii: 84

London, British Library, Cotton Titus D.xxvi+xxvii ('Ælfwine's prayerbook'): 79–80, 87n, 125n, 201n, 244, 261, 292

London, British Library, Cotton Vespasian A.xiv: 174

London, British Library, Cotton Vitellius A.vii (fols. 1–112): 163, 193n

London, British Library, Cotton Vitellius E.xii: 285

London, British Library, Harley 585: 84, 85n

London, British Library, Harley 603
    ('Harley Psalter'): 77–8, 94–6
London, British Library, Stowe 944
    (Liber Vitae of the New Minster,
    Winchester): 38n, 54n, 214, 244,
    245n
Orléans, Bibliothèque Municipale, 105
    ('Winchcombe Sacramentary'):
    112, 113n, 114, 115n, 284, 291n
Oxford, Bodleian Library, Barlow 37: 174,
    180n, 187n
Oxford, Bodleian Library, Bodley 343:
    109n, 309n
Oxford, Bodleian Library, Bodley 579
    ('Leofric Missal'): 105, 112, 113n,
    114, 115, 217n, 261n, 284, 287n,
    291n, 293n, 327n
Oxford, Bodleian Library, Bodley 718: 174
Oxford, Bodleian Library, Fairfax 17: 123
Oxford, Bodleian Library, Hatton 42: 148
Oxford, Bodleian Library, Hatton 113+114:
    49n, 51, 108n, 111n, 117n, 121
Oxford, Bodleian Library, Junius 11: 70
Oxford, Bodleian Library, Junius 121: 40,
    42, 49, 51, 108n, 110n, 174, 184,
    209n

Oxford, Bodleian Library, Laud misc. 482:
    51, 112–14, 116, 137n, 209n, 284,
    287n, 289n
Paris, Bibliothèque nationale, 943 ('Dunstan
    Pontifical'): 163, 193n, 329n
Paris, Bibliothèque nationale, lat. 3182: 174
Paris, Bibliothèque nationale, lat. 9376: 123
Paris, Bibliothèque nationale, lat. 10575
    ('Egbert Pontifical'): 272n, 323n
Rochester, Cathedral Library, A.3.5
    ('Textus Roffensis'): 195n
Rouen, Bibliothèque municipale, 274 (Y.6)
    ('Missal of Robert of Jumièges'):
    103n, 105, 112, 113n, 114, 115n,
    217n, 284, 291n, 293n
Rouen, Bibliothèque municipale, 368
    ('Lanalet Pontifical'): 113n, 114,
    163, 193
Rouen, Bibliothèque municipale, 1382:
    174, 180n
Stockholm, Kungliga Biblioteket, A.135
    ('Codex Aureus): 230
Utrecht, Universiteitsbibliotek, MS 32
    ('Utrecht Psalter'): 77–8, 95
Worcester, Cathedral Library, F. 173: 112,
    113n, 114, 115n, 116n, 284, 286, 291n

Printed in Great Britain
by Amazon

64479001R00235